HINDUTVA

VS.

SECULARISM

HINDUTVA VS. SECULARISM

WHAT DECIDES THE OUTCOME?

DIPTENDRA RAYCHAUDHURI

Vitasta

Published by
Renu Kaul Verma
Vitasta Publishing Pvt Ltd
4348/4C, Ansari Road, Daryaganj
New Delhi-110 002
info@vitastapublishing.com

ISBN: 978-81-991712-9-9

First Edition 2025
MRP ₹ 525

Edited by Reena Singh
Typeset by Shubhpreet Kaur
Cover Design by Smriti Maheshwari
Printed by Vikas Computer and Printers, New Delhi

To all who seek the Truth

Other Books by the Author

A Naxal Story

Mirchi Memsaab's House of Faith

Understanding CPI(M): Will the Indian Left Survive

Contents

Decoding 2024

Final Stamp of Change

Quite often, we humans are trapped in a web of conventional thinking that completely fogs our vision. In that haze, we forget that if we try to strip the populace of their millennia-old cultural heritage, it may generate an adverse reaction that threatens to upset the status quo.

That is precisely what is happening in India right now, where for the last three-and-a-half decades, we are witnessing a tense battle between self-described secularists and a new breed of Hindu nationalists. In essence, it is a conflict of two narratives: One that believes India is secular, and so everything rooted to a Hindu identity must be washed away, whether from the educational field or national discourse; and the other, born out of a reaction to the first, is the narrative that believes India is Hindu, and Hindu domination *must be* established in society. Both are trapped in conventional thinking and conveniently forget that India is *both* Hindu as well as secular. Its majority population is Hindu, and its dharmic philosophy, which lies at the root of Hindu and other Sanatani religions, is secular. For the convenience of the reader, certain traits of this dharmic philosophy and its manifestations in society are explained in detail in the last chapter of this book.

The genesis of this present acrimonious confrontation started with a bitter fight over Ram's birthplace, eventually culminating in the demolition of the Babri mosque in 1992. The battle has since continued, albeit in a mellowed form, between Hindu nationalism and atheist secularism, with either side winning the race to power at different times.

But, since the beginning of the second decade of the current century, a change in politics has moved forward at breakneck speed. In 2014, BJP, a Hindu party, established its monopoly over national power with just 31 per cent vote share. But it continues to hold onto power and has subsequently increased its vote share to about 37 per cent. It could not be defeated even in the 2024 general elections despite many Covid-19 blues, widespread rural distress and high unemployment.

Ever since 2014, the secular camp has pinned the blame for its defeat on rising communalism among Hindus, while the BJP reverentially credited Narendra Modi's charisma for their wins. However, such conventional analysis fails to answer two basic questions. First, why did the 'communalisation' of Hindus not award the BJP a majority in the Lok Sabha, or even around a 30 per cent vote share, either in the early days of the Ram Mandir movement or in the aftermath of the demolition of the Babri mosque in 1992? Second, if it is all due to Modi's charisma, then why despite Modi's claim that he would bag more than 400 seats in the 2024 elections, could the BJP only secure 240 seats—surviving only because of its alliance partners?

Such questions remained unanswered, but suddenly in 2024, a loud, overall consensus built up in favour of respecting Hindu religion and its religious-cultural symbols. After being elected as Leader of Opposition (LoP), Rahul Gandhi preached about the Hindu religion holding a placard of Shiva in his hand during his first speech in the Lok Sabha. Again, just prior to the elections, when the so-called secularists had decided to boycott the *pran pratistha* ceremony in the Ram Temple at Ayodhya, they had cited objections raised by some Hindu saints, including a brashly conservative and casteist Shankaracharya. Their views were splashed all over social media.

Exactly why are political parties now bringing back Hindu ideas into the national discourse, that too after a three-decade-long acrimonious confrontation on the construction of the Ram temple? The dispute was finally settled by the Supreme Court in favour of the Hindus. If the Congress was so committed to Hindu faith, why did its leaders not try to find a negotiated settlement instead of siding with the Muslims to stall the construction of the temple at Ram's 'birthplace'?

The compulsion seems to have arisen from the impression that the complete domination of the BJP since 2014 is related exclusively to political Hindutva—the use of Hindu religious symbols for political purposes. So, Congress leaders like Rahul Gandhi and Priyanka Gandhi Vadra think it will pay off if they too can show their allegiance to Hindu gods and goddesses. That was why on 31 March 2024, in their final rally at the Ramleela grounds just before the 2024 elections, Priyanka Vadra, too, invoked Ram in her speech.

However, this allegiance to Hindutva by anti-BJP politicians and intellectuals seems an outcome of utter confusion. It seems they are assuming the symptom of the cause as the cause itself. This is exactly what a large section of the pro-BJP intellectuals are doing too. But, the phenomenal rise of the BJP is not limited to merely establishing a temple or propitiating a Hindu deity. This current popularity which has the BJP riding the Hindu wave has come about more than twenty years after the demolition of the Babri mosque, and at a time when no major political Hindutva issue was raging. So, to understand it, we have to look beyond the conventional interpretations of political trends.

First of all, let's take note of the fact that many of the issues that are now being dismissed as 'Hindutvavadi' by the so-called secular brigade are actually issues that were supported by our pre-Independence icons, including Rabindranath Tagore and Mohandas Karamchand 'Mahatma' Gandhi. In fact, for decades modern secularists are trying to change the very concept of secularism by propagating themes like India is not a nation of the Hindus; all riots happen as RSS workers attack Muslims, and so on. These sets of falsehood have boomeranged, and at times punctured by leading Congress leaders. Salman Khurshid, in 2018, admitted at a gathering of Aligarh Muslim University students that Congress's hands were stained with 'the blood of Muslims'! Kamal Nath declared in 2023, that the demand to announce India as a Hindu nation was superfluous as being a nation with 80 per cent Hindu population, it was obviously so.

In the backdrop of many such false campaigns since Independence, the old orthodoxy is now being challenged and replaced. Though the political shift from a Congress-dominated electoral behaviour to a BJP-dominated one, itself, signifies a major break from the old orthodoxy, there is much more to it. The change reflects an attitudinal shift of the populace driven by a plethora of socio-cultural, economic and psychological factors, each of which will be discussed in this book.

The results of the 2024 Lok Sabha elections have confirmed this further. The argument may sound strange, as in 2024, the BJP had fallen thirty-two seats short of the magic number of 273 in the Lok Sabha, down by sixty-three from its 2019 tally, and has returned to power thanks to support from its pre-poll allies. An objective analysis, however, will point out that the number of seats it has won does not reflect the full picture. In 2014, when for the first time the BJP secured absolute majority in the lower house, it had bagged only a 31 per cent vote share. In 2024, its vote share stood at 36.56 per cent. It, of course, marked a decline of less than one percentage point from 2019, but that is negligible, particularly when one analyses it against the backdrop of the previous couple of years' disastrous experiences like Covid-19 related lockdown, economic meltdown and grand-scale rural distress. Rather, the party's pan-India footstep became more prominent in 2024, covering almost 400 Lok Sabha seats out of a total 543 for which polls took place. Five years ago, the party had won 303 seats, but came second only in seventy-three seats: so, the total number of stronghold seats was 376. In 2024, it won 240 and came second in 153, increasing the total number of stronghold seats to 393.

So, what helped Modi to come back, even when all over the world, most leaders at the helm during the Covid-19 catastrophe had either been replaced by their respective parties or had lost the elections? Why did 45 per cent of the voters, who had suffered intense miseries including loss of jobs since 2020, still vote for the National Democratic Alliance (NDA) in 2024? Forty-five per cent is the standard vote share that is bringing parties or alliances to power in India since 1952. Conventional analysis, busy with explaining where and why the BJP received a jolt, missed out on this bigger picture.

Thus, the 2024 results are definitely a confirmation of a paradigm shift in India, with a distinctive vote for replacement of the old orthodoxy that believed in commonly accepted secular-liberal doctrines, beliefs or practices. It is also to be noted that this election was held not only in the backdrop of a sharp nosedive of the economy, it also witnessed a straight fight in almost all the states between the BJP-led NDA and either partners of Indian National Development Inclusive Alliance (I.N.D.I.A.) or other non-aligned parties like BJD or YSR Congress. That the NDA secured absolute majority in this unusually tough battle is clinching evidence of a humongous change sweeping over society, in general, and political behaviour, in particular.

But what is driving this paradigm shift in the post-Hindutva era? If we analyse the different facets of the change in attitude of the Indian voters—a process that began slowly in the late eighties, reached a plateau in 2004, and then suddenly shot up to break all records since 2014, we find that the change includes three major factors: Reaction against cultural subversion that started just after Independence (cultural factor); assertion of a resurgent and self-assured India (aspiration factor); and affirmation to pro-Hindu politics (religious factor).

This book delves into the hitherto unexplained paradigm shift that took place in the minds of the Indian voter (chapter 1), and then proceeds to point out the three cardinal blunders or 'triple fault of the modern secularists' that enabled this phenomenon in chapters 2, 3, and 4. In the last chapter, the book examines and explains how cultural-religious factors have played and are still playing a defining role in India and also in different nations the world over.

The 'Paradigm Shift': How did it come about?

In his 1962 book, *The Structure of Scientific Revolutions*, the famous philosopher of science, Thomas Kuhn defines 'paradigm shift' as a radical change from the prevailing attitudes of the past, which now forms the basis of a new orthodoxy. According to him, such a shift is caused by a revolutionary discovery or innovation, or by accumulation of evidence or anomalies that challenge the status quo. In sociology, a paradigm shift denotes a major change in how a society understands and organises reality. In other words, it stands for a fundamental change in the concepts, values, thoughts and basic assumptions about society, including political society, which then motivates people to think and act differently from the past, thus breaking old patterns. In simpler terms, when society's old orthodoxy is challenged and is replaced by a new one, we call it a paradigm shift.

In India's case, a new orthodoxy is emerging and quickly replacing a narrative which had clandestinely established itself in post-Independent India by supplanting the pre-Independence Idea of India established by greats like Rabindranath Tagore, Mahatma Gandhi, and other icons. Those pre-Independence titans had suggested and emphasised a narrative of socio-cultural-political nationalism to understand 'Bharatvarsha' (the nation known as India to the world), and to organise reality accordingly. However, this cultural nationalism rooted in deep respect for the eternal values propagated from antiquity was entirely secular, as it was not targeted against any community. The essence of this 'Idea of India' is that India is a land of 'dharma' followed by Hindus and other Sanatanis, where the others are welcome to live and contribute to its civilisational values and future journey.

Back in 1900, knowledge about our civilisational journey was limited, and was believed to span only about three thousand years. It was also a time when the concocted Aryan Invasion theory, now abandoned even by the school that propagated it, was in vogue. So, our greats depended more on the philosophical depth of our ancient texts (like the Vedas, Upanishads, and the Bhagavad Gita) along with the narrations of our *itihaas* (like

Ramayana, Mahabharata, certain puranas and Kalidasa's works). The Ramayana and the Mahabharata were two firm legs of the tripod that held the Indian civilisational journey, the third being the then-still-unknown unparalleled materialistic-technical advancements of the Indus Valley Civilisation from around five thousand years ago.

The narrative or Idea of India that our greats, including those with distinct left leanings such as Jawaharlal Nehru and Subhas Chandra Bose, presented was based clearly on Hindu and other Sanatani traditions. This was naturally so, as even a thousand years ago, there existed no other religion in India other than the dharmic ones—Hinduism (with its different *panths*), Buddhism, Jainism, and the Sarna Dharma. Sikhism developed much later in the fifteenth century in Punjab. The core of such teachings, the dharma philosophy, however, had nothing to do with any religion. It was a metaphysical conceptualisation that advised human beings to act according to their conscience guided by dharma, which ultimately was focused on protecting all of creation—from the individual to the cosmos. But, Muslims in India, who gradually came under the umbrella of the Muslim League that sought Partition on the basis of religious identity and got it by resorting to unimaginable scales of violence, refused to be a part of this narrative.

After Independence, a clique suddenly clandestinely changed this narrative that had been earlier propagated by our greats. They prided themselves on being identified as secular, and by secularism they meant that nothing in public life should have any religious association or overtones. With the help of the USSR that became a guardian angel of India, they disseminated this new belief into the education system, media, films and theatres, and all other instruments that influence human thinking. In a democratic country, full draconian control of cultural and creative life is not possible, so this clique concentrated on brainwashing younger generations by introducing a curriculum that would not teach anything Hindu. They tried to supplant the pre-Independence great Indians' narrative with a new one that was by character, largely leftist, and disrespectful of India's cultural legacies developed over 10,000 years, a fact endorsed by excavations at archeological sites such as Bhimbetka and Lahuradewa.

Essentially, what they succeeded in doing was uprooting modern India's connection with its journey of over 10,000 years that gave Indians a unique unbroken cultural legacy that was distinctly Sanatani. This was further buttressed by pampering to and thus strengthening the Muslim and Christian religious elite, thus making the ordinary minority population, particularly Muslims, vulnerable to the *fatwas* issued by the fundamentalists. All this was part of the 'secular' agenda.

It began at a time when our constitution did not describe India as 'secular'. B R Ambedkar cautioned the Constituent Assembly against mentioning the word in the constitution as it would be tantamount to killing the spirit of democracy. In November 1948, K T Shah had placed before the Constituent Assembly an amendment that read, 'India shall be a Secular, Federal, Socialist Union of States'. Ambedkar had rejected it and said: 'What should be the policy of the State, how the Society should be organised in its social and economic side are matters which must be decided by the people themselves according to time and circumstances. It cannot be laid down in the Constitution itself, because that is destroying democracy altogether.' He further clarified that the constitution was inherently secular, and his opinion was accepted by the Constituent Assembly.

However, later in 1976, during the Emergency, Indira

Gandhi violated this direction to please the USSR, and added 'socialist' and 'secular' in the preamble of the Constitution at a time when democracy was suspended. And this was done when Indira Gandhi was leaning towards pro-Hindu politics as explained in chapter 4.

As the modern secular narrative that is trying to completely distance Indians from their age-old socio-cultural legacies differs from the one propagated by our traditional secularists, this former narrative can be labelled as 'neo-secular'. To summarise it in one sentence, the goal of this narrative is to prove that 'India is not Hindu; India is secular,' thus juxtaposing Hinduness with secularism. The force that is commonly referred to as 'secular-liberal' is behind this attempt, and it, therefore, makes sense to call this modern secularist force, 'neo-secularist'. It is necessary to understand that this neo-secularism, including the over-obsession with Muslim interests, is miles away from the secularism of our pre-Independence titans like Tagore and Gandhi.

Defining neo-secularism

Before proceeding further, it is pertinent to define Indian neo-secular ideology, which was linked to socialism in the past and has now grown in to a symbiotic relation with the New Left or Wokeism. This ideology is different from our traditional secularism propagated by Tagore, Gandhi, Nehru, Bose and our other pre-Independence icons, for whom pride in our age-old cultural-religious legacies lay at the root of our nationalism. Based on that legacy, secularism for them meant equal treatment of all religious communities. Neo-secularism, however, aims to deracinate Indians from their legacy of several thousand years and supplant it with an unexplainable combination of cosmetic atheist values and minoritism. Thus, by definition, neo-secularism is a distorted and politically motivated version of secularism, which under the garb of navigating the complexities of a pluralistic society, promotes religious minoritism while ignoring genuine concerns of the religious majority. How the neo-secularists exhibit these traits will be explained throughout this book.

Though Jawaharlal Nehru is criticised now as being the father of this neo-secularism, in his mind, he equated Hindus and other Sanatanis with India, and his writings and certain deeds as PM amplify this view. When Nehru decided to modernise Indian society, he brought laws known as Hindu Code Bills only applicable to Hindus and other Sanatanis, and left out Muslims, Christians and Parsis. When E V Ramasamy 'Periyar' instigated his followers to attack Brahmins, Nehru dubbed him a 'lunatic' and wrote to the Chief Minister of Madras (present-day Tamil Nadu) to put Periyar into an asylum. Indira Gandhi tried to amend neo-secular practices in the mid-1970s. The *nasbandi* (sterilisation) campaign was launched during the Emergency, overriding strong objections by the Muslims. Later, P V Narasimha Rao, who was Prime Minister from 1991 to 1996, tried to change the party's image by facilitating the construction of the Ram temple after a communal consensus, but failed. Thus, we can say, though post-Independence Congress was following the neo-secular path, still its direction was nuanced as it did not lost sight of the immediate interests of Hindus.

Meanwhile, from the mid-1980s onwards, when the first fully neo-secularised generation had reached senior and commanding positions in every walk of life, they abandoned the clandestine style followed till then, and openly started asserting hardcore neo-secular ideas. There was stiff opposition to *Vande Mataram;* the Supreme Court verdict on the Shah Bano case was reversed; Salman Rushdie's *Satanic Verses* was banned; and instead of mediating between the communities keeping in mind L K Advani's suggestion of shifting the Babri Mosque a little away, the construction of the Ram temple at Ram's birthplace was vehemently opposed. At the same time, the neo-secularists shouted hoarsely and justifiably against atrocities on Muslims or Christians, but looked the other way if Hindus were the victims. They did this even when three lakh Hindus were driven out of Kashmir Valley by militant Islamists!

Earlier, Hindus were confident that post-Partition 'Hindustan' was essentially for Hindus as opposed to Pakistan for Muslims. They had no problem with secularism as far as it meant equal treatment of all. But, when Rajiv Gandhi and his neo-secularist circle caved into the Islamists who began to call the shots in Independent India just as in Islamic countries, then Hindus began reacting. The demolition of the Babri Mosque was a fierce expression of such a reaction which could have been avoided had the Muslim side been given a push by neo-secularists to come forward to negotiate.

In hindsight, it appears that back then, neither the neo-secularists nor the Muslims had any sense of the 'paradigm shift' that was coming upon them. They challenged Hindu feelings, and now face the consequences.

It was Sonia Gandhi who led the Congress towards complete neo-secularism that eventually brought about the party's downfall. However, she cannot be solely blamed for it, for she was born and raised in a European Catholic family and had no way of knowing the great strength of Sanatan religions. Unfortunately, she was surrounded by neo-secularists, many of whom were brought into the political arena by her husband, Rajiv Gandhi. Others, who were aware of what was happening, like Pranab Mukherjee and Kamal Nath, did not dare to contradict her flawed neo-secular faith. Although Manmohan Singh was not a neo-secularist, his government from 2004 to 2014 displayed an overt anti-Hindu stance, and, as a result, the Hindu nationalist force received a major boost and succeeded in ushering in a thorough change in how Indian society understands and organises reality.

But an opportunity is still there for the Congress to gain a firm foothold back into politics. Modi and his team are now seemingly at the crossroads; they stand bereft of any agenda that can propel the advantages they had gained through this paradigm shift. Team Modi does not know that true Hindutva goes far beyond food habits and ritualistic practices or temple-hopping. It is, instead, deeply rooted in the philosophy and knowledge necessary for guiding mankind forward. As they do not know much about it, neither can they understand the need for inclusion of a secular dharmic philosophy in the educational curricula. Right now, anyone can emerge to challenge the BJP's dominance in the political arena. And if that force goes ahead of the BJP in satisfying certain features outlined in this paradigm shift, it may defeat the BJP.

Reaction against neo-secular cultural subversion

Paul W Blackstock worked for the US Army intelligence during World War II, later specialising in psychological warfare. In 1964, he described 'subversion' as an attack on public morale and commented that 'the will to resist intervention are the products of combined political and social or class loyalties which are usually attached to national symbols.' He was not writing on India, and more importantly, the idea of resisting intervention had still not become relevant to India. But his analysis describes perfectly the Indian resistance that began rolling out two decades later.

Among the cultural subversion that stood out was the

branding of a number of things our pre-Independence greats propagated as 'communal' or 'Hindutvavadi', thereby gnawing at the cultural nationalism based on the idea of an eternal India. Let's illustrate this with a few examples.

Rabindranath Tagore appealed for Hindu unity after the murder of Arya Samaji *sanyasi* and Independence activist, Swami Shraddhanand by an Islamist. Tagore demanded rewriting of Indian history as he said that the history that was (and still is) taught in school was replete with accounts of foreign invaders (from Mohammad Ghori to the British), their wars and achievements, and that there was little on the real Bharatvarsha and its many-millennia-old cultural facets. However, neo-secularists categorise the demands of Hindu unity of rewriting history as 'Hindutvavadi' interventions in education!

Again, Mahatma Gandhi had urged Muslims to chant *Ramnaam* (Ram's name); he strongly believed *Ramnaam* healed diseases and he firmly believed that cow worship was one of the greatest contributions of the Hindus to the world. After Independence, he had warned Muslims (whom he had earlier called 'bullies') that they would have to be 'loyal' to India. Gandhi also declared that he worshipped the cow and 'shall defend its worship against the whole world'. Such comments by any politician now will surely be branded as staunch Hindu communal assertions.

Tagore and Gandhi were representatives of the eternal India, and their philosophical guidance was accepted and followed by the masses as well as by top leftist Congress leaders like Jawaharlal Nehru and Subhas Chandra Bose. Bose argued that Hinduism should be propagated to the West and to Africa to portray the richness and greatness of our civilisation. If anyone were to make such a demand today, he would immediately be considered a Hindutvavadi by neo-secularists. Nehru, who has been projected as the father of neo-secularism (often called Nehruvian secularism) in India, was a strong defender of Hinduism, and he believed it was evident that Hinduism is coming down from the days of Mohenjo Daro.

Nehru once said that 'politics and religion are obsolete,' and had added, 'the time has come for science and spirituality.' Spirituality, broadly speaking, is an individual's search for the Ultimate Truth and for the sacred meaning and purpose of life. It fits in with the essence of Hinduism and Sanatan Dharma. If you belong to the neo-secularist brigade, you would definintely call Nehru, a Hindutvavadi.

Our Constitution experts asked the Indian state to ban cow slaughter and implement a Universal Civil Code, ideas that the neo-secularists abhorred and objected to. Our first Constitution signed by all the members of the Constituent Assembly had our civilisational symbols drawn on it: a Vedic gurukul, Rama's return to Ayodhya, *Geethopadesa* in the Mahabharata, Nataraja, Bhagiratha's penance and Ganga's descent, Chhatrapati Shivaji and Guru Gobind Singh. But later, the neo-secularists began preaching that the Vedas, Gita, Nataraj were all religious symbols and, therefore, non-secular! Shivaji was dismissed as an insignificant ruler who deserved no honour for fighting Aurangzeb, the emperor of India. In short, all facets of our eternal narrative were challenged and altered.

What is mentioned above is just the tip of the iceberg. Many more instances of writings by Tagore, Gandhi, Bose and Nehru are given in chapter 2.

The fundamental point here is—how what was normal and secular before Independence abruptly became communal and Hindutvavadi?

The neo-secularists know if the Idea of India propagated by Swami Vivekananda, Tagore, Gandhi, Nehru, Bose, Aurobindo Ghosh, Bal Gangadhar Tilak and such others ever comes out in the open, their alternative narrative will stand no chance to survive. With the help of a few intellectuals whom they could easily influence, they were able to hide whatever had been said by our great icons that was contrary to their neo-secular ideas. From the 1960s, the neo-secularists have been able to incentivise the entire intellectual class and assert their deep influence over the education system, intellectual discourse and the media. It is now apparent that this devious plan hid many other tentacles—some of these tentacles are identified and explained later in chapter 3.

Neo-secularism was brought, nourished and raised in India by several left-leaning politicians and intellectuals who gradually acquired control over the education system and the media by the early 1960s. They were greatly helped by the spread of Marxist 'pro-poor' idealism and the USSR's emergence as a saviour to India. Eventually, overdependence on the USSR actually crippled India, but it gave the USSR leeway to spend money to control India's political, economic and cultural sphere. Communists everywhere have attempted to distance people from their cultural legacies. So, essentially, the neo-secular narrative was to convert Hindus to anti-spiritual atheists. That is, perhaps, why Sarvepalli Radhakrishnan's suggestion about the importance of including India's religious culture in the academic syllabus was rejected by Maulana Abul Kalam Azad, the first education minister of India.

Further, the neo-secularists strongly opposed reconversion to Hinduism (now popularly known as *Ghar Wapsi*) that was strongly advocated by Swami Vivekananda in an interview to *Prabuddha Bharata* magazine.[1] But, they found nothing objectionable in others converting Hindus, thereby blatantly ignoring Mahatma Gandhi's view:

> This [Christian] proselytisation will mean no peace in the world. Conversions are harmful to India. If I had the power and could legislate, I should certainly stop all proselytising.... It pains me to have to say that the Christian missionaries as a body, with honourable exceptions, have actively supported a system which has impoverished, enervated and demoralised a people considered to be among the gentlest and most civilised on earth.[2]

Thus, evidently, whatever the neo-secularists did had a single aim—breaking Hindus through cultural subversion. Was it not a fit case to raise, as Paul W Blackstock had said, 'the will to resist intervention'? So, it was only natural that it would generate a Hindu backlash at some time in the future.

Neo-secularists of modern times have trapped themselves in cultural subversion in such a way that they no longer understand why Indians are not voting for *roti-roji* (bread and job). It propels them to think that people have turned 'communal'. The narrow vision of these rootless neo-secular leaders and intellectuals has deprived them from understanding that for the Sanatanis of this land, socio-religious-cultural legacies are as important as, if not more, than practical and mundane issues. For thousands of years, battles have been fought and lives sacrificed for protecting both our material possessions and the cultural-religious values of *sanatan samaj* (traditional society). Our history is replete with examples of people laying down their lives for protecting even their local temples.

After having lived through several such episodes spread over several hundred years, a large section of Hindus in the current century, feel that their legacies will not be safeguarded by neo-secularists. This awakening is altogether different from the anarchic mentality that brought down the Babri Masjid in 1992. In this new awakening, the internet has played an important role, as this technological wonder opened up sources of knowledge, thus demolishing the iron grip of neo-secularists over media and public discourse. It allowed a growing number of people to realise the nature and extent of damage done by the neo-secularists. What they want now is to go back to pre-Independence narratives of the Idea of India, nationalism and secularism. Being aware of the situation, and taking conscious decisions, more than half of the Hindus latched on to the ruling front despite facing hardships. This section who voted for the NDA even in 2024, and another section that might have abstained from voting as they did not approve of Narendra Modi's hubris or confrontational attitude, represent the traditional Sanatanis of the country, who attach equal or more value to their cultural legacies.

Dynamics of national aspiration and populism

Conventional thinking has missed another important point about the phenomenal rise of the BJP since 2014.

In the 1990s, during the first phase of the rise of the party, when its vote share arose from less than 10 per cent to 25.59 per cent in 1998, the BJP was led by A B Vajpayee and L K Advani, both integral to the national political elite. Their 6-year-long tenure was rooted in regular, business-type governance. So, they did not lay claim to any advantage of anti-establishment politics. Their success, too, was limited, both by the vote percentage and by longevity. By the 2009 general elections, BJP's vote share had come down to less than 19 per cent, confirming the end of the Vajpayee-Advani era.

But, in 2014, as Narendra Modi came up as the new

leader, the vote share suddenly jumped up to 31 per cent. This newcomer at the national level represented an anti-elite populist force. News about corruption scandals during Manmohan Singh's regime had by then made the people anti-elite, and in vast fields of northern, central and western India, Modi brought home rich yields from his non-elitist image. Later, his anti-corruption drives targeted at Opposition leaders broke the established impunity of the elite class, particularly the political elite, and expanded his populist appeal.

Modi's populist approach attracted the common folk who till then felt that their concerns had never resonated with the established political elite. In the Indian context, the neo-secularists (with their pro-minoritarian approach) had no connection with the masses. Perhaps they could have connected with the masses if they were rooted in the dharmic philosophy with which the masses always associated, consciously or subconsciously. Team Modi stepped in and took full advantage of this situation, attracting more and more people into their fold over the last ten years by attacking the 'fake secularists'. The new regime even utilised hate politics at times, though in limited geographical areas, thus carrying on the legacy of the Gujarat carnage of 2002 in a muted form.

Ironically, dharmic philosophy is in, itself, an antidote to hate politics. Dharmic philosophy tells us to work consciously in accordance with the Laws of Creation which is always focused on whatever protects and allows all elements of creation, whether people or the whole planet, to flourish. Dharmic philosophy further adds that dharmic acts will always be rewarded, while anti-dharmic or *adharmic* acts will be punished. So, whether in private or public life, hate must be targeted at perpetrators of adharmic acts, and to none else.

But populist politics cannot survive for long if they do not fulfil popular aspirations. Team Modi has worked consciously for creating this connection. Thus, another major facet of the paradigm shift is that it reflects the aspirations of the people, mostly of the younger generation below forty, to see India emerge as a strong, achiever nation. The younger generations believe in peace, but appreciate hitting an attacker with ten times more force; they are proud of India's past, and are ready to work for the glory of the nation; they believe in secularism, but will not tolerate appeasement politics or anti-Hindu attitudes (like being silent when lakhs of Hindus are being uprooted from their land—this silence then is viewed as encouraging the attackers). Modi, initially made some wrong moves—like going to Pakistan to appease an enemy nation—but he finally managed to win over a large chunk of the younger generation.

To some extent, these aspirational dynamics are futuristic by nature, and is associated with all the people who have worked to make India great, irrespective of their religion, caste or creed. Two such great figures to which all aspirational Indians are indebted are Homi Jehangir Bhabha and APJ Abdul Kalam. Both were not Hindus. In a broader sense, it is associated with all the people who make us proud and hold the Indian flag high in different fields—such as in science and technology, literature, philosophy, games and sports, industry and business. Their achievements have allowed Indians to rise as a confident nation, and people now want politicians who are bold enough to lead this resurgence of India, which in 1000 CE was the world's largest economy, accounting for 29 per cent of the global economy, according to a study by Angus Maddison.

In the political field, this resurgence began with Indira Gandhi's legendary victory in the 1971 war that successfully split Pakistan, the enemy in the neighbourhood, and sent out a subtle message that India could defeat even a nation protected by the mighty West. Following this, the audacious leader gave the green signal for a daring nuclear test in 1974, defying the world. P V Narasimha Rao planned a follow-up nuclear test, but had to back out as the US had learnt about it. Finally, the Vajpayee government followed up the nuclear programme with a second and more advanced test, and it was with him at the helm that India defeated Pakistan at Kargil. This helped him to bounce back in 1999 after his thirteen-month-old government had been toppled. But the same Vajpayee lost the next election in 2004 when he failed to serve exactly those constituencies that are propelling the paradigm shift now.

The point being made here is that fulfilling the aspirations of Indians for making India strong has been an idea that has been consistently rewarded since the 1970s. In contemporary times, aspirational Indians do not have faith in Opposition leaders, as they appear too compromising.

Let us consider three examples of such compromises:

First, during the last years of his reign, Manmohan Singh seemed overly interested to visit Pakistan to sign a peace deal, which was vetoed by the army as the proposed deal included demilitarisation of Siachen, which meant withdrawal of the Indian Army from the area.[3]

The UPA government was going to compromise core national interests, in the illusion that Pakistan, who was sponsoring terrorism in India, could be trusted. In contrast, Modi followed Indira Gandhi's footsteps and resorted to a surgical strike and took other measures to hit Pakistan.

In the general elections of 2014, the Congress had reached its lowest depths with a tally of less than fifty seats in the Lok Sabha, while the BJP had secured absolute majority for the first time. Again, in 2014, for the first time, the Hindu party secured a vote share bigger than that of the Congress. Why this did not happen earlier will be explained in a later section of this chapter. But for now, let us assume that in 2014, the voters had reacted like this as the election was more about nationalistic aspirations like better economic development (for which Modi was projected as *vikas purush*) and making a 'capable India' that could hit its enemies hard. It soon became a contest between a weak neo-secular government led by Manmohan Singh against the much stronger, pro-Hindu leader with a 'fifty-six-inch chest'. The contest soon became Advantage Modi as he combined populism with two aspects of India's aspirations—rapid economic development that would increase ease of living; and standing firm against evil designs of a neighbour that targets 'Hindustan'. This combination ensured the washout of the Congress.

The second example of the compromise came after the party's dismal performance. When the Modi government came up with a two-pronged strategy of the Citizenship Amendment Act (CAA) to give citizenship to Hindus, Sikhs and Christians who had fled neigbouring Muslim countries and taken shelter in India and updating of the National Register of Citizens (NRC) to identify infiltrators living in India as false Indian citizens, the Congress and other secular parties opposed both, with Mamata Banerjee being the most vocal. However, Banerjee is a regional leader and can be ignored; but this is not so with the national leadership of the Congress. What is striking is that as Opposition leader of the Rajya Sabha in 2003, Manmohan Singh had emphasised in Parliament, the need for exactly such an Act. He had said: 'After the Partition of our country, the minorities in countries like Bangladesh have faced persecution, and it is our moral obligation that if circumstances force...unfortunate people to seek refuge in our country, our approach to granting citizenship to [them] should be more liberal. I...hope that the Hon Deputy Prime Minister (L K Advani) will bear this in mind in charting out the future course of action with regard to the Citizenship Act.'[4]

Some 'invisible forces' reportedly stopped Singh from walking the talk when he became the Prime Minister; finally, when Modi brought the law, Congress opposed it. Their grounds for opposition were that the Government cannot enact laws on the basis of religion. In that case, the Hindu Code Bills passed by Nehru and various Acts conferring minority religions with some special privileges need to be annulled, too. It shows that the Congress and other neo-secular parties were protesting, and passing resolutions in assemblies where they were in majority, only to prevent Hindu refugees from getting citizenship of India.

As for NRC, the original process began in 1951, and has been updated through different mechanisms ever since. No one opposed the process then. Now, it is urgently needed as millions of Bangladeshis infiltrated into India over the last almost fifty-five years. Three Home Ministers of three consecutive decades belonging to three different parties had updated figures of such infiltrators—Indrajit Gupta (Communist Party of India) in the last decade of the last century pegged it at 10 million; Sree Prakash Jaiswal (Congress, Minister of State for Home) in the first decade of the present century pegged the figure at 12 million; and Kiren Rijiju (BJP, Minister of State for Home) put the figure down at 20 million recently. These figures are guestimates, but an indicator of the current reality. These Bangladeshis have secured voter identity cards and Adhaar cards, and ignoring Constitutional Law, Mamata Banerjee, Chief Minister of West Bengal, claimed that all those with voter cards were Indian citizens. In the national interest, the only way forward now is to stop illegal immigrants from voting in Indian elections even as they continue to live in India as permanent residents. Updating the NRC is, therefore, a must. If the Congress continues to oppose it in future too, it will prove itself to be a compromising and anti-Hindu political force interested only in enhancing its Muslim vote bank. It will lose further ground among nationalists and secular Hindus.

The third example is the opposition to the abolition of Article 370 in Kashmir. It was a Jana Sangh/BJP issue from the beginning, and one needs to remember that when the article was invoked, it was meant to be a temporary measure. But the neo-secularists cried themselves hoarse against revoking the Article; they moved the Supreme Court where they lost.

The voters endorsed such bold and nationalistic moves by Modi. Despite the 2016 demonetisation drive that turned out to be a bewildering *faux paus* which failed to unearth black money as was originally intended, in 2019 the BJP's 31 per cent vote share in 2014 grew to 37.36 per cent. Seats increased by fifty. Along with that, the NDA vote share rose to a formidable 45.3 per cent, a clear pointer that the BJP had a grip on the hearts of the people. In those five years, no major Hindutva agenda was pursued and no major communal riot with death toll in double digits had erupted. After the 2019 victory, the Modi government abolished Article 370 and implemented the CAA just before the 2024 elections, when Modi returned for the third time despite Covid-19 woes and unemployment blues. However, as a whole, the Modi government's effort on the aspirational front has now slowed down, and its national vote share has plateaued. The severe post-Pulwama attack on Pakistan was not planned, but came as a chance opportunity.

It needs to be mentioned here that earlier 'Modi's charisma' theory had sold well. The BJP was consistently securing larger chunks of the vote share in the Lok Sabha elections than in assembly elections in its stronghold states. It was happening because of two factors: the aspirational issues related to the national government and not to the states, and the fact that the state Congress leadership is often much less neo-secular than the central leadership of the party. But now, even that trend is changing. Compared to the 2022 assembly elections in UP, the NDA's vote share came down by 0.3 per cent in the 2024 general elections, while the SP and its coalition parties and Congress contested together and increased their vote share by 4.69 per cent. In Assam too, BJP's vote percentage fell by more than 2 per cent in the Lok Sabha 2024 elections than in the 2021 assembly elections. In Karnataka, the BJP+JD(S) vote percentage went down by 3 per cent in 2024 Lok Sabha elections than what they secured in the 2023 assembly elections when they had fought separately. In West Bengal, BJP's vote percentage between 2021 assembly elections and 2024 Lok Sabha elections was almost similar. The remarkable change was in Maharashtra NDA's vote share which increased by a whopping 6 per cent in the 2024 assembly elections (49.3 per cent) when in the Lok Sabha polls, it had been 43.55 per cent just a few months earlier.

In a way, the aspirational aspects about pride in the past and intended glory for the future are a continuation of the cultural nationalism of our pre-Independence greats. But if cultural nationalism can be generous and pacifist, a free nation has to be vigilant and defend itself from enemies such as a rogue Pakistan and a belligerent China. It should have zero-tolerance for the enemy's evil designs. When the Modi Government's and BJP's outlook is juxtaposed with that of the present Congress and the neo-secular brigade, a stark contrast emerges. The confident new

Indian, particularly the one who is below forty-five, does not like the timid lot who cannot hold aloft India's tri-colour. They would rather choose someone who can retaliate against Pakistanis for their wickedness and contain China, as well as keep internal trouble-makers in check. They were happy that even after rather harsh measures like abolishing J&K's special status, the Modi government was able to snuff out 'boycott' politics in Jammu and Kashmir in the 2024 assembly elections. But Pakistan has not shut down its terror factory, and the 2025 attack on the tourists at Pahalgam, targeting only Hindus, shook India once again. But, the post-Pahalgam attack by India deep inside Pakistan that once again proved India's ability to defang Pakistan's Air Force, has added to the confidence of a resurgent India.

Thus, the paradigm shift that propelled BJP's electoral success in 2014-2024 has less to do with political Hindutva, and more with fulfilling popular aspirations for making India strong. If this aspiration is labelled 'Hindutvavadi', then Indira Gandhi too was one, for it was she who stoked this aspiration in 1971 when she bifurcated Pakistan, and then dealt with Khalistani disruptions boldly. What both Indira Gandhi and Modi followed may be termed 'pro-Hindu and pro-majority politics', but the truth is that every strong nation follows similar policies.

The more the BJP government's shift away from politics based on religious symbols or ritualistic behaviour, the more they will make India strong and great. This will unwittingly strengthen the narrative of a 'Cultural Bhartiyata', which essentially is pride in the heritage plus aspirations of India to make the nation great again. This narrative will suppress Cultural Hindutva and will emerge as the true successor of Cultural Nationalism of Tagore, Gandhi and other pre-Independence icons. However, to be firmly on the path of 'Cultural Bhartiyata', Indians will have to imbibe dharmic philosophy and Upanishadic concepts, which are the most ancient and the loftiest ideas the world has ever known.

Neo-secularists contradict 'BJP is communal' slogan

The paradigm shift does not endorse communalism, but rejects the false propaganda that 'BJP is communal'. What people want to know is that if neo-secularists dub BJP as 'communal' citing the 2002 Godhra Gujarat riots, then how can they spare the Congress that planned and executed the 1984 Sikh genocide? How can we differentiate between two situations when in both of them, a community was targeted instead of the perpetrators and supporters of a crime?

Let us attack the subject from another angle: Except for the Congress, which now struggles to get even a 20 per cent vote share in the general elections, all other political parties and leaders have joined hands with the BJP and its predecessor, the Bhartiya Jana Sangh at different times. The neo-secularists of the present century—the late Mulayam Singh Yadav, Laloo Prasad, Mamata Banerjee, Naveen Patnaik and so on—have or had been in alliance with the Jana Sangh or BJP in the past. A lot of secular leaders, who spared no words against L K Advani after demolition of the Babri mosque, later joined the NDA or the BJP itself. This list includes George Fernandez, Nitish Kumar, Ram Vilas Paswan and Yashwant Sinha. Dismiss them if you think they are unimportant, but you cannot discard the likes of Ram Manohar Lohia, Jayaprakash Narayan and Biju Patnaik. Let us analyse what their attitudes towards BJS/BJP were.

Lohia was the architect of the first Opposition unity effort in 1967. After assembly elections in that year in different states, the Opposition parties, including Jana Sangh, formed governments in nine states. A decade later, with Jayaprakash acting as mentor, all the major anti-Congress parties merged to form the Janata Party in 1977. The Janata Party's electoral arrangement or the government it formed after defeating Indira Gandhi's Congress was also supported by the Left. In this government led by Morarji Desai, apart from two Deputy Prime Ministers Jagjivan Ram and Charan Singh, there was A B Vajpayee as the foreign minister and L K Advani as the information minister; Biju Patnaik was steel minister, and George Fernandez was communication minister. Among the second rung leaders of this Janata party were Mulayam Singh Yadav and Laloo Prasad.

The Janata Party broke down in 1979, and those parties who had merged into it reappeared as separate entities. The BJP appeared in 1980 as the new avatar of Jana Sangh. Another decade later, even after the BJP-initiated Ram Mandir movement, the Janata Dal ensured seat-sharing with the BJP and the Left in the 1989 Lok Sabha elections; V P Singh's government, too, was supported by both the BJP and the Left.

Yet another decade later, various politicians joined the NDA governments led by Vajpayee at different times or formed alliances with the BJP in their states. The three most prominent among them are three long-term Chief Ministers: Nitish Kumar (nineteen years), Mamata Banerjee (fourteen years) and the now-dislodged Naveen Patnaik (twenty-four years). Among others who became partners of the BJP were George Fernandez, who vehemently objected to former Jana Sangh members still keeping RSS membership during the Janata Party days. But, two decades later, in 1998, he had no qualms in being Vajpayee government's Defence Minister. All these show that dubbing the Jana Sangh or BJP as 'communal' is a matter of political convenience.

The trend continues till today. Two old allies of the BJP were Shiv Sena and the Akali Dal. Eventually, the Akali Dal parted ways with the BJP on the issue of farmers' discontent in 2020. The Shiv Sena that claims credit for the demolition of the Babri mosque left the alliance in 2019 on the issue of chief ministership, and joined the Congress-NCP alliance, though later, a large chunk of it broke away from Uddhav Thackeray and returned to the NDA fold. The neo-secularists cried hoarse when BJP formed governments by weaning away parties from the Opposition fold, but welcomed the defection of Shiv Sena that had previously won seats in alliance with the BJP in 2019. The Shiv Sena joining the Opposition further evidenced the fact that even now dubbing a party 'communal' is just a political weapon as long as a party remains a rival.

The people of this country are aware that the 'BJP is communal' is a matter of political convenience. The same flock that joined hands with the BJP at different times, later criticised it as 'communal' when they switched to the other side. It is not only about political conveniences, but it is plain political dishonesty to deceive voters through propaganda. Let us examine two other examples of such lies associated with the 'BJP is communal' propaganda by neo-secularists.

Neo-secularists had always projected that the BJP butchered Muslims while the Congress protected them. As mentioned earlier, this was busted by none other than senior Congress leader Salman Khurshid at an AMU event in 2018. The students had asked him to react to a series of old controversial communal riots in Hasanpura, Maliana, and Muzaffarnagar under Congress rule. Khurshid had said, 'I am telling you. We are ready to show the blood on our hands so that you realise that you too must not get blood on your hands. If you attack them, you are the ones who would get stains on your hands.... The Congress has Muslims' blood on its hands.'[5]

In chapter 4, the Congress's record in dealing with perpetrators of different riots, with particular emphasis on the 1969 Gujarat riots that were replicated in 2002, will be discussed. The question that the AMU students asked, and the answer that Khurshid gave and later defended emphatically, punctured the narrative that Congress was a protector of the Muslims.

The same is true about BJP being anti-Dalit while Congress is their protector. In this context, let us recall what Ambedkar said on 27 September 1951 after his resignation from Nehru's cabinet:

> I can refer to hundreds of cases where people from the Scheduled Castes round about Delhi and adjoining places have come to me with their tales of woes against the Caste Hindus and against the Police who have refused to register their complaints and render them any help.... But what I want to know is, are Muslims the only people who need protection? Are the Scheduled Castes, Scheduled Tribes and the Indian Christians not in need of protection? What concern has he (Nehru, the then PM) shown for these communities? So far as I know, none, and yet these are the communities which need far more care and attention than Muslims.... I could not contain within myself the indignation I have felt over the neglect of the Scheduled Castes by the Government.

If Ambedkar's quote is too old, check what Kumari Shelja said in 2013 after visiting the family members of a Dalit youth who was mysteriously run over by a train while in police custody: 'Is it a sin to be a Dalit in Haryana? If Dalits are not safe and the government does nothing to protect them, it is clear that it's a sin to be a Dalit in the state.... In recent years, several incidents of atrocities on Dalits were reported in Haryana. But the Hooda (Congress CM) government made no serious efforts to protect them.'[6]

It amply proved that the attitude of high-caste Congress leaders towards the Dalits was no different from the BJP's upper caste leaders.

No wonder that gradually a large section of the Dalits saw through the lies of the Congress-led neo secularists, and have started voting for the BJP. Always neglected and victims of atrocities, this segment has become aspirational now, and that too bears a sign of a resurgent India. However, the rural distress that the Modi government failed to address has gained ground, and many voters shifted away from the BJP in the rural areas of certain states, including Dalits. But, they may still return to the BJP if the Modi government addresses their concerns properly.

Amidst such a lie and communal tag, the Jana Sangh/BJP never changed track. Even when in the Janata Party, BJP leaders had refused to give up membership of the RSS, a politico-social Hindu organisation popularly considered as BJP's mentor. The Janata Party eventually formally split on this issue of 'dual membership'. During 1980-1985, when Vajpayee as president of the BJP announced Gandhian socialism as the party's ideology, most of the BJP leaders, including Vajpayee himself, still continued to be RSS members. The BJS/BJP was always a Hindu party, and all parties had joined hands with it at different times, including the Dravid parties like DMK and AIADMK.

Meanwhile, the BJP gained in strength, both vertically and horizontally, thanks also to the help provided to it by some non-Congress parties who refer to it as 'communal'. Thus, it sounds ridiculous when dwarf intellectuals and political leaders of today refer to the revolutionary-turned-Hindu Mahasabha leader and Hindutva intellectual Vinayak Damodar 'Veer' Savarkar or RSS leader M S Golwalkar as fascists and communal. Both Savarkar and Golwalkar were respected figures for the

BJS/BJP leaders both in the past and in the present. Renowned secular leaders like Ram Manohar Lohia, Jayaprakash Narayan and Vishwanath Pratap Singh took the lead, respectively in 1967, 1977 and 1989, to bring BJS/BJP together with other secular parties, including the leftists.

In 1977, when almost all the opposition non-Left parties amalgamated into a new entity called Janata Party, the BJS was its main driver. Out of the 295 seats won by the Janata Party that year, the largest chunk—ninety-three seats amounting to 31 per cent of the MPs came from the erstwhile Jana Sangh. Several socialists and others worked with members of the Jana Sangh in the Morarji Desai cabinet, and the government was supported by leftists (except CPI, who supported the Congress). Again in 1989, the VP Singh government survived its short life span with support from both BJP and the Left. So, till 1990, a Hindutvavadi force was not considered an enemy, and neo-secularists allied with them in times of need. More importantly, BJS/BJP was not considered as a force acting against our Constitution by tall, post-Independence leaders like Ram Manohar Lohia, Jayaprakash Narayan, Morarji Desai, Charan Singh, Jagjivan Ram, Madhu Dandavate, EMS Namboodiripad and Jyoti Basu.

What does this information boil down to? If BJS/BJP is communal, it was always so; if BJS/BJP was the lone slayer of the Muslims, it was always so; if BJS/BJP is anti-Dalit, it was always so. CPI(M)'s first general secretary, P Sundarayya was against joining hands with the Jana Sangh in 1967, but he was overruled by the party and in protest, he resigned from his post. This tradition of hanging out with BJS/BJP continues till today, and whenever a party has to fight the might of the BJP, it dubs it as communal. With the Opposition now facing the juggernaut of a Modi-led BJP, the 'BJP is communal' campaign has reached new heights. But, it will not cut much ice.

Before concluding this section, it must be pointed out that though the Congress never joined hands with the BJP, it always had a love-hate relation with the BJP and the RSS. Top Congress leaders often paid respect to top Hindutvavadi leaders like the Hindu Mahasabha's Veer Savarkar and RSS founder, Keshav Baliram Hedgewar. As Savarkar's birth centenary was being planned, in a message Indira Gandhi wrote, 'Veer Savarkar's daring defiance of the British Government has its own importance in the annals of our Freedom movement. I wish success to the plans to celebrate the birth centenary of the remarkable son of India.' This was in 1980, and back then, a lot of Congress leaders from Maharashtra were associated with this centenary celebration. Thereafter, thirty-eight years later, in 2018, an impeccable secular Congress leader and former President of India, Pranab Mukherjee, joined an RSS function after retiring from politics. He called for reconciliation of differing interests, for being pluralistic, and paid homage to Hedgewar, describing him as 'a great son of Mother India'.

So, stalwart Hindutva idols were 'remarkable' or 'great' sons of India according to both Indira Gandhi and her close follower, Pranab Mukherjee, though they were aware that reclamation of original sites of temples at Ayodhya, Kashi and Mathura was always on the agenda of Hindutvavadis.

Further, it is not that secular parties can produce any credible evidence that the BJP is a communal party. If they had any, it could move the Supreme Court and ban the BJP, as no communal party can participate in elections in 'secular and socialist' India.

The word Hindutva, which means Hindu-ness or essential features of Hindu religious culture, is being widely misused by the neo-secularists in a different and distorted sense of a radical and exclusivist political ideology. True that Savarkar used the term for his political convenience; but why the neo-secularists adopted and propagated it is a riddle. It seems that being ignorant of the true meaning of Hindutva, the neo-secularists have unwittingly stepped into a trap. An increasing number of Hindus are now embracing Modi's BJP assuming the party represents Hindutva, which is not true as Hindutva stands for inclusiveness, plurality, and maximum personal freedom.

But, if the secularists try to put forward the argument that only BJP is anti-Muslim, they would have to answer certain questions: Why is it that in the Indian Army for the last seventy years, Muslims form an insignificant minority of about 2 per cent? Why were the chiefs of three wings of the armed forces always been non-Muslims barring one exception, Air Chief Marshal Idris Hasan Latif who headed the IAF from September 1978 to August 1981? Why have the IB or RAW chiefs always been non-Muslims, except for Syed Asif Ibrahim? Why even neo-secular parties do not give proportional, winnable seats to Muslim candidates? Even in Bengal, where Muslims constitute 30 per cent of the voters, the TMC has only 5 Muslim MPs out of a total of twenty-nine; and nationally the Congress has only 9 Muslim MPs out of ninety-nine whereas Muslims are nationally 14 per cent of the population. Finally, why are Muslims among the poorest of the communities along with the Dalits and Adivasis? Many other points can be added to this list, and all those will prove that the attitude of all parties towards Muslims has always been the same.

Why is a paradigm shift occurring now?

Key socio-economic and psychological factors

According to sociologist Judith Kapferer, the state must bear the responsibility of protecting civilisational values in society 'including the cultural/aesthetic values that enhance the quality of life and maintain its legitimacy.'

So far, we have read how cultural and aesthetic values of Hindus and other Sanatanis, in particular, and the nationalists in general, were being trampled upon by neo-secularists ever since Independence, initially in a clandestine manner, but more openly in the second half of the eighties decade. We have also analysed the consequences that followed such attacks on Indian civilisational values. A question arises: Why did not any reaction coalesce in the sixties, like it did in the nineties, and more importantly, why did it fail to band together the majority of Hindus to reclaim their cultural legacies, like they eventually did in 2019 (when the NDA vote share rose to almost 45 per cent).

The answer lies in the sub-structural factors of society (stage of socio-economic-scientific development, cultural consciousness and the level of psychological potency of the people). Given that cultural consciousness was higher earlier than now (as constant hammering by neo-secularists affected it), we can detect a clear correlation between growth of socio-economic-scientific strength of the nation and the intensification of the reaction. As the nation crossed newer milestones in socio-economic and scientific-technological-military developments, the psychological confidence level of the people received a major boost and they reacted more vehemently than before.

The ban on cow slaughter was one of the most prominent cultural values of the Hindus, and after Independence, they thought the demand would be fulfilled as the Muslim population was down to 10 per cent. However, Nehru, and then Indira Gandhi, refused to budge. Thereafter, it snowballed into a major crisis on 7 November 1966, on *Gopashtami*, when lakhs of pro-ban activists gathered in Delhi to press their demand, together with a large number of *sadhus*.

Though, the protest began in a festive mood, keeping the festival in mind, things went haywire when some of the sadhus led by Jana Sangh MP Swami Rameshwaran decided to march towards the Parliament building. As security forces tried to stop them, chaos ensued. Police firing, large-scale damage of property, and ransacking of the homes of some Congress MPs marred the day, with the crowd turning into anarchists for a few hours. Seven demonstrators were killed in the police firing (though unofficial figures claim that many more deaths occurred). A policeman also died in the clashes.

Initially, Indira Gandhi took a belligerent stand and she ordered the arrest of all the leaders of the protesters, including the sadhus and Shankaracharyas. She also sacked pro-Hindu Home Minister, Gulzarilal Nanda. Then, as the days and weeks passed by, she started backtracking. She formed a committee (that never submitted its report) to consider a national legislation banning cow slaughter, incorporating in it M S Golwalkar, the second *Sarsanghchalak* or chief of the RSS. Soon after, on January 5, 1967, she recommended the states to consider enacting their own laws on ban of cow slaughter. One after another, the vast majority of states, including those ruled by the Congress, eventually did so, except for Bengal, Kerala and a few tiny states and Union Territories that accounted for a total of seventy-two Lok Sabha seats out of 545. The rest of the states had either completely prohibited cow slaughter or else restricted it severely to protect *gaumata* within the next two decades. Even Jammu and Kashmir, the only state in India where Muslims are in majority, banned cow slaughter by a law enacted in 1989. Even this took almost twenty-five years from 1966, the year that saw an outburst of Hindu anger. Finally, a landmark judgement delivered by a seven-judge bench of the Supreme Court on 26 October 2005 upheld the constitutional validity of anti-cow slaughter laws by various state governments, thereby putting a full stop to the debate.

That cow slaughter is now banned in about 87 per cent of the Lok Sabha constituencies of India, in itself demonstrates the political heft and popular support behind the demand. But, even in 1966, at a time when memories of the Partition killings and the mayhem created by the Muslim League was still fresh in the minds of so many millions of Indians, the slaughter ban movement did not escalate into a major agitation like the Ram Mandir movement did almost a quarter century later. Rather, the agitation died down within a few weeks.

The Bharatiya Jana Sangh (BJS) was in the forefront of the movement, but it could not reap any rich dividends except for consolidating its urban base in northern and western India. It only helped the BJS to emerge, vote percentage-wise, as the second force, but even that was not enough to cross the 10 per cent mark of vote share.

The question that has not been answered till now is why, despite having a similar agenda, the Hindutva forum's previous avatar Jana Sangh which existed from 1951 to 1977 could never get more than 10 per cent of the total valid votes polled, while the BJP, formed in 1980, crossed the milestone of 25 per cent vote share in 1998; then jumped to 35 per cent vote share in 2019. It seemed that as the nation developed and exhibited its strength, Hindu reaction too turned more resolute, and made strong overtures to establish that 'India is Hindu'.

We have to remember that from the very beginning, the Jana Sangh's agenda, like that of the BJP, was confrontational. The common political demands of the two entities, not always documented, were:

- Abolition of special status of Kashmir
- Making legal provisions for a Uniform Civil Code
- Banning of cow slaughter
- Reclaiming Kashi, Mathura and Ayodhya

These demands resonated among the Hindus even in the immediate aftermath of Independence. That was why the framers of our Constitution rejected the demand of mentioning India as 'secular' in the Preamble and elsewhere, made the special status of Kashmir a temporary measure, and asked the Union Government to make provisions for a Uniform Civil Code and ban cow slaughter.

But the new nation started its journey differently. Shyama Prasad Mukherjee, the founder of the Bharatiya Jana Sangh, demanded *'ek desh, ek bidhan, ek nishan, ek pradhan'* (one nation, one law, one flag, one Prime Minister). He died in 1953 under mysterious circumstances in a jail in Jammu and Kashmir. Sheikh Abdullah was the then Prime Minister of Jammu and Kashmir. To oppose the state's special status, Mukherjee had entered the state without a mandatory permit, and was incarcerated immediately on 11 May 1953. Just six weeks later, he was dead. The people of India were sad at Mukherjee's death, but they did not react in any notable way. Thereafter in 1959, the RSS, the promoters of the Jana Sangh, adopted a resolution to reclaim the original Biswanath temple of Kashi (now Varanasi) at the site of the Gyanvapi mosque; but even the Jana Sangh did not launch any movement in those days in support of their demand.

The Prime Ministership of Kashmir was eventually abolished in 1965. Then in 1966, Indira Gandhi's police fired upon the sadhus and pro-ban activists campaigning for legislation for banning cow slaughter, as has been previously described, but it did not produce a belligerent reaction like what followed in the nineties. On 30 April 1982, CPI(M) workers killed and burned sixteen *sadhus* and a *sadhvi* of the Anandamarg sect on Bijan Setu in Calcutta, and no one was punished for this heinous act. Even then, the Hindus did not react.

It is quite apparent from these examples that back then, people were not ready to act on a confrontational agenda, though they did take up issues aggressively and abrasively in 1992, the year the Babri mosque was demolished. So, what had changed?

Supporting a confrontational agenda involves a high degree of risk as it may invite different types of sanctions from different parts of the globe, enhancing hardships and misery for people. Such risks can be taken only when the people think their country and their leader can take on the world. In the fifties and sixties, India was weak, both economically and militarily. Back then, we had to beg for food, and survived on PL480. According to *hindubusinessline.com*, late C Subramaniam, the architect of India's Green Revolution, said a US team of experts visiting India in 1964 had predicted that an 'intractable agricultural problem' was in the offing and it 'would lead to the death of millions in the 1970s'. In 1965, during the Indo-Pak war, Prime Minister Lal Bahadur Shastri appealed to the people to 'sacrifice one meal at least a week'.

Technologically, India was at a very backward stage. As the West refused to give us the required technology, Nehru had no other option but to walk up to the USSR, for which India had to pay a heavy price as their influence ended up strengthening a neo-secular ideology. It is true that our scientists, consisting of men and women of all religious and caste denominations, had undertaken a huge effort from the late fifties to propel the nation towards technological self-sufficiency, particularly in certain critical sectors, through which technological advancement was measured. However, the news of such advancements was not disclosed before 1974.

India was in a bad shape as caste and communal tensions continued unabated, and often this had a bearing on the economic conditions of the people. Nehru was critical of the dangerous anti-Brahminical agenda of EVR Ramaswamy, *aka* Periyar, a social reformer from Tamil Nadu and founder of the DMK who championed anti-caste advocacy and spoke about killing Brahmins. To this day, Brahmins remain among the smaller communities of India according to a 2021 Pew Research Center survey, forming just 4 per cent of the population.

In a letter to Madras Chief Minister Kumaraswami Kamraj dated 5 November 1957, Nehru wrote:

> I am much distressed by the anti-Brahmin campaign continuously carried on by E V Ramaswami Naicker (another name for EVR Ramaswamy). I find that Ramaswami Naicker is going on saying the same thing again and calling upon people at the right time to start stabbing and killing. What he says can only be said by a criminal or a lunatic…this kind of thing has a very demoralising effect on the country…. Let him be put in a lunatic asylum and his perverted mind treated there.

Another expression of the caste problem was repression of 'lower' castes that ultimately provoked the Naxalites of the Maoist Communist Centre (MCC) to fight it physically in Bihar with arms, leading to a five-year-long bloody confrontation from 1996 to 2000 with the Rajput private army, Ranvir Sena.

The Naxalites problem first began in Bengal in the late sixties, and was contained there by the then Chief Minister S S Ray. But thereafter, by the eighties, it had spread to many other states.

Meanwhile, the first major communal outburst was in Gujarat in 1969, and then onwards, almost every year, communal tensions shook the nation regularly, and in a few major riots, the death toll has crossed the 1,000 mark. Among the bloodiest have been the Gujarat riots in 1969, anti-Sikh genocide in 1984, the Bhagalpur riots in 1989, Bombay riots in 1992-3 and the Gujarat riots in 2002.

In the early years, the Indian Army was weak. It conceded one-third of Kashmir to Pakistan in 1948, and the entire Aksai Chin, all 38,000 square kilometres to China in 1962. From a neutral viewpoint, the 1965 war with Pakistan was interpreted as having ended in a stalemate. Back then, India had neither money nor technology to upgrade the strength of the army, navy or air force. Even in 1965 and in 1971, Pakistan had sophisticated fighter planes like F86F Sabre fighter jets and F104 Starfighters. Comparatively, India had inferior fighter planes. It was also believed that back then, the Pakistani Army was better trained and better-equipped than the Indian Army. Moreover, the dread of the Muslims of Pakistan, who had displayed the worst of their aggressiveness and brutality towards the Hindus and Sikhs before Partition, was still fresh in Indian memory, and this severely impacted their psychological strength. The only success story in the first two decades after Independence was the liberation of Goa.

India was a new nation and still struggling from the depleted state that the British had left her with. It was weak both economically and militarily, and its image did not instil much confidence in the minds of the people to take up a confrontational agenda to assert their great cultural legacy.

However, a daring Prime Minister suddenly metamorphosed the weak, timid Indian landscape magically in 1971. Indira

Gandhi launched a war, ostensibly against the atrocities that West Pakistanis committed in East Pakistan, which had millions of refugees, mainly Hindus, fleeing to India. But obviously, what was happening in East Pakistan was Pakistan's internal matter. Indira Gandhi's real reason for waging the war was to defang Pakistan, a roguish neighbour dangerous for India's existence ever since its inception. But Pakistan was a US ally (though it had formally withdrawn from SEATO in 1968), and both the USA and Britain sent warships to teach India a much-needed lesson. However, the USSR's naval force intercepted their movement and tamed the fleets, providing India with a window of opportunity to deliver a quick and crushing blow to Pakistan, compelling its commander in East Pakistan, Gen Amir Abdullah Niazi, to surrender with his 93,000 soldiers on 16 December 1971.

With that, a new nation, Bangladesh was born even as the world looked on, stumped at India's temerity. All through this high-stake operation, Indira Gandhi not only proved India to be much mightier than Pakistan, but by uprooting the enemy from the eastern border, made India safe, strategically. Pakistan was humiliated, shaken, and defanged, and its protector, the mighty West was left speechless. Several theories did the rounds back then, including some suggesting that a plan to break Pakistan was drawn up long before 1971, and Indira Gandhi led its execution at an appropriate time.

Indira Gandhi soon followed this decisive victory with a nuclear test in 1974. A nuclear device was detonated with a yield of 12-13 Kiloton of TNT on 18 May 1974 at Pokhran, at an army test range located in the deserts of western Rajasthan. It was iconic in the sense that it was the first instance of a poor developing nation's act of defiance against the nuclear monopoly of the UN's P-5 nations. The plutonium used in the test was prepared in the Cirus reactor provided by Canada, who now froze the nuclear energy assistance agreed upon previously for building two more reactors. The P-5, consisting of China, France, Russia, United States and United Kingdom, reacted by forming the Nuclear Suppliers Group in the same year to check nuclear proliferation. Its main target was of course, India.

These two developments—the 1971 war and the 1974 nuclear test—brought out in the open, the hidden might of India that had been built carefully over the previous two decades and uplifted a hitherto weak nation to the stature of a truly developing, daring and upcoming one. It gave the Indian psyche a major boost. Almost magically, the 'Yes, we can' mentality gained root, occupying centre-stage in the geo-politics of South Asia. Moreover, it gave the Indian psyche a major boost as the 'enemy' was crushed. The two developments marked the first stage of change in the socio-psychological-cultural makeup of the nation.

But, even back then, it did not produce any belligerent 'Hindu' reaction, perhaps for three reasons. First, the vehicle of change was the Indira Gandhi-led Congress which was in power, and not the proclaimed Hindutvavadi Bhartiya Jana Sangh. Second, the belligerent Muslim fundamentalist forces, were now decidedly quiet. Third, Indira Gandhi and her son, Sanjay Gandhi, could take the lead in furthering the nationalistic and non-discriminatory secular agenda. They launched the *nasbandi* (sterilisation for population control) campaign, ignoring Muslims' objections on religious grounds, and spearheaded the demolition of several illegal colonies (including those of Muslims) in Delhi, thereby assuring the people that the reins were in the hands of leaders who were nationalist and not anti-Hindu. These developments indicated the end of the appeasement era.

Though Hindus, too, had reacted against the atrocities

committed by the ruling party during the Emergency in 1977, they condoned Indira Gandhi fast enough and brought her back into the saddle in less than three years after she had lost the elections. The development indicated Hindus had a soft corner for her and for Sanjay Gandhi as well, as it was he who led the 1980 election campaign along with his mother. However, he died tragically in a plane crash in June 1980, barely a few months after being elected.

Indira Gandhi was riding on a wave of sympathy, and this was further buttressed by her strong stand against the separatist Khalistani militants that culminated in Operation Blue Star. This was also the time when the first signs of revolt in Kashmir, leading to Maqbool Bhat's hanging, became perceptible. Indira Gandhi stood by the Hindus of Kashmir and warned the Muslims to be nationalists or face consequences. This is etched out in detail in chapter 4.

Till 1984, Indira Gandhi herself had played the role of protector of Hindu and Hindutva, while the BJP in its initial days under Atal Bihari Vajpayee's leadership had taken up Gandhian Socialism as its ideology. So, the people discarded the BJP and blessed Indira Gandhi's son, Rajiv with nearly a 50 per cent vote share in the 1984 elections held just two months after Indira Gandhi was assassinated by her Sikh bodyguards on 31 October 1984.

It is rumoured that even the RSS network voted for Rajiv Gandhi to show respect to the martyred Prime Minister. However, under pressure from his neo-secular peer circle, Rajiv Gandhi surrendered before Muslim fundamentalism on the Shah Bano case and allowed the banning of *The Satanic Verses.* These acts were seen by the Hindus as a clear departure from true secular practices, and thus instigated them to go against the

Congress, initiating a process that brought down the party's vote share to less than 20 per cent in 2014 from 49 per cent in the mid-eighties. Meanwhile, Rajiv Gandhi attempted to balance out his actions by showing that he was also sensitive to Hindu culture. He opened the gates for *Ramayana* to be telecast from the third week of January 1987 on Doordarshan, rejecting the argument that telecasting a 'Hindu' epic on the national channel was non-secular. Thereafter, he allowed the *shilanyas* of the Ram temple. But, it was too late, and his efforts could not stop the first significant rise of the BJP (from merely 2 seats in 1984 to eighty-five in 1989 with an 11.36 per cent vote share). BJP, by then, had also taken up the Ram Mandir issue. Of course, the coming together of the Janata Dal, BJP and the Left parties to defeat the Congress in 1989 helped the BJP to cross the 10 per cent mark for the first time.

Meanwhile, by the late eighties, India had come out of its worst fears. The country's economic condition was steadily improving. The food crisis was over and poverty rates were falling even in rural areas. In science and technology, including in other strategic sectors, the country was on an upward trajectory. Militarily, the groundwork done from then has enabled us to gain such superiority that stunned strategic analysts in 2025, when India decimated Pakistan's resistance in just three days, forcing Islamabad to seek Washington's help to stop India.

With preliminary attempts at decontrol initiated, from 1980 to 1989, the economy grew at an annual rate of 5.5 per cent, a distinct jump from earlier times. Industry grew at an annual rate of 6.6 per cent and agriculture at 3.6 per cent. Experts put this down to a high rate of investment that was propelling this better economic growth. Though a balance of payment crisis was looming, internally India was progressing and was in a far better shape than it was in the sixties.

This improved economic and socio-cultural status gave a further boost to the psychological makeup of the common man, inspiring the first rebellion of Hindus. No wonder that the entire mass that prided themselves on being the inheritors of India's rich cultural heritage and dreamed of a strong, resurgent India now began drifting away from the Congress as it failed to serve as a vehicle of change since Indira Gandhi's death. Though the Janata Dal was initially the biggest beneficiary of this drift, it too tried to divide Hindus on caste lines, and its implementation of the Mandal Report to ensure OBC reservation was soon perceived as an instrument to empower only the Yadavs, the dominant caste in UP and Bihar. In about twenty-five years since then, 'Mandal' completely lost out to 'Kamandalu', as the BJP became the apparent vehicle of change, acquiring long-term dynamism to re-mould the Indian polity.

In 1991, Hindus both from northern and western India started rallying around the BJP, helping its tally of eighty-five seats in 1989 to reach 120 in 1991, with its vote share crossing the 20 per cent threshold for the first time. The party had made a mark for itself and was now recognised as the main Opposition party and the second-largest party after the Congress in the Lok Sabha. The initial signs of the paradigm shift were now visible, but hardly anyone could put a name to it, much less recognise it. The demolition of the Babri mosque also worked as a major distraction. But the sub-structural factors mentioned earlier motivated a large section of people throughout the 1990s to veer towards the party that stood for resistance to the cultural deracination process. What strengthened it further was the economic reforms initiated by P V Narasimha Rao, yielding the first results as the Indian economy began growing faster, allowing more spending on technological advancement and on the social sector, and encouraging Indians to mark their footprints internationally by showing their ability to adapt to the era of information technology.

The weak and wounded nation born in 1947 had metamorphosed into a strong-willed one, ready to take on any adversary and march towards pre-eminence, by the mid-1990s. The nationalist Hindu movement, too, was steadily growing, but it was still not big enough to catapult the BJP to power, and so the party compromised on its agenda, giving up all confrontational points to attract more allies. The pro-Hindutva population supported the effort, for they too were eager to install a Hindu party at the centre to carry forward their agenda. So, after making a futile attempt in 1996, voters once again installed a BJP-led government in 1998, and then again in 1999. But over the next five years, Atal Bihari Vajpayee did little to re-establish the eternal narrative or 'Idea of India' in statecraft, and failed even to show the promised 'zero tolerance' stance on terrorism. The constituency lost faith in the BJP once more just as they had done in 1984, allowing a 10-year-long Congress regime to step in.

The point here is that the BJP did not seem to get votes for being BJP or for its leaders' image; it was getting a large share of votes because of its adherence to a nationalist Hindu agenda.

While the Manmohan Singh regime had an anti-Hindu posture, it continued its reform agenda, helping the Indian economic journey slowly spiral towards the top. In 2014, India was on the cusp of emerging as a real great economic power. It entered the club of the ten largest economies that year, and ten years later, it is the fifth largest economy of the world. India has found its place in various multilateral and minilateral economic and security forums, and is striving to become part of an alternative global supply chain. Its defiance of vested interests and search for a multi-polar world has earned it respect throughout the developing world.

India now also holds the potential to act as a bridge between the North and South, and as the world is all set to miss the UN Agenda 2030, India alone has the potential to suggest innovative, acceptable and sustainble models of development in a post-2030 world. Along with these achievements, it can even boast of having the capability to contain mighty China, besides being able to give a befitting reply to the far more developed Canada, for harbouring and encouraging Khalistani terrorists. So, naturally the focus of Hindutva politics is shifting towards a broader agenda.

With every phase of a major achievement, the Indian psyche has changed and become more confident and aspirational. Till the time of Indira Gandhi, the Congress could serve these aspirations. Thereafter, with India acquiring further might, the BJP got a chance to serve as the vehicle of change, but let it slip. The Congress government that served the nation after it, from 2004 to 2014, however failed miserably to recognise the resurgent India, and paid a heavy price. Thus, the BJP came back again when India was ready to emerge as a superpower-in-the-making. The present stage of paradigm shift, a move forward from Hindu nationalism to a more comprehensive nationalist Hindu agenda, is thus propelled by the socio-economic-strategic strides that India has made in the last two decades.

The rising confidence levels among Indians is not restricted to the political field alone, but has been seen in several other fields of life, too.

Take for example the game of cricket that is beyond popular in India. Indian cricketers till the sixties generally played a timid game, except for Mansoor Ali Khan Pataudi, but that was by virtue of his being a 'nawab' brought up in England. But in the seventies, along came Sunil Gavaskar, who was not awed by the dominant white players of developed countries at that time, and gave it back to them. In the nineties came Saurav Ganguly, who challenged the white teams on perfectly equal terms and made his defiance known across the world by taking off his jersey at Lord's. The Indian team had by then, amassed the courage of answering sledging with sledging. Finally, in the present generation of players, we have Virat Kohli, who always manages to assume a proactive role in dominating his opponents.

The rise of Virat Kohli in cricket or Narendra Modi in politics is the function of the same social dynamics.

Weakening the Congress to turn it anti-Hindu

As we study the phenomenon of a paradigm shift in Indian politics, we must remember that neo-secularism never had a solid, monolithic structure. From the beginning, it had different factions within it, and a large part of the Congress, including Jawaharlal Nehru, Indira Gandhi and P V Narasimha Rao refused to be an essential part of hardcore neo-secularism. Thus, in the last century, the Congress represented a form of nuanced neo-secularism: While it tried to erase the Idea of India and the great Hindu heritage from the minds of the people, it also often came forward to protect the Hindu interest, like modernising the community, expressing strong sentiment against divisive caste politics, allowing the states to ban cow slaughter and so on. Further, it was still a nationalist force.

At a practical level, denying Hindus any knowledge of their religion in schools or colleges was a divisive policy. It meant that while Muslims and Christians and other minorities would learn about their religion in *madrasas* and missionary schools, the Hindus would turn completely ignorant about their glorious religious-cultural heritage as they could not have their own Hindu educational institutions. This design was planned and executed by the intellectuals affiliated to CPI and the leftist clique within the Congress with active prodding by the USSR. How it was done will be explained in detail in the third chapter, and that will show how a new narrative was imposed on India after a total blackout of a part of the writings of our pre-Independence icons.

Though Congress was neo-secular, it was neither the brain behind neo-secular ideology, nor did it accept all tenets of neo-secularism in the last century. The real brain was the undivided CPI from Independence to 1964, and then onwards CPI and its offshoots like CPI(M) and the Naxalites, who could not stand any association with Hindu identity. How, over the decades, these radical neo-secularists attracted others into their fold is an interesting story.

Even before Independence, the communists had a large sway over many of the Congress leaders, as being leftist was fashionable in the days after the Bolshevik Revolution in 1917. The dreams of an egalitarian society where no one remains poor or deprived, and the instruments for achieving it—like a command economy, atheist society and internationalism in the form of unity of the working class all around the world—was revolutionising the thought process of conscious women and men, particularly in the Third World. Thus, the CPI, the only Communist Party in India till 1964, wielded much more sway over the political domain than its real political weight. Its leaders impressed upon many Congressmen to accept its different suggestions. In turn, the CPI was one of the first Communist parties in the world that pledged to work within the democratic system instead of trying to stoke an armed revolution. As they did exactly that in 1951, after crushing a revolt from within, they gained further acceptance.

Next to join the nascent neo-secularist camp were the socialists. Ram Manohar Lohia, the most politically influential socialist leader of the sixties, brought in the idea that Muslims were not to be blamed so much for the Partition. This argument was accepted immediately by the neo-secularists and was propagated widely. The Lohiaties ever since have been following the OBC+Muslim formula for garnering votes, and for that, they pursued appeasement politics more vehemently and directly than the communists or the Congress. This fact, however, strengthened the neo-secular narrative further over the years. By the eighties, the socialists' attempts to unite the Muslim vote for a certain party was held by the media as normal politics, but uniting the Hindu votes became communal 'polarisation'. The Shahi Imam of Delhi issuing a *fatwa* to vote for the Janata Dal, a platform of the socialists and some old Congressmen, became the new normal, while any Hindu religious figure doing so for the BJP was treated as unholy.

Thus, by the eighties, the socialist-communist combination firmly established the radical neo-secular narrative, and following this narrative became the new normal. The Janata Dal splintered in the nineties, giving birth to parties like Samajwadi Party (SP) in UP, Rashtriya Janata Dal (RJD) in Bihar, Janata Dal (Secular) in Karnataka, all adhering to and strengthening neo-secular ideology. Gradually, all the non-Congress parties except the BJP, Akali Dal and Shiv Sena joined the neo-secular camp. The Dravid parties had inherent anti-Brahminical bias, and they had no qualms in joining the camp. Thus, different considerations of different parties—casteism for the socialists, class theory for the communists, anti-Brahminism for Dravid parties—came together to uphold a common theme. In the process, it meant a weakening of the Hindu community.

If we look at the camp now, we will see there are four types of political forces: Communist parties like CPI(M); Socialist parties like SP and RJD; Dravid parties like DMK; and splinter formations of the Congress like TMC in Bengal, NCP in Maharashtra, and YSR Congress in Andhra Pradesh. Congress was always close to this camp, but it also fought attempts that would weaken India and thereby hurt the Hindu community, like stoking class confrontation, stoking casteist sentiments, stoking anti-Brahminism and so on.

Meanwhile, when the non-Congress neo-secular forces coalesced in the nineties, the rise of the BJP, too, had begun. It provoked some of the neo-secularists to switch camp and join the NDA. Again, some left the NDA after it was defeated. Some like Nitish Kumar and Mamata Banerjee have acted according to political convenience all through. Thus, the neo-secular camp grew or shrunk at different points of time from the beginning of this century, but its communist-socialist core (CPI-M, SP, RJD) remained intact through thick and thin. Congress succumbed to the pressure of these hardcore neo-secular camps and took an overt anti-Hindu stand after Sonia Gandhi began to lead the party.

Till the end of the last century, the neo-secular parties attacked the Congress and tried to weaken it, either as a bloc or individually. By the turn of the century, the neo-secularists succeeded to wipe out the Congress from almost 150 Lok Sabha seats in UP, Bihar and Bengal. In numbers, it means that almost a quarter of the political geography of India that was earlier dominated by the Congress, had now passed into the hands of the neo-secular parties. Later, regional parties cornered seats in other states, weakening the Congress further. The remarkable point to be noted here is that for weakening the Congress, the neo-secularists had time and again joined forces with the party that they now term 'communal' and even 'fascist'.

But why did neo-secularists try to weaken the Congress which was the main force against confrontational Hindu nationalism, and why did some of them even join forces with Jana Sangh and its later avatar, BJP in 1967, 1977 and 1989 to bleed the Congress further? The answer is quite obvious. They intended to weaken Congress's monopoly to gain a foothold, so that later they could pressurise the Congress into toeing their line. It was their way to convert the Congress into a complete neo-secular entity. Only CPI, the original Communist party that gradually became its pale shadow after CPI(M) broke away from it in 1964, stood firmly with the Congress in the seventies.

Earlier Congress leaders were rooted in cultural nationalism (as Nehru's 'will' demonstrates) and often made compromises with neo-secular ideas, all the time making sure to take decisions that would protect the Hindus. Nehru's Hindu Code Bills, Indira Gandhi's hand in splitting Pakistan and Narasimha Rao's effort to make way for Ram Mandir through negotiations were all part of the same package intended to protect the interest and serve the aspirations of Hindus. Rajiv Gandhi's decision to allow the laying of the foundation stone of the Ram Mandir, too, belonged to the same category.

In 1992, after the Babri mosque was demolished, BJP's political rise became more palpable. Had the non-BJP parties been serious about fighting Hindu nationalism back then, they could have forged a working relationship with the Congress as proposed by Saifuddin Choudhury, a CPI(M) MP and Central Committee member. But Choudhury, a loner in his own party and in the non-Congress secular brigade, was thrown out of the central committee—the highest decision-making body of the party—for his pro-Congress stance. Later, selfish political interests of non-Congress anti-BJP parties prevented them from supporting the Narasimha Rao-led Congress Party in 1996, when the Congress had won 140 seats and BJP on its own had won 161. A plethora of other parties, attached to neither Congress nor BJP had won more than 200 seats. A third force—a conglomeration of various small parties—ended up forming the government with outside support of the Congress, but it collapsed when Congress abruptly withdrew support. It could barely survive for two years even after a change of prime minister.

In the ensuing 1998 elections, the BJP formed a government with the backing of other parties, but it collapsed after just thirteen months. Sonia Gandhi visited the President of India to stake a claim to form an alternative government, but could not gather a majority as Samajwadi Party (SP) led by Mulayam Singh Yadav refused support.

Thereafter, BJP emerged victorious in the 1999 elections and completed a full term. After this severe jolt, the entire neo-secular brigade including CPI(M) adopted Saifuddin Choudhury's line, and rallied behind the Congress that had secured 145 seats in the 2004 general elections. Here, it needs to be mentioned that Narasimha Rao's Congress had won 140 seats in 1996, but the neo-secularists did not stand by him. The failure of neo-secular leaders to stand by Rao in 1996 gave the BJP its first chance of showcasing its ability to rule the country.

The turf war among the parties belonging to the non-BJP camp was their undoing. Over the past two decades, several of these non-BJP parties had been pressuring the immature leadership of the Congress to adopt neo-secularism, but the fact of the matter was that these parties, too, could not survive without the Congress. Put it down to the myopic vision of its leadership, but the Congress finally surrendered to them and this stance immensely helped the consolidation of neo-secularism and the consequent paradigm shift.

Now Congress is merely a shadow of these neo-secular parties, and is mainly a combination of the SP, RJD and the CPI(M). It attacks industrialists; expresses its anger against the likes of Veer Savarkar whom Indira Gandhi respected; and more tragically, the top leaders frequently contradict Nehru's basic principles of not compromising merit. Instead, Congress now wants to spread the reservation network and has even been demanding a caste census. The demand for a caste census finds echoes in Ram Manohar Lohia's *pichhde pabe sau me shaat* (the Backwards will get 60 per cent) ideology. Ironically, the BJP had earlier utilised the OBC issue to strengthen itself, and now may repeat the game by agreeing to have such a census.

Nehru was against caste-based reservation as it would kill merit which is ever so important for a newly independent nation. Later, when he realised that reservation was spreading its tentacles in the country, Nehru took the initiative to make economic criteria important rather than caste and wrote letters to the states about it. The Congress was, therefore, against expanding the scope of reservation for OBCs, and that is the reason why the Mandal Commission Report of 1980 was never implemented by either Indira Gandhi or Rajiv Gandhi.

The socialists had thrived on caste politics from the time of Independence, and when they were pushed into a corner by the BJP, they convinced Congress's weak leadership to join forces with them. Bereft of any imagination, the Congress now dreams of surviving on a borrowed socialist agenda by rejecting Nehru, Indira Gandhi and Rajiv Gandhi's more balanced views.

This gradual weakening of the Congress and its shift from its traditional ideological line has added momentum to the paradigm shift as the BJP now projects itself as the sole protector of the Hindus. It is what pushed the Congress to its lowest nadir of winning just forty-four seats in the 2014 national elections.

Behavioural evidence of a paradigm shift

In a democracy when two alliances vie for power, and one crosses the half-way mark, it is universally accepted as the end of the game. Even if the leading alliance fails to cross this magical mark, the trailing alliance stands aside and lets the former stake a claim to form the government. This had been the norm in India, too, till 2009, when the Congress won 206 seats, and with its alliance, UPA managed to win 262 seats (still falling ten short of the magic number). However, BJP president Rajnath Singh conceded defeat on the day of counting as the UPA had secured more seats than the NDA, and allowed Manmohan Singh to form his consecutive second government. This is normal democratic practice.

But the impact of the paradigm shift weighed so heavily on the minds of the neo-secular leaders that they forgot about such basic tenets of constitutional democracy in 2024, when the ruling pre-poll alliance NDA cleared the half-way mark smoothly with 293 seats, 21 more than the magic figure. That the BJP, by itself, did not cross the halfway mark like the earlier two times, made the Opposition and their supporting intellectuals over-jubilant, letting them gloss over the fact that they had lost the election for the third consecutive time. The liberal media made it sound almost as if Modi had lost the elections.

Rahul Gandhi did not behave maturely and even stated that the nation had rejected PM Modi and Amit Shah! Mamata Banerjee, another senior Opposition leader and Chief Minister of West Bengal, went a step ahead to claim that Modi and his Home Minister Amit Shah should resign! The Opposition even dreamed of forming a government by weaning away partners of the NDA. Unfortunately for them, their overtures were immediately rejected by the non-BJP NDA partners. Then, just a few days later, Mamata Banerjee lost her cool and said on the ABP Ananda TV channel that the government Modi was going to form was 'undemocratic and unconstitutional', and that the BJP had not emerged as the 'single largest party'! What the Opposition leaders were trying is anybody's guess.

For the record, in 2024, the BJP had contested 441 seats out of a total of 542, and won 54.42 per cent of this tally, or more than half the seats it contested. It left 129 seats for its partners, who won fifty-two of these seats, or less than 50 per cent.

Twenty-six parties had come together to form the I.N.D.I.A. grouping in a rare show of unity across the length and breadth of India except for Bengal, Kerala and Punjab. But despite this show of unity, I.N.D.I.A. could win only 240 seats and secured 41.8 per cent vote share, while the NDA romped to victory with 293 seats, securing 44.3 per cent of the vote share. The rise and fall in number of seats is a common phenomenon in a democracy. What made the Opposition and the many intellectuals who supported them forget this simple math in 2024? It was the heavy burden of working in an environment where their neo-secular partners were being rejected continuously, as a result of which a section had already moved to the BJP. What clouded their vision all the more was their inability to understand why they were losing the elections time and again.

If we analyse this further, we will find that the imbalance displayed by the Opposition in the immediate aftermath of the election results sprang from two deep psychological factors. First, without any understanding of the nature of the paradigm shift, they still believed in old, conventional ways. There was a report in *Hindustantimes.com* in which Nitin Gadkari claimed that he had been approached earlier by an Opposition leader, offering support to make him Prime Minister. This was an impossible attempt to break the BJP at the national level, for a national party cannot be split unless a crisis makes it hollow from within. Such an attempt thus reflects desperation, immaturity, and lack of rational thinking on the part of the Opposition.

Second, the fear of their ragtag 'I.N.D.I.A.' front going topsy-turvy had made the neo-secular leaders a little disoriented. Given Narendra Modi and Amit Shah's tendency to use the state machinery including investigative agencies selectively, it was mere political necessity that forced AAP, born out of anti-Congressism, to gravitate towards the Congress. However, its normal space in Indian polity is that of a third force—both anti-BJP and anti-Congress—for it has to fight both these parties to grow. Further, AAP's soft Hindu stance gives it scope to open a channel with the RSS, Hindutva's mother organisation, though BJP will always try to scuttle it. But, if AAP can grow, it may emerge as a second front of the Hindutva Brigade in the future. Another important ally, the Shiv Sena (Uddhav faction) was one of the oldest allies of the BJP, and still remains a Hindutvavadi party. Mamata Banerjee's TMC had also been an ally of the BJP in the past and seems more against Amit Shah than the BJP. The point is that there is no ideological cohesion on the I.N.D.I.A. front, and it may splinter if the BJP regains its majority in the next general election.

The neo-secularists are still following the conventional path of politics and have failed to understand that a new India, a generation of confident Indians, proud of their past and present, is rising. The generation up to age forty-five, wears this new face of resurgent India and the sooner the Opposition parties understand this, the better for them, as it will make them reject that unfounded hope they live on and enable them to see reality clearly.

Endnotes

India is a different country from the rest of the world. Despite it being 2025, it has not given up its ancient core socio-cultural-religious values. Unfortunately, the present generation of Indians, both young and old, were not taught about India's rich heritage in their school curriculum. So, truncated and corrupted ideas (like Muslims are our enemy) often surface as Hindutva, and dominate the political space.

The present paradigm shift, as explained so far, is driven by socio-economic and psychological factors. Its manifestation in the political sphere has benefitted the BJP as it stood against the neo-secular forces who tried to impose an anti-Hindu narrative in the name of secularism. This paradigm shift, however, has much less to do with divisive ideas, and much more with the revered cultural past spanning thousands of years and common futuristic aspirations (a combination that has been labelled here as Cultural *Bhartiyata*). The shift represents a break from established orthodoxy, but it has not found the ground yet to realise the pluralistic and inclusive dharmic teachings of the past. The BJP-RSS leaders or cadres are not aware of the pluralistic culture of Hindu and other Sanatani streams, as they too were not taught about it. It creates a vacuum as political Hindutvavadis have less faith in pluralism, while the neo-secularists harp on a construct that is alien to India.

Meanwhile, the Opposition is still trying to weaken the BJP by using conventional methods, and failing. The propaganda that the BJP is communal does not cut much ice with their sympathisers as all the non-Congress Opposition parties have aligned with it at some point in the past, and many Congress leaders, too, have expressed reverence to BJP-RSS stalwarts. BJP is, of course, a Hindu party, but if it is to be branded as communal, then Congress cannot escape the epithet either, as its hands too are stained with the blood of both Muslims and Sikhs. The CPI(M) has the blood of Hindu *sadhus* on their hands. The Akali Dal, AIMIM and Muslim League are also religion-based parties, but not communal. Communal elements, however, linger within all parties operating in India. Thus, the 'BJP is communal' campaign is not harming, but rather, strengthening the Hindu outfit.

But, this 'BJP is communal' propaganda has created a fear psychosis in the minds of Muslims, and when the BJP is trying to eliminate the undue advantage accrued to the Muslim community due to appeasement politics, a section of the community is showing increasing belligerence (apparent during the anti-CAA movement). This is happening at a time when globally, and in neighbouring Pakistan and Bangladesh, Islamic jihadist efforts are afoot. Unfortunately, the Muslim community, which is bearing the brunt of the faults of neo-secularists, is still being instigated by some Hindu leaders of the Congress and regional parties like the TMC in Bengal and CPI(M) in Kerala. The neo-secularist political leaders are, in the process, projecting them as anti-Hindu, further strengthening the BJP.

However, despite being the main beneficiary of the change, Narendra Modi has not yet gone for initiatives such as teaching school students the grand narrative of India, encompassing its ten-thousand-year long social, cultural, philosophical and economic journey with stress on its dharmic philosophy and pluralistic society espoused by our ancient *rishis*. Still, the trajectory of the paradigm shift strongly suggests that India has entered a mature phase where mixing religion with politics through Hindu symbols (like reclaiming Kashi, Mathura and other temples) will not yield any high political dividend any more. The BJP used Ram to unite Hindus as a political force, and thereafter adopted a strong nationalistic line. This shift succeeded in bringing more than half of the Hindus under the umbrella of the NDA.

To think logically about the present development, we need to understand that the paradigm shift is a reaction to the three cardinal faults of neo-secularists: (i) Censoring the idea of India of our pre-Independence greats from the national discourse and education system; (ii) Supplanting the narrative of Cultural Nationalism with a facile USSR-sponsored neo-secular narrative; and (iii) Imposing neo-secular governance in the present century. The goal of all these faults was the same—to create a new normal in which Tagore-Gandhi's idea of India would have no place.

As the present paradigm shift ensues from the triple fault of the neo-secularists, examining these faults will enable us to decide how we can liberate ourselves from the dual danger of our times: the dominance of either a disruptive narrative that seeks to deracinate Indians from their socio-cultural-*dharmic* past, or from a truncated version of Hindutva (Hinduness) that is non-inclusive and non-pluralist.

First Fault

Wiping out the 'Idea of India'

Adam Smith, the father of classical economics, was, for long, stamped as the proponent of the idea that 'greed is good'. But, an untruth never triumphs. Smith worked for several years on his pet theme of impulse of virtue in the actions of human agents. He was a moral philosopher at the University of Glasgow. It has been unearthed finally that his 'Wealth of Nations' was a sort of superimposition of a philosophical concept on the economic arena. His effort was far, far away from any attempt to glorify 'greed'. It was a sort of disinformation spread by using his name by those who wanted to establish that 'greed is good'. Thus, after a more-than-two-century-long abuse of Adam Smith's idea, the truth has come out to assert itself.

Throughout civilisation, the less worthy have tried to exploit the thoughts of our great thinkers, often presenting their ideas in a skewed manner to serve their petty ends. The neo-secularists of India, went far ahead in their malicious attempt to change the Idea of India established by our greats: They completely suppressed half of their writings and speeches, the half that negated the secularism they pursued, and propagated only that bit that would pop up their narrative.

How did they manage this? Here is a simple example: Let's take the following statement at face value: 'If the Muslim community joins the task of making India a strong and secured nation, there cannot be any ground for having any grudge against Muslims.' Now if you delete the part of the sentence before the comma, it fits in perfectly with the neo-secular narrative. In the same way, if you block some paragraphs of an article or some articles or some chapters of books written by Tagore, Gandhi or Nehru, the rest will fit in with their neo-secular agenda.

The ugly attempt of neo-secularists to change India's civilisational narrative was deliberately aimed at wiping out all memories of India's ancient teachings and glorious heritage. They left no stone unturned to push out of circulation those portions of the teachings of our pre-Independence greats that stood in stark opposition to their present, false narrative. Their aim was to make the present generation of post-Independent India forget their past and look up to Western values, teachings and culture as ideal. It was literally by design that generations of post-Independence Indian schoolgoers grew up dismissing everything ancient like yoga and Ayurveda and mindlessly aping the West.

The writing and teachings of our pre-Independence greats—Tagore, Gandhi, Nehru and Bose are relevant here. This list excludes Vivekananda, for he was a Hindu monk and present neo-secularists may discard his teachings and suggestions on that ground. He, however, was considered as the father of Indian nationalism by all pre-Independence greats though his definition of the Indian nation was of 'a union of those whose hearts beat to the same spiritual tune'.[1]

Highlighted in this chapter are some extracts from the writings and speeches of Tagore, Gandhi, Nehru and Bose that neo-secularists would instantly brand as Hindutvavadi or right-wing thoughts. All four had, at times, expressed their angst against the Muslim community, yet they were not anti-Muslim. They were not ready to pardon the belligerence of the community that ultimately led to the Partition.

They also criticised Hindus and especially the parochialism, casteism, and as Tagore noted, the 'non-violent non-cooperative' attitude that alienated Hindus from the outer world. More importantly, though for them Bharatvarsha was majorly a Hindu Bharatvarsha (the Hindus comprised 75 per cent of the population at that time), and Indian culture was rooted in Sanatani culture, they were strongly against targeting people of other religions. They were also not against recognising or assimilating outside elements (from the time of Ghori to the British), so long as those were not antagonistic to India's ancient culture. As a practical politician, Nehru condemned Indian communists as they were disconnected with the real Bharatvarsha and its thoughts, ideas and philosophies, but he was also not averse to accepting and assimilating the egalitarian approach of Karl Marx.

So, these great thinkers and leaders had many facets to their personality, and they must be presented as such. Their nationalism was based on their pride in Bharatvarsha's past, but they were neither isolationists nor jingoists.

The point is that these four thought leaders have suffered great injustice in our hands over these last seven decades, and it is time to resurrect them in their totality. For this reason, only small portions of their writings will be quoted in this book to unwrap other dimension of their writings that the neo-secularists have carefully kept hidden from public view. All that was needed was to wade through their entire volumes of writings to call the neo-secularists' bluff regarding these icons, and precisely that has been done here.

Tagore: Alert defender of Hinduism and Hindu unity

An article in the *Indian Express* of 8 May 2023, serves as a glaring example of the present generation's ignorance about our cultural heritage. The article was on Samarth Ramdas and proclaimed that 'various right-wing organisations have claimed that Ramdas was Shivaji's mentor and played a key role in his rule'. It was greatly amusing as the authors seemed quite oblivious that such a list of right-wingers would include none other than Rabindranath Tagore, the greatest of all intellectuals who advocated India's renewal.

Tagore in his poem *Pratinidhi* described a day when seeing his guru Ramdas begging from door to door, Shivaji was immensely irritated. He wondered why the *rajguru* should go begging when he lacked for nothing in his own home. So, Shivaji donated his entire kingdom to his guru, hoping Ramdas would not have to go begging. Ramdas accepted the donation and then asked Shivaji what he would do from then on. Shivaji replied that he would happily sacrifice his life in the service of his guru. Ramdas initially took the king with him begging from door to door, and then ordered him to rule the kingdom, not as a king, but as his *pratinidhi* (representative). It is mentioned that Tagore got the idea of this poem from Harry Arbuthnot Acworth's English translation of *Maratha Ballads*.

According to this poem, it was Ramdas who instructed Shivaji to make his attire, the saffron robe, the flag of his kingdom.

Let's discuss our national anthem. The neo-secularists being so sensitive about mixing religion with statecraft, would have come out strongly against it if they had read the full poem, the first stanza of which is now our national anthem. Here are the first lines of the third stanza:

Patan abbbhuday bandhur pantha,
yuga yuga dhabita yatri
He chirosarathi,
taba rathachakre mukharita patha dinratri
Daruna biplab majhe, taba sankhadhoni baje, sankata dukkhatrata

Translated, this reads:

Through the arduous path of the rise and fall,
the passengers are walking on from aeons
Oh, eternal charioteer,
the sound of the wheels of your chariot
resonates in the path
days and nights
In the midst of fierce upheaval,
your conch shell resounds,
the saviour from crisis and miseries.

It denotes that the whole poem is dedicated to the 'eternal charioteer'. Every Indian knows the charioteer, who can lead us through an eternal journey, and whose conch shell saves people during great upheavals, refers either to Shree Krishna or Brahman, the Supreme Being mentioned in the Upanishads. This follows that India's national anthem is dedicated to God as the eternal guide of India's civilisational journey. Nehru and other learned persons at the time of our Independence knew this; and still chose it as the national anthem as they believed in the ancient culture of Bharatvarsha.

Now let us evaluate Tagore's rejection of history textbooks, the tone and tenor of which has not been changed yet. In his 1903 article, *Bharatvarsher Itihaas,* the first Asian Nobel laureate strongly demanded rewriting of Indian history. He said:

> The history of India that we study and write in examinations after learning it by rote is only a nightmarish story of the dark nights of Bharatvarsha. Why? Because, some people came from somewhere, blood and gore followed, tussle started between fathers and sons, between brothers.... If one group somehow left, another came up—Pathan, Mughal, Portuguese, French, British, all combined to make this nightmare even more complicated over time.

He deduced:

> The real India cannot be envisaged if seen through a clouded prism of this blood-stained evolving dream sequences. Where were the Indians in it? These histories cannot provide any answer to that, as if Indians were not there, only those who resorted to clashes and hostility existed.

Perhaps, no further scathing attack can be made on our history textbooks that are being strongly defended by neo-secularists, who are opposing demands of rewriting history and dismissing it as a 'Hindutvavadi' initiative.

In this article, Tagore, who was addressed as Gurudev (the teacher) by Gandhi and Nehru, answered the question he raised: 'Where were the Indians in it?' It seemed from the history text books that Bharatvarsha was not there, and that only the roaring Mughals and Pathans were wandering from east to west and north to south. Tagore further wrote:

> But when the foreign (*videsh*) dominated, there did exist the country (*desh*), otherwise amidst all such turmoil who gave birth to Kabir, Nanak, Chaitanya, Tukaram? It was not that in those days there were only Delhi and Agra, but also Kashi and Nabadwip. The life stream that was flowing around that time

in the real India, the waves of efforts rising, the social changes happening, we don't find any description of those in history.

He commented that we are 'connected to that India that is external to our text books'. And then, in a more sombre note, he added, 'If our age-old connection with it is eliminated, our heart will not find a refuge.'

Tagore emphasised that our roots lay in Kashi (Varanasi, the 'eternal city' that had nourished our culture for thousands of years) and in Nabadwip (where the Shree Chaitanya-led Bhakti movement evolved), and places like those. So, was he Hindutvavadi? Again, Tagore categorised the invaders from Mohammad Ghori to the British as 'foreigners', and emphatically pointed out that we Indians are not 'shrubs and parasites' of this land, but 'our hundreds and thousands of roots grown through many, many centuries have occupied prime position in India.' He also lamented that while in many fortunate countries history reflects the essence of their nation, our history did not portray our nationhood. Rejecting our history textbooks as history of the darkest time of India, he wrote:

> '...in that darkness, the gems of the dancers glow in the lights of the nawabs' amusement palaces, the nawabs' wine glasses' reddish foams appear like frenzied bright eyes; in that darkness our ancient temples cover their heads, and the white marble decorated burials of fiancées of the sultans sets out to kiss the star-light.'

In simple terms, he categorically said the history that depicted Muslim rulers' wealth and might was not our history.

Such bold statements in this regard from the present right-wingers are hard to find. However, nobody could even think of calling Tagore a 'right-winger' in his days, not even Nehru, the secular icon of today. Even, he called him 'gurudev' (the teacher).

In the same article, *Bharatvarsher Itihas*, Tagore castigated those educated Indians who raised questions such as 'What do you call the (Indian) nation, where is it, where was it?' Tagore provided an answer to this that gives us deep insights into the eternal narrative of India. He argued that history was not of a singular type. If someone busy with writing the biography of Rothschild was asked to write the biography of Jesus Christ, he would first scout around for his account details, then look for office diaries and so on. After failing to get these, he could develop a sense of neglect about Christ, and might well say, 'Why write the biography of a man who did not have even a paisa'!

The way Tagore explains the cultural nationhood of Bharatvarsha by giving such a simple example, cannot be made any better. He stressed heavily on the point that India is not just about its kings and monarchs—it is more about, as Tagore said at the beginning of this article, Varanasi and Nabadwip. In other words, as Tagore explained in other articles, India is a unique nation, a cultural nation that has 'formed our inner nature', and it is not something that can be understood by the western elite. In fact, in *Bhartavarsher Itihas*, Tagore further cautioned that if we try to distort 'the way Bharatvarsha has formed our inner nature,' then we will not only fail but be embarrassed. The neo-secularists tried to distort 'our inner nature', and have been left embarrassed.

Tagore himself, in another one of his articles written in 1913, *Bharatvarsher itihasher dahara*, gave an idea about how to write the history of India, and he began his own narration from the time of Ram. The unfortunate part is that no one followed his narration even after Independence, perhaps out of fear that the neo-secularists would be upset.

Tagore, and our other greats, did not grudge the presence of Muslims in India, but they were aware that followers of Islam were aggressive and Muslims were not prepared to live along with the Hindus. The two-nation theory was first propagated by Sir Syed Ahmed Khan, the founder of Aligarh University. So, our pre-Independence titans sounded a note of caution to alert the nationalists about the nefarious designs of Islamists.

It must be acknowledged here that Tagore was a great idealist. He could not neglect the reality and decided to be candid about it. He wrote in a letter to Kalidas Nag:

> There are two religions which shows aggression against all other religions. These are Christianity and Muslim religions. They are not satisfied with following their religions, but they try to kill other religions. For these reasons, there is no other way to mingle with them except accepting their religion. About the Christians, one advantage is that they are vehicles of modern times; their mind is not hemmed in by the boundaries of the Middle Ages. Religion does not cover their entire life.

Gandhi and Nehru, too, were scathing in their criticism of Muslims. But all three—Tagore, Gandhi and Nehru did not spare the Hindus either. In the same letter to Kalidas Nag, Tagore mentioned that Hindus, too, were bound by the walls of religion. But the difference was, he pointed out, that Hindus were not aggressive and their attitude towards other religions was that of 'non-violent non-cooperation'. So, Hindus naturally kept Muslims away, and when they called Muslims to come out for the cause of the nation, the latter declined to join the movement. It shows how neutral and direct Tagore was.

Tagore had explained that when religious feelings are hurt,

the pain stays for centuries. He cautioned that whatever was achieved by sheer force, would cause a rift. In his article, *Japan Yatri* written in 1919, he wrote:

> In Delhi, where amidst the heart of ancient Hindu king's feats the Qutab Minar stands erect like the spectre of ego, or in Kashi (Varanasi) where Aurangzeb had established a mosque to insult the *puja* of Hindus, there I cannot notice beauty or welfare. But when I stand before the Taj Mahal, it does not call to mind the point whether it was a feat of Hindus, or Muslims. Then it appears as an accomplishment of human beings.

This historical perspective prompted Tagore to criticise Hindus who did not unite against foreign invaders even when their temples were demolished. It was this disunity that allowed foreigners to occupy India. This fact was painful for the great poet, for even in his time, Hindus comprised 75 per cent of the population, and their weakness reflected the weakness of the nation. In an article on Hindu social reformer, Swami Sharadhananda (compiled in the book *Kalantar*) shortly after his assassination by one Abdul Rashid on 23 December, 1926, Tagore wrote that our country has so many:

> ...miseries because the number of those who have the right to take up the vow of *satya* (truth), and who have the strength to observe the vow by offering their lives, are just a few. When the mental weakness is so deep, no need is there to describe how mournful is the death of a *veer* (hero) like Swami Shradhananda. In history, we have seen time and again that those who offer everything to take up the vow of welfare, on their foreheads, insults and assassinations draw *jaytilaka* (the victory sign) in this way.

Thereafter, in the same article, Tagore admitted that he could not provide a final answer to what was to be done immediately in that situation—should one go for retaliation or try to think about the root cause and find redressal for it? But, as a permanent solution, he suggested:

> Now we must examine where holes and sins within Hindu society are, and must attack those mercilessly.... When Muslims summon Muslim society for some purpose, they do not face any resistance—one calls in the name of one God 'Allaho Akbar'. But today if we give a 'Come Hindus' call, who will come? We have so many communities, small boundaries, so much provincialism. Who will come overcoming all those?

From the very next sentence, Tagore attempted to give a historical perspective of this disunity among Hindus and its consequences:

> So many hazards passed. But we never got united. When, from the outside world, the first harm came in the form of Mohammad Ghori, Hindus did not unite in the face of impending danger. Afterwards, when temples after temples were demolished, the idols were smashed, they fought and killed and got killed as they were disunited. We were thrashed as we were fragmented and we have proved it throughout the ages.... The sins mainly reside in weakness. If Muslims beat us and we accept the beatings meekly, then we should know that it has been possible due to our weakness—we need to overcome this weakness.... If weakness is nurtured, atrocities by others come to occupy the space naturally, no one can resist it.

Tagore advocated Hindu unity in various other articles and in letters written to his dear ones. One such letter was published in *Swastika* on 21 June 1999. The letter was reportedly written to Hemantabala Sarkar on 16 October 1933, and here, worried about the situation of the country, Tagore stated that Hindus were always divided and that was why they were suffering defeats. He juxtaposed them with Muslims who were always united in the face of danger, and concluded that the broken and divided Hindus will not be able to combat Muslims. He even predicted that Hindus will soon be humiliated by Muslims again. About 14 years later, when Tagore was no more, Muslims led by M A Jinnah did exactly so and divided the nation itself.

Can we ignore these points because to the neo-secularists these facts sound communal? Some years later, when discussions were on about the political structure of the state and proposed Communal Award, Tagore said in 1931 in an essay, *Hindu-Mussalman*, that he was prepared to accept Gandhi's formula as Gandhi was the best man to decide on it. Yet, he was also apprehensive of depending on one man's personal tolerance. He wrote:

> It has been agreed upon that the governance pattern in India will not be unitarian, but federal. It means, we cannot go as far where the mark of fixing will not be there at all.... But there still remains a knot....
>
> ...it should not be forgotten that if in distribution of entitlements one side is favoured, then general human nature will not tolerate such injustice, and the disquiet on it will ever remain prone to violence.... It is the human mind. If one string of it is tauted too much, the tune will be lost. Thereafter, despite all invoking of the sake of music, the orchestra is ruined.

If the neo-secularists had not deliberately sent all these writings out of circulation from the national discourse, they could have learnt valuable lessons on the consequences of appeasement from this strong message from Tagore.

These extracts from Tagore's writings, so far, provide us the evidence that certain facts were accepted as facts hundred years ago, and no one found anything objectionable in them. One such fact was that foreign Muslim invaders had demolished many temples during their rule. The superimposed neo-secular narrative in the post-Independence days tried to de-recognise the truth, and that is why people now ask 'what is the evidence of this fact', forgetting that evidence is available in an umpteen number of cases.

Certain observations that Tagore had about religion and culture of India are as valid today as they were back then, and are applicable to both the neo-secularists and to Hindu nationalists. In his article, *Hindu-Mussalman*, Tagore mentioned that though religion was created to unify people, it could soon degenerate into a weapon of exploitation that divided people. As an example, he cited how even non-vegetarian neighbours did not naturally accept the fish-eating Bengalis, while the Bengalis resisted the different rituals of the others. According to Tagore, the Hindu religion with all its rituals was responsible for the narrow-mindedness of people, which in turn led to 'invisible differences' that stem from 'prejudices'. He implied that over time, these prejudices become too subtle, and to that extent, more insurmountable.

We have seen how such prejudices are now being reiterated by Hindu nationalist leaders, including even by the Prime Minister, such as restrictions on eating non-vegetarian food during Navratras. But it is not that the neo-secularists are not resorting to this practice, either. Mamata Banerjee's allergy to the *Jai Shri Ram* chant is also an example of this. Just as Hanuman Jayanti gained popularity in Bengal, several ill-informed

Bengalis swarmed Facebook with posts denigrating it, thereby tarnishing Shri Ram and India's age-old culture of acceptance and inclusiveness. This age-old culture not only allows and encourages hundreds or thousands of deities and subcultures, but also teaches us to be respectful to them. What is referenced in this book as Cultural Bhartiyata represents such inclusive Sanatani values, which are both liberal and secular, and Tagore propagated these all through his life.

Tagore believed that Indian culture is all-inclusive, and one that has accepted and taken within its fold different values and cultures, all from antiquity. But despite that, it needs to establish its 'own system and own discipline for the sake of self-defense'. He believed that India's inhabitants now had to be glued together by one basic idea. He wrote, 'The instrument may come from anywhere, but the discipline has to be India's own, the basic idea should be that of India' (*Bhartvarsher Itihas*, 1903).

Tagore was a proud Indian. In another article, *Atmaparichay*[2], in 1914, he wrote:

> I respect my country from my heart, I have not found any parallel to what is the best of my country anywhere; and so I have never shown any compassion to any dust or garbage that has eclipsed the treasure of our eternal pursuit—here, time and again, my opinion has clashed with my audience and readers.... Where praise and honour is shared according to who is in my side and who is not, any honour from there is untouchable....

Tagore thought the entire Bengali ethnicity was bound by the forces of providence and no power could break it (*bidhir bandhan katbe tumi emoni shaktimaan*). But Bengali Muslims proved him wrong. Just six years after his death, they decided to split from the mainland to create East Pakistan, a Muslim nation. In his poem, *Bharat Tirtha*, where he described Bharatvarsha as a sacred land, he gave the final expression to his faith that all who have come to Bharat—Aryans, non-Aryans, Dravidians, Chinese, Shakas, Hunas, Pathans, Mughals—all have merged into one body, and they will give and take, but will never turn away (*jabe na fire*). Had he been alive in 1947, it would surely have broken his heart to see a sizeable section of Indians deciding to turn away from Bharatvarsha due to their loyalty to their religious identity.

According to Tagore, Bharatvarsha's singular effort through the ages was to forge unity in diversity, and to merge different paths to one destination. When he criticised attacks by Muslim invaders, demolitions of temples and the aggressive behaviour of Muslims, he did so because such behaviour was contrary to Indian culture. When he criticised Hindu society for casteism and for taking an isolationist attitude, or for being parochial and provincial, he did so because it went against the grain of Indian culture. At the same time, he was deeply respectful of our ancient teachings, and many of the poems and songs that he composed reflected this. Only someone who had imbibed the essence of the Upanishads could present songs with lyrics such as *anandadhara bohichhe bhuvane* (streams of joy flow through the universe) or *je rate mor duarguli* (on the night, the storm broke my doors, I did not know You had entered my room).

Symbols of Indian culture, which are inevitably Hindu symbols, were equally important for Tagore. He wrote in his introduction to *Ramayani Katha*:

> Readers must not see Valmiki's *Ramcharit* tale as a poet's creation, but must accept it as the Ramayana of Bharatvarsha. Only then you will properly understand India through Ramayana and Ramayana through India. You must remember

> that Bharatvarsha desired to hear a tale of a complete man's ideal character, and not a glorious historical story, and is listening to it till today with untiring delight. They never said it was too much, never said it was only poetry. For the Indians, their own family is not as true as Ram, Lakshman and Sita.

Again, in a letter to Soumyendranath Tagore, he wrote this about a book on Krittibas by Jogindranath Basu: 'If the young Bengali boys and girls do not read *Ramayana* by Krittibas, then that would bring in our worst deplorable fear.'

In an article (*Rabindranather rashtranoitik mat*) that Tagore wrote to clarify his political opinions after someone toned them down to shield him from public outrage, he penned:

> A lot of influences from a young age stay in life's path till the end, if not directly, its inspiration stays on.... My elders had deep respect for the age-old and universal ideals of Bharatvarsha.... In those days, those who were perturbed by contemporary, formal Hinduism, their minds used to be occupied either by a special mould of European atheism of the eighteenth century or by a tendency to adore Christianity. It is known that my family was always enthusiastic about bringing in reforms based on the best ideals of Bharatvarsha. This enthusiasm, needless to say, shaped my mind in a special mould from my boyhood days.

In another article, written in 1919, Tagore explained that in India and China, society occupied first place, with the state coming below it. It was society that educated students, fed the hungry, provided temples for the pious, and even punished criminals and honoured the greats. The character of the nation, as well as its beauty, bloomed in villages. That was why the nation was not affected by who ruled the state, or who fought with whom, and not even when foreigners occupied the throne. According to him, in a nation where the state was foremost, the nation dies with the fall of the state, just like ancient Greece and Rome did. But the India of the villages remained unaffected by such upheavals as its soul resided in its society. The rule by the westerners during the time of British rule hurt this basic mosaic of Bharatvarsha, and inundated it with miseries, poverty, lack of consciousness and *adharma*.

At this point, Tagore was close to Mahatma Gandhi who was a staunch proponent of *Gram swaraj*. Free India, however, did not pay any heed to these ideas of Gandhi or Tagore. We remain entrenched in the old, colonial system of governance, and have been unable to return all administrative responsibilities to society. Perhaps that is why the neo-secularists could think of changing the narrative using their dominance in the state apparatus that controls education, employment and a large part of social life. Though the panchayat system was introduced to strengthen society's role, greedy politicians have made panchayats and *nagar palikas* insignificant vassals of the state governments, thus killing the ideas of Tagore and Gandhi.

Before concluding this section, it is pertinent to mention something Tagore said on why Hindu-Muslim unity could not be achieved and the problem still vexes us. An article in the *Sunday Guardian* published in September 2020 referred to Tagore's interview in the *Times of India* in April 1924. He had stated:

> A very important factor which is making it almost impossible for Hindu-Muslim unity to become an accomplished fact is that the Muslims cannot confine their patriotism to any one country. I had frankly asked (the Muslims) whether in the event of any Mohammedan power invading India,

> they (Muslims) would stand side by side with their Hindu neighbours to defend their common land. I was not satisfied with the reply I got from them.... Even such a man as Mr Mohammad Ali (one of the famous Ali brothers, the leaders of the Khilafat Movement—the compiler) has declared that under no circumstances is it permissible for any Mohammedan, whatever be his country, to stand against any Mohammedan.[3]

This was Tagore, a romantic and a humanist, a nationalist and an internationalist, and an impeccable secularist who never hesitated to tell the truth as it appeared to him. Such allegiance to truth, in his case, emanated from his wisdom of the teachings of our ancient texts that proclaimed *satyameba jayate* (only truth triumphs). He appeased neither Hindus nor Muslims, and was always critical about Muslim leaders putting their *quam*, global community interest, above their allegiance to India. Further, he lamented the lack of unity among Hindus, fearing that some day, it would harm India immensely. But, at the same time, he never favoured targeting any community or attempts to establish Hindu dominance; rather he was a 'synthesist' who was open to all ideas and cultural values to make India great.

Gandhi: Traditionalist Hindu with liberal dharmic ideas

Mohandas Karamchand Gandhi, the Father of the Nation, urged the Muslims to chant *Ramnaam*, and firmly believed Muslims should have no objection to chant the name of Ram. However, he was not in favour of forcing Muslims to chant it. Further, he firmly believed that chanting *Ramnaam* healed physical diseases. He believed natural calamities occurred due to human sins. He was firm in his faith that the goal of India was to establish *Ramrajya*, and that *khadi, swaraj* and *Ramnaam* were equally important components of nation building. He felt irritated when some Congress workers saluted him with *Jai Hind* instead of *Vande Mataram*. He was also a staunch defender of cow-worship.

Thus, he would have been a perfect character to be dubbed as 'Hindutvavadi' by the neo-secularists. He was, however, hailed by them as the 'Father of the Nation', and till today every political protest of neo-secularists culminates in a sit-in in front of one of his statues. It may be called the height of hypocrisy. Gandhi was a proud Hindu who believed 'Hindu dharma is like a boundless ocean teeming with priceless gems', and that Hindu dharma is 'a way of life'. He relentlessly advocated that politics must be guided by the framework of dharma. Ironically, it was these concepts that neo-secularists have tried to demolish.

Though Gandhi once called Muslims 'bullies', he was a votary of peaceful coexistence of all religions, and was never in favour of targeting any one particular religion. But his faith in Hindu ideas and teachings was so unwavering that at times he was miles ahead of the most radical section of present-day Hindutvavadis. Let us analyse perhaps the weirdest of his ideas that no rationalist would ever dare to support. Let's also check out instances of his writings that neo-secularists would certainly have labelled as 'Hindutvavadi' if repeated today by anyone.

On 15 January 1934 at exactly 2.13 pm, a massive earthquake shook vast areas of northern Bihar and Nepal, from Purnea in the east to Champaran in the west, and from Kathmandu in Nepal in the north to Munger in the south. At least 10,000 people were killed. In the immediate aftermath, in a rally at Tinnevelly (now Tirunelveli), on 24 January, exactly 9 days later, Gandhi said:

> We who have faith in God must cherish the belief that behind even this indescribable calamity there is a divine purpose that works for the good of humanity. You may call me superstitious

> if you like; but a man like me cannot but believe that this earthquake is a divine chastisement sent by God for our sins.[4]

Then for months, he stuck to this argument in a varied way, referring to it countless times.

To us, this argument sounds illogical and unacceptable. Gandhi, on the other hand, clearly believed in the Karma theory that says bad karma would inevitably invite punishment and good karma would bring in reward. He was fearless about expressing the truth as it appeared to him—a truth that was always based on ancient Sanatani teachings. His statement was contested by Tagore, but even after this rebuttal, Gandhi did not change his views.

Gandhi also defined the sin he had referred to. In a congregation that had gathered to collect money for earthquake victims, he told his audience:

> For me there is a vital connection between the Bihar calamity and the untouchability campaign. The Bihar calamity is a sudden and accidental reminder of what we are and what God is; but untouchability is a calamity handed down to us from century to century. It is a curse brought upon ourselves by our own neglect of a portion of Hindu humanity. Whilst this calamity in Bihar damages the body, the calamity brought about by untouchability corrodes the very soul. Therefore, let this Bihar calamity be a reminder to us that, whilst we have still a few more breaths left, we should purify ourselves of the taint of untouchability and approach our Maker with clean hearts.[5]

So, even to teach Hindus an important lesson, Gandhi used his 'superstitious Hindu self' with unwavering determination. On the following day, 25 January 1934, speaking at Tuticorin,

Gandhi had said:

> I want you to be "superstitious" enough with me to believe that the earthquake is a divine chastisement for the great sin we have committed and are still committing against those whom we describe as untouchables....[6]

Tagore, deeply respectful of India's past and the teachings of Hinduism, was however a rationalist. After Gandhi's speech was reported in newspapers, he dashed off a letter to Gandhi asking whether he had indeed said this or whether he had been misreported in the media. Both Gandhi and Tagore had deep respect for each other, but did not overlook or gloss over the other's folly, as indeed they did with everyone else, whether Hindu, Muslim or Christian. Tagore had said, back then:

> It is all the more unfortunate, because this kind of unscientific view is readily accepted by large sections of our countrymen. I keenly feel the inequity of it, when I am compelled to utter a truism in asserting that physical catastrophes have their inevitable and exclusive origin in certain combinations of physical facts. Unless we believe in the inexorableness of the universal law in the working of which God himself never interferes, we find it impossible to justify his ways on occasions like the one which has sorely stricken us in an overwhelming manner and scale.

Clearly, the two titans clashed on their interpretation of dharma. Gandhi represented human morals bound by a strict and traditionalist religious framework that would appeal perhaps only to the superstitious Hindus, while Tagore represented a pious but modern view of religion (and one that has been labelled as Cultural Bharatiyata in this book). This was definitely a clash of interpreting natural phenomena within a broad Karmic framework. Tagore clearly believed that natural calamity cannot be interpreted in karmic terms, but Gandhi had said, 'We do not know all the laws of God, nor their working. Knowledge of the tallest scientist or the greatest spiritualist is like a particle of dust.'

After this exchange, Tagore did not criticise Gandhi as a Hindu fanatic, although the communists and some others certainly did, including M N Roy. Tagore even vehemently opposed such attacks against Gandhi, and invited him to Kolkata. Can we imagine exactly how neo-secularists will attack tall leaders of the present times lest they make such a comment about a natural disaster? It only proves that in pre-Independence days, even public and political figures were far more tolerant of each other and were capable of a civilised dialogue to sort out their differences.

Gandhi was deeply respectful of Hindu dharma. He wrote:

> Hindu dharma is like a boundless ocean teeming with priceless gems. The deeper you dive, the more treasures you find. In Hindu religion, God is known by various names. Thousands of people look doubtless upon Rama and Krishna as historical figures and literally believe that God came down in person on earth in the form of Rama, the son of Dasharatha and by worshipping him one can attain salvation. The same thing holds good about Krishna. History, imagination and truth have got so inextricably mixed up. It is next to impossible to disentangle them. I have accepted all the names and forms attributed to God as symbols connoting one formless, omnipresent Rama. To me, therefore, Rama described as the Lord of Sita, son of Dasharatha, is the all-powerful essence whose name inscribed in the heart removes all suffering—mental, moral and physical.[7]

At this point, it is natural to think of two questions—first, what was Gandhi's idea of Shri Ram, who the neo-secularists ridicule as an imaginary character of the epic Ramayana, and the second is what Gandhi meant by *Ramnaam* as the 'essence whose name inscribed in the heart removes all suffering'.

Gandhi himself answered the first question while replying to Muslims' opposition to chanting *Ramnaam:*

> I laugh within myself when someone objects that Rama or the chanting of *Ramnaam* is for Hindus only; how can Mussalmans, therefore, take part in it? Is there one God for the Mussalmans and another for Hindus, Parsis, or Christians? No, there is only one omnipotent, and omnipresent God. He is named variously and we remember Him by the name which is most familiar to us.... My Rama, the Rama of our prayers, is not the historical Rama, the son of Dasharatha—the King of Ayodhya. He is the eternal, the unborn, the one without a second. Him alone I worship, His aid alone I seek, and so should you. He belongs equally to all. I, therefore, see no reason why a Mussalman or anybody should object to taking his name. But he is in no way bound to recognise God as Rama. He may utter to himself Allah or *Khuda* so as not to mar the harmony of the sound.[8]

Gandhi argued on this point for months and years, together. He once declared:

> You may say you do not believe in Him. You do not know that but for His will you could not draw a single breath. Call Him Ishwara, Allah, God, Ahura Mazda. His names are as innumerable as there are men. He is one without a second. He alone is great. There is none greater than He. He is timeless, formless, and stainless. Such is my Rama. He alone is my Lord and Master.[9]

Gandhi's politics was also based on Ram. For forging Hindu-Muslim unity, he changed the original *Ramdhun* and introduced in it two new lines: *Ishwara Allah tero naam, sabko sanmati de Bhagwan.* Such mixing of religion and politics is castigated in post-Independence India by neo-secularists who brand it as Hindutvavadi. However, all around the world, politics and religion is mixed by all kinds of politicians including US secular liberals as discussed in the last chapter of this book. Some politicians around the world like Putin or Advani have used it for confrontational purposes, while others do it for cheap, ordinary gains. Gandhi, who considered dharma as providing the moral base for all other activities, and who believed Hinduism is a way of life and politics being a part of it should be guided by ethics drawn from dharma, did not hesitate to claim that:

> ...Politics bereft of religion are absolute dirt, ever to be shunned. Politics concerns nations and that which concerns the welfare of nations must be one of the concerns of a man who is religiously inclined; in other words, a seeker after God and Truth.... Therefore, in politics we also have to establish the kingdom of Heaven.[10]

So, who was Gandhi? A reactionary? Or was he superstitious? Or a plain Hindutvavadi? Neo-secularists may be provoked to answer all these questions in the affirmative though they may not dare to say it publicly, but Gandhi was the true symbol of eternal Bharatvarsha. He was, like Vishvamitra, a politician-cum-yogi, and his political decisions were guided by his *dharma*, and by his devotion to Ram. That was why he dreamt of establishing *Ramrajya*, the kingdom of Ram. He was fully aware of people's criticism of him for all his beliefs, and he announced:

> Many of my political friends despair of me because they say

> that even my politics are derived from religion. And they are right. My politics and all other activities of mine are derived from my religion.[11]

However, this dharma-based politics endeared him to such a vast chunk of Indians that we cannot imagine another politician who could sway the heart of India like he did.

Now, about the second point. What did Gandhi mean by Ram was the 'essence whose name inscribed in the heart removes all suffering'? Gandhi said:

> In the armoury of the nature curist, *Ramnaam* is the most potent weapon. Let no one wonder at it. A noted ayurvedic physician told me the other day: "All my life I have been administering drugs. But since you have prescribed *Ramnaam* as a cure for physical ailments, it has occurred to me that what you say has, too, the authority of Vagbhata and Charaka." The recitation of *Ramnaam* as a remedy for spiritual ailments is as old as the hills.... And my claim is that the recitation of *Ramnaam* is a sovereign remedy for our physical ailments also.[12]

In the same article, he also cautions his readers by writing:

> The potency of *Ramnaam* is, however, subject to certain conditions and limitations. *Ramnaam* is not like black magic. If someone suffers from surfeit and wants to be cured of its after-effects so that he can again indulge himself at the table, *Ramnaam* is not for him. *Ramnaam* can be used only for a good, never for an evil end, or else thieves and robbers would be the greatest devotees. *Ramnaam* is for the pure in heart and for those who want to attain purity, and remain pure. It can never be a means for self-indulgence.

Gandhi wrote on this point for years and answered all sorts of questions from his readers with unparalleled zeal. He wrote:

> There is no doubt that *Ramnaam* is the surest aid. If recited from the heart, it charms away every evil thought; and evil thought gone, no corresponding action is possible. The outward helps are all useless if the mind is weak. They are superfluous if the mind is pure. This must not be taken to mean that a pure-minded man can take all the liberties and still keep safe. Such a man simply will not take any liberties with himself. His whole life will be an infallible testimony to (the) inward purity. The Gita truly says that mind makes the man and unmakes him.[13]

Gandhi lamented that *Ramnaam* was not practised by the medical community, but rather, was treated as superstition. He wrote:

> I have no doubt whatsoever that the spread of *Ramnaam* and pure living are the best and cheapest preventives of disease. The tragedy is that doctors, *hakims* and *vaidyas* do not make use of *Ramnaam* as the sovereign of cures. There is no place given to it in current ayurvedic literature, except it be in the shape of a charm which will drive people further into the well of superstition. *Ramnaam* has, in fact, no connection with superstition. It is Nature's supreme law. Whoever observes it, is free from disease and vice versa. The same law which keeps one free from disease, applies also to its cure. An apt question is as to why a man who recites *Ramnaam* regularly and leads a pure life should ever fall ill. Man is by nature imperfect. A thoughtful man strives after perfection, but never attains it. He stumbles on the way, however, unwittingly. The whole of God's law is embodied in a pure life. The first

> thing is to realise one's limitations. It should be obvious that the moment one transgresses those limits, one falls ill. Thus, a balanced diet eaten in accordance with needs gives one freedom from disease.[14]

What will neo-secularists say to such a person saying these things today? Perhaps they don't realise that when they mock anyone preaching cow worship, they are actually mocking Gandhi. Let us see what Gandhi said about cow worship:

> I worship it (cow) and I shall defend its worship against the whole world.... The central fact of Hinduism is cow protection. Cow protection to me is one of the most wonderful phenomena in human evolution. Cow protection is the gift of Hinduism to the world. And Hinduism will live so long as there are Hindus to protect the cow.[15]

Interestingly, Vinayak Damodar 'Veer' Savarkar, the father of political Hindutva, was strongly against cow worship, and dubbed it as 'murder of intellect', and had argued that if human beings had to worship someone, they should worship someone existing at a higher plane, and not an animal. Savarkar was a practical politician who used Hindutva for uniting Hindus politically, but Gandhi was a saint who joined politics without giving up his core faith.

Another interesting point to note here is that it brings into focus another trait of the Mahatma that exposes the neo-secularists further. It should be noted that neo-secularists always stand by Muslims, and they object to dividing the polity in terms of Hindu and Muslim, and are quick to label all such attempts as 'Hindutvavadi'. For Gandhi, however, Hindus and Muslims were two legitimate political categories.

After Independence, Gandhi had demanded complete loyalty towards India from all Muslims. He had said:

> Let us know our own dharma. In the light of our dharma, I would tell the people that our greatest duty is to see that Hindus do not act in frenzy, nor the Sikhs indulge in acts of madness.... I appeal to Muslims that they should open-heartedly declare that they belong to India and are loyal to the Union. If they are true to God and wish to live in the Indian Union, they just cannot be enemies of Hindus. And I want Muslims here to tell Muslims in Pakistan who have become the enemies of Hindus, not to go mad: "If you are going to indulge in such madness, we cannot co-operate with you. We will remain faithful to the Union, and salute the tricolour. We have to follow the order of the Government".[16]

If someone tells Muslims today that if they 'wish to live in the Indian Union, they just cannot be enemies of Hindus', one wonders what will be neo-secularists' reaction to this? Gandhi did not hesitate to say such things loudly and clearly.

Further, Gandhi knew Muslims of India shared the same cultural legacy, and that the only difference between the two communities was that Muslims had been converted to Islam, later. So, he wrote:

> Should we not remember that many Hindus and Mahomedans own the same ancestors and the same blood runs through their veins? Do people become enemies because they change their religion? Is the God of the Mahomedan different from the God of (the) Hindu? Religions are different roads converging to the same point. What does it matter that we take different roads so long as we reach the same goal? Wherein is the cause for quarrelling?[17]

Gandhi made innumerable appeals to Muslims to shun violence and to rectify their image of being an overly aggressive community. He set off a debate in 1924 that continued over three years in the pages of *Young India* and *Navajivan*. A communal riot broke out in 1924, and a group of Muslims met Gandhi and proposed that Hindus should recognise Prophet Mohammad 'as a prophet' and Allah as almighty God, and Muslims should pay equal respect to 'Lord Ram, Lord Krishna', and accept the Vedas as divine books. Rejecting the proposal, Gandhi wrote:

> ... it would prove ineffective for the man in the street. For Hindus cow-protection and the playing of music even near the mosque was the substance of Hinduism, and for the Mussalmans cow-killing and prohibition of music was the substance of Islam.[18]

He felt synthetic solutions would not work to bring them together.

In an article also published in 1924, Gandhi wrote, 'My own experience but confirms the opinion that the Mussalman as a rule is a bully.' He explained that Muslims had become 'bullies' because there was a mystified story of Islam that established that it could not be envisaged without violence and the rule of the sword, and second, the history of imperialism associated with Islamic expansion transformed Muslims into an aggressive community. He further stated:

> 'Whatever may have been necessary or permissible during the Prophet's lifetime...cannot be defended on the mere ground of its mention in the Koran. Every formula of every religion has in this age of reason, to submit to the acid test of reason and universal justice if it is to ask for universal assent. Error

> can claim no exemption even if it can be supported by the scriptures of the world.[19]

Gandhi was a tall and fearless leader who knew how to lead, and like Tagore (as in the interview with *Times of India*) he identified the danger more than a decade before it materialised and divided the country. He was the complete opposite of our neo-secular leaders of today who gloss over all the follies of Muslims, including Islamic fundamentalism, and blame it on Hindus. So, it is only natural that the neo-secularists have tried their best to hide all these words of Gandhi from the public eye.

Gandhi, however, did not spare the Hindus either, particularly on the question of untouchability, for he was also very different from the present-day Hindu nationalist who is blindly proud of everything related to Hinduism. More importantly, Gandhi clearly spelled out that his *Ramrajya* did not denote rule by Hindus. Even after India's Independence, he felt that real victory had not been achieved, and on Diwali day, he said, 'Today there is no *Ramrajya* in India. So how can we celebrate Diwali? Only those who have Rama within can celebrate the victory.'

Like Tagore, whom Gandhi referred to as Gurudev, the Mahatma too was critical of a Hindu's lack of strength. In Noakhali, while talking to relief workers on 7 November 1946, Gandhi had declared:

> What goes against my grain is that a single individual can be converted or a single woman can be kidnapped or raped. So long as we feel we can be subjected to these indignities, we shall continue to be so subjected. If we say we cannot do without police or military protection, we really confess defeat even before the battle has begun. No police or military in the world can protect people who are cowards. Today you say thousands

> of people are terrorising a mere handful, so what can the latter do? But even a few individuals are enough to terrorise the whole mass, if the latter feel helpless. Your trouble is not numerical inferiority but the feeling of helplessness that has seized you and the habit of depending on others. The remedy lies with you. That is why I am opposed to the idea of your evacuating East Bengal en masse. It is no cure for impotence or helplessness.[20]

Further ahead in the discussion, he had said,

> '… (but these are) no consolation to the unfortunate women whose houses have been laid desolate or who have been abducted, forcibly converted and forcibly married. What a shame for Hindus, what a disgrace for Islam!'

This intrepid advocate of non-violence then told the workers gathered there:

> You will note that for the purposes of our present discussion I have not asked you to discard the use of arms. I can't provide you with arms…. You will see I am not, as I have already said, asking you just now to unlearn the use of arms or to follow my type of heroism. I have not made it good even in my own case. I have come here to test it in East Bengal. I want you to take up the conventional type of heroism. You should be able to infect others—both men and women—with courage and fearlessness to face death when the alternative is dishonour and humiliation. Then Hindus can stay in East Bengal, not otherwise. After all, the Mussalmans are blood of our blood and bone of our bone.

In a very uncharacteristic Gandhian way, he had continued:

> 'Even violence has its code of ethics. For instance, to butcher helpless old men, women and children is not bravery but rank cowardice. Chivalry requires that they should be protected even at the cost of one's life. The history of early Islam is replete with such instances of chivalry and Islam is all the stronger for them.'

It was a direct reference to the need for Hindu unity and chivalry. At this point, a worker had interjected, 'Would you permit Hindus to take the offensive?' Gandhi had then brought in the context of retaliatory attacks on Muslims in Bihar, and said:

> Use your arms well, if you must. Do not ill-use them. Bihar has not used its arms well. If the Biharis wanted to retaliate, they could have gone to Noakhali and died to a man. But for a thousand Hindus to fall upon a handful of Mussalmans—men, women and children—living in their midst is no retaliation but just brutality.

Gandhi undertook a fast when Muslims who stayed back were being attacked in Delhi by Hindus and Sikhs, and as a result, many Hindus accused him of appeasing Muslims. But even then, in his prayer meeting on January 13, 1948, he was highly critical of Muslims for their accusations against Sardar Vallabhbhai Patel:

> Muslims say that I am good, but the Sardar (Patel) is not and he must be removed. They say that Jawaharlal too is good. They say if I join the Government, it will be a good thing. They object only to the Sardar. I must tell Muslims that their argument serves no purpose, because the Government is the whole Cabinet, neither the Sardar nor Jawahar by himself.... It will not do merely to criticise him by quoting some statement or other he might have made. You must say what

> he has done. You must tell me. I meet him often and I shall bring it to his notice. Jawaharlal can dismiss him and if he does not, there must be some reason. He praises the Sardar. Then the Government is responsible for whatever the Sardar does. Therefore, I shall say that Muslims must become brave and fearless. They should also become God-fearing. They must think that for them there is no League, no Congress, no Gandhi, no Jawaharlal but only God; that they are here in the name of God.[21]

Further in defense of Patel, on the same day, Gandhi had added:

> The Sardar is blunt of speech. What he says sometimes sounds bitter. The fault is in his tongue. I can testify that his heart is not like his tongue. He has said in Lucknow and in Calcutta that all Muslims should live here and can live here. He also told me that he could not trust those Muslims who till the other day followed the League and considered themselves enemies of Hindus and Sikhs and who could not have changed overnight and suddenly become friends. If the League is still there who will they obey, Pakistan or our Government? The League's persistence in its old attitude makes him suspect it, and rightly so. He says that he no longer has faith in the bona fides of the League Muslims and he cannot trust them. Let them prove that they can be trusted. Then I have the right to tell Hindus and Sikhs what they should do.

This was Gandhi, and he was far from what the neo-secularists of today want us to believe. The fact of the matter is that Gandhi was a secular, spiritual politician deeply respectful of and deeply rooted in Indian tradition, and he took a severe stand against all communities, whenever it was needed. Both Tagore and Gandhi were true symbols of Hindu tradition and culture, and both tried to protect the glory of the eternal Indian civilisation to the hilt. Both of them, as we have seen so far, were highly critical of Muslims, but came down equally unsparingly on Hindus. Both believed that while the eternal Hindu religion was inclusive and liberal, contemporary Hinduism carried many flaws.

When India was at the doorstep of Partition due to violent uprisings by the Muslim League, Gandhi felt defeated and in a series of prayer meetings, he said he would not mind Jinnah or Muslim League turning the whole of India into Pakistan provided it was 'done by appeal to reason and not under threat of violence'.[22]

It was unacceptable to Hindus in general and the Congress leaders, in particular. Reportedly, in those days, Gandhi had also said that if 'every Hindu in East Bengal is done to death, I will not mind'. On 6 April 1947 in a prayer meeting, he had made this statement:

> Hindus should not harbour anger in their hearts against Muslims even if the latter wants to destroy them. Even if Muslims want to kill us all we should face death bravely. If they established their rules after killing Hindus we should be ushering in a new world by sacrificing our lives.

It all generated tremendous reaction among Hindus. They forgot that his words actually reflected highly critical views about Muslims; they overlooked the fact that only a man who believed that Hindus were of the highest moral standard could think of them as a community who could sacrifice their lives for a great cause. Of course, it was against the teachings of dharma enshrined in the Gita that said it is society's fundamental human duty to fight against adharma; but, at least, all Hindus should have understood the pain and the frustration that triggered such statements, and they should have stood by the man whom they called the Father of the Nation. But a section of them, though representing only extreme fringe elements, went on to assassinate the last great Indian who after Independence was carrying the torch of truth like Vivekananda and Tagore had done in the past.

Radical Hindu nationalists were accused of abetting the killer, though they denied it. However, there is no doubt that it was the politics of hatred that had provoked the killer. There is still a section among Hindu nationalists who carry that level of hatred in their minds. Such hatred is, to say the least, a major impediment in India's path of attaining the glory that it deserves to rightfully attain.

First, let us ascertain the damage that these 'criminal Hindus' achieved by killing Gandhi. The Mahatma had expressed his idea about India in his book *Hind Swaraj* published in 1909. The reader will be surprised by the similarity that he and Tagore, the two tallest men of that age, harboured in their minds about the Idea of India. Gandhi raised a question that he answered himself—whether it was not so that the British created the Indian nation? He writes, 'We were already one nation, and that was why the British could establish one government.... Our leading men travelled throughout India; learned one another's languages; there was no aloofness between them. He then asked what could be the intent of 'our farsighted ancestors who established Setubandha (Rameshwar) in the South, Jagannath in the East, and Haridwar in the North as places of pilgrimage'. He answers this question, as well, in the following way:

> They were no fools. They knew that God could be worshipped just as well at home. They had the Ganges in their own homes. They saw that India was one undivided land so made by nature

> and argued that it must be one nation. They established holy places in various parts of India and fired the people with an idea of nationality in a manner unknown in other parts of the world. And we Indians are one as no two Englishmen are.

If we analyse this thought, we will understand that he believed that the Indian nation was essentially a Hindu nation. In his prayer meeting on 13 January 1948, he mentioned: 'Muslims also must become pure and live peacefully in India.'

Gandhi was a visionary who could foresee that if a certain group of people did not intend to 'merge' with other inhabitants in India, the geographical nation would break. Let us understand his deep wisdom and prevent the country from further division.

Nehru: Proud of Indian heritage, but never a blind devotee

One distinct feature of neo-secularists is their absolute silence on the repressive practices and misdeeds of the Muslim community, and of their jubilance in condemning the illogical practices and misdeeds of Hindus. Ironically, these very same neo-secularists believe they follow Nehruvian secularism in letter and spirit! They can fool Westerners and foreign neo-secularists with such a blatant falsehood, but not Indians.

Judge for yourself by reading these lines penned by Nehru in *Discovery of India*:

> The day-to-day religion of the orthodox Hindu is more concerned with what to eat and what not to eat, who to eat with and from whom to keep away, than with spiritual values. The rules and regulations of the kitchen dominate his social life. The Moslem is fortunately free from these inhibitions, but he has his own narrow codes and ceremonials, a routine which

> he rigorously follows, forgetting the lesson of brotherhood which his religion taught him.[23]

In another passage, he writes about the Muslims:

> His view of life is, perhaps, even more limited and sterile than (the) Hindu view, though the average Hindu to-day is a poor representative of the latter view, for he has lost that traditional freedom of thought and the background that enriches life in many ways.

It is clear that India needs to reestablish the environment in which freedom of thought was possible and rediscover what Nehru describes as 'the background that enriches life in many ways'. The only way of doing this is by changing the school curriculum so that children are introduced to that knowledge and wisdom that our ancient forefathers bequeathed to us. Unfortunately, Nehru succumbed to various fears, as we will read in chapter 4, and did not get this done. Now, when India has come into its own, and we have nothing to fear, it should be done urgently.

The real secular approach lies in criticising everybody equally for their follies, as Tagore, Gandhi, and Nehru did. But over the years, the neo-secularists suppressed these bold, critical views of Nehru, in the process, almost wiping them off from public discourse. Consequently, Nehru has become the favourite whipping boy of Hindu nationalists. In Nehru's case, both sides seem to dwell on half-truths. Of course, Nehru himself provided this opportunity to Hindu nationalists as after Independence, he trudged towards the opposite direction of what he himself had proclaimed and written in the books he wrote in the pre-Independence days, particularly in *Discovery of India*.

Pre-Independence Nehru was certainly obsessed with the

true narrative of India, and fought against all those he felt would affect or alter the Idea of India, whether it was communalism, casteism, or any form of anti-India narrative.

He lashed out at the Dravid Munnetra Kazagham (DMK) and its anti-Brahminist and Dravidian campaign in the fifties and sixties. At that time, he had said:

> All the tendencies which have been so obvious in this election (of 1962), caste tendency, communal tendencies and the like which are harmful and which disintegrate the country have to be met as far as possible unitedly.... Elections upset our thinking apparatus and put passions in control of us and of others.... If it is war, it will be war, but it will not be accepted. When I find that not only the people who talk about them but others encouraging such parties and asking people to vote for them, it shows that something has gone wrong in somebody's thinking completely.[24]

Let us analyse his other writings. The neo-secularists tried hard to subtly influence our mind in believing that nationalism was bad, and they were irritated when during the Kargil proxy war and in the post-Kargil days, a mood of nationalism gripped the citizens of India. Hundreds, perhaps even thousands of articles were written and speeches delivered to caution us against the jingoism of radical Hindutva forces. This was so, because internationalism and anti-religion atheism, byproducts of the propaganda of the erstwhile USSR, were the mantras for neo-secularists all over the world. But, unfortunately for them, the BJP led by Modi quickly made nationalism a mantra and succeeded to claim a monopoly on 'nationalism'. It must be noted here that nationalism and internationalism usually coexists as long as there is no clash of material interest.

In this context, let us analyse Nehru's take on nationalism. Here is an extract from *Discovery of India:*

> A blind reverence for the past is bad and so also a contempt for it, for no future can be founded on either of these. The present and the future inevitably grow out of the past and bear its stamp, and to forget this is to build without foundations and to cut off the roots of national growth. It is to ignore one of the most powerful forces that influence people. Nationalism is essentially a group memory of past achievements, traditions, and experiences, and nationalism is stronger to-day than it has ever been.…whenever a crisis has arisen nationalism has emerged again and dominated the scene, and people have sought comfort and strength in their old traditions. One of the remarkable developments of the present age has been the rediscovery of the past and of the nation.[25]

It seems Nehru had a premonition that fifty years after his death, there would be a clash between neo-secularists and Hindu nationalists, and it was as if he was warning both of them through this passage. Neo-secularists have succeeded to 'cut off the roots of national growth' in many countries, but their effort was bound to fail in an ancient land like India. Rather, it caused such an adverse reaction that it has now almost uprooted the tree of neo-secularism.

If we examine the point of anti-religious atheism, another favourite ideal of neo-secularists, Nehru can once again guide us to show its fallibilities in India. The neo-secularists tried to train the minds of the young into accepting atheism, so that the Hindu religion could be reduced to insignificance as being unscientific, irrational and anti-humanity. But Nehru's idea of religion in India was just the opposite. He wrote:

> The bitter conflict between science and religion which shook up Europe in the nineteenth century would have no reality in India, nor would change based on the applications of science bring any conflict with those ideals. Undoubtedly such changes would stir up, as they are stirring up, the mind of India, but instead of combating them or rejecting them, it would rationalise them from its own ideological point of view and fit them into its mental framework.

Have you ever heard or read any neo-secular intellectual highlighting these statements of Nehru? They have not, and it has hurt Nehru's image more than anything else. If only they could be loyal to Nehru, if only they had the brains to understand what Nehru meant by the last two sentences of the quoted paragraph, they could have avoided their existential crisis. Indians had, as Nehru predicted, rationalised the changes that science has brought 'from its own ideological point of view', and have fitted them into their mental framework. The neo-secularists, however, thought that the teachings they had got from their master (the USSR) was more important than Nehru's teachings, and continued following it loyally long after the disintegration of the USSR.

Nehru had a very strong view about communists and about their disconnect with Indian traditions and reality. He wrote: 'I cannot speak with much knowledge of what happened elsewhere, but I know that in India the Communist Party is completely divorced from, and is ignorant of the national traditions that fill the minds of the people. It believes that communism necessarily implies a contempt for the past.' Once again, this passage is from *Discovery of India*.

It is of course true that all who advocated and still advocate neo-secularism were or are not communists, and Nehru was even harsher on them. The following passage proves that:

> It is not only the Communist Party in India that has failed in this respect. There are others who talk glibly of modernism and modern spirit and the essence of western culture, and are at the same time ignorant of their own culture. Unlike the communists, they have no ideal that moves them and no driving force that carries them forward. They take the external forms and outer trappings of the west (and often some of the less desirable features), and imagine that they are in the vanguard of an advancing civilisation. Naive and shallow and yet full of their own conceits, they live, chiefly in a few large cities, an artificial life which has no living contacts with the culture of the east or of the west. National progress can, therefore, neither lie in a repetition of the past nor in its denial. New patterns must inevitably be adopted but they must be integrated with the old.

Nehru here is referring to the essence of the civilisational journey of Bharatvarsha while emphasising the importance of the past. It is an essence that is in full consonance with what Vivekananda, Shri Aurobindo, Tagore and Gandhi believed in. Nehru further wrote:

> Sometimes the new, though very different, appears in terms of pre-existing patterns, and thus creates a feeling of a continuous development from the past, a link in the long chain of the history of the race. Indian history is a striking record of changes introduced in this way, a continuous adaptation of old ideas to a changing environment, of old patterns to new. Because of this there is no sense of cultural break in it and there is that continuity, in spite of repeated change, from the far distant days of Mohenjodaro to our own age. There was a

> reverence for the past and for traditional forms, but there was also a freedom and flexibility of the mind and a tolerance of the spirit. So, while forms often remained, the inner content continued to change. In no other way could that society have survived for thousands of years. Only a living and growing mind could overcome the rigidity of traditional forms, only those forms could give it continuity and stability.
>
> ...The essential basis of Indian thought for ages past, though not its later manifestations, fits in with the scientific temper and approach, as well as with internationalism. It is based on a fearless search for truth, on the solidarity of man, even on the divinity of everything living, and on the free and co-operative development of the individual and the species, ever to greater freedom and higher stages of human growth.[26]

If one goes through *Discovery of India*, one can tell that this was no isolated rhetoric, as the concepts are elaborated in detail in the book. It is apparent that Nehru had profound knowledge and respect for the purest form of Hinduism and respect for India's rich, cultural past.

Nehru was not only a confident Hindu proud of India's ancient Upanishadic philosophy that he felt should be propagated through our textbooks, but he also defended Hinduism strongly whenever foreigners questioned him. Today, a number of intellectuals try to convince us that Brahmanical Hindus violently attacked Buddhists and exterminated Buddhism from India by sheer brute force. Over the last half a century, there have been historians ready to embellish any such tailor-made propaganda theories, and the publishing world went all out to give the work of this section of academia full exposure. And thus, gradually, over a period of some decades, this lie eventually became 'truth'.

Nehru, tackled this controversy in *Discovery of India*. Here is what he wrote:

> It is clear that there was no widespread or violent extermination of Buddhism in India. Occasionally, there were local troubles or conflicts between a Hindu ruler and the Buddhist Sangha, or organisation of monks, which had grown powerful. These had usually a political origin and they did not make any essential difference. It must also be remembered that Hinduism was at no time wholly displaced by Buddhism. Even when Buddhism was at its height in India, Hinduism was widely prevalent. Buddhism died a natural death in India, or rather it was a fading out and a transformation into something else.... Buddhism was not only entirely a product of India; its philosophy was in line with previous Indian thought and the philosophy of the Vedanta (the Upanishads). The Upanishads had even ridiculed priestcraft and ritualism and minimised the importance of caste.[27]

Nehru was proud of India's past and of the great treasures of ancient Hinduism. But the neo-secularists have managed to misrepresent him before us and the world and he has become the convenient object of ridicule from the ruling BJP. Suffice it to say that Nehru had in-depth knowledge of Indian philosophy and of its historical role in the journey of our civilisation. He believed that even the civilisational culture of Mohenjo Daro, about which little was known in his time, proved that if taken as a whole, 'their religion is so characteristically Indian as hardly to be distinguished from still living Hinduism'. He had devoted an entire chapter of his famous book to the ancient civilisational stages of India and also the philosophies of India, titled 'The Indian Philosophical

Approach and the Six Systems of Philosophy'.

He wrote in the chapter:

> In India, far more so than elsewhere, the old concept of social organisation and the philosophy of life underlying it, have persisted, to some extent, to the present day. They could not have done so unless they had some virtue which stabilised society and made it conform to life's conditions. And they would not have failed ultimately and become a drag and a hindrance, divorced from life, if the evil in them had not overcome that virtue. But, in any event, they cannot be considered today as isolated phenomena; they must be viewed in that world context and made to harmonise with it. In India,' says Havell, 'religion is hardly a dogma, but a working hypothesis of human conduct, adapted to different stages of spiritual development and different conditions of life. A dogma might continue to be believed in, isolated from life, but a working hypothesis of human conduct must work and conform to life, or it obstructs life. The very raison d'etre of such a hypothesis is its workableness, its conformity to life, and its capacity to adapt itself to changing conditions. So long as it can do so it serves its purpose and performs its allotted function. When it goes off at a tangent from the curve of life, loses contact with social needs, and the distance between it and life grows, it loses all its vitality and significance'.

Coming to ancient Hindu philosophies that he believed formed the edifice of India, Nehru wrote:

> But, in the main, the dominating influence has been that of the six systems of Indian philosophy, or *darshanas*, as they are called. Some of these systems were themselves greatly affected by Buddhist thought. All of them are considered orthodox and

> yet they vary in their approach and their conclusions, though they have many common ideas. There is polytheism, and theism with a personal God, and pure monism, and a system which ignores God altogether and bases itself on a theory of evolution. There is both idealism and realism. The various facets of the complex and inclusive Indian mind are shown in their unity and diversity. Max Mueller drew attention to both these factors: '... the more have I become impressed with the truth...that there is behind the variety of the six systems a common fund of what may be called national and popular philosophy…from which each thinker was allowed to draw for his own purposes'.

And then, for pages together, Nehru discusses the six systems of Indian philosophy: Nyaya, Vaisheshika, Samkhya, Yoga, Mimumsa, and Vedanta. What overawes the mind is his profound knowledge of all these systems of philosophy. Readers cannot but wonder how such a practical politician such as Nehru had access to such depth of knowledge of India's past. And why is it that the present politicians know so little about the true narrative of India.

While discussing Yoga, Nehru extensively quoted Vivekananda and also Aurobindo. Here is what he wrote about Vivekananda:

> Vivekananda, one of the greatest of the modern exponents of Yoga and the Vedanta, has laid repeated stress on the experimental character of Yoga and on basing it on reason. 'No one of these Yogas gives up reason, no one asks you to be hoodwinked or to deliver your reason into the hands of priests of any type whatsoever.... Each one of them tells you to cling to your reason, to hold fast to it.' Though the spirit of Yoga and the Vedanta may be akin to the spirit of science, it is true

that they deal with different media, and hence vital differences creep in. According to Yoga, the spirit is not limited to the intelligence, and also 'thought is action, and only action can make thought of any value.' Inspiration and intuition are recognised but may they not lead to deception? Vivekananda answers that inspiration must not contradict reason: 'What we call inspiration is the development of reason. The way to intuition is through reason.... No genuine inspiration ever contradicts reason. Where it does it is no inspiration.' Also 'inspiration must be for the good of one and all; and not for name or fame or personal gain. It should always be for the good of the world, and perfectly unselfish'.

While discussing Vedanta in the same chapter in *Discovery of India*, Nehru pays tribute to Shankara (Adi Shankaracharya) in a way that suggests that he too was a devotee. He wrote:

> He strove hard to synthesise the diverse currents that were troubling the mind of India of his day and to build a unity of outlook out of that diversity. In a brief life of thirty-two years, he did the work of many long lives and left such an impress of his powerful mind and rich personality on India that it is very evident today. He was a curious mixture of a philosopher and a scholar, an agnostic and a mystic, a poet and a saint, and in addition to all this, a practical reformer and an able organiser. He built up, for the first time within the Brahmanical fold, ten religious orders and of these, four are very much alive today. He established four great *maths* or monasteries, locating them far from each other, almost at the four corners of India. One of these was in the south at Sringeri in Mysore, another at Puri on the east coast, the third at Dvaraka in Kathiawad on the west coast, and the fourth at Badrinath in the heart of the

> Himalayas. At the age of thirty-two, this Brahmin from the tropical south died at Kedarnath in the upper snow-covered reaches of the Himalayas.

And then, Nehru started searching the meaning of this journey of Adi Shankara to establish these *maths*. He wrote:

> There is a significance about these long journeys of Shankara throughout this vast land at a time when travel was difficult and the means of transport very slow and primitive. The very conception of these journeys, and his meeting kindred souls everywhere and speaking to them in Sanskrit, the common language of the learned throughout India, brings out the essential unity of India even in those far-off days.

This essential unity is what glued the population of Bharatvarsha, forging this strong cultural nationalism in pre-Independence India, for without it, we would become rootless wanderers, without direction. Nehru explains:

> Such journeys could not have been uncommon then or earlier, people went to and fro in spite of political divisions, new books travelled, and every new thought or fresh theory spread rapidly over the entire country and became the subject of interested talk and often of heated debate. There was not only a common intellectual and cultural life among the educated people, but vast numbers of common folk were continually travelling to the numerous places of pilgrimage, spread out all over the land and famous from epic times.

These two streams of India, or Hinduism—one from intellectuals who debated and discussed philosophies and foundational knowledge, and founded Sanatana Dharma; the other of the common man who carried the culture of Bharatvarsha in their hearts with piousness that often bordered ritualism—had made cultural Bharatvarsha an eternal and incomparable entity. Nehru explains it in one sentence because in his time, it was common knowledge. He did not have to explain it to his readers.

Finally, Nehru teaches us the real significance of Shankara's journey, and identifies and defines eternal India through it:

> All this going to and fro and meeting people from different parts of the country must have intensified the conception of a common land and a common culture. This travelling was not confined to the upper castes; among the pilgrims were men and women of all castes and classes. Whatever the religious significance of these pilgrimages in the minds of the people might have been, they were looked upon also, as they are today, as holiday-time and opportunities for merry-making and seeing different parts of the country. Every place of pilgrimage contained a cross-section of the people of India in all their great variety of custom, dress, and language, and yet very conscious of their common features and the bonds that held them together and brought all of them to meet in one place. Even the difference of language between the north and the south did not prove a formidable barrier to this intercourse.

Nehru was quite obviously an exponent and teacher of Hinduism and cultural nationalism. He concludes his thoughts on Adi Shankara by writing:

> All this was so then and Shankara was doubtless fully aware of it. It would seem that Shankara wanted to add to this sense of national unity and common consciousness. He functioned on the intellectual, philosophical and religious plane and tried to bring about a greater unity of thought all over the

> country. He functioned also on the popular plane in many ways, destroying many a dogma and opening the door of his philosophic sanctuary to everyone who was capable of entering it. By locating his four great monasteries in the north, south, east, and west, he evidently wanted to encourage the conception of a culturally united India.

It must be mentioned that a thousand years after Adi Shankara, another monk appeared to carry on the task of joining religion and nationalism. It was Swami Vivekananda, unanimously hailed as guru of nationalism by Gandhi, Bose, Nehru and many other eminent politicians of pre-Independence India. He was dubbed as 'the second Shankaracharya' by Bal Gangadhar 'Lokmanya' Tilak.

Unfortunately, when Nehru got the real taste of power as Prime Minister of India, he appears to have forgotten whatever he had said and written earlier, and eventually ended up building an educational system that did not teach young Indians about the basic philosophy of Vivekananda or Adi Shankara, or about the rich tradition or cultural heritage coming down to us from time immemorial. Why did he change so radically? This will be explained later in this book, where we will also discuss his 'will' that proves that while politics changed him as a politician after Independence, it still did not touch his inner core.

(All quotes in this section are from the edition of 'Discovery of India' available on the internet.)

Bose: A deeply devotional Hindu and an impeccable secularist

Most tend to think of Subhas Chandra Bose as a revolutionary freedom fighter, completely ignoring the fact that he was also a staunch Hindu nationalist. Plenty of scholars and writers have written about how deeply pious and proud he was of Bharatvarsha's past, showing him up as a nationalistic and anti-communist personality. For our subject, it is important to check his personal faith, as personal faith always has some bearing on one's political activities.

The Congress had pushed Bose to the background, bringing Nehru to the foreground as the most important and practical politician, and this appealed to the neo-secularist because Bose had joined hands with Hitler and Tojo, the sworn 'enemies' of the USSR. Thus, within forty years of Independence the hero who had contributed the most to India's freedom struggle and was a major catalyst for the British granting India its freedom, stood almost forgotten.

Shyam Benegal, a filmmaker known for his impeccable secular character, made a film on Bose in 2004, and titled it *Netaji Subhas Chandra Bose: The Forgotten Hero*. More recently, Narendra Modi can be credited with resurrecting him. It was because of him that modern researchers began projecting him from a holistic point of view to change the public perception about him.

This firebrand leader was a staunch and proud Hindu, and he had no doubt that the soul of Bharatvarsha lay in Hinduism. On 9 May 1926, he wrote in his prison notebook:

> If Hinduism is preached in Europe or America then they might change their views about Hindus—Indian philosophy might influence Western philosophy, and the glory and prestige of Indians might go up.... If two hundred lakhs of Africans embrace Hinduism, then undoubtedly the influence of Hindus and of India will be quite powerful in Africa. If India wants to be a world power, then the preaching of Hinduism will facilitate the process.

These thoughts imply that he directly equated Hinduism with cultural Bharatvarsha. From a modern neo-secularist point of view, one may conclude that he was indeed a staunch Hindutvavadi.

While travelling by the ship *S S Ganges* to Europe, he wrote on 5 March 1933, to his close friend Dilip Kumar Roy:

> To be quite frank, I am torn this side and that—between my love for Shiva, Kali and Krishna. Though they are fundamentally one—one does prefer one symbolism to another. I have found that my moods vary—and according to my prevalent mood, I choose one of the three forms—Shiva, Kali and Krishna. Of these three again, the struggle is between Shiva and Shakti. Shiva, the ideal Yogi, has a fascination for me and Kali the Mother also makes an appeal to me. You see, of late (i.e. for the last four or five years) I have become a believer in Mantra Shakti by which I mean that certain Mantras have an inherent Shakti. Prior to that, I had the ordinary rationalistic view, namely that Mantras are like symbols and they are aids to concentration. But my study of Tantra philosophy gradually convinced me that certain Mantras had an inherent Shakti—and that each mental constitution was fitted for a particular Mantra. Since then, I have tried my best to find out what my mental constitution is like and which Mantra I would be suited for. But so far, I have failed to find that out because my moods vary and I am sometimes a Shaiva, sometimes a Shakta and sometimes a Vaishnava.

From Mandalay Jail, he wrote a personal letter to Haricharan Bagchi in 1926:

> The way to conquer fear is to worship Power. The images of Durga, Kali etc. are the expressions of Power. Man can attain power by invoking any of its forms in his mind, praying to

> Her for strength and offering all his weaknesses and faults at Her feet. Infinite strength lies dormant inside us; we must bring it to life. The purpose of worship is to develop strength within one's self. You must contemplate some form of Power every day, seek strength from Her, offering all the five senses and all evil at Her feet. The five-pointed lamp symbolises the five senses. Worship of the Mother is performed with the five senses. We have eyes to see; so we worship with sweet-smelling things like incense, etc. By sacrifice is meant sacrifice of evil—because the goat is the physical form of that.[28]

Years later, when Bose was illegally incarcerated in Presidency Jail, he decided to observe a fast unto death. He announced it on the sacred day of Kali Puja on 30 September 1940 to affirm his faith. He wrote to the Superintendent of Prison: 'I repeat that this letter, written on the sacred day of Kali Puja, should not be treated as a threat or ultimatum. It is merely an affirmation of one's faith, written in all humility.[29]

It shows that Bose, unlike Nehru, was deeply pious.

On 16 February 1926, Bose wrote another letter to the Superintendent of Mandalay Jail reminding him of his earlier letter demanding allowance for observing Durga Puja, Saraswati Puja, Holi and Dol Purnima. In between the lines was this significant message: 'The pages of Indian history teem with the undying examples of martyrs who suffered and died for the sake of their religious beliefs. They died so that India may live.' According to the standards of the neo-secularists, this fits him into the category of a staunch Hindutvavadi. Then, much to the chagrin of these rootless neo-secularists of today, he wrote:

> And in spite of our misery and degradation, India still lives. She lives because of her soul is immortal—her soul is immortal

> because she believes in religion. We have lost much. Political freedom is no more. Economic independence is a thing of the past—even our national culture is being daily undermined by the subtle policy of peaceful penetration. But we still have our religion. We still claim the right to worship our God after the fashion of our glorious ancestors, and we shall sooner cease to exist than succumb to the religious domination of the West.... But Indian culture is as potent a factor today as it was thousands of years ago when some of the foremost nations of the modern world were no better than savages. And do you think, Sir, the people who have suffered so much and braved so much throughout their whole history will obsequiously acquiesce in an arbitrary infringement of their religious rights? We hope against hope that the lessons of the war of 1857 and of the Akali and Tarakeswar Satyagraha movements of yesterday have not been altogether lost on this Govt.[30]

During the British Raj, Hindus were not allowed to play music near mosques even during Hindu festivals. In the late 1920s, Satindra Nath Sen led the Patuakhali Satyagraha in Barisal, Bengal, demanding that Hindus be allowed to play music while passing through roads or paths that went past mosques. On 14 July 1930, the Calcutta High Court found Sen guilty and mentioned that it was 'a dispute between Hindus and Mohammedans because the latter objected to Hindu processions with music passing a certain mosque'. Afterwards, though the government withdrew the case, Sen was rearrested just after his release. Now Bose set off a campaign against the mistreatment of a Hindutvavadi and according to a biography of Bose and his elder brother, *Brothers Against the Raj*, he continued his campaign all through 1929.

Let us compare Bose's attitude and that of the present government of Bengal led by Mamata Banerjee. If Bose had been alive today and had led such a movement, he would surely have been branded as a communal person and a Hindutvavadi by all those who campaign for 'no vote to BJP' in Bengal. Such political campaigns become popular, but, no doubt such parties can be dubbed as following 'fraudulent practices', for while they try to project themselves as followers of Bose's secularism, they do not understand that in reality, Bose was as far away from them as he was from Hindu nationalists.

Bose was not a Hindu nationalist, for he often even took up the Muslim cause and like Gandhi, at times spoke about the greatness of Islam. All these great leaders were trying their best to convince Muslims to shun violence and become nationalists, so that all Indians could fight together against the British. However, their efforts bore no result, and the Muslim League divided the country and earned Pakistan through a bloodbath.

Bose opposed communism and outlined that it was not suitable for India on five grounds:

> There are several reasons why Communism will not be adopted in India. Communism today has no sympathy with Nationalism in any form and the Indian movement is a Nationalist movement—a movement for the national liberation of the Indian people...while many of the economic ideas of Communism would make a strong appeal to Indians, there are other ideas which will have a contrary effect. Owing to the close association between the Church and the State in Russian history and to the existence of an Organised Church, Communism in Russia has grown to be anti-religious and atheistic. In India, on the contrary, there being no association between the Church and the State, there is no feeling against

> religion as such. Further, in India a national awakening is in most cases heralded by a religious reformation and a cultural renaissance.[31]

Anyone who knew Bose closely vouched for his deep faith in the Hindu cultural legacy as the foundation of his Indian nationalism. Nirad C Chaudhuri, who worked as Bose's elder brother's secretary wrote in his memoirs, *Thy Hand! Great Anarch* that Subhas Chandra Bose's Hinduism was an essential part of Indianness. Just how essential it was can be conceived from his letter from Mandalay Jail to his sister-in-law Bivabati Bose on 26 December 1925. He wrote: 'In Durga, we see Mother, Motherland and the Universe all in one. She is at once Mother, Motherland and the Universal spirit.'

While in Mandalay Jail, in his prison notebook, there is another entry on 9 May 1926 in which he writes about India's cultural traditions:

> The culture of these Pancha Gours (Five Gours—Pataliputra, Gaur, Nabadwip, Purushottawama, Kamakhya) was fundamentally the same. What was it? Broadly speaking, this Gauriya culture was a product of a kind of synthesis between the Tantra, Vaishnavism, Nabya Nyaya with the Vedic culture. At present, the centre of this culture is in Bengal. But who can tell whether in the future, the centre of this culture will not be in Puri or Gauhati? Those who believe in the superiority of this culture should devote themselves to more historical research in this regard. To them Pataliputra, Gaur, Nabadwip, Purushottawama, Kamakhya etc., are holier than places of pilgrimage. So everybody should visit these five places of pilgrimage.[32]

Things have changed now. Forget politicians, even the cultured *babus* of Kolkata do not have any idea or knowledge of their culture, their legacy and the civilisational journey of Bharatvarsha.

Bal Gangadhar 'Lokmanya' Tilak is considered a Hindu nationalist by the neo-secularists, because he tangentially equated Gita, Shivaji Utsav and Ganpati Utsav with nationalism. But what was Bose's attitude towards him? His letter to N C Kelkar gives us a glimpse of this:

> When the order of transfer to Mandalay Jail was served on me in Berhampur Jail (in Bengal) towards the end of January last, it did not strike me at the moment that Mandalay Jail was the place where the late Lokmanya Tilak had spent the major portion of his long term of imprisonment. Not till I actually arrived here, did I realise that within the four walls of this jail amid the most dismal surroundings—the late Lokmanya wrote his famous commentary on Gita which, in my humble opinion, has placed him in the same rank with intellectual giants like Sankara and Ramanuja. All of us know about Lokmanya's imprisonment for six years. But I am sure that few are aware of the extent of the suffering, both physical and mental, which he had to undergo during that period. He was here all alone without any intellectual companion and I am sure he was not allowed to associate with other prisoners. Books were his only solace and he lived in a room by himself.... Imbued as he was with the spirit of (the) Gita, perhaps, he himself was above suffering and pain and did not, therefore, breathe a word about it to anybody else.... Only a philosopher of the type of Lokmanya endowed with a superhuman will could have overcome the emasculating effects of that incarceration, maintained peace of mind in

> the midst of suffering and bondage and have produced a monumental and epoch-making work like his commentary on (the) Gita....One has to be in jail for some time in order to realise what strength of will, depth of *Sadhana* and power of endurance—apart from intellectual ability—are necessary for producing under such adverse, depressing and enervating conditions a work so profound and so sublime as Lokmanya's *Gita Bhashya*. Speaking for myself, the more I think about the matter, the more do I lose myself in admiration and reverence. I hope our countrymen in gauging the greatness of Lokmanya will take all these facts into consideration.[33]

Here is another example of Bose's deep regard for the civilisational journey of eternal India. He wrote about his visit to Cairo in the *Modern Review* issue of April 1935:

> As compared with Egypt, India also can boast of a very ancient culture and civilisation, but one must admit that we have not been able to preserve what we constructed, owing to our comparative inefficiency in the art of preservation. Moreover, I do not think that we developed the material side of life—the arts and crafts—as much as the ancient Egyptians did. Our emphasis was not on civilisation, but on culture; not on the material side of life but on the intellectual and spiritual. Therein, we had our advantages as well as disadvantages. Owing to our superior thought-power, we could hold our own against invaders from outside even when we were vanquished physically for the time being—and in course of time, we could also absorb the outsider, while the ancient Egyptian went down before the Arab invaders and disappeared altogether. On the other hand, emphasis on the intellectual and spiritual side caused us to neglect the development of

> science and left us comparatively weak on the material and physical side of life.[34]

Such pride in our civilisational journey and achievements, yet looking at it with a critical outlook was shared by both Nehru and Bose, the two 'socialist' leaders of the Congress in the first half of the twentieth century. In the same article, Bose noted:

> The glorious periods of our history were when we were able to strike the golden mean between the demands of spirit and of matter; of the soul and of the body—and thereby progress simultaneously on both fronts. Owing to the interrelation between the soul and the body, the neglect of the body not only weakens a nation physically—but in the long run, weakens it spiritually as well.

He analyses the issue further and adds:

> India at the present moment appears to be suffering not merely from physical weakness but from spiritual exhaustion as well—the inevitable result of our neglecting one aspect of life.

These thoughts by Bose echo Vivekananda's assessment of India's civilisational journey spread over many thousand years. The sentence, 'Owing to the interrelation between the soul and the body, the neglect of the body not only weakens a nation physically—but in the long run, weakens it spiritually as well,' is very similar to Vivekananda's famous saying that at a young age, it is better to play football than studying the Gita. What Vivekananda meant was that by playing football, the body would become strong and suitable for studying the Gita, but our neo-secularists misinterpreted his comment and concluded that Vivekananda was not interested in the Gita!

Bose's attitude towards India's past was reflected in many of his writings and speeches. Here is another appropriate example:

> I am not one of those who in their zeal for modernism forget the glories of the past.... In a word, we must arrive at a synthesis. Some of our best thinkers and workers are already engaged in this important task. We must resist the cry of 'Back to the Vedas' on the one side, and on the other side the meaningless craze of modern Europe for fashion and change.[35]

His words prove that just like Nehru, he too was in favour of a balance between pride in the past and a real modern outlook. We are still looking for this balance even after a century.

Leaders like Tagore, Gandhi, Nehru and Bose were of a superior stature and completely different from the political leaders we see around us now. Our criticism of them, whether of the likes of Nehru or Veer Savarkar—is utterly futile. Bose, as the Forward Bloc supremo, aligned with Muslim League after the Calcutta Municipal polls of 1939, but before he did that, he held discussions with Savarkar's Hindu Mahasabha represented in Bengal by Shyama Prasad Mukherjee. At other times, he had criticised Hindu nationalists severely, but on 1 January 1928, in an interview with a representative of the Forward Bloc on a statement issued by the Hindu Mahasabha president, Dr Moorji, Bose had said:

> In considering the general opinion of the All-India Hindu Mahasabha, the opinion of the Bengal Hindu Sabha should not be a negligent factor. In view of the population of Hindus in Bengal and the unique part they have played not only in the struggle for India's freedom, but also in the revival of Hinduism since 1857—the opinion of Hindu Bengal should be treated

> with greater consideration than has hitherto been done. India is a huge country extending from the Himalayas to Cape Comorin and I strongly object to the prevailing practice of passing on as the opinion of Hindu India what can at best be the opinion of Hindus in a few provinces. I have heard from some important and reliable workers of Hindu Sabha that of all the provinces in India, Hindu Mahasabha has done the greater amount of work in Bengal. If this be true, it stands to reason that Hindu Mahasabha has a very large following in my province. But I know Bengal and I know at least some of the prominent Hindu Sabha workers in Bengal. And, I will tell Dr Moorji very plainly that at a very modest computation at least 80 per cent of the workers and the members of the Bengal Hindu Sabhas are nationalist to the core. I am Hindu, and though I do not agree with some aspects of the work which Hindu Mahasabha is carrying on, I sincerely admire its work in the sphere of social uplift and religious reform.[36]

Let's analyse another quote from Bose that further busts the neo-secular narrative about him. Bose in his book, *The Indian Struggle* wrote:

> History of India has to be reckoned not in decades or centuries, but in thousands of years.... Though geographically, ethnologically and historically India represents an endless diversity to any observer—there is none the less a fundamental unity underlying this diversity.... The most important cementing factor has been Hindu religion. North or South, East or West, wherever you may travel, you will find the same religious ideas, the same culture and the same tradition. All Hindus look upon India as the Holy Land.... Everywhere the same scriptures are read and followed and the epics, the

Mahabharata and the Ramayana are equally popular where ever you travel.

Thus, Bose too debunked the theory that India was never a nation by claiming that India 'on the whole' is a 'remarkable continuity of culture and civilisation'. He too believed 'the most important cementing factor' of India is that all Hindus consider it as their 'Holy Land'. It conclusively demolishes the claims of the neo-secularists about Bose. But, being inclusivist and liberal, Bose had no faith in Radical Political Hindutva either.

Endnotes

So, what was Tagore, Gandhi, Nehru and Bose's Idea of India? It centred around the following five points:

1. India or Bharatvarsha existed since antiquity; it was a cultural nation whose history deserved to be written in a way different from the conventional western tradition.
2. Hindu religion and culture shaped India and its cultural nationality from ancient times, and it was reinforced from time to time by sages like Adi Shankara.
3. The idea of India is based on the *dharmic* philosophies propagated from antiquity through the Vedas, Upanishads, Gita, Ramayana, Mahabharata, and many other texts.
4. Hindus being the overwhelming majority in this land should defend the Idea of India against foreign aggressions, while allowing the others to contribute to India's journey.
5. If Indians are not conscious and proud of their cultural, religious and philosophical heritages, they will become rootless wanderers.

These four great thinkers and ideologists were of the opinion that though the narrative and Idea of India would always be Hindu, it must accept other communities like Muslims and Christians as partners for the future, upward journey of India. Tagore summarised it in his great poem *Bharattirtha* in which he said everyone was welcome and no one should go back from this civilisational journey of India. Unfortunately, just a few years after his demise, the majority of the Muslims, mostly Bengalis and Punjabis, broke away from India, asserting that they were a different nation based on Islamic tenets.

Tagore, Gandhi, Nehru and Bose were realistic and were not at all like what the neo-secularists have tried to portray over the last few decades. In recent times, Hindu nationalists too have made a similar attempt to usurp Vivekananda, Tagore and Bose, by using only those fragments of their writings or speeches that suited them. Such attempts will eventually fail like that of the neo-secularists, as the greats supported inclusivity, and always worked towards a synthesis between warring narratives, and for reforms that would benefit all religious communities.

We need to recall that when Tagore called for Hindu unity, when Gandhi condemned the meekness of Hindus vis-à-vis Mulsims; when Nehru said Muslim's view of life was more limited and sterile than the Hindu view, or when Bose commented that in India, a national awakening is in most cases heralded by religious reformation, they were not targeting the Muslims. They knew India is essentially Hindu, and as Bose said, the 'most important cementing factor of India has been Hindu religion'. They criticised chauvinism, but they were cultural nationalists, and at the same time, had been blessed with an international outlook.

Tagore, Gandhi, pre-Independence Nehru and Bose—all of them fit in the category of what the neo-secularists now dub as Hindutvavadi or 'Hindu' Nationalists, as they all believed Hindu ideas were at the root of India and its nationalism. However, this Hindu nationalism was pluralistic and inclusive. If we call this shade of nationalism as Hindu nationalism, then it was, it is and will always be the guiding principle of India.

Second Fault

A USSR-sponsored Narrative

Politics is the perception of stakeholders about what they deserve and expect and how it can be achieved. Politics is not limited to statecraft, but is a part of life in organisations, clubs, offices and workplaces, peer groups and even in families. Many times, political disputes are managed with a change of guard or changes in the way things are run, but when it becomes unmanageable, it can break the entity itself, whether it is a nation state, a club or family. Similarly, with the overwhelming support of the Muslims, the Muslim League broke India in 1947. It was what the people expected and deserved.

After that shock, many thought the way forward was to deracinate Hindus from their socio-cultural-religious legacy of thousands of years and make them 'secular'! It was a scandalous thought, as back then in the forties, the Hindu nationalist forces—the Hindu Mahasabha and the RSS—were just fringe forces, and could not have had any significant role in pre-Partition politics. In the first Lok Sabha elections of 1951-52, the Bharatiya Jana Sangh or BJS that was formed by Shyama Prasad Mukherjee and RSS in 1951 secured just 3.06 per cent vote share and 3 seats (out of a total of 499). For the Hindu Mahasabha of 'Veer' Savarkar, it was a meagre 0.95 per cent vote share and 4 seats (thanks to their heavily concentrated small base). If we add to it, the tally of Akhil Bharatiya Ram Rajya Parishad (founded in 1948) led by Swami Karpatri Maharaj, it garnered 1.97 per cent vote share and resulted in 3 seats. Altogether, the 'Hindu' political forces received about 6 per cent votes and secured ten seats. Compared to the performance of the Congress which had 44.99 per cent vote share and 364 seats, it was really insignificant. Even the Socialist Party, the second force in Parliament that had a thinly-spread wide support base secured 10.59 per cent vote share, translating to only twelve seats.

So, there was nothing to fear from Hindu political forces in the initial decades after Independence. However, a Hindustan-Pakistan binary about the Partition did exist in the minds of the people, but it essentially meant that Pakistan was created for Muslims and Hindustan for Hindus. This perception was dangerous for the secular political parties, as they were planning to make India 'secular' in the western sense. So, they floated the idea of neo-secularism. Jawaharlal Nehru was equally invested in this idea as he was planning to make India different from Pakistan by modernising India socially through legal reforms for Hindus. To achieve it, he had to bulldoze the resistance of Hindu fundamentalists who would oppose such reforms in the name of religion.

The easiest way to make people forget this Hindustan-Pakistan binary in the short run was to loosen the grip of the Sanatan religions over the minds of the people by stopping all access to Hindutva thoughts and philosophy, and in the long run by denying that India was for Hindus.

But it was not enough to just end the binary. It was equally necessary to create a new narrative that would challenge and demolish the old Idea of India, and would absolve the Muslims of their past misdeeds—from demolishing temples, repressing and converting Hindus to dividing the nation through a bloodbath. Here, the guidance came from a communist-turned humanist, M N Roy. However, his guidance was a synthetic one, and often, completely erratic, like his advice to identify Mahatma Gandhi as a fascist who would convert India into a fascist nation. A more practical and handy idea came from the total distortion of contemporary history by Ram Manohar Lohia, the guru of present-day socialists. He gave an important cue to the neo-secularists by claiming the reason for Partition was 'Hindu hauteur'—the overbearing and proud haughtiness of Hindus as outlined in Ram Manohar Lohia's 1960 book titled, *Guilty Men of India's Partition*. Gandhi, Congress, Hindu fanatics, communal riots and others figured in his list of culprits.

The most active and dogmatic sect among the neo-secularists were the communists who were more loyal to the USSR and China rather than to India. But nationally, they remained a marginal entity till the 1980s, just like the socialists, the other pillar of neo-secularism. So, the neo-secularists clandestinely joined hands with a section of Congress leaders to monopolise the education system, as they thought that this was the best way to change the minds of Indians. Lohia's book, though critical of all other parties, including the Communist Party, inspired an institutional attempt to exonerate Muslims of all the crimes committed over the last 800 years, and to blame Hindus for everything. Text books were written accordingly, and the history that was taught during Tagore's time was further distorted to suit the purposes of these neo-secularists.

The neo-secularists thereby equated Muslim invaders like

the Delhi Sultanate and the Mughals (who cherished a desire to occupy their ancestral land till the time of Shah Jahan) with the common Muslims of India, who were always native to this land except for a miniscule minority. Being anti-Hindu by nature, the neo-secular venture went up to the ludicrous level of blaming fringe elements, like RSS and the Hindu Mahasabha, for the Partition of India. By repeating this and their whole package of untruths for decades, they had succeeded in changing the minds of a sizeable portion of the urban educated class in a few states by 1980.

The curious point is how these neo-secularists could mould this usually vocal middle class and intelligentsia to follow their diktats so faithfully to run academic institutions and the media just the way they, the neo-secularists wanted. They were able to achieve it as free India gradually relegated itself virtually to the status of a client state of the USSR out of dire necessity. The neo-secularists adopted a convenient USSR-sponsored atheist narrative that was synthetic, alien and damaging to the eternal Idea of India. It wasn't that the USSR had imposed such a narrative only on India; it imposed it on itself too, and just like in India, the narrative is now on its way out in Russia, Belarus, Ukraine and in the Central Asian Republics.

While the killing of the traditional narrative of our civilisational journey attested by the great architects of Indian nationalism was the first cardinal fault of the neo-secularists, the second one was the imposition of a shallow, atheist, narrative in a bid to 'secularise' India.

Ten salient points on the neo-secular narrative

At the onset, we encounter two basic questions: What was and is the essence of the neo-secular narrative, and how was it imposed on such a big country like India? If we seek the answer to the first question, we may find ten salient points of the neo-secular narrative, all woven together by an attitude of irreverence.

Central to the neo-secular narrative was the fixation that India was not Hindu, but was secular. While many shied away from admitting it openly, Mani Shankar Aiyar, a theoretician of the present neo-secular Congress, had the courage to make a clean breast of it. He has written repeatedly about what P V Narasimha Rao, the then Prime Minister, had told him in 1992, after the demolition of the Babri mosque: 'You don't seem to realise that this is a Hindu country.'[1] By his own admission, Aiyer was surprised as he thought India was a 'secular' nation. Aiyar belonged to the top elite, and his disconnect with the masses is understandable; but he is not alone. Millions of city-dwelling, rootless neo-secularists share his opinion. They cannot understand that India is both Hindu and secular, just as dharma and dharmic traditions are secular (though some of the pristine ideas, rituals and customs have got corrupted under pressure of aggression of foreign, adharmic forces).

1. So, the first and most important feature of the neo-secular narrative was the absurd idea that India is not Hindu, but secular. Consequently the neo-secularists had tried their best to root out all Hindu and Sanatan glory, heritage and teachings from the minds of the people.
2. The second salient point of this narrative is marked by the attempt to project Hindus as ugly aggressors and Muslims as victims. So, whenever Hindus were attacked, whether it was about driving out lakhs of Hindus from Kashmir or burning a train at the Godhra Railway station, neo-secularists either looked away, or took recourse to lies, even using a conspiracy theory to deny facts. Laloo Prasad as Railway

minister spent government money for rubbishing the Godhra incident by appointing the Banerjee Commission, whose report was thrown away by law courts. The judiciary, rather, convicted the real culprits. When V P Singh, then Chief Minister of UP, constituted a Commission to probe the 1980 Moradabad riots, Justice M P Saxena disregarded Singh's stories of implicating Hindus and was able to identify both state government and local Muslim organisations as the real culprits. The angry chief minister suppressed the report, which was finally tabled decades later by Yogi Adityanath. There are innumerable examples of such conspiracies to defame Hindus for crimes committed by the other community, and the list includes propagating the unsubstantial Hindu terror theory (later thrown out by law courts) during Manmohan Singh's tenure as PM.

3. Salient point number three is that the neo-secular narrative was always pro-minoritarian. It ensured that the Muslim cultural-religious identity would be protected, and the minorities given full freedom to practise and propagate their religious tenets. Further, Muslim institutions like the *madrasas* teaching Islamic tenets were allowed to function freely, while Hindu religious tenets were never taught in any educational institution as Hindus could not have any majority community educational institution. It is common knowledge that *madrasas* teach the Quran along with those portions of the scripture that terrorists use to promote *jihad*. Some *madrasa* teachers also inspire radicalism. To date, only one neo-secular leader has admitted this openly—Buddhadeb Bhattacharya of the CPI(M) during his tenure as Chief Minister of West Bengal. He did not retract his statement even when his party pressured him.[2]

Further, after the Congress turned fully neo-secular, party leaders like Digvijay Singh started defending Islamic terrorists, like those killed in Batla House in 2008 by Delhi Police. It was only after the Congress lost power at the Centre that the Congress officially rejected Digvijay's 'fake encounter' theory.[3]

4. Fourth, the neo-secular narrative is leftist, and by nature, anti-religion, although it is open to accept Islam. The neo-secularists blocked the way for teaching moral values guided by concepts of *paap* and *punya*, and replaced it with baseless bourgeois-proletariat class theories. Consequently, neo-secularism hit at the very root of moral values in our society, and ended up indirectly sponsoring greed, corruption, muscle power, lechery and other vices. The sense of responsibility to society also diminished as the post-Independence generations were not taught the concept of *dharma* (righteousness) and *adharma* (anti-righteousness). In a society based on dharmic values, such distortions attracted strong reactions. Anna Hazare's fast in Delhi in 2011 against corruption demanding the institution of a powerful Lokpal (defender of people) helped trigger the chain reaction that paved the way for BJP's coming to power in 2014. Unfortunately, the beneficiary Narendra Modi, too, failed to establish an independent and strong Jan Lokpal. The people's reaction found its first expression in Anna Hazare's movement and added huge momentum to this paradigm shift, for in the Indian tradition, the value of honesty and integrity is immense.
5. The fifth point about the neo-secular narrative is that it is materialistic, like all leftist narratives. It wants to make people believe that materialist concerns are the only concerns of life. The Congress and other neo-secular parties and their associated intellectuals and some 'independent' thinkers now

lament that the people are not voting for *roti-roji* (bread and job) and have instead turned 'communal'. These rootless, neo-secular leaders and intellectuals cannot understand that for the Hindus and other Sanatanis of this land, their socio-religious-cultural legacies are as important as other more practical, but mundane issues.

For thousands of years, battles have been fought and lives sacrificed for protecting both material possessions and cultural-religious values of *sanatan samaj*—traditional society. With the memory of several upheavals over centuries, a large section of Sanatanis now feel that their heritage and legacies will not be safeguarded by these neo-secularists. So, this section of people has chosen to reject them even when they feel the heat of materialistic hardships such as they did during the two worst pandemic years from 2020 to 2022. The Hindus or other Sanatanis are not afraid of the Muslims or the Christians or even the Jews because of their religious denominations; they are simply scared of attacks on their own culture and legacies.

6. The sixth salient point here is that this narrative was inspired directly by the USSR, to please whom, the economy was virtually made socialist. And USSR, on its part, brazenly took advantage of India's overwhelming dependence on it for their national security, including in the United Nations Security Council. All of India's arms and armaments requirement, including the need for a modernised fleet of fighter planes and warships was met by the USSR, at times by exerting influence in ways that were not ethical. However, it successfully projected itself as guardian angel of India, further inspiring the local population to accept its narrative. The USSR also spent huge amounts of money to manage

politicians, bureaucrats, the intelligence community and the media, all to create a sentiment in favour of the USSR and its sponsored narrative.

7. The seventh point relates to a campaign that India's Hindu past, political or economic, was not great. The narrative projected the Buddha, Buddhist kings like Ashoka, and Muslim rulers as the only symbols of unity in diversity, and references to Muslim atrocities or the role of Hindu rulers in fighting them was diligently removed from Indian history textbooks. Historical facts were further distorted—such as projecting the Buddhist emperor Ashoka as the unifier of political India ignoring the role of Chandragupta Maurya. Educators attempted to hide from students the fact that India or parts of it was under foreign rule from the mid-thirteenth century onwards for a period of 700 years. In simple words, the foreign rule had begun from the time when non-Indian languages were introduced as the official language. The neo-secularists also tried to hide that the Muslim rule was finally brought to an end not by the British, but by the Marathas, and it was because they were defeated that the British took over.
8. Next is the marginalisation of the great figures who stood as symbols of India's cultural journey. Adi Shankara, the tallest cultural figure of India reverentially referenced even by Nehru, was marginalised in the new text books prepared by the neo-seculars and instead, only the proponents of a non-combative Bhakti movement like Kabir and Chaitanya were given prominence. This was all part of a planned methodology to defang Hindus and to make them forget the spirit of fighting against adharma. It was to make them so non-violent that they would not be able to defend themselves in the future.

But looking back at these seventy-odd years, the religious core of the Hindu community and the pride they took in real Hindutva was never eclipsed, except in some metropolises and to some extent, in states like Tamil Nadu and Bengal. However, the new narrative affected loyalty to dharma and to the spirit of fighting adharma. Still, the indomitable eternal spirit of the land is largely intact and can be observed during the Amarnath Yatra, which, too has been subjected to terrorist attacks. Nevertheless, Hindu pilgrims, bound by their devotion march off towards the shrine, often with Muslim guides leading them.

9. Now, the ninth point: The narrative was to kill nationalism and replace it with socialism, and float the idea of uniting mankind across borders. The neo-secularists often quoted Tagore selectively, especially those of his works written as a reaction to Chauvinism, to bolster the anti-nationalism rhetoric. However, apart from being nationalist, Tagore was also an idealist; but his hope of the world becoming one family has not materialised even a century later. Rather, increased divisions globally have erupted in terrorism, and the danger of it deteriorating into a prolonged global war in a world where a number of countries have nuclear bombs is now very real. India, in particular, is surrounded by countries that either use terrorism as a state policy, or are obsessed with power and domination. Nehru said in *The Discovery of India* that a nation falls back on nationalism in a crisis situation. In India, the anti-nationalistic narrative was defeated when the nation faced proxy attacks by Pakistan constantly from the eighties onwards. And now, it is also under threat from its one-time 'all weather friend', China.
10. Finally, the neo-secular narrative had tried to divide the

Hindu society and weaken India on various social lines. They propagated that tribals following the Sarna faith are not Hindus, despite the many striking similarities of their rituals, symbols and faiths with Hindu sects. Many who condemned Hindu society for casteism, are now, themselves, demanding a caste census and reservations including in the private sector, thus making India totally caste-dependent.

Nehru thought reservation kills merit; Indira Gandhi in 1980 raised the slogan, '*Na jaat par na paat par, mohar lagegi haath par* (Vote for the Congress and not on caste and community lines). In the same year, in 1980, the Mandal Commission report for OBC reservation was submitted to her, but she did not accept it.[4]

After her Rajiv Gandhi not only ignored the Mandal Commission report, but when V P Singh accepted it, Rajiv Gandhi described it as an attempt to 'divide the country on caste lines'. A few lines from his speech in Lok Sabha on this are quoted in the fourth chapter.

We have so far discussed the vertical growth of this narrative, the volume and variety, which itself is mind-boggling. However, the horizontal growth of the narrative, all over India, is no less impressive. Let us examine how this was imposed and the factors that helped it to take hold. The intriguing fact is that the implementation of neo-secular ideas were never acknowledged as the official policy of the state. It was established secretively in the name of secularism amidst tremendous pressure on the government from two sections—leftist intellectuals from within and outside, and from some Muslim community leaders, who even dared that Vallabhbhai Patel be sacked from the Home Minister's post (see reference to this in Gandhi's writings in chapter 2). Together, the leftists and the Muslim leaders thwarted the introduction of Hindu values in the academic curriculum as had been proposed by Sarvepalli Radhakrishnan in the fifties. The signal was clear to the intellectuals of the academic world who accepted it quietly. Invisible pressure was then exerted successfully to shape the media in the same mould.

M N Roy: Father of the neo-secular narrative

M N Roy is perhaps the rightful claimant of the title, 'Father of Neo-secularism'. He was distinctly irreverent of India's rich religious-cultural past and its nationalistic uprising under Gandhi, even going to the bizarre extent of describing Gandhi and his path as 'fascist'. The present century's neo-secularists exhibit some of his characteristics: Deriding India's past socio-religious connections, besides mocking nationalism and the nation's achievements; and dubbing political opponents as 'fascist'.

For the record, even if the connection of fascism with economic factors is set aside, the word 'fascism', itself denotes an authoritarian ultranationalist political ideology.

Roy had set the contours of his narrative just before Independence in his 1945 book, *The Problem of Freedom*. The fourth chapter of the book, titled 'Psychoanalysis of Gandhism' begins with the following lines:

> Passionate condemnation of violence in any form is apparently, as well as ostensibly, the essence of Gandhism. In contrast to that, Fascism makes a cult of violence. Is it, then, not absurd to hold that there is any affinity between two such antithetical doctrines?
>
> Before proceeding to answer this apparently crushing question, one or two preliminary observations may be made. The exposure of the affinity between Gandhism and Fascism does not imply any doubt about the sincerity of the prophet

> of the former as regards his profession of non-violence. Fanaticism, indeed, is the highest expression of sincerity. But fanaticism, at the same time, being a highly irrational emotional state, cannot be taken as the conclusive evidence of the rationality of the cult. However, Fascism as commonly understood, is not directly equated with Gandhism. The direct relation is between Fascism and Nationalism. Nationalism cannot disown this relation without denying itself. Because, Fascism is Nationalism. On the other hand, Gandhism is the accepted ideology of Indian Nationalism. That is the relation between Gandhism and Fascism. It is not an accidental relation. There was a time when Nationalism, generally, was a progressive, liberating force. Gandhism is the antithesis of such kind of Nationalism. Gandhism supplies moral sanction to Nationalism, when it has become a reactionary force. Therefore, it is equated with Fascism.
>
> Now let us take up the question raised in the beginning. Mere appearances give rise to it. Nevertheless, it has got to be answered, not only for disposing of the question, but also because, in answering it, we shall subject Gandhi's personality as well as his doctrines to a psychological analysis which will yield otherwise interesting results.
>
> Meanwhile, let it be noted that the cultural affinity between Gandhism and Fascism, exposed by us, is not a logical deduction from hypothetical premises; much less is it a dogmatic assertion. It is a matter of fact.

In the previous chapter of the book, Roy had declared that Fascism idealises 'medieval values and mythical traditions', and then, deriding such values and tradition, he wrote, 'Things which have been, or are believed to have been, are more appealing to the unthinking than things expected to be.' He proceeded to develop the idea for pages in the fourth chapter, stating even absurd statements like 'Gandhi became the prophet of Indian Nationalism because Nationalism is denial of individual freedom.' In that chapter, he had concluded: 'The essence of Nationalism, denial of the very existence of the individual, manifests itself fully in Fascism. That is the organic relation between Nationalism and Fascism.'

It was not just Gandhian nationalism that irritated Roy. The other factor was Gandhi adhering to 'medieval values and mythical traditions'. As in the previous chapter, we had noticed Gandhi's unwavering faith in Ram, *Ramnaam*, Karmic law and cow worship, so it is not difficult to point out what Roy was alluding to by the words 'medieval values and mythical traditions'. Roy was irritated because Gandhian idealism had its root in Hindu religious culture. He further wrote in his book, *The Problem of Freedom*:

> Faith is fear of life. Gandhi preaches faith—blind, unadulterated faith amounting to unconditional submission. Those who are afraid of life, are anxious to run away from it, naturally cannot have the will to live, that is, will to be free. Because, there is no freedom except the freedom to live.... Gandhi had the advantage of practically a whole nation thinking like himself, because it has inherited an authoritarian psychology from its cultural traditions, which have not yet been repudiated by the spirit of Renaissance. That is the secret of Gandhi's success.

Interestingly, Roy did not stop here. In Chapter 5 of his book, Roy directs his attacks against Nehru for following the Gandhian way. He wrote:

> In addition to Gandhi's non-violence, there is another factor which is supposed to guarantee the purity of Indian nationalism. That is Jawaharlal Nehru the sea-green incorruptible of Indian politics. Next to the Mahatma, he is the leader of Indian Nationalism. He is moreover an avowed internationalist and a fervent Socialist. How can a movement led by such a man have anything to do with Fascism?
>
> A closer look reveals the clay-feet of this God also. Just as passionate profession of nonviolence (and passion may not vouch for sincerity) does not alter the objective fact that the Mahatma is (the) prophet of Indian Fascism, just so are Nehru's Socialism and internationalism no guarantee against his becoming the other prophet of the same cult.

Roy thus structured his argument on three pillars: First, Gandhi is fascist because he is a nationalist; second, he is a fascist because his ideas are rooted in Hindu religious myths and culture; and third, he had the ability to make 'a whole nation' think like him.

Following this construct, the communists, who had opposed Gandhi's 1942 Quit India Movement, declared that the independence India got in 1947 was a sham (*yeh azadi jhooti hai*), and Gandhi was a reactionary element. E M S Namboodiripad, a legendary communist, had to write a book in 1958—*The Mahatma and the Ism*—to wean away the communists from such daring misconceptions about Gandhi. In this book, he wrote that communists had denounced the policies and programmes of 'bourgeois leaders like Gandhi' without trying to understand those. Thus, the communists underwent a course correction from the sixties, gradually ate their words, and fully acknowledged Gandhi in the nineties when BJP's rise was palpable. The Lohiaite socialists were also critical of Gandhi's Hindu religious invocations and prayer meetings from the beginning.

So, the communists and the socialists—the early hardcore neo-secularists—came together to implement Roy's construct by opposing nationalism, by deleting Gandhi's point of view on Hindu religion, Karmic laws or cow worship from textbooks and public discourse, and most interestingly, by launching efforts to wean away the masses from the Gandhian way while praising Gandhi. As a result, present-day Indians hardly know anything about Gandhi except that he led three movements against the British. Strangely, Nehru and the later Prime Ministers never tried to resurrect Gandhi and teach the students the true narrative of his politics. As far as Roy's theory of anti-nationalism is concerned, the highest point of it was displayed in 1962 by a section of the communists (the pro-Chinese section who later formed CPI-M) who did not agree to dub China as the aggressor. In the present century, besides different vacillating regional parties, the Congress too had started following the contours of the narrative set by Roy.

Roy, a communist-turned-radical humanist, also severely criticised Gandhi's association with industrialists, and had argued that Gandhi's preaching on non-violence was a façade for protecting the ruling class. The CPI(M) followed this line of attacking top industrialists in the last century. In Bengal a common slogan that reverberated back then was *Tata-Birla kalo haath bhenge dao* (smash the dark hands of Tata and Birla). From the 1980s, another name was added to the target list: Dhirubhai Ambani, who was accused of being close to Indira Gandhi, Pranab Mukherjee and Rajiv Gandhi. All through, the socialists echoed the same sentiment, though not so virulently like the communists.

For CPI(M) things took a U-turn when Ratan Tata showed interest in having a Nano plant in Bengal. The then Chief Minister, Buddhadeb Bhattacharjee allotted the Tatas prime land in Singur, a very fertile area, and gave them a package of concessions totally opposed to what the communists had believed in the past. Meanwhile, the locals revolted against the move as the compensation for their land, which was also the source of living for them, was not adequate. Mamata Banerjee took up their cause and launched an agitation that forced Ratan Tata to leave Bengal. In the present century, after losing power in Bengal, the CPI(M) has gone back to their old track. Now, the communist-socialist combo has made Adani their new target, and for the first time, the Congress led by Rahul Gandhi has joined the chorus.

Before concluding this section, let us understand the fallacies of Roy's arguments. First, nationalism has nothing to do with fascism. Rather nationalism is a natural expression of a population of its cultural identity that validates its existence as a separate nation. It helps every nation to have its own set of aspirations based on its own heritage and culture. So, the attempt to kill nationalism is like an attempt to kill different cultures and different heritages, making the whole Indian race something like a race of robots.

The USSR, the prophet of communism, attempted it by absorbing in itself, a number of nations. That the people of the USSR eventually revolted against it showcased the point that it was a brutal attempt of an authoritarian and cruel regime to subjugate a large bouquet of independent-minded people. The fact that the erstwhile USSR is now fragmented into fifteen different nations proves the point that such synthetic anti-nationalism is bound to end in a catastrophe.

In the last century, all believers of a leftist ideology inspired by the simplistic narrative of Marxism have failed to pass the test of reality. Over time, some of them realised that nationalism is not the opposite pole of internationalism, but rather, it is an expression of cultural distinctiveness, and can help grow an ideal democratic state that believes in protecting sub-cultures and respecting the mega-culture of internationalism. One such man was Nehru. As quoted in the last chapter, he believed nationalism is 'essentially a group memory of the past achievements, traditions and experiences', and 'whenever a crisis has arisen nationalism has emerged again and dominated the scene, and people have sought comfort and strength in their old traditions'.

Unfortunately, India faced such a crisis that led to a paradigm shift in this century, and equally unfortunately, it happened as a reaction to following a course that Nehru himself had charted, forgetting his own words that one of the 'remarkable developments of the present age has been the rediscovery of the past and of the nation'. Naturally, the question that comes to mind is why, after Independence, he tried to suppress the rediscovery of India's past and the cultural heritage of India. Was he, like so many others, subconsciously influenced by the narrative of M N Roy? Perhaps, we will never know the answer to this assumption.

About the other point, dubbed as 'the medieval culture of India' by Roy, the least we can say is that it exposed Roy's complete lack of knowledge about Hindu religious culture in general, and karmic laws, in particular. He felt the Brahminical social order of Sanskritic Hinduism controlled life and that Karmic laws were deterministic, killing individual freedom. His irritation about Sanskritic Hinduism is understandable, for it stood as a bulwark against not only Islam and Christianity, but also against the facile materialistic socialist ideas that tried, time and again over the past hundred years, to wipe out the cultural heritage of several societies. What he overlooked was that the same Brahminical social order of Sanskritic Hinduism had always kept the path open for the acceptance of the new, like people of all castes working together or sharing jobs in a factory or in other urban workplaces.

For Roy, 'the Indian masses' were in a cultural trap that had as its central theme, the 'submission of man either to the will of God or to his own karma'. Attacks on Karmic law as being fatalistic exposed Roy's ignorance especially in the light of the karmic laws that Vivekananda explained in his lecture on 'Vedantism' in Jaffna. The lectures on freedom can be found in *Lectures from Colombo to Almora*. Vivekananda said that a newborn comes with 'the burden of an infinite past' (of his past births), and comes 'to work out' its 'own past deeds'. According to Vivekananda, the law of karma proposes that each of us 'is the maker of his own fate'. He said, 'If I am unhappy, it has been of my own making, and that very thing shows that I can be happy if I will.' Roy, however, was a materialist and failed to understand such sublime ideas.

Further, when Roy said that Hinduism, unchanged since the medieval ages, was instrumental in accepting a saintly leader such as Gandhi, he was both right and wrong. Gandhi represented eternal India and this was why he was widely accepted by the common folk of India. However, this eternal India with all its ingredients—literature, philosophy, ideas and concepts was changing and evolving all through, and although sometimes, it would deviate from its original path, new waves would bring it back to its original, dharmic path. Even when hereditary casteism was thrust upon it, revolts against it by the so-called lower castes and reformists like Shree Chaitanya and Swami Dayanand kept alive the process of change. Then arose figures like Vivekananda and Gandhi, who challenged it even more vehemently. Such changes, challenges and debates, empowered by ancient texts and beliefs, are the strength of eternal India and Hinduism. Roy had no idea of the fundamentals of Hinduism, and he could not fathom his own ignorance.

Roy felt that 'the religiosity of Gandhi is the psychological mainstay of authoritarianism', and that Indians were happy to accept it as they 'could not as yet think in terms of freedom'. Such contempt for the common man and eternal Idea of India is characteristic of leftists and neo-secularists in general. Believers of such ideology dub the common man who votes for the BJP as 'communal'. About Gandhi's favourite concept of *Ramrajya*, Roy cautioned against belief in an imaginary history. He wrote:'… experiences of history should dispel the illusion that Nationalism, developing in India remarkably on the classical German pattern, can lead to any different result.' The result Roy was referring to here was the rise of fascism. It was true for Roy almost eighty years ago, and it is still so for some of our opposition leaders like Rahul Gandhi and the flock of neo-secularists, who now believe in respecting Hindu symbols and nurturing nationalistic aspirations as a recipe for RSS-BJP's fascism.

M N Roy concocted an imaginary narrative of India, one that the neo-secularists still follow, without understanding that with the death of the USSR his narrative too has died a natural death. Roy failed to understand the central and progressive role of Hinduism in the development of India over centuries, and the present-day neo-secularists are equally ignorant about the role that Hindu religion and culture has played, is playing, and will always play.

(All quotes of M N Roy are from the 2000 edition of *The Problem of Freedom*, Renaissance Publishers Ltd.)

Ram Manohar Lohia: Falsehood on Partition

Ram Manohar Lohia was an erratic political leader who was looked down upon both by the Congress elite (the most by Nehru, who even described the Hindi Lohia spoke in Parliament as '*bazaari* Hindi') and socialists for his incoherent logic and unpredictable political behaviour. Ironically, it was Nehru who selected Lohia as the secretary of the foreign department of the All India Congress Committee (AICC) in 1936, and Lohia resigned in 1938. During World War II, he criticised the Congress's support to the British government in the war, stating that the latter would not grant India freedom, if the Congress cooperated with them. Nehru did not support this view, so Lohia attacked Nehru at the May 1942 session of the AICC in Allahabad. Thereafter, he worked with Gandhi and got the Mahatma's support on a few occasions.

After Gandhi's assassination, Lohia broke away from the Congress along with other socialists. They resolved to protest against the government for not doing enough to immediately integrate the princely states into India. It was a movement for a great national cause and the protest led to Lohia's arrest in January 1950. Thereafter, in 1951, Lohia attended the International Socialist Congress in Frankfurt, and till 1954, he attempted unsuccessfully to unite Asian socialists under the banner, Asian Socialist Conference. But he, himself, broke away from the Praja Socialist Party in 1955, only to rejoin the united socialist platform, Samyukta Socialist Party in 1965. Meanwhile, Lohia fought an unsuccessful electoral battle against Nehru, and afterwards, when he entered Lok Sabha after winning a by-election, *The Statesman* described his entry as 'a bull in the China shop'. Such was his image in the minds of the elite of India.

Meanwhile, the socialist influence on Indian polity remained marginal, almost static. From 1957, their vote share dropped from

10.41 per cent and nineteen seats, to 6.81 per cent and twelve seats in the Lok Sabha in 1962. Lohia's Socialist Party obtained 2.69 per cent votes and 6 seats. Lohia had realised by 1960, that unless a new agenda was found, the socialists had no great future. So, he planned a two-pronged strategy to win over Muslims and OBCs.

As far as the Muslims were concerned, the simplest way was to exonerate the Muslim League from its heinous role in the Partition, and for that, he was ready to distort historical accounts. He wrote a book, *Guilty Men of Indian Partition,* published in 1960, to implement his strategy. In it, Lohia wrote:

> …the opposition of fanatical Hinduism to partition did not and could not make any sense, for one of the forces that partitioned the country was precisely this Hindu fanaticism.… (They) have helped the British and Muslim League partition the country, if the consequences of their acts, and not their motivations are taken into account. They did nothing whatsoever to bring Muslim close to Hindu within a single nation. They did almost everything to estrange them from each other. Such estrangement was the root cause of Partition.

In the book, he mentions Jinnah as the 'architect of partition'.

Now, let us examine the claim. First of all, we need to clarify that the 'Hindu fanatics' (RSS, Hindu Mahasabha and other organisations) were a marginal force as is evident from their combined vote share (6 per cent) in the 1952 election. Naturally, the percentage was even lower before the Partition, when an additional 7 crore Muslims lived in India, making the nation's pre-Independence population, 41 crore. So, could it be so that the disparate fringe elements played an important role in Partition? Not only that, the Hindu Mahasabha led by Veer Savarkar and the Muslim League led by Muhammad Ali

Jinnah formed post-election coalitions in Sindh and North West Frontier Province in 1939. In Bengal, the Mahasabha joined a government led by Fazlul Haq, who along with his comrades shifted to East Pakistan after Independence. All these coalitions could not have been possible if the League, or other Muslim political outfits, considered the Hindu Mahasabha as an enemy. So, the estrangement was not caused by the political outfits led by any Hindu 'fanatic'. Lohia knew this well, for he lived during the turbulent time of the Partition.

The second point about the claim is that it appears that Lohia thought the Muslim League could easily have been cajoled to give up the 'two nation theory'. In that case, according to him, Partition could have been avoided. But was that really feasible? Did not Gandhi try it, even going against Nehru and Patel? Did he not propose letting Jinnah be the Prime Minister of India? The 'two nation theory' was presented by Syed Ahmed Khan, who in a speech in Benaras in 1876 predicted that 'though at present there is no open hostility between the two communities...it will increase immensely in future'.

In his book, *The Crisis of State Power*, Akmal Hussain has credited Syed Ahmed Khan for echoing the sentiments of the rising Muslim bourgeois in the post-Sepoy Mutiny decades. According to the book, which was published in 1989, he had in a speech at Lucknow on 28 December 1887, said:

> Now suppose that all the English were to leave India—then who would be rulers of India? Is it possible that under these circumstances two nations, Mohammedan and Hindu, could sit on the same throne and remain equal in power? Most certainly not. It is necessary that one of them should conquer the other and thrust it down. To hope that both could remain equal is to desire the impossible and inconceivable.

Thus, the Muslim leadership not only championed for a separate state for the Muslim nation, they also were in the game of fear mongering, predicting there would be wide-scale Hindu-Muslim clashes in the future. Such campaigns, which spread fast through the networks of mosques, made the Muslims belligerent, particularly when Gandhi bowed before them to join the Khilafat movement. History makes it clear that the Muslim League, following the basic premise of Syed Ahmed Khan, was not prepared to live under any Hindu regime. Thus, blaming Hindu fanatics for the Partition was not only a distortion of history, but a nasty game played to serve narrow political interests at the cost of the nation.

Lohia's arguments appealed to the neo-secularists, and very soon, they all started blaming Hindu fanatics for the Partition. Another thirty years later, they virtually equated Hindu fanatics with RSS-Jana Sangh and the Hindu Mahasabha. Lohia, however, wasn't so naive, for he knew that the Hindutvavadi forces were just a fringe element, and too small to influence the pre-Independence course of politics. By Hindu fanatics, he was referring to the Congress.

Lohia's list of 'right nationalists', the culprits behind the Partition, definitely included Gandhi and Nehru. He divided the rightists into two categories: those who supported the Partition and those who opposed it. He concluded, 'Right nationalism, both that supported partition and that opposed it, were barren offshoots of its parents, the main body of effete nationalism.' Do not we hear a faint echo of M N Roy's view on nationalism here?

After pointing the needle of suspicion to the Congress, he blamed the Congress's role in the post Independence days for not bridging the gap between Hindus and Muslims. 'Among the unforgivable crimes of the Congress government is precisely its failure to bring together the estranged souls, in fact, its unwillingness (to) attempt the task.' Lohia in his book further says: 'Back of this crime are the desire for vote-catching and the philosophy of cosmopolitanism.' He adds that 'almost all political elements in this land, particularly such as pride themselves on their secularity, suffer from these.' He adds that 'To obtain votes, the appeals to Hindu and Muslims are overwhelmingly separate,' and all this was 'twelve years after the country was partitioned, Congressism and *praja* socialism found it necessary once again to undertake and complete another foul act of separatism.'

Ram Manohar Lohia pointed out that all the parties, barring Jana Sangh, were separately appeasing Hindu and Muslim vote banks. He also accused the Praja Socialist Party to which he, himself, belonged till not so long ago of the same behaviour. What went on back then is exactly what the BJP now popularly dubs as 'appeasement'. But his approach was politically motivated, and he was subtly trying to inculcate a theory that except for his party, no one else had any thoughts or plans of Hindu-Muslim unity, in which lay the true well-being of all communities.

It must be noted that he was not thinking in terms of coalescing neo-secularism, as he was an ardent critic of the communists who were represented by the CPI. His criticism of the communists was even more sharper compared to what he thought of the other parties. Further, he writes in his book:

> Indian communists supported partition presumably in the hope that they would thereby gain hold in the new-born state of Pakistan, obtain influence among the Indian Muslims, and run no big risk of alienating the unformed or effete Hindu mind. Their calculation(s) have been proved to be wrong

> except in the small measure that they have acquired some pockets of influence among Indian Muslims and have roused no strong indignation among Hindus. They have therefore done no mischief to themselves, but have brought no benefit to the country.... Communist strategy in its very nature (is) such that it can bring strength to a people only if it succeeds, and must necessarily help weaken them, if it does not capture power.... To communism, no idea matters, no single principle except the total concept of worker's rule. Such a concept must necessarily weaken a nation except in certain select situations. It has been continually weakening the Indian nation.'

Lohia's political ambition and strategy become clear if we read his treatise against Hindu fanatics, whom he clearly blames for the Partition along with his call for *pichde pabe sau me shaat* (the Backwards should get 60 per cent of government jobs). This call was a clever ploy to divide Hindu society—and one used later by V P Singh, the *bête noire* of Rajiv Gandhi, when he implemented the Mandal Commission report. It did not help V P Singh politically, but the socialists of UP and Bihar led by Mulayam Singh Yadav and Laloo Prasad Yadav benefitted immensely from this policy. Thus, Lohia charted out a path for his followers in clear terms: Blame the Hindu fanatics for everything and divide Hindu society on caste lines.

Though Lohia did not come up with his package of blaming everything on Hindus and reservation for the OBCs for consolidating neo-secularism—he did it to expand his political base—his proposition enriched the narrative, and in the present century, this package has become the mainstay of neo-secularism.

Rejecting Radhakrishnan's report on education

The Congress government under Nehru, shocked and devastated by the Partition's unforeseen mayhem, killings and rapes, had, from the very beginning distanced itself from the eternal Indian tradition in which concepts like dharma and karma were essential part of everyday education and character-building. The Report of the Radhakrishnan Commission for reforms to be undertaken in the university education system, submitted in 1949, had devoted an entire chapter to Religious Education. This chapter had outlined examples from the American and Australian Constitutions, and discussed relevant themes, dimensions of the secular state and the Indian view of religion. Recommendations for religious education at the end of the chapter stated:

1. that all educational institutions start work with a few minutes for silent meditation
2. that in the first year of the Degree course, lives of the great religious leaders like Gautama Buddha, Confucius, Zoroaster, Socrates, Jesus, Samkara, Ramanuja, Madhava, Mohammad, Kabir, Nanak, Gandhi, be taught,
3. that in the second year, some selections from the scriptures of the world be studied,
4. that in the third year, the central problems of the philosophy of religion be considered.

But, the Education ministry with Maulana Abul Kalam Azad as its minister ignored these recommendations while accepting the other suggestions, particularly on the autonomy of universities.

Hindu cultural tradition, the soul of India, was not part of the syllabus even in the British period. But, before Independence, Vivekananda, Tagore, Gandhi, Aurobindo Ghosh, and Bal

Gangadhar Tilak had kept the concepts alive in the regular national and regional discourse. In the aforementioned report, Radhakrishnan attempted to show the burgeoning class of neo-secularists the cardinal fault they were committing by blocking such education:

> The abuse of religion has led to the secular conception of the State. It does not mean that nothing is sacred or worthy of reverence. It does not say that all our activities are profane and devoted to the sordid ideals of selfish advancement. We do not accept a purely scientific materialism as the philosophy of the State. That would be to violate our nature, our *svabhava*, our characteristic genius, our *svadharma*. Though we have no State religion, we cannot forget that a deeply religious strain has run throughout our history like a golden thread.

He cautioned that 'we (already) have the makings of a national faith, a national way of life which is essentially democratic and religious....'

This gross neglect could only mean either of the following: That the neo-secularists were ignorant about the national way of life which is essentially democratic and religious' and failed to understand what was being told, or that they were trapped so deeply in their alien ideology due to various enticements that they decided to ignore the warning that 'we do not accept scientific materialism as the philosophy of the State. Instead, their decision to drop all references to Indic spirituality meant that it went against our nature, our *svabhava*, our characteristic genius, our *svadharma*.

Radhakrishnan, both a great teacher and a great philosopher, had done his duty, but failed to convince Nehru or Maulana Azad. With state sponsorship, the neo-secular journey was flagged off some seventy-five years ago.

These critics of Karma, did not know that no one can evade the fruits of their karma. It has now entangled an entire nation in karmic consequences.

The R C Majumdar narrative

The neo-secularists had no clue about the extent of their mistake, and following M N Roy's preachings, they decided to teach young school students a skewed version of history. Great historians, therefore, had to be sidelined in the process of writing history and replaced by pliable ones. Here is a glaring example. When the Indian government, in 1952, set up a Board of Editors to write the history of the Freedom movement with Government sponsorship, R C Majumdar, the most famous nationalist historian of that time, was appointed Director of the project. But Maulana Azad as education minister wanted history to be written on the lines he dictated. Therefore, the two headed towards a confrontation and by the end of 1955, the Board was dissolved. A year later, the government decided to transfer the responsibility to a single scholar, an archeologist-cum-historian and academic-cum-diplomat who was then serving as the Education Advisor. For Azad, this man named Tara Chand had the right qualifications for the job, for his D Phil from Queen's College, Oxford, was on the 'Influence of Islam on Indian culture'.

Majumdar fell out with Azad as he, the tallest Indian historian of that time, was not ready to either acknowledge the backward-tending Sepoy Mutiny as the starting point of the Independence struggle, or portraying Gandhi's movement as the only stream of the national Independence movement. It is to be noted here that the Sepoy Mutiny was first described as the first War of Independence reportedly by Vinayak Damodar Savarkar. It was his attempt to glorify this as great as so many Hindu rulers were involved in it. However, there is no doubt that if those Hindu and Muslim rulers had driven away the British then, India would have not existed now, and medieval darkness would not have ended. The Hindutvavadis' obsession with Hindu rulers and the neo-secularists' obsession with the Mughals can merge at some points, like the mutiny of 1857, to disfigure and distort our sense of history. Majumdar, a professional historian, was not ready to tolerate such misinterpretation of history for the sake of eulogising Hindu-Muslim unity at some point. After falling out with the government, he wrote his multi-volume *History of Freedom Movement in India* that presented an alternative narrative.

Tragically, how governmental pressure succeeded to bend the intellectuals, themselves, was evident from Radhakrishnan's life. A few years after his failed attempt to bring Independent India back to its real consciousness, he was elected as President of India. As President, he could have ensured that the lessons of the Upanishads and the Gita, the eternal guides of dharma and karma philosophy, the essence of philosophical propositions of Adi Shankaracharya, Ramanuja, Madhvacharya, Vidyaranya, Madhusudan Saraswati and Swami Vivekananda, and the interpretations of our civilisation by Tagore and Gandhi be taught to our younger generations. But, he did not assert himself.

The way Radhakrishnan's proposal on religious education was rejected and Majumdar dropped from the government's history-writing process in the end-forties and early-fifties, sent a clear signal to the academia and the intellectuals that henceforth loyalty to neo-secularism would be the sole criteria for deciding on important assignments, postings, opportunities and for distribution of other favours. Gradually, academia devoted themselves to promote this narrative, and the media supported it, expecting its own share of favours. The effort drew further strength from USSR's long shadow looming over India in the sixties.

The KGB model of cultural subversion

What happened to India after Independence is best projected through the mighty Soviet intelligence agency KGB's modus operandi that defector Yuri Alexandrovich Bezmenov brought to the forefront. According to him, the KGB's design was to undermine the US from below by changing the psyche and values of the people. If we look at the USA of today, where confrontation between traditionalists and the Woke are threatening a society divided between extra-radicals and extra-conservatives, we understand the extent of damage done by such brainwashing. The USSR went extinct more than three decades ago, but its secret agenda affected and changed a large part of the world.

The KGB model to brainwash the populace was applied in India in a remarkably big, but subtle way. It started, rather surreptitiously, in the 1950s, and more boldly in the 1960s, coinciding with the KGB sending Bezmenov to India as a Soviet Novosti Press Agency journalist. His brief was to convert Indians to Soviet-type anti-religious, anti-tradition culture. But, as Bezmenov later admitted, he was so moved by the ancient and great culture of India that he decided not to carry out his assignment and defected to Canada in 1970. He spoke out years later, in 1984, detailing the subversion strategy of the USSR in an interview with G Edward Griffin. He claimed that the major part of KGB's strategy moved around 'a slow process which we call either ideological subversion, active measures, or psychological warfare'.

What was this strategy of 'total subversion' as explained by

Bezmenov? The answer will help us understand why the narratives of Tagore, Gandhi, Nehru or Bose were edited surreptitiously by our so-called secular intellectuals since the 1950s. According to Bezmenov, the process starts with 'demoralisation'. According to him, 'it basically means…to change the perception of reality… to such an extent that despite the abundance of information no one is able to come to sensible conclusions in the interest of defending themselves, their families, their community, and their country.' This 'great brainwashing' is done, according to him, in four stages built around:

- Weakening of religion and culture.
- Controlling the media and education process of the 'victim' nation.

In the Indian context, it meant virtually denigrating our past, including the values of Hinduism, Vedas, Upanishads, Gita, yoga, ayurveda and anything else that our ancient forefathers offered to the world and which are still considered 'sacred assets' by so many Indians and even by a section of the outer world.

This was done through school textbooks and curriculum of social sciences, and history. These texts then subtly upheld socialism in the USSR and its system as the ideal one, and preached that atheism belongs to a higher level of consciousness than religiosity and spirituality, for atheism is scientific and religiosity or spiritualism is irrational and metaphysical. Thus, a mode of rejection of the old was to be bombarded continuously, so that it would become the default mode of the brain of India's youngsters. The next sphere of influence was to make available literary and non-fiction books, films, newspaper articles and other such methods of influencing public opinion. All these were tried in India.

According to Bezmenov, the entire process is divided into four stages:

1. Demoralisation, the first stage that takes about twenty years.
2. Destabilisation, the second stage that takes about 5 years during which the economy, foreign policy, judiciary, defence and other institutions are systematically sabotaged.
3. Crisis, a stage that takes about 6 months, during which a new, pliable government is brought to power.
4. Normalisation, the last stage when the puppet government binds society down according to edicts laid down by Moscow.

In the Indian case, the second and the third stage was not required as the Indian governance was tightly controlled by the USSR from the 1960s. By that time, the USSR had already forced on India a socialistic-mixed economy, and the foreign policy, though theoretically non-aligned, leaned heavily towards the USSR. Further, the military was fully dependent on the Soviets for arms and ammunition. So, in India, instead of destabilisation and crisis, what was needed was stabilising the status quo, including the narratives and the policies.

The task in India was easier for Moscow on two counts. First, India suffered from poverty and a food crisis, and was ready for being injected with a dream of a 'revolution' that promised to change the status quo. Before and after Independence, people had revolted against inequality that had many among the poor at death's door. After Independence, the Communists tried to stage a revolution during the time of B T Ranadive that ended in a fiasco. Some years later, a radical group again tried it though they defied the Soviet diktat for peaceful change and took up the Maoist prescription for an armed revolution. This group was initially known as Naxals, and later as Maoists. Siddhartha Shankar Ray, the Congress chief minister of Bengal, ruthlessly nipped the movement in 1972, but for half a century, it has played havoc in parts of different states. Unfortunately, it corrupted the minds of a sizeable section of middle-class youth who turned into secret supporters of violence. Such concerns about the miseries of the common man helped the USSR to add a socialistic flavour with the atheist and pro-minoritarian narrative that was being imposed after Independence.

The second factor that helped the process was India's over-dependence on the USSR from the 1970s. After Independence, Nehru had knocked on the doors of the West for investments and technological knowhow, but the West was not ready to see India other than as a market for their finished goods. Under duress, Nehru thought it wise to kill the instinct of Indian entrepreneurs to curb capitalist growth and follow a socialistic state sector-led growth dependent on heavy industries. He had decided that would be the best model for India. So, he looked up to the USSR for setting up heavy industries and for technology support. Taking advantage of the situation, the KGB infiltrated deep into the Communist Party of India, leftists of the Congress, bureaucracy, media, and the IB, joining hands with them to give shape to its atheist-socialist agenda.

Nehru was aware that the KGB was pumping money into India, and tried to stop it, even bragging about catching the culprits. However, his efforts produced no significant results. Rather, taking advantage of India's heavy dependence on the USSR for survival, the KGB soon launched a drive for cultural change.

So, in short, the arrogant West that supported the creation of a Pakistan and declined technological know-how to India, pushed India steadily towards the USSR. For the USSR, it was a great opportunity on two counts: First, in those days of the Cold War, it suddenly had a 'friend' from the NAM, whom it was able to make fully dependent on it in security matters—from protecting India in the Security Council of the UN to getting India through the 1971-war situation. Its support to India in terms of arms and military supplies made India permanently crippled to take any independent decision that would harm the USSR's economic interests. The USSR had turned India into a friend by compulsion and this, no doubt, would have continued had not the USSR, itself, disintegrated into pieces because of internal pressures.

Second, in India the USSR got to manage a huge country that was home to the second-largest population of the world. Converting it to an athesist semi-communist culture from its deep-rooted religiosity was not easy. To fulfil this goal, it adopted a completely different approach than it undertook for the USA. It pampered Indians into deluding them to believe that both countries were equal partners in development. The Indians, were, therefore, happy to accept this tutelage.

Though the USSR has itself, gone extinct, its propaganda succeeded in converting a large section of the global population to the leftist social order, one that supports the weaker sections and the minorities of every sort even at the cost of interest of the others.

Over the years, India has seen an abundance of this sort of leftist-leanings and has sometimes ended up in creating undesirable moral dilemmas (like allowing Rohingyas into India). Nowhere in the world does the human race or a community, sacrifice its collective core interests for others. Such idealistic views ultimately generate confrontations that harm the weaker sections and the minorities the most.

Mitrokhin papers and other sources: Corrupting the elite

It is common knowledge that the easiest way to corrupt a populace is to corrupt its elite and its more outspoken and vocal sections. According to Vasili Mitrokhin, a former KGB man in charge of its archive, the USSR had tried it in India most elaborately.

Almost all the prominent personalities of the sixties, seventies, and even the eighties are by now dead or too old to defend themselves. So, what Soviet secret agents said or wrote about those personalities can no longer be verified or investigated from authoritative sources. Yet, certain stories that have outlasted these decades have stayed on. These stories centre around certain CPI and Congress politicians, bureaucrats, filmmakers and journalists who received money and other benefits from the Russians. We need to look at such stories for an understanding of those bygone decades, but with a pinch of salt.

One of the two books written by Christopher Andrew and Vasili Mitrokhin on the basis of claimed KGB archived documents is *The Mitrokhin Archive II: The KGB in the World*. The critics had described this book, published in 2005, as 'the biggest intelligence coups in recent years'. Many of its revelations tally with what was rumoured earlier in India. Author Vasili Mitrokhin was himself ensconced in the KGB archives, and the two chapters devoted to India list some fascinating observations such as the KGB failing to anticipate the outcome of the 1977 elections (in which Congress's *bête noire* Morarji Desai came to power), or of the Soviet agency's keenness to alter Sanjay Gandhi's open distrust of socialism. The KGB, it is reported, apparently recruited one of his close friends, codenamed PURI to impress upon Sanjay Gandhi to change his mind.

Vasili Mitrokhin writes that the KGB operations in India expanded rapidly in the fifties and sixties, but was not restricted within the geography of India. An Indian diplomat, codenamed Prokhor, stationed in the embassy in Moscow, was recruited through the common method of using a honey trap by a female KGB agent, codenamed Neverova. This man supplied the agency the embassy's codebook and other material for Rs 4,000 a month, a hefty sum in those days. The book states that two other diplomats, were also compromised. Other KGB officials have written about several such instances in their memoirs. But M K Dhar, a former IB (India) joint director, claimed that the IB identified 'four Union ministers (in Indira Gandhi's cabinet) and over two dozen MPs who were on the KGB payroll'. Among the most vulnerable were important high-ups of the Defence Ministry, particularly armed forces officers responsible for military procurement. Does it mean they were paid to make India over-dependent on Russian arms, ammunition, fighter planes and other systems? Mitrokhin pointed in that direction.

Vasili Mitrokhin was a senior officer of the KGB archives who defected to Britain in 1992, bringing along thousands of pages of top-secret KGB documents. The CIA and MI5 vouched for the genuineness of the archival material brought by him. But the papers were mainly on Europe and the US, and those materials were used for his first book. The chapters on India are in the second book that he co-authored with Christopher Andrew, an intelligence expert. The book claims that the maximum operational effort by the KGB in a Third World country during the Cold War was put into India. It is known that the Third World, particularly the non-aligned (NAM) nations were of particular importance to the USSR as almost the entire developed world—the USA and Europe, except for a few states of Eastern Europe, and Japan—was against the USSR.

The chapters on India claimed that the number of KGB agents

in India in the 1970s was higher than in any other country. KGB Major General Oleg Kalugin notes about India that 'it seemed like the entire country was for sale'. The KGB faced competition from the CIA as they too had penetrated deep within the Indian government. Both agencies were bribing the politicians and the officials of the Indian government, but the KGB was miles ahead of the CIA. No wonder, Mitrokhin writes that India was 'the model of KGB infiltration in a Third World government'. They had mines of information on India, so much so that they could decline a proposal from an Indian minister to sell classified information for US $50,000. According to the archival papers, the KGB was running over thirty high-level agents in India, with ten of these agents from Indian intelligence services in 1978.

Now let us come to the point of direct funding of the Congress and its ally, CPI (Communist Party of India). According to the KGB files, the soviet agency pumped huge money into the 1977 election campaign of twenty-one non-communist politicians in India. These included four union ministers. It is claimed that suitcases of cash regularly arrived at the Congress office, often brought in by KGB officers, themselves. Once, a secret gift of Rs 2 million (Rs 20 lakh) was sent from the Politburo to the Congress (R), the party faction led by Indira Gandhi. It was reportedly delivered personally by the KGB head in India, Leonid Shebarshin.

According to the book, both in 1962 and 1967, election campaigns of V Krishna Menon, the defence minister instrumental in buying Soviet MiGs instead of British Lightnings, were funded by the KGB. During 1975, the KGB claimed to have spent a total of 10.6 million rubles to strengthen support for Indira Gandhi and to undercut her political opponents.

The CPI was claimed to be funded in different ways, including direct transfer through car windows, something done in Delhi itself. Another revelation in the book is of the CPI general-secretary Ajoy Ghosh being asked to establish an import-export venture for trading with the Soviet bloc in 1959, a venture that showed annual profits of over Rs 3 million (Rs 30 lakh) in little more than a decade.

The fourth pillar of democracy, the media was also targeted. According to the archival papers, Rs one million (Rs 10 lakh) was given to a newspaper supporting Indira Gandhi. It also claimed that ten newspapers and one news agency were on the Soviet payroll. By 1972, the KGB boasted that they had planted more than 3,500 articles in Indian newspapers. This was done generally through the news agency because almost all newspapers subscribed to it. Sometimes, however, they approached journalists directly. The book claims that the KGB recruited one of India's most influential journalists, codenamed NOK, whose anti-US articles helped spread suspicion about the US.

At times, the KGB stoked anti-US sentiments in other, more direct ways. The book outlines how in 1969, the Politburo in Moscow was informed by the KGB that they could 'organise a demonstration of up to 20,000 Muslims in front of the US embassy in Delhi and that it would cost Rs 5,000'. Leonid Brezhnev, the then general secretary of the party, accepted the offer.

It is up to the reader to accept or reject the information in the book. There are no official records available for claims like large transactions such as money being directly sent to Indira Gandhi's residence. But this much is definitely true that a big game was on and the USSR was actively meddling in Indian politics to protect Indira Gandhi while pushing her government towards a definite direction through the CPI.

Russia's first friend was Krishna Menon, India's Defense Minister from 1957 to 1962, who was being heralded as Nehru's successor. But the defeat in the 1962 Chinese war was his undoing. So, they focused on Indira Gandhi. These things are all in the book, and we can surmise from it that the USSR was overly interested in a positive outcome of the Bangladesh liberation war, and they ensured it. Others have claimed that the USSR supported the emergency and forced the CPI to support it. These were all open secrets in those days, but could not be proven.

That the USSR made cash payments was corroborated from too many sources to be discarded. A 1985 CIA document declassified in 2011 also says that the Soviets 'provided funding to Congress-I Party coffers through kickback arrangements with Indian businesses'. However, it claimed that CPI and CPI(M) were also funded by the Soviets 'through a combination of kickback schemes, normal business transactions, and direct cash payments'. These three types of payment were certainly applicable to the CPI. It categorised these three as:

a) 60-65 per cent discount to Peoples Publishing House (PPH) accounting for three-fourths of PPH's annual sales, which as on 1985 exceeded Rs 10 million (Rs 100 lakh).
b) Soviet advertisements in CPI journals which accounted for US $60,000 in 1984.
c) Visitors' expenses, which included cash as well as air tickets for visitors to the USSR sponsored by CPI or its front groups.

It is also claimed that one woman leader, a rabid anti-Hindu politician, was supported in her 1977 election (which she lost) by East German diplomats, who financed her election campaign with US $50,000.

We have the option of taking such information with a pinch of salt, but apparently it appears that several of our politicians and political parties, including our IFS, IAS officers, and even intelligence staff, were lured by foreign money in post-independence decades.

USSR's influence over India: Skewing the economy

For over 5,000 years, from the days of the ancient Sindhu-Saraswati urban culture, our tradition had been one of unleashing the free spirit of entrepreneurship. We planted the seeds and developed an early form of *laissez faire*; and over millennia were never restricted by the *rajshakti*, the state power, in its execution. The success or failure of the forces of production and productivity was never a concern of the state which only collected revenue and facilitated the process of trade by providing basic infrastructural needs.

The process was first thwarted under colonial rule that brought in many restrictions. It was expected that in free India, the free spirit of enterprise would find liberation again, with the encouragement of political leaders. But, building upon the Bombay Plan and going to the opposite extreme, Nehru's Planning Commission fashioned the Plans upon the Soviet Planning Committee's recommendations. P C Mahalanobis, the architect of Independent India's Planning Commissions, was the main priest of this socialistic journey. The planners believed that only state-owned heavy industries would lead the growth process in India. The USSR eagerly came forward to ink an agreement on 2 February 1955 clearing the path for establishing a one-million ton per annum steel plant in Bhilai. From that point, India formally embraced the socialistic model of a mixed economy.

Thus, after Independence, India embarked on a twisted

journey, even in the economic field, one that denied traditional paths and embraced one that was hollow. It was based not on the Indian experience, but on USSR's. Such socialist economy models have been rejected everywhere in the world now, and also in India from 1991. But in its three-and-a-half decades of existence, it damaged us in two ways: First, by leashing our economic growth by frustrating the spirit of free enterprise; and second, by strengthening the neo-secular narrative as the common man was forced to believe that the socialistic mixed economy under the aegis of neo-secular leaders would liberate them from the shackles of poverty and illiteracy.

Even if we accept that theory of state-run heavy-industry-propelled development, a fundamental question remained unanswered—what was the need for blindly following Russia's economic model to stymie the private sector that even then had huge potential to contribute to economic growth? The Soviet economic model ultimately brought down the USSR itself, and left Russia so crippled that it has failed to develop a capitalist economy even now. It still remains over-dependent on the state sector that basically serves the political interests of its masters. India too had reached the end of its tether after three decades of socialistic constriction, and had to demolish it all and go in for a new economic model.

Looking back, one notices that President Nikita Khrushschev and former Communist Party secretary Nikolai Bulganin visited India in 1955, and the Soviet-type plan relying solely on heavy industry was flagged off in 1956. The plan was to first augment a process of heavy industry in-breeding further and further, and then spread the state's hand to production of consumer items, thus making India a full-fledged command economy like the USSR. All major private initiatives were nationalised to give the statist economy some stature, and almost all those steps proved counter-productive in later decades. Air India was nationalised in 1953, and after it amassed a cumulative loss of Rs 40,000 crores, a heavy drain on tax-payers' money, it was finally given back to the Tatas, the original owner, in 2022. Again, Indian Air Lines was formed by takeover and merger of many regional airlines, and finally was merged with Air India. The story of these two airlines summarises the story of the humongous failure of the state sector with the PSUs turning into white elephants.

The list of the good companies nationalised in the last century was just too long. It included Bharat Petroleum, Balmer Lawrie, Bharat Coking Coal, Braithwaite, Eastern Coalfields, Hindustan Petroleum, Hindustan Shipyard, Oil India, Western Coalfields, General Insurance Corporation of India, National Insurance and many other insurance companies and almost all the banks India had in the earlier years. The state sector could not build itself on its own strength except for a few PSUs that were established after Independence, and even those had to be reoriented later to make those profitable and to stop the drain on tax-payers' money.

In 1969, Indira Gandhi nationalised fourteen of India's largest private banks, and an additional 6 in 1980. It was done with the aim of giving loans to the farmers and to the poor, with particular focus on rural areas. But these aims were never fulfilled, as was later evident from the flourishing existence of private moneylenders (and farmers' suicide). Instead, the act of nationalisation led to another domain of corruption and exploitation of banks by private businessmen linked with politicians. This politician-businessman nexus bled not only the banks, but almost all the PSUs, where trade unions also called the shots. Thus, the socialistic structure built a system that encouraged cronyism, helped the rich including administrators and politicians, added to the quantum of black money as hefty bribes were paid to advance loans and acquire contracts. Eventually, it drained the exchequer of tax-payers' money.

This industrial policy, with corresponding restrictions on private enterprise, ruined the Indian economy. It also paved the way for the infamous license Permit Raj that further stymied investor initiatives. The Mittals, being unable to have required permissions in India, went to Indonesia in 1974 to establish a steel plant that later became ArcelorMittal, among the world's leading steel and mining company that put Lakshmi Mittal, its owner, firmly in the Forbes' richest hundred list. Ironically, India later started buying steel from Mittal's Indonesian company. Such lost opportunities damaged India for decades, but the socialistic-mixed economy pattern had become a compulsion, as any departure from it would enrage the USSR, India's Big Brother and protector. Finally, it led to the infamous balance of payments crisis around 1990, and as by this time, USSR was defunct, India could finally embark on a traditional path of economic development.

After the crisis, the Union Government launched the liberalisation drive, unshackled the private sector, and began divesting and privatising its ownership of several PSUs to rectify past blunders. However, India still suffers from the hangovers of past beliefs, and has not been able to reform the economy adequately.

Thus, the process that Nehru and Mahalanobis had initiated left its hangover even so many decades later, while bleeding India in various ways. China, a 'communist' country ruled by a Communist Party, was far wiser. Back in 1978-79, under the leadership of Deng Xiaoping, they had realised the bleakness of a command economy system, and had suitably amended it.

Since then it has moved far, far ahead of India and of many other developed nations in the world. According to media reports, Aakar Patel had said that 'The World Bank's data shows that India's per capita income in 1960 was US $82, while China's was US $89. In 1970, we were almost even, with India at $112 and China at $113. In 1980, India was $266 and China considerably behind at $194. In 2000, however, we were at $1,357 and China was at $4,450. In 2022, India was at $2,388 and China at $12,720.

Deluded by the Soviet economic model and constricted by the neo-secularists, we wasted slightly more than a decade to get onto China's path of liberalisation, and it has already done irreparable damage to us. The first-comer always enjoys a huge advantage over the second, and we are paying the price for our procrastination. Had we followed a capitalist path from the beginning with the state sector playing a supportive role, we could have reached the sky by now!

The neo-secular narrative and the socialistic mixed economy got intertwined in such a way that in the 1980s even Rajiv Gandhi could not amass the courage to break it. According to Montek Singh Ahluwalia: 'He was the first top politician to recognise that a new, aspirational middle class was emerging, with more money to spend and demands for modern consumer goods which could not be ignored. This necessitated a departure from the PC Mahalanobis strategy, which was at the core of much of Indian planning, and was based on prioritising the production of capital goods (largely produced in the public sector) while actively discouraging the production of durable consumer goods. Since the private sector was best positioned to meet the new demands, it had to be given freedom to expand and respond to these new demands. Rajiv was the first prime minister to signal a new approach to the private sector. He met representatives of the private sector much more frequently than any of his predecessors had done. He also broke visibly with tradition by taking business delegations with him on his international trips.'[5]

India's initial experiments with a socialistic economy, however, played a crucial role in strengthening the neo-secular narrative. It was presented as a means of uplifting the poor—remember the *garibi hatao* slogan and as the concept was preached by trusted leaders like Nehru and Indira Gandhi, the masses believed in its sanctity and clung on to false hopes. With a firm faith in the infallibility of this mixed economy, the huge majority of India's people had ignored even the attempts to deracinate Hindus. But the belief in the mixed economy broke down and everything was turned upside down, with the country finally following the path it had followed for thousands of years.

However, the vestiges of a socialist economy are still powerful enough to create confusion in the minds of a sizeable section of the masses who cannot understand economic logic and confuse welfare with populism. But facts are facts, and these facts show the inherent economic logic for capitalism combined with welfarism. India, condemned by global institutions for its abject poverty, had only 2-3 per cent people below the abject poverty line of $2.15 per day per head in 2022-23, according to the World Bank. The figure stood at 36 per cent when the liberalisation of the economy was initiated in 1991. The liberalisation initiated by P V Narasimha Rao unshackled the private sector and gave it the right to invest and produce as much as it could. That led to rapid growth of the industry in particular, and the economy in general, allowing the government to earn much more revenue. A sizeable part of this additional revenue could be channelised to look after the poor, and that has lifted almost the entire population from the curse of abject poverty. The Indian story shows that capitalist welfarism is more competent to serve the poor than a socialistic mixed economy.

USSR's iron grip over India: Security matters

Economic progress aside, the second most important aspect of the Indian state was security and military preparedness.

Nehru had embraced a crisis by going to the UN to resolve the Kashmir issue out of his naïve faith that the West was driven by logic and a sense of justice, and would, therefore, stand by him. But the other world leaders were not neo-secularists like him, and the general motivation behind decisions of the UN on Kashmir was based on simple logic: How could India, a Hindu nation, do justice to Kashmir, a Muslim majority province? Moreover, it suited the West to weaken India, and a US and UK-led resolution at the UNSC in 1957 called for sending a UN force to Kashmir to bring peace. It garnered support of the majority of its members, but the USSR vetoed it and saved the day for India. Thereafter, India was bereft of any option of opposing the USSR on any substantial issue, though Nehru had succeeded in projecting India as a strong proponent of the Non-Aligned Movement (NAM). From then on, the USSR continued to protect India in the UN, saving it six times in the Security Council by applying its veto power. That it was India's messiah was the image that got imprinted on to Indian minds from then, and it helped the super power to discreetly carry on with its agenda of cultural subversion in India.

In those days, India had very little military strength, but again, it was the USSR that supplied the military with *MiG-21s* along with *Ilysuhin Il-14* cargo aircrafts. Still, India was not well-equipped for emergencies. China and India were at a similar stage of development, yet India was defeated hands down by China in the 1962 war. Then, Nehru passed away in 1964. And in 1965, India was engaged in another war with Pakistan when its President, Ayub Khan sent Pakistani troops to Kashmir to lead an insurgency to 'liberate' Kashmir. Though the Kashmiris did not respond to the Pakistani call, the conflict widened with both sides capturing territories of the other and incurring heavy losses at the same time. After fighting through the months of August and September, the war was showing no decisive result. Finally, the UN interfered and a ceasefire followed. The war was considered a victory in India, as Ayub Khan's original intention was defeated. But, a 'permanent solution' was needed, and as India no longer had faith in the West, the USSR saw an opportunity to have a stronger foothold to establish its influence further in South Asia.

The dispute was finally settled in a meeting between Ayub Khan and Indian Premier Lal Bahadur Shastri in Tashkent in January 1966, and an agreement brokered by the Soviet Prime Minister Alexei Kosygin was signed by both.

India felt vindicated on many points as New Delhi had not started the war. The points for peace were based on the agreement that both countries:

i) Shall 'settle....disputes through peaceful means' and will not take 'recourse to force'
ii) Shall maintain relations 'based on the principle of non-interference in the internal affairs of each other'
iii) shall 'discourage any propaganda directed against the other country, and....encourage propaganda which promotes the development of friendly relations between the two countries

No wonder Zulfikar Ali Bhutto, Pakistan's foreign minister, rejected the proposals, but Ayub Khan went ahead and signed it, and was later blamed by his country's people for signing an unfavourable compromise. He was further blamed for miscalculating India's strength on the basis of the country's defeat at the hands of the Chinese. With that, Pak propaganda on Kashmir lost its teeth, and the USA took a little tougher stand against Pakistan for using its weapons against India.

Then came 1971. On December 6, India decided to recognise Bangladesh, and with a clear intention of intervening in favour of Pakistan, the US President Richard Nixon directed Task Force 74, part of the USA's Seventh Fleet, to advance towards the Bay of Bengal. Its junior ally, Britain, too dispatched its aircraft carrier HMS Eagle to the Arabian Sea. Their plan was simple: To attack and engage India in the Bay of Bengal and the Arabian Sea while Pakistan would attack India on land, thus ensuring India's ignominious defeat. But their well-calculated plans failed. Anticipating just this, India sought USSR's help, and immediately received a much-needed response. The Soviet Union sent its nuclear-armed Pacific Fleet led by Admiral Vladimir Kruglyakov, who intercepted the US and British warships in mid waters, blocking their advancement towards India. Consequently, the USA and UK ships had to change their routes, and before they could be in India's waters, the war had ended in a decisive victory for India.

From then on, India was over-dependent on the USSR, and indebted, a feeling not merely limited to state apparatus. The Russian support during the 1971 war turned into a household story in urban India. People were overwhelmed by the benevolent act of India's great friend, and even the Janata Party regime led by the pro-US Morarji Desai could not dent it. Later, Indians largely supported USSR's unjustified invasion of Afghanistan. From the Indian government's viewpoint, a communist Afghanistan antagonistic to Pakistan would have been a great relief for India. So, it was not surprising that the Indira Gandhi government supported the Soviet invasion of Afghanistan and backed USSR in the UN Debate in 1980. India also offered humanitarian assistance to Afghan communists after they were ousted. Their President, Mohammad Najibullah Ahmadzai, better known as Najibullah or Najib, was killed by the Taliban in 1996 after they took over Kabul. His wife and three daughters sought shelter in India.

These developments—defeat at the hands of the Chinese in 1962; Soviet Russia indirectly dishing out a favourable agreement with Pakistan in Tashkent; and the crucial Soviet intervention in 1971—pushed India strategically closer to the USSR, which turned into almost the sole supplier of arms and military equipment during Indira Gandhi's governments. At one time, almost 85 per cent of India's weapons were from USSR. Strategic experts call this a 'lock-in' effect, which means that a consumer is so strongly tied with a company that finding an alternative calls for considerable effort and expense. From the sixties to the eighties decades, India's dependence on USSR for security further strengthened the neo-secular narrative in the public imagination, and USSR was regarded as a nation actively seeking the well-being of Indians. Neither was Indira Gandhi working directly against the Hindus, and in this scenario, the Indian population stepped further into the trap of the neo-secularists. They loved their Big Brother, the USSR, not knowing that their Big Brother's policies would soon push the USSR, itself, into extinction. Even more than thirty years after the disintegration of the USSR, India does not find itself in a comfortable situation as its dependence on Russia continues. However, Russia cannot maintain the supply line of our arms and ammunition, particularly for spares. Further, it is close to China now, and may even stop supplying spares at a crucial time in the future.

The neo-secularists back then tried to portray the US and the West as villains, and they never tried to mend fences with the West, which was, to say the least, a huge diplomatic failure. This was particularly highlighted when the government had to knock on Western doors, mainly the USA, after the USSR was dissolved. Let us recall the situation that arose in 2007-2008, when the Congress was possessed by an urgency to sign a Nuke Deal with the US, and was ready to sacrifice even their own government for it. However, it is extremely creditworthy that Narasimha Rao, A B Vajpayee, Manmohan Singh and Narendra Modi contributed significantly to navigate India out of the quagmire.

India had, for too long, been a stooge of the USSR, and now that the latter had ceased to exist, India literally found itself at the crossroads, a dangerous option for a developing nation.

USSR's cultural subversion through films and literature

Every state that wants to expand its area of influence, uses its soft power to persuade other populations to accept its natural superiority. The European nations and the USA tried it aggressively, directly demonstrating their supremacy both as a donor-plus-protector and as a superior culture. But the USSR adopted a completely different approach. Indians knew English, but not Russian. So, direct imposition of supremacy was difficult, and would not have been in line with the egalitarian system they preached. Instead, they thought that sending out the message that 'you too are great and we respect you' would suit their purpose better. The USSR chose to adopt this approach, all aimed at India accepting the USSR's superior role of donor-plus-protector. The USA had the advantage of representing English literature and democratic values, while the USSR had the advantage of its egalitarian and socialistic narrative. Back in the seventies and eighties, this put the USSR at par with the USA.

At a subtler level, the Soviet strategy was to influence Indian cinema, theatre and literature by offering material benefits after India gained its Independence. The US was a democracy and could not force its theatre owners to screen or ask its publishers to publish books by Indian authors. But the Soviet system was authoritarian, and the state and the Communist Party could dictate choices to the nation's theatres and publishers. So, suddenly, Indian Bollywood films started gaining 'popularity' in Moscow from the fifties and this continued till the dissolution of the USSR. It is another matter that even today, Hindi serials and movies enjoy some level of popularity in a few Central Asian Republics because of the millennia-old cultural connections; but under the Soviet regime, the centre of false popularity was Moscow. It is interesting to note that no one ever asked for Indian films to be screened there after the dissolution of the USSR.

According to IMDb data, the USSR imported some 300 films to Moscow between 1954 and 1991, and became a reliable alternative source for earning money through scripts projecting the plight of the downtrodden especially and promoting a socio-cultural environment that was different from true Hindu culture. Back then Muslims were just 10 per cent of the population, but words like *Khudah*, and *Allah* particularly in songs sung even by Hindu characters, became more common in Bollywood than *Ishwar* or *Bhagwan*. Urdu words were given preference over Hindustani words. The producers were businessmen, and if USSR ensured good sales of tickets for 'secular' Indian films, they were happy to give in.

So, nationalistic or Hindu theme-based films lost glamour in the national formal discourse, and legendary films like *Jay Santoshi*

Ma (1975) were frowned upon by neo-secularists. For the record, *Jay Santoshi Ma,* a devotional film featuring unknown actors and made on a budget of Rs 25 lakh, grossed Rs 5 crore, which in present times would equal to Rs 150 crore. Here, we need to recollect that this figure is of a time when the Indian population was just 55 crore. Moreover, cinema tickets were far cheaper than what multiplexes charge now. As entertainment options were limited back then, movies dominated and far more people saw them in theatres than now. Further, it was competing with the iconic film *Sholay* as both films were released on the same day. Still, it became a 'cult classic' and had tremendous impact on viewers. Approximately 1 crore people saw it—the popularity of the deity Santoshi Ma increased manifold and many adopted rituals like fasting to please the goddess throughout northern India.

Summing up the contradictions between the USSR-patronised social justice films made in those days and the success of *Jai Santoshi Ma* in the cultural realm, we can conclude that on the ground, nothing had really changed, and India still remained true to its roots. However, in the absence of dharmic teachings, the common man was now being drawn solely towards ritualism. Sociologically, this development can be correlated to people's urge for seeing Ram's temple at his imagined birthplace—a demand that shook India just two decades later.

The Indian Government's cultural bosses, however, left no stone unturned, particularly in the fifties and sixties, to promote the cultural changes secretively proposed by KGB agents operating in Bollywood. It is rumoured that those who did not join this game and refused to make films championing justice for the downtrodden were discriminated against by Indian establishments. The game apparently started with the 1951 film *Awaara,* which was released in the USSR in 1954, though even before that, *Dharti Ke Lal* had been chosen by the Soviets to be screened in the USSR. However, after the Raj Kapoor-directed *Awaara* (written by Khwaja Ahmed Abbas) was released in the USSR in 1954, the strategy was formalised. The flamboyance continued till *Disco Dancer,* the 1982-blockbuster became the highest grossing Indian film in the USSR. It was written by Rahi Masoom Raza and directed by Babbar Subhash. Such attempts to control the film world, however, ended after the Emergency. During this period, *Aandhi,* another legendary film, was banned.

According to Russian film historian, Sergey Kudryavtsev, among those foreign films that sold more than 20 million tickets in the Soviet Union, fifty were Indian films. No other nation came close to it as only forty-one Hollywood films (with no patronage from the Soviet state) crossed the line. This was surprising as Hollywood films dominated all over the world in that era. In India, however, Russian films had no market, while Hollywood films like *Guns of Navarone* and *Sound of Music* in the sixties, *Enter the Dragon,* and *Star Wars* of the seventies, *First Blood* and *ET* in the eighties to recent hits like *Top Gun* and *Mission Impossible*, have always been dear to the Indian urban population. Despite this failure to popularise Russian films in India, Indian films were routinely released in the Soviet Union till the communists ruled the country, with the more popular Hindi films releasing with more than a thousand prints there, according to Sergey Kudryavtsev.

As soon as the Soviet Union collapsed in 1991, Indian films immediately disappeared from Russian cinema halls. Their exit was sudden, almost magical. It just goes to show that the Russians were never interested in Hindi films, and that the communists had artificially created a market to influence film making in India. Participation in film festivals was another means of achieving the same goal.

The environment in the sixties and seventies was such that it encouraged directors to make left-leaning films not only in Hindi but in many different languages. However, as these intellectually acclaimed films most often had no box office value, the producers were not really interested to invest in such films. However, their release in the Soviet Union guaranteed returns. Nevertheless, in the hope of changing Indian society, many producers were swayed to produce such films. A majority of these films were nothing other than sophisticated slogan-mongering, and there was no dearth of ready critics who would praise those highly. It is, therefore, not surprising that after the dissolution of the USSR, such films became almost extinct. Thereafter, films with the theme of social injustice that did survive had a good story element in them. But gradually, they too disappeared and so did the overuse of Urdu words and reference to Allah by Hindus.

Just after the USSR's demise, Bollywood films once again gave prominence to Indian traditions in its themes, and a few such films having Shahrukh Khan in the lead met with huge success. Here it must be recalled that Raj Kapoor, himself, was not a neo-secularist for he also produced films like *Satyam, Shivam, Sundaram* and *Ram Teri Ganga Maili*; nevertheless, he allowed himself to be patronised by the Russians.

The communists tried hard to make Russian films popular in India; the effort was even carried to the smaller towns, and film festivals were organised all over Uttar Pradesh—in Faizabad, Ayodhya, Darshan Nagar, Arkuna, and Bhadarsa—so that people could experience the socialistic lifestyle and culture of the USSR for themselves. Among the films shown at these festivals were *The Chronicle of October, Twice Born*, and *30 Minutes of Soviet*

Circus. These films were aimed at creating hostility against the West. As its name suggests, *The Chronicle of October* was about the October Revolution. *Twice Born* was the story of a Russian rookie's dedication who survived a shipwreck after the Germans attacked it in 1942. These films, however, failed to sway the minds of Indians and never gained popularity.

This cultural pampering was also extended to books, and Russian literature made deep inroads into India further converting young Indians into neo-secularism. The USSR heavily subsidised several beautifully produced and printed books and made them so affordable that middleclass students could buy hardbound editions. It was significant that these books were translated not just into English but in almost all other major Indian languages to reach the maximum number of Indians. These books—including some classics like those by Maxim Gorky—flooded the markets and pavements of university areas during the seventies and eighties.

Further, courses in Hindi, Bengali, and Urdu literature were conducted in Moscow, Tashkent, Tbilisi, and Leningrad universities during the Soviet regime. Russian doors were open for works of all famous authors of India such as Tagore, Premchand, Mulk Raj Anand, Nehru, and Radhakrishnan. Tagore's works sold more than three million copies.

Other methods of propaganda included cultural exchange programmes, magazines like *Soviet Land* and radio stations like Radio Moscow and Radio Sputnik broadcasting regular programmes in Hindi and Urdu. Many Indians enjoyed the interactions broadcast on these channels. The Soviet-Indian Friendship Society was another medium for cultural exchange. Universities like the North Ossetian State University in Alania, under the Soviet state's control, set up a club of Soviet and

Indian pen-friends. People's Friendship University of Russia gave special attention to India and dedicated programmes to left-leaning Indian writers like Krishan Chander and filmmaker Khwaja Ahmed Abbas. The university had a TV magazine, *Our Friend India*, and once it featured Russian girls named Indira. The first Indira had been named after Indira Gandhi when she visited Ossetia in 1955. According to media reports, Indira Gandhi was so happy about Russians being named after her that she enquired about her namesakes for several years. The *Soviet Land* wrote: 'The Indiras of Ossetia are proud to bear this name.' It goes to show that even the Prime Minister of India lapped up such propaganda.

Raj Kapoor became a cult figure in Russia and became popular as a filmmaker who stood with the underdog and rooted for them, with an individual victory becoming a symbol of a collective victory. The Soviet state actively promoted films like *Awaara*, and pushed the common man to hang his photo on their walls. Russians sang his songs for Indian guests at state functions, but all this came to an abrupt end with the collapse of the Soviet empire. It bears testimony to the fact that everything was propaganda, but ironically, for several years, Indians still believed that Raj Kapoor was hugely popular in Russia. The fact is that Russians were never interested in Hindi films; but the people of Central Asia, where 60 million tickets of *Sholay* were sold in the late seventies, loved to watch those, and they still love watching Hindi films and serials. The staged popularity of Indian films in Moscow was a glaring example of how illusions were created by the USSR to deceive unsuspecting Indians, so that the neo-secularists could take advantage of it.

This, of course, affected the common Indian, who sincerely believed that the USSR was a great nation, and that Western claims that painted Stalin out to be a mass-murderer was all false western propaganda. They also believed that the USSR's invasion of Afghanistan was justified and were shocked when the Afghans defeated the Russians and forced them to leave. The next shock came when the USSR, itself, collapsed. But by then the roots of the neo-secular narrative had gone deep, affecting education and beliefs in India.

Endnotes

The neo-secularists had already laid out the groundwork done by M N Roy, Ram Manohar Lohia, Abul Kalam Azad and others by 1950s, and it all bore fruit when the USSR turned into India's guardian angel. Under the super power's tutelage, neo-secularists spread their network far and wide. The USSR tried to brainwash Indians, as the KGB defector Yuri Alexandrovich Bezmenov pointed out, mainly through cultural subversion so that Indians forget their age-old traditions and heritage. In this process, Soviet communists utilised the opportunities provided by the economic and security-related crises of the newly independent nation. The Soviet's cultural invasion was further fuelled by a bunch of Indian neo-secularists, who utilised this situational advantage to fashion the thought that India could not survive without the USSR and its socialistic form of mixed economy. As was later seen, this mixed economy ended up harming India immensely.

The alternate facile narrative—materialistic, atheistic, pro-minoritarian and against the ethos of eternal India—could temporarily be imposed on India as this narrative was supported and at times sponsored by the guardian angel, USSR. The elite and intellectual class adopted it for their own material benefit, while the common man's mind was affected by the iilusions created by the USSR.

Three factors were at the base of this illusion. The USSR had falsely projected itself as running a poor-friendly government in the Soviet Land through a command economy, while in reality, each day, it was inching closer towards its impending doom. Second, by acting as India's protector in the international arena and empowering Indians with arms, ammunition and fighter jets, the USSR emerged as a messiah. Third, the leftist campaign further brainwashed the people to reject all truths about the Soviets as propaganda of the West, whether about its failing economy or about the killings of millions of Soviets by Stalin. Thus, USSR emerged in the Indian mind as a successful pro-poor country standing by the people of India, while being victimised by the West. It strengthened the socialist narrative and villainised the West.

The legends around the USSR were busted by the end of the century; but, by then, the neo-secular narrative had been embedded in the minds of its followers and they had succeeded in establishing that India is not Hindu. However, with the dissolution of the USSR, first Hindu reactions against the deracination attempts had become visible, and it reached its ghastly extreme on December 6, 1992, the day the Babri mosque was demolished.

From that day onwards, the neo-secular narrative was doomed to die a natural death. Surprisingly, post-Independence Congress that for fifty years had played the role of being a nuanced neo-secular party, gave up its traditional line and joined the hardcore camp in its last years. Not only that, it introduced, for the first time, a neo-secular form of governance during 2004-14, and invited the nemesis of the whole camp.

Third Fault

From Nuanced Neo-secular to Anti-Hindu Governance

The Congress was a neo-secular party as far as suppressing the traditional Idea of India was concerned, but all through the last century, its governments were never anti-Hindu. Often, the governments even safeguarded real Hindu interests ignoring the Muslims. In simple terms, it was a sort of nuanced form of neo-secularism that the Congress followed in the last century. That was why the reaction of the Hindu community was never so severe as it has been in the present century. The situation changed when the Congress ran a government from 2004-14 which displayed certain anti-Hindu characteristics. This was the third cardinal fault of the neo-seculars.

The Congress has been accused of what is now called 'appeasement of Muslims' from the time of Independence. And this, not just by the Jana Sanghis, but by other secular leaders, too. B R Ambedkar had said on 27 September 1951, in a speech in Parliament on the day he resigned from Nehru's cabinet: 'The Prime Minister's whole time and attention is devoted to the problems of Muslim.' This was in context of atrocities against the group whom we now call Dalits. His speech was like a chargesheet against Nehru's style of governance in the initial years after freedom. But, such 'appeasement' did not generate any acute reaction among the Hindus, as the socio-economic conditions after Independence would not have sustained any disruptive agenda.

A marked change in attitudes began to snowball, particularly from 1971 when India defeated Pakistan hands down in the war, ignoring threats from both the USA and UK. Curiously, during Indira Gandhi's regime lasting till 1984, no adverse Hindu reaction was visible against her. She, herself, would address the growing discontent brewing among the Hindus, particularly during 1980-1984. In 1983, her party's general secretary, C M Stephen claimed 'the wavelength of Hindu culture and Congress culture is the same'. Surely, Stephen himself a Christian, could not have said this without consulting Indira Gandhi. Abdul Ghafoor Noorani, better known as A G Noorani, a scholar and a neo-secular commentator, later wrote that had it been said by a party official during Nehru's time, he 'would have been shown the door'. But Indira Gandhi did not contradict Stephen. Rather she 'acted to prove him right', added Noorani, whose comments testify that Indira Gandhi in her last years was much less neo-secular and was trying to adjust with and assuage Hindu sentiments.

Noorani had written: 'Indira Gandhi's policy towards Indian Muslims was nothing but a cynical exploitation spread over a decade and a half. Its elements were promises galore coupled with administrative cosmetics. Both were designed to attract and also cover up unredressed and unresolved problems.'[1]

It is evident that the Muslim mind was agitated in the early eighties, as they felt their special privileges were being diluted. This will be discussed in the section on Indira Gandhi, but it seems that her sole purpose was to balance the distribution of entitlements among communities. Perhaps, from the mid-seventies, she had foreseen what was coming. It was destined to come as predicted by Tagore when he said, '…it should not be forgotten that if in distribution of entitlements one side is favoured, then general human nature will not tolerate such injustice, and the disquiet on it will ever remain prone to violence….'

Rajiv Gandhi, her son, however, vacillated between Muslim radicalism and Hindu politico-religious resurgence. When he was not in power, Rajiv Gandhi organised a party convention against communalism targeting the BJP, and planned a theme paper on communalism to be presented in the convention. He packed off Mani Shankar Aiyar and M J Akbar, his two young neo-secular lieutenants, to solicit suggestions from Narasimha Rao and V N Gadgil, two veteran Congress ideologues who had drafted numerous party documents on political, economic and diplomatic issues.

In his book, *Memoirs of a Maverick*, Mani Shankar Aiyar gives a graphic account of what happened in the meeting. 'They began, almost offensively, denigrating the traditional Congress line on secularism, saying people were not interested in listening to standard cliches.

They were seeking answers to questions about the *Tushtikaran* (appeasement) of Muslim minority. They listed the questions and asked us how we propose to answer these.' When this was communicated to Rajiv Gandhi, he dropped the idea of the theme paper, but went ahead with the convention.

The questions that Rao and Gadgil raised give an insight into the old Congress's vision on secularism and its distortion by following the neo-secularist approach. Their questions were rooted in Sanatani faith that ordains to treat followers of every religion equally. One set of their questions centred around constitutional guarantees:

- 'Why a temporary provision of Art 370 was being treated as permanent?
- Why secular India should not have a Uniform Civil Code?
- Does a government have any moral right to negate a Supreme Court verdict (such as on the Shah Bano case) by an Act of Parliament?

The other set of questions was cultural:

- Why should Muslims object to *Vande Mataram*?
- Why do Muslims cheer for Pakistan during a cricket match between India and Pakistan?
- What was the objection in shifting the Babri mosque when it had been done before in Islamic countries such as Saudi Arabia?

The questions show that these two men—Rao and Gadgil—were trying to ensure that 'the wavelength of Hindu culture and Congress culture is the same'. They were following Indira Gandhi's path, but Aiyar thought they were 'denigrating the traditional Congress line'.

Top Congress leaders from the seventies to the nineties such as Indira Gandhi, Rajiv Gandhi and Narasimha Rao were showing growing sensitiveness to Hindu concerns. However, Rajiv Gandhi, was still new to politics and often succumbed to neo-secular peer pressure. However, it was he who allowed the telecasting of *Ramayana* on DD, the only TV outlet in those days. He also arranged the foundation stone laying at Ayodhya for the Ram temple, arguably within the disputed area. Narsimha Rao tried to settle the mosque-temple dispute amicably so that a grand Ram Temple could be a reality. Once, in Parliament, he asked L K Advani not to bring Ram in between their political battle, for Ram was worshipped by all.

However, once Narasimha Rao was out, the Congress turned into a full-fledged, neo-secular party under the leadership of Sonia Gandhi. Consequently, during 2004-2014, we had the first neo-secular government, and thereafter, the marked change in attitude and confidence levels that had begun to snowball since 1971 suddenly swamped the Congress in a deluge and promoted a Hindu nationalist party.

The first fault of the neo-secularists was their attempt to wipe out the grand narrative of India propagated by Tagore, Gandhi and other pre-Independence titans. Their second fault was to supplant the Indian narrative with a facile, USSR-sponsored atheist narrative. Their third fault lay in establishing their first neo-secular government in India.

Why, and how, was the 2004-2014 Congress governance decidedly different from earlier Congress regimes? Let us examine Hindu traits of earlier Congress regimes led by Nehru, Indira, Rajiv and P V Narasimha Rao, and then take up the 2004-14 governance to show how Manmohan Singh breached the tradition.

Nehru: Vacillating between Hindu culture and leftism

Nehru was always respectful of Hindu heritage, values and philosophy. So why did he stop imparting the same values to later generations?

In a letter to his daughter, Indira, Nehru wrote that the nationalism of Swami Vivekananda was pure 'Hindu nationalism' that 'had its roots in Hindu religion and culture'. And yet he, the idol of the neo-secularists, deeply revered the Hindu monk. In another letter written in 1933, Nehru wrote:

> The general Muslim outlook was thus one of Muslim

> nationalism or Muslim internationalism, and not of true nationalism.... On the other hand, Hindu idea of nationalism was definitely one of Hindu nationalism. It was not easy in this case (as it was in the case of Muslims) to draw a sharp line between this Hindu nationalism and true nationalism. The two overlapped, as India is the only home of Hindus and they form a majority there. It was thus easier for Hindus to appear as full-blooded nationalists than for Muslims, although each stood for his own particular brand of nationalism.[2]

In this letter, Nehru describes the India of the twenties when it had three streams of nationalism—Muslim, Hindu and true nationalism. According to him, while Muslim nationalism was nowhere near true nationalism, it was not possible to 'draw a sharp line between this Hindu nationalism and true nationalism'. He added that these three kinds of nationalism 'happened to come together from 1920 to 1922, during the non-co-operation movement. He wrote:

> The three roads were separate, but for the moment, they ran parallel'. Muslim nationalism joined this stream as Gandhi joined the Khilafat movement. However, the British played their divide and rule policy and finished off the movement. In his opinion, they succeeded as divisive forces always 'succeed when there are rifts and cleavages on the other side. To say that the British Government created (the) Hindu-Muslim problem in India would be patently wrong, but it would be equally wrong to ignore their continuous efforts to keep it alive and to discourage the coming together of the two communities.
>
> ...The three different roads which had run parallel to each other began to diverge and go apart. The Khilafat question

> was out of the way. Communal leaders, both Hindu and Muslim, who had been suppressed by the mass enthusiasm of the non-cooperation days, rose again and began taking part in public life. The unemployed, middle-class Muslims felt that Hindus monopolised all the jobs and stood in their way. They demanded, therefore, separate treatment and separate shares in everything. Politically, Hindu-Muslim question was essentially a middle-class affair, and a quarrel over jobs. Its effect, however, spread to the masses.

Muslim nationalism was propagated by Sir Syed Ahmed Khan. He spelled out the reason for forwarding the two-nation theory, mainly that Indian Muslims cannot live in a democracy as that would imply Hindu rule. Nehru clearly felt that Muslim communalism gave birth to Hindu communalism, for he writes in the same letter:

> The demands of Muslim communal leaders were such as to knock the bottom out of all hope of true national unity in India. To combat them on their own communal lines, Hindu communal organisations grew into prominence. Posing as true nationalists, they were as sectarian and narrow as the others.

This highlights two points: By 1933, Nehru had virtually given up hope on Hindu-Muslim unity; and he had deduced that Hindu communalism grew as a reaction to Muslim communalism. These thoughts give us important insight into Nehru's actions after Independence just after the mayhem associated with the Partition. In the same letter, Nehru had added a very interesting point:

> These narrow communal feelings of different communities, or group nationalisms, as I have called them, were very unfortunate. And yet they were natural enough.... Non-

> co-operation had stirred up India thoroughly, and the first results of this shaking-up were these group-awakenings and Hindu and Muslim and Sikh nationalisms. There were also many other smaller groups which gained self-consciousness, and especially there were the so-called "Depressed Classes". These people, long suppressed by the upper-class Hindus, were chiefly the landless labourers in the fields. It was natural that when they gained self-consciousness, a desire to get rid of their many disabilities should possess them and a bitter anger against those Hindus who had for centuries oppressed them. Each awakened group looked at nationalism and patriotism in the light of its own interests. A group or a community is always selfish, just as a nation is selfish, although individuals in the community or nation may take an unselfish view. So each group wanted far more than its share and, inevitably, there was conflict. As inter-communal bitterness increased, the more extreme communal leaders of each group came to the front, for, in moments of anger, each group chooses as its representative the person who pitches his group demands highest and curses the others most. The conflict was aggravated in a variety of ways by the Government, especially by encouraging the more-extreme communal leaders. So, the poison went on spreading, and we seemed to be in a vicious circle from which there was no obvious way out.

This analysis by Nehru, written for his sixteen-year-old daughter, belies many points that the neo-secularists of today have concocted in the last seventy years. Rather, it records two very important points: One, because India is the only land of Hindus, it is difficult to differentiate between true nationalism and Hindu nationalism; and two, Hindu nationalism drew its strength as a reaction to Muslim nationalism. So, the narrative from 1930 to 1947 and from 1990 to 2024 is almost the same, just that Muslim nationalism has now been replaced by neo-secularism. It teaches us that whenever in India, even in modern times, if the eternal narrative of India will come under attack, Hindus will react against it.

Nehru appeared to make a *volte-face* on the issue of teaching Hindu philosophy to the younger generations. We find indications of the reasons behind this reversal in the following paragraph in his letter:

> The effect of these communal wranglings and group nationalisms was to weaken the Congress as well as the Swaraj Party in the Councils. The ideal of Swaraj went into the background, as most people thought and talked in terms of their groups. The Congress, trying to avoid siding with any group, was attacked by communalists on every side.

Was Nehru apprehensive that teaching Vivekananda, or the ancient Indian texts to the younger generations, may rile Muslims, and they may once again rally around a new avatar of the Muslim League, thus depriving the Congress of a sizeable 7 to 8 per cent vote share? That would have brought down the Congress vote to below 40 per cent, and if in reaction, a Hindu force, such as the Jana Sangh, emerged strong, it would further dent the Congress's prospects, and power might slip away from the hands of the Congress, altogether. Only this reasoning seems plausible to explain Nehru's inexplicable U-turn.

But the seeds of this idea did exist in Nehru's mind even before Independence. In *Discovery of India*, in his interpretation of Hinduism, he wrote that Indian culture could not be described as Hindu culture, and then failed to give it any other name other than Sanatani culture. Later, however, in the same book, he mentions Hindu philosophy as the fulcrum of Hindu life and describes Shankaracharya as the man who fixed the contours of Indian cultural nationalism. One interpretation is that it shows the dichotomy in Nehru's mind. On one level, he was a staunch Hindu; at another, he also wore a leftist hat.

After Independence, Nehru transformed into another person. India's cultural continuum and its civilisational journey that he was so proud of now seemed contrary to his vision of establishing a 'rational state, founded on European secular traditions'. So, finally the anglicised Nehru won over the swadeshi Nehru as soon as he tasted real power. He failed to realise that an atheist superstructure on a Hindu substructure cannot survive. This transformation of Nehru eventually led India down a perilous path of ugly confrontation.

What Nehru wrote in the thirties, eventually came true: 'The conflict was aggravated in a variety of ways by the Government, especially by their encouraging the more-extreme communal leaders.' Free India was ruled by an appeasement policy in which Muslim fundamentalist leaders, who could influence voting behaviour through the imams, were wooed. Finally, the fundamentalist Muslims became so influential that they could use the government to change a verdict of the Supreme Court, as in the Shah Bano case. The imams issued *fatwas* about whom to vote. As the BJP rose to prominence, Muslims took recourse to 'tactical voting' for the party that the imams thought would defeat the BJP. In reaction to this, the BJP made attempts to polarise the Hindu votes, and by now, more than half of the Hindus are voting for the BJP or its allies. Such polarisation and counter-polarisation has aggravated into social tensions between the two communities.

Was Nehru a true well-wisher of the Muslims? Or was he going all out to appease them because of votes? If Nehru was sincere about the future of Muslims in India, then why did he exclude them while planning to modernise India? Why did he choose to modernise only those following the religions that were indigenous to India, such as Hindus, Jains, Buddhists and Sikhs?

Nehru's vision was of a modern, refined and civilised India, and he worked towards abolishing practices and customs that were not in sync with modern times, like polygamy, depriving women of their rightful share in property and inheritance and so on. But through the Hindu Code Bills Nehru restricted the benefits to the 'Hindus, who by definition of the concerned code laws included Hindus, Jains, Buddhists and Sikhs—all the Sanatanis. It can be argued that Christians and Parsis were tiny communities, but what about the Muslims?

So who benefitted and were liberated from outdated customs and codes that allowed polygamy and a plethora of other malpractices? Here we need to keep it in perspective that Nehru made the passing of these Hindu Code Bills a major issue and campaigned extensively for them in the 1952 elections. His view was that this set of reforms was one of the basic foundations for ensuring modern India's onward journey. So, we may conclude, Nehru behaved in a majoritarian fashion when he took up the plan of modernising Indians.

Thus, the contradiction in Nehru was always prominent. It seems that he thought that by changing the Indian narrative, he would be able to make Indian Muslims true nationalists. Perhaps, he believed that as he, himself, was a Hindu, the majority community would understand why he was making all these changes. But, he forgot that he was depriving about 85 per cent of the population of their ancient cultural heritage. Thus, he laid the foundation stone of the backlash that turned into a reality two decades after his death. And yet, the same Nehru was dedicated to keep Hindu interests above everything, whether it was in modernising the majority community or liberating it from divisions based on caste.

There was abject poverty in sections of the Muslim community when India became independent, but the makers of our Constitution catered for reservations only for SC and ST Hindus and other Sanatanis. Nehru never objected to what was essentially religion-based reservation. However, in a letter written on 27 June 1961 to all the chief ministers, he had said:

> I dislike any kind of reservation, more particularly in service. I react strongly against anything which leads to inefficiency and second-rate standards.... I have referred above to efficiency and to our getting out of our traditional ruts.... The recent meeting we held here, at which the chief ministers were present, to consider national integration, laid down that help should be given on economic considerations and not on caste.

The fact that Nehru was torn between his high regard for India's illuminating past and his decision to act neo-secular was also borne by his will that he signed in 1954. The year is important, for by then, he had given the green signal to the neo-secularists to control and dominate the field of education. He wrote in his will:

> I am proud of that great inheritance that has been and is ours, and I am conscious that I too, like all of us, am a link in that unbroken chain which goes back to the dawn of history in the immemorial past of India. That chain I would not break, for I treasure it and seek inspiration from it. And as witness of this desire of mine and as my last homage to India's cultural

> inheritance, I am making this request that a handful of my ashes be thrown into the Ganga at Allahabad to be carried to the great ocean that washes India's shore. The major portion of my ashes should, however, be disposed of otherwise. I want these to be carried high up into the air in an aeroplane and scattered from that height over the fields where the peasants of India toil, so that they might mingle with the dust and soil of India and become an indistinguishable part of India.

It is, thus, doubly unfortunate that Nehru's policies and the custodians of education that he, himself, appointed deprived Indians born after Independence, from knowing what he described as that 'great inheritance that has been and is ours'. He was, by his own words of his will, conscious that 'I too, like all of us, am a link in that unbroken chain which goes back to the dawn of history in the immemorial past of India'. It is distressing to discover that Nehru, himself, stopped us from being conscious of that unbroken chain. He had promised he 'would not break' that chain, 'for I treasure it and seek inspiration from it'; but as Prime Minister he ensured that future Indians will not know about the 'chain', will not 'treasure it', and will be deprived of the opportunity to 'seek inspiration from it'.

Indira Gandhi: Socialist but pro-Hindu

On November 11 1983, the month that saw riots in Nellie in Assam and in a few places in other states, Indira Gandhi addressed a rally at the Sannihit Sarovar, at Kurukshetra, and reminded the Muslim minorities of their duties 'towards the country of their birth'. With an oblique reference to Pakistan's evil designs on Kashmir and Maqbool Bhat's attempted armed rebellion, she added that attempts were being made to create a situation 'forcing us into another *dharmayudh*. This speech came in the wake of an Arya Samaj function, where she had agreed with a speaker's theme that 'our religion and tradition' was under attack.

The neo-secular scholar A G Noorani reminded his readers that Nehru had said on 5 January 1961, that the 'communalism of a majority community is apt to be taken for nationalism'. He pitted this speech against that of Indira Gandhi's assurance to the Hindu community on 31 May 1984 that providing minorities with some privileges did not mean the government was careless or negligent towards the rights and privileges of the majority community. He concluded by saying that it was 'surely uncalled for'.

Noorani and several other neo-secular scholars opined that Indira Gandhi's apparent pro-Muslim attitude did not do any good to Muslims, and was tantamount to fostering 'a false image of pampering'. This was true of all the 'secular' governments run by the 'secular' parties of India in the last century. So, why did the neo-secularists like Noorani target Indira Gandhi? That was because Indira Gandhi was not taking any anti-Hindu posture from the second half of the 1970s. They were peeved as the Congress had even claimed that 'the wavelength of Hindu culture and Congress culture is the same'. They were afraid that their construct, 'India is not Hindu, it is secular' was tumbling down, and an alternative narrative that 'India is both Hindu and secular' was being established under the aegis of an emerging Hindutvavadi Congress.

Another neo-secular journalist and intellectual, Praveen Swami, wrote in 2022 about Indira Gandhi's agreement with the 'Hindu religion and culture are in danger' narrative, and blamed her for the rise of terrorism in India.[3] Swami, an expert on terrorism opined that Indira Gandhi's 'use of chauvinism as an electoral weapon set off a cycle of violence that claimed thousands of lives in communal riots and gave birth, in ways that are little understood, to the modern jihadists movement in India'. Such opinions reflect the core of the neo-secular mind trained to propagate the thought that in India anyone saying anything in favour of Hindus must be lashed with as much venom as possible, whether it was Indira Gandhi or Narendra Modi.

Let us move back to 1969, the year when Indira Gandhi was known as a hardcore leftist and staunch secular. It was the year when she took radical steps like bank nationalisation. It was also the year that Gujarat was devastated by a severe riot, the first big one since Independence. Later, the 2002 Gujarat riots became internationally known. However, neither the neo-secularists nor the Hindutvavadis ever mention the 1969 Gujarat riots. It happened when Indira Gandhi was the Prime Minister and Hitendra Desai of Congress was the Chief Minister of Gujarat.

The Justice Jaganmohan Reddy Commission in a 1971 report had identified instances of police inaction while Muslims were attacked and killed and their houses burnt. The Commission recorded six incidents where Islamic religious places were vandalised near police lines or police stations. Asghar Ali Engineer, in his book, *The Gujarat Carnage*, wrote that journalist Ajit Bhattacharjea accused the police of not taking any 'firm action for the first three days', and stated that 'this was not a matter of slackness but policy'. An unnamed senior Congress leader told Bhattacharjea that their government was reluctant to use force because it was afraid of losing power to Bhartiya Jana Sangh in the next elections, had they done so.

Reportedly, the riots had started after some Muslims assaulted Hindu sadhus and attacked a temple as the cows herded by the sadhus had injured them as they walked past. In retaliation, the Hindus attacked a Muslim *dargah*, and Muslim protesters attacked the temple again, leading to a breakout of mass violence. A distinctive feature of the violence, according to press reports of that time, was the attack on Muslim *chawls* by their Dalit neighbours. According to official figures, 660 people were killed, 1,074 people were injured, and over 48,000 suffered damage to their property. Unofficial reports claim as many as 2,000 deaths. The Muslim community suffered the maximum, and according to the Reddy Commission report, out of the 512 deaths reported, 430 were Muslims. It was a very significant event of that time—the first riot of such a dimension in Independent India, but Indira Gandhi did not risk any stern measures.

Indira Gandhi was known to frequently change her party's chief minister. In this case, she did nothing, letting Hitendra Desai win the assembly elections and continue as Chief Minister till 1971, after which the state plunged into political instability and the assembly was dissolved. The state then came under President's rule. Hitendra Desai, remained the state's longest serving chief minister without a break before Narendra Modi, a rare achievement for a Congress chief minister during Indira Gandhi's days. Hitendra Desai's administrative model of 1969 was followed by Narendra Modi in 2002 after he took over as the state's CM in 2001.

So, from the very beginning, Indira Gandhi was cautious about not hurting Hindu sentiment. In the initial years, she tried to build a neo-secular image for herself, but not at the cost of Hindu interest. It was in the sixties that she allowed states to have their own laws against cow-slaughter. Most states ruled by Congress followed her cue.

Despite following the socialist path as far as the economy was concerned, her actions in other fields were nationalistic and very

Hindu. She had seen the horrors of the Partition and its bloody aftermath, and always considered Pakistan, a Muslim nation, as untrustworthy and fiendish. What happened in East Pakistan in 1970-71 was an internal matter of Pakistan, and logically, India had no right to intervene. But, unlike the present neo-secularists of the Congress and other parties who believe in maintaining friendly relations with Pakistan, she saw Pakistan as an enemy that should be hurt and weakened. As some intelligence people have argued, it could not be a coincidence that RAW (external intelligence agency) was created in September 1968, and in December 1971, Pakistan was eliminated from our eastern border.

Of course, objectively, the rebellion was started by the people of Bangladesh; but they would have been crushed if the *mukti yoddhas* had not been trained and sheltered by India or if India did not intervene directly. To facilitate the intervention, Indira Gandhi made a major issue out of the huge number of Hindu refugees coming to India. This was followed by a ban on Pakistani flights over India from West to East Pakistan and pressurising Sri Lanka to stop re-fuelling of Pakistani planes. Everything was calibrated so finely that it bore the imprint of meticulous planning for many months at the highest level involving the Prime Minister. It clearly indicates that Indira Gandhi was keenly interested to weaken the enemy, the country of those Muslims who had divided India. By doing this, she rekindled nationalism and won huge popularity which has not been paralleled by any other leader so far.

After Independence, the West followed an anti-India policy, favouring Muslim Pakistan over Hindu India to create a strong rivalry in the subcontinent that would bog down India. Indira Gandhi's bifurcation of Pakistan was an apt reply to the West given by a resurgent India. International opinion on India and the mood within the nation began to change from the day the 93,000-strong Pakistani army contingent surrendered meekly in East Pakistan.

It is an interesting fact altogether that just a few years after this resounding victory, Indira Gandhi with her 352 Congress members in the Lok Sabha that then housed 521 members, emerged closer to Hindus. This journey had first manifested itself in pursuing national interest from a real secular perspective, like the *Nasbandi* programme for controlling growth in population. It was necessary in national interest, and there is no doubt that we would have been much better off if India had now harboured 120 crore people, instead of 140 crore, which could have been possible if we had adhered to the '*hum do, hamara do*' policy that was pursued strictly during the Emergency days, irrespective of religion, caste or creed. Those who talk of the demographic dividend of 140 crores forget that we cannot provide good jobs for about 20 crore young people. But the neo-secularists thought religion should be the basis of secular policies of the government and protested violently against *Nasbandi* as going against the tenets of both Islam and Christianity. Again, when Sanjay Gandhi's bulldozer drive targeted Muslim settlements of Delhi, Indira Gandhi did not intervene.

The neo-secular narrative that depicted Sanjay Gandhi as a demon succeeded temporarily as Indira Gandhi was defeated in 1977, but within three years, the people of India voted her back, knowing fully well that Sanjay Gandhi, the epitome of extra-constitutional authority from 1973 to 1977, would have a free run again. It was another matter that Sanjay Gandhi died in a plane crash a few months later. Otherwise, for sure, Sanjay, better known then as the crown prince, would have become the Prime Minister of India after Indira Gandhi. It was evident that the

Sanatanis had no objection to the Indira-Sanjay duo. But, what about Muslims? The Congress vote share increased from 34.52 per cent in 1977 to 42.69 per cent in 1980. It was a phenomenal jump, and it can be presumed that a sizeable chunk of nationalist Muslims voted for her.

After her return to power in 1980, Sanjay Gandhi was killed in a plane crash, and thereafter she did not pursue family planning as government policy, but became directly, pro-Hindu. Indira Gandhi did not stop Sanjay from being a 'Hindu' leader, and her proclivity became much more pronounced after Sanjay's death. Party leaders also initiated the process of openly advocating the cause of Hindutva. In 1983, Hindu Jagran Manch (an RSS-affiliated organisation founded by Vinay Katiyar in 1982) organised a conference in Muzaffarnagar that was presided over by Karan Singh, son of the last maharaja of Kashmir. There Karan Singh, who was himself a Hindu, said, 'We cannot even light a holy lamp at Ram's birthplace in Ayodhya. How shameful a matter is it for 80 per cent of this country's residents who call themselves Hindus?'[4]

For the record, Karan Singh never belonged to the BJP; he was always a prominent Congress leader, a long-time governor of Jammu and Kashmir, a union minister from 1967 to 1973, and a close friend of Indira Gandhi.

According to Dinesh Narayanan's book, *The RSS and the Making of the Deep Nation*, the conference was attended by veteran Congressman, Gulzari Lal Nanda, a two-time former interim Prime Minister. It is claimed that before her death, Indira Gandhi had asked to prepare various plans for the development of Ayodhya as a pilgrimage centre and was pushing through the proposals rapidly.

So, it was not only her party's general secretary, C M Stephen who claimed that the wavelengths of Hindu culture and Congress match, but different Congress leaders, too, who began voicing the demands for a Hindutva constituency by 1983. Many suggest that it was all orchestrated with Indira Gandhi's assent and that a few of the Congress leaders like Daudayal Khanna, a five-time Member of Parliament from Moradabad, was leading the Hindutva flock of the Congress Party. It was during those days that the Ram Mandir movement was gaining steam, and it got a major boost when on 4 January 1984, someone planted a Hanuman *pataka* (Hanuman's pennant) atop the central dome of the Babri mosque. Later, a two-day congegration began on 7 April 1984, and it was the first *Dharm Sansad* organised by VHP, the Hindu organisation. The organisation got permission to hold the congregation at the Vigyan Bhawan, a premier conference centre of the Government of India in New Delhi.

Indira Gandhi's Hindutvavadi acts, and her speeches at different forums provoked the neo-secularists not only to dump her, but to depict her as the root cause of Islamic terrorism in India. The CPI(M) drew her image on the walls of West Bengal as a *daini* (witch). But, she had political acumen and was visionary, so she could foresee what was coming, and tried to mend her ways as far as possible. Just as things were gaining momentum, Indira Gandhi was assassinated on 31 October 1984, when she was sixty-six. Had she been alive, perhaps she would have been a Hindutva icon, blocking the rise of the BJP and bringing in a major correction of the narrative, peacefully. No wonder then that RSS cadres were reportedly instructed to vote for the Congress in the 1984 election held just after her assassination.

The people viewed her as a true nationalist; she was so hugely popular that even after her death, the people of this country welcomed her heir, her son Rajiv Gandhi, with nearly 50 per cent votes, the highest ever for the Congress party. She had charted out a future path on two very important aspects—Pakistan and nuclear strategy. Nehru had never dared to give a green signal to make a nuclear device; Lal Bahadur Shastri sought escape routes by urging nuclear powers to provide alternative forms of security for India, but Indira Gandhi gave the green signal for a nuclear test to be conducted in 1974, and that paved the way for what India is now—a recognised nuclear power. She had given the green signal eight years before, in 1966, when political circles called her *gungi gudiya* (a dumb doll). After Pokhran-I, she had been preparing for Pokhran-II in her last term, but had to put a brake on it as uncertainty over the consequences of economic sanctions loomed large. After her, P V Narasimha Rao tried, but had to rescind his decision as the US learnt about it and threatened to impose economic sanctions on India. However, when India was no longer economically dependent on the IMF-World Bank, Atal Bihari Vajpayee went ahead with the programme, and gradually the world accepted India as a nuclear power.

As far as Pakistan is converned, the risks that Indira Gandhi took in 1971 undeniably made her the greatest Prime Minister India has ever had. She not only pushed Pakistan to the corner, but tried to normalise the Kashmir situation by weaning off a large chunk led by Sheikh Abdullah from the separatist path. The 1974 Indira-Sheikh Accord is a landmark that liberated Kashmir from its neither-here-nor-there situation and introduced parliamentary democracy in the state of Jammu and Kashmir as a viable option for the people to express their willingness to be a part of India.

Indira Gandhi was a socialist, as evidenced by her various programmes, the most important of which was bank nationalisation. It was she who inserted, almost forcibly, the words socialist and secular in the preamble. But, at the same time, she was a bold and pragmatic nationalist, and a secular Hindu leader. She believed in a strong and resurgent India, and will always be remembered that way.

Rajiv Gandhi: Indecisive under pressure from two extremes

Sonia Gandhi called Narendra Modi *Maut ka Saudagar* (Merchant of Death) after the Gujarat carnage forgetting that the epithet equally suited her husband, Rajiv Gandhi. Following the assassination of Indira Gandhi by her Sikh security guards, the Hindus led by innumerable Congress leaders and workers attacked the Sikhs. What followed was a genocide of the Sikhs (3,350 Sikhs killed nationwide, 2,800 in Delhi, according to government figures provided to the Supreme Court). The Delhi Police under Rajiv Gandhi took no action to protect the Sikhs for the first 3 days of this mayhem. Later, Rajiv Gandhi justified the anti-Sikh riots:

> We must remember Indiraji. We must remember why her assassination happened. We must remember who could be the people behind this. When Indiraji's assassination happened, there were riots in the country. We know that the hearts of the Indian people were full of anger and that for a few days people felt India was shaking. When a big tree falls, the earth shakes.

In 2015, while releasing a video of what Rajiv Gandhi had said, H S Phoolka, senior lawyer and then AAP leader, had demanded that Gandhi's Bharat Ratna be taken back. In December 2018, the Delhi High Court sentenced Congress veteran Sajjan Kumar to life; it was the first conviction of a politician in the deadly anti-Sikh riots in 1984. Pushing for a new law for speedy prosecution for genocide and mass killings, the Delhi High

Court said, 'Common to these mass crimes were the targeting of minorities and the attacks spearheaded by the dominant political actors being facilitated by the law enforcement agencies.'

What did this pogrom signify? Some pseudo-intellectuals tried to differentiate it with other riots arguing that this was a one-off incident that happened at the spur of the moment. Genocides do take some planning and there was distinct deep-rooted anger and rancour building up against the Sikh community in the first half of the 1980s when the Khalistan movement was at its peak. Though led by Congress leaders, it was not a political genocide, for the Congress workers and the others did not selectively attack only pro-Khalistani Sikhs. Instead, they indiscriminately attacked the Sikhs, many of whom were staunch Congress voters. The targets were the Sikhs as a religious community, and the attackers were Hindus.

What does the Congress say about Rajiv Gandhi? According to *Congress Sandesh:*

> Shri Rajiv Gandhi envisioned that the India of the twenty-first century should remain truly secular on the one hand, and on the other, be home to religious pluralism. Shri Rajiv Gandhi used to be deeply saddened by the communal riots taking place in the twentieth century. Although India has been considered a secular state in the Indian Constitution, yet communalism keeps taking form in one or the other parts of India. States like Uttar Pradesh, Andhra Pradesh and Gujarat etc. keep coming under the grip of communalism from time-to-time. Shri Rajiv Gandhi used to be deeply saddened by this condition of India because it not only caused loss of India's people and wealth, but also tarnished India's image in the international arena.[5]

It further quoted Rajiv Gandhi who addressed the nation from New Delhi on November 2, 1984, the third day of the genocide. He had said: 'Communal frenzy will destroy us. It will destroy all the values that India has stood for. As the Prime Minister of India, I can never allow that to happen. Don't shed blood, instead, shed hatred if you may.'

It signifies—that secularism means paying lip services to the idea and not following it in practice whenever you feel that a community has gone against Hindus, and thereby India. Then, that community should be taught a lesson. Let pundits debate it, but what we see is that there is not a single party in India which, in a broader sense (social and administrative distribution of justice and protection) is secular. The opposite is also true: No party in India is communal in a narrow sense (legislative definition and official policy of distribution of facilities). The people know it from their common and conventional sense, and that is why a very large section of Hindus and other Sanatanis are not interested in the secular versus communal debate. Muslims, on the other hand, use secularism as a shield. Perhaps, Rajiv Gandhi knew it too, and so he either encouraged, or did not stop (as did Modi in 2002), the rioters. He allowed a Hindu backlash against the Sikh community in general.

As such, Rajiv Gandhi was surrounded by two sorts of relatively younger groups of people who called the shots during his time. Some of them believed in following Indira Gandhi's Hindutva politics, and another larger group was westernised and believed in neo-secularism. Senior ministers like P V Narasimha Rao, Shankar Rao Chavan, Buta Singh and N D Tiwari did not have much say in policy decisions. It is believed that Arun Nehru proposed toeing a Hindu line and made way for constructing a temple at Ayodhya, the 'birthplace', after persuading Muslims to shift the mosque a little away from the original site. It is also said that he was instrumental in opening the gates of the Babri Mosque for Hindus through a ruling by the judiciary. But Rajiv Gandhi's neo-secular aides, who later enjoyed heavy clout when Sonia Gandhi headed the Congress, opined against toeing the Hindu line, and convinced Rajiv Gandhi that it would cause resentment among the Muslims. So, Rajiv Gandhi backed off.

But, it was during the same Rajiv Gandhi's tenure that the *Ramayana* and *Mahabharata* serials were telecast on DD, the government-controlled television network, and the significance was far-reaching, particularly of *Ramayana* that was telecast in 1987. It brought back Ram as a human being in the public's mind, helping the BJP immensely to claim his birthplace. It is said that when Ramanand Sagar forwarded a proposal to make a serial on the great epic, the top brasses of Doordarshan and the Information and Broadcasting Ministry were sharply divided on it, one section, enthusiastic, while the other section felt it would go against India's secular ethos. The proposal was being delayed because of this division of opinion. But, Rajiv Gandhi cleared the proposal, his action manifesting that he knew and respected India's culture and ethos. He was a nationalist too, and it was he who introduced and popularised the slogan *Mera Bharat Mahan* (My India is great) throughout the country.

Meanwhile, under peer pressure, Rajiv Gandhi stepped into the trap of appeasing fundamentalist Muslims when he surprisingly annulled the Shah Bano case verdict of the Supreme Court through the legislative route in 1986. Later, in 1988, he banned Indian-origin novelist Salman Rushdie's *Satanic Verses* making India the first country to ban it. Thus, under Rajiv Gandhi, India took decisions that resembled those taken in Islamic countries.

However, Rajiv Gandhi took up 'Hindu' causes again towards the end of his prime ministerial term. Allegedly under the prodding of Deoraha Baba, a Hindu saintly figure, he allowed and encouraged *shilanyas* (foundation stone laying) of the Ram Mandir on 9 November 1989. It was then a 'double engine' government of the Congress both at the Centre and in UP, and so the VHP programme was conducted smoothly. But, by then, it was too late. The next general election was just a couple of weeks away, and his fate was sealed. From nearly 50 per cent vote share in 1984, Congress's vote share plummeted down to less than 40 per cent in 1989.

The popularity of *Ramayana* and *Mahabharata* on DD was a stern reminder that India could never be uprooted from its traditional culture, values and philosophy. It also signalled that India's heartbeat is primarily Hindu. But the neo-secularists ignored it, and impressed upon Rajiv Gandhi to organise a party convention in 1990 against communalism, targeting BJP's Ram Mandir movement. Rajiv Gandhi was in the opposition then, and he agreed. It backfired and helped BJP to establish its bona fides as the only political vehicle for protecting Hindu interests.

Rajiv Gandhi tried to appease both Hindus and Muslims at the same time, but Hindus saw a red alert as they witnessed a weak Prime Minister surrendering before the unjustified demands of the Muslim fundamentalist leaders. By then, the BJP had made Ram Mandir its exclusive major issue for the elections, and also enjoyed the advantage of using the alleged Bofors scandal that was being exploited by the entire Opposition, particularly by Janata Dal led by V P Singh. It catapulted BJP from 2 seats in Parliament in 1984 to eighty-five seats in 1989, and later to 120 seats with a 20.11 per cent vote share in 1991, when it became the main opposition party for the first time. The

Hindu juggernaut had begun rolling thanks to Rajiv Gandhi's political immaturity. Since 1989, the Congress has never secured absolute majority in Parliament, while the BJP has secured it twice—in 2014 and 2019.

Indira Gandhi had already seen it coming much earlier, and had tried to preempt it by resorting to Hindu politics. Rajiv Gandhi knew it, as he was the main confidante-cum-assistant of his mother after Sanjay Gandhi's death. He was not anti-Hindu, but he did not have the political acumen to navigate his party and government through troubled waters. Neither did he have any intention of being a martyr for the neo-secular cause, as is evident from his sanction for the *shilanyas.* But his reversal of the Shah Bano case verdict by the court was perhaps his biggest failure to judge the mood of the times.

Keeping in mind today's situation, it must be mentioned that unlike his neo-secular grandson, who is now Leader of the Opposition, Rajiv Gandhi was against causing a rift in society by expanding caste-based reservation. He had followed his grandfather and mother, and that was why he did not implement the Mandal Commission report during his tenure. Later, he opposed V P Singh's decision to implement it. His speech in the Lok Sabha as Leader of Opposition on 6 September 1990, is significant. During a debate on the subject, he had said: '...where on the one hand the Prime Minister is asking the nation to be psychologically prepared for war, he is doing exactly the opposite to the nation. He is causing rift in our society so that the nation cannot be psychologically prepared to face the foreign threat of Pakistan like he has said. This is a totally irresponsible stand that the Government has taken.'

He perceived the reservation for all OBCs as a political ploy, and explained: '...We are not in favour of having such measures being cornered by one particular group within the SEBCs. The benefits must seep down to those who need them the most. ... Do we want these benefits, for example, to go to taxpayers who are obviously in the upper class of society? There will be many other such groupings. It needs to be thought out a little more deeply; is the Government looking at one particular vested interest or is the Government really looking at the socially and educationally backward classes?'

No one can surmise what policies Rajiv Gandhi would have followed, had he not been assassinated, after becoming the head of the minority government of the Congress in 1991. But the new leader chosen by the Congress, P V Narasimha Rao, was the one who tried his best to save the Congress vote bank by following Indira Gandhi's soft Hindu line that she had followed between 1980 to 1984.

P V Narasimha Rao: Last resistance to neo-secularist forces

P V Narasimha Rao became Prime Minister after the 1991 elections and initiated the process of reversing the morbid policies of the party in different fields. In the economic sphere, he ushered in a liberal regime, the opposite of the socialist economy that India had been following so far. In the realm of foreign policy, he initiated a new beginning with the US and Israel, the country hated by Muslims. Such changes were essential for India and were long overdue. In the cultural sphere, he disallowed any signal to project the Congress as anti-Hindu, and did not act against Hindus even after the demolition of the mosque. Fortunately for India, he was the right man at the right time after the dissolution of the USSR when the country needed a new direction.

Prime Minister Rao knew that his last hope was a solution for Ayodhya, and he was keen to find an answer that would have both a mosque and a temple in the area, almost a repetition of Arun Nehru's formula. In his book, *Ayodhya 6 December 1992*, Rao alleges that the BJP and the VHP sabotaged his efforts some months before the demolition of the mosque. He writes that the BJP's 'majority communal orientation' forced it to scuttle any out-of-court settlement as it was looking for a 'permanent, evergreen issue' to tantalise the Hindu voter in the form of an ongoing Ayodhya dispute. Ayodhya was not a singular issue, either. He was sure that 'more had been lined up, so that the agitation could be kept alive even if the issues of one or two specific temples were settled. The number was three (Ayodhya, Mathura, Kashi) and for good measure, in the unlikely event of all three temple issues being settled amicably (unfortunately for them), there was a never-ending store of more than 3,000 controversial temples lined up all over the country.' Rao was sure that the BJP would use the temple issue for a very long time to come.

According to Rao, the talks his party's emissaries were having with 'apolitical' *sadhus* and *sanyasis* centered on how and where a Ram temple could be built in Ayodhya 'without breaking the law or upsetting communal harmony.' The talks were proceeding well, according to Rao, till August 1992, when the VHP-backed sadhus withdrew from the talks. Rao asks in his book: 'Why did they (the sadhus) go back on their promise (to explore all avenues towards a peaceful settlement of the dispute)?' He provides the answer, himself:

> It was clear that there was a change of mind on their (the sadhus') part, or what is more likely, on the part of the political forces that controlled them. (The political force was the BJP-RSS combination.) These forces deliberately wanted to get out of a friendly situation which the sanyasis were getting into

> with me and which, if left to itself, would have made the *mandir* issue wholly apolitical.

Narasimha Rao knew that if the BJP could play Ram against the Congress, they would have a huge advantage. Once in the Lok Sabha, he had told Advani not to bring Ram into their political fight. As a true Hindu, a true Sanatani, he knew the immense force Ram contained in this land, and tried to end the dispute in a way that would end in the building of the Ram temple at Ayodhya. He wrote in his book:

> This subtle aspect of the Ram *Janmabhoomi* matter is very important and brings home the undeniable fact that while Hindu masses were swayed by their devotion to Ram and their intense desire for the temple, the political forces behind the issue could not care less for the temple—they only wanted to retain a long-term, vote-rich communal issue for as long as they could.

From personal interactions with the Advani camp (by this author), it was clear that they never wanted the mosque to be demolished. The structure was the symbol that they could exploit as the 'vote-rich communal issue'. But the others, a section within the party and the RSS, and other forces like Shiv Sena and Bajrang Dal were not interested in a long-term political game. They wanted to mark a quick victory of the Hindus over the Muslims, and they demolished the mosque to register that victory.

Rao was criticised for failing to protect the mosque on 6 December 1992 and the criticism came from those who otherwise support federalism. According to our Constitution, maintaining law and order is the responsibility of the state. Preemptive action like dissolving the state government in view of thousands of

Karsevaks converging in Ayodhya from all over India was not permissible in true democratic spirit, and the famous Bommai judgement that came a few years later echoed this spirit in a different case. Some senior bureaucrats made a plan for acquiring the disputed land, but Rao rejected it as it would serve no purpose other than shifting the responsibility from the state to the centre.

The Supreme Court was also involved in the case before the *Karsevaks* congregated on the fatal day. After they started vandalising the structure, it was not possible to stop them, as the time gap between issuing Article 356 and the action on the ground would have been fairly long, and more importantly, opening fire on the *karsevaks* could have dire consequences like the death of tens of thousands in communal clashes all over India. In his book, Rao concludes: '… there was no lapse on the part of the Central Government and that if the State Government had at least made use of the central force in time and meaningfully, the Babri structure could certainly have been saved in December 1992.'

At the cabinet meeting after the demolition, all members criticised Rao except Manmohan Singh who was eventually also asked to be quiet by M L Fotedar. In another twist, Sonia Gandhi, who arranged for an unceremonious farewell to Rao after he lost, chose Singh to head the government. Singh was uncomfortable as he was a non-political person, and found himself trying to balance between the party's heavy demand to follow rigid neo-secular principles and his own faith, for he himself believed in following traditional Congress secular policies and a capitalist economy.

The two later prime ministers—Atal Bihari Vajpayee and Manmohan Singh—followed Rao's economic liberalisation direction with the latter following it prominently. It was under his watch as finance minister that the new policy was executed in the nineties; Singh was eager to have labour reforms and voiced his thoughts publicly, but Rao had held him back. Later, when he was Prime Minister and stayed in the saddle for a decade, Singh never pushed through hard labour reforms, proving, without doubt that he still abided by the directions given by Rao earlier. Of note was Singh's Israel policy, which was a follow-up of the Rao-Vajpayee policy and was sternly anti-neo-secular.

According to experts of Indo-Israel relations, India recognised the state of Israel soon after its creation in 1948, but did not establish diplomatic relations. Nehru was inclined to set up a diplomatic office in Israel, but was dissuaded by Maulana Azad. After the 1967 war, India, however, took a pro-Arab stance during Indira Gandhi's regime. However, as Pakistan was establishing contact with China and North Korea, Indira Gandhi sent R N Kao, Indian spymaster and head of RAW, to reach out to Mossad. As a member of the UNSC, India's backroom negotiations culminated in Resolution 242 asking Israel to withdraw only from 'territories occupied' in the Six-Day War, but not from all occupied territories. That was one of Indira Gandhi's shrewd balancing acts. But, after the Bangladesh War, she leaned towards the Palestine cause further, a measure meant to appease the Muslims. However, it is claimed that clandestine contact with Israel was maintained all through, and that Israel had even supplied armaments during the Bangladesh war and after.

The Morarji Desai government adopted a much more liberal attitude towards Israel. But Rajiv Gandhi followed his mother's policy, and after the PLO announced the formation of Palestine in 1988, accepting a two-state solution, India was the first non-Arab nation to recognise it. It was Narasimha Rao who established full diplomatic relations, discarding the opposition's view by claiming that the Muslim community in India were nationalists and would not react negatively. Thereafter, the Vajpayee government expanded India-Israel relations in several fields, including defence, and Israel supplied ammunition to India during the Kargil War. However, it was the Manmohan Singh government that vastly expanded relations with Israel, affecting India's stand on Palestine.

Chinmaya Gharekhan, India's special envoy for West Asia in those days, claimed that though India still voted in favour of the UN resolutions, it was no longer co-sponsoring such resolutions. Neo-secularists during Manmohan Singh's time as PM saw Israel-Arab relations through the prism of religion and not of India's national interest, and cried themselves hoarse against Israel as a pro-Muslim stance is at the centre of their ideology. But like Rao, Manmohan Singh gave preference to national interest, discarding a rootless ideology.

Thus, Narasimha Rao had deeply impacted those Congress leaders who looked at India's national interests. Manmohan Singh was one of them. Another such was Pranab Mukherjee. Rao was both a nationalist and a pragmatic. He knew he was not strong enough to introduce Indian religious-philosophical studies in the school and college curriculum, and he did not try it. But, he was always focused on protecting Hindu culture.

By the eighties, *Vande Mataram* was not heard in public forums. Rather, another poem by Muhammad Iqbal, who had inspired M A Jinnah to demand Pakistan for Muslims, was unofficially replacing it. The song was *Sare jahanse achha*, and the music was provided by Pandit Ravishankar at the request of a leftist cultural organisation. But, as the BJP was fast filling the vacuum of nationalistic space and gaining popularity, the P V Narasimha Rao-led Congress once again assumed its old nationalistic hues. When BJP leader Ram Naik demanded singing both *Vande Mataram* and *Jana-Gana-Mana* in Parliament sessions, the government acceded to the demand, and since 1992, *Vande Mataram* is played at the beginning, and *Jana-Gana-Mana* at the end of each session of Parliament.

2004-14: Anti-Hindu governance

The six-year-long BJP rule (1998 to 1999, and again from 1999 to 2004) created the fear of 'fascism' in the minds of the neo-secular intellectuals, but political parties did not think the regime mattered much as Vajpayee had not launched any anti-corruption drive. Vajpayee, a part of the elite, ran his government as usual, barring the nuclear test and Murli Manohar Joshi's attempts to resurrect cultural traditions and change textbooks. The BJP government's return in 1999 was also aided by the Kargil incursion, but during its second run, it did not promote either the Hindu nationalist or Cultural Bharatiyata narrative. It even surrendered meekly before the Islamic terrorists in the Kandahar Hijack episode. So, support for the government diminished and it eventually lost power in 2004.

But, the opposition looked upon it as a defeat of Hindutva and victory of neo-secularism. Manmohan Singh did not and could not assert himself as Prime Minister except in the fields of finance and external affairs, for he was not chosen by the people. He ran the government more as a chief executive officer, rather than as a political authority. So, he quietly toed the neo-secular line dictated by Sonia Gandhi and her team. Going against Congress tradition, Manmohan Singh even presided over the first anti-Hindu governance in India bent upon defaming and weakening Hindus.

The ugliest attempt by the Singh government to strengthen the neo-secular narrative was in their attempt to establish a story of unfounded 'Hindu terror', an attempt to taint Hindus internationally with a terrorist tag to encourage Hinduphobia. No other government since Independence had been so openly anti-Hindu.

Their mindset was clear. In 2006, at the National Development Council meeting, Manmohan Singh had said:

> I believe our collective priorities are clear: agriculture, irrigation and water resources, health, education, critical investment in rural infrastructure, and the essential public investment needs of general infrastructure, along with programmes for the upliftment of SC/STs, other backward classes, minorities, and women and children.... We will have to devise innovative plans to ensure that minorities, particularly Muslim minority, are empowered to share equitably in the fruits of development. They must have the first claim on resources.

The following day, the media reported that Manmohan Singh had said that the minorities had the first claim on the nation's resources. A furore followed and by the next day, the PMO issued a clarification to claim that the PM had not referred to only the minorities, but to all sections mentioned earlier in his speech (including programmes for the upliftment of SCs, STs, OBCs, women and children and minorities). The Godi media accepted the diktat and fell silent. But, even if we accept this argument, the statement remains objectionable.

First, a natural question follows—why should the rich families of the minority communities have preference in the government's eyes over poor, upper caste Hindus (who were not mentioned in the speech)? Second, from the point of view of constitutional jurisdiction, can religion be a criterion for development? Can any government say the first claim on resources belongs to any particular religion like Muslim, Christian, Parsi or Hindu? All other categories that Manmohan Singh mentioned—SC/ST, Other Backward Classes, women and children—were valid categories, but not the 'minorities'. Third, when the category OBCs includes the backward classes of the minorities, why were the minorities mentioned separately? Was it also intended to include rich Muslims as a special category within this list? Last, governance is a serious business, and this statement did not measure up to the standards expected from a PM such as Manmohan Singh. The categories he had mentioned virtually included more than 90 per cent of the population, excluding only upper caste male Indians!

The only appropriate category here having first claim on resources, should have been the 'poor', irrespective of caste, creed or religion. It would have included a third of our population if the 'poor' are properly defined. Muslims are one of the poorest communities, along with the STs and SCs, and they should be looked after. Similarly, the poor of the upper castes, the only category that the Prime Minister excluded from having 'first claim on resources', also needed addressing.

The statement was regarded as being politically motivated, with the government wanting to send a signal that for them, Muslims were a special priority class, for whom the government 'will have to devise innovative plans to ensure' that they are 'empowered to share equitably in the fruits of development'. Note, even the STs and SCs were excluded from this penultimate sentence of the quoted paragraph, reeking of a blatant attempt at appeasement at the cost of equally poor Hindu categories. There were two aspects to this statement: One was appeasement of Muslims, and the other was targeting the upper caste Hindus, thereby dividing Hindu society. The government had then managed to silence the Godi media but the collective memory of Hindus proved more effective at a time when social media was emerging as an alternative to traditional media.

During Manmohan Singh's regime, a theory of Hindu terrorism was construed centering around two incidents, both of which, the courts threw away as baseless charges against Hindus. The term 'Saffron terror' was used by journalist Praveen Swami after the 2002 riots in Gujarat, but he failed to categorise the Islamic terrorists who had attacked the train at Godhra railway station or those who drove away 3 lakh Hindus from Kashmir Valley. This seemed natural on the part of the neo-secularists who were anti-Hindu and bent on somehow glossing over the crimes committed by Muslims. However, the term Hindu terror got traction after the Congress leader, and prominent neo-secularist, Digvijay Singh, used it for the 2007 *Samjhauta Express* bombing. The term was further popularised by Congress leaders close to 10, Janpath after the Malegaon blasts. The then Home Minister P Chidambaram asked cops to watch out for 'saffron terror' during a meeting with state police chiefs in New Delhi in August 2010. The investigators of the *Samjhauta Express* bombing and Malegaon cases used the words 'Hindu terror' in their press notes. Curiously, the Malegaon blast happened in 2006, and back then, the Maharashtra ATS blamed it on SIMI (Students' Islamic Movement of India); but the chargesheet changed in 2013 after the NIA (under control of the Central Government) joined the investigation, and shifted the blame onto Abhinav Bharat and Pragya Thakur, both of whom were later released by the court for lack of evidence.

Thus, it was a concerted effort to make light of Islamic terror by showing Hindus were capable of being terrorists too, and to malign Hindus and create some Hinduphobia internationally.

According to a 2018 book, titled *The Myth of Hindu Terror: Insider Account of Ministry of Home Affairs*, by RVS Mani, a former officer in the Internal Security division of the Home Ministry, the UPA government had forced Home Ministry officials to invent a narrative of 'Hindu terror'.

According to Mani:

> At a time when we had the best team in the IS (internal security) division, the attitude of the government in power and intent to cover every terror incident as 'saffron' and the ambivalence in acting against the real perpetrators of the terror attacks was making this country a cannon fodder for those with evil designs against India.
>
> ...In every case assigned to NIA, they overlooked the first set of evidences and replaced it with the evidences supporting (the) Hindu terror narrative.

He had said that since Chidambaram had taken charge of the ministry, the NIA was given the role of big brother in security matters.

While reviewing this book, journalist Abhinandan Mishra wrote in *The Sunday Guardian*: 'It is worthwhile to mention here that senior officials with the NIA, with whom this correspondent used to interact during the UPA times, have admitted off the record that they had no evidence of any organised Hindu terror.'[6]

Later developments have confirmed what Mani claimed and Abhinandan endorsed. It is pertinent to point out that both Digvijay Singh and P Chidambaram were very close to 10 Janpath. However, for the common man, it does not matter whether the directions came from Sonia Gandhi. What matters is that the responsibility of allowing this anti-Hindu narrative to germinate lies squarely with the then Prime Minister, Manmohan Singh, for it was his government. These desperate attempts were made mostly in the second term of Singh's governance. Though the mainstream Godi media blacked out the news of this conspiracy, it spread through social media and word of mouth, inviting the wrath of the Hindus.

This time around, the Congress pressured the government to build better relations with Pakistan, though the Pakistani establishment continued with their conspiracies to weaken India. The neo-secular Congress was walking towards the opposite direction which Indira Gandhi had led it to, as it almost equated Indian Muslims and Pakistan, a gross insult to nationalist Muslims. It was overly eager to improve people-to-people relationships, allowing Pakistani actors, singers and entertainers in India even after the 2008 attack in Mumbai. If Kasab had not been arrested, the attack could even have passed off as one done by others, and not Pakistan, or even as acts of Hindu terror. Indian gestures lured Pakistanis to trap India once again as it offered the status of 'most favoured nation' to India in 2011.

Despite Pakistan showing no remorse for the 2008 attack, Manmohan Singh acted like a Pakistan-lover when he suddenly invited Pakistan's then Prime Minister, Yousaf Raza Gilani to the 2011 World Cup cricket semi-finals at Mohali. The latter immediately agreed, seeing a huge opportunity to have another season of good relations with India that would give them enough scope to prepare for another deadly terrorist attack. Soon, both countries began serious bilateral engagement talks in April 2011, and the commerce secretaries of both countries met in Islamabad. And then, in a surprise move, Manmohan Singh decided to visit Pakistan in 2013, but the decision was stalled at the end of 2012, fearing tremendous reaction from the people at a time when national elections were less than two years away. Later, information trickled down that the army too had opposed the idea, fearing the visit would end in demilitarising the Siachen Glacier, and could give Pakistan another opportunity to repeat a Kargil-type operation to occupy Siachen.

Atal Bihari Vajpayee had invited Pakistan President Pervez Musharraf after the Kargil incursion, and this had been a major reason for the gradual decline in his popularity. Narendra Modi had also visited Pakistan, perhaps to show his liberal face hoping it would help wash away his 2002 image. It could have ended up harming him gravely had he not mended his image by his highly publicised 2016 surgical strikes. Singh, however, did not have time to undo the damage caused by his expressed intention to visit Pakistan.

Ironically, after the Modi government's 'surgical strike', the Congress claimed that such operations had been undertaken during Singh's regime, too. If so—and there is evidence to suggest that it was really so—what had prevented the then government from publicising their action? Who were they scared of, and why? Was the government scared of the reaction of the party high-command, or of the reactions of the Indian Muslims, which was again tantamount to denigrating the nationalist Muslims of India?

Many such questions pop up, like why police operations against Islamic terrorists were often criticised by the party. Why did it seem that neo-secularists like Digvijay Singh were always ready to exonerate Muslim terrorists? Even after the 2008 Batla House encounter, by the Delhi Police that was under the Central Government, Digvijay Singh and other neo-secularists had concocted a fake encounter theory. They dared to do it even though a bold officer Mohan Chand Sharma was martyred there. It shows how adventurous a section of the neo-secularists had turned during Manmohan Singh's regime. It is only that they did not know that by doing so, they were virtually inviting their own nemesis. Another important question is: When the Manmohan Singh government knew huge money was making its way into India mainly from the Gulf countries to radicalise Indian Muslims, why did it not make any effort to stop this inflow? That it could have been stopped if Singh had political will was later proved by Narendra Modi, the Hindu nationalist, who achieved it by improving relations with Muslim countries.

Manmohan Singh's actions were tantamount to killing the Idea of India that Tagore and Gandhi had, and perhaps that is the reason why it created tremendous reaction among Hindus and nationalist Muslims and Christians of India. Though such trends began before 2009, the people seemed willing to give Manmohan Singh another chance as they were wary of Advani, who was fickle and vacillating. Five years later, they found a far better candidate in Modi, and threw out the neo-secular Congress completely. Congress hit its three lowest scores after Independence in three consecutive national elections between 2014 to 2024, failing to reach even a three-digit tally thrice in a row. It seems the Congress leadership has not yet understood why they are not being accepted, as they are still under the influence of neo-secular intellectuals.

The neo-secularists also compelled Singh's government to go slow on urgent decisions related to national security. The government dithered on signing the three foundational agreements that Washington demanded—The Basic Exchange Cooperation Agreement (BECA), Communications Compatibility and Security Agreement (COMCASA), and the Logistics Exchange Memorandum of Agreement (LEMOA)—because of pressure from a large number of neo-secularists.

All these agreements were signed later by the Narendra Modi government, and consequentially we have improved relations with the US, the West, Israel, Australia, and Japan, and all these nations are working together in strategic matters, especially against a rogue nation like China.

The delaying tactics impacted the purchase of state-of-the-art warplanes that the Air Force sorely needed. The ten years of Congress regime under Manmohan Singh failed to buy a single fighter jet despite the dwindling stock of it in India. It confirms the fact that the neo-secular narrative tries to keep India weak. Accordingly, Rahul Gandhi started a crusade against the purchase of Rafale fighter jets by the Modi government. It was based on frivolous questions on pricing, which depends on attachments and add-ons that cannot always be disclosed in the interest of national security. It appears that Rahul Gandhi was instigating the Modi government to reveal those details, thereby weakening India's defence preparedness.

Many such neo-secular follies pushed Manmohan Singh's government into a political quicksand. The proverbial last straw came in the guise of unparalleled corruption. On one level, all sorts of amoral acts had been encouraged for decades by promoting a non-dharmic code that did not link destiny to one's karmas.

But, on another level, large sections of our population, mostly rural and semi-rural, were still rooted in the civilisational values of fighting a-dharma. It is no wonder that Anna Hazare's anti-corruption fast demanding a Lokpal system made the ruling Congress so uncomfortable. It eventually paved the way for a victory of the BJP in 2014. It also rekindled memories of *satyagraha*, as the site of the dharna resonated with Mahatma Gandhi's favourite *bhajans* like *Raghupati Raghava Raja Ram* and *Vaishnava Jan to tene kahiye je*. Anna Hazare's fast at Jantar

Mantar in April 2011 was the first definite pointer that the pot had reached its boiling point. The new India, based on its evergreen culture and values, was awakening, and Modi reaped full benefit of this phase.

Post 2014: Same neo-secular trends

Neo-secular intellectuals and politicians saw the end of secularism in Modi's presence and participation in the *pran pratishtha* ceremony for the Ram Mandir. They cried themselves hoarse that the Prime Minister's participation in the *pran pratishtha* ceremony violated the Constitution's secular principles. Their arguments, however, did not stand the scrutiny of rationalism. Secularism is tested by the government's actions, and not by an individual's (including the PM's) private faith. Just after Independence, the Somnath temple was rebuilt under the aegis of Deputy Prime Minister Vallabhbhai Patel, and the consecration was attended by the then President, Rajendra Prasad. Many of the later Prime Ministers, including Indira Gandhi, have attended *pujas* in various temples. It is outrageous to think that our Constitution's integrity can be compromised by a Prime Minister attending a *puja* in a temple.

Prime Minister Modi did not deliver any political speech from Ram Mandir. However, the last US president, Joe Biden from the Democratic Party that the Wokes support, had used the church for wooing his voters, and no American secularist had ever criticised it. So what were our secular liberal intellectuals trying to preach? If a secular icon like Mamata Banerjee drawing the eyes—the *chakshu daan*—of the Durga idol and inaugurating Durga *puja* are secular acts, if her building a Jagannath temple at Digha with government money is a secular act, then how could Narendra Modi's presence in the

Ram Mandir *pran pratishtha* ceremony be non-secular?

However, the electorate did not bother about the temple, reflecting the maturing of the constituency of Cultural Bharatiyata. But neo-secularists rejoiced when the BJP lost its Ayodhya seat to the Samajwadi Party. It only betrayed their lack of understanding of the dynamics of the paradigm shift that showed that the electorate had finally matured and did not regard religion as a necessary component of good governance. It in no way meant that the voters were now ready to entertain a neo-secular agenda.

This present stage of the paradigm shift is good news for neo-secularists as it will provide opportunities to the opposition to claim a larger share of the political pie, if only they are able to correct their course to become proud nationalists having respect for Sanatan values. It is good for democracy too, as a strong opposition will not only check the Prime Minister's hubris, but also guard against violation of liberties. But, much depends on whether the Opposition can rectify their 'Triple Faults' and propose governance strategies that will treat everyone as equals irrespective of caste or religion. That calls for ending appeasement of any community, whether minority or majority, and deciding everything on merit. So far, neo-secularist politicians have not shown any sign of mending the course, except for trying to prove that they too are pious Hindus. But that will not help them much now, as the electorate has become much, much more matured than the voters in the eighties and nineties.

The Opposition's fortunes will not turn around until they find a suitable agenda for their vision of a new India. What India needs is a skills census, not a caste census as that will only divide the population further. A skill census, on the other hand, is positive and inclusive. However, the Modi government has already announced a caste census, for it is interested primarily in winning elections. It is not known whether the neo-secularists will acquire power someday to extend reservation to the private sector. But one thing is certain: If any future government does so, flight of capital will follow and tear down the development story of India.

Attacking industrialists for political gain, as Rahul Gandhi and some of the neo-secularists have been doing regularly after being defeated in elections again and again, is also tantamount to targeting India's growth. Capitalists not only contribute to the state's revenue, but also provide employment to millions of people. An anti-capitalist socialistic stance is a recipe for killing anti-poverty measures and employment generation opportunities. Luring people with the promise of unsustainable money transfers is another myopic idea, as it can never happen unless the government earns huge revenue thanks to robust growth of sectors like industry and service.

Thus, setting the agenda right is important for sustaining progress and success. Rahul Gandhi's slogan of *Jitni abadi utna hak* (entitlement according to population), is an echo of Ram Manohar Lohia's sixties slogan of *Pichhde pabe sau me shat* (the Backwards will get 60 per cent). This neo-secularist demand is an attempt to shackle India's progress by killing merit and dividing Hindu society.

Nehru believed that reservations will kill merit, and in his last years had been thinking of changing caste-based reservations to economic criteria-based reservation. At present, there is no scope of any trade-off between merit and uplift of the downtrodden. Sacrificing merit will make India weak, while neglecting the downtrodden will exclude meaningful participation of a section in the nation's onward journey. The dream of tiny political gains is diverting the Opposition to a path that will harm them and the nation.

Most importantly, the Opposition has not been able to distance themselves from their image of habitually choosing a course of action that actively brings appeasement to the Muslims. The Congress's and the neo-secularists' support for the right of Muslim women to wear the *hijab* is also another example of naked appeasement of minorities, and it shows support only to a repressive and backward tradition. An important aspect of modern India is the march towards modernity initiated by Nehru. Progressive Muslim women intellectuals in India and other countries have been fighting against wearing of the *hijab* for decades. And if the *hijab* comes back, it won't be long before the *ghunghat* also makes a comeback, and we will soon go back to the medieval ages.

Why should young Muslim women be asked to cover their faces and be denied opportunities necessary for their progress? Fundamentalists all over the world are trying to deny women equal rights and are opting to reduce them to faceless entities. Even if some women are being persuaded by them and opting to wear the *hijab*, civil society needs to educate them that this is a practice of the middle ages and it goes against women's liberty. Instead, neo-secular parties and intellectuals are exploiting the Muslim community and pushing them backwards to strengthen their own vote base; in the process, they have ended up trampling over the rights of young Muslim women.

Post-2014, it seems the less neo-secularists talk about Indian culture, the better for them. The diversity of India could not be explained more frivolously by anyone other than Sam Pitroda, who said in a podcast: 'We could hold together a country as diverse as India—where people on East look like Chinese, people on West look like Arab(s), people on North look like maybe Whites and people in South look like Africans. It doesn't matter. We are all brothers and sisters.' The Congress might have distanced itself from such a bizarre explanation after BJP jumped in to ridicule them, but it only exposes the ignorance of the neo-secularists about India and its culture. If you travel across non-elite India, you will come across fair and dark people everywhere. Our skin colour cannot be subjected to racial mapping, for that appears to be a result of ignorance and uncultured arrogance. For the record, Sam Pitroda was an adviser to both Rajiv Gandhi and Sonia Gandhi, and he now heads the Congress's overseas wing and advises Rahul Gandhi.

Interestingly, while trying to prove them as devotees of various deities, the neo-secularists have not been able to shed their inherent anti-Hindu attitude. As soon as a debate on the Gyanvapi *shivlinga,* a symbol of Shiva, and the character of the structure erupted, radical Hindus immediately concluded that it was a temple, while the neo-secularists announced that it was not one. They ridiculed the Radical Hindu demand and claimed the disputed *shivlinga* was only a fountain. How could they say this for sure? Was it only a reflex action based on their neo-secular beliefs? Is superstition guiding both sides? The logical thing to do would be to let archaeological experts determine the findings. But, even before the report had come, both sides had reached their conclusions. Eventually, the radical Hindus won and the neo-secularists lost, as the 839-page ASI report stated that 'there existed a large Hindu temple prior to the construction of the existing structure' and that various parts of the temple were then used to build the mosque. Thus, the neo-secularists again proved themselves to be anti-Hindu. However, after the court allowed Hindus to offer *puja* in the southern cellar of the Gyanvapi mosque, Congress was silent, while both the SP and RJD criticised the verdict.

Another example of a strong anti-Hindu bias was the neo-secular opposition to the Citizenship (Amendment) Act (CAA). It is relevant to quote Gandhi and Nehru to show how present neo-secular Congress leaders were contradicting them while opposing the move to confer citizenship on Hindus who had fled neighbouring Islamic nations to avoid persecution. Gandhi had said, 'If people flee their homes in Sindh and other places out of fear and come here, shall we turn them away? If we do so, with what face shall we call ourselves Indians? How can we chant the slogan *Jai Hind*? Welcome them saying, this too is your country just as that is your country' (Discourse of 10 July 1947). Gandhi also spoke of accepting persecuted 'nationalist Muslims' (those who were against Partition), and India has done this, too, since decades. Jawaharlal Nehru said in a speech on 5 November 1950: 'There is no doubt that the affected people who have come to settle in India are eligible for citizenship. If there is no appropriate law, then the law should be amended.' That amended law is now the CAA.

At present, we see not only a divided polity, but also a divided media, divided judiciary, divided intellectuals and propagandists who do not see things from a neutral and principled position. Of course, it is true that none of us can be completely neutral, as subjectivity creeps in without us knowing it. But if too much bias is found, then it creates a major problem. Ironically, neo-secular intellectuals now use yardsticks like totalitarian tendencies, unjustified arrests, and so on to attack the BJP; however, they never use the same yardstick for their own camp. At present, two autocratic governments are running in UP and West Bangal. Both use the police for enhancing political muscle. In UP, criminals belonging to the BJP get a long rope, and in Bengal, criminals attached to the TMC enjoy the same advantage. In both states, dissenting voices of the common man are muzzled, and justice to the ordinary man denied in many cases. Though the neo-secularists severely criticise the UP government, they remain silent about Bengal. On the other hand, the BJP and its allies criticise Bengal and keep mum about UP. Both have thus proven themselves to be two sides of the same coin.

The Modi government that had tightened mechanisms to punish the corrupt, such as enforcing the *Benami* Property Act and the ED Act, does not target corrupt elements associated with their own BJP network. Similarly, the neo-secularists do not attack innumerable instances of corruption in states ruled by the opposition like Bengal. So, nobody cares for the neo-secularists when they portray themselves as victims of 'political vendetta'. On 18 April 2024, during the election campaign in Kerala, Rahul Gandhi mentioned two Chief Ministers who were in jail, asking why the Kerala Chief Minister Pinarayi Vijayan had not faced similar consequences. For the record, the Congress and CPI(M) are not only in the same I.N.D.I.A. bloc at the national level, they even team up to fight elections together in West Bengal. Rahul Gandhi's words prove that he adjusts his speeches according to political expediency, and there is no principle involved in it.

Altogether, the neo-secular camp has not changed its old political lines and orientations that made them face their nemesis. A significant change, however, is not expected from non-Congress parties as they follow alien leftist narratives. But, if the Congress fails to change, the BJP may have a very long run at the centre in the future. That will not be good for the nation, as absolute power corrupts absolutely.

Endnotes

To conclude this chapter, let us recall President Sarvepalli Radhakrishnan's farewell address to the nation on All India Radio (12 May 1967). He had said:

> Despite the apparent lowering of standards and increase of lawlessness and indiscipline, my faith in our people is unshaken. The culture which we have inherited is an ancient one and it has faced many waves of invasion of Yavanas, Sakas, Hunas, Pathans and Mongols, among others, and is still enduring. It is not only the quality of antiquity—*pracinata*—but also of enduring vitality—*mrtyuizjayata*— which has enabled it to last all these centuries. The secret of this staying power is the quality of tolerance and understanding. The saints and sages have been the great integrators of our society....
>
> Democracy is more than a system of government: it is a way of life and a regime for civilised conduct of human affairs. We are not truly democratic if we only possess the outward trapping of representative institutions but fail to be loyal to the qualities of strength of the democratic spirit. Unseemly wrangles and alliances of convenience, prejudices of caste and creed, personal aggrandizement, lack of cleanliness in administration, these are not calculated to inspire faith in representative government.[7]

If the Congress leaders of the present century had read these lines and taken proper lessons, they would have avoided meeting their nemesis.

Congress was a nuanced neo-secular party from the days of Nehru, but it never ignored Hindu sentiments in the last century. The governments run by Nehru, Indira Gandhi, Rajiv Gandhi and P V Narasimha Rao had often equated Hindus with the nation while trying to modernise the country and in their attempts to make it stronger. It was in the present century that the Congress-led government at the Centre began to display explicit anti-Hindu characteristics, and eventually paid a heavy price for that.

Even now, it is up to the Congress whether they will learn lessons from Nehru's efforts to modernise India; from Indira Gandhi's attempts to put the nation first irrespective of considerations of religion; of Rajiv Gandhi's attempt to propagate the basic heritage of India (like the Ramayana); of P V Narasimha Rao's effort to negotiate between Hindus and Muslims to solve disputes amicably; or whether to remain loyal to their new-found love for neo-secularism. This will decide whether they will slide down the tapering path that awaits neo-secular forces in India or ride the tide that promises to benefit all Indians, collectively.

The Way Forward

Religion, Politics and Dharma

'Religious ideas, supposedly private matters between man and god, are in practice always political ideas,' wrote Christopher Hitchens in his book *The Monarchy: A Critique of Britain's Favorite Fetish*.

Eight decades of post-Independence India have witnessed continuous efforts by neo-secularists to hold back Hindu religious ideas from emerging as political ideas in India. To achieve the goal, they curbed the narratives and Idea of India propagated by Tagore, Gandhi and other icons; developed an alternative atheist narrative and imposed it through intellectuals and academics; and finally, they ran an anti-Hindu government. But all their efforts have failed, and as Hitchens said, Hindu religious ideas have emerged as political ideas, ushering in a paradigm shift in the country.

In the light of the paradigm shift, now it is time to focus on how we can liberate ourselves from a disruptive and anti-Hindu neo-secular narrative and also from a fanatic, extreme Hindu nationalist narrative born as a reaction to the former. Let us underline a keynote here: While religion and politics are intertwined in almost all the modern nations of the world, it has a deeper significance in India where it crosses the limiting spheres of religion to spark off a discussion on dharma. It is time to remember Mahatma Gandhi who said in *Young India*:

> For me, politics bereft of religion are absolute dirt, ever to be shunned. Politics concerns nations, and that which concerns the welfare of the nations must be one of the concerns of a man who is religiously inclined, in other words, a seeker after God and Truth....Therefore, in politics also we have to establish the Kingdom of Heaven.

It was evident that by religion, Gandhi meant dharma as interpreted by dharmic philosophy.

In India, an overwhelming majority of the population still follows the basic concepts of dharma, the basic moral values of life including harbouring belief in *paap-punya* and *karmafal* or fruits of karma. But under tremendous pressure especially during the rule of the Turks and Mughals, from the time of colonialism, and in post-Independent India, much of the grand narrative of that model life has weakened. Consequentially, the problem now is that the philosophy is being wrongly interpreted and is being equated with religion. Earlier, through teachers in neighbourhood Sanskrit schools, ballads about the past sung by folk singers and bards, *kathas* recounted by priests, and the writings of our greats had kept the ancient flame burning. With increasing urbanisation, and our reliance on Western values, this philosophy is in danger of dying faster even in smaller cities and towns.

Dharma has played a role for millennia in organising society, economy and polity, and continues to be relevant as the foundation for a secular society. That explains the urgent necessity of making it a part of our education system.

Now, we will attempt to understand what role the dharmic construct and Sanatani religions have played in the past, and this last chapter will explain this. We will also analyse whether religion and politics exist as two separate chambers in more developed nations like the USA, USSR and China. But, before that, let us first dissect the reality about Hindu-Muslim tension and its causes, as we need to solve this dilemma first by following a dharmic path.

The formation of the Hindu-Muslim rift

The ordinary citizen learns about the world beyond their reach from the media, from articles and books written by intellectuals, and now, also from social media. But when some sort of code of silence is imposed on media persons and intellectuals, the common man's understanding of reality becomes increasingly lopsided with each passing year and decade. The Italian term, *omerta,* in India was about suppressing the real facts of communal divisions and tensions, as everybody's view was that this was the best way to promote communal amity. Often, there was ubiquitous censorship of incidents where Hindus or other Sanatanis were the victims, while full freedom was given to reporting on incidents in which Muslims or Christians were attacked. This led to total lack of understanding on communal relationships, the objects of fear and hatred, and the scope of reconciliation.

Everytime a riot broke out somewhere, the media would dish out a romantic tale of Hindu-Muslim 'brotherhood' like Muslims donating for a temple and so on. The media has been doing this for decades, but these futile attempts have failed to ensure peace. Now that social media has become the main source of information with its over-reliance on rumours and targeted campaigns, it is necessary to break the *omerta*.

If we speak out the truth like Salman Khurshid did on the Delhi 1984 incidents, it will go a long way to chart out a futuristic, right path. On the 1984 Sikh genocide that followed Indira Gandhi's assassination, the famed lawyer and prominent neo-secular leader of the Congress wrote in his book, *At Home in India*: 'There was also a terrible satisfaction amongst Muslims, who had not completely forgotten the Partition's unpleasant aftermath. Hindus and Sikhs were alike paying for their "sins". They were paying for the blood they had drawn in 1947.' While he was criticised for writing this, he had exposed the deep-rooted rancour that is a reality between India's many religious communities.

Let me add my own observations on the communal situation in the country, on the basis of my encounters as a journalist with thousands of commoners from both communities, particularly in Delhi, UP, Rajasthan and Bengal, where I have been covering politics for decades. Here are some observations:

- Hindus or Muslims are generally not fearful of the other community and neither do they hate individual members of the other community. But they are fearful of the 'collective' group from the other religion. In other words, problems start when a large number of people get together as either Hindus or Muslims.
- The fear or hatred essentially centres around religious symbols like temples and mosques, about *aajan* from the mosque and *bhajans* from temples, and about the people wearing clothes specific to their religion. It boils down to a fear of the unknown.
- Communal tension grips groups of people when religious cries like *Allah hu Akbar* and *Har Har Mahadev* and *Jai Shri Ram* rent the air. Each community is scared of extreme

fundamentalism on either side—the Hindus of Muslim belligerence, and the Muslims of chants like *Jai Shri Ram* and the *trishul* (trident) that symbolise Hindu resurgence.

- At the root of this fear is the collective memory of clashes between the two communities for about a thousand years, and this deep-rooted thought cannot be weeded out from the minds of the people. It all started with invaders coming down from Turkey and Central Asia who not only defeated the Indians, but also demolished their temples, something that was unknown to the local population before that period.
- However, for the most part, both the communities collaborate with each other in places where they benefit mutually like in the bazaar, in offices and factories, in hospitals and so on.

Why is there no such animosity between Hindus and Christians or Muslims and Christians? The reason is that Christianity never took recourse to large-scale violence to convert Hindus (except in Goa), the last terrible instance of which was Noakhali in 1946-47. Moreover, Christians never demolished Hindu temples or converted them into Churches. They, too, attacked Hinduism, but did so subtly by introducing a westernised education system that eventually helped us to navigate the modern world.

Lord Macaulay, who introduced the education system that continues to govern the Indian mind even today, had said in his speech on 2 February 1835 in the British Parliament:

> …such wealth I have seen in this country (India), such high moral values, people of such calibre that I do not think we would ever conquer this country, unless we break the very backbone

> of the nation, which is her spiritual and cultural heritage, and therefore I propose we replace her old and ancient education system, her culture, for if the Indians think that all that is foreign and English is good and greater than their own, they will lose their self-esteem, their native culture, and they will become what we want them, a truly dominated nation.

He summarised his goal twenty months later in his letter to Zachary Macaulay written on 12 October 1836—'No Hindoo who has received English education ever continues to be sincerely attached to his religion.'

Lord Macaulay and the neo-secularists of post-Independence India worked with the same goal, trying to impose a foreign narrative targeting the Indians, particularly the Hindus and other Sanatanis. But, as the present paradigm shift shows, all such attempts failed. Instead, our eternal narrative was rediscovered and propagated as Cultural Nationalism by our pre-Independence icons. Those who challenged it with alternative ones like the Islamic narrative, too have failed miserably. Pakistan is now a failed state that has turned rogue, and Bangladesh is following in its footsteps. Neo-secularists, too, are losing their hold on India. Now is perhaps the time to unite the nation with the narrative of Cultural Bhartiyata.

As the neo-secularists followed and used Macaulay's education system to deracinate Hindus, their narrative was eventually targeted by Hindu nationalists. Ironically, the target became the Muslim community as Muslim invaders had attacked Hindu symbols and culture, too. That the Muslim fundamentalists were being appeased by the neo-secularists added further fuel to this movement. This diverted focus needs to be corrected immediately to facilitate the adoption of Cultural Bhartiyata, which is an advanced form of our pre-Independence Cultural Nationalism.

There is, however, a significant difference between pre-Independence Cultural Nationalism and Cultural Bhartiyata. This difference reflects the dissimilarities in the approach of the great minds of a nation under occupation and the attitude of a nation which is independent, but somehow still entangled with enemies: at present the enemy is our twin nation (Pakistan) that has gone rogue and is bent upon destroying India by aligning with China.

The pre-Independence narrative was based on lofty ideals: It was liberal; it was internationalist; it was based on non-violence. It needed to impress the whole world with its idealism. But a free nation also has to act for itself. It has to defend itself; and at times, it has to stoop to harm the enemy, both external and internal, particularly if they are linked. So, it is cultural nationalism coupled with the need for doing whatever it takes to catapult the nation to the top again. All the communities that are an intrinsic part of India will have to understand this futuristic narrative and prepare themselves to act accordingly.

Building up a workable coexistence between Sanatan religions and Islam in India is the first step towards fortifying the narrative of Cultural Bhartiyata. India has reconciled differences while being guided by the dharmic philosophy from antiquity, and its people today will have to follow the same path again. The Muslim community will have to understand that no community in India can ask for special privileges, and that every community will have to embrace nationalistic values. On the other hand, the Hindu community will have to be inclusive, and ensure that all communities are partners in the journey to the top.

The only way to ensure this is to teach all Indians the Vedantic, dharmic philosophy; it is the eternal guidance for resolution of conflicts. It was also the main socio-cultural-political driver of Bharatvarsha since long, and it still is.

Pillars of Hindutva: Dharma, Karma and *Dharmayuddha*

Language often fails to communicate meanings, and a glaring example of it is the word, 'Hindutva'. The word is similar to Christianity, which according to the Oxford dictionary means the 'beliefs and practices' of the Christian religion, or 'Christian quality or character'. Similarly, Hindutva denotes beliefs and practices of Hindu and Sanatani religions, or Hindu quality or character. A Bengali scholar, Chandranath Basu first used the term in 1892. Later, Vinayak Damodar Savarkar used the word while propagating the idea of a radical Hindu political nation. Since then, both in India and in the outer world, the word 'Hindutva' has become a victim of a cultural construct. From it, the term 'Hindutvavadi' has been formed to denote radical Hindu majoritarianism.

Why is the term 'Hindutva', looked upon with suspicion? That's because large sections of neo-secularists and the world cannot understand that the word stems from the philosophy of dharma. The problem has been further compounded by the fact that even many Indian languages translate 'religion' as 'dharma'. But, dharma and religion is not the same. Any religion that stakes a claim that it is the only 'true religion' fails to qualify as dharma, because that statement points to the fact that it believes in forcible conversion. Let's take the example of Islam and Christianity. Both religions believe that their God is the only Supreme God and that no other God of another religion is true. Dharma, instead, invites one to introspect and find one's own path to connect with the forces behind Creation.

A religion seeks loyalty to a set of codes, rituals, and concepts or their imagined manifest forms (deities) from its followers. Thus, all religions, including dharmic religions, seek to control, but dharma lets individuals create their own religion. That was how in the past, the Hindu religion successfully amalgamated hundreds of sects into its fold over thousands of years. But, under existential threat for the last thousand years, Hindu and other Sanatani religions have copied traits of other, more aggressive religions, and have also become conservative and dependent on rituals.

This tells us how a political force that only uses the symbols of the Hindu religion for political power, and which imposes control to demolish diversity, the soul of dharma, has now come to be known as Hindutvavadi. However, a very large chunk of its supporters do not agree with the hate part of its ideology or efforts to impose vegetarianism and other forced ideas.

Another facet of the narrative that Hindu nationalists often put out—that Islam is responsible for the woes of Hindus—is also not true. The degeneration of Hindus began long before Muslims invaded and conquered large parts of India. Hindu kings and elites of Bharat did not respond to the call of the Persians (*Ballad of Vahram*) when Persia was being conquered by Islamic forces; neither did Hindu kings respond when Hindu kings of Afghanistan were being conquered by Muslim invaders or when large sections of the population were being converted to Islam. Most Hindus remained indifferent, while some meekly surrendered before the invaders. When Rana Pratap was fighting against the Mughals, another Rajputana king was marrying off his daughter to Akbar.

The invaders could easily defeat Hindus because they were fragmented and meek, and only looked at their own petty and parochial self-interest. Contrary to Hindu nationalist narratives, there was nothing glorious about Hindus in the last millennium. Vivekananda, Tagore, and Gandhi, had lamented this meekness of the Hindus. There were only a very few glorious exceptions.

It is quite surprising that it was only after Indira Gandhi's death, somewhere in the late eighties, that the radical political Hindutva factor began to unite the Hindu/Sanatani populace. One reason for this could be the strengthening of a political democracy that liberated people from the mandatory loyalty to kings and elites. Democracy, like dharma, allows everyone to choose one's path and evolve with time. If we compare the political parties that fought the first general election, we notice that most of those parties are extinct, or have split. This is because people exercised their free choice. It seems this democratic process and free choice eventually drove a large section of Hindus to unite and fight as one unified group.

The second reason is that during the last 1,500 years—the period of Bharat's degeneration—the concept of dharma was still very much alive in non-elite societies who earlier had no power to assert themselves politically. As democracy opened the gates of liberty, and as economic development of the nation led to economic empowerment, these scattered groups began to exert their rights. Essentially, taking the two points together, we may say that democracy and economic development have allowed the masses to rally together for their faith.

Now, let us delve into some basic features of their dharmic philosophy. As said earlier, dharma is not a religion, and stands far above the confines of religion. If religions can be compared to different, fertile swathes of land, dharma is the infinite sky, which believes that all honest efforts for seeking the Ultimate Truth are worthy. It encourages dissent, with resolution and reconciliation coming through debates. Such debates have continued for thousands of years (like on *dvaita* or dualism and *advaita or* monism). Organised religions of the world try to control the mind and the brain, but dharma is a quest for the Ultimate Truth of existence, and it encourages all to participate in their own, exclusive way.

Rigveda expressed this eternal truth like this: The ultimate truth of existence is one, but the wise men call it by different names (*Ekam sat, vipra bahudha badante*).The word dharma too is in use from the time of Rig Veda, which was composed at least 6,000 years ago (as it does not mention any urban civilisation in the Sapta Sindhu area where, as modern archeological evidence shows, urban civilisation developed more than 5,000 years ago and shifted eastward as the land turned arid).

This dharmic philosophy is based on a network of eternal truth and has three pillars: Dharma, the laws of Karma, and *dharmayuddha* (fighting for establishing righteousness).

The literal meaning of the word 'dharma' is—'that holds'—a reference to holding creation and all its ingredients, from the individual to the Cosmos. Within creation are human beings, who have to act constantly throughout life, or perform their Karma. Our good karma protects creation and all within it, adding to our positive points (*punya*). But, if our karma disturbs or destroys any ingredient of creation, whether a human life or free functioning of Nature, we earn negative points (*paap*) and are punished for that. Rewards and punishment for our karma do not always manifest before our eyes; but when we damage Nature, the consequences are obvious, like the present climate disaster that will unsettle human life to some extent in the coming decades of this century. Dharmic philosophy proposes the Law of Karma to protect and let prosper.

By logical derivation, it means fighting *adharma*—the forces that oppose dharma. The root cause of *adharma* is greed for wealth, amoral happiness, amoral fame, for forcibly acquiring partners for sex and for getting favours. Excessive pride in one's self, obsession for animate or inanimate objects and so on are further aspects of this form of *adharma*. Whenever such *adharmic* forces dominate, we are supposed to fight it and establish a righteous realm. This is *dharmayuddha*. Those who are weak and unable to fight mighty *adharmic* forces, must socially boycott such individuals. If one follows the righteous path, one is rewarded with happiness in life; otherwise one is punished with sorrow. By logical derivation, it also entails rebirth as the fruit of karma cannot end in one's present lifetime.

Dharmic philosophy is entirely secular and has no relation to any particular religion. At times, adharmic forces grip people and they end up harming a lot of families and communities. The only way out is to resort to *dharmayuddha*, or battle for establishing justice and righteousness. It is not comparable to *jihad* or crusade, for its goal is not the victory of any religion, but the victory of benevolence over malevolence.

Any attempt to deracinate Hindus and Sanatanis from this cultural association of dharma is, therefore, adharma. Differentiating between citizens for granting special entitlements is adharma too. Similarly, targeting a religious community for their religion is also not a dharmic action. In the Indian context, the role religion has played in politics was always based on the construct of dharma. Efforts to impose a certain religion was a distraction from this dharmic path. To build the narrative of Cultural Bhartiyata, it is essential that this secular construct of Dharma is taught to school students.

Sadhus in Indian politics

Ignorance of one's own cultural background is nothing to be proud of and could have dangerous consequences. Here is one example from Bengal, the land of India's renaissance. During the 2024 campaign, Mamata Banerjee criticised some *sadhus* including Kartik Maharaj for supporting the BJP, asking why *sadhus* and monks should be involved in politics. In protest, the *sadhus*, except those of the RK Mission, marched on Kolkata roads on 25 May 2024, just when Lok Sabha election fever was high. Incidentally, Kartik Maharaj belonged to Beldanga, where the local TMC MLA Humayun Kabir had threatened the local Hindu population while campaigning for former cricketer Yusuf Pathan. The local Hindus who are only 30 per cent of the population there were threatened with dire consequences by the TMC MLA, but Mamata Banerjee's police did not take any action against him, just like the BJP governments in various states do not take action against hate speeches by BJP leaders.

Mamata Banerjee was, however, spinning a new yarn about *sadhus* by claiming they must not participate in politics. In Bengal, a state where a leftist mindset still dominates, this narrative sold well. But was it ignorance, or calculated propaganda? Famed author Bankim Chandra Chatterjee wrote two novels *Anandamath* (the original work in which *Vande Mataram* appears as a poem) and *Devi Choudhurani* in 1875 and 1884 respectively. Both novels were written with the backdrop of the *Sannyasi* Rebellion in the late eighteenth century under the leadership of Pandit Bhabani Charan Pathak. The rebellion was centred around Murshidabad (where Kartik Maharaj supposedly works to protect local Hindus) and in the Baikunthapur forests of Jalpaiguri. If modern Bengalis do not know these facts, then it is no doubt that elite India has forgotten the role that *sadhus* played in politics, including in the

Age of Mythologies and in the historical past.

Neo-secularists may wish away the traditions that began in antiquity with Vishvamitra, but they cannot deny the role of the Naga *sadhus* and of the Nath yogis in the historical period. In 1952, during the first general election in Phulpur constituency, Jawaharlal Nehru had a face-off with an independent candidate, Prabhudutt Brahmachari, a Hindu religious teacher who opposed Nehru's modernisation attempt through the Hindu Code Bills. While Nehru secured 38.33 per cent vote, Brahmachari got 9.41 per cent. In 1964, after the Vishwa Hindu Parishad (VHP) was established, this Hindu fundamentalist, played an important role in arranging the Kumbh Mela. Nehru never questioned his bona fides to have a role in politics. In 1966, Karpatri Maharaj, another Hindu saint who founded Ram Rajya Parishad, a political party, and the Shankaracharya of Puri played an important role in organising rallies demanding ban on cow slaughter.

Mahadev Sadashivrao Golwalkar, the second *sarsanghchalak* of the RSS, abandoned his law career in 1936 and joined the Sargachi Ramkrishna Mission ashram in West Bengal to become a *sanayasi.* He had Swami Akhandananda, a disciple of Ramakrishna and brother monk, Swami Vivekananda, as his guru, and reportedly received *diksha* from him in January 1937. When his guru died in the same year, he left the ashram in a state of depression, and was picked up by the then *sarsanghchalak* Keshav Baliram Hedgewar who impressed upon him to dedicate himself to work for the society through the RSS, a quasi-political organisation.

This tradition of *sadhus* taking up political roles is, therefore, an integral part of our culture. The Naga Sadhus, according to James G Lochtefeld's book, *The Illustrated Encyclopaedia of Hinduism*, formed the last line of Hindu defence and fought fiercely against Aurangzeb to defend the original Kashi Vishwanath temple in 1664. Reportedly, they defeated the Mughal emperor's army. Some Naga *sadhus* like Rajendra Giri and his disciple Anoop Giri ruled over Rohilkhand, making alliances with both the Mughals and the Marathas.

When Ahmed Shah Abdali invaded India for the fourth time (he attacked India 8 times), an Afghan general Sardar Khan defeated the Jats and advanced towards Gokul after killing many in Mathura and Vrindavan. There, he encountered resistance from the Naga *sadhus*.[1] In the Battle of Gokul in 1757, a 4,000-strong Naga *sadhu* army, with warriors smeared in ash and carrying swords and cannons, defeated a much larger Afghan army. This account can be read online and is also found in *The Naga Warriors: The Battle of Gokul*, a historical novel by Akshat Gupta. The Hindu traditionalists of Vrindavan still recount the story. Interestingly, though Gokul is a Vaishnav site, the Shaivite Naga ascetics (believed to have become warriors under the influence of Adi Shankara) laid down their lives to protect it.

The Sikh Nihangs had also fought bravely against Abdali. There is a long tradition of them fighting to protect their religion. Jarnail Singh Bhindranwale, who was part of the Khalistani rebellion against India, too was a *sant* (saint). Many Sikhs still remember him with devotional attachment. Thus, the relation between religion and the nation is a complicated one in this country, as the *sadhus* and *sants* have a long tradition of participating in battles and wars for fighting the enemy.

The Gorakhpur Math, established in the eleventh century, also played an important role in influencing politics, both in the past and also in modern India. The *mahants* of this math were associated with Veer Savarkar's Hindu Mahasabha and later with the BJP. Mahant Digvijay Nath was instrumental in placing the

Ram idol in Ayodhya in 1949; his successor Mahant Avaidyanath was a Hindu Mahasabha MP, while his successor, Yogi Adityanath is the present and longest serving Chief Minister of UP.

Thousands of sadhus had worked with the Mahasabha, the RSS, the Jana Sangh, the BJP, the VHP and the entire Hindu political fold over the last few decades to strengthen the Hindu identity and the Ram Mandir movement. However, it is not as if they always stood by the BJS/BJP. Before the 2018 assembly elections, a large number of *sadhus* in Madhya Pradesh took to the streets to defeat BJP's Shivraj Singh Chouhan, the then chief minister. Namdeo Das Tyagi, a high-profile *sadhu* popularly known as Computer Baba, was at the forefront of this rebellion. After a massive conclave of Hindu religious leaders on the banks of River Narmada (Narmada Sansad in Jabalpur on 23 November 2018, attended by over a thousand *sadhus* from across the state, he told *The Caravan*, 'All we want is protection of Narmada River and the cow, but Shivraj Singh Chouhan is not willing to listen.... He is anti-Narmada and anti-cow and wants to fool the ascetic community by patronising *sadhus* who enjoy the backing of the RSS.'[2]

Thus, the belief that religion and politics do not go together and is not in consonance with age-old Hindu traditions is clearly a misconception. One Mission or the odd ashram may decide to stay away from politics or voting, but that does not alter anything. The relation between religion and politics is strong in this country, and the BJP has used religion blatantly for political purposes.

For centuries, Hindu *sadhus* have protected Hindus whenever they felt that Sanatan Dharma was in danger. The Bengal rally of the *sadhus* after Mamata Banerjee's tirade against Kartik Maharaj was not reported widely, as large sections of modern Indians are not even aware of the probable fallout of such a development. The fact is that it has the potential to lead to greater upheaval and may alter the political paradigm again.

Dharma, culture and society: The Indian journey

India has a long history of being guided by great teachers like Yagnavalkya, Adi Shankara and Vivekananda, all spiritual monks. Various reform movements like Buddhism and Bhakti and several ancient and medieval kings have helped India play a leading role in the global stage. This narrative has driven society since antiquity, with the state playing a supportive role.

Indian history cannot be like the history of other Western countries. As Tagore explained, it was Indian society that occupied centre-stage, and not kings or emperors. Thus, how much land Ashoka or Akbar annexed is not of much consequence, as what was more important was the cultural ethos of India and its society that was organised according to dharmic cultural values. This socio-cultural history of India was composed of two streams—spiritual and materialistic. The former has two elements in it, one, philosophical, the other, devotional. The first led to the establishment and development of dharmic philosophy over many thousand years, while the second kept it alive through folk, ritualistic and devotional forms. Together, these two streams formed our cultural nation. To establish this point, Nehru gave the example of Adi Shankara establishing four *maths* at four corners of India to delineate the idea of a cultural nation to the common man.

The materialistic part was about becoming the largest economy of the ancient world (as Angus Maddison and other economic historians had shown), about trade and commerce through land and sea, and continuous development of science and engineering from more than 5,000 years (evident in the artefacts found in the Indus Valley Civilisation).

What it pointed out was that our ancient society was very organised. The village panchayats worked as the local government with full authority with caste problems being deliberated upon by caste panchayats of a broader area. Practices for devotion, such as which deities were to be worshipped and so on were decided by society, in consultation with caste panchayats. Apart from general deities, most places also had their local deities, often along with a holy jungle, holy hill and so on.

Indian civilisation is believed to have developed over 10,000 years, with its civilisational centres—Lahuradewa, Bhirrana, and Mehergarh—maturing as early as 6,000 BCE. Though our mythologies record this journey, it remains unique because its socio-religious-cultural core remained intact all through. India faced innumerable invasions, but eventually the invaders took up Indian nationality and further enriched our cultural heritage. This civilisational journey had suffered no break till just before foreign invasions by people of Abrahamic religions such as Muslims and Christians. Despite the invaders, three-quarters of Indians survived the calamity to continue with their rich, cultural journey. This unique Indian civilisation stemmed from its societal organisation based on dharma.

The neo-secularists are always attacking Brahminism and the caste system, because they know that it was these two strong features that helped India have an unbroken journey through several millennia. All other ancient nations, barring India and to some extent, China, have given up their old culture and religious faith. India could achieve this as a society organised on the foundation of caste-based division of labour and dharmic traditions carried forward by the Brahmins who provided extensive freedom to evolve and adapt. The *rishis* developed the scriptures, but its interpretations were given by the priests of local temples and by teachers of local Sanskrit schools. New interpretations evolved, matching the needs of the time. In this way, rituals and interpretations began to differ across regions, giving birth to different ritualistic practices. However, such heterogeneity and pluralism did not weaken India, but further strengthened it as the fulcrum of the Indian journey was its dharmic philosophy.

Dharmic society also played an important role in augmenting production and productivity by honing traditional skills of different castes. Society nurtured the whole structure through division of labour that it had devised based on justice to all according to their skillsets. The Brahmins were at the top of the ladder, and they allowed the Sankritisation process of the caste structure to incentivise innovation. In simple terms, whenever a professional caste innovated some primitive technology to increase productivity, it went up the ladder of the caste structure. For example, those who first started using two bullocks (*di-baladia*) instead of one (*ek-baladia*) for extracting oil, moved up a notch in the caste structure. The concept of purity, in its original form, was contemplated as a mechanism to encourage lessening human labour and thereby increasing volume of production. Later, it lost its original meaning and became an instrument for maintaining ritualistic religious purity.

The caste system was a complicated form of division of labour, and gradually it became rigid in the Current Era. But, even during the Current Era, the system was run under the guidance of the Brahmins. The Brahmins being a small community were amenable to societal pressure, particularly when exerted by other so-called higher castes. Yet they tried to work for the betterment of the entire population, and seldom were part of any caste riot even in modern times. Cultural India, from the days of the Rig Veda, had sought materialistic advancement. Brahmin-dominated structures of ancient times supported free enterprise and continuous development of the production process. It placed Indian society at the top of the world as the leading economic power. Even in the medieval age, following Chanakya's guidelines, Hindu states did not intervene in the production process. Muslim invaders, when they settled down as rulers, followed the same policy and encouraged further growth.

The dharmic path is open to all, irrespective of one's religion, caste, creed, colour of skin or such divisive criteria. Hindu and Sanatani religions accept all within their fold, even atheists, and also people of other religions if they agree to live, not just believe in, a dharmic life. This allowed ancient society to accept outsiders or new-comers readily. It is said that when the Parsis came and settled down in India, the locals were initially hostile to them, but when they saw the new entrants worship fire, they accepted them as new neighbours.

However, such liberal ideas and societal practices were lost and ritualistic excesses for preserving 'purity' crept in when India faced non-dharmic aggression from foreign invaders. It led the priestly class to close doors not only to other religions, but even for a section of Hindus who had lost their 'purity'. These people were then designated as 'untouchables' and were allotted menial jobs. Such practices went against dharmic principles, and such adharma was punished as many of these untouchables converted to Islam to protest against the treatment meted out to them. In the past, whenever such adharmic practices had crept in, the people of Bharat weeded them out through *dharma-yuddha*. But in more recent centuries, Hindu society appeared confused under Muslim rule and no such effort was made.

In ancient India, non-Brahmins could become scholars and

even avatars like Ram and Krishna. A *shudra* could even become a king. It, perhaps, became strictly hereditary after Buddhism emerged as a 'Protestant' form of Hinduism and received large-scale state endorsement. Such change was not good, but the critics must remember that heredity creeps in due to various reasons as is seen in the modern world. Even under capitalism, industry and business follows hereditary patterns and politicians and even the members of judiciary often use the hereditary ladder to reach their posts.

For similar reasons, professional categories maximised their skills in their hereditary profession in India from antiquity. It was also a way of protecting weaker sections by making their professions their exclusive right. However, when the scope for new professional jobs like working in factories, mills and offices emerged in the British era, the Brahminical system allowed all castes to participate in it, and no sanctions were imposed on anyone for availing such opportunities.

Thus, the caste system acted as the mainstay of Hindu society for thousands of years, and its guardians, the Brahmins, were and still are highly respected by traditionalists. The Brahmins are just about 3 per cent of the population and could run their socio-religious writs as the Hindu population looked up to them as guides. Even today, when Mayawati, the leader of the Dalit community (the lowest in the caste structure) wanted to expand her political base beyond her community, she approached the Brahmins. Rahul Gandhi, the Congress icon, when challenged about his Hindu credentials, retorted that he was a Brahmin with *yagnapabita*.

Democratic concepts of freedom have once again focused attention on social evils like rigid, inhuman casteism, thus pushing the society again on to a dharmic path. All these need to be taught in school to young ones to prevent misguidance and wrong impressions about the past. Only then they will understand what Shri Aurobindo had said in his Uttarpara speech:

> Other religions are preponderatingly religions of faith and profession, but the Sanatana Dharma is life itself; it is a thing that has not so much to be believed as lived. This is the dharma that for the salvation of humanity was cherished in the seclusion of this peninsula from of old. It is to give this religion that India is rising. She does not rise as other countries do, for self or when she is strong, to trample on the weak. She is rising to shed the eternal light entrusted to her over the world. India has always existed for humanity and not for herself and it is for humanity and not for herself that she must be great.... This Hindu nation was born with the Sanatana Dharma, with it, it moves and with it, it grows. When the Sanatana Dharma declines, then the nation declines.

Hindu ideas dominate in Independent India

Those from the Congress who are rooted in Indian soil—like Kamal Nath a veteran politician and many times Lok Sabha MP, Union Minister and former Chief Minister of MP—still agrees with the old Congress idea that 'India is Hindu'. When, in 2023, he was asked to react on Dhirendra Shastri's (a godman whom Kamal Nath and his son Nakul Nath revered) demand of Hindu Rashtra, the then Madhya Pradesh Congress chief had said, 'What is the point of making it a Hindu nation when 82 per cent are Hindu here? In a country where there is such a huge percentage, is it a matter of debate? What is the need to announce a Hindu nation, the figures state.'

Kamal Nath's reply was widely reported in various newspapers and websites on 8 and 9 August 2023, particularly because the assembly election was just three months away. He did not lose 'secular' votes for saying it straight, rather gained in quantum as evident from the total count of votes the Congress got in Madhya Pradesh in 2018 (1,55,95,696) and in 2023, (1,71,88,236). It shows that despite neo-secular machinations for so many decades, basic Hinduness in polity is alive as it always was.

If the moot question is that of mixing religion and politics, or if political Hindutva is an ideological red line, then how is it that so many leaders from so many neo-secular parties regularly cross over to the BJP? For them, the various political parties are just alternative forums to fulfil their aspirations. They all know that no real ideological barrier exists between them, and for the political parties, this is just a matter of convenience. In the last century, a leading example of such a *dal-badlu* politician was Yashwant Sinha. Now, we can cite the example of leaders like Jyotiraditya Scindia, Himanta Biswa Sarma and Suvendu Adhikary who have fitted in as comfortably with the BJP and its political Hindutva as they were earlier with their neo-secular parties. Among these new additions to the BJP, especially Himanta Biswa Sarma, the present Chief Minister of Assam, and Suvendu Adhikary, the present leader of Opposition in Bengal, are more vocal about Hindu and Sanatani issues than even the old BJP leaders.

It proves that the dividing line between these political parties is not ideological, but merely a function of opportunism. For example, Mamata Banerjee, now a neo-secular icon, had re-joined the NDA after the 2002 Gujarat riots that had shaken the conscience of the nation. It also means that the present fight is basically against Modi, a distinct non-Lutyens' figure in Indian politics, and not so much against the BJP. Again, in recent years, governments by AAP and TMC have taken steps that can be branded as mixing of religion and politics, or Hindutvavadi.

After boycotting the *pran pratishtha* ceremony at Ayodhya, Mamata Banerjee has built a Jagannath temple at Digha, that too with tax payers' money.

There is also a large section of non-confrontationist Hindus, who are proud of their Hindu-Sanatani civilisational journey and achievements, but do not like constant confrontation on religious issues. The post-Independence old Congress had many such leaders, including former Prime Minister Morarji Desai. A Congress leader and the first elected chief minister of Bombay state, Desai was later inducted into Nehru's cabinet as finance minister though he was openly pro-business and favoured pro-enterprise reforms. As a PM, Desai went to the US, and in an interview with Dan Rather for *CBS*'s weekly news magazine *60 Minutes*, the eighty-two-year-old had said, '…in Hindu philosophy… cow's urine has been considered holy, and it is prescribed in every ceremony. People must drink it.'[3]

This generation of inclusivist and proud Hindus includes Pranab Mukherjee who was elected as President of India. After his tenure as President ended, he attended an RSS function as a guest in 2018. He stood on the balcony of the birthplace of Keshav Baliram Hedgewar, the founder of the RSS, garlanded his statue, and wrote in the visitors' book: 'I came here to pay my respects to a great son of India.' He knew the *swayamsevaks*' 'red book' *Patheya* by Hedgewar had these lines:

> *Sangh swayamsevak* should fearlessly proclaim, "Hindusthan of Hindus". Remove all narrow-mindedness. We do not say that others should not live here. But they should be aware that they are living in Hindusthan of Hindus. (Like others would realise, if they were living there, that they are living in France of French people, or Germany of Germans, or Spain of Spanish people). Others cannot infringe on the rights of Hindus here.

Pranab Mukherjee's comment was reminiscent of Indira Gandhi admiring Vinayak Damodar 'Veer' Savarkar as a 'remarkable son of India' in 1980. She had donated for Savarkar's memorial. Savarkar, has unfortunately become the favourite villain of present-day neo-secularists, particularly of Rahul Gandhi. His grandmother, Indira had said, 'Veer Savarkar's daring defiance of the British government has its own important place in the annals of our freedom struggle.'

Another prominent Congress leader, Jagjivan Ram, the Dalit face of the Congress for decades, had performed the *bhoomi pujan* of the memorial, named Swatantryaveer Savarkar Rashtriya Smarak in Bombay. Other Congress stalwarts associated with it include Rajni Patel, who was inspired by Nehru and was close to Indira Gandhi, and former chief ministers of Maharashtra, Vasantdada Patil, Babasaheb Bhosale, Sushil Kumar Shinde, and former Congress union cabinet minister, Murli Deora.[4]

So, when Pranab Mukherjee praised Hedgewar, he sent a strong message that he belonged to the old generation of secular Congress leaders who were raised before the advent of 'neo-secularism'. Mukherjee spoke about our great ancient period, our unbroken history of 5,000 years, and then mentioned the foreign invaders under whom Bharat or Hindustan had suffered an 800-year-long foreign rule. Was he a Hindutvavadi? If so, then almost all leaders of the Congress born before Independence were or are Hindutvavadis. It only proves the point that a lot of things the neo-secularists brand as Hindutvavadi are integral parts of our traditional secularism. It also proves that there is a sizable section of our population that does not vote for the BJP, but is not averse to their Hindu ideology. That Indira Gandhi too belonged to this camp has already been detailed in a previous chapter.

However, taking pride in Cultural Bhartiyata is not the

monopoly of Hindus alone. Oscar Fernandez, a Christian, and a senior leader of the Congress extolled yoga, Indian medicinal systems, and even the healing power of cow urine in a parliamentary debate on two bills for setting up the National Commission for Homeopathy and Indian System of Medicines in 2020. He revealed that after he was advised to go for a knee replacement, he was cured by practising *vajrasana.* Fernandez also stated that he had met a person who claimed to be cured of cancer by cow urine treatment.

Many Muslim leaders of pre-Independence days, as pointed out by Naghma Sahar and Rashid Kidwai in an article in *The Print,* had demanded a ban on cow slaughter. The list included Maulana Mohammad Ali, Hakim Ajmal Khan, Mian Haji Ahmed Khatri, Mian Chhotani, Maulana Abdul Bari and Maulana Hussain Ahmad Madani. All of them had actively participated in the Mahatma Gandhi-led Khilafat movement of 1919. Later, a group of aggressive Muslims had incited riots in Malabar and a tense communal situation with Muslims and Hindus continued for years. In the thirties, riots had marred peace in many places. Then came the carnage by Muslim League in the name of Direct Action, the Noakhali genocide of the Hindus, and the Partition. Strangely, after Partition, the aggressiveness of Muslims was encouraged and the issue of banning cow slaughter was labelled as a communal issue by the neo-secularists, though the Constitution mandated through Directive Principles to prevent killings of 'cows and calves and other milch and draught cattle'. It proves that Hindu ideas are ingrained in our Constitution.

Most of the states had banned cow slaughter in past Congress regimes, and in recent years, the first Indian state that bought *gomutra* (cow urine) was Congress-ruled Chhattisgarh during the Hareli festival on 8 September 2022. The last Congress

Chief Minister of the state, Bhupesh Baghel was buying *gomutra* on behalf of the government. In a report published in *Congress Sandesh*, it was stated that the Chhattisgarh government has been continuously working towards making cows productive along with focusing on cow protection. The report stated that in the previous two years, more than Rs 300 crores have been transferred into the accounts of cow dung vendors, *Gauthan* (shed) committees and women's groups.[5]

'Cow protection' was earlier an agenda of Hindu nationalists. Another prominent hardliner Muslim leader of Assam, Maulana Badruddin Ajmal appealed to Muslims not to sacrifice cows during Eid-ul-adha for 'respecting the sentiments of Hindus', reminding them that 'our forefathers were all Hindus.[6]

Maulana Badruddin Ajmal heads the All India United Democratic Front (AIUDF) and the Assam State Jamiat Ulama, an organisation of Islamic scholars belonging to the Deobandi School.

Across the board, there is a sentiment that comes under the broad umbrella of Cultural Bhartiyata; it is well-ingrained in Indian society, cutting across religions. A part of this constituency does not vote for the BJP for they do not like the party and the violence it advocates in the name of Hindutva politics. Yet another part of the constituency votes not for the BJP in the Lok Sabha elections, but for the Congress or the other parties in the assembly elections.

This voting behaviour of the state clearly manifests that the voters have faith in the state leaders of the Congress, but not in Rahul Gandhi who for years has stood up as a hard-liner believing in neo-secularism.

This constituency of Cultural Bhartiyata recognises that

India is Hindu and also secular, and that India's past glories must be respected and highlighted.

Religious culture and global powers

Dharma and Hindutva are integral parts of our civilisational journey, and have helped Hindu radicals to assert its validity. But India isn't the only country guilty of mixing religion and politics. Look at how the two intermix in three nations—Russia, China, the USA—and all three nations are among the most prominent in world affairs.

Emerging great power China and established global player Russia have both incorporated new forms of cultural and religious outreach to shape and influence those parts of the world deemed to be strategically significant for them. Russia is busy mobilising internal and external public opinion through projection of religious and value-based identities. China, on the other hand, despite being a socialist country is desperately using Confucianism for internal consumption and is highlighting its Buddhist heritage to emerge as a classical soft power in countries along the route of the Belt and Road Initiative in the south, particularly Sri Lanka and Thailand. As far as the US is concerned, even Presidential candidates use the church to woo voters.

Putin's Christian narrative

What Putin is stressing on is the fact that a country with a strong religious affiliation cannot be deracinated from its religious culture. Western experts opine that Putin is winning elections by going back to Russia's religious roots and using it to his advantage. At his first inauguration, Putin had arranged for the Patriarch of the Russian Orthodox Church, who presented him with religious relics and blessed him with a personal prayer. In return, Putin announced that the Russian nation owed the Church a huge debt of gratitude for preserving Russia's 'century-old traditional spiritual and moral values, which would have been otherwise lost, irretrievably'.[7]

It was a resurrection of the deep connection among the Russian people, the state, the Church, and its shared cultural unity and history. Putin strengthened it further by his own 'integration propaganda', and passed a plethora of anti-LGBTQ laws and regulations along with measures to censor Western culture and postmodern values. By supporting and strengthening the Russian church, he has renewed the Russian identity that is helping him validate his authority as the protector of traditional values.

In an address on 21 February 2022, Putin attacked former Soviet leaders for repressing Russia's people and their religious values. He described it as 'not just a mistake, but...worse than a mistake', for it attempted to deprive Russians of their historical destiny. A year later, he came down on the Western elite for their attempts leading to the destruction of the family, of cultural and national identity, perversion and abuse of children, including paedophilia, 'all of which are declared normal in their life'. Declaring that he would not allow the Western elite to influence the hearts and minds of the Russian people, he concluded his speech by quoting Jesus Christ: 'Father, forgive them, for they know not what they do.'[8]

His target audience was not only the Russians, but also pious Christians of the West. Putin had claimed in a 2022 speech, that 'millions of people in the West realise that they are being led to a spiritual disaster' by liberal elitist governments. Soon after, in late February 2022, America's First Political Action Conference and some commentators supported his views.

The Ukraine War is another example of adding a moral validity to an apparently unjustifiable war. Putin had factored in Orthodox Christian religion as the necessity for Ukraine's geopolitical alignment with Moscow. To validate his argument, he referenced the tenth century Christianisation of Kievan Rus (a pan-Slavic kingdom centered in modern-day Ukraine, perceived as a precursor to modern Russia). But as the Ukraine government did not respond, the branch of the Orthodox Church in Ukraine, the UOC-MP (the Ukrainian Orthodox Church-Moscow Patriarchate), declared that Russia was the guardian of Christian civilisation and traditional family values while many European nations favoured Western efforts to export feminism and LGBTQ rights. Soon after, Russia attacked Ukraine. The dominant church in Ukraine, however, did not support this argument.

Russia's electoral outcomes might be inflated, but all neutral assessments indicate that Putin would emerge victorious even in a free and fair environment. He remains immensely popular due to a combination of factors, the use of religion perhaps being the most important among those. His twenty-year rule has marginalised the communists, the main opposition.

In India, Modi is the driver of a vehicle that has been in use for the last seventy years (first as Jana Sangha, then as BJP), while Putin himself is the inventor of the vehicle that powers Russia. Before him Boris Yeltsin, the first Russian president, had begun the process by joining the Russian Orthodox Church in 1992, but the Christian narrative began touching the Russian people only after 2000, with the beginning of the Putin era. In that sense, Putin's achievements far exceed Modi's. But, unlike Modi, he does not attack Muslims or any other community. He only attacks the 'neo-secular' narrative of Russia, while propagating a Christian narrative. Putin knows his task better and implements it with superb finesse. It is also noteworthy that Muslims of Russia, who are 9.5 per cent of the total population, do not resent this initiative as they are not being targeted.

Russia's connection with the orthodox Christian faith dates back to 988 CE, when Vladimir, King of Rus, accepted Christianity and established a Christian nation over present-day Ukraine. So, Putin is only using a 1,000-year-old narrative to promote glory, world leadership and restoring an old, domestic cohesion. In this attempt, disruptions created by the communists have helped him immensely. He has not only washed out the communists' atheist narrative, but has successfully re-established the old Christian narrative, thus unifying the domestic population and igniting cultural friction in the West.

China's U-turn from non-religiosity

China, taking a cue from Putin, is also slowly moving away from a non-religious regime and is resurrecting Confucianism that remained buried from the time of Mao Zedong and his Cultural Revolution—a revolution aimed at deracinating the Chinese population from their ancient legacies. Earlier, the communists had destroyed Confucian temples, burnt religious texts, and reportedly desecrated the sage's tomb. But, President Xi Jinping has now taken a U-turn, accepting and recognising Confucianism as the root of Chinese culture and is attempting to merge it with Marxist ideology.

Internally, Xi Jinping's thoughts have led to the production of a tele-serial, *When Marx Met Confucius*, a propaganda instrument aimed at reconciling communist views with China's cultural heritage. According to *conversation.com*, it had received 8 million views in the first two weeks after it was released online in October 2023. This integration of Marxism and traditional culture in a communist country stemmed from Xi's original idea of 'second integration' introduced in July 2021. The serial provided Confucius (551 BCE-479 BCE) and Marx equal stature and scripted an imaginary dialogue between the two, showcasing the similarities between them to promote validation for the communist regime.

Both in Russia and China, the long suppression of their internal cultural heritage failed to deracinate the people, and now a desperate attempt is being undertaken in China to gain legitimacy by proving that the Communist Party is following and protecting their ancient traditional culture.

Will our neo-secular leaders learn from these examples? Will they realise that they can regain legitimacy only if they amend their thoughts and relate it directly to the Indian cultural heritage? For the record, Confucius was very close to ancient Hindu thoughts of dharma, karma and *dharmayuddha* or waging a battle to establish righteousness. Early Confucian tradition had put stress on doing the right thing at the right time while maintaining existing norms to perpetuate the social fabric The guiding principle is *yi*, which means righteousness.

China has also started promoting 'Buddhism in BRI' (B-BRI) and is now trying to influence Buddhist countries, particularly Sri Lanka and Thailand, using Buddhism as a cultural resource. This is a new diplomatic ploy to attract Buddhist countries to go closer to China and participate in its failing Belt and Road Initiative (BRI), a global infrastructure development strategy adopted by the Chinese government in 2013. These overtures by Russia and China for the outside world are similar to what Turkey is doing in parts of East Africa with its significant Muslim population—building transportation infrastructure and new mosques. In

Brazil, conservative groups linked to former President Jair Bolsonaro had expanded their ties with like-minded evangelical and Pentecostal groups in Portuguese-speaking African nations. This use of traditionalism for furthering politico-diplomatic goals has become a common feature all over the world.

Religion and church in politics in the USA

Despite a ban on the church for endorsing candidates, Pastor Brandon Burden of KingdomLife Church in the Dallas suburbs openly announced support for a political candidate. Pastor Brandon did so claiming that God was working through his North Texas Congregation to take the country back to its Christian roots. He was not alone. In 2022, eighteen churches were identified by different news organisations, who, over the previous two years, openly violated the ban known as the Johnson Amendment, named after former President Lyndon B Johnson who had introduced it.[9]

In 1960, Johnson was elected as Vice President as the running mate of John F Kennedy, and in 1963, after Kennedy's assassination, he was sworn in as President. He vowed to build 'a great society' for the Americans, and introduced a slew of welfare measures, besides curbing pastors' influence in politics. However, some pastors even now go as far as to paint candidates they oppose as 'demonic'.

It is not as if pastors express their opinion only in local or state elections. The tradition continues in presidential elections, too. On 20 December 2021, Church leaders reported that on that very day, Donald Trump had delivered a special address to worshippers at the First Baptist Church in Dallas, Texas. The report mentioned that the 'megachurch' was pastored by Robert Jeffress, 'who is a frequent contributor to Fox News and served on Trump's faith advisory team during the 45th president's tenure'. It further reported that Trump had read not only from a prepared speech, but had also diverted from it to add extempore remarks on Afghanistan, inflation and police reforms. The service was streamed live on First Baptist Dallas' Youtube page. After delivering a speech on 'what if there were no Christmas', the pastor 'effusively' complimented Trump and invited him to speak, even though it was known that Trump was eyeing another presidential term in 2024.[10]

What will be the reaction in India if priests of a renowned temple invite Modi or Yogi Adityanath to deliver a speech from their podium and the invited leader then delivers a political speech which is streamed live? There was criticism in the US, but without the hullabaloo such an action would have invited in India.

According to news items, President Biden, too, delivered speeches from various churches, with the tone and tenor of his speeches having a definite political undertone. In one such speech in January 2024, he extolled the existence of Black churches, saying the world would be a different place if these churches were not around to show people the 'power of faith' during dark times. The speech, delivered at St John Baptist Church, South Carolina, with a definite aim of wooing the Black voters, was reported extensively by the media.[11]

Trump belongs to the Republican Party and Biden to the Democratic Party. They both used the church for political gain, but no one has made a big issue out of such mixing of religion with politics.

The Christian US, though theoretically secular like India, does not hesitate to express solidarity with Christians of other countries, and the White House does not think twice before issuing statements such as: 'This year, we are keeping the many Orthodox Christian communities in war-torn regions of our globe close to our hearts. Every human being is created in the image of God and deserves to be treated with dignity and respect. We mourn every innocent life lost and continue to counter persecution and discrimination against any group because of who they are, what they believe, or how they practice their faith.... We are grateful for the invaluable contributions that the Orthodox Christian community makes to our own country and to nations around the world, and we join together in praying for peace in the year ahead.' This statement was issued by Biden's White House on 7 January 2024.

We know what will happen if Modi issues a statement saying the the government is 'grateful for the invaluable contributions that the Hindu community makes to our own country and to nations around the world', But such statements with religious overtones are common in Europe and America. So, are Indian intellectuals oversensitive about the relationship between religion and politics? Or do they just use it for propaganda purposes to demean the Hindu religion and Indian culture?

Understanding the paradigm shift will help these radical secularists and radical Hindutvavadis to change their course and work for cultural Bhartiyata. The neo-secularists must acknowledge that India is Hindu, and the political Hindutvavadis should accept that India is secular, that too since thousands of years. BJP still has time to make amends as it is the only vehicle of change till now; but time is running out for the neo-secular parties. Their triple fault has come back to haunt them, as it was destined to do.

Endnotes

A handful of well-known intellectuals are still trying to denigrate India internationally, instead of promoting its great achievements. Take the example of neo-secularists like Economics Nobel laureate Amartya Sen. *The New Yorker* published a long interview of Sen on 6 October 2019, in which Sen categorically claimed that the communal situation is much better in Bangladesh than India. Sen made this statement even when he definitely knew that in Bangladesh, the percentage of the minority Hindu population had come down to half of what it was in 1971, when the state was born. But even after the Islamist-initiated forcible regime change in 2024, he has not cared to issue a clarification and has instead stated that Bangladesh should continue its 'admirable commitment to secularism'.[12, 13]

Such blatant falsehoods by prominent personalities create tremendous reaction among nationalist Hindus, and consequently harms the nationalist Muslims in India. The Hindus react by concluding: 'Oh, then we have to bring down the Muslim percentage of population in India to half of it to prove our 'admirable commitment to secularism'. This creates a dangerous cycle of action and reaction.

Fortunately, Sen is not so well-known outside Bengal, and so the reaction remains limited. It is anybody's guess why intellectuals like Sen love to disparage India internationally; but their attempts vitiate the atmosphere much more than the reckless talks of politicians like Rahul Gandhi abroad, who has been given a befitting reply in poll after poll. Such a false narrative ultimately strengthens Hindu nationalists, and delays the journey towards Cultural Bhartiyata.

What these intellectuals and politicians fail to understand is that India's ten-thousand-year long cultural journey cannot be derailed so easily. Attempts spanning hundreds of years have already been undertaken to do so; but all those have failed. Neither is it so easy to distort the truth that ultimately triumphs.

The neo-secularists forget that India's dharmic journey is not only about love, devotion and peaceful coexistence, but also of crushing the forces of adharma, as did Ram and Krishna.

While neo-secular narratives that are false and either demeaning for India or harmful for national integration need to be crushed, the focus has instead shifted to fighting the Muslim community. This needs to be stopped immediately, because this is injurious to the future journey of India.

There is no denying the fact that hundreds or thousands of temples were demolished and many of them converted to mosques all over India a few hundred years ago. Similarly, it is also true that after the eclipse of Buddhism in India, Hindus too occupied many Buddhist shrines. We may not find any evidence of such occupations before 500 BCE, as no dharmic religion had any permanent structure like a temple or a monastery in those days. However, our *itihaas* provides us details of clashes between dharmic sects. When our ancient stories talk about clashes between Kal Bhairav and Brahma, or Shiva and Daksha, metaphorically they tell us about battles between sets of believers. What it shows is that cultural-religious clashes have been part of the journey of India for thousands of years.

It is to be noted that such clashes before the advent of the 'Turki' Muslims were finally amicably settled through a process of reconciliation. Through this process, various Sanatan dharmic sects merged to form what we call Hinduism now. But the same process failed to work with the non-dharmic religions, mainly Islam and Christianity, as its followers believed that theirs was the 'only true religion'. But the demand of the modern times is revival of the dharmic path to unite different communities. In this endeavour, all the communities need to come forward with an open mind.

If we want to create a secular society, the Muslims will have to acknowledge that their forefathers belonged to this land, and were once partners in India's civilisational journey from the time of Lahuradewa-Birrana-Mehergarh and Bhimbeeta, all evidencing the beginning of our civilisational journey from 8000 BCE or even before. Indian Muslims will also have to acknowledge that Hindu temples were indeed destroyed by Muslims, but that those who did such heinous acts were invaders from Turkey and Central Asia. Similarly, Hindus too will have to acknowledge that demolishing a mosque or targeting innocent Muslims for some of the confrontational crimes is unpardonable. Only then will a truly secular India be born.

In the same vein, the neo-secularists will have to acknowledge that their attempt to deride Hindu/Sanatan culture and suppressing the eternal Idea of India are sinful acts. Similarly, Hindu nationalists will have to abandon their anti-Muslim narrative and acknowledge their failure to understand the essence of true dharmic culture, which is liberal and pluralistic. Such confessions by all the warring sides will facilitate our journey towards Cultural Bhartiyata, leading to prosperity of all.

Three ingredients of Cultural Bhartiyata

(i) A deep respect for our socio-cultural heritage of the past 10,000 years,

(ii) A determination for collective effort to put India at the top again,

(iii) A resolution that whoever will challenge this two-pronged agenda, whether Hindu, Sikh, Muslim, Christian or whoever will ultimately be crushed by a grand alliance of all the communities. Similarly, any foreign power that will challenge India should be crushed too.

The time has come when, for attaining the great future that awaits this land, its people need to follow the path of its eternal journey that took it to the top of the world in economic, spiritual, and cultural fields thousands of years ago, and kept it as *numero uno* for millennia. Economic historian Angus Maddison and others agree that India was the largest economy in 1 CE and continued to be number one or two till just before the onset of the British colonial era.

Max Muller, who once thought India needs to be conquered again, later proclaimed: 'If I were asked under what sky the human mind has most fully developed some of its choicest gifts, has most deeply pondered over the greatest problems of life, and has found solutions of some of them which well deserve the attention even of those who have studied Plato and Kant, I should point to India.'[14]

It is also well documented that India was the first example of conquering a large part of the world with its soft power which does not coerce, but coopts through socio-cultural-religious wisdom.

We, Indians, need to reestablish India on that highest pedestal again through our economic strength and soft power. To achieve that, our young generations deserve to have in-depth knowledge of our 10,000-year-long journey, particularly the dharmic philosophy and great achievements of the past, including yoga and Ayurveda. The education field needs to be tapped for it, as that remains the easiest way to reach this knowledge to young learners. Whoever will take the lead in this will not only put the last touches on this ongoing paradigm shift, but will also be remembered for paying the richest tribute to Bharatvarsha.

References

Chapter 1

1. Reprinted by RK Mission in *The Complete Works of Swami Vivekananda,* vol 5, p 233)
2. *The Collected Works of Mahatma Gandhi*. Vol XXIV. p 476
3. Report in the September 21, 2012, issue of *TOI*, under the heading, 'Army chief opposes PM's trip to Pak'.
4. https://www.thehindu.com/opinion/op-ed/a-tale-of-two-demands
5. Congress hand stained with Muslim blood: Salman Khurshid, April 24, 2018, https://economictimes.indiatimes.com
6. It's a sin to be dalit in Haryana, Oct 18, 2013, *Times of India*

Chapter 2

1. https://vivekavani.com/common-bases-hinduism-swami-vivekananda/
2. 'Who was Samarth Ramdas and what was his relationship with Chhatrapati Shivaji Maharaj, *Indian Express*, May 8, 2023
3. https://sundayguardianlive.com/opinion/tagore-khilafat-hinduism-can-relieve-world-meanness

(The article is in Bengali and has been translated by the author)

4. *Collected Works of Gandhi,* 1999, volume 63, p. 38
5. Ibid pp. 39–40
6. Ibid, p. 40
7. *Harijan*, issue of 2 June 1946
8. Ibid, issue of 28 April 1946
9. Ibid, issue of 24 November 1946
10. *Young India*, issue of 18 June 1925, p. 214
11. *Harijan*, issue of 2 March 1934
12. *Harijan*, issue of 7 April 1946
13. *Harijan*, issue of 12 May 1946
14. *Harijan*, issue of 19 May 1946
15. https://www.mkgandhi.org/momgandhi/chap81.php
16. *Collected Works*, vol. 89, p. 176
17. *Hind Swaraj*, 1909
18. *Collected Works*, vol. 29, p.187
19. Ibid, vol. 30, p. 312
20. *Harijan* issue of 1 December 1946
21. *Collected Works,* vol. 90, p. 413
22. *Collected Works,* vol. 94, pp. 209-210
23. *Discovery of India*, p. 520
24. https://indianexpress.com/article/explained/how-nehru-won-a-third-term-despite-growing-challenge
25. *Discovery of India*, p. 515
26. *Discovery of India* p. 517
27. The Discovery of India, Chapter 5
28. Correspondence 1926-1932, *Netaji Collected Works*, vol. 4)
29. *The Alternative Leadership*, p. 187-189
30. *Netaji Collected Works*, vol. 3
31. *The Indian Struggle (1920-1942)*, p. 352

32. The Call of The Motherland: Writings and Speeches 1923–1929, Netaji Collected Works, vol. 5
33. Correspondence May 1923-July 1926, *Netaji Collected Works*, vol. 3
34. India's Spokesman Abroad, Collected Works, vol. 8
35. The Call of The Motherland: Writings and Speeches 1923–1929, Collected Works, vol. 5
36. Ibid

Chapter 3

1. https://www.indiatoday.in/india/story/narasimha-rao-first-bjp-pm-congress-leader-mani-shankar-aiyar-2425694-2023-08-23
2. https://economictimes.indiatimes.com/buddhadev-not-to-interfere-in-anti-terror-drive/articleshow/603265.cms?from=mdr
3. https://www.hindustantimes.com/india/congress-distances-itself-from-digvijaya-singh-on-batla-house-statement/story-m8afic4ZSXI7rNqW65sivL.html
4. https://www.indiatoday.in/india-today-insight/story/the-story-of-two-slogans-from-indira-gandhis-fight-against-caste-politics-to-rahul-gandhis-fight-for-it-2441790-2023-09-28
5. https://www.theweek.in/theweek/cover/2021/05/20/rajiv-gandhi-opened-the-doors-for-1991-reforms-montek-singh-ahl.html

Chapter 4

1. https://www.jstor.org/stable/4396930
2. Glimpses of World History, p 720
3. https://theprint.in/opinion/security-code/indiras-hinduism-in-danger-to-karnataka-hijab-what-jihadists-want/828621/
4. theprint.in/pageturner/excerpt/indira-gandhi-wanted-to-give-ayodhya-a-facelift-to-show-she-wasnt-just-courting-muslims/474671/

5. https://inc.in/congress-sandesh/tribute/rajiv-gandhi-s-vision-of-religion-in-the-twenty-first-century
6. https://sundayguardianlive.com/culture/book-mha-officer-reveals-upa-manufactured-hindu-terror-narrative
7. https://archive.org/details/presidentradhakr02radh/, p 94, 96

Chapter 5

1. https://indianexpress.com/article/research/bare-souls-boundless-spirit-decoding-the-naga-sadhus-9782126/
2. https://caravanmagazine.in/politics/madhya-pradesh-elections-computer-baba-rss-vhp-congress-narmada-sansad
3. indianexpress.com (Did Morarji Desai drink his own urine?)
4. news18.com, 'Remarkable Son of India': How Indira, Other Top Congress Leaders Backed Savarkar's Ideology
5. Congress Sandesh (online edition: https://inc.in/congress-sandesh)
6. www.ndtv.com, 8 July 2022
7. http://en.kremlin.ru/events/president/news/38090
8. Vladimir Putin, "Presidential Address to Federal Assembly Address, 21 Feb 2023
9. www.texastribune.org/2022/10/30/johnson-amendment-elections-irs
10. https://churchleaders.com/news/413046-trump-addresses-dallas-first-baptist.html
11. https://apnews.com/article/biden-black-churches-south-carolina-primary-59db36dad46d0bece5152eecc8fa4626
12. https://www.newyorker.com/news/the-new-yorker-interview/amartya-sens-hopes-and-fears-for-indian-democracy
13. https://theprint.in/opinion/amartya-sen-read-bangladesh-wrong-faith-in-yunus-revive-country-misplaced/2559771/
14. India: What Can It Teach Us

Hadrat Umar Farooq

Hadrat Umar Farooq

(Allah's Blessings be upon him)

By
Prof. Masud-ul-Hasan

KITAB BHAVAN
1784, Kalan Mahal, Daryaganj,
New Delhi-110 002 [INDIA]

KITAB BHAVAN
Publishers, Distributors, Exporters & Importers
1784, Kalan Mahal, Darya Ganj,
New Delhi - 1100 02 (India)

Phones : (91-11) 23277392/93, 23274686, 32906494
Fax : (91-11) 23263383

Website : www.kitabbavan.net
: www.kitabbavan.com

Email : nasri@vsnl.com
: nusrat@bol.net.in

1ST Published in India : 1997
4th Edition : 2015

ISBN : 81-7151-229-1
Book Code No. : H00179

Printed & Published in India by :
Nusrat Ali Nasri for KITAB BHAVAN
1784, Kalan Mahal, Darya Ganj,
New Delhi - 1100 02 [India]

Contents

Subjects ***Pages***

Subjects ***Pages***

Preface

I have the pleasure to present to my readers this exercise in the shape of "Life of Hadrat Umar Farooq (R. A.). This book seeks to project the life story of Umar the Great (R. A.).

About a hundred years ago, Allama Shibli Numani wrote in Urdu a biography of Hadrat Umar (R. A.) under the title "Al-Farooq". The book was translated in English in the fiftees of the twentieth century.

Since then no remarkable work on the life of Hadrat Umar (R. A.) has appeared in any language of the world. It is surprising that no original work on Hadrat Umar (R. A.) has appeared in English so far.

In the annals of mankind, Hadrat Umar (R . A.) occupies a unique position. Human history is studded with the names and exploits of great conquerors, empire-builders, administrators, and statesmen, but Hadrat Umar (R. A.) is the greatest of them all. During the short space of ten years, Hadrat Umar (R. A.) succeeded in building the largest empire in history. Under his leadership the Muslims emerging from the deserts of Arabia overthrew the empire of Persia in the east and shattered the empire of Byzantium in the west.

Hadrat Umar (R. A.) set standards of republican and democratic behaviour which have not been surpassed so far. He was the Head of the largest State in the world, and yet he lived the life of a common man. Of simple habits, austere and frugal, he was always accessible to the meanest of his subject, and yet he was cause of terror for the wrong doer. He would wander about at night to enquire into the condition of the people without any guard or escort. He did not live in any palace, and yet the rulers of the day trembled at the very mention of his name.

The greatness of Hadrat Umar was acknowledged by the Holy Prophet of Islam (S. A. W.) when he said that if there were to be any Prophet after him it would have been Hadrat Umar (R. A.). Verily Hadrat Umar (R. A.) was not a prophet, but he did things which a prophet would have done.

Hadrat Umar (R. A.) is one of those extraordinary personalities who made history. His brilliant conquests, his benevolent administration, his far-reaching reforms, and the integrity of his sterling character mark him as one of the greatest men of all times.

In view of the greatness of Hadrat Umar no apology is needed for writing his life story. By undertaking such an exercise we hardly add anything to the greatness of the great man; by recounting some of the prominent features of his greatness we merely seek to inspire ourselves and make our lives sublime.

In the case of Hadrat Umar, a matter of regret is that the number of books written so far about him is very meagre, and in no way commensurate to his greatness. The Orientalists boast of having produced a number of books on Islam, but they have not produced any book on Hadrat Umar, presumably the greatness of Hadrat Umar has been too dazzling for the western scholars to take notice of.

I long pondered over the point as to what was the reason that inspite of the fact that Hadrat Umar (R. A.) was one of the greatest men of all times, no original work in English had been produced about him. Perhaps the western scholarship was in no mood to project his greatness. Presumably they wanted to suppress his greatness. That prompted me to undertake an exercise in writing the life story of Hadrat Umar (R. A.). After working on the project for some three years, I have produced a book on Hadrat Umar

PART I

The Pre-Caliphate Period

THE FAMILY

The exact date of the birth of Hadrat Umar is not known. The concensus of opinion, however, is that Hadrat Umar was born at Mecca around 580 A.D. He was younger than the Holy Prophet of Islam by about ten years.

Hadrat Umar belonged to the Adi clan of the Quraish. It was one of the ten clans of the Quraish who inhabited Mecca.

The pedigree of Hadrat Umar was : Umar the son of Khattab; the son of Nufail; the son of Abul Uzza; the son of Riza; the son of Ribah; the son of Qurat; the son of Adi; the son of Ka'b.

The pedigree of the Holy Prophet was: Hadrat Muhammad (peace be on him) the son of Abdullah; the son of Abdul Muttalib; the son of Hashim; the son of Abd Munaf; the son of Qussay; the son of Kulab; the son of Ka'b.

In the case of Hadrat Abu Bakr and the Holy Prophet, Murrah in the eighth degree was their common ancestor. In the case of the Holy Prophet and Hadrat Umar, Ka'b in the ninth degree was their common ancestor.

Among Hadrat Umar's ancestors, Adi rose to prominence as a diplomat, and the clan came to be known after him. Whenever the Quraish of the day had to negotiate any settlement with any other tribe, Adi represented the interests of the Quraish as an ambassador. Even in the case of disputes among the Quraish themselves, Adi acted as the arbitrator. After the death of Adi the two offices of diplomatic representation and arbitration became hereditary in his descendants.

Hadrat Umar's grandfather Nufail arbitrated in a dispute between Abdul Muttalib, the grandfather of the Holy Prophet and Harab bin Umayyah over the custodianship of the Ka'bah Nufail gave his verdict in favour of Abdul Muttalib. Addressing Harab bin Umayyah he said:

> " Why do you pick a quarrel with a person who is taller than you in stature; more imposing than you in appearance; more refined than you in intellect; whose progeny outnumbers yours and whose generosity outshines yours in lustre? Do not, however, construe this into any disparagement of your good qualities which I highly appreciate. You are as gentle as a lamb, you are renowned throughout Arabia for the stentorian tones of your voice, and you are an asset to your tribe."

This address is indicative of Nufail's skill in diplomacy and his highly developed sense of judgment.

Khattab the father of Hadrat Umar was among the prominent members of the Banu Adis. The Banu Adis had some feuds with Banu Abdul Shams. The Banu Abdul Shams were stronger in power and position, and the Banu Adis as a safety measure had to seek alliance with some other clan. They allied themselves with Banu Shams. On this alliance, Khattab composed the following verses:

> "How can Abdul Shams still threaten us,
> When other men of mettle espouse our cause?
> In the halls of Banu Shams there are mighty warriors,
> Whose hospitality and protection we enjoy."

The house in which Hadrat Umar was born in Mecca was situated midway between Safa and Marwah. During the period of his caliphate, Hadrat Umar had the house dismantled, and the site was turned into a camping ground.

Hadrat Umar's mother was Khantamah who was the daughter of Hisham bin al-Mughira. Al-Mughira was a personage of high rank among the Quraish. In the event of war he marshalled the Quraish troops and led them to war. Hisham the maternal grandfather of Hadrat Umar and al-Walid the father of the renowned General Khalid were brothers. Khalid was thus a cousin of Hadrat Umar's mother and his maternal uncle.

Abu Jahl whose personal name was Amr bin Hisham bin al-Mughira was a brother of Hadrat Umar's mother, and his maternal uncle. One of the sisters of Hadrat Umar's mother, Umm Salma was married to the Holy Prophet of Islam.

Hadrat Umar had several brothers and sisters. The most well known out of these were: Zaid and Fatima. Zaid and Hadrat Umar were step brothers, their mothers being different. Nevertheless the two brothers were devoted to each other. When Zaid was later martyred at the battle of Yamama during the caliphate of Hadrat Abu Bakr, Hadrat Umar was highly grieved. He used to say, "Whenever the wind blows from Yamama, it brings me the fragrance of Zaid."

Fatima was the real sister of Hadrat Umar. She was married to her cousin Saeed bin Zaid bin Amr. She played an important role in the conversion of Hadrat Umar to Islam.

Amr, a brother of Khattab was a paternal uncle of Hadrat Umar. Zaid the son of Amr, and a cousin of Hadrat Umar was among the distinguished persons of the Quraish, who before the advent of Islam gave up idolatry, and came to believe in the unity of God. Zaid was a poet. One of his poems reads:

"I believe in one God,
I cannot believe in a thousand gods.
I ignore the idols of Lat and Uzza,
A wise and cautious man can do no more."

Khattab the father of Umar persecuted Zaid for his religious beliefs. Zaid died before the Holy Prophet of Islam announced his prophetic mission. When the Holy Prophet proclaimed his prophethood, Saeed the son of Zaid who had married Hadrat Umar's sister Fatima, was among the early converts to Islam.

HADRAT UMAR IN THE DAYS OF IGNORANCE

No account is preserved about the early life of Hadrat Umar during the days of ignorance. Hadrat Umar belonged to an ordinary family of average means and there was nothing conspicuous about Hadrat Umar or his family during the days of ignorance to be recorded or chronicled. We can merely pick up stray accounts here and there, and try to weave them into a readable narrative.

It appears that Hadrat Umar grew up as a typical Arab—a tall young man with a fine physique and impressive personality. When he was a child his father put him to the task of grazing camels. Khattab was a hard taskmaster, and Hadrat Umar often recalled how his father belaboured him mercilessly whenever there was a lapse on his part. Hadrat Umar also recalled that when he was a child he used to graze the flocks of goats and sheep of his maternal aunts who doled out pittance to him in the shape of dates.

As a child, Hadrat Umar used to graze the animals under his charge in the grazing ground Dajnan, about ten miles from Mecca. When Hadrat Umar became the Caliph, he happened to pass through Dajnan. Turning to his companions he said:

> "Gracious heavens ! There was a time when I used to roam about this desert as a camel-herd, wearing a felt jacket, and whenever I sat down tired my father beat me. Now the times have changed. There is now none save God as my superior."

Among the Quraish of those days, reading and writing was not in vogue. In spite of that Hadrat Umar received education in reading and writing. It is related that among the Quraish of Mecca only seventeen persons could read and write, and Hadrat Umar was one of them. That has to be acknowledged as a great attainment.

Hadrat Umar's father was an authority in tracing genealogies. Under the guidance of his father, Hadrat Umar also acquired matchless skill in the matter of the study of pedigrees. Hadrat Umar knew intimately as to who was who among the Quraish. He was also well versed in the knowledge of the history of Arabia.

Hadrat Umar was blessed with a strong physique. He could undergo great rigours. He could travel on foot for miles. He was an athlete and a wrestler. He participated in the wrestling matches on the occasion of the annual fair at Ukaz, and he won in most of such matches. From the accounts that have come down to us it appears that Hadrat Umar had attained perfection in the art of wrestling.

Some first hand descriptions of the physical appearance of Hadrat Umar have come down to us. Ibn Saad and al-Hakim have recorded a description of Hadrat Umar as Abu Miriam Zir, a native of Kufa described him. Zir said:

> "I went forth with the people of Madina on a festival day, and I saw Umar walking barefoot. He was advanced in years, bald, of a tawny colour—a left handed man, tall, and towering above the people."

Ibn Umar described the physical appearance of Hadrat Umar as follows:

> "He was a man of fair complexion, a ruddy tint prevailing, tall, bald and grey."

> Ubayd bin Umayr described Hadrat Umar as follows: "Hadrat Umar used to overtop the people in height."

> Salima bin al-Akwa'a said about him:

> "Hadrat Umar was ambidexter; he could use both his hands equally well."

Ibn Asakir records on the authority of Abu Raja al-U'taridi that:

"Umar was a man tall, stout, very bald, very ruddy with scanty hair on the cheeks, his moustaches large, and the ends thereof reddish."

Hadrat Umar was a skilful rider. He could successfully manage even the wildest of horses. He would literally jump on the back of the horse, and sit with such ease and steadiness that he appeared to be a part and parcel of the horse he rode.

He was very intelligent and shrewd. He was a good public speaker. He was gifted with an uncommon degree of tact and judgment, and on several occasions he successfully undertook ambassadorial missions on behalf of the Quraish.

By all accounts he was self-respecting, broad-minded and sincere. He was a man of strong convictions, a good friend, and a bad enemy. Like the rugged hills around him, he was harsh and stern, violent in temper, but very good of heart. He was always prepared to stand up against the oppressor and espouse the cause of the weak.

He followed the profession of a trader. He undertook journeys to Syria, Iraq, Yemen, and elsewhere for the purposes of trade. He was a successful trader, and he made good money as a result of these commercial journeys. When Haurat Umar migrated from Mecca, according to his own account, he was one of the richest Quraish merchants.

In his books, *Akhbar-ul-Zaman*, and *Kitab-ul-Ausat* the celebrated historian Masudi is understood to have related the incidents of the travels of Hadrat Umar. Masudi states that Hadrat Umar paid visits to several Arabian and Persian princes. These books of Masudi have, however, been lost, and the details of these journeys are no longer available to us.

Before his conversion to Islam, Hadrat Umar had three wives. His first wife was Qariba bint Abi Umayya al-Makhzumi. She belonged to the same clan as the mother of Hadrat Umar. She was one of the most beautiful women of Mecca of the day. His second wife was Zainab bint Mazaun. She was the sister of Usman bint Maz'un an early companion for whom the Holy Prophet had great regard. She was the mother of Abdullah and Hadrat Hafsa. His third wife was Malaika bint Jarul al-Khuzai. She was also called Umm Kulsum.

HADRAT UMAR AND ISLAM

When the Holy Prophet (peace be on him) proclaimed his apostlehood, the reaction among the Quraish was violent. Hadrat Umar, a young man of strong convictions, held the new faith to be a sacrilege of the idols of Ka'bah. Young, well-built, and fiery-tempered as he was, Hadrat Umar was in the forefront in opposition to Islam.

Some accounts have come down to us showing Hadrat Umar's attitude to Islam in the days before his conversion. Hadrat Umar has related that in the days of ignorance he was one day standing by an idol with a number of Quraish when an Arab sacrificed a calf. From the belly of the calf the following cry was heard:

"O blood red one,
The deed is done.
A man will cry
Besides God, none."

This corroborated what the Holy Prophet (peace be on him) said. Hadrat Umar, however, dismissed the cry as sheer hallucination.

It is on record that along with some Arabs Hadrat Umar went to a soothsayer, and asked him to look into the matter of Hadrat Muhammad (peace be on him) who had proclaimed a new faith. The soothsayer looked to the heaven for a long time. Then he leapt and said:

"O men, God has honoured and chosen Muhammad,
Purified his heart and bowels.
His stay, among you, O men will be short."

Hadrat Umar cursed the soothsayer and returned home very cross and upset.

Lubna, a maid servant of Hadrat Umar, accepted Islam. When Hadrat Umar came to know of her conversion, he beat her violently and asked her to retract. She said that he might kill her, but she would not leave Islam. Thereafter it became the wont of Hadrat Umar that he would beat her every day and would stop beating till he Himself felt exhausted. In spite of that, the slave girl remained steadfast.

Umm Abdullah bint Khatamah, a lady related to Hadrat Umar, also accepted Islam. Hadrat Umar was very furious at her conversion. As she along with her husband Amar bin Rabiah and other early converts decided to migrate to Abyssinia, Hadrat Umar felt moved. He visited her and said, "Umm Abdullah are you going ?" She said, "By God, you have made our living in Mecca very difficult. There is no option with us but to migrate elsewhere." Inadvertently Hadrat Umar said, "Umm Abdullah, may God protect you; go in peace." At that time Umm Abdullah felt that in spite of Umar's opposition to Islam, he would one day accept the new faith.

We have it on the authority of Hadrat Umar Himself that one day he came across the Holy Prophet in the Ka'bah. The Holy Prophet was reciting verses from the Holy Qur'an and as Hadrat Umar listened to these verses he felt that it was the work of some poet. Then the Holy Prophet recited, "This is the revealed word of God; it's not the work of any poet. Yet you people do not believe". Thereupon Hadrat Umar felt that if this was not the work of any poet it would be the work of a soothsayer. Thereupon the Holy Prophet recited the verses, "And this is not the word of any soothsayer; it is divine word communicated through Gabriel." Hearing these verses Hadrat Umar stood transfixed for some time. In his heart of hearts he thought that perhaps truth lay with Hadrat Muhammad (peace be on him).

Hadrat Umar, however, dismissed these feelings and soon he was his former self very hostile to Islam. He went to the Quraish and participated in their counsels. They felt concerned that the venom of the new faith was spreading and the only remedy was that Muhammad (peace be on him) sould be killed. All present at the meeting agreed that

Muhammad (peace be on him) should be killed. Then the meeting invited volunteers who would kill the Prophet. Hadrat Umar volunteered to kill the Prophet, and vindicate the faith of their forefathers.

TA HA

One hot sultry day in the year A.D. 616, Hadrat Umar buckled his sword and set out to kill the Holy Prophet (peace be on him). In the way, Hadrat Umar met Nuaim bin Abdullah. He was a friend of Umar. He had been converted to Islam, but Hadrat Umar did not know of that.

Noticing the dark frowns on his face, Nuaim asked Umar what he was up to. Umar said that he was going to slay Muhammad (peace be on him), and thus vindicate the gods of Ka'bah. Nuaim said, "Beware if you harm Muhammad (peace be on him) you will not be safe from the fury of Banu Hashim. Desist from such a course in your own interest". Umar ejaculated angrily: "It appears you have also become a Muslim." Nuaim said, "Umar, do not bother about me, but take care of your sister and brother-in-law who have been converted to Islam, and who may be reading the Qur'an at this very moment."

That made Hadrat Umar pause. Instead of going to the Holy Prophet, he went to the house of his sister. His sister was Fatima and her husband was Saeed bin Zaid. Umar loved his sister. He had never thought that his brother-in-law or his sister would have the audacity to accept Islam. This was news to him. He could not believe it, but he thought it advisable to verify the facts.

As Hadrat Umar stepped into the house of his sister, he found that both Fatima and her husband were reading the Qur'an from a leaf. Seeing Umar, his sister hid the leaf. Fatima rose to welcome her brother with a smile. But there was a dark frown on the face of Umar. "What were you reading", he thundered. "Nothing", replied Fatima.

Hadrat Umar caught his brother-in-law by the throat and said, "So you have apostasised from the faith of your forefathers". Saeed retorted, "Rather we have abandoned falsehood for truth." Thereupon Hadrat Umar was about to strike Saeed when Fatima intervened saying, "Hands off from my husband. If you have anything to say, say it to me, but do not touch my husband." Hadrat Umar asked, "Is it a fact that you have become Muslims." She replied, "Yes we have become Muslims. You may kill us if you like, but we will not waver in our faith".

Umar stayed his hands and desired that the leaf from which they had been reading should be shown to him. Fatima said that he could not touch the sacred leaf until he had washed his hands. Umar washed his hands, and the sacred leaf was handed over to him. It was the Sura *Ta Ha*. It read:

> *"Ta Ha*
> We have not sent the Qur'an to thee,
> To be an occasion for thy distress,
> But only as an admonition to those who fear God.
> A revelation from Him,
> Who created the earth and the heavens on high.
> God most gracious,
> Is firmly established on the throne of authority.
> To Him belongs what is in the heavens and on earth,
> And all between them and all beneath the soil.
> If thou pronounce the word aloud, it's no matter
> For verily He knoweth what is secret
> And what is yet hidden.
> Verily there is no god but He
> To Him belongs the most beautiful names." (20: 1—8)

As Hadrat Umar read the verses over and over again, he felt as if these verses were addressed to him in person, and the mysterious *Ta Ha* referred to Umar—the Man. Hadrat Umar shuddered with the fear of God, and he felt as if his conscience was upbraiding him, "Umar, how long would you stay away from the path of truth. Has not the time come for you to follow the truth?"

And then Hadrat Umar resolved that he would lose no time in following the truth. Turning to his sister and brother-in-law he said, "I came to you as an enemy of Islam; I go from you as a friend of Islam. I had buckled this sword to slay the Prophet of Islam; I now go to him to offer him allegiance."

Fatima and Saeed cried "Allah-o-Akbar".

The episode has been dramatised by Allama Iqbal in his poem "Secrets of the Self". He has exhorted the Muslim women to be like the sister of Umar. He says:

"O Muslim women ;
Out of the evening create a new dazzling morn.
To the true lovers of God,
Recite the Holy Qur'an
And enthusiastically translate
Its spirit into action.
Don't you know that such recitation
Changed altogether Umar's fate."

AL-FAROOQ

From the house of his sister, Hadrat Umar proceeded to the house of Arqam at the foot of the Safa hill, where the Holy Prophet was lodged.

Hadrat Umar knocked at the door of the house of Arqam.

"Who comes", enquired the guard.
"Umar bin al-Khattab", said Umar.

As the guard peeped through the door he saw that Umar had buckled his sword. The guard therefore hesitated to open the door.

Hadrat Hamza said to the guard, "Open the door; if he comes in peace he will be welcome. If he is bent on mischief, we are enough to overpower him".

Hadrat Umar was admitted. Hadrat Hamza caught him by the hem of his cloak and said, "Umar, what brings you here?" The Muslims with drawn swords surrounded Umar, so that he could be overpowered if he showed any signs of violence.

Hearing the noise, the Holy Prophet came out of his cell. Addressing Hamza the Holy Prophet said, "Leave him. Let him come forward".

As Hadrat Umar stepped forward the Holy Prophet said, Umar, how long will you stray from the path of Islam. Has the time not come for you to see the truth?"

Hadrat Umar said, "Verily the time has come for me to see the truth. I have come to profess my faith in Islam".

The Holy Prophet stretched his hand. Hadrat Umar held the hand with reverence and said, "I declare that there is no god but Allah, and that Muhammad is the Messenger of God".

In joy the Muslims shouted "Allah-o-Akbar". The Holy Prophet embraced Hadrat Umar. The other Muslims embraced Hadrat Umar one by one. Hadrat Umar was the fortieth person to become a Muslim.

That day even Gabriel congratulated the Holy Prophet on the conversion of Hadrat Umar. Gabriel said:

> "O prophet of God, the dwellers in Heaven rejoice at the conversion of Umar and offer you their congratulations".

Intoxicated with the joy of having become a Muslim, Hadrat Umar proceeded to various parts of Mecca to announce that he had become a Muslim. He first went to the house of his maternal uncle Abu Jahl. He knocked at the door of the house of Abu Jahl.

"Who comes", asked Abu Jahl.

"It's Umar", said Hadrat Umar. Abu Jahl opened the door and said,

"Welcome nephew". Hadrat Umar said,

"Uncle do you know, I have become a Muslim." Abu Jahl said,

"Do not talk like that. I know that a man of your views can never become a Muslim". Umar said,

"No, uncle it is a fact that I have become a Muslim." Abu Jahl thereupon said,

"If what you say is true then be damned". Saying this Abu Jahl shut the door in the face of Hadrat Umar.

Thereafter Hadrat Umar went to see some other Quraish chiefs. He told them of his conversion to Islam. Like Abu Jahl they damned him and shut the doors of their houses against him.

Then Hadrat Umar proceeded to the Ka'bah. There he saw Jamil bin Ma'mar al-Jamahi who enjoyed reputation for spreading reports in Mecca. Hadrat Umar told him that he had accepted Islam. Jamil rose from his seat, and cried at the top of his voice:

"O ye Quraish, know that Umar bin al-Khattab has been converted to Islam, and apostatised from the faith of his forefathers."

On hearing this some Quraish youth gathered at the Ka'bah. Hadrat Umar said,

"What Jamil said is not correct. I have not apostatised: I have seen the truth and accepted Islam". Thereupon the Quraish youth rushed at Hadrat Umar with a view to beating him. A Shaikh dressed in Yemeni robes Al-Aas bin Wail passed that way, and enquired what was the matter. The Quraish said that Umar had apostatised, and they wanted to punish him for straying from the faith of his forefathers. The Shaikh said,

"A man should be free to choose whatever religion he likes. Why beat him for that ?" Abu Jahl also happened to come that way. Seeing the Quraish, he said,

"I offer protection to my nephew". Hadrat Umar said,

"Uncle, I do not need your protection. For me the protection of God and the Holy Prophet is enough".

Then Hadrat Umar went to the Holy Prophet and told him that he had publicly announced his conversion. Heretofore those who were converted to Islam kept their conversion to Islam secret for fear of the oppression of the Quraish. They also prayed in secret. Hadrat Umar submitted to the Holy Prophet:

"O Messenger of God are we not in the truth?" The Holy Prophet said,

"Why not, we are verily in the truth".

"Then why should we not pray in the public ? Has not the time come for us to declare our faith publicly ?" said Hadrat Umar. Hadrat Umar tried to prevail on the Holy Prophet that the truth of Islam should become manifest. The Holy Prophet agreed with Hadrat Umar.

The following day all the Muslims emerged from the house of Arqam and proceeded to the Holy Ka'bah, in two lines, one led by Hadrat Umar, and the other by Hadrat Hamza. At the Ka'bah the Muslims prayed openly. The Quraish watched the Muslims pray and said, "Verily by the conversion of Umar to Islam, the Muslims have taken the revenge from the Quraish".

After the Muslims had prayed in the Ka'bah, the Holy Prophet conferred on Hadrat Umar the title of "Al-Farooq," for on that day through the efforts of Hadrat Umar, the truth of Islam had become manifest.

MIGRATION FROM MECCA

In A.D. 622, the Holy Prophet decided that the Muslim should migrate from Mecca to Madina. The Muslims were required to proceed to Madina in batches.

Abu Salmah Abdullah bin Ashhal was the first Muslim to migrate from Mecca to Madina. He was followed by Bilal and Ammar Yasir. Thereafter Hadrat Umar migrated from Mecca.

While most of the other Muslims left Mecca in secret, Hadrat Umar publicly declared that he was proceeding to Madina. He even challenged the Quraish that if any one of them had the courage to stop him from going to Madina, he was welcome to try his strength with him. No Quraish of Mecca could have the courage to prevent the migration of Hadrat Umar, and no one accepted the challenge to measure strength with him.

According to Ibn Asakir, Hadrat Ali commented on the migration of Hadrat Umar in the following terms:

> I never knew any one migrate unless secretly except Umar, for he, when he resolved on migration, girt on his sword and slung over his bow and grasped in his hand its arrows, and went to the Ka'bah where in its quadrangle were the chiefs of the Quraish, and he went round about it seven times, then prayed two *raka'ts* at the station of Abraham, and went to each, one by one, in their circle and said, "May the face be foul of such as desire that his mother be bereaved of him and his child be left an orphan and his wife a widow, and if there be such a one, let him meet me behind this valley", but no one followed him.

In *Sahih Bukhari* it is stated that some twenty Muslims accompanied Hadrat Umar on the occasion of his migration from Mecca. His companions included Zaid bin Khattab the brother of Hadrat Umar ; Said bin Zaid, the nephew of Hadrat Umar and Khunais bin Hudhaifah the son-in-law of Hadrat Umar (the husband of Hadrat Hafsa). Other persons who accompanied Hadrat Umar included: Amr b. Suraqah; Abdullah b. Suraqah; Waqid b. Abdullah Tamimi; Khaula b. Abi Khaula; Malik b. Abi Khaula; Ayas b. Bukair; Aqil b. Bukair; Amir b. Bukair and Khalid b. Bukair.

Ayyash b. Abu Rabiah al-Makhzumi and Hisham b. Al-Aas b. Wail al-Sahmi also decided to migrate with Hadrat Umar. They made an appointment to meet at the thorn tree of Adat of Banu Ghifar about ten miles from Mecca. It was decided that if any one of them failed to turn up at the appointed place by sunrise on the day of departure fixed before hand it would be construed that he was not coming and had been held back by force.

Hadrat Umar with his companions and Ayyash arrived at the appointed meeting place according to schedule. Hisham did not turn up and was held back by the Quraish.

The party arrived at Quba on the outskirts of Madina and there they stayed with Banu Amr bin Auf.

One day Abu Jahl and al-Harith rode to Quba and contacted Ayyash who was their cousin. They told Ayyash that his mother had vowed that she would not comb her hair, nor take shelter from the sun until she saw Ayyash.

Hadrat Umar told Ayyash that this was nothing but an attempt to seduce him from his religion. Hadrat Umar added that if the lice disturbed his mother she would of her own accord comb her hair, and if the heat of Mecca oppressed her, she would herself take shelter.

But Ayyash felt inclined to go. He said:

"I may go for a short while. I will clear my mother of her vow. I have also some money to recover from the people in Mecca which I would like to get."

Hadrat Umar said:

"I am one of the richest of the Quraish and if you do not go with them, you may have one half of my money."

Ayyash, however, persisted in his wish to go to Mecca once.

Thereupon Hadrat Umar said:

"If you must go, then take this camel of mine. She is well bred and easy to ride. Don't dismount, and if at any stage you suspect them of treachery, you may well escape on this camel. Then Ayyash left for Mecca on the camel of Hadrat Umar. After they had proceeded some distance, Jahl said to Ayyash:

"I find my beast hard to ride. Will you not mount me behind you ?"

Ayyash agreed, and when they made their camels kneel to make the change over, Abu Jahl and al-Harith fell on Ayyash and bound him securely. They brought him to Mecca bound and said:

"O men of Mecca deal with your fools as we have dealt with this fool of ours".

When the Holy Prophet came to know how Hisham had been held back and how Ayyash had been abducted, he said:

"Who will bring me Ayyash and Hisham ?"

Al-Walid b. al-Mughira volunteered to undertake the mission. Al-Walid rode to Mecca and there he came to know that Hisham and Ayyash were kept in custody in a house which had no roof. One night al-Walid climbed the wall and contacted the prisoners who were in fetters. Al-Walid cut the fetters with the strokes of his sword. Then al-Walid led Ayyash and Hisham to Madina.

EARLY DAYS IN MADINA

Having arrived in the neighbourhood of Madina, Hadrat Umar and his party chose to stay at Quba, a suburb of Madina. Hadrat Umar had about twenty persons with him including his brother Zaid, Khunais bin Hudhaifah his son-in-law; Waqid bin Abdullah al-Tamimi, and Ayyash. At Quba Hadrat Umar and his party were the guests of Rifa'a bin Abdul Mundhir of Banu Amr. Hadrat Umar and his party were accommodated in a few independent houses where they were lodged comfortably. There was already a mosque at Quba and here Hadrat Umar prayed at the appointed hours.

At Quba all the Muslims waited eagerly for the Holy Prophet to come. Parties of men would go out for some distance on the route to Mecca and there wait for the Prophet to come. Several days passed away and the Holy Prophet did not come. Hadrat Umar felt uneasy and he thought of going to Mecca to ascertain why the Holy Prophet was late in coming.

Then one noon the Holy Prophet accompanied by Hadrat Abu Bakr arrived at Quba. As they arrived the people crowded round them. As the people had not seen the Holy Prophet before, it was difficult for them to know as to who out of the two was the Holy Prophet. Seeing this predicament of the people, Hadrat Abu Bakr stood up and shielded the Holy Prophet with his mantle. Hadrat Umar arrived at the spot and rushed to meet the Holy Prophet. The Holy Prophet embraced Hadrat Umar and the chiefs of Quba who had come to welcome him.

The Holy Prophet stayed at Quba for a few days and led the prayers in the mosque. Then the Holy Prophet proceeded to Madina. Hadrat Umar followed in the train of the Holy Prophet. At Madina the Holy Prophet and the emigrants from

Mecca were given a royal reception. The maidens of Madina mounted the roof tops of their houses and sang:

The full-moon has arisen on us
From the Thaniyat il- Wada'.
Thanksgiving is incumbent on us
So long as an invoker may invoke God.
O thou Divinely sent among us,
Thou hast brought a commandment that shall be obeyed!

The world of Madina was quite different from the world of Mecca. At Mecca the Muslims were a persecuted people; at Madina they were the masters of their destiny. The life at Madina was a complete break with the past. The days of trials, tribulations and torture were over; they were now set on the path of fulfilment. They were now to build a new commonwealth and a new ideal society.

At Madina, the Holy Prophet had a mosque built. The Holy Prophet Himself participated in the construction of the mosque. Hadrat Umar used to go every day from Quba to Madina to participate in the construction of the mosque. As the Muslims laboured they chanted:

"There is no life but the life of the next world,
O God have mercy on the Mohajreen and the Ansar."

To rehabilitate the emigrants from Mecca in the society of Madina the Holy Prophet established a fraternity among the Muslims of Mecca and those of Madina whereunder each migrant was paired with an Ansar of the corresponding status. The brotherhood thus established was unique in the annals of mankind. So strong and cordial were these bonds that these even surpassed the relationship of blood. In this roll of brotherhood, Hadrat Umar was paired with Itban bin Malik of Banu Al-Khazra.

The climate of Mecca was dry, but the climate of Madina was damp. The change adversely affected the health of the emigrants. On arrival at Madina most of the emigrants fell sick. Hadrat Umar was blessed with a robust constitution, and he was one of the few emigrants who did not suffer due to the change in climate.

In Mecca Hadrat Umar was a trader. He had brought ample amount with him from Mecca. In Madina he started business afresh. He had his store at Quba and from there goods were supplied to the market at Madina. No details about the business of Hadrat Umar are available. Hadrat Umar was a shrewd businessman, and we have reasons to hold that his business flourished at Madina as it did at Mecca. After attending to business, Hadrat Umar spent his spare time in the company of the Holy Prophet. The Holy Prophet consulted Hadrat Abu Bakr and Hadrat Umar on all important matters. When Hadrat Abu Bakr and Hadrat Umar held different views on a matter, the Holy Prophet took both the views into consideration before taking his decision. When Hadrat Abu Bakr and Hadrat Umar agreed on a point that view was invariably accepted by the Holy Prophet.

> We have it on the authority of Abdur Rahman-bin-Ghanam that the Holy Prophet said to Hadrat Abu Bakr and Hadrat Umar that "if you two are agreed upon a counsel, I would not oppose you". (Suyuti 'History of the Caliphs').

BATTLE OF BADR

The first battle between the Muslims and the Quraish of Mecca took place at Badr sixty miles from Madina on the trade route to Syria. A divine revelation had prepared the Muslims for *Jihad*. The revelation was:

> "Fight in the way of God, with those who fight against you; but transgress not, for God loveth not the transgressors."

It was a cold day in January 624 A.D. when the Holy Prophet and his army reached the valley of Badr. Intelligence was brought that the Quraish army was encamped beyond a sandhill at the other end of the narrow plain.

The Muslims hastened to take possession of the only stream of water in the valley. The Muslims prayed to God for help. The Holy Prophet prayed, "O Lord, forget not Thy promise of assistance, for if this little band were to perish; there will be none to offer Thee worship."

The Muslim army consisted of 313 men. They had only two horses and 70 camels. The Quraish army consisted of a thousand persons, and they had a cavalry of 200 horsemen and 700 camels. The Muslims were poorly equipped, but the Quraish were well armed.

The battle began early in the morning. The heralds of the Quraish stepped forward and poured insults and abuses on the Muslims. The Muslims replied with the shouts of "Allah-o-Akbar."

Then three of the Quraish leaders Utba, Shaiba, and Walid stepped forward and challenged the Muslims to single combat. The challenge was accepted by Ali, Ubaidah and

Hamza on behalf of the Muslims. In the duels that followed Ali killed Walid; Ubaidah killed Shaiba; and Hamza killed Utba. The Quraish army was stunned at the death of its three chosen leaders.

Then the general battle began. The ground on which the Muslims stood was hard and firm, being the sloping ground of a hill, while the Quraish were encamped on a sandy soil. Rain had fallen during the previous night. It had softened the ground where the Quraish stood and hardened the ground under the Muslims. The Quraish found the soil difficult to tread upon, and this was a great handicap for them. The Quraish were cut off from all water, as the only stream and the source of water was in the occupation of the Muslims. When the battle began the sun stared in the face of the Quraish warriors, which greatly confused them. The Muslims fought with the sun at their back, and this was a great advantage for them.

When the battle was at its height, the Holy Prophet picked up a handful of pebbles and threw them in the direction of the enemy saying, "Confusion seize them !"

And then a dust storm arose. It blew into the faces of the Quraish warriors. At this stage the Holy Prophet ordered a general charge. The Muslims rushed forward borne on the crest of the dust storm. Soon the hard-pressed Quraish fled in disorderly rout. The battle ended in the victory for the Muslims. Seventy men of the Quraish lay dead on the battle field. Only fourteen Muslims were martyred. Seventy persons from among the Quraish were captured alive. The rest of the Quraish escaped and fled to Mecca. The booty that the Muslims were able to capture comprised 115 camels, 14 horses, and considerable equipment and armour.

Throughout this battle Hadrat Umar was the right hand of the Holy Prophet. Among the Quraish who took part in the battle all tribes of the Quraish were represented except the Banu Adi the tribe to which Hadrat Umar belonged. No person from the Banu Adi fought against the Muslims at the battle of Badr, and this was attributed to the great regard in which

Hadrat Umar was held by his clan. On the other hand many persons belonging to Banu Adi who had been converted to Islam fought on the side of the Muslims under the leadership of Hadrat Umar.

Among the Quraish who fought against the Muslims was Asi bin Hisham bin Mughira a respectable Quraish noble. He was a brother of the mother of Hadrat Umar and his maternal uncle. Hadrat Umar maintained that all ties of relationship had ceased to exist between the Muslims and the polytheists. He singled out his maternal uncle and killed him in the battle.

The first person to be martyred in the battle was Mahja, a slave of Umar. Hadrat Umar thus came to claim the honour that the first Muslim to be martryred in the cause of Islam was a slave who belonged to him.

The Muslims returned to Madina along with the Quraish captives. Out of the prisoners many were eminent Quraish nobles. These included Abbas an uncle of the Holy Prophet; Aqil a brother of Hadrat Ali ; Abul Aas and Walid bin al-Walid. The sight of these chieftains coming as humble prinsoners was very touching. On seeing them Hadrat Saudah a wife of the Holy Prophet observed, "You come as prisoners; why did you not die on the battle-field?"

The Holy Prophet consulted his companions as to how these captives should be treated. Hadrat Umar took the strong line and urged that unless these persons accepted Islam they should be killed. He suggested that each Muslim should kill his own kinsman among the prisoners ; that Hamzah should kill Abbas and Ali should sever the head of Aqil.

Hadrat Abu Bakr took the softer line. He suggested that they should be set free on ransom.

The Holy Prophet said that as God had given them victory, it was necessary for them to show mercy to the fallen enemy. He, therefore, agreed to set the captives free on ransom.

CAPTIVES OF BADR

About the fate of the captives of Badr, Hadrat Abu Bakr and Hadrat Umar held contrary views. Hadrat Abu Bakr took the lenient view, while Hadrat Umar took the sterner view.

After taking into consideration both the views, the Holy Prophet said:

> "Almighty God softens the hearts of some people—softer than milk. And He hardens the hearts of some people—harder than stone."

Turning to Hadrat Abu Bakr who had counselled a lenient view, the Holy Prophet said:

> "Abu Bakr you are like Abraham who said, 'He who follows me is one of us, and he who disobeys me, then O God, You are gracious enough to forgive'. And Abu Bakr you are also like Jesus who said, 'If you punish them they are Your servants, and if You forgive them, You are All Powerful, Mighty and Wise."

Turning to Hadrat Umar, the Holy Prophet said:

> "Umar, you are like Noah who said, 'O God, do not leave on the earth a single unbeliever.' And Umar you are also like Moses who said, 'O God destroy their properties and harden their hearts so that they are not converted till they have suffered punishment."

The Holy Prophet accepted the advice of Hadrat Abu Bakr and acted accordingly.

The following day, Hadrat Umar visited the Holy Prophet, and saw that both the Holy Prophet and Hadrat Abu Bakr were weeping.

Hadrat Umar addressing the Holy Prophet said:

"What is it that makes you weep. Tell me, so that if there is any matter to be grieved over, I may also weep with you."

The Holy Prophet said:

"Umar, there is nothing for you to be grieved over. On the other hand you should rejoice that God has upheld the view that you had taken about the captives of Badr, and admonished those who had taken a contrary view."

Hadrat Umar's curiosity was awakened and he wanted to know what exactly was the revelation. The Holy Prophet recited the verses that had been revealed :

"It is not fitting for an Apostle
That he should have prisoners of war,
Until he has thoroughly subdued the land.
Ye look on the temporal goods of this world,
But God looks to the Hereafter,
And God is Exalted, Mighty, and Wise." (8:67)

UMAYR BIN WAHB

Umayr bin Wahb was one of the leaders of the Quraish of Mecca who used to molest the Holy Prophet and his companions while at Mecca, and caused them considerable distress.

In the battle of Badr many of the relatives of Umayr were killed, and one of his sons Wahb was taken prisoner.

After the battle of Badr, while one day Abu Sufiyan and Umayr sat in the Ka'bah at Mecca and exchanged views about the battle of Badr, Abu Sufiyan referring to the Quraish discomfiture said, "By God, there is no good in life now that they are dead."

Umayr said, "You are right. Were it not for a debt outstanding against me which I cannot discharge, and a family I cannot afford to leave unprovided for, I would ride to Madina and kill the Prophet."

Abu Sufiyan said, "If you have such noble thoughts I undertake to discharge your debt. I also undertake to take care of your family, and all that I have shall be theirs."

The pact was struck, and Umayr undertook to ride to Madina and kill the Prophet. Umayr took his sword, sharpened it, smeared it with poison and rode to Madina.

One day while in the Prophet's mosque at Madina, Hadrat Umar was talking with some of his friends about the battle of Badr and mentioning how God had honoured them in giving them victory over the Quraish, he suddenly saw Umayr alight at the door of the mosque, girt with his sword.

Seeing him, Hadrat Umar said, "This dog, the enemy of God is Umary bin Wahb. By God he has come with some evil purposes."

Then Hadrat Umar went to the Holy Prophet and said "O Prophet of God! this enemy of God, Umayr bin Wahb, has come girt with his sword." The Holy Prophet asked Hadrat Umar to let Umayr come in.

Hadrat Umar came to Umayr, and seizing his bandoleer he gripped him round the neck with it. He called the Muslims who were in the mosque, and asked them to sit around the Holy Prophet and watch the rascal Umayr carefully for he was not to be trusted.

When the Holy Prophet saw Hadrat Umar grasping Umayr's bandoleer round his neck he told Hadrat Umar to leave Umayr and let him advance.

Umayr came up and according to the pagan way said, "Good morning."

The Holy Prophet said, "God has honoured us with a better form of greeting O Umayr. It is 'Salaam', the greeting of the inhabitants of the paradise."

After a while, the Holy Prophet asked Umayr what had brought him to Madina.

Umayr said, "I have come about the release of my son."

"Then why have you a sword round your neck," asked the Holy Prophet.

Umayr said, "God damn these swords. Have they done us any good ?"

"What has brought you ?" asked the Holy Prophet again.

Umayr said that he had come to secure the release of his son.

The Holy Prophet said, "Did you not make a pact with Abu Sufiyan? Did he not undertake the responsibility to discharge your debt and look after your family ? Did you not sharpen your sword and smear it with poison ?"

"That's enough" said Umayr, "All this was secret known to no one. God alone must have told you of that. You are verily the Prophet of God".

Thereupon Umayr declared the article of faith and was converted to Islam. His son was released, and he too was converted to Islam.

Thereafter Umayr returned to Mecca, and he called the Quraish to Islam for that was the true faith.

THE CALL TO PRAYER

When the Holy Prophet was settled in Madina, some basic reforms were introduced. These included the institution of prayer, the levy of alms tax, the ordaining of fasting, the prescription of punishments; and the specification of the lawful and the unlawful.

In the early days the practice was that the faithful gathered in the mosque for prayer at the appointed time of their own accord without being summoned. The Holy Prophet, however, felt that with the spread of Islam, and the growth in the number of the Muslims, some method for the summoning of the faithful to prayer would have to be adopted.

At first the Holy Prophet thought of using a trumpet to summon the Muslims to prayer as the Jews did. On second thoughts he felt that it would not be advisable to imitate the Jews. Then an idea occurred to him that a clapper should be beaten to summon the faithful to the mosque.

One night a companion Abdullah bin Zaid had a dream which indicated the way for the summoning of the Muslims to prayers. Abdullah came to the Holy Prophet and narrated his dream in the following terms:

> "In the dream I saw a holy man wearing green garments. He held a clapper in his hand. I asked him to sell the clapper to me. He asked what for I needed the clapper, and I told him that I needed it for summoning the Muslims to prayer. He said that the clapper would not serve the purpose. I then asked him as to what method should be adopted, and he said 'Let some one with a loud voice stand at a suitable place in the mosque, and give the call 'God is great. I bear witness that there is no god but Allah. Come to prayer."

The idea appealed to the Holy Prophet. When it was the time for prayer, the Holy Prophet summoned Bilal and asked him to give the call to prayer, in the terms of the formula indicated by Abdullah bin Zaid.

As the stentorian call resounded in the city of Madina, the faithful felt elated and electrified, and they rushed to the mosque in response to the summons. Hadrat Umar heard the call in his house, and he hastened to the mosque dragging his cloak on the ground. He waited on the Holy Prophet, and enquired as to how the idea of the call to prayer had occurred to him. The Holy Prophet thereupon narrated the dream of Abdullah bin Zaid, and added that, as the vision appeared to be inspired, he had accepted it, and had the call given accordingly. Hadrat Umar said that he too had a similar vision, but was happy that Abdullah bin Zaid had anticipated him. Hadrat Umar said that there was however one difference between the formula proposed by Abdullah and the one that he had heard in his dream. The Holy Prophet anxiously enquired as to what was the difference. Hadrat Umar said:

> "According to the formula of Abdullah bin Zaid we are only to witness that there is no god but Allah. In the call that I heard in my dream there were also the words 'I bear witness that Muhammad is the Messenger of God."

Thereupon the Holy Prophet instructed Bilal that in the call to prayer, the expression "I bear witness that Muhammad is the Messenger of God" should be included.

Turning to Abdullah bin Zaid, and Hadrat Umar the Holy Prophet said, "Praise be to God. There are men among my followers to whom truth is revealed in dreams."

WHEN HADRAT UMAR SLEW THE MAN WHO APPEALED TO HIM

When the Holy Prophet came to Madina, all the people except the Jews were converted to Islam. Most of them were sincere and earnest in their faith in Islam. Some of them in spite of their profession of Islam were hypocrites and indulged in activities hostile to Islam. There were some among them on whom Islam sat lightly and who did not fully realise the spirit of Islam or the status of the Holy Prophet.

It is recorded on the authority of Abul Aswad that two persons of Madina who professed Islam but did not realise its full significance had a dispute among themselves and took the matter to the Holy Prophet for decision. After hearing both the parties, the Holy Prophet gave his decision in favour of one person. The other person felt dissatisfied, and at his instance both of them went to Hadrat Umar and the aggrieved person lodged an appeal with Hadrat Umar against the decision of the Holy Prophet.

After hearing both the parties, Hadrat Umar said to the man who had filed the appeal: "So you are dissatisfied with the decision of the Holy Prophet, and want me to reverse his decision."

"Yes, that is so," said the man
"And are you a Muslim," enquired Hadrat Umar.
The man said, "Yes, I am."

Thereupon Hadrat Umar said, "Wait for a while. I will soon give my decision that would satisfy you."

Hadrat Umar went inside the house and brought his sword. With the sword Hadrat Umar smote the appellant saying, "Woe to you, you regard yourself a Muslim and yet choose to appeal to me against the decision of the Holy Prophet. You are an infidel, and the penalty for your infidelity is death."

The other man went to the Holy Prophet and complained that Hadrat Umar had killed his companion.

The Holy Prophet summoned Hadrat Umar and put him to explanation. Hadrat Umar said, "The man wanted me to hear an appeal against the decision of the Holy Prophet, and for this impudence he deserved the punishment of death."

The Holy Prophet deferred the decision on the case till God gave some light on the matter.

Soon God revealed that he who had no confidence in the Holy Prophet was no believer. As such Hadrat Umar was justified in killing the man who had by his action expressed want of faith in the Holy Prophet.

The Holy Prophet accordingly absolved Hadrat Umar of the charge of murdering a believer.

BATTLE OF UHUD

The battle of Uhud was an extension of the battle of Badr.

The Quraish of Mecca came with a force of 3000 men to avenge the defeat of Badr. The Muslims could muster a force of 1000 persons only, and out of these three hundred persons under Abdullah bin Ubbay a hypocrite withdrew at the last moment thus leaving only 700 persons to face the hostile Quraish.

The Holy Prophet arranged his force in battle array and posted a small contingent of archers to guard a vulnerable passage in the rear. The archers were instructed that they were not to leave their positions at any cost unless otherwise directed by the Holy Prophet.

With the Quraish was a contingent of women. They beat drums and sang songs to excite their men to action. They sang:

"We are the daughters of the morning star;
We tread on carpets;
If you advance we embrace you;
If you turn back we leave you."

The Quraish charged with full force, but the Muslims held fast. Then in the counter attack the Muslims broke the enemy's line, and the Quraish fell back. At this stage the contingent of the Muslim archers, contrary to instructions, left their position in order to plunder the camp of the retreating Quraish. Khalid who was still a non-Muslim, and was fighting on the side of the Quraish rushed with his contingent and occupied the position vacated by the Muslim archers. The Quraish rallied, and launched an attack on the Muslims both from the front as well as the rear. In the confusion that followed, many Muslims were martyred. Even the Holy Prophet was wounded seriously, and he fell in a pit where many of his followers lay dead. Thereupon a cry rose from the ranks of the enemy that they had killed the Prophet of Islam.

When the news of the Holy Prophet's death got wind, panic seized some of the Muslims, and thinking that all was over, they fled to Madina. According to tradition when Hadrat Umar heard the news that the Holy Prophet had died, he flung his arms declaring that it was no use fighting any longer.

It is related that Anas b. Nadar passing by Hadrat Umar asked him how it had fared with the Prophet. Hadrat Umar replied that he had heard that the Prophet had been killed. Anas observed that the Prophet's death should not prevent him from fighting in the way of Allah, for Allah was alive. Saying this Anas rushed at the infidels, and was martyred after having received seventy wounds.

Later, the Holy Prophet was found lying in a pit. At this stage Ali, Abu Bakr, Umar, Talha, Zubair, and Harith gathered round the Prophet, and removed him to a place of safety.

Abu Sufiyan the leader of the Quraish climbed a hillock and shouted, "Is Muhammad there ?" The Holy Prophet asked his companions to remain quiet.

Abu Sufiyan then called for Abu Bakr and Umar. No reply was made, and thereupon Abu Sufiyan shouted, "All of them have been killed."

At this Hadrat Umar could not restrain Himself, and shouted in reply, "O enemy of Allah, all of us are alive."

Abu Sufiyan in a mood of exultation cried, "O Hubbal glory to thee."

Hadrat Umar retorted, "Only Allah is Most High and Great."

Abu Sufiyan said, "We have Uzza with us, and you have no lord."

Hadrat Umar retaliated, "Allah is our Lord, and you have no lord."

When the two armies withdrew from the battle-field, seventy Muslims lay dead on the battle-field. In the battle the Quraish had the upper hand. They felt satisfied that they had avenged their defeat at Badr. The Quraish were in no mood to press their advantage to march to Madina. They chose to return to Mecca.

THE MAN WHOM HADRAT UMAR ENVIED

Wahab bin Qabus was a shepherd who lived in a village near Madina. One day he came to Madina to see the Holy Prophet. He was accompanied by his nephew, and his herd of goats.

In Madina, Wahab came to know that the Holy Prophet had left for Uhud where he was fighting against the Quraish. He left his nephew and his goats at Madina, and Himself proceeded to Uhud.

When he reached Uhud, the battle was at its thickest. A group of the Quraish was at the time advancing to attack the Holy Prophet. It was a critical situation, and turning to his companions the Holy Prophet said:

> "He who disperses these people will be my companion in the Paradise."

Hearing the call, Wahab rushed at the advancing Quraish. Some were killed and the rest were put to flight. The Holy Prophet watched Wahab overpower the Quraish group single handed. When Wahab after the flight of the Quraish came to the Holy Prophet, he was given the tidings of Paradise. Wahab was intoxicated with pleasure at these tidings.

As soon as he heard these tidings, Wahab took his sword, and rushed to the enemy line. He dashed against the enemy as a hill torrent would dash against the rock making its way. Killing right and left he penetrated deep into the enemy line. He was surrounded by the enemy on all sides. He received many wounds but he went on playing havoc in the ranks of the enemy. The blood flowed profusely from his wounds, and then he fell dead on the battle-field.

When the battle was over, and the Muslims collected the dead bodies of all the martyrs, the Holy Prophet stood by his dead body and said:

> "O Wahab, you have pleased me. May Allah be pleased with you."

Although the Holy Prophet was Himself wounded, he led the funeral prayer of Wahab, and put him in the grave with his own hands. Hadrat Umar who was present said that in the battle of Uhud none surpassed Wahab in bravery.

Thereafter Hadrat Umar used to say often:

> "I never envied anybody more than Wahab. I wish I could appear before Allah with a record as good as his."

HADRAT HAFSA

Hadrat Hafsa was the daughter of Hadrat Umar. Her mother was Zainab, a sister of Usman bin Mazun an eminent Companion. Hadrat Abdullah was a real brother of Hadrat Hafsa.

In Mecca, Hadrat Hafsa was married to Khunais bin Hudhaifah of the Banu Sahm clan of the Quraish. Khunais was one of the early converts to Islam. He participated in two migrations, migration to Abyssinia and the migration to Madina, and was blessed by the Holy Prophet.

In Madina, Khunays participated in the battle of Badr. He also fought in the battle of Uhud. He was wounded in the battle of Uhud. These wounds proved fatal, and he died shortly after the battle of Uhud. Hadrat Hafsa thus became a widow at a very young age.

Hadrat Umar felt much distressed at the grief of his daughter. After the period of *'Iddat* was over, Hadrat Umar thought of re-marrying her. Like her father, Hadrat Hafsa was hot of temper. Hadrat Umar felt that it would be advisable if she was married to an elderly man of a sober temperament.

Hadrat Umar's choice fell on Hadrat Abu Bakr. Hadrat Umar went to Hadrat Abu Bakr, and offered him the hand of Hadrat Hafsa. Hadrat Umar had hoped that Hadrat Abu Bakr would enthusiastically welcome the proposal. Hadrat Umar was, however, disappointed, for Hadrat Abu Bakr remained quiet and evaded the issue. Hadrat Umar felt distressed that his friend Hadrat Abu Bakr had not grasped the hand of friendship that he had extended to him.

Hadrat Umar next went to see Hadrat Usman. Hadrat Usman had been married to Ruqayya, a daughter of the Holy

Prophet. Ruqayya had died. Hadrat Umar offered him the hand of Hafsa. Hadrat Usman asked for some time to consider the matter. When Hadrat Umar saw Hadrat Usman a few days later, Hadrat Usman said that his grief over the death of Ruqayya was so overwhelming that he did not contemplate another marriage.

Hadrat Umar felt very angry at the rejection of his proposal by Hadrat Abu Bakr and Hadrat Usman. Brimming with rage, Hadrat Umar went to see the Holy Prophet. The Holy Prophet greeted him with a smile and asked tenderly what was worrying him ? Hadrat Umar poured out the grief of his heart, and complained against Hadrat Abu Bakr and Hadrat Usman who had turned down the hand of friendship that he had extended to them.

The Holy Prophet addressed Hadrat Umar with great affection and said, "Umar, I know of your worries and I also know of your services to Islam. Rest assured, Hafsa will marry a man better than Usman, and Usman will marry a lady better than Hafsa."

This meant that the Holy Prophet Himself wanted to wed Hafsa. Hadrat Umar was overwhelmed with joy at this great honour beyond his aspirations. Hadrat Umar reverently kissed the hand of the Holy Prophet in token of his gratitude. He hurried home, and told Hafsa of the happy news.

Then he went to Hadrat Abu Bakr. From the face of Hadrat Umar radiating happiness, Hadrat Abu Bakr judged of the developments. Addressing Hadrat Umar he offered apologies and said, "The Holy Prophet had spoken to me about Hafsa, and as such I could not accept your proposal. But for that it would have been a great honour and pleasure for me to agree to your proposal."

Hadrat Umar then went to Hadrat Usman. Hadrat Usman offered apologies and said, "The Holy Prophet had talked to me over the matter. He had offered me the hand of his younger daughter Umm Kulsum, and he had expressed the desire to marry Hafsa Himself. Under these circumstances I could not accept your proposal."

In A.D. 625 Hadrat Hafsa was married to the Holy Prophet. That elevated the status of Hadrat Umar and brought him at par with Hadrat Abu Bakr, as both of them enjoyed the unique privilege of being the fathers-in-law of the Holy Prophet.

THE JEWS

In Madina there was a considerable number of Jews. They were wealthy and commanded influence. The Holy Prophet followed the policy of 'live and let live'. He accordingly entered into a treaty with the Jews. According to the terms of the treaty the Jews were to enjoy religious freedom and there was to be no interference in the religious affairs of the Jews by the Muslims. The Muslims and the Jews were to be on friendly terms and were to help each other in the promotion of objects of mutual interest. It was stipulated that the Muslims and the Jews would help each other in case of an attack by an enemy. No party was to give protection to the Quraish, and in case the Quraish invaded Madina both the Muslims and the Jews were to join in the defence of the city.

The Jews knew that in their holy books there were references to the advent of a prophet in Arabia. They were under the impression that the prophet would rise from their midst. When the Holy Prophet appeared from the ranks of the Quraish in Mecca, the Jews recognised in him all the signs of prophethood foretold in their sacred books. When the Holy Prophet came to Madina the Jews thought that he would be subservient to them. When the Holy Prophet followed an independent policy, the Jews embarked on a campaign of ridiculing Islam, and resorted to activities hostile to the Muslims.

Hadrat Umar knew Hebrew, and he could talk with the Jews in their own language. Hadrat Umar was a trader, and he had business contacts with the Jews. Out of the Muslims, Hadrat Umar was popular with the Jews. One day the Jews gave him a copy of the Torah. Hadrat Umar brought the copy to the Holy Prophet and said, "Messenger of God, this is a copy of the Torah". Other companions including Hadrat Abu Bakr were sitting with the Holy Prophet. The Holy Prophet paid no attention to what Umar had said. When Hadrat Umar received no reply he began to read some passages from the Torah to the obvious displeasure of the Holy Prophet. Turning to Hadrat Umar, Hadrat Abu Bakr said, "Confound you, do you not see how God's Messenger is looking ?" Hadrat Umar looked at the Holy Prophet and said "I seek refuge in God from the anger of God and His Messenger. We are satisfied with God as Lord, with Islam as religion, and with Muhammad as prophet". Then the Holy Prophet said, "By Him in Whose hands Muhammad's life is, were Moses to appear to you, and you were to follow him and abandon me, you would err from the right path. Were he alive and come in touch with my prophetic mission, he would follow me." And then referring to the Jews the Holy Prophet said, "The Jews betrayed their own prophet; how can they be your friend?"

Hadrat Umar asked some of his Jew friends whether there were any references to the Prophet Muhammad (peace be on him) in their scriptures. They answered the question in the affirmative. "Then why don't you accept him" asked Hadrat Umar, and they said, "God sends him messages through Gabriel and Gabriel is our enemy." Hadrat Umar told of this talk to the Holy Prophet. A few days later, God revealed to the Holy Prophet:

> "O Apostle tell them,
> Whosoever is the enemy of Gabriel,
> Let him be so at his peril.
> Verily God is the enemy of infidels." 2:97—98

After this revelation, Hadrat Umar broke up all contacts with the Jews.

When one of the Jewish tribes in Madina, Bani Qainuqa violated the terms of the treaty with the Muslims, the Holy Prophet consulted his companions as to the action to be taken against the Jews. Some of the companions were in favour of conciliation, but Hadrat Umar counselled that they should be expelled from Madina. They were accordingly expelled from Madina.

The Jews of the Banu Nadir clan affected to be submissive, and they were allowed to remain in Madina. Some time in A.D., 626 the Holy Prophet along with Hadrat Abu Bakr and Hadrat Umar went to the Banu Nadir Jews to claim blood money for a man murdered by a Jew. The Jews affected great humility, spoke words of flattery, and assured the Holy Prophet that they would comply with any order that he issued. As such they assured that the blood money demanded would be paid. Secretly the Jews deputed a man to climb on the roof of the house where they were sitting and from there hurl a stone on the head of the Holy Prophet, as if it was an accident. It was revealed to the Holy Prophet that the Jews meant mischief.

The Holy Prophet accordingly rose from the place where he was sitting and returned home. His companions followed suit. The next day the Holy Prophet deputed Hadrat Umar to tell the Jews that they should evacuate Madina. They hesitated. There followed a skirmish in which the Jews were overpowered. They were accordingly departed from Madina. Some of them went to Khyber and some went to Syria.

BATTLE OF THE TRENCH

In A.D. 627 the Muslims had to face the combined opposition of the Quraish, the Jews, and some other tribes. The Quraish and their allies mustered a force ten thousand strong and marched to Madina.

The Holy Prophet was advised that a face to face fight against such a large force was not possible for the Muslims, and the safest course for them was to remain on the defensive. It was accordingly decided that a deep and wide trench should be dug round Madina for protective purposes.

The entire Muslim community in Madina was turned to dig the trench. When the Muslims dug the trench the following war song was on their lips:

> "By God, had not Allah guided us, we would not have seen the right path, nor given *Sadaqah*, nor offered the prayers;
> May Allah bestow on us confidence and calmness of mind, and make our steps firm to face the enemy.
> The enemy has risen against us, and he intends insurrection, but we refuse to submit.
> O God there is no welfare except that of the next world;
> Shower Thy Grace on the Ansars and the Muhajirs".

The site for the trench was demarcated by the Holy Prophet. He allotted ten yards of trench to be dug by each party of ten persons. One of such parties was led by Hadrat Umar. Later a mosque known as Umar Masjid was constructed near the site where Hadrat Umar and his party had dug the trench.

When the Quraish and their allies arrived they found that a wide and deep trench which could not be crossed lay between them and the Muslims. This was a mode of warfare with which the Quraish were not familiar. They camped beyond the trench and decided to besiege the Muslims.

The Holy Prophet divided the trench into a number of sectors and a contingent was posted to guard each sector. One of such contingents was under the command of Hadrat Umar. One day the Quraish assaulted the sector commanded by Hadrat Umar, and tried to carry the entrenchment by storm. Hadrat Umar reinforced by Hadrat Zubair beat back the enemy with a heavy hand and many Quraish were killed.

On another occasion Hadrat Umar's contest with the Quraish was so prolonged that the time for the afternoon prayers passed away. After making the enemy beat a retreat, Hadrat Umar came to the Holy Prophet, and told him how the enemy had kept him so hotly engaged that he had missed his afternoon prayers. The Holy Prophet said that he Himself had not offered his afternoon prayers by that time. Then the Holy Prophet led the prayers and Hadrat Umar and other companions offered their prayers.

The siege prolonged for a month, and the Muslims were subjected to great hardships. Food ran short, and subsistence became a problem. The Muslims nevertheless persevered and hoped that God would come to their relief.

And God did come to the relief of the Muslims. There were dissensions in the camp of the enemy. Provisions with lifted ran short. Above all a strong storm lashed the countryside. The Muslims were safe in their houses in Madina, but the Quraish who had to bear the brunt of the storm in the open were unnerved. Abu Sufiyan ordered that the seige should be lifted, and the Quraish should withdraw to Mecca. Their allies also left.

The Muslims had the upper hand on account of their unusual perseverance against heavy odds and the inspired leadership of the Holy Prophet.

TREATY OF HUDAIBIYA

Early in A.D. 628 the Holy Prophet decided to proceed to Mecca to perform the pilgrimage. He was accompained by companions about fourteen hundred in number. Hadrat Umar also accompanied the Holy Prophet. In order to convince the Quraish that the Muslims had no war-like intentions against them, the Holy Prophet decided that they would carry no arms.

When the Muslims halted at Zul Hulaifah six miles from Madina, Hadrat Umar waited on the Holy Prophet and submitted that no reliance could be placed on the Quraish and accordingly it was unsafe to proceed to Mecca without arms. Hadrat Umar urged that for self-defence the Muslims should be armed. The Holy Prophet accepted the advice of Hadrat Umar, and some persons were sent to Madina to bring in arms.

When the Quraish of Mecca came to know that the Muslims were coming to Mecca they sent Khalid bin Walid and Ikramah bin Abu Jahl with two hundred horsemen to intercept the Muslims, and prevent their advance to Mecca. Finding the way to Mecca barred the Holy Prophet consulted his companions as to what course of action they should adopt. The consensus of opinion was that they should go ahead. If they were stopped they would fight; otherwise not.

The Holy Prophet enquired of his companions whether any one out of them could lead the Muslims to Mecca by a path other than the main route barred by the enemy. One of the companions volunteered to show an alternative way. He led the Muslims on a way full of rough rocks through the ravines of Mudniya. After a weary march the Muslims reached Hudaibiya on the lower side of Mecca and within the sacred territory.

The Muslims encamped at Hudaibiya, and here Urwa bin Masud came to see the Holy Prophet on behalf of the Quraish. He talked in diplomatic language, and tried to impress that the Quraish were strong and would not allow the Muslims to visit Mecca. He also insinuated that at the time of crisis the followers of the Holy Prophet were likely to leave him. Thereupon the companions of the Holy Prophet said, "May God curse you; how dare you think that we will abandon the Holy Prophet. Rest assured we will fight to the last for him".

When Urwa returned to the Quraish, he gave his impressions about the Holy Prophet and the Muslims in the following terms:

> "O people of the Quraish ! I have seen kings but by God I have never seen a king as I have seen Muhammad amongst his companions. If he makes his ablutions they would not let the water fall on the ground; if a hair of his body falls they pick it up. They will not surrender him for anything in any case, do what you may."

As among the Quraish, the Adis specialised in diplomatic skill the Holy Prophet wanted Hadrat Umar to go to the Quraish to negotiate. Hadrat Umar submitted that he was a *persona non grata* with the Quraish, and his mission was not likely to be successful. He advised that Hadrat Usman who was soft spoken and was popular with the Quraish should be sent on the mission. The advice was accepted and Hadrat Usman was accordingly sent to the Quraish to negotiate regarding the Muslim's entry into Mecca and performing the pilgrimage.

When three days passed away, and Hadrat Usman did not return from Mecca a rumour got afloat that he had been killed by the Quraish. Hadrat Umar donned his arms and accoutrements and waited on the Holy Prophet. He submitted that if the Quraish had killed Hadrat Usman, the Muslims should fight the Meccans to the bitter end. The Holy Prophet asked all his Companions about 1,400 in number to assemble and take a vow binding themselves to *Jihad* against the infidels. The Holy Prophet sat under a tree, and all the Companions took the oath turn by turn. God approved of this measure, and the following verse was revealed to the Holy Prophet:

"Verily Allah was pleased with the faithful that they swore allegiance to thee under the tree."

In view of the pleasure of God, this oath later came to be called *'the Bait-ul-Rizwan'*—the oath that pleased God.

A little later Hadrat Usman returned from Mecca along with some emissaries from the Quraish. After some further negotiations the terms of a pact between the Muslims and the Quraish were hammered out. These terms were:

(1) There was to be a truce between the Muslims and the Quraish for a period of ten years.
(2) If any tribe wanted to enter into treaty with the Muslims it could do so, and whoever wished to enter a covenant with the Quraish was likewise free to do so.
(3) If any one from the Quraish came to the Muslims without the permission of his guardian, he was to be returned to the Quraish. On the other hand if a Muslim sought refuge with the Quraish, he was not to be delivered to the Muslims.
(4) The Muslims were to withdraw that year without performing the pilgrimage. They were free to perform the Hajj the following year when they could stay in Mecca for three days.

Prima facie these terms favoured the Quraish and Hadrat Umar felt very bitter about them. He waited on the Holy Prophet and submitted:

"O Prophet of God ! Are you not the Messenger of God?"
"Certainly I am", said the Holy Prophet.
"Are not our enemies idolatrous polytheists?" asked Hadrat Umar.
"Undoubtedly they are", rejoined the Holy Prophet.
"Why should then we disgrace our religion?" added Hadrat Umar.

The Holy Prophet said, "I am the Messenger of God, and I do not act in contravention of His commandments."

This silenced Hadrat Umar, but he felt these terms to be humiliating to the Muslims. He saw Hadrat Abu Bakr, and wanted him to persuade the Holy Prophet to revise the terms. Hadrat Abu Bakr said:

> "The Holy Prophet knows things better than we do. What the Holy Prophet has done is in the interests of the Muslims. Have faith in God. Do not be critical and hold fast to the stirrup of the Holy Prophet."

Thereafter the pact which came to be known as the Hudaibiya pact was duly signed between the Muslims and the Meccans. On behalf of the Muslims, the pact was among others signed by Hadrat Umar.

After the pact had been signed Suhail's son Abu Jandal who had accepted Islam and was a captive with the Meccans escaped from the captivity and came to seek refuge in the Muslim camp. Suhail followed his son and demanded that in accordance with the Hudaibiya pact his son should be returned to him. Hadrat Umar advocated that as Abu Jandal did not want to return, it was unfair to force him to return. The Holy Prophet said that they had entered into a pact with the Meccans and as Muslims they could not go back upon their word. He allowed Suhail to take away his son. Turning to Abu Jandal the Holy Prophet said, "Abu Jandal be patient. God in His bounty will Himself devise some way to facilitate your return to the Muslims". Hadrat Umar went some distance with Abu Jandal and Suhail. He kept goading Abu Jandal with his sword, and the idea was that he should take the sword and kill his father. Abu Jandal was too depressed and confused to follow the clue. When Suhail and his son rode off to Mecca, Hadrat Umar returned to the Muslim camp crest fallen.

The Muslims struck camp, and started on the return journey to Madina. Hadrat Umar felt unhappy. He was bitter that in this deal the Quraish had had the upper hand. In the way, Surah *Al-Fath* was revealed to the Holy Prophet.

"Verily, We have opened wide for thee the gates of victory." The Holy Prophet called for Hadrat Umar and told him that God had that day revealed to him that the Hudaibiya pact would lead to the victory of the Muslims. That made Hadrat Umar rejoice.

Hadrat Abu Bakr assessed the treaty of Hudaibiya in the following terms:

> "No victory of Islam has more importance than the treaty of Hudaibiya. Men are always for hurrying things on, but God lets them ripen. Previously there had subsisted a wall of partition between the Muslims and the rest of the men; they never spoke to each other, and wherever they met they began to fight. Subsequently hostility died down, and security and mutual confidence took its place. Every man of even moderate intelligence who heard of Islam joined it, and the twenty-two months in which the truce subsisted the number of conversions was greater than throughout the whole of the previous period, and the faith of Islam diffused itself in all directions among the people."

POST HUDAIBIYA-PACT DEVELOPMENTS

In the wake of the Hudaibiya pact there took place developments which affected Hadrat Umar personally.

At the time of Hudaibiya pact it was undertaken that if any person from the Quraish accepted Islam such a person was to be returned to the Quraish. Some men from among the Quraish accepted Islam and sought shelter with the Muslims. In accordance with the terms of the pact these persons were returned to the Quraish.

Later a crisis developed when some Quraish women accepted Islam against the wishes of their parents and husbands and sought refuge with the Muslims. The Quraish wanted such women to be returned to them. The Holy Prophet refused to return such women to the Quraish as in the meantime God had revealed:

> "Believers, when believing women came to you as refugees, examine them. Allah knows the state of their faith. If you find them to be true believers do not return them to the unbelievers. They are not lawful to the unbelievers, nor are the unbelievers lawful to them. You shall, however, give to their former husbands what they have spent on them. And you will be doing nothing unlawful after you have given them dowries." 60:10

Another verse on the same subject provided:

"Do not marry idolatresses until they embrace the faith. And do not marry your women to idolators."

Hadrat Umar had three wives, namely:

(1) Zainab bint Mazaun Jamiah;

(2) Malaika bint Jarul Khuzai; and
(3) Qariba bint Abi Umayya Makhzumi.

Out of these three, only Zainab bint Mazaun had accepted Islam and migrated to Madina. The other two ladies did not accept Islam and did not choose to migrate. After the Hudaibiya pact, Hadrat Umar divorced Malaika as well as Qariba. After being divorced by Hadrat Umar, Malaika married Abu Jahm bin Hudhaifah while Qariba married Abdur Rahman son of Hadrat Abu Bakr who was still an infidel.

After the Hudabiya pact the first Muslim woman who fled from the Quraish and sought refuge with the Muslims was Sabiha bint al-Harith. Her husband did not accept Islam. When the Quraish came to demand the restoration of Sabiha, the Holy Prophet refused to return her to the Quraish saying that the condition in the pact applied to men only and not to women. The Holy Prophet had Sabiha married to Hadrat Umar.

In Madina, Hadrat Umar married an Ansar lady Asiah bint Sabat Ansari. On marriage Hadrat Umar changed her name to Jamila. Hadrat Umar resided with her at Quba. It is reported that for some years she was Hadrat Umar's favourite wife. A few years later, Hadrat Umar divorced her and shifted to Madina. The reason why Hadrat Umar divorced her is not known.

RAID ON AL-MUSTALIQ

Some time in A.D. 628, news was brought to the Holy Prophet that the Banu Al-Mustaliq were gathering together against the Muslims. The Holy Prophet decided that before the enemy could gather strength the Muslims should fall upon and break their power.

The Holy Prophet led the campaign personally. The Muslim force that accompanied the Holy Prophet included Hadrat Umar. It also included Abdullah bin Ubayy, an Ansar chief whose loyalties to Islam and the Holy Prophet were doubtful.

A confrontation with the Banu al-Mustaliq took place at Muraysi on the road to the sea. The Banu-Mustaliq were defeated with heavy losses, and the Muslims captured considerable booty including many captives both men and women.

After the Banu al-Mustaliq were overpowered and put to flight, the Muslim force halted at a watering place. Here Jahja bin Masud a servant of Hadrat Umar led his horse to the watering place. There a quarrel arose between him and Sinan b. Wabar al-Juhani, an Ansari. In the quarrel Sinan called the men of the Ansar to his aid, while Jahja invoked the assistance of the Muhajreen.

The incident was exploited by Abdullah b. Ubayy, and he spoke unbecoming words against the Muhajreen. He said:

> "The Muhajreen dispute our priority. They want to overpower us in our own city. Nothing fits us and the vagabonds of Quraish as the ancient saying 'Feed a dog and it will devour you'."

Zaid b. Arqam an Ansar boy who heard Abdullah bin Ubayy indulge in such talk reported to the Holy Prophet what he had said. Hadrat Umar who was sitting with the Holy Prophet asked for the Holy Prophet's permission to kill Abdullah bin Ubayy. The Holy Prophet said:

> "Umar be calm and patient. If I permit you to kill Abdullah, will not the people say that Muhammad kills his own followers?"

The Holy Prophet immediately ordered a march to Madina. It was noon, an unusual time to travel, but all concerned complied with the order thinking that something unusual had happened and the Prophet of Allah knew what was best.

Abdullah bin Ubayy saw the Holy Prophet, and denied having said what had been reported against him. There were others even among the Ansars who held that Abdullah bin Ubayy had said what he should not have said. The Holy Prophet, however, chose to be silent.

When the party reached Madina, the unfortunate episode became the talk of the town. According to the consensus of opinion, Abdullah b. Ubayy was to blamed. When the son of Abdullah b. Ubayy came to know of what his father had said, he waited on the Holy Prophet and said:

> "I have heard that you want to kill my father for what you have heard about him. If you intend to kill him, then order me to do so, and I will bring you his head. I am afraid that if you order some one else to kill him, my soul will not permit me to see his murderer walking among men, and I shall kill him thus killing a believer for an unbeliever and so I would go to hell."

The Holy Prophet said, "Thank God there are persons among the Muslims who would be prepared to kill their fathers for the sake of Islam."

Turning to the son of Abdullah b. Ubayy the Holy Prophet said:

> "Thank you for your offer. I do not contemplate any such action against your father."

The son of Abdullah praised the Holy Prophet for his magnanimity. After he had left, the Holy Prophet turned to Hadrat Umar and said:

> "Now Umar what do you think. Had I allowed you to kill him on the day you wanted me to permit you, his people would have risen in his support. Today you see, his own son is prepared to kill him."

Thereupon Hadrat Umar replied:

> "Verily I know not what you know. Your vision is certainly penetrating and blessed."

HADRAT AYESHA AND HADRAT UMAR

The raid on al-Mustaliq led to another unfortunate episode which was a cause of great concern to the Holy Prophet and his companions for some time. Each time the Holy Prophet went on a campaign, one of his wives accompanied him, and the decision was always taken by the drawing of lots. On the occasion of the raid of Mustaliq, Hadrat Ayesha accompanied the Holy Prophet. On return from the campaign she travelled on the back of a camel in a closed litter. On account of the regrettable behaviour of Abdullah bin Ubayy, there was considerable tension in the atmosphere. As the caravan travelled at an unusual time, there was considerable upsetting of the programme. The party halted for the night at some distance from Madina. At early dawn the call to move was given. Hadrat Ayesha went to the desert to answer the call of nature, and on return occupied her litter. There she noticed that the necklace of Yemenite agates which she wore was no longer around her neck. Hurriedly she left the litter, and went to the desert where she found the necklace. When she returned to the camp the spot was deserted, and the caravan had left. The men in charge of her camel, seeing the litter closed, and thinking it occupied, had placed it on the camel and departed with it. Hadrat Ayesha called aloud, but no one responded to her call. She decided to sit down, hoping that some body would come to fetch her. Soon she fell asleep, wrapped in her cloak.

"We belong to God and to Him we return." These words fell on the ears of Hadrat Ayesha, and she awoke with a start. A young man stood before her holding a camel by its reins. Safwan bin Al-Muthal following the army in the rear had notice a young woman asleep in the desert, and upon approaching her, recognised her as the wife of the Holy Prophet (peace be on him). Hadrat Ayesha quickly covered herself with her veil. Safwan adjusted the camel's saddle-girth and made the beast kneel. Hadrat Ayesha thereupon mounted the camel. Holding the camel by the bridle, Safwan resumed the road. After a tiring journey they reached Madina at noon, a few hours after the arrival of the Holy Prophet. That provided an opportunity to Abdullah bin Ubbay and some other hypocrites to whip up a campaign of slander against Hadrat Ayesha. The Holy Prophet consulted his friends about divorcing Hadrat Ayesha. Hadrat Ali advised that Hadrat Ayesha should be divorced. When Hadrat Umar was consulted he said, "O Prophet of God, I know for certain that the hypocrites are speaking malicious lie." The Holy Prophet asked Hadrat Umar as to the grounds with him for holding that the hypocrites were speaking lies, Hadrat Umar said:

> "By reason of God not allowing a fly to settle upon thy blessed skirts, because it alights also on impure things and soils its feet. How then would He not preserve thee and thy name from a worse defilement ?"

Hadrat Umar further said that he was sure that God Himself would cause the innocence of the young lady to become manifest." He further said:

> "If God does not allow thy shadow to fall upon the ground, lest it might be polluted, or a person step thereon, will He not restrain thy honoured spouse from committing impropriety?"

Later, as anticipated by Hadrat Umar, the Holy Prophet had a revelation in which God Himself bore witness to the purity and innocence of Hadrat Ayesha. When the ordeal was over, the Holy Prophet thanked Hadrat Umar for his support during the crisis. Hadrat Ayesha paid for this kindness many years later when she allowed Hadrat Umar to be buried in her chamber by the side of the Holy Prophet and Hadrat Abu Bakr.

PURDAH FOR WOMEN

In Madina the Muslim women did not observe any purdah. They freely moved among men. The majority of men in Madina were men of great faith, and they were very careful in their conduct to women. There were some hypocrites among Muslims from whom any mischief could be expected. There were also some Jews from whom no good could be expected. Hadrat Umar felt that if God forbidding any hypocrite played any mischief with regard to the women of Muslims that would be very damaging.

Hadrat Umar expressed these views to the Holy Prophet, and suggested that women should be required to stay at home. Hadrat Umar said that the wives of the Holy Prophet should particularly stay at home, for their prestige and honour were a matter of great concern for the Muslim community.

On hearing this advice of Hadrat Umar, Hadrat Zainab a wife of the Holy Prophet said:

> "Umar you have started in interfering in the domestic affairs of the Prophet as well. The revelation comes to our house, and you come up with suggestions of your own."

The Holy Prophet, however, appreciated what Umar had said. He said that he was awaiting revelation, and action would be taken in accordance with the injunctions of God.

And then came a detailed revelation on the subject. The revelation was:

> "Prophet say to your wives: 'If you desire the present life and its beautiful things, come and I will give you your dowries and send you away in a handsome manner. And if you desire Allah and His Prophet and the next world,

remember that Allah has in store a great reward for those of you who are righteous." 33:28

Another verse provided:

"O wives of the Prophet ! Whoever of you commits flagrant indecency will have your punishment twice over. Indeed it is easy for Allah to double your punishment. As for those who are obedient to Allah and His Apostle and act righteously We shall give them their reward twice over. We have rare gifts in store for them." 33: 30

And yet another verse said:

"O wives of the Prophet, you are like no other women. If you fear Allah do not be soft spoken, for it will tempt the man who has a disease in his heart. Speak in a dignified tone, stay in your homes, and do not display your beauty as in the days of ignorance. Observe prayer, give alms, and obey Allah and His Apostle. Members of the house of the Prophet ! Allah only intends to rid you of your uncleanliness and to purify you completely. Women keep in mind the revelations of Allah and the words of wisdom which are recited in your houses. Benign is Allah; All-Aware." 33: 32

These verses corroborated what Hadrat Umar had said. When the Holy Prophet informed Hadrat Umar of these verses he felt satisfied that God had ordered in the way he had desired. Turning to Hadrat Umar the Holy Prophet said, "Umar, rejoice for once again Allah has spoken through your tongue."

EXPEDITION TO TURBAH

Banu Howazin was a tribe which inhabited the Turbah valley at two days march from Mecca. The tribe had indulged in some hostile activities against Islam, and in 629 A.D., the Holy Prophet decided to take punitive action against the tribe.

The Holy Prophet commissioned Hadrat Umar to lead the expedition against Banu Howazin. The instructions of the Holy Prophet were that the tribe should be called to Islam, and in the event of their refusal, force should be used against them, and they should be driven away from the Turbah valley.

The Muslim expeditionary force consisted of thirty men. They had with them a guide of the Banu Hilal, who showed them the way, and led them to Turbah valley through unfrequented paths.

When the Muslim force reached the Turbah valley, they found that on hearing the approach of the Muslim force, the Banu Howazin had evacuated the valley and fled elsewhere with their animals and other belongings. The Muslim force stayed in the valley for some days. Scouts were sent in various directions to find some clue of the whereabouts of the Banu Howazin. No clue was found, and as the object of driving away the hostile tribe from the neighbourhood of Mecca had been achieved without firing a shot, the Muslim force decided to return to Madina.

When on the return march, the Muslim force reached Zi-Aljaza, about six miles from Madina, the Banu Hilal guide said:

> "As on the expedition against Banu Howazin you have had no booty, and if you want to return to Madina carrying some booty I can guide you against some other tribes. Banu Khusham have been afflicted with famine.

> I have seen them going that way. If you think of attacking them and getting some booty, I can take you by a path to such a place from where you could launch a surprise attack on them. In spite of famine conditions they have ample wealth with them which you could appropriate."

Thereupon Hadrat Umar said:

> "The Holy Prophet merely sent us against Banu Howazin, and the object was to promote the cause of Islam and not to get booty for ourselves. As the Holy Prophet did not authorise me to attack any other tribe, I am afraid I can not attack any other tribe just for the sake of booty, without the express instructions of the Holy Prophet."

When on return to Madina, Hadrat Umar submitted his report to the Holy Prophet, and stated how he had not accepted the advice of the guide to attack Banu Khusham, the Holy Prophet said, "Umar you did well. If you had attacked them, I would have been unhappy."

BATTLE OF KHYBER

After having been driven away from Madina, the Jews settled at Khyber. The Jews were a cunning and crafty people, and they involved themselves in intrigues against the Muslims.

The pact of Hudaibiya brought truce with the Quraish for a period of ten years. This meant that the Quraish could no longer openly aid the Jews against the Muslims. In spite of this situation, there was no diminution in the hostility of the Jews against the Muslims, and they began to work for the formation of an another coalition against the Muslims.

To forestall the evil designs of the Jews, the Holy Prophet marched to Khyber in 629 A.D. with a force of 1,400 Muslims. The Jews shut themselves in their forts. Some of these forts were very formidable with frowning walls built of the living rock.

The Jews had ample provisions, and there was no shortage of arms with them. They were offered to accept Islam, but they spurned the offer. Thereupon the Holy Prophet ordered an offensive against the Jews.

On the first day the Muslims led the attack against the Jews under the command of Hadrat Abu Bakr. The Jews remained locked up in their forts and there was no confrontation.

The following day, Hadrat Umar commanded the Muslim forces. The Jews remained shut up in their forts and there was no fight.

On the third day, Hadrat Ali commanded the Muslim forces. Surprisingly, the Jews came out of their forts that day and fought in the open. In a hand to hand fight the Jews were overpowered and they capitulated.

According to the terms of the settlement, the Jews agreed to submit to the suzerainty of the Muslims, and to pay them a land tax equivalent to one half of the land produce.

The battle of Khyber had far reaching consequences. It established the paramountcy of Islam in the Arabian peninsula. The Jews now became the subjects of the Muslim State. As the Quraish thereby lost the support of the Jews, the battle of Khyber paved the way for the conquest of Mecca.

At Khyber, Zainab bint Harith a Jewish lady invited the Holy Prophet and his companions to a feast. Hadrat Abu Bakr sat by the side of the Holy Prophet, and next to Hadrat Abu Bakr sat Hadrat Umar.

The Holy Prophet took a morsel of meat and after chewing it threw it away saying, "The meat is poisoned." Hadrat Abu Bakr and Hadrat Umar had so far held their hands. Bishr bin Bra who sat next to the Holy Prophet on the other side ate a good deal of meat, and after a few moments he was dead.

The feast ended in confusion, Zainab was put to explanation, and she admitted her guilt. She pleaded that she had poisoned the meat thinking that if Muhammad (peace be on him) was a prophet he would find that it was poisoned, and if he was not a prophet, the world would get rid of him..

Accounts of subsequent proceedings differ. According to one account Zainab became a Muslim and was forgiven. According to another account she was beheaded.

A tradition has come down to us on the authority of Hadrat Umar Himself that on the day of Khyber some of the companions of the Holy Prophet stated that so and so were martyrs. When they came to a man about whom they said, "So and so is a martyr" the Holy Prophet declared, "By no means, I have seen him in hell in a cloak which he took dishonestly." The Holy Prophet said to Hadrat Umar "Go, Ibn al-Khattab and announce among the people three times that only the believers will enter Paradise." In compliance with these instructions Hadrat Umar went out and announced three times, "Only the believers will enter Paradise."

THE CONQUEST OF MECCA

According to the terms of the treaty of Hudaibiya the Arab tribes had the option to be allied with the Quraish or the Muslims. As a consequence the Banu Bakr joined the Quraish, and the Khuza'ah joined the Muslims.

In disregard of the treaty, Banu Bakr attacked the Khuza'ah and even when the Khuza'ah sought the sanctuary of the Ka'aba, many persons of the Khuza'ah were chased and put to death.

The Khuza'ah wanted the Muslims to come to their aid in accordance with the terms of the treaty. The Holy Prophet gave an ultimatum to the Quraish making three alternative demands, i.e.

(1) to pay the blood money for the victims;
(2) to terminate their alliance with Banu Bakr; or
(3) to consider the Hudaibiya pact to be abrogated.

In a fit of arrogance the Quraish replied that they would neither pay blood money, nor terminate their alliance with Banu Bakr, and that they were prepared to consider the Hadaibiya pact as having been abrogated.

The Muslims in general and Hadrat Umar in particular were happy that the Hudaibiya pact of which they were critical had been abrogated by the Quraish themselves.

The Quraish soon realised that they had imprudently abrogated the treaty. Abu Sufiyan the leader of the Quraish visited Madina to arrive at some amicable settlement. He wanted his daughter who was a wife of the Holy Prophet to plead for him with the Prophet but she refused. Abu Sufiyan waited on Hadrat Abu Bakr and Hadrat Ali but they did not listen to him. He sought the help of Hadrat Umar, and Hadrat

Umar made him understand that there could no longer be any reconciliation with the Quraish unless they accepted Islam. The peace efforts having proved futile, Abu Sufiyan returned to Mecca.

After Abu Sufiyan had left Madina, the Holy Prophet ordered preparations to be made for a foray. As Hadrat Umar came to see his daughter Hadrat Hafsa, he saw that she was packing some goods. He enquired whether Holy Prophet had ordered her to get things packed up, and she said that he had. Later the Holy Prophet took Hadrat Umar into confidence and told him that he was leading an expedition to Mecca, and that he was also to accompany him.

The Holy Prophet mustered a force over ten thousand strong and marched to Mecca. Having reached the neighbour-hood of Mecca the Muslim army encamped at Marr al-Zahran.

The Holy Prophet sent Hadrat Abbas to Mecca on a diplomatic mission. Hadrat Abbas met Abu Sufiyan and advised him that the best course for him and the Quraish was to place themselves at the mercy of the Holy Prophet. Abu Sufiyan agreed to wait on the Holy Prophet to get terms.

Hadrat Umar saw Hadrat Abbas and Abu Sufiyan proceeding to the camp of the Holy Prophet. Hadrat Umar strode forward hurriedly, and addressing the Holy Prophet said, "Permit me to behead Abu Sufiyan the enemy of Islam." The Holy Prophet said, "Umar, wait for a while and see."

At the Muslim camp, Abu Sufiyan was converted to Islam. That was the end of the Quraish opposition.

The following day the Muslim army marched triumphantly into Mecca. One of the contingents was led by Hadrat Umar.

The triumphant entry of the Muslims in Mecca marked the vindication of the truth of Islam. The city which ten years ago had treated the Muslims cruelly, and had driven them to seek refuge with strangers, now lay at the feet of the Muslims.

In the hour of triumph the Holy Prophet forgot every evil suffered, and forgave every injury that had been inflicted on him. He granted general amnesty to the people of Mecca.

The Holy Prophet along with his companions visited the Ka'ba. The idols were broken, and one by one the stone gods were destroyed. Thereupon the Holy Prophet recited the verse from the Holy Qur'an:

> "Say the Truth is come and falsehood gone;
> Verily faslehood is ever vanishing."

The people assembled at the Ka'aba, and the Holy Prophet delivered the following address:

> "There is no god but Allah. He has no associate. He has made good His promise that He held to his bondman and helped him and defeated all the confederates. Bear in mind that every claim of privilege, whether that of blood or property is abolished except that of the custody of the Ka'aba and of supplying water to the pilgrims. Bear in mind that for any one who is slain the blood money is a hundred camels. People of Quraish, surely God has abolished from you all pride of the time of ignorance and all pride in your ancestry, because all men are descended from Adam, and Adam was made of clay." Then the Holy Prophet turning to the people said:
>
> "O ye Quraish, what do you think of the treatment that I should accord you.?"
>
> And they said, "Mercy, O Prophet of Allah. We expect nothing but good from you."
>
> Thereupon the Holy Prophet declared:
>
> "I speak to you in the same words as Joseph spoke to his brothers. This day there is no reproof against you; Go your way, for you are free."

The announcement was received with greatest joy and applause. Then accompanied by Hadrat Umar the Holy Prophet ascended the brow of the Safa to initiate the people to the vow of allegiance to Islam. The people came in large numbers to be converted to Islam. After the oath-taking ceremony of men was over, the Holy Prophet directed Hadrat Umar to take the oath of allegiance from women on his behalf. All the Quraish ladies in Mecca took the oath of allegiance to Allah, the Holy Prophet and Islam at the hands of Hadrat Umar.

BATTLES OF HUNAIN AND TAIF

After the fall of Mecca, the neighbouring tribes of Howazin and Sagef had to choose between Islam and war against Muslims. They chose the war path, and the two tribes along with their allies mustered in considerable strength at Autas to the west of Mecca. The coalition was led by Malik bin Auf a fiery commander of considerable skill.

When the Holy Prophet came to know of the hostile intention of the tribes, he decided to take action against them. On a cold day in January 630 A.D. the Muslim forces set out from Mecca. The army consisted of 12,000 persons fully armed. Out of these 10,000 were from Madina who had attacked Mecca and 2,000 were the newly converted Muslims from Mecca.

As on the way to Autas the Muslim army passed through the valley of Hunain, some eleven miles north east of Mecca, a rain of arrows fell on the Muslims let loose by a group of archers of the hostile tribes who lay hid in the mountain pass. Taken unawares the advance guard of the Muslim army fled in panic. There was considerable confusion, and camels, horses and men ran into one another to seek cover.

The Holy Prophet stood firm. There were only nine companions around him including Hadrat Umar. All the rest had fled. Under the instructions of the Holy Prophet, Hadrat Abbas shouted at the top of his voice, "O Muslims, come to the Prophet of Allah".

The call was heard by the Muslim soldiers, and they gathered round the Holy Prophet. When the Muslims had gathered in sufficient number, the Holy Prophet ordered a charge against the enemy. In the hand to hand fight that followed the tribes were routed and they fled to Autas.

The Holy Prophet posted a contingent to guard the Hunain pass, and led the main Muslim army to Autas. In the confrontation at Autas, the tribes could not withstand the Muslim onslaught. Finding the resistance useless the tribes broke the camp and retired to Taif.

From Autas the Muslim forces set out for Taif. The tribes shut themselves in the fort and refused to come out in the open. The Muslims employed catapults to throw stones in the town, but this did not lead to any tangible results. The Muslims tried the testudo device whereunder a group of soldiers shielded by a cover of cowhide advanced to set fire to the gate. The enemy threw red hot scraps of iron on the testudo which made it ineffective.

The siege dragged on for two weeks, and still there was no sign of the fall of the fort. The Holy Prophet held a council of war. The companions including Hadrat Umar advised that the siege might be raised and that God would Himself make arrangements for the fall of the fort.

The advice was accepted, and in February 630 the siege of Taif was raised, and the Muslim army returned to Mecca. A few days later, Malik bin Auf came to Mecca of his own accord and became a Muslim. Thus God Himself arranged for the surrender of Taif to Islam.

EXPEDITION TO TABUK

In A.D. 630 the Holy Prophet decided to lead an expedition to Tabuk on the Syrian border. In order to finance the expedition the Holy Prophet invited contributions and donations from his followers.

Hadrat Umar had then considerable wealth with him, and he thought that was the occasion for him to excel Hadrat Abu Bakr in the matter of donation in the way of God.

Hadrat Umar went home and he returned loaded with considerable wealth. When the Holy Prophet asked him how much he had left for Himself and his family, he said that he had given one half of his wealth in the way of Allah, and had left one half for Himself and his dependents. The Holy Prophet was much pleased at the contribution, and he thanked Hadrat Umar profusely.

Then Hadrat Abu Bakr came carrying his contribution, and the Holy Prophet put him the same question as to how much wealth he had left for Himself and his family. Hadrat Abu Bakr said, "I have brought all that I had. I have left Allah and His Prophet for myself and my family."

This episode has formed the theme of one of the poems of Allama Iqbal. The last verse of the poem reads:

> "For the moth the lamp, and for the nightingale the flower,
> For Siddiq, God and His Prophet alone suffice."

The call to arms was given at a very inconvenient time. The weather was burning hot. Crops were ripe and ready for harvesting. The journey to the Syrian border was long and arduous. Many persons preferred to stay back. In spite of obstacles and difficulties, an army of thirty thousand persons was raised.

The Muslim army reached Tabuk after a weary march. There was no Byzantine force to meet the Muslims. On coming to know of the advance of the Muslim army, the Byzantines had withdrawn their army well within Syria. The Muslims achieved their object without firing a shot.

The Byzantines who had at one time threatened to invade Arabia were no longer in the mood to measure swords with the Muslims. The tribes in the region which were under the paramountcy of the Byzantines transferred their allegiance to the Muslims.

At Tabuk, the Holy Prophet delivered a classical address which as passed into history. He said:

> "Verily the most veracious discourse is the Book of Allah.
> The most trusty stronghold is the word of piety.
> The best of religions is the religion of Islam.
> The best of the precedents is the precedent of Muhammad.
> The noblest speech is the invocation of Allah.
> The finest of the narratives is the Qur'an.
> The best of the affairs is that which has been firmly resolved upon.
> The worst in religion are those things which are created without sanction.
> The best of the ways is the one trodden by the Prophets.
> The noblest death is the death of martyr.
> The most miserable blindness is the waywardness after guidance.
> The best of the actions is that which is beneficient.
> The best guidance is that which is put into practice.
> The worst blindness is the blindness of the heart."

RUMOUR OF DIVORCE BY THE HOLY PROPHET

In Madina, Hadrat Umar lived in an elevated part of the city. His neighbour was Banu Umayya bin Zaid Ansari. The practice was that one day Hadrat Umar attended the Holy Prophet, and informed his Ansari firend about all that had happened in the Prophet's Mosque. The other day Banu Umayya attended the Prophet's Mosque and on return informed Hadrat Umar of all that had happened that day.

Hadrat Umar felt that while in Mecca the Quraishites dominated over their women, in Madina things had changed, and the women asserted themselves. One day Hadrat Umar was cross with his wife on some matter, but instead of being quiet she retorted, "How is it that you feel annoyed at my remonstrance. Go and see that the wives of the Holy Prophet remonstrate with the Holy Prophet. To-night one of his wives quarrelled with him all the night."

Hearing this, Hadrat Umar went to his daughter Hadrat Hafsa and enquired of her whether she had quarrelled with the Holy Prophet. She said that she had quarrelled with the Holy Prophet as she had a grievance. Thereupon Hadrat Umar said, "Hafsa you are incurring loss. Don't you know by annoying the Holy Prophet you invite the wrath of God." After reprimanding here in severe terms, Hadrat Umar returned home.

At night the Ansari neighbour of Hadrat Umar knocked at his door, and as Hadrat Umar went to see what was the matter, his friend told him that something very grave had happened. Hadrat Umar thought that perhaps Banu Ghassan whose attack was expected had invaded Madina. Hadrat Umar enquired whether Banu Ghassan had launched the attack.

Banu Umayya said, "No. Something more serious than that has happened". When Hadrat Umar pressed him to tell what had happened he said that the Holy Prophet had divorced his wives.

Hadrat Umar was very much upset at the news. He spent the whole night in prayer. Early in the morning next day, Hadrat Umar went to Hadrat Hafsa. He found her weeping. He enquired of her whether the Holy Prophet had divorced her. She said that she did not know. Hadrat Umar rebuked her saying, "Did I not warn you before hand that by annoying the Holy Prophet you would be inviting trouble?" Thereupon Hadrat Hafsa burst into violent sobs. Hadrat Umar left her weeping and went to the Prophet's Mosque. There the people were sitting in groups here and there and were lamenting that the Holy Prophet had divorced his wives.

The Holy Prophet was in the cell attached to the Mosque. Hadrat Umar went to the cell, and asked the slave at the door to seek the Holy Prophet's permission to his admittance. The slave returned to say that he had sought the requisite permission from the Holy Prophet but he had kept quiet.

Hadrat Umar returned to the main hall of the Mosque, and sat in a corner in a dejected mood. After some time he rose and went again to the cell of the Holy Prophet. Once again he requested the slave to get permission for his admittance. The slave returned to say that the Holy Prophet had made no reply.

Hadrat Umar returned once again to the main hall of the Mosque. He was highly upset and he prayed to God for mercy. Then once again he went to the cell of the Holy Prophet. This time he was allowed permission. Entering the cell, Hadrat Umar said:

> "O Messenger of God, I have not come to plead for Hafsa. If that is your pleasure I would wring her neck with my own hands."

That softened the Holy Prophet and he smiled at the words of Hadrat Umar.

Hadrat Umar further said, "I find that in Mecca our ladies were docile ; the climate of Madina has made them assertive. O Prophet of God if because of the impudence of your wives, you have divorced them, God, His angels, and all your followers are with you."

The Holy Prophet smiled and said, "Be assured, I have not divorced my wives. I have only decided to remain separate from them for a period of one month."

"Then may I tell so to Hafsa", said Umar.
The Holy Prophet said. "You may, if you like'.

Hadrat Umar cast a glance across the room. The Holy Prophet lay on a bare mat. There was no furniture in the room. There was hardly anything for the Holy Prophet to eat, but a barley bread. Seeing this extreme state of austerity, tears began to trickle from the eyes of Hadrat Umar.

The Holy Prophet said, "Ibn-i-Khattab, what makes you weep?".

Hadrat Umar said, "You are the Prophet of God and you are living in such straitened circumstances. The people of Persia and Byzantine live in luxury. O Prophet of God why don't you pray to God that he should bestow wealth on you?"

The Holy Prophet said, "Do you think He Who made me His Prophet could not make me wealthy. Indeed He offered me the keys of all treasures in the world, but I refused them in return for the treasures in the next world. Surely treasures in the next world are to be preferred to petty wealth in this world. And as for the riches of Persia and Byzantine rest assured all such wealth will lie at the feet of the Muslims. I will not be alive then, but in your lifetime, both Persia and Byzantine will be overpowered by the Muslims."

THE FUNERAL OF ABDULLAH BIN UBAYY

Abdullah bin Ubayy was an Ansar chief of Madina. Abdullah bin Ubayy had the ambition to wear the crown of Madina. When the people of Madina invited the Holy Prophet and the Muslims to migrate to Madina and accepted the Holy Prophet as their ruler the designs of Abdullah bin Ubayy were frustrated. As all the Arabs of Madina accepted Islam, Abdullah also became a Muslim as a measure of expediency. Islam, however, sat lightly on him, and he often indulged in activities hostile to Islam.

In the battle of Uhud, he betrayed the Muslim trust and withdrew his contingent at the last moment. On the occasion of the raid of Al-Mustaliq he said unbecoming things against the Muhajreen including the Holy Prophet. In the sad episode of *False Allegation* he was responsible for calumny against Hadrat Ayesha. Hadrat Umar sought the permission of the Holy Prophet to kill Abdullah bin Ubayy, but the Holy Prophet, kind-hearted as he was, did not give the permission.

Even Allah had taken notice of the hypocrisy of Abdullah bin Ubayy, and in a revelation to the Holy Prophet it was said that even if he prayed for the hypocrites seventy times his prayer would not be accepted.

When Abdullah bin Ubayy died, the Holy Prophet attended his funeral and decided to lead the funeral prayer. At this stage Hadrat Umar waited on the Holy Prophet, and tried to dissuade him from leading the funeral prayer of Abdullah bin Ubayy. Hadrat Umar recounted the various hypocricies of Abdullah, and also referred to the revelation whereunder God had said that the hypocrites would not be forgiven even if seventy prayers were offered.

The Holy Prophet said:

> "Umar, get behind me and let us offer the prayer. In this matter God has given me the choice, and I have decided to adopt a magnanimous attitude."

Thereupon Hadrat Umar joined the ranks and the funeral prayers were offered under the leadership of the Holy Prophet. The Holy Prophet remained in the graveyard till Abdullah was buried. Then the Holy Prophet prayed over the grave of Abdullah before returning home.

A few days later, the following verses were revealed to the Holy Prophet:

> "And never pray for any of them at his funeral,
> And do not stand by his grave,
> For they disbelieved in God and His Apostle." 9 : 13

When the Holy Prophet informed Hadrat Umar of these verses, Hadrat Umar felt happy that Almighty Allah had confirmed his point of view.

WHEN GABRIEL APPEARED IN THE SHAPE OF A MAN

Hadrat Umar stated that one day when he and some other companions were with God's Messenger, a man with very white clothing and very black hair came up. Sitting down beside the Holy Prophet, leaning his knees against his, and placing his hands on his thighs he said, "Tell me Muhammad about Islam."

The Holy Prophet said,"Islam means that you should testify that there is no god but Allah; that Muhammad is God's Messenger; that you should observe the prayer, pay the Zakat, fast during Ramadan, and make the pilgrimage to the House of God, if you have the means".

The visitor said "You have spoken the truth. Now tell me about faith."

The Holy Prophet said, "It means that you should believe in Allah, His angels, His books ; His Apostles, and the last day, and that you should believe in the decreeing both of good and evil."

The man said that that was true. He then asked, "Now tell me about doing good."

The Holy Prophet said, "It means that you should worship Allah as if you are seeing Him, and if you are not seeing him (percieve) that He is in fact seeing you.

The man accepted the statement as correct. He next asked, "Now tell me about the Hour".

The Holy Prophet said, "The one who is asked about is no better informed than the one who is asking".

Thereupon the man said, "Then tell me about its signs".

The Holy Prophet replied, "The signs are that a maid servant should beget her mistress, and that you should see barefooted, naked poor men and shepherds exulting themselves in buildings."

The visitor felt satisfied. Then he sought leave to depart and as soon as leave was given he disappeared. Hadrat Umar who was present wondered who was the visitor.

Turning to Hadrat Umar, the Holy Prophet said, "Do you know who was the visitor ?"

Hadrat Umar replied that he did not know.

Thereupon the Holy Prophet said, "He was Gabriel, who came to you to teach your religion."

TIDINGS OF PARADISE

It is related by Hadrat Abu Huraira that once he along with other companions including Hadrat Abu Bakr and Hadrat Umar were sitting with the Holy Prophet. The Holy Prophet rose from their midst and went to the garden of Ansar Banu Najjār.

The return of the Holy Prophet was delayed, and his companions felt anxious. Hadrat Abu Huraira was the first to proceed to the garden of Banu Najjār. There he found no gate. He managed to go inside the garden through a drain.

Seeing him, the Holy Prophet said, "Abu Huraira what brings you here ?"

Abu Huraira said, "You took long to return and we felt worried. So we have come after you".

Thereafter the Holy Prophet gave him his shoes and said, "Go carrying these shoes outside the garden, and whomsoever you meet who declares the article of faith with the sincerity of heart, give him the tidings of Paradise."

As Hadrat Abu Huraira came out of the garden carrying the shoes of the Holy Prophet, the first person to meet him was Hadrat Umar.

Hadrat Umar said to Hadrat Abu Huraira, "Why are you carrying the shoes of the Holy Prophet ?"

Hadrat Abu Huraira said, "I am carrying these shoes under the command of the Holy Prophet. I have been commissioned to give the tidings of Paradise to whomsoever I meet, while carrying these shoes, who declares that he believes in the article of faith with sincerity of heart."

Hadrat Umar felt angry. He handled Hadrat Abu Huraira rather violently and said, "No such tidings are necessary. Abu Huraira go back."

As Hadrat Abu Huraira went back to the Holy Prophet, he complained against Hadrat Umar, and said that Hadrat Umar had obstructed him in the performance of the mission that the Holy Prophet had entrusted to him.

In the meantime Hadrat Umar also turned up. Seeing him, the Holy Prophet said, "Why did you behave rudely to Abu Huraira?"

Hadrat Umar said "May my parents be a sacrifice to you Holy Prophet. The truth of the matter is that he intended to give the tidings of Paradise to all Muslims irrespective of their conduct. That would have been repugnant to the injunctions of Islam which makes admission to Paradise contingent by doing good. Holy Prophet, do not issue permits for the Paradise. Let the people do their duties. If they are assured of Paradise before hand there is the danger that they would relax in the performance of their obligations."

The Holy Prophet said, "Alright, let the Muslims perform their obligations."

THE FAREWELL PILGRIMAGE

Early in A.D. 632 the Holy Prophet decided to proceed to Mecca to perform the Hajj. The pilgrimage was planned on a large scale. Messengers were sent to all parts of Arabia asking the Muslims to collect at Madina for the purpose of the pilgrimage. In response to this call over one lakh persons assembled in Madina.

Then the caravan of over one lakh persons started for Mecca. The Holy Prophet rode at the head. All his wives accompanied him. Then followed Hadrat Abu Bakr and Hadrat Umar accompanied by their families.

At Dhul Hulaifa the Holy Prophet and all his followers put on the Ihram. The Holy Prophet gave the signal call "*Labbaik, Allahumma Labbaik*—here I am at Thy service O Lord." This cry was repeated by all the one lakh persons in the congregation.

The party reached Mecca on the 4th of Zul Hajj, after a journey of nineteen days. On the 8th of Zul Hajj the party left Mecca for Mina and passed the night there. Next day the party proceeded to Arafat. After mid-day prayers on the 9th of Zul Hajj the Holy Prophet delivered his historic address.

After giving praise to God, the Holy Prophet said:

"O people, listen carefully to my words for I may not be among you next year, nor ever address you again from this spot. O people just as you regard this month as sacred, so regard the life and property of every Muslim as a sacred trust. Return the goods entrusted to you to their rightful owners. Hurt no one so that none may hurt you. Usury is forbidden. Satan has despaired of leading you astray in big things, so beware of obeying him in small things. Women have rights over you and you have rights over them. Be good to them. You may soon have to appear before God and answer for your deeds. So beware. Do not go astray after I have gone. O people no prophet will come after me, and no new faith will be born. Worship your God, say your prayer, fast during the month of Ramadan, and give your wealth in charity. All Muslims free or enslaved have the same rights and the same responsibilities. None is higher than the other unless he is higher in virtue. Feed your slaves as you feed yourselves; clothe them as you clothe yourselves. Do not oppress them, nor usurp their rights."

Having spoken thus the Holy Prophet turned his face to the Heaven and said:

"Be my witness O God, that I have conveyed Your message to Your people."

And then all the people said:

"Yes, you have done so."

After the Holy Prophet had delivered his address, God revealed to him the verses:

"This day have We perfected for you your faith,
And completed Our blessing upon you
And have accepted for you Islam as religion."

As Hadrat Umar heard these verses, he felt happy that God had perfected the faith for them. Hadrat Umar called on Hadrat Abu Bakr and found him very sad. Hadrat Umar asked Abu Bakr the reason for his sadness when God had sent the tidings that their faith had been perfected. Hadrat Abu Bakr said that the implication of these verses was that the mission of the Holy Prophet had been completed, and that the day when the Holy Prophet would depart to meet his Lord was not far off. Hadrat Umar could not, however, share the fears of Hadrat Abu Bakr that the Holy Prophet would not live long in their midst.

The party left Arafat in the evening and passed the night at Muzdalifa. The following day they went to Mina, and sacrificed the animals. The Holy Prophet sacrificed 63 animals, one for each year of his life. Hadrat Umar sacrificed 52 animals. The men next shaved their heads and the Hajj was completed. Thereafter the Holy Prophet and his followers returned to Madina.

PASSING AWAY OF THE HOLY PROPHET

A short time after returning from the 'Farewell Pilgrimage', the Holy Prophet fell sick. The poison which a Jewess had given to him at Khyber had slowly penetrated into his system, and began to show its effects. The Holy Prophet felt that having fulfilled his mission his earthly life was to end and he was to meet his Master.

One night the Holy Prophet went to the graveyard and there prayed for the souls of his companions who had fallen at the battle of Uhud. Then he returned to the apartment of his wife Maimuna. The fever became violent. The Holy Prophet assembled all his wives and told them that on account of his sickness it would not be possible for him to visit each wife in turn. He wanted their permission to stay in the apartment of Ayesha till he recovered. All the wives gave their consent, and the Holy Prophet supported by Ali and Abbas moved to the apartment of Ayesha.

A day later there was some relief and the Holy Prophet took a bath. Refreshed by the bath the Holy Prophet went to the Mosque to offer the noonday prayer. After the prayer had concluded, the Holy Prophet took his seat on the pulpit and addressed the people:

> "There is a servant whose Lord has given him option between this life and the next nigh unto the Lord and the servant has chosen the latter. O People it has reached me that you are afraid of the approaching death of your Prophet. Has any previous Prophet lived for ever among those to whom he was sent so that I would live for ever among you ? Behold, I am about to go to my Lord. You too will go sooner or later."

After the address the Holy Prophet retired to the quarter of Hadrat Ayesha. His condition did not improve. The night following the seventh June 632 A.D. lay heavy upon him. He was overheard praying constantly to Allah for his blessings. The morning of the eighth June brought some relief. Fever and pain abated to some extent. Moving the curtain of his apartment the Holy Prophet saw the Muslims praying in the Mosque. The Holy Prophet supported by Ali walked to the Mosque. After the conclusion of the prayer, the Holy Prophet took his seat on the pulpit and addressed his followers thus:

> "By the Lord ! As for myself, I have not made lawful anything excepting that which God has declared lawful; nor have I prohibited aught but that which God has forbidden."

Thereafter the Holy Prophet returned to the apartment of Hadrat Ayesha. The condition of the Holy Prophet grew worse, and within a few hours he passed away.

The faithful had assembled in the Mosque. They sat in groups here and there. There was an air of uneasiness in the atmosphere. There was a whispering that the Holy Prophet was dead. There were suppressed sobs and sighs. Many persons were weeping. What would happen to the Muslims when the Great Prophet was to be no longer in their midst was the thought that disturbed every one.

All eyes were turned to the quarter of Hadrat Ayesha. The faithful had the fond hope that the door of the chamber would open any moment and the Holy Prophet would emerge with his face radiating divine light.

In the courtyard of the Mosque. Hadrat Umar moved among the people saying:

> "Who says that the Prophet is dead. I testify that he is alive and has gone to Allah like Moses, and would return to us after some time."

The door of the chamber of Hadrat Ayesha opened and a thin frail old man walking stoopingly moved towards the courtyard of the Mosque. He had the look of a patriarch. He was Abu Bakr. As he stood among the people, his furrowed face and tear stained eyes betrayed the grief within him. In measured words he said:

> "Listen to me, ye people. Those of you who worshipped Muhammad know that he is dead like any other mortal. But those of you who worship the God of Muhammad know that He is alive and would live for ever."

A hushed silence fell on the gathering. They were stunned with the shock. Hadrat Abu Bakr wiped the tears from his eyes and turning to the people recited the following verses from the Holy Qur'an:

> "Muhammad is but a Messenger,
> Messengers of God have passed away before him.
> What, if he dies or is killed ?
> Will you turn back upon your heels ?
> And whosoever turns back upon his heels
> Will by no means do harm to Allah,
> And Allah will reward the thankful."
> Hadrat Abu Bakr added:
> "Muhammad the Great Prophet was a mortal;
> From Allah he came, and to Allah he has returned."

The effect of Hadrat Abu Bakr's address was electrical in character. It appeared as though the people did not know that this verse of the Holy Qur'an had come down until Hadrat Abu Bakr had recited it that day. Hadrat Umar said:

> "By God when I heard Abu Bakr recite these words I was dumb founded so that my legs would not bear me, and I fell to the ground knowing that the Holy Prophet was indeed dead."

ELECTION OF HADRAT ABU BAKR AS THE FIRST CALIPH

When the dead body of the Holy Prophet of Islam was being prepared for burial, the Ansar assembled at their meeting place *'Saqifa-i-Bani Sa'dah'* to discuss the question of succession to the Holy Prophet. The Holy Prophet was the last of the prophets, and there could be no prophet after him. He was also the Leader of the Muslims, and it was necessary that after him there should be some one who should be the head of the community.

At the meeting at Saqifa-i-Bani Sa'dah, Sa'd bin Ubadah made a passionate plea that the successor to the Holy Prophet for managing the temporal affairs of the community should be chosen from among the Ansars. He argued that they were the people who had protected Islam, and had offered a home for the Holy Prophet and his companions when they were persecuted by their own people. It was through their efforts that Islam had spread and grown. When Sa'd completed his speech he was applauded by the audience and it appeared as if the Ansars were going to choose him as their Leader in succession to the Holy Prophet.

While the meeting was being held at Saqifa-i-Bani Sa'dah some one reported to the Muhajreen assembled at Masjid-i-Nabvi that the Ansars had assembled to choose a successor to the Holy Prophet. It was a critical situation. The burial of the Holy Prophet was a matter that needed priority, but the question of choosing a successor to the Holy Prophet was a question of life and death for the Muslim community and if any wrong decision was taken at that stage, the future of Islam was likely to be jeopardised. Hadrat Umar accordingly prevailed upon Hadrat Abu Bakr to proceed to Saqifa-i-Bani

Sa'dah to negotiate the matter with the Ansars before it was too late.

When Hadrat Abu Bakr, Hadrat Umar, and Hadrat Abu Ubaidah reached the Saqifa-i-Bani Sa'dah, the Ansars were on the verge of electing Sa'd bin Ubadah as the successor to the Holy Prophet. Hadrat Abu Bakr took the stage and explained that the Quraish were the custodians of the House of God at Mecca, and as such it was necessary that the successor to the Holy Prophet should be chosen from among the Quraish. Addressing his appeal to the Ansar he said:

> "O Ansar, none can deny the superiority of your position, or the greatness of your eminence in Islam. You were chosen by Allah as the helpers of His religion and His Apostle. To you the Prophet was sent on his emigration from Mecca and from among you come the majority of his companions and his wives. Indeed, in position you are next only to the earliest companions. Therefore it would be fair if we take the Amirate and you accept the Wazirate. You should not be obstinate in your stand. We assure you that we will do nothing without consulting you."

This did not satisfy the Ansars. Habab bin Mandhar rose to say that the Amirate was the right of the Ansars and they could not forego that right. He added that the utmost concession that they could make in favour of the Muhajreen was that they could have two Amirs, one from the Ansars and the other from the Muhajreen.

Hadrat Umar said that this would create a division between the Ansars and the Muhajreen and that would be against the interests of Islam. Islam stood for unity—one God, one Prophet and one Qur'an. It followed as a necessary corollary that the Muslim community should remain united and should have one Amir. If the proposal of having two Amirs from the Ansars and Muhajreen was accepted, other tribes would later lay claim to the election of their Amir as well. Such multiple Amirates would lead to the disintegration of Islamic polity. Hadrat Umar emphasised that in the interests of the solidarity of Islam they should not have more than one Amir and that such Amir should be chosen from among the Quraish, the tribe of the Holy Prophet.

There was some further exchange of hot words between Habab and Hadrat Umar. Hadrat Abu Bakr took the stage again and said:

> "God is my witness that we are not pressing the claim of the Quraish because of any selfish interest. The proposal is prompted in the interest of the solidarity of Islam. To give you a proof positive of our sincerity I declare before you that I do not covet the office. Here are Umar and Abu Ubaidah. You may choose any one of these."

This appeared to have some effect on the Ansars. Zaid bin Thabit an eminent Ansar said:

> "In fact the Holy Prophet was from the emigrants. Hence it is necessary that the Imam is also selected from among them. God chose us as Helpers, and we should continue to help the successor of the Holy Prophet in the same way as we helped the Holy Prophet Himself."

Supporting him, Bashir bin Sad another Ansar leader said:

> "O Ansar ! if we have secured a position of superiority in the holy wars against the polytheists and gained precedence in matters of religion, it was with the object of pleasing our Allah and obeying our Prophet. It is not proper to make this as a ground for self aggrandisement. We should leave our reward to Allah. We must realise that the Holy Prophet came from the Quraish, and that the Quraish have strongest claims for his successorship. We should not quarrel with the Quraish on this issue."

That turned the tables, and the Ansars now appeared to be inclined to choose the Leader from among the Quraish. Thereupon Hadrat Abu Bakr repeated his proposal that they might choose any one out of Umar and Abu Ubaidah.

Hadrat Umar rose to say :

"O Abu Bakr, how can I or Abu Ubaidah be preferred to you.

You were the second of the two in the Cave. You were appointed as Amir-ul-Hajj. During his illness the Holy Prophet appointed you as the Imam to lead the prayers. Of all the Companions you were the dearest to the Holy Prophet, and so you are dearest to us. Stretch your hand so that we may offer our allegiance to you."

Hadrat Umar made Hadrat Abu Bakr stand, and he was the first to touch the hand of Hadrat Abu Bakr reverently in token of allegiance. Hadrat Abu Ubaidah was the next to offer allegiance. Thereafter the Ansars except Sa'd bin Ubadah advanced turn by turn to offer allegiance to Hadrat Abu Bakr.

INSTALLATION OF HADRAT ABU BAKR AS THE CALIPH

On the day following the burial of the Holy Prophet, all the Muslims assembled in the Prophet's Mosque.

Hadrat Umar addressed the people as follows:

"O ye men of faith ! Yesterday I had said to you 'Who says that the Holy Prophet is dead'. I am afraid what I said was not correct. In the Holy Book of God there is nothing to indicate that the Holy Prophet was to live for ever. The Holy Prophet Himself never gave an indication to the effect that he was to live for ever. I was cf the impression that the Holy Prophet was to live in our midst and guide us. But this impression was not correct. The Holy Qur'an itself provides that the Holy Prophet was a mortal liable to death. The Holy Prophet had come from God and to God he has returned. He has returned after fulfilling the mission entrusted to him. God has perfected our religion. God has given us a Book through which He guided His Messenger, and through which He will continue to guide the faithful. Our task is to hold steadfast to the Book of God, and to follow His injunctions. We miss the Holy Prophet. But the Holy Prophet was a messenger. He has delivered the message, and after fulfilling his role returned to his Master. The message remains with us in the form of the Holy Book. Those who worship Allah let them know that Allah lives and is not subject to death. The Holy Prophet was a mortal and has gone to His Master. We must follow in the footsteps of the Holy Prophet, and get used to life without his physical presence. In his absence our people must have a leader who would guide us. For this task who can be more competent than Abu Bakr, the life long friend of the Holy Prophet, whom God has referred to as 'Second of the Two'. O ye faithful, rise and offer allegiance at the hand of Hadrat Abu Bakr."

Having made this address, Hadrat Umar requested Hadrat Abu Bakr to take his seat on the pulpit. Hadrat Abu Bakr took his seat on the pulpit, a step below that which was used by the Holy Prophet. Thereafter all the Muslims present swore their allegiance.

Thereafter Hadrat Abu Bakr after praising Allah and the Holy Prophet addressed the people:

> "O people ! I swear by Allah that I never coveted the Amirate either by day or by night, nor had I any inclination towards it. I never prayed to God openly or in secrecy to confer the Amirate on me. But I certainly feared that some mischief might arise at this critical juncture in the history of the Muslims. In fact a big task has been assigned to me which is beyond my power to fulfil except with the help of the Almighty Allah. I wished to see the strongest of men in my place today. Now, it is beyond doubt that I have been elected your Amir, although I am no better than you. Help me if I am in the right; set me right if I am in the wrong. Truth is a trust; falsehood is a treason. The weak among you shall be strong with me till God willing his rights have been vindicated, and the strong among you shall be weak with me till, if the Lord will, I have taken what is due from him. Obey me as long as I obey Allah and His Prophet. When I disobey Him and His Prophet, then obey me not."

Hadrat Umar played an important role in the election of Hadrat Abu Bakr as the first Caliph of Islam. During the caliphate of Hadrat Abu Bakr, Hadrat Umar remained as the principal Adviser of the Caliph.

USAMAH'S EXPEDITION TO SYRIA

After assuming the Caliphate the first issue that Hadrat Abu Bakr was called upon to decide was whether the expedition to Syria which the Holy Prophet had directed to be sent under the command of Usamah should proceed to its destination, or should the expedition in view of the change in circumstances be abandoned.

The background of the expedition was that in 639 A.D. the Holy Prophet had sent an expedition against the Syrians under Zaid bin Harith. In the confrontation that had taken place at Mutah, Zaid had been martyred. The command had thereafter been taken over by Jafar bin Abu Talib and he had also been martyred. Abdullah bin Rawaha who had next taken the command had also been martyred.

At that critical stage, Khalid bin Walid had taken over the command. By his skillful tactics and superb strategy he had succeeded in retrieving the position and bringing back the Muslim forces safely to Madina. For this act of heroism, Khalid bin Walid had received from the Holy Prophet the title of 'Saifullah'—the Sword of Allah.

In 632 A.D. on return from the 'Farewell Pilgrimage', the Holy Prophet ordered a detachment to be sent against the Syrians under the command of Usamah the son of Zaid bin Harith. Some persons objected to the command of Usamah, a mere youth of twenty when other veteran commanders were available. The Holy Prophet overruled the objection, and declared that Usamah was worthy of the command.

When the Holy Prophet fell ill the detachment of Usamah was camped at Jorf a few miles from Madina on the road to

Syria. On account of the serious illness of the Holy Prophet, Usamah delayed his departure. When the Holy Prophet died, Usamah returned to Madina, and sought further orders from the new Caliph.

Most of the Companions were of the view that at that critical stage in the history of Islam when most of the tribes had apostatised from Islam, and Madina itself was surrounded by hostile tribes it was dangerous to send the army outside the country. They were further of the view that if the expedition was necessarily to be undertaken, there should be a change in the command and some veteran soldier should be appointed as the commander instead of Usamah. The companions chose Hadrat Umar as their spokesman to represent their view point before Hadrat Abu Bakr.

Hadrat Umar saw Hadrat Abu Bakr, and represented the case with considerable vehemence. As regards the issue whether the expedition should or should not be undertaken Hadrat Abu Bakr said that as the Holy Prophet had insisted on sending the expedition, it would be a breach of faith on his part to reverse the orders of the Holy Prophet. Hadrat Umar tried to argue that if the army was sent, the city of Madina would be exposed to attack by the enemy, and the Caliphate itself would be in danger. To this Hadrat Abu Bakr replied:

> "Who am I to withhold the army that the Holy Prophet had ordained to proceed? Come what may, let Madina stand or fall, the Caliphate live or perish, the command of the Holy Prophet shall be carried out."

As regards the issue about the change of command Hadrat Abu Bakr said:

> "This objection had been raised before the Holy Prophet as well and he had rejected the objection. How can I as the susccessor of the Holy Prophet accept an objection which the Holy Prophet had in his wisdom rejected ?"

Hadrat Umar said:

> "O the Caliph of the Holy Prophet, you are wiser than us all. You are right. May God bless you and your decisions".

Thereafter Hadrat Umar explained to the companions the decisions of Hadrat Abu Bakr, and the justification therefor.

The army under Usamah was accordingly directed to proceed to its appointed task. On the eve of the departure of the army, Hadrat Abu Bakr addressed the soldiers and gave them instructions regarding their conduct and responsibilities. Hadrat Umar was also included among the soldiers in the army of Usamah. Turning to Usamah, Hadrat Abu Bakr said:

> "I beg one favour of you. Do not take Umar with you. Leave him here to help me."

The army of Usamah marched from Jorf to Syria. Hadrat Umar was left at Madina to serve as an Adviser to Hadrat Abu Bakr.

DEFENCE OF MADINA

Madina was surrounded by a ring of tribes whose attitude to Islam was unfavourable if not hostile. The Bani Asad had their concentration at Sumairah, the first stage on the way to Mecca. The Bani Ghatafan had their concentration in the south of Madina. The Banu Tha'lba, the Banu Harrach and the Banu Abas had their stronghold at Abraq. The Banu Dhunayn had their headquarter at Dhul Qissa the first stage on the route from Madina to Nejd.

When Usamah's army left Madina for the Syrian front, the tribes around Madina sent a deputation to wait on Hadrat Abu Bakr. The tribes were prepared to own Islam, but they refused to pay Zakat. Hadrat Abu Bakr consulted the companions. Almost all of them advised that as the Muslims were hemmed in by danger from all sides, allegiance of such tribes to Islam should be accepted by foregoing the claim to Zakat, so that there should be no further secession from the fold of Islam.

According to Suyuti's *History of the Caliphs*, Abu Bakr Ahmad bin Ibrahim al-Ismail, a scholar of the Shaafii school has preserved an account of what happened in the words of Hadrat Umar Himself. The account reads :

> "When the Apostle of God died, some of the Arabs fell from the faith and they said 'we will perform the prayers, but we will not pay the poor rate'. I went to Hadrat Abu Bakr and said 'O Vicegerent of the Apostle of God conciliate the people and be indulgent to them for they are not, on a level with brute beasts'. Hadrat Abu Bakr replied 'I hoped for your help, and you have come withholding your aid. You were stern in the time of ignorance. Why have you become dissipated and disspirited in Islam ? How can I conciliate with them by

ignoring the injunctions of Islam? If God and the Holy Prophet had left the matter to the discretion of the community, I could have accepted your advice and allowed concession in the matter of poor rate on the basis of expediency. But where the orders of the Holy Prophet and Allah are conclusive and definite, how can I or you modify such orders, in spite of the gravity of the situation. Alas the Holy Prophet is dead, and divine inspiration is no longer available to us. As the representative of the Holy Prophet it devolves on me to enforce the order passed by the Holy Prophet, and not to modify or amend such order.' Thereupon I realised how correct was Hadrat Abu Bakr. I congratulated him on his resolve and assured him of my full support".

When the delegation of the tribes waited on Hadrat Abu Bakr, Hadrat Abu Bakr explained to the delegates that if they professed Islam, they had to observe all the injunctions of Islam in toto. There was no half-way house in Islam, and it was not permissible for them to pick and choose according to their wHems in the matter of religion. Islam had either to be accepted or rejected, and there was no room in Islam for any compromise on fundamentals. Zakat being a fundamental injunction of Islam had to be paid, and any refusal to pay Zakat implied apostasy. Addressing the delegates, Hadrat Abu Bakr declared in unequivocal terms:

> "Under the circumstances, if with reference to Zakat you withhold even as much as a string to tie a camel, as a Caliph of the Holy Prophet, it will be my duty to fight for it whatever the consequences."

Hadrat Umar sat by the side of Hadrat Abu Bakr as the delegates met the Caiiph. Thus rebuffed the recalcitrant tribes decided to accept the challenge. As the main Muslim army under Usamah was out of the country, the tribes felt that Madina was vulnerable and would easily fall to any attack. The tribes held a council of war among themselves and decided to attack Madina. One night the tribes marched to Madina and opened the attack.

Hadrat Abu Bakr and Hadrat Umar were alive to the gravity of the situation. They took precautionary measures and every able bodied male adult in Madina was called upon to come forward for the defence of the city. With all the forces that could be mustered the Muslims marched to face the invaders. The invaders threw inflated water skins in the path of the Muslim army. That frightened the camels on which the Muslims were riding, and the camels ran towards Madina. The tribes felt jubilant at the retreat of the Muslims.

Hadrat Abu Bakr and Hadrat Umar rallied the Muslim forces. In the late hours of the night, the Muslim forces marched out of the city and led a violent attack. The tribal forces were taken unawares and were cut to pieces. Those who survived fled in confusion. Before the day dawned the Muslims had won the victory and the threat to Madina was over.

HADRAT UMAR AND KHALID BIN WALID

Khalid bin Walid who was a cousin of the mother of Hadrat Umar was the hero of the apostasy wars conducted during the caliphate of Hadrat Abu Bakr. While Hadrat Umar appreciated Khalid's skill as a General he was critical of Khalid's moral conduct.

Having defeated Taleaha at the battle of Buzakha, and reduced the tribes in the north Khalid bin Walid decided to march against the Bani Tamim who lived on a plateau bordering on the Persian Gulf. The Bani Tamim had accepted Islam during the life time of the Holy Prophet. After the death of the Holy Prophet when the wave of apostasy spread over the Arabian peninsula, the Bani Tamim were also affected. The tribe came to be divided into two sections. One section remained faithful to Islam while the other section apostatised.

When Khalid gave his army the order to march to Bataha the headquarter of the Bani Tamim a section of the army objected to the order on the ground that the Caliph had not sanctioned any action against the Bani Tamim. The objection was overruled by Khalid.

The orders of Hadrat Abu Bakr were that if any tribe professed faith in Islam, no action was to be taken against it. If a tribe did not profess faith in Islam, it was to be invited to accept Islam, and operations were to be undertaken against it only in the event of refusal. The strategy laid down was that if on reaching a settlement the residents pronounced Adhan, it was to be understood that the people were Muslims. In the absence of such response it was to be presumed that the people were hostile to Islam.

Before the Muslim army reached Bataha, delegation from Bani Tamim waited on Khalid. They brought with them the necessary amount of the tax payable to the Muslims. Khalid took the amount, but continued his advance to Bataha. When the forces of Khalid reached Bataha there were no forces of the Bani Tamim to oppose the Muslims. The position was confused. Malik the chief of Bani Tamim neither came forward to offer his submission, nor did he come forward to oppose the Muslims.

Khalid directed his soldiers to forage in the neighbourhood. Malik and his wife Laila were taken captive and brought before Khalid. Malik's wife Laila was known far and wide for her breath-taking beauty. Her long glossy hair flowed upto her knees. She had gorgeous legs and she carried herself with peculiar grace and charm. In Khalid's camp Malik was killed and Khalid married Laila.

This led to considerable scandal. In some quarters it was held that Malik was indeed a Muslim and that he had been killed because Khalid coveted his beautiful wife Laila. Some of the Ansars in the army of Khalid led by Abu Qatadah withdrew from the army of Khalid. Abu Qatadah along with Mutamim the brother of the late Malik set out for Madina to lodge a complaint against Khalid. Mutamim was a distinguished poet, and he composed a heart rending elegy mourning the death of his brother. The elegy became very popular in Madina, and those who listened to it felt sympathy for Malik.

Khalid was summoned to Madina and put to explanation. Khalid's defence was that if according to the Holy Prophet he was the 'Sword of Allah' how could such sword fall against the neck of a Muslim ? Hadrat Umar was highly critical of the conduct of Khalid and held that he was guilty of murdering a Muslim to marry his beautiful wife. As the false prophet Musailma had defeated the Muslims twice, and Khalid's services were required to defeat Musailma, Hadrat Abu Bakr took a lenient view, and decided that blood money should be paid out of the Baitul Mal to the heirs of Malik. Hadrat Umar did not feel happy over the decision.

Khalid fought against Musailma in what came to be known as the battle of Yamama. It was a great trial of strength and though the Muslims won a victory, this was achieved at a heavy cost. Over 14,000 followers of Musailma died in the battle. Twelve hundred Muslims fell as martyrs in the battle, and though the number was very much less than the number of dead of Banu Hanifa, the tribe of Musailma, yet the Muslim loss was quite heavy. Among the martyrs was Zaid the brother of Hadrat Umar. Hadrat Umar felt much grieved at the death of his brother. He used to say "Whenever the breeze blows from Yamama it brings to me the fragrance of Zaid".

Terms with the Banu Hanifa were negotiated by Khalid with Maja'a. Maja'a had a beautiful daughter and one of the terms stipulated by Khalid was that Maja'a should marry his daughter to him. Maja'a hesitated but Khalid forced him to marry his daughter to him the same day that the treaty was signed. Hadrat Umar was critical of the conduct of Khalid, and complained to Hadrat Abu Bakr. Hadrat Abu Bakr wrote a letter to Khalid reprimanding him in the following terms:

> "O son of the mother of Khalid. What has gone wrong with you ? You are out to wed women when the land around your camp is still drenched with the blood of over a thousand martyrs."

In Iraq, in the battle of Daumatul Jandal fought in 633 A.D. Khalid married the beautiful daughter of the chief Judi bin Rabee'a. Hadrat Umar spoke critically of this marriage to Hadrat Abu Bakr. Hadrat Abu Bakr disposed of the matter with the remarks:

> "Khalid has a soft corner in his heart for beautiful women. He is the victor, and he may well have Bint Judi as his prize, if that is his pleasure."

At the battle of Muzayyah in Iraq fought under the command of Khalid two Muslims, Abdullah and Labid were killed. Khalid was criticised for killing two Muslims. Hadrat Umar was very bitter and pressed for action against Khalid. Hadrat Abu Bakr again took a lenient view. He held that such things were likely to occur when Muslims chose to live in the midst of non-Muslims against whom military operations were undertaken. Hadrat Abu Bakr paid blood money out of the Baitul Mal to the heirs of the two persons who had been killed.

HADRAT UMAR AS ADVISER

During the Caliphate of the Hadrat Abu Bakr, Hadrat Umar was the principal Adviser of the Caliph.

A story is on record showing the great esteem and regard that Hadrat Abu Bakr had for Hadrat Umar and his opinion.

It is related that once Ayanayah bin Hassan and Aqrah bin Habas two tribal chiefs waited on Hadrat Abu Bakr, and requested that an estate be awarded to them. They suggested that close to their settlement there was a rock waste land which produced nothing, and that that wasteland might be gifted to them so that by their efforts they might make it productive.

Hadrat Abu Bakr consulted the people around him. They suggested that it was a good proposition for thereby the wasteland would become productive. Hadrat Abu Bakr accordingly agreed to award the land in question to them. A document was drawn up. Hadrat Umar was not present and Hadrat Abu Bakr advised the grantees to get it witnessed by Hadrat Umar.

The grantees thought that such witnessing by Hadrat Umar was merely formal and that there would be no difficulty in obtaining his signature, on the document. The grantees went to Hadrat Umar and requested him to affix his signatures to the document as it had been approved by Hadrat Abu Bakr.

After reading the document, Hadrat Umar returned it to the grantees saying that he could not be a party to the deed.

The grantees in a fit of anger went to Hadrat Abu Bakr and reported what Hadrat Umar had said.

Hadrat Abu Bakr remained quiet. Thereupon the grantees turning to the Caliph said "Are you the Caliph, or is Hadrat Umar the Caliph ?"

Hadrat Abu Bakr said "You may very well take Hadrat Umar to be the Caliph".

Then Hadrat Umar came to the Caliph. Hadrat Abu Bakr enquired what was the reason for his refusal to sign the document.

Hadrat Umar asked "Is the land which you have gifted your property or is it a trust with you on behalf of the Muslim community".

Hadrat Abu Bakr said "It is not my personal property; as such it should be a trust on behalf of the Muslim community."

Hadrat Umar said "If that is the position, how can you extinguish the trust by gifting it to A or B. They may take it on lease subject to terms, but it must remain the State property."

Turning to the applicants, Hadrat Abu Bakr said "Umar has spoken the truth. I cannot deviate from the law."

Turning to Hadrat Umar, Hadrat Abu Bakr said "I had already requested you to take over the office of the Caliph, but you thrust the burden on my shoulders. I may not be with you for long and ultimately this responsibility will have to be shouldered by you."

HADRAT ABU BAKR AND HADRAT UMAR

Between the Holy Prophet and Hadrat Abu Bakr, the latter was "The Second of the Two'. A similar equation obtained between Hadrat Abu Bakr and Hadrat Umar. When Hadrat Abu Bakr became the Caliph, Hadrat Umar was decidedly the 'Second of the Two'. The attachment and friendship between the two was of an exceptional character. Each preferred the other to Himself. After the death of the Holy Prophet Hadrat Abu Bakr wanted Hadrat Umar to be the Caliph, and Hadrat Umar took steps to have Hadrat Abu Bakr elected as the Caliph. The Holy Prophet often came to the mosque flanked by Hadrat Abu Bakr on one side, and Hadrat Umar on the other.

Hadrat Umar and Hadrat Abu Bakr vied with each other in doing good. In this connection some stories have come down to us which highlight the equation between Hadrat Abu Bakr and Hadrat Umar.

In 633 A.D. the Holy Prophet decided to lead an expedition, to Tabuk on the Syrian border. In order to finance the expedition, the Holy Prophet invited contributions and donations from his followers. Hadrat Umar had then considerable money with him. He thought that that was the occasion when he might excel Hadrat Abu Bakr in the doing of good. Hadrat Umar went home and brought his donation. The Holy Prophet enquired of Hadrat Umar as to what he had left behind for Himself and his family. Hadrat Umar stated that he had donated one half of his wealth in the name of Allah and had left one half for Himself and his family. Then Hadrat Abu Bakr came with his donation and the Holy Prophet put him the same question as to how much he had left for Himself and his family. Hadrat Abu Bakr said that he had donated all that he had in the name of Allah, and that he had left Allah and His Prophet for Himself and his family. This episode has formed the theme of one of the poems of Iqbal. The poem provides;

> "For the moth the lamp and for the nightingle the flower;
> For Sidiq, God and His Prophet alone suffice."

On that account Hadrat Umar realised that it was difficult to excel Hadrat Abu Bakr in the doing of good.

Abu Yala records from Ibn Masud that he said "I was in the mosque praying when there entered the Apostle of God and with him were Hadrat Abu Bakr and Hadrat Umar. He found me praying and said 'Ask and it shall be granted unto thee'. Then he said 'Whosoever wishes to read the Qur'an in a fresh and joyous manner let him read it with the reading of lbn Masud'. Then I returned to my house and Hadrat Abu Bakr came to me and gave me the good tidings regarding what the Holy Prophet had said. Then came Hadrat Umar and he found Hadrat Abu Bakr going forth having already been before him, and he said 'Verily Abu Bakr is the foremost in good'."

Even when Hadrat Umar was not the Caliph, it was his practice to move about in Madina and help persons in distress.

In one of the suburbs of Madina there lived a blind old women who had no one to help her. Hadrat Umar used to go in disguise to the house of the old woman, but was always surprised to find that some one else had anticipated him, and supplied the wants of the old lady.

Hadrat Umar felt much distressed that in this noble task of helping a lady in distress his efforts were always frustrated by some other person. Hadrat Umat felt curious as to who that person could be who beat him in the field of social service.

One day, Hadrat Umar went to the house of the old woman earlier than usual and hid Himself to watch as to who was the person who attended to the wants of the old woman.

Hadrat Umar did not have to wait long for soon a man arrived who attended to the needs of the old woman, and this man was none other than the Caliph Hadrat Abu Bakr.

Hadrat Umar felt relieved that if in the matter of social service he had been beaten by any one, such person was the Caliph Hadrat Abu Bakr who was decidedly superior to him.

PART II

The Caliphate of Hadrat Umar

NOMINATION OF HADRAT UMAR AS THE CALIPH

On the seventh Jamadi-ul Akhir of the 13th A.H. (8th August 633) which was a cold day, Hadrat Abu Bakr took a bath and caught a chill. That developed into a high fever.

Hadrat Abu Bakr was confined to bed, and he appointed Hadrat Umar to lead the prayers during the period of his illness. His illness prolonged, and when his condition worsened, he felt that his end was near. It was suggested to him that a physician be called. He said "Now all is over."

Realising that his end was drawing near, Hadrat Abu Bakr felt that he should nominate his successor, so that the issue might not be a cause of dissension among the Muslims after his death. Hadrat Abu Bakr summoned Abdul Rahman bin Auf, and asked for his opinion about the nomination of Hadrat Umar. Some other Companions were also consulted.

The general concensus was that Hadrat Umar was the fittest person to be appointed as the Caliph. It was, however, felt that Hadrat Umar had too fiery and tirascible temper, and he might not be able to show moderation so necessary for the Head of the Community.

Hadrat Abu Bakr observed that Hadrat Umar's display of severity was meant to counteract his (Hadrat Abu Bakr's) leniency. Hadrat Abu Bakr felt confident that when the full responsibility of government devolved upon Hadrat Umar he would become more moderate in his opinions.

Hadrat Abu Bakr elaborated.

"I can say from my personal experience that Hadrat Umar had always cooled me down whenever I lost my temper with any one just as whenever he felt me to be too lenient he counselled greater severity. For this reason I feel certain that with time, Umar will achieve that moderation you desire."

Taleah objected to the nomination of Hadrat Umar and said,

"O successor of the Prophet ; You know full well how harsh Umar has been towards us all during your regime and God only knows how he will dear with us when you are gone. You know that you are leaving us for ever, and yet you are content to leave us in the hands of a man whose fierce and ungovernable rages are well known to you. Think O Chief, what answer will you give to your Lord for such a behest."

At this, Hadrat Abu Bakr who was lying prostrate in his bed, rose up with considerable effort and said:

"Have you come to frighten me? I swear that when I meet my Lord, I will gladly tell Him that I appointed as ruler over his people, the man who was the best of all mankind."

Thereupon Hadrat Ali, who was also present, rose to say that he would acknowledge no other Caliph save Hadrat Umar. Hadrat Abu Bakr was much impressed with the selflessness of Hadrat Ali for not pressing his own claim, and for putting the interests of the Muslim community above personal interests. Turning to Hadrat Ali, Hadrat Abu Bakr said:

"You are indeed a prince in the most exalted sense of the term, for others are mere men."

Then Hadrat Abu Bakr sent for Hadrat Umar, and informed him that he had appointed him as his successor.

Hadrat Umar said : "But I have no desire for the office." Thereupon, Hadrat Abu Bakr said:

"But the office needs you. I have prayed to God to direct me rightly in the choice of my successor, and my choice is fundamental for the unity and strength of the Muslims."

Hadrat Umar acquiesced, and Hadrat Abu Bakr dictated the testament to Hadrat Usman appointing Hadrat Umar as the Caliph in succession to Hadrat Abu Bakr.

The testament having been drawn up. Hadrat Abu Bakr, supported by his wife Asma walked up to the door, and A.D. dressed the people who had gathered there. He told them that he had appointed Hadrat Umar as his successor, and they said "We approve."

After obtaining the approval of the people in general terms, Hadrat Abu Bakr lay on the bed and prayed to God ;

"O Lord ! I have made this testament for the welfare of the community in order to counteract discord among them. What my intentions are, yoú know full well. I have spared no pains in making the best selection. O God, I entrust the Muslims to your care. O Allah keep their ruler on the right path. O God, make my successor the most pious of rulers and confer peace on the Muslims."

HADRAT UMAR'S INAUGURAL A.D. DRESS

After the assumption of office as the Caliph, Hadrat Umar A.D. dressed the Muslims who had assembled in the Prophet's mosque. In the course of the A.D. dress, Hadrat Umar said:

"O ye faithful ! Hadrat Abu Bakr is no more amongst us. After having led us for about two years, he has returned to His Maker. He has the satisfaction that he has successfully piloted the ship of the Muslim state to safety after negotiating the stormy sea. He successfully waged the apostasy wars, and thanks to him, Islam is now supreme in Arabia. Islam is now on the move and we are carrying Jihad in the name of Allah against the mighty empires of Byzantine and Persia.

After Hadrat Abu Bakr, the mantle of Khilafat has fallen on my shoulders. I swear it before God that I never coveted this office. I wished that it would have devolved on some other person more worthy than me. But now that in national interest, the responsibility for leading the Muslims has come to vest in me, I assure you that I will not run away from my post, and will make an earnest effort to discharge the onerous duties of the office to the best of my capacity in accordance with the injunctions of Islam.

In the performance of my duties, I will seek guidance from the Holy Book, and will follow the examples set by the Holy Prophet and Hadrat Abu Bakr. In this task I seek your assistance. If I follow the right path, follow me. If I deviate from the right path, correct me so that we are not led astray.

Now brothers I offer a few prayers and you say Amen to them.

O Allah I am hard, make me soft to promote the Truth, to comply with your injunctions and to aspire to a better life in the world hereafter.

O Allah make me hard for the enemies of Islam and for those who create mischief so that their designs against Allah come to naught.

O Allah I am miser ; make me generous in the promotion of the good.

O Allah save me from hypocrisy. Strengthen my resolves so that whatever I do, I do for the sake of winning Your approbation.

O Allah soften my heart for the faithful so that I attend to their needs with a sense of dedication.

O Allah, I am careless, make me responsible enough so that I do not lose sight of You.

O Allah I am weak in offering my obedience to You ; make me active and fortify my faith.

O Allah bestow on me faith, and the power to do good.

O Allah give me the power of self-criticism and self-assessment.

O Allah bestow on me the insight into the meaning of the Qur'an and the strength to act in accordance with what the Qur'an says.

O Allah You are capable of doing anything : bless us with Your favour.

Amen.

HADRAT UMAR'S A.D. DRESS ABOUT HIS CONDUCT

After the assumption of office as Caliph, Hadrat Umar soon realised that he was more feared than loved. Hadrat Abu Bakr his predecessor was tender and soft hearted. Whenever he appeared in the streets of Madina, the children ran to him saying "Father, Father." He caressed and patted them. When Hadrat Umar became Caliph, the children would run away at his sight saying "Here comes Umar, let us run away."

On the occasion of the first Friday prayer after his assumption of office as Caliph, Hadrat Umar A.D. dressed the faithful assembled in the mosque in the following terms:

> "Brethern, it has come to my notice that the people are afraid of me. They say 'When the Holy Prophet was alive, Umar was harsh to us. During the Caliphate of Hadrat Abu Bakr, Umar was hard and stern. Now that he has become the Caliph himself, God knows how hard he will be. Whoever has said this is not wrong in his assessment.

The truth of the matter is that I was the slave and servant of the Holy Prophet. The Holy Prophet was most kind hearted, liberal and generous. In contrast I was hard and harsh so that I was like a naked sword. It was for the Holy Prophet to use the sword or sheathe it at his option. On occasions he sheathed the sword, and sometimes he used it. My purpose was to point to the Holy Prophet the other side of the picture. The decision rested with him. Sometimes he ignored my point of view. There were occasions when he agreed with me. Till the death of the Holy Prophet that remained the equation between him and me. Thank God, the Holy Prophet was pleased with me. Though the Holy Prophet sometimes accepted my A.D. vice, and sometimes turned it down, yet he approved of my conduct.

During the caliphate of Hadrat Abu Bakr my role remained the same. Hadrat Abu Bakr was most soft hearted and tender. It as my business to bring the other side of the picture to his notice. He always took my point of view into consideration, but the ultimate decision lay with him. Sometimes he agreed with me, and I acted as his agent to enforce a decision which appeared to be harsh. Sometimes he did not agree with me, and I had to remain quite. I am happy that throughout the period of his office, Hadrat Abu Bakr approved of my conduct, and ultimately nominated me as his successor, although I did not covet the office.

Now that the entire responsibility has come to vest in me, know ye brethern that you will feel a change in me. I will no longer be hard and stern in all matters. For those who practise tyranny and deprive others of their rights, I will be harsh and stern, but for those who follow the law, and are devoted to religion, I will be most soft and tender. I will not tolerate any person make any excess. He who commits any tyranny, him I will sternly call to book. I will be harsh and stern against the aggressor, but I will be a pillar of strength for the weak and the meek. They will find in me their best friend.

Friends you have some rights on me, and I tell you of these rights, so that you may be in a position to call me to account. These rights are :

firstly, that I should not exact any tax or other levy from you not authorised by law ;

secondly, that whatever taxes are lawfully realised from you are spent in your best interests :

thirdly, it is incumbent on me that I should protect the frontiers of your land ;

fourthly, it is my duty to promote your prosperity and look after your interests ; and fifthly, it is my obligation to do justice.

O servants of God, continue to fear God. Suppress your selfish motives and work for the solidarity of the Muslims as a whole. In running the State, you are my partners. Help me with your sound A.D. vice. If I follow the right path laid down by God and His Prophet follow me. If I deviate, correct me. Strengthen me with your A.D. vice and suggestions. Let us pray for the glory of Islam."

AMIRUL MUMININ

When the Holy Prophet died, and Hadrat Abu Bakr succeeded him he was called "Khalifa tul Rasul", i.e. the representative of the Prophet.

When Hadrat Abu Bakr died and Hadrat Umar succeeded him he called himself 'Khalifa', but the question arose whose Khalifa or representative he was. It was pointed out that strictly speaking he was not the Khalifa of the Rasul. He was the Khalifa of the Khalifatul Rasul. Hadrat Umar felt that this was a cumbersome title, for in that case, those who followed him would have to be designated by an endless chain of Khalifas

Hadrat Umar accordingly felt that the Head of the Muslim State should be known by a simpler title which should reflect the Islamic character of the State. Hadrat Umar asked the people around him to ponder over the matter, and if they could think of some suitable title they should bring such title to his notice.

One day Labid bin Rabia and A.D. i bin Hatim came to Madina from Kufa. They alighted at the Prophet's mosque and there coming across Amr b. Al-Aas asked him to announce their arrival to the Amir-ul-Muminin.

Amr b. Al-Aas was struck by the novelty of the term 'Amir-ul-Muminin'. He asked Labid and A.D. i as to how they referred to Hadrat Umar as 'Amir-ul-Muminin'. They said "We all Muslims are Momins and Hadrat Umar is our Commander. He is thus 'Amir-ul-Muminin".

Amr b. Al-Aas said "Wonderful. You have hit upon a beautiful term. God bless You".

Amr b. Al-Aas hastened to Hadrat Umar and there said "Amir-ul-Muminin, two persons have come from Kufa, they seek permission to see you."

Hadrat Umar became curious at being A.D. dressed "Amir-ul-Muminin". He asked Amr b. Al-Aas as to how he had coined the term 'Amir-ul-Muminin'. Amr b. Al-Aas said that the visitors from Kufa had used that term, and as he was attracted by the term he had used it.

Hadrat Umar said "We were in search of some suitable term to signify the office I hold, and here is a term which is attractive." He asked Amr b. Al-Aas as to what he thought of the title.

Amr b. Al-Aas said "I am attracted by the term. It is God sent. We all are Muslims and your are our Amir. The term is very attractive and significant."

After Hadrat Umar had seen the visitors from Kufa, he convened a meeting of his consultative assembly, and there the question was discussed whether he should A.D. opt the title of 'Amir-ul-Muminin' for the office that he held. The Assembly approved the title.

Henceforward Hadrat Umar came to be A.D. dressed in his official capacity as Amir-ul-Muminin.

HADRAT UMAR'S ALLOWANCE

Before becoming the Caliph Hadrat Umar lived by trade. After assuming the Caliph he could no longer carry on charge as his business. He accordingly agreed to accept a daily allowance from the Baitul Mal. Different amounts of daily allowance were suggested by different people. Hadrat Umar sought the A.D. vice of Hadrat Ali as to the amount of the allowance he should accept. Hadrat Ali suggested that he should take as much amount as might moderately suffice for an average Arab, neither too much, nor too little. Hadrat Umar accepted this suggestion and a modest amount of allowance was settled for him. The exact amount of the allowance thus settled is, however, not reported in any history.

Later on some companions including Hadrat Ali, Usman, Zubair, and Talha thought of increasing the allowince of Hadrat Umar as it was not sufficient to meet the minimum requirements of Hadrat Umar. These companions could not have the courage to broach this subject to Hadrat Umar direct. They accordingly approached Hadrat Hafsa the daughter of Hadrat Umar, and asked her to ascertain Hadrat Umar's reaction to the proposal.

When Hadrat Hafsa talked about the matter of Hadrat Umar, he became angry and wanted to know who were the persons who had made that suggestion. Hadrat Hafsa said that before she could tell who were the persons concerned she wanted his reaction to the proposal.

Thereupon Hadrat Umar wanted Hadrat Hafsa to tell what was the Holy Prophet's best dress in her house. She said that it was a pair of clothes of red colour which the Holy Prophet wore on Fridays or when receiving envoys.

Hadrat Umar then asked what was the best of food that the Holy Prophet took. She said that the Holy Prophet's food was simple barley bread. Hadrat Umar next asked as to what was the best bedding that the Holy Prophet ever used. She said that it was a piece of thick cloth. In summer it was spread in four layers and in winter in two, half he spread underneath, and with the other half he covered himself.

Thereupon Hadrat Umar said:

> "Hafsa, go and tell the people who have deputed you that the Holy Prophet has set a standard by his personal example. I must follow him. My case and that of the Holy Prophet and Hadrat Abu Bakr is like the case of three men travelling on the same road. The first man started with a provision and reached the goal. The second followed the first and joined him. Now the third is on his way. If he follows their way he will also join them, otherwise he can never reach them."

When Hadrat Hafsa told of Hadrat Umar's reaction to the proposal to the companions who had deputed her they said: "May God bless Umar. He excels all of us in the matter of virtue."

EXPULSION OF JEWS AND CHRISTIANS FROM ARABIA

At the time of his death the Holy Prophet had expressed the view that in Arabia there should be only one religion, namely Islam. During the lif-time of the Holy Prophet, all the tribes in Arabia had accepted Islam. There were only a few pockets of non-Muslims, the Jews in Khyber, and the Christians in Najran.

During the caliphate of Hadrat Abu Bakr, many tribes who had accepted Islam apostatised. As a result of the apostasy wars, all the apostate tribes were defeated and they once again accepted Islam. During the brief period of his office, Hadrat Abu Bakr allowed the status quo to continue with regard to the Jews and the Christians.

At the time of the conquest of Khyber, a treaty was executed with the Jews whereunder they were allowed to clutivate the lands on the payment of one half of the produce to the Muslim state at Madina. The treaty also provided that the Jews could be turned out of Khyber, whenever the Muslim state deemed it necessary.

When Hadrat Umar became the Caliph he deputed his son Abdullah to Khyber to collect the revenue. As Abdullah lay sleeping on the roof of a house in Khyber at night, his bed was overturned by the Jews causing him an injury in the arm. Hadrat Umar investigated the matter and found that the Jews were bent on mischief. Hadrat Umar accordingly passed orders expelling the Jews from Khyber. They migrated to Syria. They were allowed to carry their movable belongings with them. Their immovable property in Khyber was distributed among the Muslims.

The Christians of Najran near Yemen had a pact with the Holy Prophet whereunder they were allowed to live in peace unless they indulged in any hostile activities against Islam. It was also stipulated that they would not indulge in usury. When Hadrat Umar became the Caliph it was brought to his notice that the Christians of Najran had violated the peace pact in as much as they were indulging in usury, and were also guilty of activities hostile to Islam.

Hadrat Umar summoned the representatives of the Christians of Najran, and apprised them of the charge of violating the terms of the treaty. In a vainglorious mood the deputationists said "If that was that, they might be expelled." Hadrat Umar accordingly passed orders for their expulsion. Arrangements were made for their settlement in Iraq. They were allowed to carry their entire movable property with them. Their immovable property was acquired by the State on payment.

Hadrat Umar instructed his officers in Iraq that all possible assistance should be provided for the settlement of the refugees from Najran in Iraq. The Christians were exempted from the payment of Jizya for the first two years.

With the expulsion of the Jews and the Christians from Arabia, the country became an exclusively Muslim land. Hadrat Umar has thus the distinction of being the first ruler under whom Arabia became the exclusive preserve for Islam.

TARAWIH

In the month of the Holy Ramdan, it was the practice with the Holy Prophet that he would stay in the mosque after the Isha prayers, and offer extra prayers. One night as the faithful saw the Holy Prophet offering extra prayers, they also prayed as the Holy Prophet did. The following night more Muslims stayed in the mosque after the night prayer to offer extra prayers. On the third night there was a still larger gathering of the Muslims to perform the extra prayers. On the fourth night when a large number of the faithful assembled to offer the extra prayers, the Holy Prophet did not offer the extra prayers and retired to his house immediately after the Isha prayers. For the following nights as well the Holy Prophet retired immediately after the night prayers, and gradually the number of Muslims who offered the extra prayers diminished. Then one night the Holy Prophet offered the extra prayers again. When the Holy Prophet was asked about the reason for the break in the extra prayers for some nights he said that he had avoided these prayers lest the Muslims might take them to be an obligation under law, and that might become a burden for the Muslims. The Holy Prophet explained that such prayers were not compulsory, but if any one offered them voluntarily, he would have the blessing of God. Thereafter it became the practice that some Muslims offered the extra prayers during the month of Ramdan on their own account, while others did not, and retired to their homes after offering the night prayers.

When Hadrat Umar became the Caliph, he saw that many Muslims gathered in the Prophet's mosque to offer extra prayers after the night prayers. Each person prayed according to his own discretion, and there were no specifications about the number of *Rakaats* to be offered. Hadrat Umar felt that it would be a reform in the proper direction, if the prayers were offered in congregation and the number of *Rakaats* was fixed. After consulting the Companions, Hadrat Umar issued instructions in 635 A.D. that such extra prayers should be offered in congregation under the imamate of a Qur'an reader who should recite a considerable part of the Qur'an each night, so that the entire Qur'an was completed during a week or so. It was laid down that these prayers should comprise ten *taslima's* each containing two *rakaats* and that after every four *rakaats* there should be a *'rawih'* or a pause. Because of such pauses these extra prayers came to be known as *'Tarawih'*.

These instructions were circulated throughout the Muslim dominions. There were some who felt that as the Holy Prophet had not prescribed such prayers, it was unlawful to prescribe such prayers after the death of the Holy Prophet. Hadrat Umar explained that he was not prescribing these prayers as compulsory ; it was open to any one to offer or not to offer these prayers at his discretion. If any one offered these prayers that would be to his credit, but if any body did not do so that would not bring him any discredit. He also elucidated that his instructions being of an A.D. visory character only were in no way repugnant to Islam. If he had instructed the Muslims to do what Allah or the Holy Prophet had prohibited that would have been repugnant to Islam, but if he wanted the Muslims to do anything at their option which was intrinsically good and had not been prophibited, that was not repugnant to Islam, but was on the other hand in consonance with the spirit of Islam.

HADRAT UMAR AND THE HOLY QUR'AN

The Holy Qur'an was revealed to the Holy Prophet in parts from time to time spread over a period of 23 years. Whenever the Holy Prophet received the revelation he would dictate it to one of his *Katibs* who would record it on some piece of leather, date skin, or even bones and stones.

The principal scribe of the Holy Prophet was Zaid bin Thabit. Many companions committed the entire Qur'an to memory and these *'Huffaz'* could recite the entire Qur'an any time. The Holy Prophet kept all the pieces of leather, date skins another materials on which the verses of the Holy Qur'an had been written in his custody.

During the lif-time of the Holy Prophet, revelation was a continuous process, and there was no occasion for giving them the form of a book. After the death of the Holy Prophet, the process of revelation came to close, and now the need of some sort of compilation to preserve the Word of God was felt.

In the battle of Yamama, most of the Companions who had learnt the Holy Qur'an by heart were martyred. Hadrat Umar was the first to feel that if those who had committed the Holy Qur'an to memory were dead, there was the danger that there would be none left who could be relied upon as the repository of the Qur'an. There was also the danger that with the lapse of time there might be some interpolations in the text inadvertently or even deliberately.

Hadrat Umar suggested to the Caliph Hadrat Abu Bakr that the Holy Qur'an should be suitably compiled under the authority of the State. Hadrat Abu Bakr was reluctant to undertake the project. His plea was that as the Holy Prophet had not felt the necessity for such a compilation, it did not behove him as the successor to the Prophet to take any initiative in the matter.

Hadrat Umar, however, continued to press his point. Hadrat Umar argued that during the lif-time of the Holy Prophet the process of revelation was continuous, and as the Holy Prophet himself was the repository of all revelations, there was no occasion for such a compilation. After the death of the Holy Prophet, the position had changed, and unless the Holy Qur'an was compiled, there was the danger that the Qur'an might be lost. In the absence of an authentic text, there was also the danger that some unscrupulous persons might A.D. d to or vary the text to suit their interests. The argument appealed to Hadrat Abu Bakr, and when other prominent Muslims were consulted, they also endorsed the views of Hadrat Umar. Hadrat Abu Bakr accordingly undertook the project for the compilation of the Holy Qur'an.

Zaid b. Thabit was commissioned by Hadrat Abu Bakr to collect all the verses of the Holy Qur'an and compile them in a book form.

Zaid's immediate reaction to the proposal was that if he had been asked to remove a mountain from its original site, and place it elsewhere, he would have considered such a task easier than the task of collecting the Holy Qur'an. Hadrat Abu Bakr and Hadrat Umar appreciated the gravity of the problem, but observed that as the Word of God had to be preserved for the guidance of the coming generations, the task had to be undertaken whatever the odds. Zaid thereupon set to the task of collecting the verses.

A proclamation was made that whosoever had learnt any portion of the Qur'an from the Holy Prophet should produce such portion. Two witnesses had to be produced in each case to establish the genuineness of the verse. When all the verses had been collected a Committee was set up of which Hadrat Umar was a member. This Committee supervised the compilation of the Holy Qur'an. Sad b. Al-Aas dictated, and Zaid bin Thabit wrote the Holy Qur'an. These was checked by the members of the Committee including Hadrat Umar.

When the work was completed it was further checked by Hadrat Abu Bakr, and the finally approved copy was kept by Hadrat Abu Bakr in his personal custody. The sacred compilation was given the name of *'Mashaf'*.

During his Caliphate, Hadrat Umar took steps to ensure that the teaching of the Holy Qur'an was spread extensively, and that a large number of persons learnt the text by heart so that there could be no possibility of any corruption in the text.

Under the orders of Hadrat Umar, hundreds of schools were opened throughout the length and breadth of the Islamic world for the teaching of the Holy Qur'an. Highly qualified teachers were appointed for the purpose, and they were given good salaries.

Such Companions who had learnt the Holy Qur'an by heart were sent to distant places to teach the Holy Qur'an. Muadh b. Jabal ; Ibada b. Al-Samit ; and Abu Darda were prominent companions who knew the Holy Qur'an by heart. They were sent to Syria where Ibada headed the school at Hims : Abu Darda at Damascus; and Muadh at Jerusalem. It is related that Abu Darda held his classes in the Jamia Masjid at Damascus and the enrolment in his class was 1600.

Hadrat Umar took pains in promoting and popularising the study of the Holy Qur'an. All the Muslims were required to learn at least five Suras by heart. Special stipends were granted for the learning of the Holy Qur'an. In his instructions to the Army, Hadrat Umar exhorted the men to read and memorise the Holy Qur'an.

Hadrat Umar was very particular about the use of correct vowels and the correct pronunciation of the words in the Holy Qur'an. In his instructions to the teachers of the Holy Qur'an, Hadrat Umar said :

"Teach them the vowels of the Qur'an, as you teach its leaning by heart."

Hadrat Umar also instructed that along with the teaching of the Holy Qur'an, the study of the Arabic language and literature should be made compulsory so that the readers of the Holy Qur'an should themselves be able to distinguish between right and wrong vowels.

Hadrat Umar also laid down that no one who was not versed in Arabic lexicology should be permitted to teach the Holy Qur'an.

HADRAT UMAR AND MOSQUES

As the Islamic dominions extended progressively, Hadrat Umar ordered that mosques should be built in all conquered territories.

In the newly founded cities of Kufa and Basra, Jami Masjids were built in the centre of the city and smaller mosques were built in each tribal quarter.

In the case of smaller towns in Iraq and Syria, a mosque was required to be constructed in each town. According to one account as many as 4000 mosques were constructed during the caliphate of Hadrat Umar.

Hadrat Umar had the sacred mosque at Ka'aba extended. In 739 A.D. Hadrat Umar purchased the surrounding houses at state expense. These were demolished, and the area under them was included in the mosque. Heretofore there was no wall round the mosque. Hadrat Umar had a wall constructed for the first time. Heretofore the mosques were not lit. Hadrat Umar provided lights for the mosques for the first time.

Formerly the cover of the Ka'aba was of ordinary cloth. Hadrat Umar had the cover made of a superior and finer cloth manufactured in Egypt.

The bounds of the Haram, the sanctuary of the Ka'aba extended to three miles in one direction, and seven to nine miles in other directions. The boundaries were not defined, and there was the risk of this area being encroached upon. Hadrat Umar had the area surveyed, and the boundaries were demarcated. Stone pillars called *Ansab* were fixed to mark the boundaries.

Hadrat Umar extended the Prophet's Mosque at Madina as well. In 739 A.D. , the same year as the Ka'aba was extended,

Hadrat Umar purchased the houses that surrounded the Masjid-i-Nabvi. After demolishing them, the area was utilised for the extension of the mosque.

Hadrat Abbas whose house also surrounded the mosque refused to sell his house. He sued the state in the Court of the Qazi Ubayy b. Kab. The Court gave its verdict against the state, and held that the property could not be acquired compulsorily. Hadrat Umar accepted the verdict of the Court. Thereupon Hadrat Abbas voluntarily gifted his house for the extension of the mosque. Hadrat Umar accepted the gift gratefully, and provided alternative accommodation to Hadrat Abbas.

As a result of extension the length of the mosque rose from 100 to 140 yards while its width rose from 60 to 80 yards.

Hadrat Umar was the first to provide lights for Masjid-i-Nabvi. Hadrat Umar also made arrangements for the burning of the incense in the mosque. The floor of the mosque was paved and covered with mats.

THE HIJRI CALENDAR

Some time in 638 A.D. , Abu Musa Asha'ari, the Governor of Basra wrote:

> "Amir-ul-Mominin, we receive instructions from you every now and then, but as the letters are undated, and sometimes the contents of the letters differ, it becomes difficult to ascertain as to which instructions are to be followed."

That set Hadrat Umar thinking. In the meantime, he received from Yemen a draft for some money which was encashable in Shaban. Hadrat Umar thought that the practice of merely mentioning the month in such cases was defective for one could not be sure whether the month referred to was of the current or the following year.

Hadrat Umar convened an assembly to consider the question of calendar reform.

Some one suggested that the Roman calendar should be A.D. opted. After discussion the proposal was rejected as the Roman calendar dated from too remote an era and was cumbersome.

It was next considered whether the Persian calendar might be A.D. opted. Hormuzan explained the salient features of the Persian calendar called 'Mahroz'. The consensus of opinion was that such a calendar would not be suitable for the Muslims.

The general opinion was that instead of A.D. opting any alien calendar, the Muslims should have a calendar of their own. This was agreed to, and the point next considered was from when should such an era begin?

Some one suggested that the era should begin from the date of birth of the Holy Prophet. Some suggested that it should begin from the death of the Holy Prophet. Hadrat Ali suggested that it shoutd begin from the date the Muslims migrated from Mecca to Madina. After discussion, Hadrat Ali's suggestion was agreed to.

The Holy Prophet had migrated in the month of Rabi-ul-Awwal, when the year had already run two months and eight days. Next the question arose from which month should the new era start.

Some one suggested that the calendar should start with the month of Rajab as in the pre-Islamic period this month was held sacred. Some one proposed that the first month should be Ramdhan as that is a sacred month for the Muslims. Another proposal was that the first month should be 'Zul Hajj' as that is the month of the pilgrimage.

Hadrat Usman suggested that as in Arabia the year started with Muharram the new era should also start with Muharram. This suggestion was accepted. The date was accordingly pushed back by two months and eight days, and the new Hijri calendar began with the first day of Muharram in the year of migration rather than from the actual date of migration.

Hadrat Umar accordingly issued instructions to all concerned regarding the enforcement of the Hijri calendar.

HADRAT UMAR AND DRINKING

Drinking was very common among the Quraish. Some accounts say that during the days of ignorance even Hadrat Umar was a wine bibbler. When Hadrat Umar became a Muslim, he never touched wine. Hadrat Umar was a great thinker. He thought that as under the influence of drink one becomes oblivious of his duties and responsibilities, drink must be prohibited by an injunction from God. Hadrat Umar often talked to the Holy Prophet on the subject, and prayed for an injunction to enforce prohibition.

At Madina the following verse was revealed to the Holy Prophet:

> "They ask you about wine and games of chance. Say, 'They lead to great sin, and have some use for men. But the sin inherent in them exceeds their usefulness." (2: 219)

The Holy Prophet informed Hadrat Umar of this revelation. Hadrat Umar said : "Holy Prophet, this is not enough, pray to God for a specific injunction."

Some time later came another revelation, namely :

> "Believers ! wine, games of chance, idols, and diving arrows are abominations which are the handiwork of the Devil. Avoid them so that you may prosper." (5: 90)

When Hadrat Umar was informed of this revleation, he said:

> "Holy Prophet ; this is a negative provision. Pray to God to give some positive injunction."

Then another verse was revealed which provided :

> "The Devil intends that by means of wine, games of chance, he should provoke enmity and hatred among you; and stop you from remembering Allah and saying your prayers. Will you not keep them away from them?"
> (5: 91)

This verse provided the necessary sanction for the prohibition of drinking. In spite of this injunction many Muslims continued to indulge in drinking.

When Hadrat Umar became the Caliph, and the Muslim conquests extended east and west, bringing prosperity to the Muslims, Hadrat Umar felt that in order to safeguard the purity of faith some hard and fast policy about drinking should be laid down. While the Holy Qur'an provided specific punishments for some offences, no penalty was specified in the case of drinking. That made some of the wine bibblers take the plea that if God intended prohibition, the penalty for the offence would have been prescribed.

Hadrat Umar convened a meeting of his Consultative Assembly to consider the question. The first question that was taken up for consideration was : whether the drinking of wine was lawful or unlawful. The verdict was that it was unlawful.

The next question was : if it was unlawful what should be the penalty therefor. Hadrat Umar agreed that no penalty in this behalf had been laid down in the Holy Qur'an, but he held that a penalty therefor could be laid down on the basis of analogy keeping in view the penalty provided for offences of kindred character.

Hadrat Ali argued that the offence of drinking was of the same species as calumny for under the influence of drink one was apt to say many things which he should not have otherwise said. In the case of calumny the Holy Qur'an provided punishment as follows :

> "Give eighty lashes to each one,
> Of those who accuse honourable women ;
> But do not support their accusation with four
> witnesses.

> Do not accept their testimony,
> For it is they who break the law."

Hadrat Ali A.D. vised that for drinking the same penalty i.e. eighty lashes should be provided.

This A.D. vice was accepted by Hadrat Umar. Hadrat Umar issued orders to all concerned to the following effect :

> "Drinking is banned under the Holy Qur'an. If any Muslim drinks and pleads that this was lawful then cut off his head for what he says is a violation of the Holy Word. If he says that it is unlawful but that he fell into error then give him eighty lashes publicly."

These instructions were enforced vigorously, and the Muslim society was practically rid of the evil of drinking.

SLAVERY

When Islam appeared on the world stage, the world economy was based on slavery. Islam was the first religion to raise its voice against slavery. Among the early converts to Islam, many were slaves. Indeed one of the reasons for the hostility of the Quraish against Islam was that they saw in Islam a hostile force to slavery on which the economy of Mecca was based.

When Hadrat Umar became the Caliph of Islam, he took particular measures to eliminate the evils of slavery as far as possible. He took a very bold step when he declared that no Arab could be a slave. Arabia was thus the first country in the world, which under the impact of Islam abolished slavery. During the apostasy wars many Arabs had been taken captive and made slaves. Hadrat Umar emancipated all such slaves.

Hadrat Umar also decreed that slave women who had borne a child to her master stood emancipated.

The Holy Qur'an laid down :

"If you see good in them (slaves), make agreement with them."

Hadrat Umar implemented this injunction and laid down that a slave could make an agreement with the master that he would pay so much within the specified period to secure his freedom. Anas had a slave Sirin by name. The slave wanted to enter into an agreement with his master, but Anas refused. When the matter was reported to Hadrat Umar, he made Anas enter into an agreement with his slave.

In the matter of stipends allowed by the state, Hadrat Umar made no distinction between the master and the slave.

The slaves were given the stipends on the same scale as their masters.

Hadrat Umar issued orders that slaves could not be separated from their kindred. Under these orders the child was not to be separated from its mother. If there were two brothers it was obligatory that both of them should be purchased by one master.

Hadrat Umar was considerate that when some very highly placed person was taken captive, he should be ransomed and not kept as a slave. When in Syria the daughter of the empreror Heraclius was taken captive, she was returned to her father. When in the battle of Babylon, Armanusa the daughter of Maqauqas was taken captive she was returned to her father.

In order to raise the status of slaves, Hadrat Umar enjoined that the master should generally take meals with their slaves. Occasionally Hadrat Umar invited slaves to dine with him.

Hadrat Umar said :

> "The curse of God be upon those who feel ashamed to sit to meals with slaves."

Hadrat Umar laid down that if a Muslim slave gave protection to a non-Muslim such protection was to be honoured like the protection given by any other Muslim.

Hadrat Umar took pains to provide facilities to slaves to rise to position of importance in the State. During the caliphate of Hadrat Umar Ikramah who came to be regarded as an Imam of Hadith was a slave. Nāfi who was the teacher of Imam Malik was a slave. There were many other slaves who became eminent during the caliphate of Hadrat Umar.

HADRAT UMAR'S CONTROL OF SEXUAL LAXITY

In the days of ignorance sexual laxity was the order of the day. Islam stood for reform in the moral and social fields, and condemned sexual laxity in all forms. Under Islam a limitation was placed on the number of wives one could marry. Such number was not to exceed four, and it was enjoined that all the wives should be treated alike with due justice. Lapidation was provided as the punishment for those found guilty of A.D. ultery.

When Hadrat Umar became the Caliph he took further steps to rid the society of sexual laxity.

In the days of ignorance poetry was pressed into service as an instrument of moral laxity. The poets indulged in ribald poems. They named their sweethearts in their poems and by indulging in poetic licence compromised the honour and integrity of ladies. Then where ladies were no party to love the poets in their imagination made their beloveds return their love in passionate terms. Such poetry did considerable social harm, and disturbed domestic peace in many a home. Hadrat Umar took cognisance of this unsocial practice. He commanded the poets not to mention the names of ladies in their poems. He also issued directions that the poets should not indulge in any versification calculated to encourage moral depravity. Where some poets inadvertently or otherwise contravened these instructions they were flogged or punished.

Mutah in some form or the other was permissible or at least not expressly forbidden before the time of Hadrat Umar. Hadrat Umar felt that *Mutah* whereunder a man married a woman for a specified number of days amounted to disguised prostitution and this led to moral laxity. Hadrat Umar accordingly passed an order prohibiting *Mutah*. He declared that it was open to a person to divorce a woman after regular marriage for any valid reason, but a marriage which was stipulated to be dissolved after a specified number of days was repugnant to the spirit of Islam which stood for stability of domestic homes. Hadrat Umar elaborated that the purpose of marriage was to set up homes with a view to getting children and *Mutah* negated such objects. Moreover in the case of *Mutah* the children born of such union were to be subject to social disability which was detrimental to social order.

Under the Islamic law divorce was permissible. The Holy Prophet however took pains to explain that divorces which disrupted family life were distasteful to God. People were enjoined not to be hasty in the matter of divorce. Divorce could be effective only when three divorces were given. The idea was to provide some opportunity for reconciliation. When under Hadrat Umar more countries were conquered and women from other countries became available for the Muslims, some Muslims resorted to the practice of announcing three divorces simultaneously. In order to put a stop to this unsocial practice Hadrat Umar laid down that if a person gave three *talaqs* simultaneously such divorce would be irrevocable.

With the conquest of Iraq and Syria, Iraqi and Syrian women became available to the Muslims. Attracted by the beauty of these women, the Muslims divorced their Arab wives. That created a social crisis which led to sexual laxity. Hadrat Umar accordingly ordered that marriages with foreign ladies should be permitted under exceptional circumstances. Hudhaifah was the A.D. ministrator of al Madina and he married a Christian beauty of Iraq. When this was brought to the notice of Hadrat Umar he required Hudhaifah to divorce the Christian beauty. Hudhaifah said that he would not comply with the order unless he was told whether his marriage was unlawful or else; the Caliph referred to the authority under which he wanted him (Hudhaifah) to divorce his legally wedded wife. Hadrat Umar wrote to say that the marriage he had contracted was not unlawful, but he had been A.D. vised to divorce the Christian beauty as it was bound to A.D. versely affect the interests of Arab ladies. Moreover if the Muslims married non-Muslim ladies merely for their beauty that would encourage sexual laxity. Thereupon Hudhaifah divorced his Christian wife.

Besides four lawful wives Islam permitted any man to take over any number of slave girls to bed. These slave girls were to be the property of the Master and he could sell them any time. With the extension in conquests the number of available slave girls increased and Hadrat Umar felt that this would promote sexual laxity. He ordered that Umm ul Walad that is such slave girls who bore children to their masters would stand emancipated. This had the effect that such women could no longer be treated as concubines and were to be given the status of regular wives or divorced when they could, as free women, marry other persons.

SATIRES AND LAMPOONS

During the days of ignorance, satires and lampoons were the common device to discredit one's A.D. versaries. Poets were hired to write satires and lampoons ridiculing one's rivals and A.D. versaries. As poetry was a popular pastime, such satires would get swift publicity and led to many disputes and much mischief.

Hadrat Umar felt that such poems which ridiculed and caricatured certain sections of the society and were abusive and divisive in character were repugnant in Islam which stood for social solidarity. Hadrat Umar declared the writing of satires a criminal offence and warned the poets that if they indulged in such unsocial activities they would be punished.

Tamim and Najashi were two poets. Tamim complained before Hadrat Umar that Najashi had satirised him. Hadrat Umar wanted the verse objected to be quoted. The verse provided :

"If God were to hate the mean and the ignoble ;
Then may Banu Ajlal hate Tamim bin Muqbal."

Tamim argued that the implication of the verse was that he (Tamim) was mean and ignoble and that his tribe should hate him. Hadrat Umar had other verses of the poem read as well and came to the conclusion that these verses were defamatory in character and amounted to a satire. Najashi was accordingly punished.

Hutayya was a well known satirist of the age. He ridiculed Zabarqan bin Badr and the later lodged a complaint against Hutayya in the court of Hadrat Umar. Zabarqan was asked to quote the verse to which he objected. The verse ran :

"Do not aspire to do great deeds,

For in the matter of sustenance you are a burden on others."

Hadrat Umar summoned Hassan bin Sabit the poet laureate of the time to give evidence whether this verse amounted to a satire. Hassan said that the verse implied that Zabarqan depended for his sustenance on others and was not capable of doing anything good. That amounted to a satire.

Hutayya explained that satirising was his profession, indeed so much so that he satirised his own mother and even himself. Hadrat Umar wanted to know how he had satirised his mother. He said that he had composed the following verse about his mother :

"Begone, be away from me
May God save the world from you."

Hadrat Umar then wanted to know how he had satirised himself and he quoted the following verse :

"Today I will not say anything against any one,
For I have seen my own ugly face in the mirror."

Hadrat Umar gave him some money and warned him that he should not satirise any one again.

In the time of the Holy Prophet when they saw that all their weapons against the Prophet and Islam had failed they hired poets to satirise the Holy Prophet. In retaliation the Holy Prophet permitted Hassan bin Sabit to satirise the Quraish. Hassan's poems remained in currency even after the Quraish had embraced Islam. When Hadrat Umar became the Caliph he ordered that such poems should no longer be recited as these had become out of context and revived memories of ancient enmity.

THE DHIMMIS

In the conquest of non-Muslim countries by the Muslims, the population which did not embrace Islam were guaranteed life, liberty, and property and were called "Ah Al-Dhimma" or "Dhimmis" i.e. the People of the Covenant or Obligation.

In the treaties with the non-Muslims executed during the caliphate of Hadrat Umar it was invariably provided that the life, liberty, and property of the non-Muslims who accepted to pay Jizya was guaranteed.

In the treaty with the Christians of Jerusalem it was provided : "The protection is for their lives, and properties, their Churches and Crosses. Their Churches shall not be used for habitation nor shall these be demolished, nor shall injury be done to their Crosses."

Hadrat Umar took pains to uphold the principle that there is no compulsion in religion. Those non-Muslims who chose to become Muslims of their own accord were welcome, but there were no compulsory conversions. The Muslims were forbidden to interfere with the religious freedom of the Dhimmis.

The Dhimmis were treated as full citizens of the State. There was to be no discrimination between a Muslim and non-Muslims in the eyes of law. If a Muslim killed a Dhimmi he was subject to the same penalty as if he had killed a Muslim. The lands of the Dhimmis were left in their possession. Hadrat Umar issued strict instructions that all assessments in the case of Dhimmis should be fair.

The Dhimmis were required to pay Jizyah, but this was in lieu of their exemption from military duty. Where the Dhimmis performed military duty, Jizya was not taken from them. When any non-Muslim was too poor to pay Jizya he was exempted from the levy.

Hadrat Umar allowed the Dhimmis to follow their own personal laws. In order to maintain the integrity of the Dhimmis Hadrat Umar ordered that they should wear the dress which they used to wear before the conquest of their country by the Muslims. They were required not to imitate the Muslims in the way of dress or otherwise. This order was issued not with a view to humiliating the Dhimmis in any way but to maintaining their cultural identity.

The Dhimmis were free to follow their religious practices but they were enjoined in their own interest not to carry such practices in any way offensive to the Muslims. The Christians were free to ring bells in their churches but in the interests of enmity between the two communities they were asked not to ring the bells at the time when the Muslims were offering prayers. The Christians were allowed to take out their crosses in processions but they were A.D. vised that such processions should avoid routes passing through settlements populated by Muslims. These restrictions did not in any way interfere with the liberty of the Dhimmis. These were in their direct interests inasmuch as thereby the risk of any conflict with the Muslims on sentimental grounds was eliminated.

Hadrat Umar issued strict instructions to his officers that the covenants with the Dhimmis should be enforced in letter as well as in spirit. These instructions provided :

"Forbid the Muslims to do any injustice to the Dhimmis. No harm should be done to them in any way."

Even on his death bed, Hadrat Umar thought of the State's responsibility to the Dhimmis. In his bequest to his successor he said:

> "My bequest to my successor is that covenants with the Dhimmis should be observed faithfully. They should be defended against all invasions. No injustice should be done to them. They should be treated as full fledged citizens and should enjoy equality before law. Their taxes should be fair, and no burden should be imposed on them which they cannot bear."

ALLOWANCES AND STIPENDS FOR THE MUSLIMS

After the battles of Yermuk and Qadissiya the Muslims won heavy spoils. The coffers at Madina became full to the brim and the problem before Hadrat Umar was as to what should be done with this money. Some one suggested that money should be kept in the treasury for the purposes of public expenditure only. This view was not acceptable to the general body of the Muslims. Concensus was reached on the point that whatever was received during a year should be distributed.

The next question that arose for consideration was as to what system should be A.D. opted for distribution. One suggestion was that it should be distributed on A.D. hoc basis and whatever was received should be equally distributed. Against this view it was felt that as the spoils were considerable that would make the people very rich. It was therefore decided that instead of A.D. hoc division the amount of the allowance to the stipend should be determined before hand and this allowance should be paid to the person concerned regardless of the amount of the spoils. This was agreed to.

About the fixation of the allowance there were two opinions. There were some who held that the amount of the allowance for all Muslims should be the same. Hadrat Umar did not agree with this view. He held that the allowance should be graded according to one's merit with reference to Islam.

Then the question arose as to what basis should be used for placing some above others. Suggested that a start should be made with the Caliph and he should get the highest allowance. Hadrat Umar rejected the proposal and decided to start with the clan of the Holy Prophet.

Hadrat Umar set up a Committee to compile a list of persons in nearness to the Holy Prophet. The Committee produced the list clan wise. Bani Hashim appeared as the first clan. Then the clan of Abu Bakr was put and in the third place the clan of Hadrat Umar was put. Hadrat Umar accepted the first two placements but relegated his clan lower down in the scale with reference to nearness in relationship to the Holy Prophet.

The members of the clan of Hadrat Umar objected to the order of Hadrat Umar but he rebuked them saying; "You desire that you should stand on my neck and deprive me of my good deeds. I cannot permit that."

In the final scale of allowance that was approved by Hadrat Umar the main provisions were ;

(1) The widows of the Holy Prophet received 12,000 dirhams each ;
(2) Hadrat Abbas the uncle of the Holy Prophet received an annual allowance of 7,000 dirhams ;
(3) The grandsons of the Holy Prophet Hasan and Hussain got 5,000 dirhams each ;
(4) The veterans of Badr got an allowance of 6,000 dirhams each ;
(5) Those who had become Muslims by the time of the Hudaibiya pact got 4,000 dirhams each ;
(6) Those who became Muslims at the time of the conquest of Mecca got 3,000 dirhams each ;
(7) The veterans of the apostasy wars got 3,000 dirhams each.
(8) The veterans of Yermuk and Qadissiya got 2,000 dirhams each. In announcing this scale Hadrat Umar said ;

"I have decided the scale according to merit by entry into Islam and not by position."

In this award Hadrat Umar's son Abdullah got an allowance of 3,000 dirhams. On the other hand Usama got 4,000. Abdullah objected to this distinction and Hadrat Umar said :

" I have given Usama more than you because he was dearer to the Holy Prophet than you and his father was dearer to the Holy Prophet than your father."

FAMINES

During 640 A.D., Arabia suffered from serious draught. There were no rains, and as such there was no cultivation. That led to serious famine. There was not a blade of grass to be found anywhere, and as such there was nothing for the animals to graze upon. Because of serious famine conditions the people were involved in great distress. Black dust storms blow over the countryside and that A.D. ded to the distress of the people. The people from the interior flocked to the cities. There was practically no grain in the market. Ghee, butter and meat disappeared from the markets. It became a serious problem to feed the people.

Hadrat Umar rose to the occasion. He wrote to the provincial governors asking them to send food-grains to Arabia. Camel loads of foodgrains and other necessities of life came from Syria, Iraq, and Egypt. Foodgrains were received from Egypt through the sea as well.

Hadrat Umar distributed foodgrains and other necessities among the people family wise. Meals were cooked at the State level and all persons from interior of the desert who took refuge in Madina were fed daily at state expense. According to one account as many as 40,000 persons were fed every day.

In view of the resources of his disposal, Hadrat Umar could afford to have dainty food but he vowed that as long as the famine lasted he would eat only what was available to an Arab of ordinary means. He refused to eat meat, ghee or butter during the period of famine. He ordered that his meal should be cooked with oil. He would eat only the coarsest of food. As a consequence of eating nutritionless food his colour took a blacker hue. His stomach would rumble, but he said: “O stomach you may rumble as much as you like, but as long as the famine persists I cannot allow you anything dainty". One day some ghee came to the market and his servant purchased the ghee for him. When Hadrat Umar came to know of that he refused to have anything to do with such a luxury. A son of his cooked some meat one day and offered him the dish. He refused to eat it. So strict was Hadrat Umar that during the period of famine he refused to go near his wives.

At night he would move about from street to street to see for himself that all had been fed. Whenever any case of hardship came to his notice he would rush relief immediately. He would in most cases carry the relief goods on his own back. After taking his rounds, Hadrat Umar would pray to God till late hours of the night. He would then wake up in the early hours of the morning, and again pray before going to the mosque to lead the morning prayer.

Addressing the congregation Hadrat Umar would say :

> "I cannot say whether this calamity is because of the lapses of the Caliph or the sins of the people. Whosoever is to be blamed let us repent, and pray to God for, relieving us of this misery."

There is a story on record that one Bilal bin Harith of the Mazni tribe slaughtered a goat. There was nothing but bones in the corpse. Bilal had the bones ground and fed on them. At night he saw the Holy Prophet in a dream. The Holy Prophet asked him:

> "Go and give Umar my message. He is firm in the way of religion. He should further press religion into service for the aversion of this distress."

Bilal bin Harith called on Hadrat Umar and delivered him the message of the Holy Prophet. Hadrat Umar could not exactly follow what exactly was the significance of the message. He felt that perhaps the Holy Prophet was referring to some lapse on his part. That made him shudder with the fear of God. Hadrat Umar went to the mosque and enquired whether they had noticed any deficiency in him. They said that they had not seem any weakness in him. They enquired as to what was the occasion for the question. Thereupon Hadrat Umar asked Bilal to narrate his dream. After Bilal had narrated his dream, one of the Companions stood up to say : "Amirul Muminin there is nothing against you in this message. The Holy Prophet prescribed the prayer of Istisqa for praying to God for being relieved of any calamity. The message of the Holy Prophet is that you offer special Istisqa prayers."

Hadrat Umar fixed a day for the offering of Istisqa prayers. The faithful were required to offer the special prayer on the specified day throughout the Muslim dominions. On the day fixed all the Muslims in Madina assembled in a plain outside Madina and offered the Istisqa prayers. In the sermon on this occasion Hadrat Umar said:

> "We have erred. Let us repent and ask of forgiveness from God. O Allah Thee alone do we worship and from Thee alone do we ask help. O Allah forgive us for our sins. Have mercy on us, and be pleased with us."

It is related that within a week of the special prayer clouds appeared on the sky and there were heavy rains. Hadrat Umar then led a thanksgiving prayer. After the rains things changed for the better and the famine was over. Hadrat Umar led the people during the crisis of the famine with considerable credit.

HADRAT UMAR'S CRITERIA FOR APPOINTMENT AS GOVERNORS

In order to maintain the integrity of A.D. ministration, Hadrat Umar laid down very difficult criteria for the selection of candidates for appointment as Governors. Some accounts have come down to us which show how scrupulous was Hadrat Umar in choosing his Governors.

It is related that once Hadrat Umar decided to appoint a Governor. The Governor-designate came to Hadrat Umar to get his orders of appointment. Hadrat Umar asked his Secretary to draft the order. As the order was being drafted a younger son of Hadrat Umar came and sat in his lap. Hadrat Umar caressed the child. Thereupon the Companion said, "Amir-ul-Muminin your children come to you freely, but my children do not dare to come near me". Thereupon Hadrat Umar said, "If your own children are afraid of you, the people will be still more afraid of you. The oppressed will hesitate to bring forward their complaints to you. As such you are not fit to be a Governor, and the orders about your appointment as Governor stand cancelled."

Once Hadrat Umar thought of appointing a companion as Governor. Before the orders of appointment were issued that Companion called on Hadrat Umar and solicited appointment as a Governor. Hadrat Umar said :

> "I was going to appoint you as a Governor on my own account, but now that you have yourself asked for this appointment, I think you are not fit for the office. As you have asked for the office I fear you will use it as an office of profit and I cannot allow that. I would appoint

only such men who regard such office as a burden to be entrusted to them in the name of Allah."

The appointment of Governor for Kufa became a matter of great headache for Hadrat Umar. If he appointed a man who was harsh and stern the people complained against him. If he appointed a soft hearted man, the people took A.D. vantage of his leniency. Hadrat Umar wanted his comrades to A.D. vise him regarding the selection of a right man for the office of the Governor of Kufa. One man rose up to say that he could suggest a man who would be the fittest person for the job. Hadrat Umar enquired who was he, and the man said, "Abdullah bin Umar" Hadrat Umar said, "May God curse you, you want that I should expose myself to the criticism that I have appointed my son to a high office. That can never be".

Around Hadrat Umar there were such prominent persons as Usman, Ali, Zubair, Talha and others. Hadrat Umar did not offer them any office. Some one asked Hadrat Umar why did he not appoint such prominent persons as Governors. Hadrat Umar said, "These notables occupy a high status because of their virtues and other qualities. I do not appoint them as Governors lest for any lapse they may lose the prominence they enjoy at present."

Once the post of the Governor of Hims fell vacant, and Hadrat Umar thought of offering it to Ibn Abbas. Hadrat Umar called Ibn Abbas and said, "I want to appoint you as the Governor of Hems, but I have one misgiving." "What is that", asked Ibn Abbas. Hadrat Umar said, "My fear is that some time you would be apt to think that you are related to the Holy Prophet, and would come to regard yourself above the law." Ibn Abbas said, "When you have such a misgiving I would not accept the job." Hadrat Umar then said, "Please A.D. vise me what sort of man should I appoint." Ibn Abbas said, "Appoint a man who is good, and about whom you have no misgiving".

Some one asked Hadrat Umar, "What is your criterion for selecting a man for appointment as a Governor ?" Hadrat Umar said, "I want a man who when he is among men should look like a chief although he is not a chief, and when he is a chief, he should look as if he is one of them."

POLITICAL A.D. MINISTRATION

Under Hadrat Umar the country was divided into number of provinces. Historians differ about the exact number of provinces. Some say that the number of provinces was eight, while there are others who give a higher figure.

From the information that has come down to us, it appears that:

(1) Arabia was divided into two provinces, Mecca and Madina;
(2) Iraq was divided into two provinces, Basra and Kufa;
(3) In the upper reaches of the Tigris and the Euphrates, Jazira was a province;
(4) Syria was a province;
(5) Hadrat Umar divided Palestine in two provinces Ayla and Ramlah;
(6) Egypt was divided into two provinces, Upper Egypt and Lower Egypt;
(7) Persia was divided into three provinces, Khurasan; Azarbaijan and Fars.

Each province was in turn divided into districts. The exact number of districts is not known. In Persia alone the number of districts was 47. The total number of districts in the country must thus be around 100.

Each province was under the charge of a Governor or Wali. Other officers at the provincial level were :

(1) Katib, or Chief Secretary ;
(2) Katib-ud-Diwan ; Secretary, Army ;
(3) Sahib-ul-Kharaj ; Revenue Collector ;
(4) Sahib-ul-Ahdath ; Police Officer ;

(5) Sahib-ul-Bait-ul-Mal, Treasury Officer
(6) Qadi, the Chief Judge.

In some districts there were separate military officers, though the Wali was in most cases the Commander-in-chief of the army quartered in the province.

During the Caliphate of Hadrat Umar some of the notable Governors were :

(1) Abu Ubaidahh was the Governor of Syria.
(2) Yazeed b. Abi Sufyan became the Governor of Syria after the death of Abu Ubaidahh.
(3) Amir Mu'awiyah became the Governor of Syria after the death of his brother Yazeed.
(4) Amr b. Al-Aas was the Governor of Egypt.
(5) Saad b. Abi Waqqas was the Governor of Kufa.
(6) Utba b. Ghazwan was the Governor of Basra.
(7) Abu Musa Ashari succeeded Utba as the Governor of Basra.
(8) Itab b. Usaid was the Governor of Mecca ;
(9) Ayyad b. Ghanam was the Governor of Jazira.

For every district, there were two main office holders, namely

(1) Amil who was the main executive and responsible for the general A.D. ministration ; and
(2) Qadi responsible for the A.D. ministration of justice.

Every appointment was made in writing. On appointment every officer was given an instrument of instructions in which his powers and duties were specified. On arrival at the headquarters of his charge, the officer in question was required to assemble the people and read the instrument of instructions before them. In this way the public became aware of the powers and obligations of the officers concerned, and could call them to account for any sins of omission or commission.

Hadrat Umar's general instructions to his officers were:

"Remember, I have not appointed you as commanders and tyrants over the people. I have sent you as leaders instead, so that the people may follow your example. Give the Muslims their rights and do not beat them lest they become abased. Do not praise them unduly, lest they fall into the error of conceit. Do not keep your doors shut in their faces, lest the more powerful of them eat up the weaker ones. And do not behave as if you were superior to them, for that is tyranny over them."

At the time of appointment, every officer was required to make the promise :

(1) that he would not ride a Turkish horse ;
(2) that he would not wear fine clothes ;
(3) that he would not eat sifted flour ;
(4) that he would not keep a porter at his door ; and
(5) that he would always keep his door open to the public.

At the time of appointment a complete inventory of all the possessions of the person concerned was prepared and kept in record. If there was an unusual increase in the possessions of the office holder, he was immediately called to account, and the unlawful property was confiscated by the State.

The principal officers were required to come to Mecca on the occasion of the Hajj. In public assembly Hadrat Umar invited all who had any grievance against any office to present the complaint. In the event of complaints inquiries were made immediately and grievances redressed on the spot.

Explaining the functions of the officers, Hadrat Umar said:

"Brethren, officers are appointed not that they should slap you in your faces and rob you of your properties, but in order that they should teach you the way of the Prophet of Allah. So, if any officer has acted contrary wise, tell me that I might avenge it."

A special office was established for the investigation of complaints that reached the Caliph every now and then against the officers of the State. The Department was under the charge of Muhammad b. Maslama Ansari a man of undisputed integrity. In important cases Muhammad b. Maslama was deputed by Hadrat Umar to proceed to the spot, investigate the charge and take action. Sometimes an Inquiry Commission was constituted to investigate the charge. On occasions the officers against him complaints were received were summoned to Madina, and put to explanation by the Caliph himseif.

In order to minimise the chances of corruption, Hadrat Umar made it a point to pay high salaries to the staff. Provincial governors received as much as five thousand rupees a month besides their shares of the spoils of war.

LAND ADMINISTRATION

As a consequence of conquests on a large scale in Iraq and Persia and elsewhere a question arose as to the administration of land in the conquered territories. The Arabs followed the maxim, "Spoils belong to the victors". On this basis all spoils that were won as a result of any victory were distributed to the extent of four-fifth among the conquering army, and one-fifth was sent to Madina as the State share. On this analogy the army insisted that all agricultural lands should be distributed among the conquering army, and the inhabitants should be made their serfs and slaves.

Hadrat Umar convoked a special assembly at Madina to consider the question from all aspects. Eminent companions like Abdur Rahman b. Auf and others supported the viewpoint of the army. They argued that the lands belonged to the conquerors, and future generations had no right to them. Bilal was so vehement in the support of the demand of the army that Hadrat Umar had to exclaim "May Allah save me from Bilal."

At the assembly Hadrat Umar argued that as the conquering army had already had the spoils distributed among them that was enough and the land should belong to the State. Hadrat Umar advanced the argument that if the lands in the conquered territories were divided up among the army, wherefrom would they get the necessary finance for the raising and equipment of the armies in future for defence against foreign aggression and for the maintenance of law and order within the country.

Hadrat Ali, Hadrat Usman, and Hadrat Talha supported Hadrat Umar but still no decision could be reached. Then Hadrat Umar recollected Sura Al-Hashr which spoke of the poor who had fled, and of those to come thereafter. From these verses Hadrat Umar inferred that lands were assets in which even the coming generations were interested and as such these should be the property of the State. These verses proved decisive and a concensus was reached :

(1) that the lands conquered would be the property of the State and not that of the conquering forces ;
(2) that the former occupants of lands would not be dispossessed ;
(3) that they should continue in possession of the lands and pay specified taxes to the State.

That was a wise decision attributable to the genius of Hadrat Umar. Hadrat Umar took settlement operations in a scientific way. In Iraq his Settlement Commissioners were Usman b. Hanif and Hudhaifah b. al-Yaman. These Settlement Commissioners measured land in Iraq with such care and precision as one measures cloth. Iraq measured 375 miles long and 240 miles wide with a superficial area of 30,000 square miles. The royal dynasty's estates, endowments of fire temples, and the estates of those who had died heirless or fled the country were declared state property. The rest of the lands were left in the possession of their former occupants and assessed to land revenue per jarib according to the nature of crops sown. These rates were : wheat two dirhams per jarib per year ; barley one dirham ; sugar cane six dirhams ; cotton five dirhams ; grapes ten dirhams ; date palm gardens ten dirhams and so on. In the first year the income from State land amounted to seventy lakh dirhams. Land revenue assessment under private occupation worked out at 86 million dirhams.

The whole settlement was carried out in such a way that fresh lands were extensively brought under cultivation, and the land produce increased extensively. In the year following the settlement the land revenue increased from 86 million dirhams to 100 million dirhams.

In other conquered countries no special settlements were carried out. In such countries the existing systems continued and the records in existence were adopted. In Iraq and Persia the records were kept in Persian. Hadrat Umar allowed the records to be kept in Persian even after their conquest by the Muslims. In Syria the previous records were kept in Latin, and in Egypt in the Coptic. In all such cases status quo was allowed to continue.

Under the Pharaohs taxes on land in Egypt could be paid in cash or kind, and the settlement was for a period of four years at a time. When the Romans occupied Egypt the same system continued but besides the normal land revenue they levied additional levies whereunder large quantities of grain were collected for presentation to the authorities at Constantinople. Hadrat Umar abolished the additional levies and the system in vogue under the Pharaohs was allowed to continue. The rules about the method of collection were made simpler and milder. In the time of Hadrat Umar the land revenue collected from Egypt amounted to twelve million dinars.

In Syria the annual collection of land revenue in the caliphate of Hadrat Umar was fourteen million dinars.

ARMY

In the early days of Islam there was no standing army. On the occasion of any battle contingents were raised from the various tribes and these were disbanded when the battle was over. No regular salaries were paid. Those who fought were compensated by distributing the spoils of war among them.

Hadrat Umar was the first Muslim ruler to organise the army as a State Department. This reform was introduced in 637 A.D. A beginning was made with the Quraish and the Ansars and the system was gradually extended to the whole of Arabia. A register of all adults who could be called to war was prepared, and a scale of salaries was fixed.

The scale was :

(1)	Those who had fought in the battle of Badr.	5,000 dirhams
(2)	Those who had fought in the battle of Uhud.	4,000 dirhams
(3)	Those who had migrated before the conquest of Mecca.	3,000 dirhams
(4)	Those who had embraced Islam at the time of the co-nquest of Mecca.	2,000 dirhams
(5)	Those who had fought in the battles of Yermuk or Qadissiya.	2,000 dirhams
(6)	For the Yamanites.	400 dirhams
(7)	Those who had fought after the battles of Yermuk and Qadissiya.	300 dirhams
(8)	The rest.	200 dirhams

All men registered were liable to military service. They were divided into two categories, namely :

(1) those who formed the regular standing army ; and
(2) those who lived in their homes, but were liable to be called to the colours whenever needed.

For the purpose of army administration, Hadrat Umar established Military Centres which were called 'Jund'. These Centres were set up at Madina ; Kufa ; Basra ; Mosul ; Fustat; Damascus ; Jordan ; and Palestine. At these centres barracks were built for the residence of troops. Big stables were constructed where four thousand horses fully equiped were kept ready for service at short notice at every Military Centre. All records pertaining to the army were kept at Military Centres. Food stores of the commissariat were kept at these places and therefrom sent to other places.

In addition to Military Centres, cantonments were established in big towns and places of strategic importance.

Under the Army Department, there was a separate Commissariat Department. All the food stores were collected at one place, and from there disbursed on the first of every month.

Pay and Bhatta were disbursed at different times. The pay was paid in the beginning of the Mohurram. The Bhatta was paid in spring and some extra allowances were paid during the harvesting season.

Every tribal unit had its leader called Arifs. Such units under Arifs were grouped and each group was under a Commander called Umar-ul-Ashar.

Promotions in the army were made on the strengh of the length of service or exceptional merit.

Expeditions were undertaken according to seasons. Expeditions in cold countries were undertaken during the summer, and in hot countries in winter. In spring the troops were generally sent to lands which had a salubrious climate and a good pasturage.

Much thought was given to climate and sanitation in the lay out of cantonments and the construction of barracks.

Special provisions were made for roads and streets in cantonments, and Hadrat Umar issued instructions prescribing the width of roads and streets.

When the army was on the march, it always halted Fridays. When on march, the day's march was never allowed to be so long as to tire out the troops. The stages were selected with reference to the availability of water and other provisions.

Leave of absence was given to army men at regular intervals. The troops stationed at far off places were given leave once a year and some time twice.

Each army corps was accompanied by an officer of the treasury, an Accountant, a Qazi, and a number of interpretors besides a number of physicians and surgeons.

Hadrat Umar issued instructions laying stress on the teaching of four things to the soldiers, namely : horse-racing; archery; walking barefoot, and swimming.

On the battlefield the army was divided into sections. These sections were :

(1) Qalb or the centre ;
(2) Maqaddamah or the vanguard ;
(3) Maimanah or the right wing ;
(4) Maisarah or the left wing ;
(5) Saqah or the rear ;
(6) Rid-extreme rear.

Other components were :

(1) Talaiah or patrols to keep watch over the movements of the enemy ;
(2) Ra'id or foraging parties ;
(3) Rukban or the camel corps ;
(4) Farsan or the cavalry ;
(5) Rajil or the infantry ;
(6) Ramat or the Archers.

According to instructions every soldier was required to keep with him several things of personal need. These included among other things needles, cotton, twine, scissors, and a feeding-bag.

Catapults were used extensively in siege operations. Under Hadrat Umar another machine employed in siege operations was Dabbabah. It was a wooden tower which moved on wheels and consisted of several storeys. The tower was wheeled up to the foot of the fort under siege, and then the walls were pierced by stone throwers, wall-piercers and archers who manned the Dabbabah.

Under the instructions of Hadrat Umar, suitable arrangements were made for the clearance and construction of roads, and bridges. These operations were usually performed by the conquered people under the supervision of the Muslim army.

A remarkable feature of the army organisation under Hadrat Umar was that he had complete control over the army at all times as if he were present in person at every field. The control was facilitated because of the sense of awe and majesty that the person of Hadrat Umar inspired. The espionage and intelligence services in the army were well organised. Reporters were attached to every unit, and they kept the Caliph fully informed about everything pertaining to the army.

Under Hadrat Umar vast conquests were made in Iraq, Persia, Syria, and Egypt and this speaks for the efficiency of the army and the military organisation.

JUDICIAL ADMINISTRATION

Hadrat Umar took particular pains to provide effective and speedy justic for the people. He set up an effective system of Judicial administration, whereunder justice was administered according to the principles of Islam.

Qadis were appointed at all administrative levels for the administration of justice. Hadrat Umar was the first ruler in history to separate judiciary from the executive. The Qadis were chosen for their integrity and learning in Islamic law. High salaries were fixed for the Qadis so that there was no temptation to bribery. Wealthy men and men of high social status were appointed as Qadis so that they might not have the temptation to take bribes, or be influenced by the social position of any body. The Qadis were not allowed to engage in trade. Judges were appointed in sufficient number, and there was no district which did not have a Qadi.

Hadrat Umar issued 'Farmans' from time to time laying down the principles for the administration of justice. In one of the Farmans issued to Judicial Officers, Hadrat Umar laid down the following principles :

> "Praise to God.
>
> Verily justice is an important obligation to God and man. You have been charged with this responsibility. Discharge the responsibility so that you may win the approbation of God and the goodwill of the people.
>
> Treat the people equally in your presence, in your company, and in your decisions, so that the weak despair not of justice, and the high-placed have no hope of your favour.

The onus of proof lies on the plaintiff. He who denies must do so on oath. Compromise is permissible, provided it does not turn the unlawful into lawful, and the lawful into unlawful. Let nothing prevent you from changing your previous decision if after consideration you feel that the previous decision was incorrect.

When you are in doubt on a question and find nothing about it in the Qur'an or in the Sunnah of the Prophet, think over the question over and over again. Ponder over the precedents and analogous cases, and then decide by analogy.

A term should be fixed for the person who wants to produce witnesses. If he proves his case, get him his right. Otherwise, the suit should be dismissed.

All Muslims are reliable, except those who have been punished with flogging, or who have borne false witness or are doubtful in integrity."

History has preserved the names of some of the eminent persons who held judicial office during the caliphate of Hadrat Umar.

Zaid bin Thabit was appointed by Hadrat Umar as the Qadi of Madina. He was well versed is Syriac and Hebrew, and was an expert in civil law.

Ka'b-b. Sur al-Azdi was the Qadi of Basra. He was a man of keen insight and wide learning. Many of the dicta laid down by him became classical and were reported by Imam Ibn Sirin.

Ibada b. al-Samat was the Qadi of Palestine. He was one of the five men who had memorised the Holy Qur'an in the lifetime of the Holy Prophet. Hadrat Umar held him in great esteem.

Abdullah b. Masud was the Qadi of Kufa. He was a man of great scholarship and judicial acumen. He is considered the Father of the Hanafi law.

Qadi Shuraih succeeded Abdullah b. Masud as the Qadi of Kufa. He was well known throughout the country for his intelligence and keen sense of judgment. He was regarded as a model Judge. Hadrat Ali used to call him 'Aqd-ul-Arab'—i.e. the most judicious of all the Judges of Arabia.

About Qadi Shuraih's appointment as a Judge there is a story on record. It is related that Hadrat Umar purchased a horse on approval, and gave it to somebody to try it. The horse got hurt in the ride, and Hadrat Umar wanted to return it, but the owner refused to take it back. In the dispute that arose as a consequence, Shuraih was chosen as the arbitrator. He gave the verdict that if the horse was ridden with the permission of the owner it could be returned ; otherwise not. Hadrat Umar said that that was the right decision and at once appointed Shuraih as the Qadi of Kufa.

PUBLIC TREASURY & COINS

In the time of the Holy Prophet there was no public treasury. Whatever revenues or other amounts were received were distributed immediately. There were no salaries to be paid, and there was no state expenditure. Hence the need for the treasury at public level was not felt.

In the time of Hadrat Abu Bakr as well there was not treasury. Hadrat Abu Bakr earmarked a house where all money was kept on receipt. As all money was distributed immediately the treasury generally remained locked up. At the time of the death of Hadrat Abu Bakr there was only one dirham in the public treasury.

In the time of Hadrat Umar things changed. With the extension in conquests money came in larger quantities. Hadrat Umar also allowed salaries to men fighting in the army. In 536 A.D., Abu Huraira who was the Governor of Bahrain sent a revenue of five lakh dirhams. Hadrat Umar summoned a meeting of his Consultative Assembly and sought the opinion of the Companions about the disposal of the money. Most of the Companions advised immediate distribution of the money. Hadrat Usman advised that the amount should be kept for future needs. Walid bin Hisham suggested that like the Byzantines separate departments of Treasury and Accounts should be set up.

After consulting the Companions Hadrat Umar decided to establish the Central Treasury at Madina. Abdullah bin Arqam was appointed as the Treasury Officer. He was assisted by Abdur Rahman and Muiqib. A separate Accounts Department was also set up and it was required to maintain record of all that was spent.

Later provincial treasuries were set up in the provinces. After meeting the local expenditure the provincial treasuries were required to remit the surplus amount to the central treasury at Madina. According to Yaqubi the salaries and stipends charged to the central treasury amounted to over three crore dirhams.

In most of the histories of the Muslim period it is stated that among the Muslim rulers, the Umayyad Caliph Abdul Malik bin Marwan was the first to strike coins. Further historical research has established that Hadrat Umar has the distinction of being the first Muslim ruler to strike Islamic coins.

It is stated in Maqrizi's *Kitab-ul-Nuqad ul-Islamia* and Mawardi's *Al-Ahkam us-Sultaniyah* that Islamic coins were first struck by Hadrat Umar. Hadrat Umar struck the coins of dirhams. The coins of Hadrat Umar resembled the coins of Anusherwan. These, however, bore the legends "Praise to Allah" ; "Muhammad is the Apostle of Allah" ; and "There is no god but Allah".

According to Mawardi when Persia was conquered three types of coins were current in the conquered territories, namely Baghli of 8 dang ; Tabari of 4 dang ; and Maghribi of 3 dang. Hadrat Umar made an innovation and struck an Islamic dirham of 6 dang.

PUBLIC WORKS

Hadrat Umar stood for simplicity and austerity. Consequently he did not believe in any large scale programme of public works involving extravagance. Nevertheless as a consequence of the extension of the Muslim rule to distant lands, the undertaking of works of public utility became imperative.

As Muslim conquests extended east and west, and more people embraced Islam, it became necessary to construct mosques. The mosques were not mere places for offering prayers ; these were community centres as well where the faithful gathered to discuss problems of social and cultural importance. During the caliphate of Hadrat Umar as many as four thousand mosques were constructed extending from Persia in the east to Egypt in the west. Hadrat Umar enlarged and improved the Prophet's mosque in Madina. He also paved the Holy Ka'aba.

During the caliphate of Hadrat Umar many new cities were founded. These included Kufa, Basra, and Fustat. These cities were laid in according with the principles of town planning. All streets in these cities led to the Friday mosque which was sited in the central chauk. Markets were established at convenient points. The cities were divided into quarters, and each quarter was reserved for particular tribes. In the construction of houses, strict instructions were laid down prohibiting the construction of palatial buildings. The houses were to be single storeyed, not exceeding specified dimensions. These instructions were vigorously enforced, and if any body constructed a double storey in violation of these instructions, such double storeys were invariably demolished. The houses did not reflect the opulence or poverty of the owners. These were symbolic of the egalatarian society of Islam, whereunder all were equal.

Many buildings were built for administrative purposes. In the quarters called "Dar-ul-Amarat" Government offices and houses for the residence of officers were provided. Buildings known as 'Diwans' were constructed for the keeping of official records. Buildings known as 'Bait-ul-Mal' were constructed to house public treasuries. For the lodging of persons suffering sentences as punishment, prison houses were constructed for the first time in Muslim history. In important cities Guest Houses were constructed to serve as rest houses. Roads and bridges were constructed for public use. On the road from Madina to Mecca, shelters, wells, and meal houses were constructed at every stage.

Military cantonments were constructed at strategic points. Special stables were provided for cavalry. These stables could accommodate as many as 4,000 horses. Special pasture grounds were provided and maintained for Bait-ul-Mal animals.

Canals were dug to irrigate fields as well as provide drinking water for the people. Abu Musa Canal was a nine mile long Canal which brought water from the Tigris to Basra. Another Canal known as Maqal Canal was also dug from the Tigris. A Canal known as the Amirul Mumnin Canal was dug to join the Nile to the Red Sea. During the famine of 639 A.D. foodgrains were brought from Egypt to Madina through this Canal and the sea. Saad Canal dug from the Euphrates brought water to Anbar. Amr bin Al-Aas the Governor of Egypt even proposed the digging of a Canal to join the Mediterranean to Red Sea. The proposal, however, did not materialise, and it was 1200 years later that such a Canal was dug in the shape of the Suez Canal.

HADRAT UMAR AND HADITH

During his lifetime the Holy Prophet pronounced on various matters. When any one met with a problem he went to the Holy Prophet for his verdict. Such decisions remained known to the persons concerned and were not publicised. As such the decisions of the Holy Prophet remained wide spread. The traditions were not compiled in any compendium and as such the sources remained scattered. In view of the diffusion of resources there grew the risk that some traditions reported might be spurious or coloured with the views or prejudices of the narrator.

Hadrat Umar was the first to realise the necessity of the proper sifting of the traditions. Hadrat Umar accordingly founded the science of Hadith. The practice with Hadrat Umar was that if any new problem cropped up, Hadrat Umar announced in the public assembly the point at issue, and inquired if any of them remembered any tradition of the Holy Prophet on the subject. Those who narrated any tradition were required to produce some witnesses in support of the tradition. If such statement was duly corroborated and was in accordance with the spirit of the Holy Qur'an as well as common sense it was adopted and applied to the facts of the case in hand. In this way a rich corpus of Hadith was built up. These were recorded and copies were supplied to all provinces for guidance. Hadrat Umar deputed experts in Hadith to various provinces to educate the provincial officers in Hadith.

Hadrat Umar classified the traditions in two broad categories. One category of traditions pertained to religious, moral and social affairs pertaining to the community at large. These matters emanated from the prophetic mission of the Holy Prophet. The other traditions revolved round the person of the Holy Prophet and pertained to his words and deeds as a human being. Hadrat Umar distinguished between these two categories and took care to ensure that these two categories did not get mixed up. All matters falling in the first category were binding and had the status of law. The matters falling in the second category remained as ideals to be followed, but these did not have the status of law. Hadrat Umar took particular care to disseminate all traditions falling in the second category. The traditions in the second category were sparingly reported or publicised.

Hadrat Umar was alive to the danger that whatever was ascribed to the Holy Prophet, right or wrong would obtain currency and venerable acceptance. Hadrat Umar evolved principles on the basis of which the traditions were to be accepted. The basic principles were :

(1) The report should be literally faithful ;
(2) Every Hadith narrated should carry with it the name of the narrator and the chain of narrators ;
(3) The narrators must be men of proven faith and integrity;
(4) In judging the veracity of a report the occasion and circumstances involved should be taken into consideration;
(5) The report should not be repugnant to the Holy Qur'an;
(6) The report should be rational.

There was some dispute about the number of takbirs to be said in funeral prayers. Sufficient evidence was adduced to the effect that the Holy Prophet offered four takbirs. It was accordingly laid down by Hadrat Umar that in funeral prayers four takbirs should be said. The matters regarding bath for sexual impurity, Jizya to be levied on Magians and other allied matters were decided in the light of authentic traditions of the Holy Prophet.

It is related that Abu Musa Ash'ari the Governor of Basra once came to see Hadrat Umar and by way of permission said "Assalamulaikam". Hadrat Umar was busy and did not pay attention to Abu Musa. Abu Musa repeated the greetings thrice and then went away. Hadrat Umar had him recalled and enquired why he had gone away. Abu Musa said that he had heard the Holy Prophet say, "Ask permission thrice, and if you do not get permission go away". Hadrat Umar asked for corroborative evidence in support of the tradition. Abu Musa produced the evidence and the tradition was accepted as a guide.

In the time of Hadrat Umar a question arose whether a woman who had been divorced but the divorce had not become effective could remain in the house of her husband. A lady Fatima bint Qais stated before Hadrat Umar that she had it on the authority of the Holy Prophet that such woman could no longer lodge with her husband. The Holy Qur'an clearly provided that such woman could lodge with her husband till the divorce became effective. Hadrat Umar accordingly ruled: "We cannot abandon the Book of Allah on the word of a woman, for we do not know whether she remembers the tradition correctly or has forgotten it."

Lest the people should make mistakes in reporting Hadith direct from the Holy Prophet, Hadrat Umar forbade the Companions to report direct from the Holy Prophet. Hadrat Umar also enjoined that Hadith should not be mixed with the Qur'an. Lest there might be mistake in reporting. Hadrat Umar enjoined, "Report sparingly from the Holy Prophet". When Hadrat Umar was asked to quote traditions he would usually say "Had I not feared that I might make a mistake in reporting Hadith I would have quoted one." Hadrat Umar emphasised that extra care should be taken to ensure that there was no mistake in reporting. The checks and restraints imposed by Hadrat Umar on the reporting of traditions and the high standard of accuracy required by him paid dividends and all the traditions that were accepted and publicised were free from flaw.

TRADITIONS ON RELIGIOUS MATTERS

Hadrat Umar was very close to the Holy Prophet. He was very careful and cautious in reporting traditions. Over five hundred traditions are on record which are said to have been reported exclusively on the authority of Hadrat Umar.

Some of the traditions on religious matters reported by Hadrat Umar are noticed hereunder. The account is based on 'Sahih Bukhari'.

Hadrat Umar said that he heard the Holy Prophet say:

"God created Adam, then passed His right hand over his back and brought forth from it his offspring saying 'I have created these for paradise and they will do the deeds of those who go to paradise'. He then passed his hand over his back and brought forth from it his offspring saying 'I have created these for hell and they will do the deeds of those who go to hell'." A man asked what was the good of doing anything. The Holy Prophet replied:

"When God creates a man for paradise He employs him in doing the deeds of those who will go to paradise, so that his final action before death is one of the deeds of those who go to paradise, for which He will bring him into paradise. But when He creates a man for hell He employs him in doing the deeds of those who will go to hell, so that his final actions before death are the deeds of those who go to hell, for which He will bring him into hell."

Hadrat Umar stated that on the day of Khybarsome of the companions of the Holy Prophet stated that so and so were martyrs, but when they came to a man about whom they said "So and so is a martyr", the Holy Prophet declared "By no means. I have seen him in hell in a cloak which he took dishonestly."

The Holy Prophet asked Hadrat Umar : "Go, Ibn al-Khattab and announce among the people three times that only the believers will enter paradise."

In compliance with these instructions, Hadrat Umar went out and announced three times "Only the believers will enter paradise."

Hadrat Umar reported the Holy Prophet as saying :

"Do not sit with those who believe in freewill and do not address them before they address you."

The Holy Prophet, according to Hadrat Umar said :

"If any one performs the ablution completely, then says 'I testify that there is no god but God, and that Muhammad is His servant and messenger', the eight gates of paradise will be opened for him, and he may enter by whichsoever of them he wishes."

Hadrat Umar said, "The Prophet saw me standing and passing water and said Umar do not pass water standing" and I never did it again."

The Holy Prophet said, "Do not wash in water which has been exposed to the sun for it produces leprosy."

The Holy Prophet said :

"If four persons give a good testimony about any Muslim, God will cause him to enter paradise."

The Holy Prophet was asked whether this would apply if three testified and he said it would they further asked if it applied if two testified and he said it would but they did not ask him about one.

Hadrat Umar reported the Holy Prophet as saying:

"Should any one fall asleep and fail to recite his portion of the Qur'an or a part of it, if he recites it between the dawn and the noon prayer, it will be recorded of him as though he had recited it during the night."

Hadrat Umar said :

"I heard Hisham b. Hakim b. Hizam reciting Sura al-Furqan in a different way from my way of reciting it—the way that God's Messenger had taught me. I nearly spoke sharply to him, but I delayed till he had finished, and then catching his cloak at the neck I brought him to God's Messenger and said : 'Messenger of God, I heard this man reciting Sura al-Furqan in a manner different from that in which you taught me to recite it'. The Holy Prophet told me to leave him, and then turning to him asked him to recite. When he recited it in the manner in which I had heard him recite it, God's Messenger said, 'Thus was it sent down'. He then asked me to recite it, and when I had done so, he said 'Thus was it sent down'. I was surprised and the Holy Prophet said, 'The Qur'an was sent down in seven modes of reading, so recite according to what comes most easily."

About the Holy Qur'an, Hadrat Umar reported the Holy Prophet as saying :

"By this Book, God exalts some people, and lowers others."

Hadrat Umar said that God's Messenger used to seek refuge in God from five things, namely :

(1) Cowardliness ;
(2) Niggardliness ;
(3) Evils of old age ;
(4) Evil thoughts ; and
(5) Punishment of the grave.

Hadrat Umar reported the Holy Prophet as saying:

"Among God's servants there are people who are neither prophets nor martyrs but whose position in relation to God will be an object of desire by the prophets and martyrs on the day of resurrection."

The people wanted to know who were such people and the Holy Prophet said :

> "They are people who have loved one another by reason of God's spirit, and were giving gifts to one another without being related or having common property. I swear that their faces will be light, and they will be placed upon light, neither fearing when men fear, nor grieving when men grieve."

Hadrat Umar said that the Holy Prophet sent to Najd an expedition which took much booty and came back quickly.

A man who had not gone out said, "We have never seen an expedition return more quickly or bring finer booty than this one."

Thereupon the Holy Prophet said :

> "Shall I not indicate to you people who have most excellent booty and a most excellent return ? They are people who have been present at the morning prayer, then sat mentioning of God till the sun rose. They have the quickest return and the most excellent booty."

Hadrat Umar stated that he heard God's Messenger say:

> "Four rakaat before the noon prayer after the sun has passed the meridian are reckoned equivalent to a similar number at the dawn prayer. There is nothing which does not glorify God at that hour."

Hadrat Umar said that then the Holy Prophet recited:

"Their shadows turn round from the right and the left prostrating themselves to God."

Hadrat Umar said that he asked the Holy Prophet about the injunction:

"You may shorten your prayer if you fear those who are infidels may afflict you."

About this the Holy Prophet elaborated :

"It is an act of charity which God has done to you, so accept His charity."

About the call to prayer, Hadrat Umar reported the Holy Prophet as saying :

"When the Muezzin says 'God is most great, God is most great', and you make the response 'God is most great, God is most great', then says 'I testify that there is no god but God', then says I testify that Muhammad is God's Messenger', and you make the response 'I testify that Muhammad is God's Messenger', then says 'Come to prayer', and you make the response 'There is no might and no power except in God', then says 'Come to salvation', and he makes the response 'God is most great ; God is most great', then says 'There is no god but God', and if you say this from heart, you will go to paradise.

TRADITIONS OF ETHICAL IMPORTANCE

Some traditions of the Holy Prophet of ethical importance have been reported by Hadrat Umar.

Hadrat Umar reported that the Holy Prophet said :

"Deeds are to be judged only by intentions, and a man will have only what he intended. When one's emigration is to God and His Messenger his emigration is to God and His Messenger, but when his emigration is to a worldly end at which he aims or to a woman whom he marries his emigration is to that to which he has emigrated".

Hadrat Umar reported God's Messenger as saying:

"If any one says, on seeing some one who is suffering affliction 'Praise be to God Who has kept me free from the affliction He has brought on him and has shown me favour above many whom He has created, that affliction, whatever it may be, will not smite him."

Hadrat Umar said that he had heard the Holy Prophet say:

"An oath or a vow to disobey the Lord or to break ties of relationship or about something over which one has no control is not binding on you."

Hadrat Umar stated that he heard the Holy Prophet say "Give the road its due". He was asked what was the road's due. The Holy Prophet replied :

"Lowering the eyes ;
Removing anything offensive ;

Returning salutations ;
Recommending what is reputable ;
Forbidding what is disreputable ;
Helping the sorrowful ;
Guiding people on their way."

Hadrat Umar reported that the Holy Prophet taught him to say:

"O God make my inner nature better than my outer, and make my outer nature good. O God I ask Thee to give me some of the abundance Thou givest to men, in family, property and children, which neither strays nor leads astray."

Hadrat Umar stated that he heard the Holy Prophet say:

"He who is humble for God's sake will be exalted by God, for though he considers himself lowly he is great in the eyes of men ; but he who is proud will be abased by God for though he considers himself great he is lowly in the eyes of men to such an extent that he is of less value in their estimation than a dog or a pig."

Hadrat Umar reported the Holy Prophet as saying :

"In the last days my people will be afflicted with distresses from their rulers from which no one will escape but a man who knows God's religion and strives on its behalf with his tongue, his hand and his heart, that being the one who will have surpassing felicity in Heaven ; a man who knows God's religion and believes in it ; and a man who knows God's religion but keeps quiet about it, who if he sees some one doing good loves him for it ; that one will escape for all that he kept concealed in his heart."

Hadrat Umar stated that once he went to see the Holy Prophet and found him lying on a reed mat without any cover. The marks of the mat were on the body of the Holy Prophet. The room was bare and there was no sign of any comfort.

Hadrat Umar said to the Holy Prophet :

> "O Messenger of God supplicate God to enrich your people for He has enriched the Persians and the Byzantines, and yet they worship him not."

The Holy Prophet replied, "Is that how you feel, Ibn-ul-Khattab? These people have been given their good things in advance in the present world. Are you not pleased that they should have the present world, and we should have the next?"

Hadrat Umar said that he went one day to the Prophet's mosque, and in the way found Mu'adh b. Jabal sitting on the Prophet's grave weeping. Hadrat Umar asked him what was making him weep and he replied that it was something which he had heard from God's Messenger. He had heard him say, "A little hypocrisy is polytheism, and any one who is hostile to a friend of God has gone forth to fight with God. God loves the upright, pious and retiring ones who are not missed when they are absent, and are not given invitations or treated with honour when they are present. Their hearts are the lamps of guidance and they come forth from every dusty and dark place."

HADRAT UMAR & FIQH

Hadrat Umar was the founder of Fiqh or Islamic jurisprudence. Over one thousand juristic pronouncements of Hadrat Umar are on record. All the four schools of law in Islamic jurisprudence follow the law laid down by Hadrat Umar. The pronouncements of Hadrat Umar are cited in the *Musannaf* of Ibn Abi Shaiba. These are also found in Shah Wali Ullah's book *Faruq's Fiqh*.

Hadrat Umar not only declared the law ; he also established principles of inference and construction and formulated rules therefor. He distinguished between the acts of the Holy Prophet performed in pursuance of his prophetic mission and the acts that he performed as an ordinary man. All that the Holy Prophet did in the first capacity was held by Hadrat Umar to be binding and a basic source of law. In matters falling in the second category room remained for devising new laws to suit the changing conditions and circumstances.

Hadrat Umar also laid down the principle of Qiyas or logical deduction. According to this principle when the Qur'an and the Hadith did not mention the details of law on any point, such law could be arrived at by logical deduction. In his instructions to his judicial officers Hadrat Umar said :

> "When you do not find a judgement on an issue in the Qur'an or Hadith and you are in doubt about it, ponder over the question and ponder again. Then look for dicta on like and similar issues, and decide accordingly."

In addition to these fundamental principles Hadrat Umar enunciated numerous rules about inference and generalisation of laws which form the basis of Islamic jurisprudence.

When some one asked Hadrat Umar's verdict on a mere academic question which had not actually arisen, Hadrat Umar forbade people raising hypothetical propositions.

Hadrat Umar held that one should not urinate standing.

Hadrat Umar was asked whether one could perform the ablution with sea water. Hadrat Umar answered the question in the affirmative.

Hadrat Umar was asked whether one could perform ablution with water taken from a non-Muslim. Hadrat Umar found no objection to such ablution.

Hadrat Umar was asked whether one who has had sexual intercourse could perform Tayammum and offer prayers. Hadrat Umar said that for him bath was essential.

Hadrat Umar was very strict about the offering of prayers. He issued instructions to the provincial Governors that their foremost duty was the offering of prayer.

Hadrat Umar was asked as to the time for the morning prayer. He said "In the shadow of the twinkling stars".

Hadrat Umar held that the prayer of Zuhr should be delayed as far as possible and the prayer of Isha should be offered as early as possible.

Hadrat Umar was asked : if the meals are ready and it is also the time for prayers, which should be given priority. Hadrat Umar said "First take your meals".

When Hadrat Umar saw a person offering prayer by the roadside he was advised to pray in the mosque.

Hadrat Umar forbade the people to talk loudly in the mosque.

Hadrat Umar enjoined that one should not come to the mosque having eaten some thing which produces a bitter smell.

Hadrat Umar was very particular that when offering prayers in congregation the lines should be straight.

Hadrat Umar held that journey on a Friday was not forbidden.

Hadrat Umar enjoined that around a person on death bed one should recite the article of faith.

When one of the wives of Hadrat Umar died Hadrat Umar led the funeral prayers himself.

Hadrat Umar held that in one's shroud three sheets were enough.

Hadrat Umar ruled that on the occasion of a funeral prayers four Takbirs should be offered.

Hadrat Umar held that in a garden those trees the fruit whereof was reserved for distribution among the poor were exempt from Zakat.

Hadrat Umar held that if any thing was given as Sadaqa it could not be repurchased whatever the price or consideration.

Hadrat Umar held that when a man was under debt, he should offer Zakat on the value of his property after deducting the amount of the debt.

Hadrat Umar held that one should not fast unless he had seen the moon of Ramadan and he should not fast after he had seen the Eid moon.

Hadrat Umar advised the people to keep a fast on the tenth of the Muharram.

Hadrat Umar insisted that in the month of Hajjj priority should be given to the Hajjj and not to Umra.

Hadrat Umar prohibited the sale of wine.

Hadrat Umar held that one should not purchase anything already mortgaged with him.

Hadrat Umar held that if one passed through a garden he could pick up fruit that had fallen on the ground.

Hadrat Umar forbade Mut'ah.

Hadrat Umar held that where three talaqs were announced simultaneously such divorce would be irrevocable.

Hadrat Umar held that a slave woman who bore children to her master stood emancipated.

Hadrat Umar held that justice should not be delayed.

Hadrat Umar enjoined his officers to despatch the State business expeditiously.

Hadrat Umar held that in the court the Judge should not be praised.

All acts should be judged according to the test of public interest.

Any act which did not harm any one and was otherwise not forbidden under law was permissible.

In the famous Fidak case Hadrat Umar held that the property which vested in the Holy Prophet vested after him in the State and not in his heirs.

MATTERS ABOUT FIQH

Hadrat Umar said :

"I provided a man with a horse to ride on God's path, but as he who had it did not look after it well, I wanted to buy it, and I thought he would sell it at a cheap price. I therefore asked the Prophet, but he said 'Do not buy it, and do not take back what you gave as Sadaqa even if he gives it to you for a Dirham, for the one who takes back what he gave as Sadaqa is like a dog which returns to its vomit."

Hadrat Umar said :

"Once, captives came to the Holy Prophet among whom was a woman whose breast was oozing with milk. She was running and when she found a child among the captives she took him, put him to her breast and suckled him. Then the Prophet said to us 'Do you think this woman will cast her child into the fire ?' We replied 'Not so long as she is in a position not to do so'. He said 'God is more merciful to His servants than this woman to her child."

Hadrat Umar reported the Holy Prophet as saying :

"Gold for gold is usury unless both hand over on the spot; silver for silver is usury unless both hand over on the spot; wheat for wheat is usury unless both hand over on the spot; barley for barley is usury unless both hand over on the spot; dates for dates is usury unless both hand over on the spot."

Hadrat Umar reported the Holy Prophet as saying :

"He who brings goods for sale is blessed with good fortune, but he who keeps them till the price rises is accursed."

Hadrat Umar also reported the Holy Prophet as saying:

> "If any one keeps grain from the Muslims waiting for the price to rise, God will smite him with tubercular leprosy and insolvency."

Hadrat Umar said :

> "God sent Muhammad with the truth and sent down the Book to him, and the verse of stoning was included in what God Most High sent down. God's Messenger had people stoned to death and we have done it also since his death. Stoning is a duty laid down in God's Book for married men and women who commit fornication when proof is established, or if there is pregnancy, or a confession."

Hadrat Umar said that a man called Abdullah whose nome-de-plume was 'ass' used to make the Prophet laugh. The Prophet had beaten him because of wine drinking, but when he was brought to him one day and he gave orders and had him beaten, and then one of those present said, "O God curse him; how often he is brought', the Prophet said, "Do not curse him. I swear by God that for all I know he loves God and His Messenger."

Hadrat Umar reported the Holy Prophet as saying : "When you find that a man has been unfaithful with regard to spoils in God's way, burn his goods and beat him."

Hadrat Umar stated that the Holy Prophet reserved three things exclusively to himself namely the Banu an-Nadir: Khybar; and Fidak. The Banu an-Nadhir property was kept wholly for his own purposes. Fidak was kept for travellers. Khybar was divided into three sections, two for the Muslims and one for the maintenance of his family. If anything remained after meeting the needs of his family, that was divided among the poor MuHajjreen.

THE LAND OF FIDAK

When during the lifetime of the Holy Prophet, the Muslims conquered Khybar, the Holy Prophet deputed Mahisa bin Masud Ansari to Fidak a neighbouring township to invite the inhabitants to Islam. The township was a Jewish settlement, the chief being a Jew Yusha bin Nun. After the fall of Khybar, the Jews of Fidak were in no mood to offer resistance. The Jews submitted, and offered to surrender one half of their land.

> About the disposal of the land in Fidak, God revealed:
> "What Allah has made this people (the Jews) to deliver,
> To conquer which you did not lead any force,
> Vests in the Apostle,
>
> And Allah empowers His Apostles over whom He pleases."

The Holy Prophet accordingly reserved the land for himself. The proceeds from the property were utilised by the Holy Prophet for the maintenance of His family. These were so utilised for charity, and for the relief of those in distress.

After the death of the Holy Prophet Hadrat Fatima as the successor of the Holy Prophet claimed the land at Fidak. Hadrat Abu Bakr did not concede the claim. Hadrat Abu Bakr declared that He had heard from the Holy Prophet that prophets leave no inheritable property and that all that they have is public trust.

Hadrat Fatima died during the caliphate of Hadrat Abu Bakr. After the death of Hadrat Abu Bakr, Hadrat Ali and Hadrat Abbas lodged before Hadrat Umar a claim to the land of Fidak. Hadrat Umar upheld the decision of Hadrat Abu Bakr. He held that the land was a reserve of the Holy Prophet, but it was a reserve for public purposes, and after his death the reserved vested in the State, and could not be claimed by his successors as if it was his personal property.

On this occasion, explaining his decision, Hadrat Umar said:

> "The Holy Prophet used to take from the land of Fidak the maintenance of his family for the year. The rest he spent in the way of Allah. This was the Holy Prophet's practice as long as he lived. When the Holy Prophet, on whom be peace and blessings, died, Hadrat Abu Bakr said 'I am the successor of the Apostle of Allah'. So he took possession of land and used it as the Holy Prophet had used it. Then Hadrat Abu Bakr died. Now I am the successor of Hadrat Abu Bakr, and I have had the land in my possession for two years, and have done with it as the Holy Prophet, and Hadrat Abu Bakr had done before."

The upshot of Hadrat Umar's decision was that the land at Fidak was a public trust to which the ordinary law of inheritance did not apply.

FAY

When after the battle with Banu Nadir the lands of the Jews were occupied the question arose as to how such lands were to be distributed. To solve this issue, the following verse was revealed to the Holy Prophet :

> "Whatever lands fall to you from the people of the town, they belong to Allah and the Apostle and orphans and the needy and the wayfarer and the poor among the MuHajjreen who were driven from their homes, and for all those who come after."

During the caliphate of Hadrat Umar when extensive conquests were made in Iraq and Syria, the combatants demanded that all agricultural lands left by the enemy should be distributed among them.

Hadrat Umar convened an assembly at which this question was discussed. Abdul Rahman bin Auf, Zubair bin Al-Awam and Bilal bin Rabah among others were strongly of the view that such lands should be distributed among the soldiers.

Hadrat Umar observed that there were various aspects of the question and each aspect had to be taken into consideration carefully.

The economic aspect of the question was that if such lands were distributed no assets would be left with the state to provide the source of revenue for the future. Under the circumstances the best course was that such lands should be state property so that income accruing therefrom could be utilised for meeting the future needs.

The social aspect was that if such lands were distributed some people would get rich, while the others would remain poor. Those who have fought on various fronts would on that basis get lands in various countries and that would create great disparity among the ranks of the Muslims. That was repugnant to Islam.

Hadrat Umar emphasised that in the verse of the Holy Qur'an on the subject (quoted above), the words 'and those that will come after,' were of particular significance. The implication was that such lands should remain state property so that the coming generations might also profit therefrom.

Hadrat Umar elaborated :

"These lands belong to the coming generations and are therefore the property of the nation. How can I then distribute them among those who are present and deprive those who will come after."

The debate lasted for several days, and ultimately the concensus of opinion emerged in favour of the view advanced by Hadrat Umar. According to the four schools of law that emerged subsequently three schools upheld the view taken by Hadrat Umar. The school of Imam Shaf'i, however, insisted that the conquered lands should have been divided among the combatants.

USHR

Hadrat Umar was the first Muslim ruler to levy Ushr. Ushr as the name implies was an import duty levied at ten per cent on the value of goods imported.

When the Muslim traders went to foreign lands for the purposes of trade they had to pay a ten per cent tax to the foreign states. Ushr was levied on reciprioal basis on the goods of the traders of other countries who chose to trade in the Muslim dominions.

Hadrat Umar issued instructions that Ushr should be levied in such a way so as to avoid hardship. The tax was levied on merchandise meant for sale. Goods imported for consumption or personal use but not for sale were not taxed. The merchandise valued at two hundred dirhams or less was not taxed.

The instructions provided that the tax should be charged only on goods which were brought in openly, and the personal luggage was not to be searched.

When the citizens of the State imported goods for the purposes of trade, they had to pay the customs duty or import tax at lower rates. In the case of the Dhimmis the rate was five per cent and in the case of the Muslims 2½ per cent. In the case of the Muslims the rate was the same as that of Zakat. The levy was thus regarded as a part of Zakat and was not considered a separate tax.

A story is told that a certain Christian of the Banu Taghlib tribe and a citizen of the Muslim state imported a horse. The horse was valued at 20,000 dirhams, and being a Dhimmi the import tax on the horse was assessed at 5 per cent, i.e. 1,000 dirhams. He paid the tax but then went out of the country on business riding that horse. He returned after some time, and the taxing authorities demanded the Ushr on the horse again. He represented that as he had already paid the tax, it was a case of hardship to pay the tax for the second time.

The Christian waited on Hadrat Umar at Madina, and represented his case. Hadrat Umar after hearing the case merely said, "Alright, you can go." The man thought that Hadrat Umar had probably not agreed with his view point. He accordingly went to the tax authorities and expressed his willingness to pay the tax. The taxing authorities told him that they had already received instructions from Hadrat Umar that when any goods had been subjected to Ushr, these should not be subjected to the tax on re-import within a year.

Hearing of this order, the Christian trader said, "How just is Umar ; verily the religion that he follows is the Truth." Thereupon he declared the article of faith and became a Muslim.

KHUMS

Before Islam, the usage in Arabia was that whatever spoils were won in a battle these were distributed among the combatants, subject to the condition that one-fourth of the share was given to the chief of the tribe. This implied that whatever spoils fell into the hands of a combatant belonged to him.

The first battle fought by the Muslims was the battle of Badr. After the victory some Muslims went in pursuit of the enemy and gathered some booty. They took the plea that whatever they had obtained belonged to them. Those who had stayed behind to guard the Holy Prophet argued that as they had taken part in the war, they had the right to an equal share in the booty.

To solve the matter, the following verse was revealed to the Holy Prophet :

> "People ask thee about the spoils,
> Say, they belong to the Allah and the Apostle."

This verse abrogated the principle that the spoils were the exclusive right of the combatants. The verse, however, did not indicate how the spoils were to be distributed. To settle that issue, another verse was revealed as follows :

> "Whatever spoils of war you capture ;
> One-fifth of them belongs to
> Allah and the Apostle and to the near of kin,
> And the poor and the wayfarers."

In accordance with this injunction the practice with the Holy Prophet was that four-fifths of the spoils were distributed among the Muslims at large, and one-fifth was retained by the Holy Prophet for his personal use and for the use of persons closely related to them. A part was used for providing relief to the poor, the widows, and the orphans.

This one-fifth was known as 'Khums'. This became a subject of controversy in the time of the caliphate of Hadrat Umar. Hadrat Ali, Hadrat Abbas, and other Uashmites pleaded that even after the death of the Holy Prophet, 'Khums' should be distributed among those who were related to the Holy Prophet.

Hadrat Umar did not accept this view. He distributed four-fifths among the warriors participating in the war, and the 'Khums' was credited to the Baitul Mal for the use of the Muslims at large.

Hadrat Umar argued that the Holy Prophet himself declared that the prophets leave no inheritance, and as such the relatives of the Holy Prophet could claim no preference in the matter of distribution of the spoils of war. The entire Muslim community was the heir of the Holy Prophet, and as such the 'Khums' was to be used for the benefit of the entire Muslim community, and could not be earmarked as a privilege for any particular section.

Hadrat Umar's view was that as with his death, the Holy Prophet lost his share of the 'Khums', his relatives lost that special privilege as well. After the death of the Holy Prophet, the relatives of the Holy Prophet and the other Muslims were to be treated at par. Thus they could have their share as Muslims and not on the basis of relationship with the Holy Prophet.

Hadrat Umar also argued that if it was held that the relatives of the Prophet were to enjoy a special privilege even after his death, this would imply that this practice should continue for ever. Such a course would be irrational. That would imply the creation of a privileged group within the Muslims, a sort of Brahmins with born privileges and that would be repugnant to Islam.

During the caliphate of Hadrat Umar, the Hashmites felt unhappy at the decision of Hadrat Umar though they did not challenge it. Among the four schools of the law that developed among the Muslims, the school of Imam Shafi argued vehemently in favour of special privilege for the relatives of the Holy Prophet. The other schools upheld the decision of Hadrat Umar.

IMRA-UL QAIS

Imra-ul-Qais was a great poet of Arabia of the pre-Islamic period. His grandfather was King Harith of Kinda, the antagonist of Mundhir III, king of Hira. King Harith was killed in a battle against Hira. On the death of Harith, his kingdom was split up into a number of principalities. One of such principalities, the Banu Asad was ruled by Hujr who was the father of Imra-ul-Qais.

There is a story that Imra-ul-Qais was banished by his father who despised him for being a poet, and was enraged by the scandals of the adventures of his love. Imra-ul-Qais led a wild life, and came to be known as the 'Vagabond prince.'

Hujr was killed by an enemy. When the news of the death of his father reached Imra-ul-Qais, he cried "My father wasted my youth, and now that I am old, he has laid upon me the burden of avenging his death. Wine to-day, business tomorrow." Seven nights he indulged in carouse. Thereafter he swore not to eat flesh, or drink wine, nor use ointment, nor wash his head until he had avenged the death of his father. He visited the oracle in the valley of Tabala north of Najran, and drew the omen by drawing an arrow. The arrow that he drew was to the effect that such vengeance was forbidden. He broke the arrow and dashed it against the face of the idol saying "If your father had been killed, you would not have hindered me."

Thereafter he set out for Constantinople, where he was favourably received by the Byzantine emperor Justinian, who desired to see the power of Kinda re-established as a counterpoise to Hira which was subject to Persia. At Constantinople Imra-ul Qais was involved in a love affair with a Byzantine princess. In order to get rid of him, the emperor appointed him the Governor of Palestine. He was awarded an official robe which he was required to wear throughout his journey. The robe was poisoned, and Imra-ul-Qais died of the effects of the poisoned robe in the course of the journey around 540.

In *Stray Thoughts*, Iqbal has assessed the poetry of Imra-ul-Qais in the following terms :

> "Of the poet Imra-ul-Qais who flourished about 40 years before Islam, our Prophet is reported to have said, 'He is the most poetic of all poets and their leader to hell'. Now, what do we find in the poetry of Imra-ul-Qais. Sparkling wine, enervating sentiments and situations of love, heart rending moans over the ruins of habitations long swept away by stormy winds, superb pictures of the inspiring scenery of silent deserts—and all this in the choicest expression of old Arabia. Imra-ul-Qais appeals more to imagination than to will', and on the whole acts as a narcotic on the mind of the reader. The Prophet's criticism reveals this most important art principle—that the good in art is not necessarily identical with the good in life. It is possible for a poet to write fine poetry and yet lead his society to hell. The poet is essentially a seducer ; woe to the people if instead of making the trials of life look beautiful and attractive he embellishes decadence with all the glories of health and power, and seduces the people to extinction. Out of the richness of his nature he ought to lavish on others something of the super-abundance of life and power in him, and not steal away, thief-like, the little they already happen to possess."

Hadrat Umar admired the excellency of the poetry of Imra-ul-Qais and the originality of his themes. It is related that Abdullah bin Abbas once asked Hadrat Umar of his opinion about Imra-ul-Qais, when he said :

> "He was the foremost. He brought fresh water from the well of poetry and gave sight to blind themes."

NABIGHA AL-DHUBYANI

Nabigha was an Arabic poet of the pre-Islamic period. He flourished at the court of the princes of Hira.

Numan III the ruler of Hira was a tyrant. He loved his step mother Mutajarrida who was a famous beauty of the age. She did not return his love but he forced her to marry him.

Nabigha wrote some beautiful poetry in the praise of Mutajarrida. He was accused of being in love with the Queen, whose beauty and charm he described in minute detail in his poems. To escape the vengeance of Numan III, Nabigha fled from Hira and sought refuge in the court of the Ghassanid kings in Syria.

Hadrat Umar admitted the poetry of Nabigha. He was fond of quoting verses from Nabigha.

The following verses of Nabigha were quoted by Hadrat Umar on different occasions :

"Remember Sulaiman when God said to him ;
Stand up on the earth and mark out a portion for yourself."
"I come to you in rugged clothes,
Lest you should entertain evil notions about me."
"I have sworn and have left no room for doubt in your heart;
And for a man there is no way beyond Allah."
"Whatever has been told to you about me is false ;
If I am dishonest the man who has been backbiting
Against me is fraudulent and false."
"If you do not reform your brother
You will have to forego him."
"Crooked thorns tied in strings,

When such strings are in your hand
These attract me to you."
"Like night, you will get hold of me,
If I ever think that leaving you I can go anywhere."
"Towards Ibn Muhariq I led my dromedary
When the world was asleep."
"I saw that the trust had not been betrayed,
Likewise Nuh did not betray his trust."

ZUHAIR BIN ABI-SALMA

Zuhair bin Abi Salma was a poet of the pre-Islamic period. His most well known work is *Mu'allaqa.* In his poems he preached the principles of noble conduct for individuals and society. He belonged to a family which produced great poets. These included ; his father-in-law Aus bin Hajjr ; his sister Salma; his daughter al-Khansa ; and his son Ka'b.

In his *Mu'allaqa* he praised the magnanimity of the chiefs of Dhubyan who brought about peace among the tribes after so many years of bloodshed.

He warned the tribesmen against vengeance and hatred. He said :

"Then cannot hide their guilt from God,
It will be recorded and punished on the day of retribution
Or avenged in this life,
They know war and its bitterness,
They should not revive that monster
Which brings only woe and destruction."
Talking about his patrons and his poetry he said :
"Your gifts have vanished, but my poems are still alive;
They are robes of honour which do not become worn out by time."

Hadrat Umar had great admiration for the poetry of Zuhair. He used to call him the most poetical of all poets. Once Abdullah bin Abbas asked Hadrat Umar the reason for his admiration of the poetry of Zuhair. Hadrat Umar said that he admired Zuhair because he did not use rare words. His poems were free from complexity. He dealt with only such subjects in which he was at home. When he praised any one, he spoke only of those virtues which the person praised really possessed.

Hadrat Umar quoted the following verses of Zuhair to establish his point:

> "Qais bin Ghailan has attained the height of nobility;
> Now if anybody tries to exceed him, he will only come to shame.
> If praise could have given immortality to a man,
> Thou wouldst never have died,
> But people's adulations never make one immortal."

Hadrat Umar admired Zuhair because his poetry was chaste, and though he belonged to the pagan period, his language was so refined that he gave the impression of being a poet of the Islamic period. He used simple language and did not indulge in exaggeration.

Zuhair's patron was an Arab chief Harm b. Sinan. Once a son of Zuhair and a son of Harm met Hadrat Umar. Hadrat Umar asked the son of Harm to recite some poems of Zuhair composed in the praise of Harm. Thereupon Harm's son recited some poems. Hadrat Umar said that Zuhair wrote well in the praise of Harm and his family. Harm's son said 'He was paid well for that'.

Thereupon Hadrat Umar said, " What your father gave has perished, but what Zuhair gave lives."

Then turning to Zuhair's son, Hadrat Umar asked where were the robes of honour that Harm had bestowed on his father. He said that those had perished. Thereupon Hadrat Umar said, "Time will never destroy the robes that Zuhair bestowed on Harm".

AGHLAB & LABID

Aghlab and Labid were two well known poets of the time of Hadrat Umar. They resided at Kufa. They were allowed by Hadrat Umar a stipend of 2,000 dirhams each.

When Mugheera bin Shaaba was the Governor of Kufa, Hadrat Umar asked him to call these poets and hear from them the poetry they had written after conversion to Islam.

Mugheera called Aghlab and asked him to recite some verses which he had written since his conversion to Islam. He recited :

"Do you want a battle song or a panegyric,
Verily you have made a simple demand."

Then Mugheera called Labid, and asked him to recite some verses.

He said :

"If you like I could recite for you the verses that I wrote during the period of ignorance."

Mugheera said :

"No, let us hear something which you have written during the Islamic period."

Thereupon Labid recited some verses from the Holy Qur'an and said :

"Since I have become a Muslim, the Holy Qur'an is my poetry."

Mugheera reported to Hadrat Umar what Aghlab and Labid had said.

Thereupon Hadrat Umar wrote to Mugheera reducing the stipend of Aghlab from 2,000 dirhams to 1,500 dirhams, and raising the stipend of Labid from 2,000 dirhams to 2,500 dirhams.

Aghlab felt grieved and he wrote the following verses to Hadrat Umar:

> "Hadrat Umar asked me to recite my verses
> I complied with his order
> There was nothing wrong with my verses
> But Umar reduced my stipend
> That was a strange reward
> For compliance with the orders of the Caliph."

Hadrat Umar regretted the reduction in the stipend of Aghlab and passed orders for the restoration of the stipend of 2,000 dirhams to Aghlab. The stipend of Labid was not touched and he continued to enjoy the stipend of 2,500 dirhams.

WHEN HADRAT UMAR WAS PUT TO EXPLANATION

It was noon of a Friday. The faithful at Madina had gathered in the Prophet's mosque to offer the Friday prayers.

Hadrat Umar, the Caliph arrived to lead the prayers. He said his preliminary prayer and then proceeded to deliver his address to the congregation. He began by reciting some verses from the Holy Qur'an. Then addressing the congregation he said "Now listen".

A young man from the congregation stood up to say, "We will not listen to you, until you give us the explanation that you owe to us."

The people were startled at this audacious interference. Hadrat Umar paused for a moment, and then turning to the young man said, "Explanation for what ?"

The young man said "The other day each one of us obtained a piece of cloth from the Baitul Mal. Today I find two pieces of cloth on the person of the Caliph. I want to know what right had the Caliph to get a share twice the share of an ordinary Muslim ?"

Before Hadrat Umar could explain, Abdullah the son of Hadrat Umar rose up and said, "Friends, the truth of the matter is that like every other person my father and myself obtained a piece of cloth each from the Baitul Mal. My father is so tall that the piece of cloth that he got from the Baitul Mal did not suffice him. So I gave him my piece of the cloth".

This explanation satisfied every one. The young man who had interrupted the Caliph said, "We are satisfied. You can now proceed with your address. We will listen to you and obey your commands."

Turning to the audience Hadrat Umar said, "What will you do, my friends, in case I deviate from the truth one day?"

Thereupon a man rose up and said, "When you wilfully deviate from the truth, we will withdraw our allegiance to you and I for one would feel it my duty to kill you with my sword."

The Caliph said with an apparent show of anger "Man, do you know to whom you are speaking ?"

The man said, "Yes, I am talking to Hadrat Umar, the Commander of the Faithful."

"Then how dare you threat him with your sword" said the Caliph.

The man said, "You are our Caliph and Commander as long as you follow the truth. When you deliberately deviate from the path of the truth you no longer command our allegiance. Then we have the right to kill you, because you lead us in the wrong way."

At this the face of Hadrat Umar lit up, and a smile of satisfaction played on his lips. Raising his hands towards the heaven he said in a voice choked with emotion "Great Allah, I offer you my thanks that there is no dearth of men among the faithful who have the courage to lift the sword even against the head of Umar when he deviates from the Truth."

Turning to the faithful, Hadrat Umar said : "I enjoin you to follow me as long as I follow Allah and his Prophet. When there is any deviation on my part correct me. If I deliberately deviate from the Truth do not follow me. Pray that you and I may steadfastly keep to the path of the Truth enjoined by Islam."

HADRAT UMAR & SELF REMORSE

Once Hadrat Umar was busy with some important affairs of the State, when a person came to him and, complaining about some petty grievance, asked for immediate redress.

Thus disturbed, Hadrat Umar felt very much annoyed. He took the lash and struck the man saying :

> "When I sit for redressing the grievances of the common men you do not come, and when I am engaged in other important work you come with your grievances to disturb me."

The person walked away in a sullen mood. When the man went away, Hadrat Umar felt struck with remorse for having treated the man shabbily.

Hadrat Umar ran after the man, and overtaking him handed him his lash and said :

> "I have been hard on you and lashed you. You take this lash, and strike me so that the account may be squared."

The man was overwhelmed with the sense of justice of Hadrat Umar. He said :

> "O Commander of the Faithful, how can I raise my hand against you. I seek no revenge. I forgive you. May Allah forgive you."

Hadrat Umar went home and offered a special prayer of repentance. He upbraided himself loudly :

> "O Umar, you were low but Allah elevated you. You were wandering astray but Allah guided you. You were base

> but Allah ennobled you and gave you sovereignty over the people. Now one of them comes and asks you for requital for the harm done to him, and you beat him.
>
> What answer would you give before Allah?"

Hadrat Umar kept chiding himself long. Holding a straw in his hand he said :

"I wish, I were a straw like this." Turning to himself he said, "I wish my mother had not given birth to me."

FRIENDS WHO COULD STRAIGHTEN HIM

True to the title 'Al-Farooq', Hadrat Umar was an embodiment of truth. He did not hesitate to speak the truth, in the best interests of the Muslim State. Such truth was sometimes bitter, and the people held him in awe.

Some people understood him, and appreciated his sterling qualities of courage, conviction, and truthfulness. Some people misjudged him and felt that he was unduly hard and harsh with the people.

Hadrat Umar knew that he was more feared than loved. Under a stern exterior, Hadrat Umar had a heart full of the milk of human kindness. Whenever Hadrat Umar came across a person who was in distress or was in any way oppressed, Hadrat Umar was all sympathy for him, and he did all he could to alleviate his distress.

Hadrat Umar did often reflect and ponder over the responsibilities that had come to vest in him and the way he discharged them. He did not feel very happy with the equation between himself and the people. He regretted that the people did not understand him properly.

Hudhaifah a prominent companion has left on record that one day he went to see Hadrat Umar and found that he was feeling much perturbed. Seeing the disturbed state of the mind of Hadrat Umar, Hudhaifah enquired as to what was the matter.

Hadrat Umar said :

"I was feeling unhappy that the people have awe of me. They generally avoid me, and hesitate to bring my shortcomings to my notice. I was just thinking as to what would happen if I were to fall in erroneous ways, and because of the awe that the people have of me, no one comes forward to restrain me."

Thereupon Hudhaifah said :

"Your awe is because of the truth at your command. If you deviate from the path of truth, the people will not be afraid to call you to account. Verily if I see that you are in the wrong, I will fix you up, and straighten you."

At this Hadrat Umar felt very happy. He said :

"Thank God, there are friends who will straighten me when I err. If I have such friends around me, I need have no fear of falling into error."

THE MAN WHO CAME TO MURDER BECAME A CONVERT

By 638 A.D., the whole of Syria was under the occupation of the Muslims. Heraclius the Byzantine emperor had left Syria and withdrawn his forces. His parting words were :

> "Farewell Syria, never again will I come to this beautiful land. What a fine country I am leaving for the enemy."

Some of the Christian Arabs felt grieved at the discomfiture of the Christians at the hands of the Muslims. In a spirit of fanaticism they vowed vengeance against the Muslims. Having failed to defeat the Muslims on the battlefield they decided to resort to underhand means and murder some high ranking Muslims. A Ghassanid Arab Wasiq by name undertook to murder Hadrat Umar the Caliph of Islam.

Wasiq waited on Heraclius at Constantinople, and volunteered to rid the Byzantine emperor of his enemies. The scheme appealed to Heraclius. He paid Wasiq a huge sum and promised to pay much more when he succeeded in his mission. Thus patronised, Wasiq decided to proceed to Madina.

Arab as he was, Wasiq found no difficulty in coming over to Madina in cognito. He posed himself as a Muslim coming from the interior of the desert to pay a visit to Madina. Wasiq carried a poisoned dagger carefully hidden in the folds of his cloak. Having reached Madina, he was on the look out for a suitable opportunity when he could come face to face with the Caliph of Islam, and kill him with his dagger in an unguarded moment.

He had thought that the ruler of the Muslim state would be surrounded by heavy body-guards at all times and it would be difficult to reach him. He was surprised to learn in Madina that there were no body-guards around the Caliph of Islam. Wasiq felt happy that unguarded as the Caliph was, he could easily get an opportunity to fulfil his mission.

Wasiq waited for a suitable opportunity. One day at noon Wasiq found Hadrat Umar sleeping under a tree, all alone and without any guard. There was no body near at hand. Wasiq thought that this was a golden opportunity for him and he could despatch the Caliph of Islam without any difficulty.

Cautiously with measured steps and hushed breath Wasiq stepped upto Hadrat Umar and took his sword. He was about to plunge his sword in the body of Hadrat Umar when his eyes fell on the face of Hadrat Umar. The sight of the unadorned majesty of the pious Caliph sent a shudder through the body of Wasiq, and the sword dropped from his trembling hands. With the noise of the dropping of the sword, Hadrat Umar opened his eyes. He was quick to take hold of the fallen sword and then rising up faced his would be assassin.

Wasiq fell at the feet of the Caliph, implored his forgiveness and embraced Islam.

CRITICISM AGAINST HADRAT UMAR

One day in a Friday address Hadrat Umar said that he had tried to serve Islam and the Muslims to the best of his capacity. He added that being a human being he was apt to make mistakes. He requested the faithful to point out his mistakes if any, so that he may correct himself.

After the prayers Umman bin Sawad stepped upto Hadrat Umar and said that he wanted to apprise him of his mistakes. Hadrat Umar invited him to come along to his house where they could talk over the matter at leisure.

Umman bin Sawad said that he had no intention of criticising the Caliph ; as a well wisher he merely wanted to bring some points to his notice. Hadrat Umar said that such observations and counsels were most welcome to him.

Umman bin Sawad said that he had four objections and these were :

(1) That Hadrat Umar had prohibited Umra in the month of Hajjj ;
(2) That Hadrat Umar had declared Mut'ah unlawful.
(3) That Hadrat Umar had emancipated slave girls who bore their masters children.
(4) That Hadrat Umar was harsh and stern.

Hadrat Umar enquired whether these were all the objections against him or whether there were any other objections as well. Umman said that these were the only points of criticism against him.

About the first charge Hadrat Umar said:

"I have not prohibited Umra. My only instructions are that in the month of Hajjj priority should be given to

Hajj over the Umra. Some of the persons were prone to think that when they had performed the Umra that was enough and that thereafter Hajjj need not be performed. Such a course was derogatory to Hajjj and in order to preserve the integrity and sanctity of Hajjj I have merely instructed that in the month of Hajjj, the pilgrims should concentrate on the Hajjj. In the other months it is open to them to perform Umra."

About the Mut'ah, Hadrat Umar said :

"Mut'ah was an ancient practice with the Arabs. The Holy Prophet did not like the practice though he tolerated it on some occasions due to special circumstances. Even then on at least two occasions he prohibited the practice. God has spoken of the sanctity of the marriage ties, and if the marriage is held sacred on one side and Mut'ah is allowed on the other that would be inconsistent. If Mut'ah is allowed that would be a sort of sanctioned prostitution. That is repugnant to Islam. If any person marries the idea is to establish a home. If a person marries for a few specified days that is foreign to the establishment of a home. Mut'ah is thus repugnant to Islam. If any person wants to dissolve the marriage after a few days it is open to him to give the divorce in the usual way. I have prohibited Mut'ah in the interests of the sanctity and integrity of Muslim homes. That is a social reform. There is no express injunction allowing Mut'ah and by disallowing it I have not contravened any provisions of Islamic law."

As regards the emancipation of slave girls, Hadrat Umar explained :

" We have already laid down that no Arab can be a slave. If the slave girls were not emancipated there would have been the anomaly that while the children were free their mother was not free. Moreover for every marriage there is a dower. In the case of slave girls the dower is that when they become mothers they would be emancipated. This is a humanitarian reform strictly in accordance with the spirit of Islam."

As regards the fourth charge Hadrat Umar said :

"I am harsh and stern only for the wrong doer, the tyrant and the oppressor. For the weak and the meek I am never harsh or stern."

After hearing these explanations Umman bin Sawad said:

"Verily Umar you have spoken the truth. You have done well in whatever you have done. You have acted in the interests of Islam. May God bless you. No blame rests on you."

THE EID MOON

Uqba bin Farqad was the Governor of Azarbaijan. It was the month of the Ramadan. When 29 fasts were over the faithful gathered to sight the Eid moon, but no moon was seen. Uqba bin Farqad accordingly ordered that the fast should be kept for the thirtieth day of the Ramdan as well.

The next day Uqba kept the fast, and went on tour in the interior of the country. The Governor said the noon prayers and then retired to rest. When he woke up, he was told that the new moon was visible in the sky. Uqba went out and he saw that though there were yet a few hours for the sun to set, the moon was visible in the sky.

On sighting the moon, the Governor summoned the Ulema and sought for their opinion about the observance of the fast and the Eid. The concensus of opinion was that after the moon had been sighted the observance of the fast was not lawful. In deference to this opinion Uqba broke the fast before sunset and other Muslims did likewise.

A difficulty, however, arose about the celebration of the Eid. It was so late in the day that Eid could not be celebrated that day. After consulting the Ulema Uqba decided that though the fast was to be broken, the Eid was to be celebrated the following day.

As the issue involved an important question of religious law, Uqba referred the case to Hadrat Umar for the final verdict in matters concerning the sighting of the moon in day light and the celebration of the Eid.

When the case was referred to Hadrat Umar, he gave the following decision :

"When you see the moon in the earlier part of the day you should break the fast and celebrate the Eid. A moon appearing in the earlier part of the day is indicative of the fact that it actually appeared on the horizon the previous night, but for some reason could not be seen. When you see the moon in the later part of the day keep the fast and celebrate the Eid on the following day. Sometimes the moon is bigger and it becomes visible before the evening, but it is not a moon of the previous day. It is really for the day to follow. Moon seen in the earlier part of the day belongs to the previous day and the moon seen in the later part belongs to the following day."

HADRAT UMAR'S ATTITUDE TO SINNERS

Some time in 639 A.D. the year of the famine and the plague some Muslims in Syria drank wine. When called to question, they argued that in the Holy Qur'an, no definite punishment was prescribed for drinking and as such they were not liable to any punishment. Abu Ubaidah reported the matter to Hadrat Umar.

In reply, Hadrat Umar instructed Abu Ubaidah to call the delinquents to the mosque and there before the congregation ask them whether they considered drinking lawful or unlawful. If they considered it lawful they should be deemed to have apostasised and in that case they should meet the penalty for apostasy namely death. If they held that drinking was unlawful then they should be inflicted eighty lashes. Hadrat Umar explained that although the Holy Qur'an did not provide the penalty for drinking, it did not forbid the prescription of such penalty. The State could therefore in public interest prescribe a penalty. The State had after due deliberation provided a penalty of 80 lashes and this was in no way repugnant to Islam.

When the instructions of Hadrat Umar were received at Emessa, Abu Ubaidah called the delinquents to the mosque. These included Zarrar bin Azwar and Abu Jandal. There before the congregation Abu Ubaidah put them the question whether they regarded drinking as lawful or unlawful. They held that they regarded it unlawful. Abu Ubaidah then said that if they had done an unlawful thing they exposed themselves to punishment. They argued that no punishment was due as none had been prescribed by the Qur'an. Abu Ubadia explained in the terms of the instructions of Hadrat Umar that when a person was guilty of an unlawful act, the State could prescribe a penalty. Abu Ubaidah accordingly inflicted on the delinquents the punishment of eighty stripes.

The delinquents took the punishment to heart. Abu Jandal was particularly very disconsolate. He locked himself in his house and refused to come out and face the people. Abu Ubaidah felt for him and reported the matter to Hadrat Umar. Thereupon Hadrat Umar wrote a conciliatory letter. He wrote:

> "It is a fact that when you violate the principle of the unity of God, and create rivals to Allah the sin is too serious to be forgiven. Allah does not forgive this sin. As regards other sins God in His Mercy and Kindness forgives such sins when one is repentant. Allah says 'O my people, if you transgress and then repent do not despair of the mercy of Allah for He is Forgiving and Merciful."

In the letter Hadrat Umar advised Abu Jandal to seek the forgiveness of Allah and come out of his house and attend to the affairs of the world as usual. To the general public Hadrat Umar advised in the letter :

> "Do not exult over the sins of others. Do not ridicule them. If they are repentant help them in the process of repentance so that Allah may forgive them."

When the letter of Hadrat Umar was received, Abu Ubaidah called Abu Jandal and other delinquents to the mosque and there read the letter of Hadrat Umar before the gathering. The letter had the necessary solacing effect. The delinquents repented and then applied for being sent to some expedition on Jihad. Abu Ubaidah sent them to fight and they fought with a sense of dedication.

ABU SUFIYAN AND HADRAT UMAR

Before the conquest of Mecca, Abu Sufiyan was the leader of the Quraish in Mecca. He was very hostile to Islam. He led the Quraish at the battle of Uhud. He was the leader of the Quraish at the battle of the Ditch. The Muslims suffered considerably at the hands of Abu Sufiyan. Umm Habiba a daughter of Abu Sufiyan, however, accepted Islam and was married to the Holy Prophet.

As Abu Sufiyan was the bitter enemy of Islam, Hadrat Umar was very bitter against him. At the time of the conquest of Mecca when Abu Sufiyan came to the Muslim camp for negotiation, Hadrat Umar sought the permission of the Holy Prophet to kill Abu Sufiyan. The Holy Prophet asked Hadrat Umar to wait and watch further developments.

Thereafter Abu Sufiyan and all the Quraish of Mecca became Muslims. As Abu Sufiyan was an aristocrat, even after becoming a Muslim he could not get rid of his past arrogance.

In Madina a complaint was lodged before Hadrat Umar against Abu Sufiyan. It was complained that Abu Sufiyan had constructed a house, and blocked the drainage so that the drainage water was diverted to the houses of neighbours thereby creating a nuisance and damaging such houses.

Hadrat Umar decided that when he visited Mecca on the occasion of the Hajjj he would see the site, and pass the necesisary orders on the spot. When Hadrat Umar came to Mecca he visited the site. It transpired that Abu Sufiyan had placed some stones in the drain in such a way that the flow of the sullage in the proper direction was obstructed and was instead diverted to the houses of the neighbours. Hadrat Umar felt convinced that the conduct of Abu Sufiyan was not fair.

Hadrat Umar summoned Abu Sufiyan and asked him to remove the stones so that the sullage should flow unobstructed. Abu Sufiyan contended that he had acted within right and as such was not going to comply with the orders of the Caliph. Hadrat Umar flourished his whip and said, "Abu Sufiyan I command you to remove these stones forthwith, otherwise I will whip you, your status not wit standing."

Without further contention, Abu Sufiyan removed the stones in the manner desired by Hadrat Umar.

Thereupon turning his face to the Ka'aba Hadrat Umar said:

"Praise be to God, Who, because of the power of Islam, made an ordinary man like Umar dominate over a chief like Abu Sufiyan."

Abu Sufiyan said :

"All praise is due to God Who blessed me with the light of Islam which has shown me the true path, and made me bow before the truth".

Hadrat Umar said :

"Abu Sufiyan ! Congratulations, for Islam has shown you the true path."

HADRAT UMAR'S WIFE ACTS AS A MIDWIFE

It was the usual practice of Hadrat Umar that he would patrol the streets and suburbs of Madina to watch the interests of the people, and attend to their needs.

One day Hadrat Umar noticed a tent pitched in an open space outside Madina. A person was sitting outside the tent, and some one inside the tent was groaning.

Hadrat Umar went to the man, greeted him, and wanted to know who he was.

The man said that he was a man of the desert, and had come to Madina to wait on the Commander of the Faithful and seek his assistance.

Umar next asked who was groaning inside the tent. The man said that inside the tent his wife was groaning with labour pains. He said that he was a stranger in Madina and did not know what to do. Hadrat Umar enquired whether he had any woman to look after the confinement of his wife. He said that there was none.

Hadrat Umar said, "Do not worry. I will make the necessary arrangements."

Hadrat Umar came home, and asked his wife Umm Kulsum to accompany him on a mission of service. Umm Kulsum got ready and took with her such things as might be needed for the purposes of confinement. Hadrat Umar took with him some provisions for the purposes of cooking a meal.

Hadrat Umar returned to the camp with his wife. Umm Kulsum went inside the tent to attend to the woman in pain, while Hadrat Umar sat outside the tent with the Bedouin and began cooking some meals for him.

After an hour or so when the meals had been cooked, Umm Kulsum from inside the tent addressed Hadrat Umar : Amirul Mominin ! Congratulate your guest on the birth of a son."

Hearing this the Bedouin felt much embarrassed. Turning to Hadrat Umar he said, "Amirul Mominin, why did you not reveal your identity ? You have overwhelmed me with your benevolence."

Hadrat Umar put all his fears to rest saying : "That's all right. There is nothing to worry about. Thank God I have been of some service to you at the time of your need. You may come to me tomorrow and I will see what can be done further to help you".

It was late at night when Hadrat Umar and Umm Kulsum left. The Bedouin thanked God and said : "God be praised. I came to seek the Commander of the Faithtul, and God sent the Commander of the Faithful to seek me."

ATIKA BINT ZAID

Atika was the daughter of Zaid bin Amr bin Naufal. Zaid was the uncle of the Hadrat Umar. Atika was thus a cousin of Hadrat Umar.

At Madina, Atika was married to Abdullah the son of Hadrat Abu Bakr. Atika was very beautiful and Abdullah was much enamoured of her. He was so much lost in her love that he failed to participate in the various expeditions undertaken by the Muslims. He even neglected to offer his prayers in the mosque.

The love of Abdullah and Atika became proverbial. Abdullah felt that Atika was the most valuable thing in the world. When Hadrat Abu Bakr came to know that Abdullah had not taken part in the various expeditions and had even neglected his prayers, he put him to explanation. He had no explanation to offer. The matter of fact position was that he was so much overwhelmed by the love of Atika that he could not attend to other duties.

Hadrat Abu Bakr gave vent to anger and told his son in plain words that his failings and shortcomings were too grave to be passed over. Abdullah placed himself at the mercy of his father, and Abu Bakr decreed that Abdullah should divorce Atika within three days.

Abdullah was torn between two minds. At times he thought that he should be faithful to his love. On second thought he felt that the command of his father should be obeyed whatever the cost. After three days Abdullah divorced Atika. This decision made Abdullah deranged. He would neither eat nor drink. He sobbed and sighed and sang heart rending verses giving expression to his great grief over the loss of his beloved.

The divorce of Atika became the matter of talk in Madina. When the Holy Prophet came to know of the matter, he felt sympathy for Abdullah. The Holy Prophet revoked the divorce, and the two lovers were reunited.

Abdullah was very particular thereafter to ensure that the love for Atika did not stand in the way of his duty to God. In all the campaigns that were undertaken by the Holy Prophet thereafter, Abdullah took part therein, and fought valiantly. In the battle of Taif, Abdullah was wounded, and later he died of such wounds at Madina.

Atika bitterly mourned the death of Abdullah, and in a touching elegy she said :

> "Abdullah I have sworn that my eyes
> Shall not cease grieving over thee ;
> And my body shall ever remain,
> Covered with dust."

Atika resolved that after Abdullah she would not marry any one. She kept her resolve for four or five years. Hadrat Umar felt for her. He felt distressed that one so young and beautiful should remain a widow. Hadrat Umar advised her that she should marry. When Hadrat Umar became the Caliph, he himself offered to marry. After some hesitation, Atika accepted the proposal.

After the consummation of the marriage, when Hadrat Umar held the marrige feast, Hadrat Ali congratulated Hadrat Umar, and sought his permission to talk to the bride. Hadrat Umar permitted and Hadrat Ali reminded Atika of her resolve not to marry any one after Abdullah. Thereupon Atika burst into weeping. Hadrat Umar consolingly said :

> "Atika do not be grieved. All women do like that. May God bless you. By re-marriage you have conformed to the injunctions of Islam."

Of Hadrat Umar, Atika had a son "Ayaz".

UMM HAKIM

Umm Hakim was the daughter of Harith bin Hisham who belonged to the Makhzun tribe of the Quraish. Her mother was the sister of the famous General Khalid bin Walid.

Umm Hakim was married to Ikramah the son of Abu Jahl. The family was known for its opposition to Islam, and Umm Hakim opposed Islam tooth and nail. In the battle of Uhud she was with the Quraish of Mecca who fought against the Muslims.

When the Muslims conquered Mecca, the Quraish were converted to Islam. At that time Umm Hakim also became a Muslim. Her husband Ikramah being afraid of the wrath of the Muslims fled to Yemen.

Umm Hakim waited on the Holy Prophet, and prayed for amnesty for her husband. Seeing her fidelity, the Holy Prophet acceded to her request. She went to Yemen in person, and brought Ikramah to Madina, where he was converted to Islam.

Thereafter Ikramah became a staunch Muslim, and he participated in all the campaigns undertaken by the Muslims. In the time of the caliphate of Hadrat Abu Bakr, Ikramah fought in the apostasy wars. Later he went to Syria and fought against the Byzantines. Umm Hakim went with Ikramah to Syria and remained in the military camp. Ikramah was martyred at the battle of Ajnadin.

After the death of Ikramah, Umm Hakim stayed in Syria. Khalid bin Saeed sent her the proposal of marriage. She accepted the proposal, but said that the marriage should be held after the war against the Byzantines was over. Khalid bin Saeed said that he had a feeling that he was not going to survive the battle, and as such he wanted the marriage to be held immediately. Thereupon Umm Hakim gave her consent and the marriage was celebrated.

The marriage was consummated in the military camp at Marjal-Saffar outside Damascus. The next day Khalid bin Saeed went to fight and he was martyred. The tent of Umm Hakim was surrounded by the enemy. Though dressed in bridal clothes, Umm Hakim showed great presence of mind. She plucked the poles from the camp, and struck to death all the Byzantine soldiers who attempted to seek admittance to the camp. In the resultant confusion she escaped and sought safety in the midst of the Muslim forces.

Then she returned to Madina. She was a cousin of Hadrat Umar and Hadrat Umar condoled with her over the deaths of Ikramah and Khalid b. Saeed. Hadrat Umar was much impressed with her heroism in killing nine Byzantine soldiers with the poles of the tent at the time when she was dressed as a bride.

Hadrat Umar saw that she was feeling disconsolate. Hadrat Umar proposed marriage and after some consideration Umm Hakim accepted the proposal. Hadrat Umar and Umm Hakim were married in the third year of the caliphate of Hadrat Umar.

Of Umm Hakim, Hadrat Umar had a daughter who was named Fatima.

HADRAT UMAR MARRIES A MILKMAID TO HIS SON

One night, Hadrat Umar as usual went in disguise with his comrade Ibn Abbas to see the condition of the people. They strolled from one quarter to another. At last they came to a colony where very poor people lived.

While passing by a small hutment, the Caliph heard a whispering talk within. The mother was telling her daughter that the amount fetched by her that day on account of the sale of milk was very little. She told her that when she was young, and used to sell milk, she always mixed water with milk, and that led to considerable profit. She advised her daughter to do the same.

The girl said, "You adulterated milk, when you were not a Muslim. Now that we are Muslims, we cannot adulterate milk."

The mother said that Islam did not stand in the way of the adulteration of milk.

The daughter said, " Have you forgotten the Caliph's order? He wants that the milk should not be adulterated."

The mother said, "But the Caliph has forgotten us. We are so poor, what else should we do but adulterate milk in order to win bread ?"

The daughter said "Such a bread would not be lawful, and as a Muslim I would not do anything which is against the orders of the Caliph, and whereby other Muslims are deceived."

The mother said, "But there is neither the Caliph nor any of his officers here to see what we do. Daughter you are still a child. Go to bed now and tomorrow I will myself mix the milk with water for you."

The girl refused to fall in with the plan of her mother. She said, "Caliph may or may not be here, but his order is order, and it must be obeyed. My conscience is my Caliph. You may escape the notice of the Caliph and his officers, but how can we escape the notice of Allah and our own conscience ?"

Thereupon the mother remained quiet. The lamp was extinguished and the mother and the daughter went to sleep.

The next day, Hadrat Umar sent a man to purchase milk from the girl. The milk was unadulterated. The girl had kept her resolve.

Hadrat Umar turned to his companion and said, "The girl has kept her resolve in spite of the exhortation of her mother. She deserves a reward. What reward should I give her?"

"She should be paid some money" said Ibn Abbas.

Hadrat Umar said, "Such a girl would become a great mother. Her integrity is not to be weighed with a few coins ; it is to be measured in the scale of national values. I shall offer her the highest award in my gift, and which shall also be in the highest interest of the nation."

The Caliph summoned the daughter and the mother to his court. The mother trembled as she stood before the mighty ruler. But the girl faced the Caliph boldly and with great equanimity. She was beautiful, and there was an impressive dignity about her.

Then before the gathering, Hadrat Umar related how he had overheard the mother and the daughter, and how in spite of the exhortations of the mother the daughter had kept her resolve.

Someone suggested that the mother should be taken to task. The Caliph said that ordinarily he would have punished the mother, but he had forgiven her for the sake of her daughter. Turning to the girl the great Caliph said, "Islam needs daughters like you, and as a Caliph of Islam it devolves on me to reward you by owning you as a daughter".

The Caliph called his sons, and addressing them said, "Here is a gem of a girl who would make a great mother. I desire that one of you should take this girl as wife. I know of no better bride than this girl of sterling character. In matters of wedlock, it should be the character, and not the stature in life that should count."

Abdullah and Abdur Rahman the elder sons of the Caliph were already married. Asim the third son was yet unmarried, and he offered to marry the girl. Thereupon with the consent of the milkmaid and her mother Asim was married to the girl, and the milkmaid became the daughter-in-law of the Caliph.

From this union was born a daughter Umm Asim, who became in due course the mother of Umar bin Abdul Aziz. Umar bin Abdul Aziz became a Caliph in due course.

While other Caliphs of the Umayyad dynasty revelled in luxury, Umar bin Abdul Aziz as a Caliph set up standards for austerity and simplicity following in the footsteps of Hadrat Umar the second Caliph of Islam. It is said that if ever there was a noble Caliph after the 'Rightly guided Caliphs', such a man was Umar bin Abdul Aziz. And he inherited the noble qualities of the milkmaid who married the Caliph's son, and those of Hadrat Umar Farooq who had the eye to discern the nobler qualities of sterling character in a poor girl.

HADRAT UMAR FLOGS HIS SON TO DEATH

Abu Shahma was a son of Hadrat Umar. He fought in the battles in Egypt. After the conquest of Egypt he built a house for himself in Fustat.

One day in the company of a friend he inadvertently drank wine and became unconscious. The following day he went with his friend to Amr bin Al-Aas, confessed their guilt, and wanted to be punished. Amr bin Al-Aas said that as they had drunk the wine inadvertently, and were feeling repentant, that was enough and no further punishment was called for.

Abu Shahma did not wish to avail of the benefit of inadvertence. He insisted that he should be punished according to law, failing which he would bring the matter to the notice of the Caliph. Thereupon Amr bin Al-Aas inflicted the usual punishment of lashes in the compound of his house. Abu Shahma's head was also shaved off in the house of the Governor.

The Reporter reported the matter to Hadrat Umar, and Hadrat Umar addressed a letter to Amr b. Al-Aas in strong terms as follows :

> "O Amr bin Al-Aas it has come to my notice that you have been derelict in the performance of your duty. You have shown undue favour to Abu Shahma by awarding him punishment in your house rather than at a public place. You were apparently moved by the consideration that he is my son. You should know that in such matters I cannot tolerate any concession to a person on the ground that he is related to me. As soon as you get this letter send Abu Shahma to Madina on a naked camel."

Amr bin Al-Aas complied with the instructions and despatched Abu Shahma to Madina. In the way Abu Shahma fell sick and when he reached Madina he could hardly walk.

Hadrat Umar was furious, and he ordered that Abu Shahma should be lashed in the public. Abdul Rahman b. Auf pleaded that the boy had already been lashed in Egypt and no further punishment was called for. Abu Shahma said that he was suffering, and the punishment should be deferred till he was recovered.

Hadrat Umar brushed aside these pleadings. Abu Shahma was flogged publicly. Abu Shahma could not withstand the ordeal. He fell senseless after a few stripes had been inflicted. He remained in a state of agony for a few days and then died a martyr to the highly developed sense of justice of his father.

THE WOMAN WHO PINED FOR HER HUSBAND

In the wars that were conducted during the rule of Hadrat Umar, the soldiers on the front remained absent for considerable periods. Hadrat Umar introduced the reform that leave should be granted to every soldier after he had served on the front for four months. A story is recorded as to how this reform was brought about.

It is related that one night Hadrat Umar went on his round in Madina as usual. It was the dead of night, and every where was quiet. From one of the houses in the street, Hadrat Umar heard a lady lamenting. She said :

"The night is wearisome and keeps me sleepless ;
For I have none to keep me company.
I fear Allah, Who keeps watch over our souls,
And would not take another companion,
But who could tell Umar,
That he should not be so cruel,
As to keep my husband away from me,
For such a long period."

Hadrat Umar knocked at the door, and when the lady came to the door he said :

"I have heard, what you wanted to be conveyed to Umar. How long has your husband been away."

The lady said, "About a year."

Hadrat Umar said, "Rest assured your husband would come back to you shortly."

Hadrat Umar consulted Hadrat Hafsa as to the maximum period for which a man might remain separate from his wife. She suggested a period of four months. Hadrat Umar accordingly issued orders to the effect that unless a man of the armed forces could take his wife with him, he should be allowed a spell of leave after every four months of active service on the front.

HADRAT UMAR AND HIS WHIP

It is related that once while riding a camel, the whip of Hadrat Umar dropped. Many persons who saw the whip fall rushed to pick up the whip to hand it over to the Caliph. Hadrat Umar asked them to mind their own business, and not to bother about his whip. Hadrat Umar dismounted and picked up his whip himself.

Iqbal has dramatised the episode in his classic poem The Secrets of the Self'. Iqbal exhorts :

"Like Umar, come down from the camel,
Beware of incurring obligations, beware' "

From this episode, Iqbal deduces a code of conduct, the highlights whereof are :

"Do not incur the obligation of any person,
Do not debase yourself by receiving benefits.
Self is weakened by asking ; asking disintegrates the Self,
By asking, poverty is made more abject.
By begging, the beggar is made poorer,
Even if you are poor and overwhelmed by affliction,
Do not seek your bread by the bounty of another."

Iqbal further elaborates :

"God loves a man that earns his living ;
Woe to him that accepts bounty from another's table.
The more your hands are empty, the more you are master of yourself.
Seek no favours and walk with your head erect like the pine.
Sweet is a litlle dew, gathered by one's own hand,
Be a man of honour, and like the bubble
Keep the cup inverted even in the midst of the sea."

HADRAT UMAR'S CARE FOR THE POOR

It was the year of the famine. Hadrat Umar took pains to ensure that adequate relief reached all people, and that there were no persons in the city who went to sleep hungry.

One night as usual Hadrat Umar went on his round. He was accompanied by his slave Aslam. As he strolled from street to street all was quiet and the people seemed to be asleep. Hadrat Umar thought to himself, "Thank God, there is no one in this city whom the famine has afflicted."

Then as he turned a corner he saw a cottage where light was burning, and from where the sound of the weeping of the children was heard. Hadrat Umar went to the cottage. He saw that the lady of the house was cooking something on the hearth, and the children were crying.

Hadrat Umar knocked at the gate, and addressing the lady of the house Hadrat Umar enquired why were the children crying. She said that they were crying because they were hungry. "And what are you cooking", asked Umar. The lady said that in the kettle there was only water and stones. That was to while away the children that food was being cooked for them. She hoped that exhausted the children would go to sleep.

Hearing this tale of woe, Hadrat Umar felt guilty. He had thought that because of the arrangements made by him, no one was afflicted in the city and here was a family which was starving. Hadrat Umar said to the lady that he would arrange relief for her family immediately.

Hadrat Umar went to the Baitul Mal. There he put the necessary provisions in a bag and carried the bag to the cottage. His slave insisted that he would carry the bag, but Hadrat Umar said that he would carry his burden himself. Hadrat Umar handed over the bag of provisions to the lady. Hadrat Umar sat by the hearth and helped the lady cook the meals. When the meals were ready the children were awakened and served with the delicious meals. As the children ate to their fill and were satisfied they smiled the smile of happiness. Seeing the destitute children smile Hadrat Umar also felt happy.

Hadrat Umar enquired of the lady whether there was none to support. She said that the father of the children had died, and there was no body to support. Whatever little was in the house had been gradually used up and they were starving since the last three days.

Hadrat Umar asked the lady why she had not brought her distress to the notice of the Caliph. The lady said that in spite of her poverty she had some sense of self-respect and she could not go and beg the Caliph for any favour. She added that it was incumbent on the Caliph to ascertain that there was no one in his charge who was starving.

Hadrat Umar said, "You are right. Please excuse me for the remissness in the past. For the future it will be my responsibility to see that your wants are satisfied."

And when the lady realised that the man who had come to her relief was the Caliph himself, she felt satisfied that the Caliph had discharged his onerous responsibilities creditably.

STIPENDS FOR CHILDREN

When Hadrat Umar opened the register for public allowances, and allowed stipends for children as well, he laid down the condition that the children were not to get any allowance until they were weaned.

In their desire to get allowances for the children, the parents cut down the period of weaning.

One night Hadrat Umar went on his rounds as usual. As he was patrolling a street, he heard the voice of a baby crying. Hadrat Umar stood outside the house for some time, but the baby did not stop crying.

Hadrat Umar knocked at the door and was admitted inside the house. He saw that a woman held a small baby in her lap and the baby continued to cry.

Hadrat Umar turned to the lady and said, "What sort of mother you are. The baby is crying, and you do not feed it with your milk."

The woman said, "Go and ask Umar as to what sort of Caliph he is. He has ordained that a child would not get a stipend until it was weaned. In order to secure the stipend for our child we are trying to wean it."

Hadrat Umar argued that it was cruel to wean a baby at such an early age.

The woman retorted, "The blame for such cruelty rests on Umar who has created artificial distinction between child and child. Justice demands that every child should get a stipend, weaning or no weaning."

Hadrat Umar said, "All right. Feed your baby with your milk, and rest assured you will get the stipend for your baby even though it is not weaned."

The following day Hadrat Umar passed orders that stipends would be allowed for children from their date of birth. These orders were given a retrospective effect and the previous orders were rescinded.

HADRAT UMAR FINDS CLUE TO MURDER

Once the dead body of a beardless youth was found in an isolated place in Madina. Hadrat Umar wanted the relatives of the dead boy to take care of the body and give it a burial. No one came forward to claim the body. Hadrat Umar had the body buried. Thereafter he initiated an inquiry to trace the murder, but the murder could not be traced. Hadrat Umar prayed to God that he may facilitate his task by providing some clue to trace the murder.

After about nine months, a new born baby was found at the same site where the dead body of the young man had been found. Hadrat Umar entrusted the foundling to a wet nurse at state expense. He instructed the nurse that if any lady came to enquire about the baby, or caressed it, he should be informed. Hadrat Umar felt sure that ere long the mystery of the dead young man would be solved.

After a few months the nurse reported that a lady so and so had come to see the baby, and caressed it as if she was its mother. Hadrat Umar noted the name and address of the lady, and after having girded his sword went to see the lady.

It transpired that the lady was unmarried and was the daughter of a respectable Ansar chief. Hadrat Umar took the chief into confidence, and said that he wanted to talk to her daughter as he suspected her to be guilty of murder.

Hadrat Umar went inside the house and then branding his sword said, "You are according to my investigation guilty of murder. If you have any defence to offer, let me hear what you have to say."

The girl said, "It is true that I mudered the young man. You may listen to my story, and then you may pass whatever verdict you may pass".

Hadrat Umar said, "Yes. You may narrate your story. But mind you, speak nothing but the truth".

The girl said, "A few years ago I engaged an old woman as a maid servant. She was very kind and affectionate. She treated me as a daughter, and I looked to her as a mother. Some time later she said that she would be going to her village but would like to leave her young daughter with me." She brought her daughter and left her with me. The girl was of my age, and we soon became intimate friends. She would sleep in the same room as myself and we would talk of pleasant things till late hours in the night.

One night we talked of love and allied matters till midnight. Then feeling heavy with sleep I dozed while she kept sitting on my bed. After some time I found to my horror that whom I had taken to be a girl was a boy, and was doing foul action with me. In the heaviness of sleep I did not know what had happened, but when I regained my senses and found that I had been betrayed I took the dagger and killed the boy. Thereafter I had thrown the dead body at a solitary spot.

Nine months later a baby was born. I did not kill it but had it thrown at the spot where the dead body of its father had been thrown previously."

After hearing the story, Hadrat Umar said, "You have spoken the truth. You were betrayed and in killing the boy you vindicated your honour. You acted within the bounds of law, and I pronounce the verdict of 'Non-guilty'. You can even keep the baby with you, if you like."

JABALA BIN AIHAM

Jabala bin Aiham was a Ghassanid prince. He became a convert to Islam and came to Madina. At Madina, Jabala stayed as the personal guest of Hadrat Umar. A few days later Hadrat Umar and Jabala travelled to Mecca for the purposes of pilgrimage. In Mecca too, Jabala was the State guest.

As Jabala was circumambulating the Holy Kaaba, his pilgrim scarf was accidentally trodden by a poor Arab of the Banu Fazara. That aroused the wrath of Jabala. Without waiting to listen to any explanation, Jabala buffeted the Arab in the face bruising him severely in the nose.

The Arab lodged a complaint with Hadrat Umar. Hadrat Umar sent for Jabala and asked him whether the charge levied against him by the Arab was true. Jabala answered haughtily "This rascal trod on my reverence for the Kaaba and, but for the prohibition to shed blood within the sacred premises, I would have slain the man on the spot, instead of merely thrashing him."

Hadrat Umar put the Arab to explanation and he said on oath that due to extraordinary rush, he trod on the scarf of Jabala accidentally.

Turning to Jabala, Hadrat Umar said, "Do you agree that what happened was accidental, or did this man deliberately offend you."

Jabala said, "I am not concerned with that. It might have been accidental but the fact remained that he trod on my scarf thereby uncovering me. It must be borne in mind that I am a prince while he is a commoner."

Hadrat Umar said, "In Islam there is no distinction between a prince and a commoner. You could not take the law in your own hands merely on the ground that you are a prince, and he is a commoner."

Jabala felt annoyed and said, "I had thought that Islam would add to my dignity and prestige, and here Islam is becoming an instrument for my humiliation".

Hadrat Umar said, "Law must have its own course, and I am obliged to do justice. There are two alternatives. Either patch up with the man and satisfy him, or be prepared to face my verdict."

When Jabala saw that Hadrat Umar was serious in invoking the penal provisions of law he said, "Give me one day to ponder over the matter".

Hazrat Umar deferred his judgement for one day. That very night Jabala left for Syria secretly along with his retinue. From there he proceeded to Constantinople. In Constantinople he become a Christian. He said, "I denounce Islam because it does not discriminate between a peasant and a commoner."

When Hadrat Umar came to know on the following day that Jabala had slipped away, he allowed the poor Arab adequate compensation from the Bait-ul-Mal.

HADRAT UMAR AND NASR B. HAJJAJ ALSALMI

It is related that when one night, Hadrat Umar was on his usual round in the streets of Madina, he heard a girl in a house singing :

"Can I get some wine to drink ;
Can I ever find access to Nasr bin Hajjaj
A young man known for his beauty, youth and manners,
He who is of noble birth,
He whose company was a matter of joy".

Another girl friend sitting by her enquired who was Nasr.

The girl said, "Nasr is the most beautiful young man in Madina. I long that he should spend a night with me, when he and I should be alone."

The following day, Hadrat Umar summoned Nasr. When he saw him he wondered at his beauty. Undoubtedly he was the most beautiful young man in Madina. He had beautiful curly hair. Hadrat Umar called a barber and had the hair of Nasr cut.

Thereupon Nasr composed the following verses :

"Umar could not see my curls,
My hair which when combed waved like a chain ;
He made that head bald where once there were profuse hair ;
He who was bald headed felt jealous of him who had hair,
As he could not be proud of his hair, he deprived me of his hair. "

Hadrat Umar called Nasr again. Even though deprived of his hair he looked still more attractive. Hadrat Umar ordered that he should wear a turban.

Hadrat Umar called him again, and with turban he looked more manly and attractive. Thereupon Hadrat Umar said :

"You cannot live with me in this city where women long for you."

He ordered that Nasr should go to Basra.

When Nasr went away to Basra the girl Zulfa who had sung about him felt worried about her fate. She wrote verses to the effect that she had sung of wine and Nasr only in an imaginary mood ; otherwise she was a girl of excellent character, and did not actually crave for wine or Nasr.

Hadrat Umar made enquiry about the girl, and it transpired that she commanded good character. Hadrat Umar assured her that he proposed no action against her, but warned her that as a good girl she should not think of things forbidden by law."

At Basra, Nasr became the guest of Mujasha bin Masud. When Mujasha's wife Shameela saw Nasr she felt attracted. Nasr reciprocated her love. When Mujasha came to know of this clandestine love affair he turned out Nasr from his house and divorced his wife.

From Basra, Nasr wrote a letter to Hadrat Umar supplicating that the orders of his exile should be rescinded, and he should be allowed to come to Madina. Nasr's mother waited on Hadrat Umar and said, "Your sons are with you, but you have exiled my son. That is not fair." Hadrat Umar said, "Your son is a source of danger to the morals of the maidens of Madina. As long as I live, I would not allow him to come, and tempt innocent maidens with his looks."

When Hadrat Umar died, Nasr returned to Madina.

PUNISHMENT FOR ILLICIT LOVE

Abul Siara was a native of Madina. He fell in love with a beautiful lady who was the wife of one Abi Jandab. Abul Siara saw the lady and pressed his suit vehemently. The lady warned him to desist from such a course. She told him that if her husband came to know of his approach he would murder him. In spite of the warning, Abul Siara continued his suit. The lady reported the matter to the younger brother of Abi Jandab. He warned Abul Siara in strong terms, but he took no heed and persisted in his erroneous course.

Exasperated, the lady reported the matter to her husband Abi Jandab. Abi Jandab laid down a trap for catching Abul Siara. He gave out that he was going out for the grazing of his camels, and he would return after a few days. At night thinking that Abi Jandab was not at home, Abul Siara knocked at the door of his beloved. The lady asked him to go away as she was married and could not reciprocate his love. He sighed and sobbed and made declarations of love in pathetic terms. He said that he was so much lost in her love that he would even welcome death. Apparently moved by the frenzied state of her lover, the lady admitted Abul Siara to her house. She advised him to hide himself in the room. In the meantime she would decorate herself and then come to him.

As soon as Abul Siara entered the room, Abi Jandab who was already there started beating Abul Siara with sticks and whips. Abul Siara cried and shrieked. The lady asked the younger brother of Abi Jandab to intervene lest the man might be killed. At his intervention, Abi Jandab withdrew his hand. Badly bruised with his bones broken, Abul Siara was carried out and thrown in the way of camels. When Abul

Siara came to consciousness and the people asked as to what had happened he said that he had fallen from a camel and broken his bones.

The matter came to the notice of Hadrat Umar. He sommoned the parties and recorded their statements. The lady stated how Abul Siara tried to seduce her and how she resisted his love. Abi Jandab stated how a trap had been laid to catch Abul Siara red handed. Abul Siara confessed his guilt. Hadrat Umar highly praised the conduct and character of the lady. He absolved Abi Jandab of the charge of violence against Abul Siara. Abul Siara was pronounced guilty and awarded punishment.

DISMISSAL OF A GOVERNOR FOR WRITING POETRY

Al-Numan was the son of Adiy. Adiy was an early convert to Islam. He migrated to Abyssinia under the instructions of the Holy Prophet and died there. Al-Numan was born in Abyssinia. Later he returned to Madina. He was a good poet.

During the caliphate of Hadrat Umar, he was appointed the Administrator of the district of Maisan in Iraq. He had a beautiful wife Al-Hasna who stayed at Madina.

In a poetic vein, Al-Numan composed some verses and sent them to his wife at Madina.

The verses read :

"Hasn't Al-Hasna heard that her husband in Maisan
Is drinking from glasses and jars ?
If I wished the chief men of the city would sing to me
And the dancing girls whirl in ecstasy.
If you are my friend, give me a drink in the largest cup,
Don't give me the half-filled cup,
Perhaps the Commander of the Faithful will take it amiss
That I am indulging in the drinking of wine."

Al-Hasna showed the letter of her husband to some of her girl friends. They appreciated the verses of Al-Numan. The verses got popular and Hadrat Umar also came to hear them. Hearing the verses, Hadrat Umar said :

"He is right. By God I do take it amiss, and I will call him to account."

Hadrat Umar forthwith dismissed Al-Numan from his office.

Al-Numan came to Madina. He saw Hadrat Umar and pleaded that he had never acted in the way that his verses implied. He urged that he was a poet who wrote in an exaggerated way.

Hadrat Umar said, "The penalty for writing in an exaggerated way is dismissal ; if you had acted in the way the verses implied I would have lashed you in the public. Know that I want the rulers to have a balanced view of things, and if they write in an exaggerated way, poetry or otherwise, they are not fit to hold administrative offices."

SAEED BIN AAMIR

Hadrat Umar appointed Saeed bin Aamir as the Governor of Emessa in Syria. Saeed was highly advanced in piety and led a very austere life. Hadrat Umar had a very high opinion about his integrity.

When Hadrat Umar went to Syria, he asked the people of Emessa whether they had any complaint against their Governor. The people said that they had four complaints against the Governor.

Hadrat Umar summoned Saeed bin Aamir, and then in his presence asked the complainants to state their complaints.

The first complaint was that he came out of his house very late in the morning. Hadrat Umar put Saeed to explanation and he said, "We have no servant. I and my wife are alone. On rising up in the morning we offer our prayers, then read the Qur'an. Thereafter my wife cooks the meals and I help her. That takes time."

The second complaint was that at night he did not attend to any body. When asked to explain, Saeed said, "I have reserved the day for the people, and the night for God. As I attend God during the night I cannot attend to any person when I am attending God."

The third complaint was that once a month, he came out of his house very late in the afternoon. Saeed said, "I have only one change of clothes with me. I wash them once a month myself. Washing and drying the clothes takes time, and that is why once a month I am held up in my house till the afternoon."

The fourth complaint was that sometimes he fell into fits of unconsciousness. Saeed said that in Mecca he had witnessed how Khabib a convert to Islam was tortured to death by the Quraish of Mecca. The Quraish, offered him safety and wealth if he disowned the Holy Prophet. He spurned their offer. He was asked whether he would not like Muhammad (peace be on him) to be tortured in his place. Khabib replied that he could not suffer even a thorn pricking the Holy Prophet. Thereupon the Quraish hung him dead downward along a date tree and did him to death. Saeed added, "At that time I was an infidel and did not do anything to come to the relief of Khabib. I recall how Khabib died calling 'Muhammad'. Now whenever I recall that tragic event, I am overwhelmed with remorse, and I swoon."

Hadrat Umar dismissed the complaints. He said : "Thank God, my opinion about Saeed has been confirmed by this trial. Verily he is a great Muslim, and those who complain against him their ignorance owe him an apology."

UMAIR BIN SAAD

Umair bin Saad held the office of the Governor of Emessa for some time during the caliphate of Hadrat Umar. Umair was more of a saint than a statesman. Instead of amassing wealth he distributed all that he had in the way of Allah.

For a year Umair remitted no revenue to Madina. Hadrat Umar felt suspicious that Umair had misappropriated the revenues. He issued instructions calling upon Umair to come over to Madina.

As soon as the instructions of the Caliph were received Umair started for Madina. He took a tiffin carrier for carrying the meals, and a small waterskin for carrying water. He took a staff in his hand and started for Madina on foot. When he reached Madina he waited on Hadrat Umar.

Hadrat Umar enquired how did he do.
Umair said, "You can see for yourself."

Looking at his strange appearance, Umar enquired whether he had come all the way from Emessa to Madina on foot.

Umair answered the question in the affirmative.

Umar then asked why did he not hire an animal for the purposes of the journey.

Umair said that he had no money to pay for the hire. Some persons offered him a free ride in consideration of the office held by him, and such offers were rejected by him.

Umar then enquired about the revenues. Umair said that all the revenues were spent for the use of the people.

Umar wanted him to go back to Emessa, and ensure that in future the State share of the revenues was sent to Madina.

Umair said that he was not fit to be a Governor and that some one else should be appointed in his place.

Hadrat Umar prevailed upon him to take back his resignation but Umair said that his decision was irrevocable.

Umair took leave of the Caliph, and retired to his village which was a few miles from Madina.

Umar was surprised at the behaviour of Umair. He thought that Umair had affected such austerity to cover up the misappropriation of revenues. Hadrat Umar deputed a man to go to the house of Umair and submit a report. Hadrat Umar instructed, "Go to the house of Umair and there be his guest for three days. Watch him carefully. If you see any signs of opulence about him, furnish me a report. Take this bag of money. If you find that he is in straitened circumstances make him a gift of this money."

The man deputed by Hadrat Umar went to the house of Umair and there lodged with him as his guest. There he found that Umair subsisted on bare barley bread and there was no sign of opulence about him. When the agent of Hadrat Umar was about to depart he presented him the bag of money. Umair refused to accept the money.

When the report was submitted to Hadrat Umar, he said that Umair was a great man.

MUGHEERA BIN SHU'BA

Mugheera bin Shu'ba belonged to the tribe of Thaqeef of Taif. He was converted to Islam in 628 A.D. He took part in the battle of Yamama. He was a brave fighter. In one of the battles he lost an eye.

When Utba b. Ghazwan was the Governor of Basra, Mugheera was his deputy. In 639 A.D., Utba left for Mecca and Madina for performing Hajj and left Mugheera as the acting Governor of Basra.

At Madina, Utba waited on Hadrat Umar and wanted to be relieved of the office of the Governor. Hadrat Umar did not agree and Utba was required to return to Basra in national interest. On the way to Basra Utba fell off his camel and died from the fall. On the death of Utba, Hadrat Umar confirmed Mugheera in his appointment as the Governor of Basra.

Mugheera b. Shu'ba was known for his weakness for women. He would marry women and would divorce them after some time to make room for more beautiful faces. In this way, he married no less than 80 wives, taking steps to ensure that at a time his wives were not more than four, the limit prescribed by the Shariah.

In those days at Basra, there was a beautiful woman Umm Jamil. She belonged to the same tribe as that of Mugheera. Her husband had died and she became notorious for loose morals. Mugheera was attracted by her and she visited him often.

Some Muslims in Basra became critical of the conduct of Mugheera. Among them was Abu Bakra Thaqeefi whose house across the street faced the house of Mugheera. One day a strong wind blew and the windows of the houses of

Abu Bakra and Mugheera got opened through the force of the wind.

Abu Bakra saw through his window that in this house Mugheera was locked up in an uncompromising state with a woman. He thought that the woman was Umm Jamil. He had some friends with him, and they also saw Mugheera involved with a woman.

Abu Bakra Thaqeefi wrote to Hadrat Umar accusing Mugheera of adultery. The report was endorsed by four witnesses who had seen Mugheera in an uncompromising state with a woman.

Hadrat Umar took prompt action. Hadrat Umar appointed Abu Musa as the Governor of Basra and removed Mugheera from the office. Mugheera was summoned to Madina to face the trial. Abu Bakra and the other witnesses who had made the complaint were also summoned to Madina.

At the trial, Mugheera pleaded not guilty. His defence was that the woman in question was his wife and not Umm Jamil. With great indignation he averred that Abu Bakra and the men with him had no right to interfere in his privacy.

Abu Bakra on the other hand maintained that the woman was Umm Jamil. Three other witnesses corroborated the statement of Abu Bakra. The fourth witness Ziyad stated that he had seen the event, but he had not seen the face of the woman and did not know who she was. The other witnesses were cross examined, and it was found that there were some weak points in their evidence. They were asked whether the woman had her back or her face toward them. They said that she had their back to them. They tried to make out that even from her back she could be identified as Umm Jamil. They argued that the scandal of Mugheera and Umm Jamil was very common in Basra, and that lady was none else but Umm Jamil.

Under the Qur'anic law in order to press the charge of adultery definite evidence of four witnesses was necessary. As in this case the fourth witness was not sure of the identification of the woman, Mugheera was given the benefit of doubt and acquitted. Abu Bakra and his companions who had levelled the charge were punished with lashes for making a charge which could not be established.

In spite of his acquittal, Mugheera was not restored to the office of the Governor, and was detained in Madina. Mugheera made some show of indignation at having been treated shabbily in a case which was false. Hadrat Umar called him to his presence and issued the warning :

> "O Mugheera offer thanks to God that full evidence was not forthcoming against you, and you have been saved from disgrace by a technical flaw. Grounds of suspicion against you were very much there, and I have given you the benefit of doubt. Remember that if the evidence was complete, you would have been stoned to death."

ABDULLAH BIN QART

Abdullah bin Qart was appointed by Hadrat Umar as the Governor of Emessa. When Hadrat Umar went on a tour of Syria, he enquired of the people of Emessa as to how was their Governor. The concensus of opinion was :

> "He is a good man, but he has some pride and haughtiness about him, and he has constructed a double storeyed house for himself, while the houses of all other Muslims are single storeyed."

Hadrat Umar deputed an agent to verify whether Abdullah had in fact built a double storeyed house. The agent was further instructed that if the house was in fact double storeyed the door on the upperstorey should be burnt as indicative of the displeasure of the Caliph. The agent found that a double storeyed house had actually been constructed. He, therefore, in compliance with the order of Hadrat Umar had the door burnt. Abdullah watched the burning of the door with a sense of hurt pride. This was reported to Hadrat Umar.

When Hadrat Umar returned to Madina, he summoned Abdullah bin Qart to Madina. Having arrived at Madina, Abdullah bin Qart waited on Hadrat Umar. Hadrat Umar did not see him for three days and kept him waiting.

When after three days, Abdullah was admitted to the presence of Hadrat Umar, Hadrat Umar asked him whether he had built the second storey with his own money, or with money procured through unlawful means. Abdullah produced accounts to show that the house had been constructed with his own money. Hadrat Umar showed his satisfaction on that count. Thereupon Abdullah behaved haughtily and asked "When the house was constructed with my own money, where lay the offence."

Hadrat Umar cast a searching look at Abdullah and then said with some show of anger, "As a Governor of a Muslim state, you had to set a standard of equality among the Muslims. You have violated this principle by constructing a double storeyed house for yourself, thus placing yourself above the people."

Hadrat Umar ordered Abdullah to see him at Harrah the following day. Harrah was the state pasture a few miles from Madina. When Abdullah appeared at Harrah, Hadrat Umar ordered him, "Take off your costly clothes, and don this dress of a shepherd. Till further orders you have to look after the camels in this pasture". Abdullah reluctantly complied with the orders. Hadrat Umar visited Harrah a fortnight later and asked Abdullah as to how he felt. Abdullah said, "I feel repentant". Thereupon Hadrat Umar said, "A Muslim Governor cannot be haughty or proud. If you are repentant I send you back as Governor. I hope you have learnt the lesson that a Governor is not superior to the people ; he is only one of them, with great responsibilities."

Abdullah returned to Emessa a changed man.

ABU MUSA ASH'ARI

Abu Musa Ash'ari was the Governor of Basra. He held the chief command of the operations in Persia. After the victory of Isfahan Abu Musa sent a delegation of sixty persons to Madina. A young man Zaba bin Mahsin waited on Abu Musa and desired that he should also be included in the delegation. Abu Musa regretted his inability as persons more deserving than Zaba had been included in the delegation. Zaba felt dissatisfied and he held out a threat of complaining to the Caliph. Abu Musa informed Hadrat Umar of the threat of Zaba.

Zaba went to Madina and there lodged a complaint against Abu Musa. Hadrat Umar recorded the complaint and summoned Abu Musa to Madina. When Abu Musa came to Madina, Hadrat Umar showed him the list of charges against him and asked for his explanation.

The first charge was that out of the captives he had kept sixty captives for himself. Abu Musa explained that these captives had applied for being ransomed and he had kept them with him till they were ransomed. Hadrat Umar held that the charge was not established.

The second charge was that he had paid one thousand dirhams to a poet. Abu Musa said that he had paid the amount out of his money. Abu Musa presented the accounts. Hadrat Umar felt satisfied and this charge was dismissed.

The third charge was that Abu Musa had a maid Aquila who was given two shares. Abu Musa explained that there was something curious with the maid as her consumption of food was twice that of an average adult. As such she had to be given two shares.

The fourth charge was that Abu Musa had entrusted most of his work to a young man Ziyad. Abu Musa explained that he had done so in public interest as Ziyad was most intelligent.

Hadrat Umar summoned Aquila and Ziyad to Madina. He verified that Aquila actually consumed food twice the normal food of an adult. By questioning Ziyad Hadrat Umar felt convinced that Ziyad was highly intelligent and that it was in public interest to avail of his intelligence.

Abu Musa acquitted of the charges, and was asked to resume his office at Basra.

On another occasion a person came to Hadrat Umar, and complained against Abu Musa. He said that at the time of the distribution of spoils Abu Musa gave him a smaller share. He protested and urged that he should be given the full share due to him. Thereupon Abu Musa felt annoyed, struck him with twenty lashes and had his hair shaved. Hadrat Umar asked the complainant to return to Basra and there level the charge against Abu Musa before a congregation. If the charge was established he could have his revenge from Musa. Hadrat Umar gave the complainant the necessary authority in this behalf. The complainant returned to Basra and there in the mosque levelled the charge against Abu Musa. There were many in the congregation who came forward to support the charge. Abu Musa turning to the complainant said, "You can have your revenge. You may beat me, or accept some money from me at your option." Thereupon the complainant said, "Now I feel satisfied and I forgive you in the name of Allah."

TRIAL OF SAAD BIN ABI WAQAS

Saad bin Abi Waqas was the victor of Qadisiyya. He was a prominent companion and a maternal uncle of the Holy Prophet. Hadrat Umar appointed him as the Governor of Kufa. In spite of his very high position, Saad could not escape from the scrutiny of Hadrat Umar and had to face a trial.

It was reported to Hadrat Umar that Saad had constructed a palace, and had provided a door which could be shut at his option. The orders of Hadrat Umar were that where the Governors sat to meet the people or attend to their complaints there should be no door so that all people could have access to the Governor at all times.

Hadrat Umar deputed Muhammad bin Masalma to hold an enquiry on the spot and if he found that a door had in fact been constructed it should be burnt. Muhammad went to Kufa and found the door. Saad argued that as a market adjoined his house the door was necessary to shut down the noise. This explanation was not accepted and Muhammad burnt the door.

On the eve of the battle of Nihawand when Saad was commanding the operations Jarah bin Sanan Asadi lodged some complaints against Saad. It was a critical time when all attention had to be concentrated at mobilising forces for confrontation with the Persians. In spite of critical situation, Hadrat Umar decided to hold the enquiry. The complainant along with his witnesses was summoned to Madina. Saad was also summoned to Madina to face the trial.

The charges against Saad were :

(1) that in the battle-field he did not fight personally:

(2) that he did not make fair distribution ; and

(3) that he did not offer the prayers correctly.

Saad explained that he could not fight personally as there were boils on his body. Nevertheless he directed all field operations personally and God made the Muslims victorious. Hadrat Umar accepted the explanation and absolved Saad of the charge.

As regards the charge of unfair distribution, Saad presented the entire record. Hadrat Umar scrutinised the record and agreed that the distribution in all cases had been made according to merit. He was accordingly absolved of this charge.

Hadrat Umar asked Saad as to how he offered prayers. Saad explained in detail how he offered his prayers. Hadrat Umar was satisfied that there was nothing wrong with the way in which he offered his prayers.

Hadrat Umar accordingly absolved Saad bin Waqas of all the charges against him. He said that he knew that the charges were baseless but he had held the enquiry to establish the integrity of Saad.

In the enquiry Jarah bin Sanan Asadi had lodged the complaint and Asama bin Qatada had given evidence against Saad. After the enquiry Saad cursed Jarah as well as Asama. His curse fell on these two persons. Jarah became blind and was afflicted with poverty. Asama was killed by his own people.

AMR BIN AL-AAS

Amr bin Al-Aas was the conqueror of Egypt. He enjoyed a high position but in spite of that he did not escape from the scrutiny of Hadrat Umar.

It was reported to Hadrat Umar that Amr had amassed much wealth. Hadrat Umar wrote to Amr :

"It has come to my notice that you have amassed considerable wealth. Originally you were a man of ordinary means. Whence comes such wealth ?"

Amr explained that he owned some land which brought good income, Moreover the salary that he got was ample which he could invest in business.

Hadrat Umar was not satisfied with the explanation. He had half of the wealth of Amr confiscated to the State. Hadrat Umar reprimanded Amr in the following terms :

> "O ye Governors you have sat on the springs of wealth. Nothing stands in your way in amassing wealth. You people are playing with fire."

Amr bin Al-Aas had a pulpit for himself in the Juma Mosque at Fustat. Hadrat Umar rebuked Amr for that in the following terms :

> "I cannot approve that the Muslims should sit low while you should sit above them. Do away with the pulpit."

Amr bin Al-Aas complied with the orders.

Once on the occasion of the Hajj in the presence of all the Governors, Hadrat Umar addressed the people :

> "O ye people, I have not sent the Governors so that they may maltreat you or deprive you of your lawful possessions. I have sent them so that they may be a source of inspiration to you in leading life according to the Islamic way. If any Governor violates these terms, please inform me and I would take action."

A man rose up from the congregation to enquire whether a Governor could on his own account beat a Muslim. Hadrat Umar said that if any punishment was inflicted as a result of a judicial trial the man could be punished ; otherwise not. The man complained that Amr bin Al-Aas the Governor of Egypt had inflicted eighty stripes on him without any judicial trial. Amr said that he had beaten the man to enforce discipline .Hadrat Umar said that unless the man was judicially tried and found guilty no punishment could be inflicted on him. Hadrat Umar asked the complainant that as Amr beat him without authority, he could strike him with a similar number of lashes to vindicate himself. Amr begged for Hadrat Umar's permission to conciliate the man. Hadrat Umar agreed, and Amr bin Al-Aas conciliated the man after paying him a substantial amount.

On one occasion Amr called a man 'Munafiq'. The man came to Hadrat Umar and complained. Hadrat Umar gave the complainant the authority to return to Egypt, confront the Governor with the charge before the public and if it was established claim indemnity. The man returned to Egypt and confronted the Governor with the charge in the main mosque. Amr denied the charge but the man asked the men in the congregation to say on oath whether they had heard the Governor on such and such a day calling him 'Munafiq'. Many persons stood up to corroborate the statement. Thus cornered Amr said to the complainant, "You may take your revenge". Thereupon the complainant said, "Now I forgive you."

On another occasion an Egyptian complained before Hadrat Umar that in a horse race his horse was leading but Muhammad the son of Amr beat him and had his own horse to be the winner. When the matter was brought to the notice of Amr he put the complainant in prison. The complainant escaped from the prison and came to Madina to lodge his complaint with Hadrat Umar. Hadrat Umar summoned Amr and his son to Madina. They were apprised of the complaint against them. They could not offer a satisfactory explanation. Hadrat Umar ordered that the complainant should beat Muhammad the son of Amr in the same way as Muhammad had beat him. The complainant beat Muhammad the son of Amr accordingly and felt satisfied.

HARITH BIN WAHB YASHI

Harith bin Wahb Yashi was a prominent companion. Hadrat Umar appointed him as a Governor of a province.

Hadrat Umar had an intelligence service in each province and this department was under the direct control of Hadrat Umar himself. This Department was required to report from time to time about the activities of the officers in the province.

The Intelligence Department reported to Hadrat Umar that Harith bin Wahb Yashi the Governor had sold some camels for one hundred dinars.

Hadrat Umar summoned Harith bin Wahb Yashi to Madina and put him to trial.

He was asked whether it was a fact that he had sold some camels for one hundred dinars.

He admitted that he had sold some camels for this amount. He was next asked, ' From where did you get the camels".

He replied that these camels were the share of his spoils.

"What profit did you earn from the sale of the animals", was the next question put by Hadrat Umar.

Harith bin Wahb said that he could not be sure as to the exact amount of the profit, but it might be fifty dinars.

Thereupon Hadrat Umar gave the verdict :

"I sent you as a Governor and not as a trader. Deposit the amount of the profit in the public treasury, and do not indulge in trading activities as long as you hold the office of the Governor."

Harith bin Wahb deposited the amount in the public treasury and submitted his resignation. He said :

"By God, I will not serve under you."

Hadrat Umar said :

"By God, I will not appoint you as Governor again."

QADAMA BIN MAZAUN

Qadama was the son of Mazaun who was one of the earliest converts to Islam. The Holy Prophet had great regard for Mazaun. A sister of Qadama, Zainab was the wife of Hadrat Umar. Qadama was the maternal uncle of Abdullah and Hadrat Hafsa.

Hadrat Umar appointed Qadama as the Governor of Bahrain. Qadama was a good administrator and he ruled his province well. Hadrat Umar had his intelligence service in Bahrain and the Department reported that though Qadama was honest and a good administrator he was apt to indulge in drinking.

Once a companion Jarud came from Bahrain and he reported to Hadrat Umar that Qadama had drunk and he had seen him in an unconscious state.

Hadrat Umar asked whether he could produce a witness. Jarud said that Abu Hurairah be summoned as a witness.

Hadrat Umar called Abu Hurairah, and asked him whether he could give any evidence on the point whether Qadama had drunk.

Abu Hurairah said : "I did not see Qadama drinking, but I saw him in an unconscious state."

Hadrat Umar summoned the wife of Qadama Hind bint Al-Walid who was a sister of Khalid and was related to Hadrat Umar. Hind was asked to give evidence on the point whether her husband drank. She gave evidence against her husband.

Hadrat Umar summoned Qadama from Bahrain and put him on trial.

When faced with the evidence of his own wife, Qadama did not choose to rebut the charge. He took the stand that drinking was not specifically prohibited.

Hadrat Umar said, "Qadama I put you the question whether you regard drinking as lawful."

Qadama said, "I would not say that it is lawful, but I do maintain that drinking is not punishable."

Hadrat Umar said, "You are not correct that drinking is not punishable. I will inflict on you the usual punishment. I cannot make any exception in your case on the ground that you are my brother."

Hadrat Umar inflicted the punishment on Qadama. Qadama resigned the office and refused to be on speaking terms with Hadrat Umar. He also divorced his wife who had given evidence against him.

When Hadrat Umar went on Hajj he had a dream in which he was asked to reconcile with Qadama. Qadama happened to be in Mecca. Hadrat Umar went to Qadama, and sought his conciliation. After some discussion both the sides decided to forgive and forget. Qadama said that he would not serve again under Hadrat Umar but he promised that he would not drink again.

DISMISSAL OF KHALID

Some time in 637 A.D., Khalid had a special bath in which he rubbed his body with a certain substance which had an ingredient of alcohol in it. This was reported to Hadrat Umar, who reprimanded Khalid as follows :

> "It has come to my notice that you have rubbed your body with alcohol. Lo Allah has made unlawful the substance of alcohol as well as its form, just as He has made unlawful both the form and substance of sin. He has made unlawful the touch of alcohol in a bath no less than the drinking of it. Let it not touch your body for it is unclean."

Hadrat Khalid explained that the drug had been boiled before use and all alcohol therein had evaporated. Hadrat Umar did not accept the explanation, but he chose to take no action.

After the battle of Marash in 638 A.D., Athath bin Qais a Kinda chief and poet wrote a panegyric in the praise of Khalid. Khalid gave the poet a reward of 10,000 dirhams. When this was reported to Hadrat Umar, he commanded Abu Ubaida :

> "Bring Khalid in front of the congregation, tie his hands with his turban and take off his cap. Ask him from which funds he gave such a high award to Athath, from his own pocket or from the spoils acquired in the expedition of Marash. If he confesses to having given the award from the spoils, he is guilty of misappropriation. If he claims that he gave the money from his own pocket, he is guilty of extravagance. In either case dismiss him and take over the charge from him."

The command of Hadrat Umar was carried to Abu Ubaida by Hadrat Bilal, the Muezzin. Bilal arrived at Emessa and handed over the Caliph's letter to Abu Ubaida for compliance. Khalid who was then at Qinissrin was summoned to Emessa.

At Emessa when Khalid called on Abu Ubaida, he was informed of the Caliph's charge against him. Abu Ubaida asked Khalid whether he was inclined to confess his guilt. Khalid wanted some time to consider the matter and this was allowed. Khalid consulted his sister who was at Emessa. She advised him against confession. Khalid accordingly told Abu Ubaida that as he was not guilty, there was nothing to be confessed.

A congregation of the Muslims was held in the principal mosque at Emessa. Here Bilal faced Khalid and enquired, "O Khalid, did you give Athath ten thousand dirhams from your own pocket or from the spoils ?" Khalid was astounded, and for some time he was quiet. Bilal walked upto him ; took off his turban and tied his hands therewith. Bilal said that he had done so in accordance with the orders of the Caliph. He repeated his question as to from where ten thousand dirhams had been paid to Athath. After some time Khalid found his voice and said that he had paid the money from his own pocket.

Abu Ubaida took over the charge from Khalid and instructed him to proceed to Madina to see the Caliph.

Khalid arrived at Madina as an embittered man. When Khalid met Umar, Umar paid him a tribute : "Khalid you have done what no other man has done ; but it's not the people who do ; it is Allah Who does".

Khalid protested against the treatment meted out to him. Hadrat Umar said, "Whence comes all this wealth ?"

Khalid said, that it was the share of his spoils Khalid estimated that his wealth did not exceed 60,000 dirhams. He offered, "Whatever exceeds 60,000 dirhams is yours."

Hadrat Umar had the possessions of Khalid checked and evaluated. The assessment worked out to 80,000 dirhams.

Hadrat Umar accordingly confiscated Khalid's possessions valued at Rs. 20,000. After this transaction, Hadrat Umar said to Khalid :

> "That settles the case. I have no more charge against you. I assure you that you are honourable in my eyes, and you are dear to me. After this day you will have no further cause of complaint against me."

Khalid felt bitter. After staying in Madina for a few days, Khalid left for Syria. Many people gathered to bid farewell to the General. The people felt that Khalid the hero of their dreams had been treated with injustice.

After Khalid had left, the people of Madina waited on Hadrat Umar and wanted him to return to Khalid his property which had been confiscated. Hadrat Umar did not accept the appeal. He said, "I do not trade with what belongs to Allah and the Muslims". The issues which agitated the public mind were : Whether Hadrat Umar had taken such drastic action because of his personal ill will against Khalid or whether Khalid was really dishonest. Hadrat Umar clarified :

> "I have not dismissed Khalid because of my anger or personal ill will against him. I have not dismissed Khalid because he was dishonest. I have dismissed him because the people glorified him and were misled. I feared that the people would rely on him. I want the people to know that it is Allah Who does all things ; and that there should be no wavering in the faith of the people in Allah by attributing success in any field to any human being."

AYAD BIN GHANAM

Ayad bin Ghanam was the conqueror of the Jazira, the land between the Tigris and the Euphrates in the upper part of Iraq. He served as the Governor of Jazira for some time. Later he was transferred to Egypt.

One day a Bedouin came to Hadrat Umar and said, "Umar, beware of the fire of hell."

Hadrat Umar enquired what was the matter.

The Bedouin said, "You have enjoined upon your Governors to lead a simple life and be accessible to the people at all times. But do you know that Ayad your Governor of Egypt is living a luxurious life and he is not accessible to the people."

Hadrat Umar noted the complaint and assured the complainant that suitable action would be taken thereon. He deputed an agent to Egypt to verify the complaint. He instructed further that if the complaint was correct, Ayad should be summoned to Madina.

On reaching Egypt the agent deputed by Hadrat Umar felt satisfied that the Governor dressed himself in fine clothes, and that he was not easily accessible to the public. The emissary of Hadrat Umar accordingly summoned Ayad to Madina.

When Ayad was presented to Hadrat Umar, the latter could not recognise him. When he was told that he was in fact Ayad, he said :

> "When I sent you as Governor you were neither so white nor so fat as you are now. *Prima facie* you have abused your position."

Hadrat Umar asked him to take off his fine clothes, wear the dress of a shepherd and look after the goats of the Baitul Mal in the State pasture. Iyad complied with the order. A few days later Hadrat Umar went to the State pasture and enquired of Ayad as to how he felt. Ayad said, "My father was a shepherd, and I feel no humiliation in following in the footsteps of my father."

Thereupon Hadrat Umar said, "If that is so, it means that your conscience is not guilty. I have checked your accounts and these have been found in order. You are not corrupt but you have indulged in luxury. You became arrogant because of the office held by you. I hope you are now rid of your pride and arrogance. What sort of man will you be if I send you back to your office."

Ayad said, "I have no desire for the office, but if that is your command, I will do as you ordain."

Hadrat Umar said, "That is well said. I order you to resume charge as the Governor of Egypt. Dress yourself as a simple man and avoid wearing Egyptian finery. Let there be no guard at your door, and see that you are accessible to the people at all times."

Ayad said, "The orders of the Caliph will be complied with strictly."

Ayad returned to Egypt, a changed man. He strictly complied with the orders of Hadrat Umar both in letter and spirit.

PART III

Conquest of Iraq and Persia

ABU UBAID AS COMMANDER-IN-CHIEF IN IRAQ

During the caliphate of Hadrat Abu Bakr under the command of Khalid bin Walid the Muslims conquered a greater part of Iraq. In June 634 A.D., Khalid was asked to proceed to Syria, and Muthanna was left in command of the Muslim forces in Iraq.

With the departure of Khalid to Syria there was a lull in fighting on the Iraq front. Roughly the position was that the Persians held the territory to the east of the Tigris while the Muslims held the territory to the west of the Euphrates. The position about the territory between the two rivers known as the "Suwad" was somewhat obscure. It was no man's land. Sometimes parts thereof were occupied by the Persians and sometime by the Muslims. The people of the region thus kept shifting their loyalties, sometimes to the Persians and sometimes to the Muslims.

In July 634 a battle was fought between the Persians and the Muslims in the 'Suwad', somewhere near ancient Babylon. The Persians were under the impression that with the departure of Khalid and a diminution in the strength of the Muslim forces, it would be easy for them to defeat the Muslims. The battle of Babylon belied these hopes. Muthanna rose to the occasion, and after a violent battle the Persians were defeated.

Soon after there was a revolution in Persia. The Persian king was killed, and a lady Puran Dukht ascended the throne of Persia. The veteran General Rustam became the Commander-in-Chief of the Persian forces and he undertook to drive away the uncouth Arabs from the fertile land of Iraq.

Anticipating a Persian offensive on a larger scale under the new set up Muthanna felt that the Muslims should get ready for such a war, and for that more reinforcements were needed. In the third week of August 634 Muthanna went personally to Madina to get reinforcements for the Iraq front.

When Muthanna reached Madina, the Caliph Abu Bakr lay on the death bed. Muthanna waited on the dying Caliph, and apprised him of the situation in Iraq. He stated that the Persians were going to launch a big offensive, and that the Muslim forces in Iraq were too inadequate to meet the challenge. He made a strong plea for further reinforcements.

Hadrat Abu Bakr though dying listened to Muthanna very carefully. He then sent for Hadrat Umar the Caliph-designate and when he came addressed him thus :

> "Listen O Umar to what I say to you and act upon my words. I hope to die this very day and when I am dead let not the evening come upon you before you have exhorted the people to go with Muthanna. And if I survive till nightfall, let not the morning come before you have exhorted the people to go with Muthanna."

Hadrat Abu Bakr died that night, the 21st of August 634. He was buried the same night. After the funeral prayers, Hadrat Umar exhorted the assembled Muslims to join Muthanna in the Iraq campaign.

On the morning of 22nd August the Muslims assembled to take the oath of allegiance to the new Caliph. After the ceremony was over Hadrat Umar once again exhorted the Muslims to volunteer themselves for war on the Iraq front. Again there was no response. The Muslims were ready to join war in Syria but they hesitated in participating in a campaign against the Persians in Iraq. Although the Persians had been defeated in some campaigns, they were still held in awe, and the Muslims felt that the Persians were a hard nut to crack.

In his heart of hearts, Hadrat Umar felt much upset at this want of response from the Muslims. He decided that whosoever was the first to offer his services for fighting on the Iraq front would be made the Commander-in-Chief of the Muslim forces in Iraq.

On the 23rd August, the Muslims were once again exhorted to Jihad in Iraq. Seeing the hesitation of the people, Muthanna took up the stage, and spoke eloquently of the need of pushing the war in Iraq to a successful conclusion. He said:

> "Ye Muslims, listen to me ! You should have no fear of the Persians. I have tested the courage of the fire worshippers and discovered that they are not at home on the battle-field. Years of luxury have made them easy going, and it would not be difficult for us to overpower them. We have already conquered most of the important districts of Iraq, and humiliated the Persians. With a little more effort and with the help of God we can become the masters of the whole of Iraq. It is incumbent on us to take the message of Allah and His Messenger to these fire worshippers and offer them the true faith of Islam."

Then Hadrat Umar delivered a thrilling speech highlighting the mission of Islam. That appeared to move the audience. Then the Caliph asked for volunteers. Abu Ubaid the chief of the clan of Thaqafi rose up to offer his name. Hadrat Umar welcomed the offer and said, "Abu Ubaid, I appoint you as the Commander-in-Chief of the Muslim forces in Iraq.

Then other people offered their names. By 25th August over 1,000 Muslims were ready to proceed to the Iraq front. Thereupon Muthanna left for Iraq. Abu Ubaid and his contingent were to follow.

Abu Ubaid was a man of great courage and dash, but he had no experience of actual fighting in any war. Hadrat Umar was advised that for such an important campaign some veteran companion of the Holy Prophet seasoned in war should be appointed to lead the campaign.

Hadrat Umar said:

"The Companions are entitled to such precedence because of their courage and love for Jihad. Here I have been giving the call to Jihad ever sinee we buried Hadrat Abu Bakr, and I have had no response from the companions. Now that a young man who is not a companion has given the lead, I am determined to appoint him as the Commander-in-Chief. The Companions have lost this precedence by their own fault, and they should serve under a man who has given a greater show of courage."

Hadrat Umar however appointed a few Companions as the advisers of Abu Ubaid. Abu Ubaid was instructed by the Caliph that he should act on the advice of these advisers.

After a few days when the necessary preparations had been made Abu Ubaid left Madina with aforce of one thousand fighting men. He was further instructed that as he proceeded to Iraq he should recruit more fighting men from the tribes on the way.

BATTLE OF NAMARAQ

Muthanna returned from Madina to Hira in September 634 A.D.

The Persians commissioned two forces to fight against the Muslims. One was placed under the command of Narsi and it was stationed at Kaskar. The other army under the command of Jaban was required to march to Hira. Heralds were sent to various parts of Iraq to foment an insurrection against the Muslims by appealing to their sense of religious honour.

Seeing the Persians to be in an offensive mood, Muthanna decided to remain on the defensive. All Muslim outposts in Suwad were pulled back and all Muslim garrisons were withdrawn to the west of the Euphrates. As Jaban marched through Suwad, he met no resistance from the Muslims. As Jaban approached Hira, Muthanna evacuated Hira and moved to Khaftan closer to the desert. The strategy was to tempt the Persians come as near the desert as possible.

Abu Ubaid set off from Madina in September 634 with a force of one thousand fighting men. In the way he recruited more fighting men from the tribes, and when he reached Khaftan early in October he had a force of 4,000 fighting men with him.

Jaban crossed the Euphrates and camped at Namaraq near the site of modern day Kufa. Abu Ubaid moved with the Muslim forces from Khaftan, and came to Namaraq. At Namaraq the two armies were deployed for battle. The Persians led the attack, but the Muslim ranks held fast. Then the Muslims led the charge, and the Persians had to fall back. The Muslims redoubled the charge, and the Persians retreated in confusion. The battle ended in the defeat of the Persians, who lost heavily. Jaban himself was captured by a Muslim soldier. Jaban did not reveal his identity and he bargained with his captor that if he was released he would offer two Persians in his place. The unsophisticated Muslim warrior agreed to the bargain, and Jaban was set free.

Later it was found that Jaban was the commander of the Persian forces and that he had escaped due to a stratagem. The matter was reported to Abu Ubaid. Abu Ubaid felt satisfied that a Muslim soldier had in fact given the promise to Jaban, and the Muslims could not go back on that promise.

This episode has been versified by Allama Iqbal in his poem.

"The Mysteries of Selflessness" as an illustration of Muslim brotherhood.

The poem reads :

"A certain general of King Yazdjurd
Became a Muslim's captive in the wars ;
A fire worshipper he was, inured to every trick
Of fortune, drafty, cunning, full of guile.
He kept his captor ignorant of his rank
Nor told him who he was, or what his name,
But said, "I beg that you will spare my life
And grant to me the quarter Muslims gain."
The Muslim sheathed his sword. "To shed thy blood,"
He cried "is forbidden for me."
When Kaveh's banner had been rent to shreds,
The fire of Satan's sons turned all to dust."
It was disclosed the captive was Jaban
The Commander of the Persian host.
Then was his fraud reported,
And his blood petitioned from the Arab General.
But Abu Ubaid the Muslim Commander
Answered their request
"Friends, we are Muslims, strings upon one lute
And of one concord.
Ali's voice attunes with Abu Dharr's,
Although the throat be that of Qanbar or Bilal.

Each one of us is trustee to the whole community
And one with it in malice or in truce.
As the Community is the sure base
On which the individual rests secure,
So is its covenant his sacred bond.
Though Jaban was a foeman to Islam,
A Muslim granted him immunity ;
His blood, O followers of the best of men
Cannot be spilled by any Muslim sword."

BATTLE OF KASKAR

After the battle of Namaraq, the defeated Persian force who survived sought refuge with Narsi at Kaskar. Narsi was a cousin of the Kisra Puran Dukht and Kaskar was his estate. Kaskar was the Tigris downstream of Ctesiphon the capital of Persia. It was about two hundred miles from Namaraq across the entire Doab between the Euphrates and the Tigris.

Narsi had a good concentration of force at Kaskar. With the coming of the Persian forces who had been defeated at Namaraq the strength of the Persian forces at Kaskar further increased. The Persian Commander-in-Chief promised to send some more Persian forces under the command of Jalinus to Kaskar. With these forces at his disposal, Narsi felt secure at Kaskar. Kaskar was so far away from the Muslim camp that Narsi felt that no Muslim attack could be imminent.

Abu Ubaid, the Muslim commander, thought otherwise. He thought that it would have a good psychological effect if in the wake of the battle of Namaraq the Muslims rushed to Kaskar and deal with the Persian forces there before the forces under Jalinus could come to their assistance. Abu Ubaid accordingly ordered a march across the Suwad to Kaskar. Dashing across the Suwad the Muslim forces appeared before Kaskar. The two forces met at Saqatia a few miles from Kaskar. The strategy of the Persians was to defer action till the arrival of the force under Jalinus. The strategy of the Muslims was to press the attack and force immediate decision.

The right wing of the Persian army was commanded by Banduyah and the left wing by Tairuyah. Both of them were the cousins of Kisra. Abu Ubaid launched the attack. The battle was hotly contested. No details about the battle are available. All that we know is that the Persians were defeated, and those who survived retreated to Ctesiphon. Immense booty fell to the Muslims. The most prized possession that the Muslims got was the Narsi garden which was known throughout Persia for its delicious fruit. The fruit of the garden were heretofore reserved for Narsi, and he sent occasional gifts to the Kisra. On getting hold of the garden the Muslims distributed the fruit among all soldiers. Some fruit was also sent to Hadrat Umar to taste.

Abu Ubaid stayed at Kaskar but he sent Muslim contingents in the adjoining areas to bring the people under Muslim rule. Muthanna was sent with his force to the region of Barosma. Walid was sent against Zawabi. Asim was sent against Nahrjubar. No resistance was offered anywhere. The chiefs of these places waited on Abu Ubaid at Kaskar and offered submission. They also offered him some delicious food. He asked whether this food was meant for the entire Muslim army. The chiefs stated that the food was meant for him and his officers and that they would give a feast for the army later. Thereupon Abu Ubaid refused to accept the food and returned it with the remarks that as the General of the Muslim army he could only eat what the common soldiers ate.

In the meantime the Persian force under Jalinus advanced. While the Persian force was still in the territory of Barosma, Abu Ubaid advanced from Kaskar to meet it. The two forces met at Baqsiasa. After a hot contest the Persians were defeated and they retreated after leaving many soldiers dead on the battlefield.

Abu Ubaid wrote to Hadrat Umar a detailed report of the battles of Kaskar and Baqsiasa. Hadrat Umar in reply advised Abu Ubaid in the following terms :

> "You have entered the land of trickery and guile, dishonesty and oppression. You have marched against a people who love evil and know it well and abjure goodness of which they are ignorant. So be on your guard and watch your tongue. Reveal not your secrets for those who guard their secrets are secure against unpleasantness and loss."

BATTLE OF THE BRIDGE

The Muslims under the command of Abu Ubaid had won a few initial successes against the Persians. That emboldened Abu Ubaid.

The Persians now sent another force under Bahman. Bahman was a veteran General of considerable standing, and he undertook to drive away the Arabs from the soils of Persia.

Bahman marched with his army towards Hira and camped at Quss Natif on the east bank of the Euphrates some distance north of Hira, and little below the site of Kufa.

When Abu Ubaid came to know of the movements of the Persian army, he marched the Muslim forces from Hira and camped with 9,000 men on the west bank of the Euphrates at the village called Marauha.

Now the river Euphrates lay between the two forces, Bahman sent an emissary to Abu Ubaid with the message "Either you cross and come over to our side ; or we will cross and come over to your side."

Abu Ubaid was advised that he should ask the Persians to cross. The Persian emissary played on the emotions of Abu Ubaid, and said that in the Persian camp the general belief was that the Muslims were afraid of the might of Persia. Abu Ubaid made him understand that one Arab was equal to ten Persians. The emissary said that if such claim was not an empty boast, the Muslims should substantiate it by taking the initiative and crossing over to the Persian side. In a vainglorious mood Abu Ubaid declared, "We will cross the river ; go and tell your Commander accordingly."

As soon as the Persian emissary had left, Abu Ubaid ordered that the Muslim forces should prepare for crossing the river. Saleet bin Qais who had been appointed by Hadrat Umar as the Adviser to Abu Ubaid told Abu Ubaid that his decision to cross the river was not sound. Abu Ubaid retorted "Saleet, you are frightened. Have trust in God."

Muthanna who commanded the cavalry also tried to persuade Abu Ubaid reconsider his decision. Abu Ubaid remained adamant and he removed Muthanna from the command of the cavalry. In his place he appointed his cousin Abu Mihjan to the command of the cavalry.

Some other veterans in the Muslim army said to Abu Ubaid, "O Commander do not cut your means of escape, and do not make yourself a target of the Persians." Abu Ubaid said that such were the counsels of the chicken-hearted, and that those who were fighting in the way of God should have the courage and boldness to beard the lion in its den.

The previous night, Dauma the wife of Abu Ubaid who was with him in the camp had a dream. In the dream she had seen a man come down from heaven with a vessel from which Abu Ubaid drank. Thereafter his brother Al-Hakam drank from it. Next his son had a drink from it, and then some other members of the tribe of Abu Ubaid drank from the vessel. After all had drunk the person concerned carried the vessel back to the heaven.

When Dauma related her dream to Abu Ubaid, he interpreted it to mean that he and all the other people who had drunk from the vessel would be blessed with martyrdom. That did not in any way unnerve Abu Ubaid. On the other hand he felt happy at the prospects of martyrdom.

A bridge of boats was thrown across the river, and the Muslim army marched along the bridge on the morning of 28th November 634 A.D. The Persians watched the Muslim army cross the river. They, however, remained arrayed in battle order in light formation.

As the Muslim army crossed over to the other side of the river they found that the space at their disposal was circumscribed, and there was no room for any manoeuvres or outflanking movements.

Immediately after crossing, the Muslims formed themselves into battle formation and faced the Persian hosts. The Persian army had with them a large number of war elephants. Each elephant carried a howdah in which sat soldiers armed with javelins and bows. To each howdah branches of palm trees were tied to give the illusion of size Bells were tied round the neck of the elephants, and these appeared to produce an unearthly din.

When the battle began the Muslim cavalry advanced to the charge. At the sight of the monster elephants the Arab horse shied, turned, and bolted. That led to confusion and the Muslim cavalry was disorganised.

Seeing this confusion in the Muslim ranks, Bahman ordered an advance by the Persian forces. As the Persian forces advanced the noise from the bells of the elephants became louder. The Persians seated in the howdahs of the elephants made good use of their bows and arrows and drove several wedges in the Muslim front.

At this stage Abu Ubaid ordered the Muslim cavalry to dismount and attack on foot. Abu Ubaid himself led the attack. He exhorted his men to attack the elephants and cut their girths. In the attempt many Muslims were killed, but some Muslims succeeded in cutting the girths of some elephants. Abu Ubaid rushed at the leading elephant, a white monster elephant, with his javelin. The beast was blinded in one eye. Then Abu Ubaid got under the elephant and cut its girth bringing down the howdah and its occupants. In the scuffle that followed the elephant knocked down Abu Ubaid and trampled him under its heavy foot.

Al-Hakam the brother of Abu Ubaid rushed to the spot. He shot the animal dead. He picked up the standard and led fighting. After some time he too fell fighting and the command was taken over by Jabr the son of Abu Ubaid. The battle waged with unrelenting fury and one after another all the Muslim commanders were martyred. All those whom Dauma the wife of Abu Ubaid had seen drink from the vessel brought from the heaven tasted martyrdom.

The Persians increased the violence of their attack and the Muslims fell back. At this stage Abdullah bin Marthad who belonged to the clan of Abu Ubaid cut off the boat bridge and to those who sought the bridge he shouted "O people die for what your Commanders have died." Some people turned back to fight and fell dead at the battle-field. Others plunged in the river and were drowned.

The Muslim forces were at this stage without a Commander, and the Persians increased the violence of their assauits. At this critical moment Muthanna took command of the army. He ordered the bridge to be rebuilt, and when it was ready he organised a rear guard action. With a select force he faced the Persians, and asked the others to cross calmly without being panicky. Muthanna and his reserves remained at their posts until the entire army had crossed. Muthanna was the last to cross. In guarding the bridge he had received innumerable wounds and as he reached the Muslim camp he fell exhausted.

As the Muslim forces assembled at Marauha on the other side of the Euphrates, only 3,000 persons assembled out of the total strength of 9,000. Some 2,000 persons fell fighting, some 2000 persons were drowned in the river, and some 2,000 persons fled away to Madina and elsewhere.

The immediate worry of Muthanna was pursuit by the Persians. If in the wake of their victory the Persians had crossed the Euphrates, all that had been left of the Muslim army would not have been able to face the Persians. Bahman felt elated at his victory over the Muslims. He had demonstrated that the Persians were still a mighty force. He had a mind to pursue the Muslims across the Euphrates but at that crucial moment there was a revolt against Rustam at the Persian capital, and Rustam recalled Bahman to Al-Madain to help in putting down the revolt.

When the scouts brought the news that the Persians were marching back to Al-Madain Muthanna felt relieved. Hira was now unsafe for the Muslims. Muthanna accordingly abandoned Hira and marched with his weary army to Ulleis.

Abdullah bin Zaid carried the news of the tragedy of the Battle of the Bridge to Madina. Hadrat Umar felt grieved at the reverse of the Muslims, but the disaster did not unnerve him in any way.

In this moment of crisis Hadrat Umar rose to great heights of leadership. Instead of apportioning blame, he said:

> "O Lord every Muslim is in my charge and I am a refuge for all Muslims. May Allah bless Abu Ubaid. Having crossed the river he should have secured his position by the side of a hill. I wish he had not crossed, and sought his death, but had returned to me."

Some persons who had fled from the battle-field and had returned to Madina wept bitterly at the disaster. To them, Hadrat Umar consoled with the following words :

> "Do not weep. I am your refuge, and you have returned to me."

To Muthanna at Ulleis, Hadrat Umar sent the message: "Stay at your post. Help will soon come."

BATTLE OF BUWAIB

After the disaster of the Bridge the Muslim army under Muthanna was stationed at Ulleis. Both Hadrat Umar and Muthanna sent heralds and emissaries to all parts of Arabia inviting the Arabs to participate in the war against the Persians.

In response to this call volunteers came from all parts of Arabia. Makhnaf b. Salim the chief of the Azd tribe came with 700 horsemen. A contingent of a thousand men of the Banu Tamim came under the command of Hasin b. Mabid. Adi the son of the legendary Hatim Tai came with a large contingent of his tribesmen. Contingents also came from the tribes of Rabab, Banu Kinanah, Khath'am, Banu Hanzalah, and Banu Dabbah. The Christian Arabs of the tribes of Namr and Taghlab also joined to reinforce the Muslim war effort. To the clan of Bajeela led by Jareer bin Abdullah, Hadrat Umar offered an additional share of the booty, out of the Khums—the state share.

After having received reinforcements, Muthanna moved to Zu Qar a few miles south of Qadissiya. When the Persians came to know of the preparations of the Muslims they decided to send a strong force against the Muslims led by Mihran. Mihran had been in Arabia and was regarded as an expert in the Arabian way of war. The Persian army under Mihran marched to the Euphrates and camped on the east bank opposite he site of modern Kufa.

Muthanna with the Muslim army advanced from Zu Qar, and arriving on the west bank of the Euphrates camped at Nakheila. At Nakheila a stream Buwaib took off from the Euphrates.

Mihran sent a message to Muthanna whether the Muslims would like to cross the Euphrates, or whether they would like the Persians to cross over to their side. The Muslims have had a bitter experience of crossing the river in the 'Battle of the Bridge', and so Muthanna said to the Persian emissary "You cross."

The following day, the Persians crossed the river, and Mihran arranged his forces in battle order with display of much splendour and pomp.

One wing of the Muslim army was led by Adi b. Hatim, and the other wing was led by Jareer. Masud, a brother of Muthanna held the command of the infantry. Muthanna mounted his horse 'Shams', and rode from one end to the other. Addressing the army he said :

> "Brave soldiers ! beware, lest, on account of you, the stigma of dishonour should fall to the Arabs."

The Persians dashed forward roaring like thunder. Muthanna shouted to his men not to pay any heed to such noise, as it was mere sound signifying nothing. He asked the wing commanders to stick fast, as he was going to make a rush on the Persian forces.

With the shouts of Allah-o-Akbar the Muslim army rolled forward, and such was the overwhelming impetuosity of their onslaught that they rent asunder the serried ranks of the Persian right flank, and penetrated the Persian centre. The Persians reeled before the terrible onset, but they rallied and fought so desperately that the Muslim ranks began to waver.

Seeing some Muslims turn back, Muthanna thundered: "O Muslims, whither are you going. I am here ; come to me. Muthanna rallied his forces and ordered a fresh attack. Masud the brother of Muthanna received many wounds, and fell down. That made the Muslims lose heart. Turning to the Muslims, Muthanna said :

> "O Muslims, never mind if my brother is killed. Valiants always die like that. See that the standard that you carry is not lowered."

Masud himself while dying cried, "Let not my death make you lose heart ; you must forward to your task."

Anas b. Hilal, a Christian commander fighting with the Muslim forces fell fighting heroically. Muthanna took him up in his arms, and laid him alongside his brother Masud. Many Muslim officers of note were killed, but Muthanna wanted his men to persevere. Mihran the Commander-in-Chief of the Persian army fought heroically. Muthanna asked his men to advance, and make Mihran their target. A youthful warrior of the Taghlab tribe rushed forward with great courage and intrepidity, and penetrating the Persian ranks slew Mihran with his sword. The youth proclaimed :

"I am a young men of the Taghlab tribe ;
"I have killed Mihran, the Persian Chief."

The death of Mihran turned the tide of the battle. The Persians lost nerve, and fled in disorder. Muthanna at once made a dash for the bridge and captured it. That prevented the Persians from recrossing the river. The Muslims made mincemeat of the Persians. According to the annals, no battle had ever left so many corpses for its sanguinary souvenir as were strewn on the battle-field of Buwaib. For years thereafter the travellers in the region witnessed the grim spectacle of heaps of bones scattered in all directions.

The battle of Buwaib was the reply of the Muslims to the battle of the Bridge. In the battle of the Bridge a greater part of the Muslim army managed to escape ; in the battle of Buwaib the entire Persian army was annihilated.

At the conclusion of the battle, Muthanna said :

"I have fought Arabs and Persians. I have fought them in the time of Ignorance and again in the time of Islam. By Allah during the days of Ignorance a hundred Persians were stronger than a thousand Arabs, but to-day a hundred Arabs are stronger than a thousand Persians."

The battle of the Buwaib was fought in April 635.

CAMPAIGNS IN SOUTH IRAQ

Uballa on the Persian Gulf was the key of South Iraq. When Khalid bin Walid began his campaigns in Iraq he started with Uballa and occupied it without much resistance. Later as the Muslims won victories after victories in Iraq the focus shifted north west to Hira.

When Khalid bin Walid went to Syria very few Muslim forces were left in Iraq. Consequently the Muslims abandoned many posts in Iraq including Uballa. Uballa was re-occupied by the Persians. A small Muslim force under Qutba bin Qatada, however, continued to be stationed in the nighbourhood of Uballa to protect the routes to Arabia.

When Hadrat Umar sent Abu Ubaid on the main Iraq front, he felt that it was necessary to send some reinforcement to the southern sector as well. Hadrat Umar accordingly sent a contingent under Shareeh b. Amr to reinforce Qutba. Qutba was instructed to raid deeper into Persia.

Qutba sent Shareeh across the Tigris to raid Ahwaz. In the way at Daris, Shareeh was intercepted by the Persian forces and killed.

After the battle of Buwaib, Qutba wrote to Hadrat Umar asking for more aid for intensifying activities in the southern sector.

Hadrat Umar realised the importance of the southern sector. He sent for Utba b. Ghazwan an early Companion and offered him the command of the southern sector. Addressing him the Caliph said :

> "Allah Most High and Mighty has given Hira and what is around it to your brothers who have subdued the

> region of Babylon. Many of the Persian nobles have been killed. I feel that the Persians from the south will go to the help of the Persians in the north west. My strategy is to prevent the Persians on one side from helping the Persians on the other. Go to the region of Uballa and keep the people of Ahwaz and Fars and Meisan occupied so that they do not help their comrades in the Suwad.
>
> Fight them in the hope that Allah will give you victory. March with faith in Allah and fear Allah. Be fair in judgement; say your prayers at the appointed times and remember Allah much."

Utba bin Ghazwan set off from Madina with 2,000 men and arrived in the neighbourhood of Uballa in June 635. He took over the command of the sector. The Muslims were encamped at a site twelve miles from modern Basra amidst the ruins of an ancient town.

The Commander of the Persian forces of the district of Furat marched to battle. His strategy was to fall upon the Muslims unawares and thereby crush them. When the Persian forces arrived they found the Muslims ready for War. In the battle that followed the Persians were defeated. The Muslims pursued the defeated Persians to Uballa. No resistance was offered to the Muslims at Uballa which was occupied by the Muslims in September 635 A.D.

With Uballa as the base, Utba sent a force across the Tigris which occupied the district of Furat. The Muslim forces next marched into the district of Meisan. The Persians contested the advance of the Muslims but they were defeated and the entire district of Meisan was occupied by the Muslims. Another Muslim force advanced further afield and occupied the district of Abarqubaz. Another column captured Mazar. After subjugating these areas the Muslim forces returned to Uballa. The southern sector was now under the command of the Muslims, and the Persian supply line from Fars was cut off.

A little later the Governor of Abarqubaz revolted. Utba sent a column under Mugheera b. Shu'ba to deal with the revolt. The two forces met at Marghab. The Persians were defeated, and their Commander Feelhan was killed.

Next, there was a revolt in the district of Meisan. A column under Mugheera marched against the rebels and the revolt was successfully suppressed.

By November 635 A.D. the Muslim hold in the southern sector was quite firm. Utba went on a short leave to Madina, where he died. Hadrat Umar appointed Mugheera b. Shu'ba to the command of the Muslim forces in South Iraq.

S'AAD BIN ABI WAQAS

Another revolution in Persia brought Yazdjurd to the throne of Persia. He was young and intelligent, and on coming to the throne his principal concern was to take effective steps to drive away the Arabs from the soil of Iraq.

Heretofore some battles had been fought on the soil of Iraq, but these had not been decisive. The Muslims had occupied some areas, but their hold had not been firm. In the counter movements of the Persians the Muslims were pushed out of such areas. The Muslims retaliated and occupied such areas again. And again they abandoned them either of their own accord for strategical reasons or were pushed back. This to and fro process had been repeated several times, and this had led to political instability in the Suwad, the fertile area between the Euphrates and the Tigris.

Yazdjurd decided to organise things in a big way, and mobilise the resources of his empire for a titanic struggle with the Arabs. The Persians mustered a strong force under the veteran General Rustam. The force fully armed and equipped was cantoned at Sabat near Al-Madain.

When these developments were reported to Hadrat Umar, he realised that the scanty Muslim forces in Iraq under the command of Muthanna were exposed to great danger. The Caliph ordered Muthanna to abandon Hira and other advanced posts in Iraq and to withdraw to the edge of the desert. Muthanna pulled back his forces and stationed them at Sharaf close to the edge of the desert. In the southern sector the Muslims also pulled back and encamped in the hills of Ghuzayy.

The entire Suwad and all the main cities of Iraq were once again under Persian occupation. The war against the Persians, had to start once again from the periphery. Hadrat

Umar gave the call to Jihad. Throughout the Arabian peninsula messages were sent to the Governors and the chiefs of tribes to muster in full strength at Madina. The command of Hadrat Umar was:

> "Leave none who has weapons or a horse or strength or intelligence. Take him and send him to me. Hurry, O hurry!"

The response to the call was encouraging. Volunteers began to pour into Madina. Hadrat Umar organised the camp at Sirar three miles from Madina on the route to Iraq. In March 636 A.D. the first concentration of troops was complete, and Hadrat Umar moved in person to the camp at Sirar leaving the administration at Madina to the charge of Hadrat Ali.

Hadrat Umar addressed the troops mustered at Sirar, apprised them of the situation in Iraq, and invited their reaction. The congregation said with one voice, "Go, and we go with you for the glory of Islam." Hadrat Umar said, "Prepare for war, and I will go with you unless some better counsel comes forth."

Hadrat Umar summoned a council of war at Sirar to which leading Companions were invited. The council was required to advise whether the campaign in Iraq should be led personally by Hadrat Umar, or should some one else be appointed to the command.

Hadrat Ali said, "Go yourself for that will have a greater psychological effect both upon the Muslims as well as the enemy". Talha endorsed this view.

Abdur Rahman bin Auf said, "Stay, and send the army, and the will of Allah in respect of your wishes will be manifested in the fortunes of your army. If it is defeated, it will not be your defeat; but if you are killed or defeated, it would be a humiliation and a terrible blow to Muslim prestige."

After discussion, and the weighing of the pros and cons the consensus emerged in favour of the view advocated by Abdur Rahman bin Auf.

The Caliph next sought advice to the person who should be appointed as the Commander-in-Chief of the Muslim forces in Iraq. Abdur Rahman bin Auf proposed the name of S'aad bin Abi Waqas.

S'aad bin Abi Waqas was at that time the Governor of Nejd. He was one of the earliest converts to Islam. He was among the 'Ashra Mubashara', the Ten Companions who had been given the news of Paradise in their life time. He was the only man to whom the Holy Prophet had said, "I sacrifice my father and mother to you." He was the maternal uncle of the Holy Prophet.

Hadrat Umar said, "I know that S'aad is a brave man. He fought at Badr and Uhud. My only anxiety is that he does not have sufficient knowledge about the strategy of war."

Hadrat Usman said, "S'aad should be appointed to the command, and he should be instructed to seek counsel from men of experience and knowledge of war, and not act without their advice." This view was endorsed by all and ultimately agreed to.

The following day Hadrat Umar ordered a congregation of the army at Sirar, and addressed them as follows :

> "Lo ! Allah Most High and Mighty has gathered his people to Islam and has joined their hearts and made them brothers one to another. The Muslims are like one body of which the entire body suffers, if any part suffers.
>
> It is incumbent upon the Muslims to decide their affairs in a council of men of judgement. The troops must follow the one appointed to command by mutual agreement and consent ; and the one appointed to command must accept the decision of men of judgement in the strategy of war.
>
> O people, I am just one of you, but men of judgement have dissuaded me from going with you. I have decided to remain here, and send another person in command; and I have consulted all in this matter."

S'aad was called from Nejd, and as he appeared before Hadrat Umar, the Caliph said :

> "I have appointed you Commander of the war in Iraq. Remember my words for you are proceeding on a difficult and fearful mission in which right can only prevail."

In May 636 A.D., S'aad bin Abi Waqas marched from the Sirar camp with an army of 4,000 men. At the time of departure Hadrat Umar prayed for the success of the mission they had undertaken. His parting instruction to S'aad was :

> "Stop when you get to Zarud and disperse in the region. Urge the people there to join you and take all who have courage, intelligence, strength and weapons."

Hadrat Umar promised that he would send more and more of help. He said that he would hurl every chief, every noble, and every warrior in Arabia against the Persians.

As the army under the command of S'aad marched past Hadrat Umar, the Caliph raised his hands in prayers and said:

> "O Mighty Allah ! These people are going to fight in your way. Bless them with victory."

CAMPS AT ZARUD AND SHARAF

S'aad arrived with his force of 4,000 at Zarud and went into camp. The troops were spread in the region, and couriers were sent to all the tribes in Northern Arabia calling the tribesmen to war in the name of Allah. As a result of these efforts about 7,000 warriors were recruited from the tribes particularly the Bani Asad and Bani Tamim. Among those who joined the Muslim forces was Taleaha who had during the apostasy campaigns of the time of Hadrat Abu Bakr claimed to be a prophet and had fought against the Muslims. He had escaped to Syria where he was converted to Islam. Those who had once apostated were not allowed by Hadrat Abu Bakr to be recruited to the Muslim forces. Hadrat Umar, because of the large scale campaigns to be undertaken lifted the ban. Availing of this concession Taleaha and his tribesmen joined the Muslim forces in Iraq in large numbers.

Hadrat Umar sent another force of 4,000 men to join the main army at Zarud. The strength of the army at Zarud now rose to 15,000. Muthanna with 3,000 men was stationed at Sharaf some sixty miles from Zarud on the main route to Iraq.

From Zarud the main Muslim army marched to Sharaf, and they arrived there in July 636 A.D. Before S'aad arrived, Muthanna was dead. In his will Musanna had desired that S'aad bin Abi Waqas should marry his widow Salma bint Khasfa. He also left a message for S'aad which ran as follows:

> "The Muslims should not fight the Persians when they are concentrated in their homeland, but should fight them on the boundary near the desert. Thus if Allah should give the Muslims victory, they will have whatever lies behind the Persians, and if the result is otherwise,

they can withdraw into a region the routes whereof they know best and of which they are masters--until Allah decides that they should return to battle."

S'aad prayed for the soul of Muthanna. He paid rich tributes to his bravery. In fulfilment of the will of Muthanna, S'aad married his widow Salma. He was impressed with the parting advice of Muthanna, and decided to follow it. He reported this advice to Hadrat Umar who approved of it.

Hadrat Umar instructed S'aad as follows :

"Organise the army into tens and let the men know their units.
Appoint the commanders of the corps and let them see and know their men.
Give the contingents Qadissiya as the meeting point.
Get Mugheera bin Shu'ba to join you with his cavalry.
Comply with these instructions and then write to me."

S'aad organised the army in accordance with the instructions of Hadrat Umar. From the Uballa sector Mugheera bin Shu'ba joined S'aad with his cavalry of 800 horse.

Hadrat Umar next instructed S'aad as follows :

"March with the Muslims from Sharaf towards the Persians.

Place your faith in Allah and seek His help, and know that you are advancing against a people whose numbers are vast, whose equipment is superb, whose strength is great and whose land is difficult. Even its plains consist of rivers and heavily watered land. When you meet them or any of them, attack them fiercely, but beware of facing them if they are all together. Let them not trick you, for they are wily plotters and their ways are not your ways.

When you get to Qadissiya, remain there and leave not your place. They will find your continued stay intolerable and will come out against you with all their strength of horse and foot. And if you stand fast against them, you shall overcome them, and should they ever assemble again in great numbers, they shall do so without hearts.

And should the result be otherwise, you will have the desert behind you and can withdraw into a region which you know and control and of which they are ignorant and afraid. And there you should stay until Allah decides victory for you and you return to battle."

TO QADISSIYA

In July 636 A.D. the main Muslim army marched from Sharaf to Qadissiya. Qadissiya was on the west bank of the Ateeq, a branch of the Euphrates. It was the last staging camp in Arabia on the route to Iraq. Hira lay about thirty miles ahead.

After establishing the camp, organising the defences, and securing the river heads, S'aad sent parties inside the Suwad to conduct raids. In one of these raids the Muslims captured the bridal procession of the daughter of Azazbeh the Persian Governor of Hira. A large booty was captured including the bride and other Persian damsels.

From Qadissiya, S'aad wrote to Hadrat Umar :

"The enemy has sent no one against us and has not appointed, so far we know, anyone to command the campaign. When we get the information, we will report to you and seek Allah's help."

To this Hadrat Umar replied in the following terms :

"Strengthen your heart and your army with sermons and right intentions and worthiness ; and as for those who forget, remind them. Steadfastness and again steadfastness!—for help comes from Allah according to one's intentions and His reward according to one's deserts. Caution and again caution!—for grave is the matter upon which you are embarked. And pray to Allah for his blessings.

Write to me when you know of the concentration of their army and who commands it, for in the absence of knowledge about their army and its commander I am not able to give you much guidance.

Describe the place where you are and the land between you and Madain. Describe it so clearly that I may see it with my own eyes, and become one of you.

Fear Allah and in Him rest your hopes."

S'aad sent the required topographical information. The intelligence reports of the spies were also forwarded to Hadrat Umar. S'aad stated that all the people of the Suwad who had entered into pacts with the Muslims had gone back on their pledges. They were collaborating with the Persians and were preparing for war against the Muslims.

S'aad wrote :

"The Commander of the Persian army is Rustam, and he has some other top-ranking Generals.

They seek to weaken us and pounce upon us and we seek to weaken them and attack them. The command of Allah is as good as bone and His decision will be according to whatever He wishes for us or against us. We beseech Allah for the best of decisions and the best of judgements."

In reply, Hadrat Umar instructed :

"Remain where you are until Allah fixes your enemy for you.

And if Allah should give you victory, pursue them until you fall upon Madain, which Allah willing will be destroyed."

A week later, Hadrat Umar further instructed:

"My heart tells me that when you meet the enemy you will God willing defeat him. So dispel all doubt from your mind, and if any of you gives a promise of peace to a Persian, with sign or speech, even if he does not understand it, let him fulfil the promise.

Beware of jesting, faithfulness and again faithfulness. Errors committed in good faith are acceptable but

> deliberate unfaithfulness leads to destruction. In it will lie your weakness and your enemy's strength, the depression of your courage and the elevation of the courage of your enemy.
>
> I caution you not to bring dishonour to the Muslims, nor be a cause of their disgrace."

S'aad reported about the large strength of the forces of the Persians. To this Hadrat Umar replied as follows :

> "Let not the information which you get about the enemy distress you. Seek Allah's help, and in Him place your trust."

Hadrat Umar also desired that a delegation of some intelligent persons should be sent to the emperor of Persia to call him to Islam.

After the battle of Yermuk some forces were released from the Syrian front and sent to Iraq under the command of Ath'ath bin Qais. The strength of S'aad's army at Qadissiya now rose to 29,000.

The Muslim forces intensified their raiding activities. The entire Suwad now became a hunting ground for the Muslim raiders. These raids were undertaken partly to gather supplies for the Muslim army, and partly to demoralise the Persians.

The inhabitants of the Suwad appealed to the Persian emperor to do something urgently to save them from the raids of the Muslims. The emperor Yazdjurd assured them that he was sending a large force under Rustam against the Muslims, and he would crush the Arabs.

ADVENTURES OF TALEAHA

Taleaha bin Khuwalid was an adventurer. He was the chief of the Bani Asad. He was a poet and a soothsayer, and commanded respect in Arabia during the days of ignorance.

When the Holy Prophet declared his mission, Taleaha became a vicious enemy of Islam. In the Battle of the Ditch Taleaha sided with the Quraish, and commanded a contingent of the Bani Asad in the coalition of the infidels who fought against the Muslims.

In the battle of Khybar he sided with the Jews but was worsted. In 631 A.D. when all other Arabian tribes accepted Islam, he also became a convert to Islam. In 633 A.D. he renounced his allegiance to Islam, and declared himself to be a prophet. He introduced a new way of prayer in which there were no prostrations. Many clans of Central Arabia joined him, and soon he became a powerful enemy of Islam.

In the apostasy campaigns, Taleaha was defeated by Khalid bin Walid in the battle of Buzakha. From Buzakha Taleaha fled to Syria. When Syria was conquered by the Muslims, Taleaha once again became a convert to Islam.

Later he returned to Arabia, and joined the war against the Persians. In the camp at Qadissiya, S'aad bin Abi Waqas deputed Taleaha to go to the Persian camp and gather some intelligence.

Taleaha crossed the Ateeq and proceeded in the direction of Najaf. He had hardly gone four or five miles when he came upon the Persian camp at Kharara.

The men with Taleaha decided to return, but Taleaha moved on and went into the Persian camp. He soon came upon a beautiful white tent, outside which a beautiful horse stood tethered. Taleaha took the horse. He cut the ropes of the tent, which collapsed upon the sleeping inmate. A little further he came across another good horse and a fine tent. He took that horse as well. Here again he cut the ropes of the tent which fell on the man who slept inside.

A little further there was another horse and a tent. This time again he took the horse, and by cutting the ropes made the tent collapse. It transpired that these tents lodged gladiators, called 'Hazar Mard', each gladiator being deemed equal in strength to a thousand men.

Taleaha now outside the Persian camp mounted his own horse and began his return journey leading the three captured horses. He had not gone far when the three gladiators caught up with him.

Undaunted, Taleaha turned to his pursuers. One of the gladiators challenged him to personal duel, and Taleaha agreed. The gladiator charged at Taleaha with his lance, but Taleaha side stepped and avoided the charge. As the Persian hurled past him, Taleaha swung round in his saddle, and plunged his spear in the back of his adversary who fell down dead.

Next the second Persian champion grappled with Taleaha. He attacked and Taleaha side stepped. Then Taleaha charged and the Persian champion fell dead.

Then the third champion came forward, and over-powering him, Taleaha rode with him as a captive to the Muslim camp. Before dawn Taleaha was back in the Muslim camp with three Persian horses and a 'Hazar Mard' as a captive.

The Persian captive was presented to S'aad bin Abi Waqas, and he gave much useful information about the Persian moves. The Persian champion said on oath that he had seen war ever since he was a boy and had defeated and killed many champions in his lifetime but he had never seen such a fighter as Taleaha.

Taleaha offered the Persian champion Islam, and he accepted the faith of Islam. In the war that followed the Persian 'Hagar Mard' fought valiantly by the side of Taleaha.

THE MUSLIMS CARRIED THE EARTH OF PERSIA

In compliance with the instructions of Hadrat Umar, S'aad bin Abi Waqas sent a delegation of twelve Muslims to offer Islam to Yazdjurd the emperor of Persia. The Muslim delegation included Numan b. Muqarrin, Muthanna bin Haritha, Asim b. Amr, and Mugheera bin Zurara.

The Muslim delegation rode to Ctesiphon or Al-Madain the capital of Persia. The Muslims dismounted outside the palace of the emperor. A large crowd of the Persians gathered to stare at the shaggy horses and stern faced hard sons of the desert.

The delegation was ushered into the presence of the emperor Yazdjurd surrounded by interpretors and couriers. The Persians used to prognosticate events by omen. In a playful mood Yazdjurd asked the Muslim envoys what a mantle was called in Arabic. They said that it was called "burd". "Burd" in Persian meant to carry away, and the emperor felt that the Arabs were to carry away Persia.

Then he asked what was the Arabic name for a whip and they said that it was 'Saut'. He construed it as 'Sokht', which in Persian meant "burned". The emperor felt in his heart that the Muslims were going to burn Persia.

Yezdjurd next asked, "What compels you to invade our land. Is it because we have left you in peace that you have grown so bold ?"

Numan b. Muqarrin speaking on behalf of the delegation said that Allah had been kind to them. God had sent a prophet to them who had shown them the right way. Under the leadership of the Prophet they had been transformed. They were the chosen people of God, and God had entrusted to them a mission, the mission of spreading the true faith.

Numan added :

"In pursuance of our mission, we call you to our faith. If you accept our faith we will leave you with the Book of God, and leave you to your land. If you are not agreeable to join our faith you should accept our overlordship and pay us 'Jizya'. If this alternative is also not acceptable to you, then the sword will decide the issue between us."

Yazdjurd retorted :

"Don't you recollect that you were the most wretched and most miserable people that the world ever saw. Whenever you showed signs of recalcitrance we had only to issue orders to the commanders of our frontier outposts and they crushed your mutinous spirit."

Thereupon Mugheera bin Zurara said that what the emperor said about the Arabs was true in the days of Ignorance; after the advent of the Prophet things had changed and they were no longer wretched or miserable. It was not hunger or misery that had brought them to Persia. They had come carrying the message of the new faith for them. If the message was accepted they would be happy and treat them as brothers. If they were not inclined to accept the new faith or pay Jizya, then there was no option but fight.

The emperor was enraged at these bold words of the Muslims. He shouted, "But for the fact that envoys are not killed, I would surely have killed you. Know that we are a great people whose history extends over ages and such people are proud of their faith which they would not change. And as regards Jizya, I would put dust in your mouth. And as regards the fight know that we are not afraid of you. Tell your Commander that I am sending Rustam against him with a large force, who will teach you a bitter lesson."

Then Yazdjurd asked a court attendant to fetch a basket of earth. When the basket was brought, addressing the Muslim envoys he said, 'Here is the Jizya for you ; carry it".

Asim b. Amr stepped forward, and carried the basket on his head. Turning to the emperor he said, "You have of your own accord handed over your land to the Muslims. We accept your gift."

Thereafter the Muslim envoys rode back at great speed to the Muslim camp carrying the basket of the earth of Persia.

Immediately thereafter Rustam saw Yazdjurd, and the emperor told him that he had given the Muslim envoys dust to carry. Rustam said that was a bad omen for it signified that the Muslims had carried away Persia.

Rustam sent off a group of horsemen to pursue the Muslim envoys and get the fateful basket containing the dust of Persia back from them. To these horsemen Rustam said, "Proçeed with the speed of lightning and snatch your mother-earth from the Muslims. If you recover the basket our land will be safe ; if you fail then we are doomed."

The Persian party set off at a brisk pace in pursuit of the Muslim envoys, but they could not catch the Muslims. The Muslims crossed the Ateeq bridge to safety long before the Persians could arrive at the bridge head. The Persians returned crest fallen to report to Rustam the failure of their mission.

In the Muslim camp, there was rejoicing. Presenting the basket containing the dust of Persia to S'aad b. Abi Waqas Asim b. Amr said :

> "Commander Allah has given us the keys of their kingdom. Rejoice for this is a sign that we are going to conquer their land."

In the Persian camp, Rustam sulked and muttered to himself :

> "The enemy has snatched away the keys of our kingdom."

RUSTAM AND MUSLIM EMISSARIES

At the head of the Persian army Rustam marched against Qadissiya and encamped on the east bank of the Ateeq. The Muslim forces lay entrenched at Qadissiya on the west bank of the Ateeq.

Rustam the Commander-in-Chief of the Persian forces sent a message to the Muslim Commander S'aad asking him to send on emissary for talks. S'aad dupeted Rabi bin Amir as the envoy. Rabi crossed the bridge and made for the camp of Rustam. Rabi appeared before Rustam wearing a coat of shining mail over which was wrapped a coarse woollen cloak. Around his head was a veil held by the thongs of a camel's girth. His sword hung at his side in a sheath of coarse cloth. In his right hand he carried his spear. Rabi mounted on a shaggy horse arrived at the edge of the carpet at which Rustam and his couriers were seated.

The Persians wanted Rabi to lay aside arms. Rabi said, "I have not come to you to lay down my weapons. You invited me, and I have come, if you do not wish me to come the way I like, I shall return."

Rustam asked his men to let the Muslim come in the way he wished.

Rustam asked Rabi as to what was thier mission. Rabi said that their mission was to spread Islam. He said, "If you accept Islam we are brothers and there is peace between us, if you refuse we fight you and leave things to God."

"What do you expect in return", asked Rustam.

Rabi said, "Victory if you we survive, and Paradise if we die fighting in the way of Allah."

Rustam said that he should be allowed some time to think over the matter further.

Rabi said that according to a tradition of the Holy Prophet he could give him a time of three days.

"Are you thier chief", asked Rustam.

Ribi said, "No, but the Muslims are like one body, and the lowest is equal to the highest."

The next day Rustam asked again for an emissary. This time S'aad deputed Hudhaifah bin Mihsan. He rode over the carpet to Rustam's throne, and remained seated on his horse throughtout the talks.

Rustam wanted to know why the envoy of the previous day had not come. Hudhaifah said, "Our Commander treats us equally in enjoying favours and bearing hardships. This time it is my turn."

"What do you expect of us", asked Rustam.

Hudhaifah said, "We would expect you to become Muslims or pay Jizya."

Rustam said, "What if we do not agree to both these alternatives."

Hudhaifah said that in that case the arbitration would rest with the sword. Saying that Hudhaifah rode back from the Persian camp.

For the third time Rustam asked for another envoy. This time Mugheera bin Zurara was chosen as the Muslim emissary. Mugheera rode forward and sat on the throne beside Rustam. The Persians wanted to unseat him, but he held fast, and Rustam said, "Let him remain seated."

Looking at the short light arrows which protruded from the quiver of Mugheera, Rustam said, "O Arab what do you do with these spindles?"

Mugheera said, "We shoot them."

"And why is your sword wrapped in rags", asked Rustam.

Mugheera said, "It is clothed in rags but it strikes like steel."

Rustam said that it was perhaps thier hardship that had brought the Arabs to Iraq. He said :

"I shall give your commander a set of clothes, a mule and 1,000 dirhams, and to every man among you two garments and a bag of dates. And you shall go away from us for I have no desire to kill you or take you in captivity."

Mugheera said that times had changed, and because of Islam the Arabs were no longer fighting because they were poor or were subject to any hardship. They were fighting in the way of Allah, and they did not stand in need of any gifts from the Persians.

Rustam thereupon said, "This means that there can be no peace between us. When we go to the battle, we will slay the whole lot of you."

Thereupon Mugheera walked away from the Persian camp.

The following day a delegation consisting of four Muslims namely Busr b. Abi Ruhm ; Arfaja b. Harsama, Qirfa b. Zahir and Mazur b. Adi went to see Rustam.

This time Rustam talked in parables. He said :

> "We are like the man who had a vineyard and saw a fox in it one day. He said one fox did not matter. But the fox called other foxes to the vineyard. When they had all gathered in it, the owner closed the hole in the wall of the vineyard through which they had entered, and then killed all the foxes.
>
> And you are like the rat who found a jar of grain with a hole in it and went through the hole. His friends called to him to come out but he refused and went on eating the grain until he became fat. Then he felt a desire to

show his friends how beautiful he looked, but found that because of his bulk he could no longer get through the hole. So he complained to his friends of his trouble and asked for their assistance. They asked him to starve himself so that he might become as thin as before. The rat starved itself but in the meantime the owner of the jar came to know of it and killed it."

Rustam further said :

"And you are like the fly that saw a bowl of honey and said to his friends, 'Whoever gets me to that honey shall have two dirhams'. The other flies tried to stop him, but he went on to the honey and then into it. As he began to drown in the honey he cried out 'Whoever gets me out of the honey shall have 4 dirhams."

Rustam narrated another parable. He said :

"You are like the fox who came into a vineyard, thin and starving and began eating as God wished. The owner of the vineyard saw him and pitying his condition, let him stay. But when the fox had been there for some time and grown big and fat, he turned wicked and started to destroy more grapes than he consumed. This angered the owner, who along with his servants, took a big stick and came after him. The fox dodged them and ran to the hole in the vineyard wall through which he had come, but that hole was big enough for him only when he was thin, and now he was too fat to get through it. So the owner and his servants caught up with him and beat him with sticks until he was dead.

O Arabs you came when you were thin, and now you are fat. See how you get out."

The Arabs said that these parables were idle narrations which carried nowhere. They reiterated their usual demands, Islam, Jizya or sword.

Exasperated Rustam said, "If that is that, let the sword decide."

He asked, "Will you cross the river to our side, or shall we cross to your side."

The Muslims said, "You cross to our side."

When the Muslim envoys returned they apprised S'aad of the proceedings. Thereupon the Muslim Commander-in-Chief sent word in the Muslim camp that they should get ready for war.

THE BATTLE OF QADISSIYA

The Persians crossed the Ateeq on the 16th November, 636 A.D. The previous night Rustam had a dream in which he had seen Umar seal the arms of the Persians. As Rustam woke he said to himself : "This Umar has eaten my heart. May God burn him."

As Rustam saw his warriors cross the river and take up their positions for battle, he felt over-confident. He remarked to an Officer, "With this army we will shatter the Arabs into pieces." The Officer added the words, "If God wills it." Rustam was in a defiant mood and he retorted, "Even if He does not will it."

The Persian army was deployed with five corps holding the front and one corps in reserve, each corps having a depth of 13 ranks. The centre was commanded by Rustam himself. The other Commanders were : Left Centre : Beerzan ; Right Centre: Jalinus ; Left Wing : Mihran ; and Right Wing : Hormuzan. The reserve was commanded by Bahman.

The Persian army had a strength of 60,000 men. There were 33 war elephants in the Persian army each mounted by several men armed with javelins and bows.

At an elevated seat shaded by a canopy near the west bank of the river sat Rustam wearing his armour. By his side waved the Dirafashe-Kavian the standard of the Persians.

The Muslim Commander-in-Chief S'aad b. Abi Waqas was suffering from sciatica, and there were boils all over his body. In Qadissiya there was an old royal palace which stood at the extremity of the battle-field. S'aad took a seat in the upper storey of the palace where he lay propped up by pillows. From this seat he directed the war operations. He appointed

Khalid b. Arfatah as his Deputy, who maintained liasion with the army, and carried out whatever instructions were issued by S'aad from time to time.

In the centre of the Muslim army the infantry was commanded by Hammal b. Malik. The other Commanders were : Left Centre : Asim bin Amr ; Right Centre : Zuhra b. Al-Hawiyya ; Left Wing : Shurahbeel b. As-Samit ; Right Wing: Abdullah b. Al-Mut'im. The reserve was commanded by Salman bin Rabee'a.

When the Muslim forces were arrayed in the order of battle, poets and orators addressed them, and with their stirring declamations inspired the warriors to action.

One of the orators said ;

> "O warriors, turn your swords into an impenetrable wall of steel ; rush upon your antagonists like so many roaring lions; don the panoply of dust and turn your eyes downwards. When you have done with swords then let the arrows fly, for the swords cannot reach where arrows find their way."

Readers of the Qur'an recited verses from the Holy Qur'an on the subject of 'Jihad' with forceful cadence which stirred the hearts of the warriors.

The battle began with personal duels. The first duel was between Ghalib b. Abdullah of the Bani Asad and the Persian General Hormuz. Hormuz was overpowered and brought to the Muslim camp where he was locked as a prisoner of war. From the Persian ranks a Persian officer stepped forward and gave a challenge. This was accepted from the Muslim ranks by Amr b. Madi Karib. They wrestled for some time when Amr threw his adversary and cut off his head. Amr then turned to his men and shouted : " When a Persian has dropped his javelin he is useless". Then another Persian stepped forward. Amr closed up and lifted the Persian off his horse, and then cut his throat. Then he shouted, "When a Persian has lost his bow, he is useless". The Arab champion returned to his ranks, and turning to his companions shouted, "I am Abu Thaur.

Do as I do." To this his admiring companions replied : "O Father of the Bull, who can do as you do."

There was another combat between Asim b. Amr and a Persian Officer. When the Persian got near Asim, he lost nerves, and galloped back to the Persian army. Asim followed him to the Persian line, but no Persian stepped forward to meet the challenge of Asim. Asim found a mule loaded with two saddle bags. Asim took the reins of the mule and led it to the Muslim camp. The saddle bags were found full of date cakes and honey. S'aad gifted this trophy to the men belonging to the contingent of Asim.

After the duels were over, Rustam struck at the Muslims with his elephants and his wings. The Persians attack began with heavy showers of arrows. The Muslim archers shot their arrows in return, but these were light, and the Persians derisively said that the Muslim arrows were mere spindles.

After the Persian archers had gained the upper hand, Rustam ordered an attack on the Muslim right. The elephants led the attack and advanced upon the contingent led by Jareer b. Abdullah. As the elephants advanced, the Muslim horses broke out of control and fled from their position thereby leaving the infantry unsupported. As the elephants advanced the Muslim infantry was thrown into confusion, and began to fall back.

S'aad seated upstairs in the Qadissiya palace saw this confusion. He was writhing in an agony of pain, and was impatiently tossing from side to side. His wife Salma the widow of Muthanna was seated close to him. Seeing the confusion in the Muslim ranks Salma exclaimed, "What a pity, Muthanna is not here to-day." Cut to the quick, S'aad slapped her on the face saying, 'What could have Muthanna done even if he were present ?" Salma retorted "I wonder the cowards have also a sense of honour". Then she walked away inside the house.

S'aad sent orders to Ath'ath b. Qais who commanded the Kinda in the right centre, and to Hammal b. Malik who commanded the infantry of the centre to attack the Persian corps which were pursuing the Bajeela contingent. Using javelin and sword the Muslims arrested the Persian advance. Then the advancing Persians were attacked from the front as well as the flank. That made the Persians withdraw.

Rustam now ordered his right wing under Jalinus to advance against the Muslims on their front. The elephants of the Persian right and right centre moved forward. The Persian archers came into action and let loose a rain of arrows. The Muslim horses on the left and centre became unmanageable and fled from their positions. S'aad sent word to Asim b. Amr who commanded the Bani Tamim to do something about the elephants.

Asim ordered his men to pick off the Persians on the elephants' backs with arrows, to get behind the elephants and then slip in and cut the girths of the howdahs. Bani Tamim rushed forward to their task, and soon the girths of all the howdahs had been cut. Many Persian elephant-riders were killed as they fell, and the rest beat a hasty retreat making the elephants retire to the position behind the front line.

By afternoon the Persian attacks on the Muslim wings were beaten back. Now S'aad ordered a counter attack. The Muslim front at once moved forward. The Muslim cavalry charged with full force. That made the Persians reel back. The Muslim infantry then advanced. The javelin-men hurled their javelins, and the swordsmen rushed forward brandishing their swords. About sunset the Muslims were able to create several gaps in the Persian front. Through one of such gaps the Muslim warriors charged and got very near Rustam the Persian Commander-in-Chief. Rustam plunged into the foray personally and repulsed the Muslim attack though he received several wounds on his person.

The fighting ended at dusk. The battle was inconclusive. There was considerable confusion and loss on both the sides. In the Muslim chronicles the first day of the battle of Qadissiya came to be known as "The Day of Disorder."

BATTLE OF QADISSIYA THE SECOND DAY

As soon as it was day, S'aad had all the dead bodies of the Muslims evacuated from the battle-field, and carried on camels to Uzeib where these were buried in a small valley.

The Persians had suffered heavy casualties the previous day. All their elephants were wounded, and on the second day there were no elephants in the Persian fighting force.

The battle began with the ususal duels, Jalinus the Persian general threw a challenge for single combat which was accepted by Taleaha from the Muslim side. The two champions grappled with one another. After sometime Taleaha struck his sword on the head of the Persian General. The sword hardly cut the helmet of the Persian's General but did him no physical harm. Unnerved Jalinus beat a hasty retreat.

There was a dual beteen Ilba b.Jahash and a Persian Officer. The Persian was killed. Ilba also received some fatal wounds, and his intestines came out of his belly. He put the intestines into his belly and began to crawl to the Persian front. With his last breath he said :

"I look for merit with our Lord
I was of those who fought the best."

Thereafter he fell dead just in front of the Persian front.

There was another duel between A'war b. Qutba and the Persian noble Shahryar. In this duel both the Muslim and his Persian adversary were killed.

At noon a small cloud of dust rose in the horizon on the way leading to Syria. Out of the cloud emerged a contingent ledy by Qaqa b. Amr. Hadrat Umar had written to Abu Ubaidah the Commander of the Muslim forces in Syria that whatever forces he could spare from the Syrian front should be sent to Iraq. After the fall of Yermuk Abu Ubaidah sent a force of 1,000 men to Iraq under the Command of Hashim b. Utba who was a nephew of S'aad b. Abi waqas. When Hashim neared Qadissiya he sent an advance guard under Qaqa. As Qaqa arrived at the battle-field he gave the cry of 'Allah-o-Akbar', and this cry was taken up by the other Muslims who were thrilled at his arrival. Qaqa was a brother of Asim b. Amr.

Qaqa rushed into the battle-field and gave the challenge for a duel. The challenge was accepted by the Persian General Bahman the man who had commanded the Persians at the battle of the Bridqe. In a few rounds Qaqa killed Bahman. Qaqa threw another challenge. This was accepted by the Persian General Beerzan.

In the duel that followed Beerzan was killed by Qaqa. Thereafter Qaqa returned to the Muslim lines. Addressing his men he said:

> "O Muslims greet the enemy with the sword. Only with sword do men kill. Do as I do."

Then S'aad ordered a general attack. The Muslim forces swept forward, but the Persians stood firm and repulsed every attack. Ultimately the Muslims pulled back to their original position. Qaqa now resorted to an ingenious device. The camels were camouflaged to look like weird monsters. These monsters moved to the Persian front and seeing them the Persian horses turned and bolted. With the disorganisation of the Persian cavalry, the Persians became vulnerable. S'aad ordered the Muslims to intensify the attack. Some of the Persian units reeled under the Muslim attack and fell back to the river bank. Through the gaps in the Persian army, the Muslims penetrated deep towards the rear of the Persian army. Qaqa led a group of men through the Persian centre towards Rustam'a headquarters. Rustam drew his sword and personally led a counter attack against the Muslims.

Fighting was hard and fierce. It continued till night had set in. Then the two armies pulled back to their camps. The battle of Qadissiya was not over, but the Muslims had certainly established their supermacy over the Persian forces.

EXPLOITS OF ABU MIHJAN

Abu Mihjan belonged to the Saqeef clan. He was a cousin of Abu Ubaid who had commanded the Muslim forces in Iraq and was martyred at the battle of the Bridge.

The home town of Abu Mihjan was Taif. When the Muslims under the Holy Prophet besieged Taif after the fall of Mecca, Abu Mihjan fought against the Muslims. His arrow mortally wounded Abdullah son of Hadrat Abu Bakr.

Later when the Saqeef submitted to the Holy Prophet and accepted Islam, Abu Mihjan also became a Muslim. He was staunch in his faith in Islam, but he had weakness for liquor, and sometimes secretly drank wine.

At the battle of the Bridge, Abu Mihjan was the commander of the cavalry. He drove back the elephant which had crushed Abu Ubaid to death. After the disaster of the battle of the bridge, Abu Mihjan stayed on with Muthanna at Ulleis for some time. Then he returned to Madina.

At Madina, Hadrat Umar caught him drinking and as a punishment he was exiled to Yemen. Later he was forgiven and was allowed to join the Muslim forces in Iraq under S'aad. In camp, Abu Mihjan drank again, and on discovering his offence S'aad had him whipped and thrown into a cellar in fetters. His cell was in the palace at Qadissiya where S'aad was lodged and from where he commanded the war operations.

From his cellar, Abu Mihjan saw the battle waging in great fury. Abu Mihjan was a born soldier, and when the other Muslims were locked up in life and death struggle, he pined to be free to wield the sword against the enemy. He approached S'aad, and asked for permission to fight. S'aad rebuked him and ordered him back to his cellar.

While returning to his cellar, Abu Mihjan met Salma the new wife of S'aad. He wanted her to help him, but Salma was not inclined to interfere.

Back in his cellar, Abu Mihjan burst into pathetic verses:

"It is sufficient sorrow when you see a cavalier,
Deprived, abandoned and bound in shackles,
While I stand these fetters detain me,
While others are fighting.
I was once a man with wealth and kinsmen,
But I am now left entirely alone.
By Allah, I give the pledge,
If freed, I will never drink again."

Salma heard the song and was moved. She wanted to know what she could do for him. He said :

"Release me so that I may go and fight. I promise that if I am not killed I will return to the cellar at night. Lend me a horse so that I may ride to the battle-field."

Salma released him. She also got for him the horse of S'aad. Fully armed Abu Mihjan rode to the battle-field. He rode through the Muslim ranks and then with the cry of "Allah-o-Akbar" hurled himself at the Persian front killing a man. He galloped back to the Muslim ranks and after a while again dashed at the Persian front killing another man. He thus went to and fro and killed about a dozen Persians.

The Muslims marvelled at the sight of Abu Mihjan. "Who is this warrior" they asked. S'aad saw him from the top storey of his palace. He thought that the man was Abu Mihjan but then he knew that Abu Mihjan was in the cellar. He felt that the horse that the unknown warrior rode appeared to be his own horse, but he dismissed the thought as he knew that his horse was in the stable.

At night after his triumph at the battle field, Abu Mihjan returned to his cellar and his fetters. Back in the cellar, Abu Mihjan burst into song :

"Have you ever known the Saqeef without honour ?

I am the finest of them with the sword
And the most steadfast of them.
On the night of Qadissiya they did not know me
Or of my escape from the prison to the battle-field."

When the battle of Qadissiya was over and Salma and S'aad were reconciled Salma told S'aad how she had released Abu Mihjan and how Abu Mihjan after performing daring exploits at the battle-field had in keeping with his promise returned to the cellar. Now S'aad recalled that the unknown warrior whom he had seen performing wondrous exploits and riding S'aad's horse was indeed Abu Mihjan.

S'aad was in a mood of appreciation. He released Abu Mihjan and said, "By Allah, after seeing what you did at the battlefield I will not whip you again."

And Abu Mihjan said, "I shall never drink again."

BATTLE OF QADISSIYA THE THIRD DAY

On the third day of the battle of Qadissiya, the elephants were once again in the front of the Persian army. That altered the situation to the advantage of the Persians, and Rustam pressed this advantage into service. He ordered an attack, and the Muslims had to remain on the defensive.

The Persians let loose a rain of arrows against the Muslims, and that led to considerable damage to the Muslims. The Muslim archers shot their arrows in reply, but these were not very effective.

The Persian elephants moved forward supported by their infantry and cavalry. At the approach of the Persian elephants, the Muslim horse got panicky and that led to confusion in the ranks of the Muslim cavalry. The Persians pressed the attack, and the Muslims fell back.

Through the gaps that had appeared in the Muslim ranks as a result of the Persian advance, some Persian cavalry pressed forward to capture the old palace where S'aad the Commander-in-Chief of the Muslim forces was stationed. The strategy of the Persians was that the Muslim Commander-in-Chief should be killed or taken captive with a view to demoralising the Muslims.

The Muslims realised the danger that beset their Commander-in-Chief. A strong cavalry contingent of the Maslims rushed to the spot, and drove away the Persians.

S'aad now directed that the elephants should be overpowered by blinding them and severing their trunks. Qaqa and his brother Asim took with them a strong group of the Bani Tamim, and moved towards the elephant which was causing the greatest havoc among the Muslim ranks. The Bani Tamim charged with cries of Allah-o-Akbar, struck at the Persians who surrounded the elephant, and moved forward through the gap created by their attack. Thereupon the Persians rushed to the flanks and rear of the elephant. There being no Persian in front of the elephant, Qaqa and Asim stole to the front and threw their javelins at the elephant. The javelins pierced the eyes of the elephant. The beast writhed with pain, and the Howdah that it carried came tumbling down. Qaqa and Asim fell on the Persians who had fallen with the Howdah and killed all of them. Then they severed the trunk of the elephant with strokes of their swords. In an agony of pain, the elephant turned and bolted away trampling the Persians under its feet.

Hammal b. Malik and Ribbel b. Amr of the Bani Asad led a similar attack against another elephant. That elephant also lost its eyes and trunk, and retired from the battle-field writing with pain.

Amr b. Madi Karib with his men rushed at another elephant and the elephant blinded and mutilated galloped away from the battle-field. Other groups of Muslim warriors also rushed at the elephants adopting similar tactics and succeeded in mutilating the monsters. The mutilated beasts rushed through the Persian ranks and made for the river. The other elephants seeing their leaders leave the field, also turned tail and fled to the river. By noon no elephant was left on the battle-field. The flight of the elephants caused considerable confusion in the Persian ranks.

At this stage, S'aad ordered an assault. The Muslims moved forward and the two armies clashed. In spite of the Muslim pressure, the Persians held the ground. After some fierce fighting the Muslims pulled back.

After a little break the battle was resumed in the afternoon. In the absence of Persian elephants, the Muslims once again brought camels camouflaged as monsters. The trick did not work and the Persian horse stood their ground.

The Muslims charged again, but though the Persians suffered heavy casualties, they held the ground and refused to yield. When the dusk set in both the armies were locked in life and death struggle.

The third day of the battle of Qadissiya proved to be the hardest day of the war. There were heavy casualties on both sides, and the battle-field came to be strewn with dead bodies of fallen warriors, both Muslims and non-Muslims. When the battle began and the elephants were brought to the front all advantages lay with the Persians, and Rustam felt that the collapse of the Muslim army was imminent. At one stage the Muslim Commander-in-Chief ran the risk of being killed or captured alive.

Later the Muslims succeeded in driving away the elephants. The Muslims then launched the assault. In spite of the violence of the Muslim attack, the Persians held the ground and refused to yield. Thus at the end of the third day the battle of Qadissiya was still inconclusive.

BATTLE OF QADISSIYA THE LAST DAY

On the third day of the battle even at night there was no break in fighting. It was a moon-lit night, and in spite of fatigue after three days' strenuous battle, the armies continued to fight.

It was now a war of stamina. Both sides were on the verge of human endurance, and whosoever could be steadfast for some time more was likely to win. Both the sides hoped that they were likely to win.

In the matter of stamina the refined Persians could be no match for the hardy Arabs. The strategy of S'aad was to wear down the Persians, and snatch away the victory from them.

The battle waged all the night long. About midnight, Qaqa shouted:

> "We have strangled the enemy,
> The enemy is now on the verge of collapse."

There were heavy casualties among the Persians, but they stood firm.

At sunrise the fighting ceased, but still the result was inconclusive. That was now the fourth day of the battle, and it was felt that it might be the last day of the battle. Qaqa addressed his men:

> "If we fight for an hour or so more, the enemy will be defeated.
> So, warriors of the Bani Tamim make one more attempt and victory will be yours."

Other Chiefs spoke in similar terms to their contingents. The Muslim warriors shouted "If you attack we are with you."

Qaqa hurled his contingent against the Persians with great violence. Seeing the Bani Tamim launch the attack, other Muslim contingents followed suit. The Persians too exhausted after continuous war for twenty-four hours were taken unawares at the resumption of battle. They stood up in battle formation to resist the Muslim charge, but now there were signs of weakness among the Persian ranks. The right wing of the Persians under Harmuzan was pushed back. After withdrawal they reformed and again stood their ground. By noon Qaqa and his men were able to pierce through the Persian centre. They dashed towards the Persian Headquarters to get hold of Rustam, the Commander-in-Chief of the Persian forces.

At this time a strong dust storm lashed the battle-field. The storm blew in the faces of the Persians, and aided the onward advance of the Muslims. The canopy and the throne of Rustam were blown away by the dust storm and thrown in the Ateeq. Rustam was alone. He moved back and sought shelter behind a mule which carried in saddle boxes his personal belongings. A Muslim warrior Hilal b. Ullafa saw the mule and struck at the saddle boxes with his sword. Owing to poor visibility, Hilal could not notice Rustam, nor was Rustam able to see Hilal. The saddle box fell on Rustam. He cleared the box and ran towards the river. Hilal now saw Rustam, and ran after him. Rustam plunged in the river. Hilal jumped in the river after him. He dragged him to the bank, where drawing his sword he struck several blows at Rustam and killed him. Then he dragged the corpse of Rustam and threw it under the feet of the mule. Hilal exultant at having killed the Commander-in-Chief of the Persian forces shouted:

"By the Lord of the Ka'aba,
I have killed Rustam,
I am Hilal bin Ullafa."

The Persians were not aware of the death of Rustam, and they went on fighting doggedly.

When S'aad came to know that Rustam had been killed, he ordered the Muslims to make one more attack and drive away the Persians. In the afternoon the Muslims mounted another attack. By this time even the Persians knew that their Commander-in-Chief had been killed. That demoralised the Persians and after putting up a last heroic resistance, the Persian front collapsed. With the collapse, the Persian warriors fled in panic to the river.

The chained Persians arrived at the bank of the Ateeq anxious to fly to safety. The victorious Muslims followed at their heel. Some Persians were picked up by the Muslims with their long spears. Those who plunged in the river, because of the heavy weight of their armours and chains were unable to cross to the other bank and were drowned.

At this stage Jalinus took command of what was left of the Persian army. He got control of the bridge head, and succeeded in getting a section of the Persian army cross the bridge safely.

The battle of Qadissiya was now over. Out of 60,000 Persians who had taken the field, only 20,000 survived to tell the story of the disaster that they had met at the battle-field of Qadissiya. 40,000 Persians were killed or drowned. The Muslim casualties numbered 6,000 out of a total force of 30,000. In the case of the Persians, out of every three persons only one survived: in the case of Muslims out of every five Muslims four survived to rejoice at the victory.

S'aad sent parties to pursue the fleeing Persians. The main Persian force commanded by Jalinus proceeded to Najaf. The pursuing Muslim party led by Zuhra caught up the Persians half way between Kharara and Seilahun. Brought to bay Jalinus choose to fight. He threw a challenge for a personal duel. The challenge was accepted by Zuhra. In the duel Jalinus was killed. Thereupon the Persians fled. They were pursued upto Najaf, and the stragglers that the Muslims met in the way were put to sword. When it was night, Zuhra and his party returned to Qadissiya.

Other parties sent in various directions also caught up flying Persians. Most of them were killed or taken captives.

The booty that the Muslims captured was vast. After setting aside the State share of one fifth, the rest was distributed among the men who had participated in the battle of Qadissiya. Each infantry man received 7,000 dirhams, and each cavalryman 14,000 dirhams as his share.

NEWS OF THE MUSLIM VICTORY CARRIED TO HADRAT UMAR

As soon as the battle of Qadissiya was over, S'aad sent a report of the victory of the Muslims to Hadrat Umar. In the report, S'aad observed:

> "Allah the Mighty has given us victory over the enemy after prolonged and fierce battle. The enemy was in great number and strength, but Allah in His Mercy has granted victory to the Muslims. For this Allah and His Prophet be praised."

The report was accompanied by a list of casualties as well as the immediate spoils that had fallen in the hands of the Muslims.

The report was sent through a special messenger. The courier selected for the mission was S'aad b. Umeila of the Bani Fazara, a clan that lived to the north of Madina.

The courier was provided a fast camel. He was also given provisions for the journey. He was commissioned to ride post haste to Madina, and tell the Caliph and the Muslims the happy news of the victory of the Muslims at the historic battle of Qadissiya.

From Qadissiya, Madina was about a thousand miles Riding day and night, with very short spells of rest, S'aad b. Umeila covered the distance in a fortnight. The sun had just risen when the courier reached the outskirts of Madina.

When about two miles from Madina, the courier came upon a man sitting by the roadside who stood up a the approach of the camel rider and asked him from where did he come. S'aad b. Umeila said that he was coming from Iraq.

The man who accosted the camel driver was Hadrat Umar. So keen was Hadrat Umar about getting the news of the result of the battle of Qadissiya that Hadrat Umar would every day in the morning walk for a few miles from Madina on the way to Iraq hoping that some courier would come carrying the news. For the last one week this was the usual practice with Hadrat Umar. When the sun rose high, and no traveller from Iraq appeared the Caliph would return to Madina. At Madina day and night the faithful prayed for the victory of the Muslims in the battle of Qadissiya.

When S'aad b. Umeila said that he was coming from Iraq, Hadrat Umar did not reveal his identity to him. Excitedly he asked, "What news do you carry about the battle of Qadissiya." S'aad said exultantly, "God has given the Muslims victory."

Hadrat Umar 's face lit up with joy as he heard the news of the victory of the Muslims. He did not tell the courier that he was the Caliph and that the report that he carried was meant for him.

The courier quickened the pace of the camel so that he might reach Madina as early as possible. Hadrat Umar started running alongside the camel, and kept on asking the camel rider the details about the Muslim victory, S'aad furnished the necessary details. When S'aad had related all that he could tell, Hadrat Umar exclaimed "Glory be to Allah", and S'aad also said, "God be praised."

By this time they had reached Madina, and seeing Hadrat Umar, the Madinites gathered round him and greeted him as "Amir-ul-Mominin." Thereupon the courier felt embarrassed and turning to Hadrat Umar said, "O Commander of the Faithful, why did you not reveal your identity to me ?"

Hadrat Umar said, "Brother, be at rest. No blame rests on you."

S'aad then handed over the report of S'aad b. Abi Waqqas. As Hadrat Umar read the report, tears of joy trickled from his eyes. All the Muslims of Madina gathered in the Prophet's Mosque. There Hadrat Umar read the report of S'aad b. Abi Waqqas to the congregation. Then the Muslims led by Hadrat Umar offered a special prayer of thanksgiving to God for the victory of the Muslims at the battle of Qadissiya.

AL-KHANSA

Al-Khansa was the daughter of the great poet Zuheir. She was the distinguished poetess of Arabia during the early Islamic period. Even the Holy Prophet of Islam admired her verses. She accepted Islam along with the other members of her tribe .

The elegy that she wrote on the death of her brother is regarded as one of the best elegies in Arabic. She said:

> "The herald of the dead announced the loss
> Of the most generous man, Sakhr;
> And he cried it so loud
> That far and wide he was heard.
> It wounded me so painfully
> That in my misery I looked like a drunken person.
> Every morning when I awaken,
> The first rays of the sun remind me of him
> And every evening when the sun sets
> I mourn for him."

She was not only a poetess; she was very brave and valiant as well. When the Muslims fought against the Persians in the battle of Qadissiya she was present at the front with her four sons. On the eve of the battle by a fiery and inspiring speech she exhorted her sons to fight for the glory of Islam. She said:

> "My sons, I have borne you with pain and brought you up with great care. I have brought no dishonour to your family and no slur to your tribe. I have wrought no indignity to your father's prestige, and there can be no doubt about the sanctity of the character of your mother. Now, therefore, listen to me. Remember the great merit of fighting for defending your faith; remember

the Qur'anic injunction of adopting patience in the midst of distress. Tomorrow morning, rise from your bed hale and hearty and join the battle with fearless courage. Go into the midst of the thickest of the battle encounter the boldest enemy and if necessary embrace martyrdom."

The four sons of Al-Khansa joined the battle with fearless courage. The words of their mother kept ringing in their ears and they plunged themselves heroically in the thick of the battle, and encountered the boldest enemies. They put many Persians to sword and were rewarded with the crown of martyrdom.

The Muslims won the battle of Qadissiya, but Khansa lost all her sons. When the news of the death of her sons was brought to her, she wanted to know what was the result of the battle. When she was told that the Muslims had won, she thanked God for the martyrdom of her sons, and said, " Who dies, if Islam lives."

When she saw the dead bodies of her sons, she did not weep. She burst into an elegy:

"My sons I bore you with pain
And brought you up for care;
You have fallen today in the cause of Islam,
Who says you are dead;
You are very much alive, and alive with honour.
I feel proud to be the mother of martyrs."

When Khansa returned to Madina, Hadrat Umar went to her house to condole with her over the death of her sons. Khansa merely said:

"Congratulate me, Amirul Mominin,
For verily I am the mother of martyrs."

Hadrat Umar loaded her with gifts, and as long as she lived, she got the allowances due to her sons. The shares of her sons in the spoils of war arising out of the battle of Qadissiya were also paid to her.

BATTLE OF BURS

With the victory at Qadissiya, the road to Ctesiphon called Al-Madain by the Muslims) the capital of Persia lay open to the Muslims. Ctesiphon was on the Tigris, a few miles downstream of the present day Baghdad.

The battle of Qadissiya shook the Persian rule in Iraq to its foundations, but that was not the end of the Persian rule in Iraq. As long as the Persians held their capital Ctesiphon, there was always the danger that at some suitable moment they would make an attempt to recover what they had lost, and drive away the Arabs from Iraq.

Hadrat Umar accordingly sent instructions to S'aad that as a sequel to the battle of Qadissiya, the Muslims should push forward to Ctesiphon and wrest it from the Persians.

Some time towards the end of November 636, S'aad bin Abi Waqqas issued orders to the Muslim forces under his command to march to Ctesiphon. S'aad reorganised his army into five corps, and each corps was placed under the command of a veteran General. The commanders were:

(1) Zuhra bin Al-Hāwiyya;
(2) Abdullah bin Muta'm;
(3) Shurahbeel bin Al-Samit;
(4) Hashim b. Utba; and
(5) Khalid bin Urfula.

The entire army consisted of cavalry.

From Qadissiya, the main stages on the route to Ctesiphon were Najaf, Burs; Babylon; Sura; Deir Kab; Kusa; Sabat; and Ctesiphon.

The corps of Zuhra b. Al-Hāwiyya set off as the advance guard. It occupied Najaf and stayed there till the other corps reached Najaf. Then Zuhra with his corps crossed the Euphrates and proceeded on the road to Ctesiphon. He reached Burs on the western bank of the Hilla branch of the Euphrates.

At Burs the advance of Zuhra was resisted by a Persian force under the command of Busbuhra the Mayor of Burs. The troops on both sides were deployed for action. Busbuhra stepped forward and gave the challenge for a personal duel. Zuhra accepted the challenge. Zuhra inflicted heavy wounds on Busbuhra. Profusely bleeding he retired. There was some fighting, but the Persians were no match for the Muslims. The Persian army withdrew and crossing the Hilla branch proceeded to join the main Persian army at Babylon. At Babylon, Busbuhra died of the wounds.

After the withdrawal of the Persian force, the people of Burs approached Zuhra with the offer of peace, which was accepted. Zuhra stayed at Burs for some time to attend to administrative matters. In the meantime other Muslim corps also arrived at Burs.

BATTLE OF BABYLON

Babylon was across the other bank of the Euphrates. It was a place of historic importance having been at one time the capital of Iraq. It was also a place of strategic importance and was the gateway of the Suwad, the land between the Euphrates and the Tigris.

About two years earlier the Muslims had fought a battle at Babylon under Muthanna when they had occupied Babylon. Later on the eve of the battle of Qadissiya when the Muslims withdrew from all advance posts in Iraq, they abandoned Babylon. Having won the battle of Qadissiya, the Muslims now advanced to re-conquer Babylon.

Some time in the middle of December 636, the Muslims crossed the Euphrates and camped outside Babylon. There was a big concentration of the Persian forces at Babylon commanded by the veteran Generals, Feerzan, Hormuzan, Mihran and Nakheerzan.

There was a battle at Babylon. The details of the battle have not been recorded in any history. It appears that there was disunity among the Persians, and they could not put up a stiff resistance against the Muslim charge. Hormuzan with his forces withdrew to his home province Ahwaz. On his withdrawal, the other Generals also pulled back their forces and withdrew northward.

After the Persian forces had left, the citizens of Babylon formally surrendered. They were afforded protection under the usual terms. They volunteered to cooperate with the Muslims in their fight against the Persians. They furnished a good deal of useful information about the disposition of the Persian forces. Some Babylonians were employed in the construction of roads and bridges.

BATTLE OF SURA AND DEIR KAB

While the main Muslim army remained at Babylon, Zuhra was commanded by S'aad to pursue the Persians who had retreated from Babylon. The Muslim advance guard under Zuhra followed the Persians, and caught the Persian rear-guard at Sura. The Persian rear-guard deployed themselves for action and after a short clash their resistance broke down and they with drew to Deir Kab.

Zuhra next marched to Deir Kab. There was large concentration of Persian forces at Deir Kab commanded by the General Nakheerzan. The two sides deployed their forces for combat. Then the Persian commander Nakheerzan stepped forward to throw a challenge for a personal duel.

From the Muslim side Zubair bin Salim a lieutenant of Zuhra stepped forward to accept the duel. In an exciting duel, Nakheerzan was overthrown and killed. Then the battle began. For some time the Persians put up a stiff resistance, and all Muslim attacks were repulsed. Then by a flanking movement Jareer bin Abdullah was able to capture the bridge at the rear of the Persians. From there he raised the shout of "Allah-o-Akbar'. At this the Persians lost heart, and they withdrew in great disorder after suffering heavy losses. Deir Kab was occupied by the Muslims, and the people were afforded protection under the usual terms.

BATTLE OF KUSA

Early in January 637, the Muslim advance guard under Zuhra reached Kusa. It was only ten miles from Ctesiphon. There was a sizable detachment of the Persian forces here commanded by Shahryar. He was a huge camel-like man, very haughty and arrogant.

As the two forces were deployed for action, Shahryar stepped out of the Persian ranks, and gave the challenge for a personal duel in very arrogant terms. He said:

> "Who can dare come forward to measure strength with me. Verily, whoever comes to fight with me, comes to meet his death ."

> Zuhra the Commander of the Muslim forces said:

> "I would have come to fight with you personally, but in view of your arrogance I am deputing a slave to fight you."

Under the orders of Zuhra, Nail bin Jushan emerged from the Muslim ranks and proceeded to have a duel with Shahryar. As the two antagonists faced each other mounted on horseback, Shahryar saw that Nail was a lean thin man whom he could overthrow in no time.

The duel began. They first fought with lances, then with swords. Thereafter the two champions dismounted from the horses and a hand to hand fighting ensued. In such a fight, Shahryar in view of his bulk appeared to have an upper hand. Shahryar overthrew Nail, and was about to draw his dagger to kill Nail, when the Arab with his strong teeth crushed the thumb of Shahryar. That made Shahryar lose his balance. Nail rose immediately, and thrust his dagger in the body of Shahryar. The camel-like man fell on the ground dead.

Seeing their commander fall, the Persians lost nerve, and choosing discretion as the better part of valour, they withdrew to Ctesiphon. Thereafter the Muslims occupied Kusa. A deputation of the citizens waited on Zuhra, when the usual terms were offered to them, and they accepted them without argument.

After the victory, Zuhra stayed at Kusa for some time. In the meantime all the Muslim forces reached Kusa. Kusa was a place of historic importance. It was the place where Nimrod imprisoned the Prophet Abraham, and where he was thrown in burning fire, out of which he had emerged unharmed. The Muslims visited all these sites and offered prayers for the soul of Abraham. S'aad wrote of the Muslim victories to Hadrat Umar, and also about the sanctity of Kusa.

In reply Hadrat Umar wrote:

> "Just as the Prophet Abraham emerged out of the ordeal of fire unharmed, thus I have the faith that in the battle of truth that you are waging against the Persians, you will, with the grace of God, triumph. Now Al-Madain awaits you. Go ahead, and let the Muslim flag flutter over the palace of the Chosroes. May God bless you. Have faith in God, for such faith would give you the courage to fight against heavy odds,"

BATTLE OF BAHRSEER

In the second week of January 637, Zuhra advanced with his corps and reached Sabat four miles from Ctesiphon. It was a Persian cantonment, but there was no garrison there. The Mayor of Sabat, Sheerzad waited on Zuhra and offered allegiance to the Muslims. The residents were given protection on the usual terms. Now the entire land upto the very gates of Ctesiphon belonged to the Muslims.

Ctesiphon the capital of Persia was not one city; it was a conglomeration of several cities. Indeed the Arabs called Ctesiphon 'Al-Madain', meaning the cities. The main city lay on the eastern bank of the Tigris. One of the cities forming part of 'Al-Madain' lay on the western bank of the Tigris and was known as Bahrseer.

Bahrseer had been prepared for defence and a deep ditch had been dug round the perimeter of the suburb. As the Muslim advance guard approached Bahrseer, the Persian garrison within the fortified city hurled stones at the Muslims through ballistas and catapults. The Muslims pulled back beyond the range of the stones and decided to lay siege to the city.

The siege began in January 637, and dragged on for two months. The supplies from the countryside on which Bahrseer depended were entirely cut off, and the citizens were reduced to eating cats and dogs. Things for the Persian force became still worse, when some of the Persians who had accepted the Muslim rule, built for the Muslims engines which could throw stones. Equipped with these engines, the Muslims were able to answer the Persian military fire, stone for stone. That caused considerable havoc among the besieged citizens.

One day in March 637, cut to sore straits, the Persian garrison called forth from the city in the determined effort to break through the Muslim ranks. The Persian forces were led by a fierce lion which had been specially trained for war. The lion rushed at the Muslim front, and the Muslim horses bolted causing considerable harms. Hashim who was commanding the vanguard of the Muslim forces rushed at the lion with his sword and dealt it such a well directed blow that it fell dead. S'aad the Commander-in-Chief of the Muslim forces stepped forward to kiss Hashim bin Utba on the forehead as a mark of admiration for his act of unparalleled heroism.

The Commander of the Persian force gave a challenge for a personal duel. The challenge was accepted by Zuhra bin Al-Hāwiyya. In the exciting duel that followed, Zuhra killed the Persian Commander. Then the two armies clashed, and the fight continued till the night set. In the battle an arrow struck Zuhra, the hero of the march to Ctesiphon, and the great hero died. He was buried with full military honours.

After the break in fighting, a Persian emissary came to the Muslim camp to convey a message from the Persian emperor. The Persian emissary said:

> "Our emperor asks if you would be agreeable to peace on the condition that the Tigris should be the boundary between you and us, so that whatever is with us on the eastern side of the Tigris remains ours and whatever you have gained on the western side is yours. And if this does not satisfy your land hunger, then nothing would satisfy you."

S'aad the Muslim Commander-in Chief told the emissary that the Muslims were not hungry for land; and that they were fighting in the name of Allah. He added that if the Persian emperor wanted peace it was open to him to accept Islam, or to pay Jizya. If both the alternatives were not acceptable then peace was out of question, and only the sword could decide the issue between them.

When the day dawned, it was found that the Persians evacuated Bahrseer. In withdrawing the Persian garrison had destroyed all bridges on the Tigris. They had also taken away all the boats-from the western bank of the Tigris, and anchored them on the eastern bank.

The Muslim forces occupied Bahrseer. The town was empty. All the residents had during the night managed cross over to Ctesiphon on the other bank of the Tigris.

CAPTURE OF AL-MADAIN

After the occupation of Bahrseer, only the Tigris half a mile wide lay between the Muslims and Ctesiphon. The river was in flood and there were no means with the Muslims to cross it. In their withdrawal from Bahrseer the Persians had taken away all the boats. The approaches to Ctesiphon were heavily guarded by the Persians. It was reported that there was considerable Persian force in Ctesiphon under the command of Generals Mihran and Khurrazad. Khurrazad was a brother of the General Rustam who had been killed in the battle of Qadissiya.

Some Persians who had accepted the Muslim rule volunteered to show S'aad a site downstream where the river could be forded. S'aad saw the site, but was not sure whether it was fit for crossing. The Arabs were land warriors and they hesitated to negotiate water. That night S'aad had a dream in which another site was indicated to him which the Muslims could cross.

The next morning S'aad asked for volunteers who could cross the river on horseback. Asim was the first to volunteer. Then others offered themselves. S'aad went to the site which he had seen in the dream, and after invoking the blessings of God asked the six hundred warriors led by Asim to plunge into the river and cross over to the other bank.

The Muslim horses plunged in the river and slowly proceeded to the other bank. When the Persians saw that the Muslims were coming, the Persian horses also plunged in the river to hold back the Muslims from crossing the river. When the Muslims were hardly half way in the river they faced the Persians. A river battle ensued. In the hand to hand fight that followed the Muslims were able to kill many Persians and the rest fled away. As the Muslims landed on the eastern bank of the Tigris, a cry went around the Persian camp, "The Muslims have come: they are not men—they are devils and jinns. Who can fight them?"

After the first band of six hundred volunteers under Asim, other contingents crossed the river, and this process went on till all the Muslim forces had crossed over to the other side of the Tigris. When the Persian Generals came to know that the entire Muslim force had crossed over to Ctesiphon in spite of the flood in the river, they decided that they should evacuate Ctesiphon as further resistance was futile. The Persian army evacuated the city. The Persian emperor Yazdjurd retreated to Hulwan. While withdrawing the Persian emperor carried away as much of the imperial treasure and other valuable possessions as he could carry.

From the river bank the Muslim forces marched to the city of Ctesiphon. The march was led by the column of Asim. He was immediately followed by the column of Qaqa. Then other columns marched in military order. At one place a few Persian soldiers offered resistance but they were soon cut off. The Muslim columns marched through the heart of Ctesiphon. All business premises were closed. No Persians were seen, and the Muslims met no resistance. The Muslims got to the White Palace the seat of the Persian Government. A small Persian regiment stationed there offered some resistance. Salman the Persian who was with the Muslim troops advised the Persian regiment to submit in its own interest as they could no longer face the Muslims. The garrison surrendered, and the White Palace was occupied by the Muslims.

After occupying the city, S'aad announced amnesty to all Persians who were in the city. A delegation of the representatives of the people waited on S'aad. They sought terms, and the usual terms being offered they agreed to the imposition of Jizya. A regular peace pact was drawn up, and the citizens were called upon to follow their normal avocations. Without any large scale fighting the Muslims had conquered Ctesiphon, the capital of the once mighty Persian empire.

S'aad moved into the White Palace and established his headquarters there. The great courtyard of the palace was converted into a mosque where S'aad led a mass victory prayer.

S'aad next sent out columns in several directions to deal with the Persian stragglers. One column took the route to Hulwan. They caught up some Persians at Nahrawan and recovered the valuable goods that they were carrying. These included the fabulous crown of Persia, the imperial regalia and several ornaments. The booty comprised enough gold and precious stones to purchase a kingdom. Another column operating in another sector recovered some swords and other valuable armour. Another Muslim column captured some chests which contained a horse of gold studded with sapphires and emeralds.

Within Ctesiphon the Muslims found a pavilion containing a large number of sealed baskets. These baskets contained utensils of gold and silver. From the imperial treasury the Muslims got cash of over a billion dirhams.

When the booty was distributed among the soldiers the share of each man came to 12,000 dirhams. Among the booty was a grogeous carpet found from the White Palace. It was a huge bulky affair 900 meters square. It was worked with gold and gems. It represented a garden with glades, trees and flowers. The branches of the tree were that of gold, the leaves were of silver, and the fruit were of gems. It was one of the wonders of the world. As it could not be distributed among the soldiers, S'aad sent it to Madina along with the usual one fifth State share.

HEIRLOOMS OF PERSIA

After the occupation of Ctesiphon, one-fifth of the booty gathered from Al-Madain was sent to Hadrat Umar at Madina. These included vast riches comprising rare and priceless heirlooms. These comprised besides cash, the gorgeous carpet; the gem studded crown and royal robes, bangles of the Persian kings, and other curios.

On receiving the news of the subjugation of the capital of the Persian empire, Hadrat Umar led a thanksgiving prayer. The Holy Prophet had prophesied that the Muslims would one day overpower the mighty empire of Persia and this prophecy had been fulfilled only within six years of the death of the Holy Prophet .

As Hadrat Umar surveyed the vast riches that had been brought to Madina, he wept. These were tears partly indicative of his joy and partly of his fear lest such wealth might turn the head of the Muslims.

Hadrat Umar sought the advice of the Companions as to what should be done with the carpet. The general view was that it might be retained by the Caliph. Hadrat Umar asked for the opinion of Hadrat Ali. Hadrat Ali said, "What they say is right, but if you set this precedent to-day, tomorrow there will be those who will claim such trophies without deserving them." Hadrat Umar said, "Ali you are right; verily, you have given sound advice. "The carpet was cut into small pieces and distributed among the people. Hadrat Ali got one average piece, and he was able to sell it for 20,000 dirhams.

In Madina there was a man Muhallam by name who was cast in royal mould, and was known for his dignity, grace, and symmetry of body. On seeing him the Holy Prophet had said that he would one day wear the robes of the kings of Persia.

When in the spoils the robes of the Persian kings came to Madina, Hadrat Umar called Muhallam and had him dressed in the robes of the kings of Persia. All the people of Madina came to see him thus dressed. In this way the prophecy of the Holy Prophet was fulfilled.

There was another man in Madina Saraqa by name about whom the Holy Prophet had said that one day he would wear the bangles of Chosroes. There was an interesting background to the story of Saraqa. When the Holy Prophet and Hadrat Abu Bakr escaped from Mecca with a view to migrating to Madina, the hostile Quraish of Mecca announced a reward of one hundred camels to any one who captured the Holy Prophet. Saraqa bin Jusham was a Quraish. Some one reported to him that he had seen three persons travelling on the road to Madina. Thinking that such persons were the Prophet and his party Saraqa decided to pursue them with a view to winning the reward of hundred camels. Saraqa rode on a swift horse and he ultimately came in sight of the Holy Prophet and Abu Bakr. As he drew near them his horse stumbled and he fell down. He drew arrows from his quiver to divine the course of action for him. The omens forbade the pursuit. In spite of that Saraqa rode again to pursue the fugitives. This time the horse stuck up in the loose sand and could not come out. Once again he cast the arrows in the process of divination, and once again he received a negative answer. He now felt convinced that some supernatural power protected the Prophet. He shouted to the Holy Prophet and Hadrat Abu Bakr to stop and listen to him. They stopped and as he came to them Saraqa said that he had come to pursue them but after what had happened to his horse he had changed his mind. He said, "You may go to Madina in peace. I will return to Mecca and I will see that you are not pursued. Give me in writing an assurance that when the time comes my services would be recognised." The Holy Prophet asked Hadrat Abu Bakr to give a document to that effect to Saraqa.

When Mecca was conquered, Saraqa presented that document and was allowed amnesty. He was converted to Islam and came to Madina. In Madina the Holy Prophet had said, "Saraqa ! a time will come when you will wear the bangles of Chosroes." Hadrat Umar called Saraqa and gave him the bangles of Chosroes as a reward for the services that he had rendered to the Holy Prophet. As Saraqa wore the bangles, Hadrat Umar said, "Thank God, the prophecy of the Holy Prophet stands fulfilled."

BATTLE OF TAKREET AND MOSUL

When the Muslims occupied Ctesiphon the capital of Persia it did not mean that Persia had completely abandoned Iraq. In the north-east of Ctesiphon, the Persian forces gathered in great strength at Jalaula. Still further upstream the Tigris there was a concentration of the Persian forces at Takreet and Mosul.

When the Persian forces gathered at Jalaula, the Persian Governor of Mosul, Intaq by name collected some Persian forces and marched with them from Mosul to Takreet. He also collected large contingents from the Christian Arab tribes of Iyad, Taghlib and Namr. At Takreet he had a sizable Persian army. He dug a ditch round the city.

Takreet lay north-west of Jalaula, and the strategy was that the contingents from Takreet could be sent to the help of the Persian army at Jalaula. It was also believed that in the event of Persian defeat at Jalaula, the Persians could take a stand at Takreet.

S'aad b. Abi Waqqas reported this situation to Hadrat Umar. Hadrat Umar issued the following instructions to S'aad b. Abi Waqqas:

> "Send Abdullah b. Mut'am to deal with Intaq. The Commander of his advance guard will be Ribi b. Al-Afkal, of his right wing Haris b. Hassaan, of his left wing Furat b. Hayan, of his rear-guard Hani b. Qais, and of his cavalry Arfaja bin Harsama."

Hadrat Umar further instructed:

> "If Allah defeats the two armies, the army of Mihran and the army of Intaq, send Qaqa b. Amr forward so

that he is between the Suwad and the hills. on the boundaries of the Suwad, to act as the guard of the Muslims. May Allah preserve the Suwad for you."

Some time in May 637 A.D., Abdullah b. Mut'am marched from Ctesiphon with a force of 5,000 men, and arriving at Takreet invested the city. Abdullah made several attempts to break the defences but the Persians held the ground.

With the Persians inside the city of Takreet there was a considerable strength of the Christian Arabs. Abdullah sent his agents to contact the Arab tribes in the city, and tried to persuade them not to support the Persians. He suggested that they should join the Muslim Arabs against the Persians. These overtures were successful and the Christian Arabs became lukewarm in their support of the Persians. The Persians soon noticed that the Arab tribes were not active in the war effort and avoided war. Thereupon the Persians decided to evacuate secretly.

These developments were reported to Abdullah by the agents of the Christian tribes. The Christian Arab tribes offered to join the Muslims in case suitable terms were offered to them. Abdullah said that if the Christian tribes were sincere they should declare that there was no God but Allah and that Muhammad was the Messenger of God. The agents carried this message to their tribes inside the city. These agents returned after some time to tell Abdullah that the Christian Arabs agreed to accept Islam.

Abdullah decided that the main Muslim army would start the attack from the east across the ditch and would announce it with 'Takbir'. The Arabian tribes within the city were required that as soon as they heard the Takbir, they should raise the Takbir and secure the western side of the city on the river front.

At night the Persian soldiers made preparations to embark in the boats. At that time they heard the call of Allah-o-Akbar. The Persians were frightened and they thought that the Muslims had landed on the west edge of the city and cut their line of retreat. The Persians accordingly rushed eastward to escape from that side. Here they ran into the Muslim army which struck them with violence. The Persians pulled back and in the rear they were attacked by the Christian Arabs who had been converted to Islam. The Persians found themselves entrapped and they were killed in large numbers.

With the annihilation of the Persian army the Muslims occupied Takreet. As all the residents had accepted Islam there was great rejoicing at the occupation of the city by the Muslims .

Two days later, Abdullah sent a strong detachment of the army under Rabi bin Al-Akfal to Mosul. When the Muslims reached Mosul, the Persian garrison came out to fight. The Persians could not stand the Muslim attack and the Persians chose to surrender on the payment of Jizya in return for the safety of their lives and property.

Thereafter Abdullah also moved from Takreet to Mosul, and made arrangements for the administration of the area. After things had settled down Abdullah returned to Ctesiphon and left a garrison at Mosul under the command of Muslim bin Abdullah.

With the victories of Jalaula, Takreet, and Mosul, the Muslim hold on northern Suwad became firm.

BATTLE OF JALAULA

After withdrawal from Ctesiphon, the Persian armies gathered at Jalaula north-east of Ctesiphon. Jalaula was situated in the neighbourhood of what is modern Baghdad. It lay on the main road to Khurasan. Jalaula was a place of strategical importance from where routes led to Iraq, Khurasan and Azerbaijan.

The Persian forces at Jalaula were commanded by General Mihran. His deputy was General Khurrazad a brother of General Rustam. The Persians made great preparations for a large scale battle against the Muslims. The entire town was converted into a fortress. A deep ditch was dug round the city. Various fortifications were constructed behind the ditch. In front of the ditch caltrops were strewn in large numbers with a view to laming the horses of the advancing enemy. The Persian troops took an oath by the sacred fire that they would die fighting rather than retreat. The town was stocked with provisions, and the Persians prepared themselves with grim determination for a long siege.

When S'aad came to know of the preparations that the Persians had made to defind Jalaula he reported the intelligence to Hadrat Umar and asked for his orders. Wilh the Persian army quartered at Jalaula the Muslim hold on Ctesiphon could never be firm. The Caliph, therefore, ordered that steps should be taken to capture Jalaula. He directed S'aad b. Abi Waqqas that Hashim b. Utba should be sent on the expedition against Jalaula at the head of a force of twelve thousand men. The Caliph further ordered that the vanguard should be commanded by Qaqa; the right wing by Musir b. Malik; the left wing by Amr b. Malik; and the rear-guard by Amr b. Marrah.

Some time in April 637 A.D., Hashim marched at the head of 12,000 troops from Ctesiphon, and arriving at Jalaula found that the Persians were in a strong position with fortifications, entrenchments, deep ditch, and a belt of caltrops. Hashim established his camp and decided to lay a siege to Jalaula.

The siege dragged on for seven months. There were occasional skirmishes but these led no where. The Persians continued to get reinforcements from Hulwan. Some time in November heavily reinforced the Persians decided to launch an offensive and drive away the Muslims. This suited the Muslims. Hashim pulled back his arrny so that the entire Persian army might be brought in the field.

The action began with a heavy attack by the Persians all along the front. The Muslims withstood the ground but as the Persians intensified their pressure some Muslim units were pushed back, and they were exposed to the danger of a collapse. Hashim dashed forward to such units, and exhorted them to hold fast. He assured them that the battle of Jalaula was going to be the last battle and it had to be won at all costs. The fight continued with considerable violence. The battle was carried with arrows; then with javelins, spears and lances; and thereafter with swords and maces.

In the afternoon there was a short break in fighting. When the fighting was resumed, the Muslims launched the attack. Qaqa with his reserve made a flanking movement and reached the ditch in the rear of the Persian army. Late in the afternoon a storm began to blow. So severe was the dust storm that the land became dark. The storm blew in the faces of the Persians, and helped the Muslims rush forward with greater momentum. The fighting was savage and each side fought with fanatical fury. When the combat was going on violently, Qaqa raised the cry from behind the Persian forces, "O Muslims I am here. I have captured the ditch. Come to me."

At this call, the Muslim forces attacking the Persians from the front increased the violence of their attack. As the Persians moved back they had to face the attack from the rear by the men of Qaqa. The storm also gained in virulence.

In the face of these hostile circumstances the Persian resistance broke and they dispersed in all directions. The Muslims pursued them, and the Persians were slaughtered in large numbers. According to Tabari one lakh Persians were killed in the battle of Jalaula. Even though this figure might be somewhat exaggerated, the Persian loss was colossal. Mihran found safety in flight to Hulwan.

The Muslims occupied Jalaula. As the Persian army had withdrawn, the residents surrendered on the usual terms of Jizya. The spoils of war collected were valued at 30 million dirhams. After setting aside the usual one-fifth state share, the rest was distributed among the warriors. The share of each warrior came to 9,000 dirhams.

The State share of the booty was sent to Madina through Ziyad. A public assembly was convened and the faithful gathered in the Prophet's mosque to hear an account of the Muslim victory at the battle of Jalaula. Ziyad gave such an eloquent and graphic description of the battle that Hadrat Umar admiringly said, "This is what an orator should be." Ziyad said that the credit for such narration was due to the heroic deeds performed by the warriors of Islam.

The property brought in booty was stored in the courtyard of the mosque and Abdul Rahman b. Auf and Abdullah b. Arqam kept watch over the property during the night. In the morning under the supervision of Hadrat Umar the mantle that covered the goods was drawn aside, and it was found that besides vast property and goods there were vast sums in gold and silver.

Hadrat Umar ordered the immediate distribution of the property among the Muslims. As the property was distributed tears trickled from the eyes of Hadrat Umar. the faithful gathered round Hadrat Umar enquired as to the reason for his weeping. Hadrat Umar said, "God be praised for showering so much wealth on the Muslims. I weep because I am afraid that where riches appear, envy and jealousy are bound to follow in their wake."

CAMPAIGNS OF KHANIQEEN AND HULWAN

After the conquest of Jalaula, a Muslim force under Qaqa marched in pursuit of the Persians.

The Persian army that escaped from Jalaula took its position at Khaniqeen fifteen miles from Jalaula on the road to Iran. The Persian force at Khaniqeen was commanded by General Mihran. His deputy was Feerzan. The force at Khaniqeen was joined by some reinforcements from Hulwan.

When Qaqa arrived at Khaniqeen he deployed for battle. Mihran and Feerzan also arrayted their army for battle on the plain outside Khaniqeen.

The battle began with a duel between Qaqa and Mihran. In this duel Mihran was killed. With the death of Mihran, the Muslims launched the attack with considerable violence. The Persians put up a defence but it did not last long. Feerzan and the force he commanded found safety in flight.

With the withdrawal of the Persian army Khaniqeen was captured by the Muslims. A good deal of booty was captured by the Muslims which was distributed after setting aside the state share of one fifth. In this battle a large number of Persian women was captured by the Muslims. These were also distributed among the Muslim soldiers.

When Yazdjurd the Persian emperor came to know of the defeat of the Persians at Khaniqeen he left the defence of Hulwan to a general named Khusro Shanum, and himself fled to Qum.

From Khaniqeen Qaqa marched to Hulwan. At Hulwan the Persian forces under Khusro Shanum offered resistance.

On a cold January day in the year 638 A.D., the Muslim and the Persian forces clashed on the battle-field. The Muslims fought with great vigour and violence. The Persians put up a stiff resistance but they felt that the Muslims were devils and jinns and they could be no match for them. The Persians lost heart as well as the battle. Khusro Shanum and his forces found safety in flight.

With the withdrawal of the Persian forces the citizens of Hulwan formally submitted to Muslim rule and agreed to pay Jizya. Hulwan was a large city and Qaqa stayed there to restore law and order and administer its affairs.

A considerable booty was captured by the Muslims. It was distributed in the usual way and the one fifth state share was sent to Ctesiphon and Madina.

Qaqa sent a report of the victory of Hulwan to S'aad. He chose to stay at Hulwan pending receipt of further orders. Qaqa suggested that he should be allowed to continue his advance to North Persia in the pursuit of the defeated Persian army. He also desired that if such advance was to be made further reinforcements should be sent.

S'aad transmitted the report to Hadrat Umar at Madina. He recommended that the Muslim forces should be allowed to march further inland in Persia.

Hadrat Umar thanked God for the victory of the Muslims at Hulwan. He took counsel with the Companions whether the Muslim forces should continue their advance in the heart of Persia. Hadrat Umar was of the opinion, and this view was endorsed by the Muslims in Madina, that there should be halt to further advance .

Hadrat Umar accordingly wrote to S'aad bin Abi Waqqas that there should be no further advance. He wrote:

> "I wish that between the Suwad and the Persian hills there were a wall which would prevent them from getting to us, and prevent us from getting to them. The fertile Suwad is sufficient for us; and I prefer the safety of the Muslims to the spoils of war."

In view of this policy of no further advance Qaqa was withdrawn from Hulwan to rejoin the main force at Ctesiphon.

Qaqa left Qubas b. Abdullah as the Commander of the Muslim garrison at Hulwan. The garrison was to guard the frontiers of Islam. Jareer b. Abdullah withdrew from Jalaula leaving a small Muslim force there.

By February 638 there was a lull in fighting on the Persian front. The Suwad, the Tigris valley, and the Euphrates valley were now under the complete control of the Muslims. The Persians had withdrawn to Persia proper. It appeared as if this was going to be the dividing line between the Arabs and the Persians.

CONQUEST OF MASABZAN

After the battle of Jalaula, the Persian forces scattered in various pockets. One of such pockets was Masabzan. As Hashim b. Utba was returning from Jalaula to Madain, he was informed in the way by his army scouts that some of the Persian forces which had escaped from Jalaula had assembled in the territory of Masabzan at the base of the hills under the command of Azeen the son of Hormuzan. When Hashim reached Madain, he communicated this information to S'aad. S'aad in turn wrote to Hadrat Umar and sought his instructions, particularly when he had ordered that there should be no further advance in Persia.

Hadrat Umar wrote to say that while he was against any advance into Persia proper, he was not against the liquidation of Persian pockets in Iraq which might be a threat to Muslim dominions. We accordingly desire that in the interests of the safety of Iraq, an expedition should be led to Masabzan which should be occupied and cleared of the Persian forces. Hadrat Umar appointed Zarrar b. Khattab of the tribe of Maharab to the chief command of the force to be led against Masabzan. Ibn Hazil Asadi was appointed as the commander of the advance guard. Abdullah bin Wahb Rabi was appointed to the command of the right wing, and Musarab al-Ajaali was appointed as the commander of the left wing.

Some time in January 638 A.D. a Muslim force under the command of Zarrar marched to Masabzan. At Hindaf the two forces clashed. The Persians under Azeen fought desparately, and in spite of heavy pressure of the Muslims held their ground. Azeen directed the operations from an elevated place in the rear of the Persian army. Zarrar withdrew the Muslim army to some distance, and the Persians thinking that they had won the day rushed forward. The Muslim army counter charged and the Persians could not withstand the charge. In the meantime some Muslim warriors managed to reach the camp of Azeen and captured him alive. With the capture of Azeen the war was over, and whatever remained of the Persian army took to flight.

From Hindaf the Muslim army marched to Sirwan. No resistance was offered. The city had been evacuated and the Persian army as well as the citizens of Sirwan had fled to the Hills. Zarrar occupied Sirwan and established his headquarters there .

He announced general amnesty, and asked the people to return to their homes. The offer was availed of and the citizens returned to their homes. A peace treaty was drawn up and the inhabitants agreed to pay Jizya. Considerable booty was obtained which was distributed according to the usual formula.

After the restoration of peace, Zarrar stayed in Sirwan as the Governor. He organised the administration, appointed Muslim Officers in the districts, and collected taxes. Later when Kufa was founded as the capital of Iraq, Zarrar moved to Kufa leaving Ibn Hazil Asadi as his successor in Masabzan.

CAMPAIGNS OF HEET AND QIRQASSIA

After the conquest of Jalaula in December 637 A.D. Hashim sent a contingent under Qaqa b. Amr to pursue the Persians to Hulwan. Hashim left a garrison of 4,000 men under Jareer b. Abdullah at Jalaula to guard against hostile moves from the north. With the remainder of the army, Hashim returned to Ctesiphon.

In spite of the fall of Ctesiphon and Jalaula, there were some Persian pockets upstream the Tigris and the Euphrates. After the fall of Jalaula, S'aad undertook campaigns in the Tigris valley at Takreet and Mosul.

For the Euphrates valley, S'aad organised an expeditionary force and sent it under the command of Amr b. Malik to deal with the Persian pockets at Heet and Qirqassia.

In the last week of December 637 A.D. the Muslim forces under Amr b. Malik arrived at Heet. Here they found that the Persians had dug a ditch round the town. Amr pitched his tents beyond the ditch, and decided to lay siege to the town.

The Persians remained shut in the town and remained on the defensive. Further upstream at Qirqassia at the junction of the Khabur and the Euphrates there was another Persian cantonment. The Persians at Heet continued to receive provisions from Qirqassia through the river.

Amr b. Malik waited at Heet for some time, but no engagement took place. Amr thought that in order to force the Persians at Heet into submission, their source of supply from Qirqassia should be cut.

Amr decided to pounce upon Qirqassia, take them unawares and thereby cut the source of supply to Heet. Amr left the Muslim camp at Heet standing occupied by a detachment under Haris b. Yazeed. With the rest of the army Amr marched off at night for Qirqassia. The Muslim force appeared suddenly at Qirqassia. The Persians offered some feeble resistance, but being no match for the Muslims the Persian garrison surrendered. The representatives of the inhabitants of Qirqassia waited on Amr and sought for terms. The usual alternatives of Islam or Jizya were offered and the inhabilants agreed to pay Jizya.

With the surrender of Qirqassia the source of supply to Heet was completely cut. Amr sent a fast courier to Haris at Heet instructing him to inform the defenders of Heet that Qirqassia had submitted and agreed to pay Jizya. If the people of Heet agreed to submit on similar terms their safety lay in such a course. Amr further instructed Haris that if the people of Heet did not surrender he should construct another ditch outside the ditch of the Persians. In that case he would be returning from Qirqassia to resume the offensive against Heet.

The people of Heet came to know of the fall of Qirqassia from their own resources as well, and they felt that after the fall of Qirqassia they could not hold long against the Muslims. The people of Heet were mostly Christian Arabs, and they felt that the Persian forces were no longer strong enough to protect them.

When Haris called upon the people of Heet to surrender on the usual terms they accepted the offer and agreed to pay Jizya. In the second week of January the Persian forces withdrew from Heet. The inhabitants of the town opened the gates of the town to the Muslims. Thereupon the Muslim forces marched in and occupied the town.

With the occupation of Qirqassia and Heet, the Muslim hold in the Euphrates valley became firm. After restoring order Amr left garrisons at Qirqassia and Heet and himself returned to S'aad at Ctesiphon.

KUFA, BASRA AND MOSUL

In Iraq the Persians had their capital at Al-Madain. Al Madain was situated across the Euphrates and the Tigris and was situated on the eastern bank of the Tigris. After the occupation of Al-Madain, the city served as the provincial capital for the Muslims. The climate of the city was damp, malarious and unhealthy for the Arabs used to the dry climate of the desert. When the Muslim officers from Al-Madain waited on Hadrat Umar at Madina he was struck by the fact that such persons by residence in Al-Madain had lost in health. Hadrat Umar looked into the causes for the decline in the health of the people and he came to the conclusion that that was due to the unhealthy climate of Al-Madain. Hadart Umar accordingly desired that another city should be founded as the capital of Iraq. His instructions were:

(1) Only that site would suit the Arabs as would suit their camels. The new site should be such where the climate is dry.

(2) As far as possible there should be no water between you and me. Choose a site for the new capital which is to this side of the Euphrates and the Tigris.

Salman and Hudaifa were accordingly commissioned to select a new site for the provincial capital. For this purpose they selected the site of Kufa. It was at some distance from the western bank of the Euphrates and the climate was dry. Before Islam, Numan bin Mundhir had his capital here. In the neighbourhood there were some buildings of the period of Numan. Arab flowers like Uqehawan, Shaqaiq, Qaisum and Khazami grew here in abundance. The Arabs called the site "Khadd-ul-Azra"—The Beloved's Cheek. The soil was sandy and gravelly and suited the Arab temperament.

Hadrat Umar approved of the site, and because of the sandy and gravely nature of the soil, the place was named Kufa.

Hadrat Umar ordered that houses should be constructed in the city to accommodate 40,000 persons. Each Arab tribe to be settled in the city was to have a separate quarter. The town was laid out under the supervision of Hayaj bin Malik. Hadrat Umar gave instructions about the laying out of roads and streets. The main roads were to be 40 cubits wide. The subsidiary roads were to be 30 cubits wide. The streets were to be 20 cubits wide, and the side lanes were to be 7 cubits wide. The Jamia Masjid was constructed in the centre. Adjoining the mosque was the central market. Then a few public buildings were provided of public character such as Government House, the Treasury, the Guest House etc. The town was divided into two dozen quarters. Each quarter was inhabited by one tribe. Each quarter had its own mosque. All houses were to be single storeyed and no house was to contain more than three rooms.

Within a year the new town was completed and the Muslim forces moved from Al-Madain to Kufa. Hadrat Umar called Kufa, 'the Glory of Islam'.

At the time Kufa was built in Central Iraq a new city was built in Southern Iraq near Uballa a port on the Persian Gulf. Utba bin Ghazwan was commissioned to select a site. He selected the site of Karibah where there were some ruins of ancient times. The land was gravelly. Water and pasture were available. The climate was dry. Hadrat Umar approved the site and the town was named Basra. According to one version the town was so named because of the gravels that abounded on the site. According to another version 'Basrah' meant 'Bis Rah' i.e. many roads, and was so named because of its strategic importance.

The city was town planned on lines similar to Kufa. The Friday mosque was provided in the centre. From the central square roads radiated in all directions dividing the city into various quarters. Each quarter was populated by one tribe and each quarter had a mosque.

Originally most of the houses both in Kufa and Basra were of wood. A year after the foundation of the towns these houses caught fire and were burnt. Hadrat Umar then ordered that houses of bricks should be constructed. It was laid down that no house should consist of more than one storey and no house was to comprise more than three rooms.

In Upper Iraq a town was laid out outside the fort at Mosul. The town of Mosul was laid out under the supervision of Harthama bin Arfaja. The same design as at Kufa and Basra was adopted. At Mosul there was a considerable population of the Christian Arabs and some quarters were exclusively earmarked for the Christian Arabs.

All the three cities namely Kufa, Basra, and Mosul rose to great importance. Kufa became the capital of Iraq. Basra rose to importance as a seat of learning. Mosul rose to importance as a trading centre. According to a saying that got current at the time while Nishapur was the gateway of the east, and Damascus was the gateway of the west; Mosul was the pathway of the east and the west, for when proceeding from the east to the west or from the west to the east one had to pass through Mosul.

CAMPAIGN OF AHWAZ

Ahwaz was a place of strategic importance. It lay on the east bank of Karun river north east of Basra. It was the estate of Hormuzan one of the seven great chiefs of Persia.

Hormuzan had led a Persian contingent at the battle of Qadissiya. When the Persians were defeated at the battle of Qadissiya, Hormuzan managed to escape from the battle-field

When the Muslim army under S'aad b. Abi Waqqas advanced to Ctesiphon the capital of Persia, the Muslim advance was resisted by the Persian force stationed at Babylon. One wing of the Persian force at Babylon was commanded by Hormuzan .

When the Persians were defeated at Babylon, the main Persian army withdrew to Ctesiphon, but Hormuzan with his contingent retired to Ahwaz.

When the Muslims captured Ctesiphon and later laid siege to Jalaula, Hormuzan with his base at Ahwaz sent raiding parties to different parts of Iraq occupied by the Muslims. These raids had sufficient nuisance value. One of the raids was led by Azeen the son of Hormuzan. In this raid Azeen was captured by the Muslims and killed.

After the death of Azeen, Hormuzan intensified his raids. These raids were conducted from two bases, namely Ahwaz and Manazir. The raids were conducted in the territory under the charge of Utba b. Ghazwan the Governor of Basra. As the raids were intensified, Utba asked for reinforcement from Ctesiphon. S'aad sent a force under Noman b. Muqarrin. Meanwhile Utba recruited more warriors from the local Arabs.

Having received reinforcement, Utba declined to take the offensive against the raiding parties of Hormuzan.

Two Muslim contingents advanced to the Persian bases Ahwaz and Manazir. One of these contingents was led by Noman and the other by Salma. The two Muslim forces launched a coordinated plan of attack, and the Persian force pulled back from the forward posts .

The Muslim detachments followed the retreating Persians and secured the right bank of the river Karun. The Persian forces stood on the left bank.

As the two forces faced each other on either bank of the Karun, the usual pre-war parleys began and emissaries went to and fro. The Muslims offered the usual three alternatives, conversion to Islam; payment of Jizya, and settlement through sword.

Hormuzan gave these alternatives due consideration. With his experience of Qadissiya and Babylon Hormuzan felt that the Persians were no match for the hardy Arabs. Settlement through the sword was likely to result in the defeat of the Persians. Hormuzan was therefore inclined to avoid war. Although Hormuzan believed in his heart of hearts about the truth of Islam, for political and other reasons he felt that at that stage he could not publicly accept Islam. He, therefore, agreed to the alternative of the payment of Jizya.

A treaty was executed between Utba and Hormuzan in November 638 whereby the entire princedom of Ahwaz came under the control of the Muslims. Hormuzan was to continue as the Governor and he was to pay a Jizya to the Muslims. The part of Ahwaz already occupied by the Muslims was to remain under the direct military rule of the Muslims. This area included the district of Manazir.

With the conquest of Ahwaz, the approach of Persian to the north of the Persian Gulf was completely cut off. The Muslims had now their firm hold on the delta area of the Tigris, the Euphrates, and the Karun.

CONQUEST OF AHWAZ AND DAURAQ

According to the treaty of Ahwaz, while some parts of the province of Khuzistan were under the direct rule of the Muslims, Ahwaz proper and the rest of the province were ruled by Hormuzan as a vassal of the Muslims.

Restored to power, Hormuzan tried to build up a force in a bid to have another contest with the Muslims. He recruited a large number of Kurds from his ancestral district of Mihirjanqazuf. He even incited the Persians in the Muslim zone to join him so that another effort might be made to overthrow the Muslims.

The Muslim commander Salma reported of these develop-ments to Abu Musa the Governor of Basra who had taken over after the death of Utba. Abu Musa in turn asked for the instructions of Hadrat Umar. The Caliph ordered that the Muslims should capture Ahwaz.

Abu Musa the Governor of Basra marched with the Muslim forces to Ahwaz. For some time the two opposing forces lay encamped on either side of the Karun, and there was the usual exchange of emissaries. The negotiations broke down, and it was decided that an engagement should be risked.

Hormuzan gave the Muslims the option to cross the Karun and come over to the side of the Persians, or let the Persians cross and come over to the side of the Muslims. Heretofore the Muslims generally refrained from crossing the river, and generally asked the Persians to cross over to their side. That was the stage when by way of abundant caution the Muslims wanted to remain as close to the desert as possible. Now things had changed, and the Muslims had advanced too far inland, and the question of proximity to the desert no longer arose. Abu Musa accordingly decided that the Muslims would cross over to the Persian side of the river. After crossing the river, Abu Musa took special steps to ensure that the bridge by which they had crossed remained heavily guarded.

After the Muslims had crossed, the forces of the two sides were deployed for action. For some time the contest was fierce, and there were casualties on both sides. The Muslims increased their pressure, and the Persians could not hold the ground. They began to fall back and Hormuzan found safety in flight. Hormuzan with his force withdrew to Ram Hormuz.

After the withdrawal of the Persian forces, Ahwaz was occupied by the Muslims. Abu Musa sent a pursuit column under Juzz b. Muawia to follow the retreating Persians. The Muslims caught up with the retreating Persians, but Hormuzan resorted to rearguard action avoiding a decisive engagement.

The Muslims occupied Dauraq the chief city of the district of Surraq. Hormuzan retired east of the river at Arbuk and here he took a stand. The Muslims prepared for battle, but Hormuzan sent an emissary and sued for peace. Juzz reported the developments to Abu Musa and Abu Musa in turn referred the matter to Hadrat Umar.

Hadrat Umar gave orders that the offer of peace be accepted. According to the peace terms the districts of Ahwaz and Dauraq were annexed by the Muslims. The rest of the princedom of Hormuzan was left to him and he shifted his capital from Ahwaz to Ram Hormuz. Hormuzan cleared the arrears of Jizya and undertook to pay Jizya regularly in future. At Ahwaz and Dauraq a considerable booty fell to the share of the Muslims. After distributing four-fifth, the rest of the booty was sent to Hadrat Umar as the state share.

BATTLE OF TUSTAR

Although peace with Hormuzan had been accepted for the second time, it proved to be shortlived. Hormuzan was smarting under the disgrace of repeated defeats, and the loss of a greater part of his princedom. He had lost Ahwaz which was the main city of his dominions, and he held his court at Ram Hormuz which was a small mofussil town to the east of Ahwaz.

After the conquest of Ctesiphon the capital of Persia by the Muslims, the emperor Yezdjurd shifted to Hulwan. He had hoped that the Persian forces concentrated at Jalaula would hold up further advance of the Muslims in Persia. These hopes were not realised and the Persians suffered another defeat at Jalaula. That made Hulwan unsafe for the emperor and he fled to Qum. Khaniqeen and Hulwan were captured by the Muslims the emperor fled to Kashan and then to Isfahan. The emperor became a fugitive in his own kingdom and the court had to move from town to town. The Persian administration collapsed to such an extent that the Persians had no capital, and very little of governmental organisation.

Yazdjurd, however, continued to make strenuous efforts to rally the Persians for another confrontation with the Muslims. He appealed to the Persians in the name of their religion and their country to line up for another major effort to defend their homeland. The Persians assured him that they would stand by him. At this juncture the emperor felt that Hormuzan could suitably act as the vanguard of Persian resistance against the Muslims. Yazdjurd appealed to the patriotism of Hormuzan and prevailed upon him to spearhead the Persian struggle against the Muslims. The emperor assured him of full support.

Hormuzan accordingly undertook to make another effort to drive away the Muslims from the Persian soil. Hormuzan was thus once again on the war path. He built a strong force. The emperor placed the resources of Persia at his disposal. The Persians took the oath by the sacred fire that they would win or die.

The war preparations in the Persian camp were reported to Abu Musa the Governor of Basra. Abu Musa reported to Hadrat Umar that trouble could be expected from Hormuzan any moment. Hadrat Umar ordered that before Hormuzan should gather further strength the Muslim forces should advance against him, and take him to task for breaking his pledges repeatedly. Hadrat Umar also wrote to the Governor of Kufa that a column should be sent from Kufa to reinforce the Muslim forces in the Basra sector.

The action began with the advance of a Muslim column under Noman bin Muqarrin from Ahwaz to Ram Hormuz. The Muslim force crossed the river near Ram Hormuz at Arbuk and confronted the Persian force arrayed on the east bank. A sharp engagement followed which resulted in the flight of the Persian force from the battle-field. Hormuzan with his army left Ram Hormuz undefended and retired to Tustar north of Ahwaz.

The Muslims occupied Ram Hormuz and the residents surrendered on the usual terms. After leaving a garrison at Ram Hormuz the Muslim force marched northward to Izaj at the base of the Zagros mountain. That was the easternmost district of the province of Khuzistan. No reistance was offered and Izaj was occupied by the Muslims.

Tustar which Hormuzan had occupied lay west of Izaj. Intelligence was brought that Hormuzan had fortified himself at Tustar. Abu Musa felt that the Muslim forces should not march to Tustar unless these were further reinforced. Leaving a garrison at Izaj the main Muslim force returned to Ahwaz. A detailed report was submitted to Hadrat Umar and his further instructions were sought.

Yazdjurd had sent some forces for the help of Hormuzan. When Hormuzan was defeated at Arbuk and fled to Tustar, a contingent of the Persian force under General Siyah crossed over to the Muslim camp and accepted Islam. That was a welcome addition to the Muslim force.

Hadrat Umar wrote to Abu Musa that he was sending help and that when he was reinforced he should march to Tustar. Hadrat Umar asked Ammar bin Yasir the Governor of Kufa to despatch a detachment from Kufa to augment the strength of Abu Musa's army. Ammar b. Yasir despatched a force of 1000 men under Jareer b. Abdullah. In compliance with further instructions from Hadrat Umar, Ammar himself marched with half of his army to the aid of Abu Musa. Ammar left Abdullah b. Masud as his deputy at Kufa.

After having received reinforcements, Abu Musa decided to launch the attack; against Tustar. In 640 A.D. a Muslim column under Noman bin Muqarrin marched from Ram Hormuz to Tustar. The rest of the Muslim army including the contingents from Kufa met at Ahwaz and from there marched to Tustar.

Tustar lay to the north of Ahwaz upstream the Karun. The Muslim forces marched through the Karun valley and without any encounter reached Tustar.

Tustar was a walled city with battlements in the walls. Inside the city there was a strong citadel. The town had its water supply from a canal from the Karun river. Outside the city, Hormuzan had a deep ditch dug. The town was stocked with provisions adequate to last for a year. A large Persian force was quartered inside the city. As Hormuzan surveyed the arrangements made for the defence of Tustar he felt assured that the city was unassailable and invulnerable. Hormuzan felt strong enough to fight in the open. His strategy was to drive away the Muslims before they could settle to a regular siege.

As soon as the Muslim forces arrived at Tustar, Hormuzan challenged them to action. The two forces met in the plain south east of Tustar. The Persians fought desperately, and for some time they appeared to have the initiative. Then the Muslims charged heavily and the Persians were forced to withdraw to the safety of the ditch.

Thereafter the Muslims besieged the city. Detachments of Muslim forces were stationed at key points, and all routes of access and escape for the Persians were closed.

The siege dragged on for several months. There were skirmishes every now and then, but these were not conclusives and no side could claim success. After some months the Persians made a desperate sally. In the fierce fight that followed the Persians lost ground and hastily withdrew. The Muslims followed close on their heels and were able to capture the ditch. The Persians having lost the protection of the ditch shut them selves in the walled city.

The Muslims now closed round the walls of the city with the ditch at their command. With the tightening of the siege, the Persians within the city got demoralised. There were dissensions among the Persians. A Persian Seena by name escaped from the city, and waiting upon the Muslim Commander offered to show the Muslims an easy way to capture the city. The offer was accepted and the Persian accepted Islam. One night, Seena led a band of Muslim warriors inside the city through the main sewer. The guards at the main gate of the city were overpowered, and the gate was thrown open for the Muslim force to enter.

The Persians were taken by surprise, but they nevertheless put up a stiff fight. With sword in hand, Hormuzan fought desperately. He killed two eminent companions Baraa bin Malik and Majza'a bin Saur. As the Muslim forces increased their pressure, the Persians withdrew to the citadel. Now the city was in the hands of the Muslims, but Hormuzan and his forces were in the fort. The Muslims besieged the fort. The residents of the city deprived of the protection of the Persian army surrendered.

The following day Hormuzan hoisted the flag of peace on the citadel. He mounted the roof of the citadel and said that he was prepared to surrender on the condition that Hadrat Umar himself decided the case. The offer was accepted, and the Persians formally surrendered. The Muslims were now the masters of Tustar.

The booty was collected and distributed. Each cavalryman received a share of 3,000 dirhams while a footman had a share of 1,000 dirhams. The usual one fifth state share of the booty was despatched to Madina. Hormuzan was sent under escort to Madina for the decision of his case by Hadrat Umar.

BATTLE OF SUS

After the conquest of Tustar it was found that some Persian soldiers from the army of Hormuzan had escaped to Sus, and there they had collected under the command of Shahryar, a brother of Hormuzan.

After settling the affairs at Tustar, Abu Musa left a garrison there and with the rest of the army marched to Sus. Sus lay to the north west of Tustar. Like Tustar, Sus was also a walled city. When the Muslim forces reached Sus some time in January 641, the Persians shut the gates of the city, and remained on the defensive. The Muslims set up posts around the city and tightened up the arrangements for the siege.

The Persians made occasional sallies to break through the Muslim lines, but they were driven back to the city. The Muslims made attacks to break through the gates of the city, but failed to achieve their object.

One day a Persian priest appeared on the wall of the city and addressing the Muslims said:

> "O Arabs we know from the prophesies in our holy books that Sus will not be taken except by Dajjal, or by a people among whom there is a Dajjal. If you have Dajjal among you, you will conquer us; if not, do not bother to besiege us."

Abu Musa brushed away this prophesy as a superstition. Siyah the Persian General who had crossed over to the Muslim camp at Ahwaz told Abu Musa that as he had abjured the Persian faith, he was the Dajjal in Persian terminology, and as he was in the midst of the Muslims, they were destined to conquer Sus. Siyah said to Abu Musa:

"Leave the capture of Sus to me. I will do so through a stratagem of which Dajjal alone could be capable."

Abu Musa let Siyah have his way.

The following day when the Persian priest once again appeared on the walls of the city, and wanted to know whether any Dajjal was there, Siyah responded to the call and said that Dajjal was very much there and as such the state of Sus was sealed. When the Persians came to know that a Dajjal had appeared outside their city they were demoralised, and felt that under the circumstances any further resistance was futile.

One day as the first light of dawn appeared the Persian sentries on the wall by the main gate saw a Persian officer with his uniform stained with blood lying on the ground near the gate. There had been fighting at this spot the previous night, and the Persian soldiers thought that a wounded Persian officer had lain there all the night. The Persian soldiers rushed to the aid of the wounded Persian officer. They opened the gate and carried a bed to lift the wounded officer.

As the Persian soldiers approached the wounded officer, he sprang to his feet, and falling upon the soldiers with the speed of lightning killed all of them. This hero was Siyah, the Dajjal. The Muslim soldiers lurked near the gate, and as soon as the gate was opened and the sentries had been killed the Muslims led by Siyah rushed forward in the city carrying havoc. Siyah shouted at the top of his voice:

"O ye Persians, surrender, for the Dajjal has come."

The Persians taken by surprise rallied in a desperate bid to measure swords with the advancing Muslims. The Persians, however, fell back. Soon word went from house to house in the city "Dajjal" of whom our holy books prophesied has appeared." As the sun rose, more Muslim forces rushed in through the gates, and the Persian resistance broke down. The Persians surrendered. Thanks to the genius of Siyah, the historic city of Sus was conquered by the Muslims. Turning to Siyah, Abu Musa said:

"O one eyed one; you and your comrades are not as we thought you were." Siyah accepted the compliment.

Abu Musa reported the conquest of Sus to Hadrat Umar. In his despatch, Abu Musa referred to the prophesy about Dajjal and the role that Siyah had played as Dajjal. Abu Musa also reported that in one of the temples of Sus they had come across the coffin of the Prophet Daniel. Considerable booty was captured at Sus, and the usual one-fifth share of the booty was sent to Madina. The rest was distributed among the soldiers on the spot.

Hadrat Umar appreciated the services of Siyah and his comrades and desired that their pay should be doubled. Hadrat Umar also desired that the remains of the Prophet Daniel should be buried with due ceremony. Siyah and his comrades felt happy at the recognition of their services by the Caliph of Islam. In compliance with the orders of Hadrat Umar, Abu Musa arranged for the burial of the remains of the Prophet Daniel. Abu Musa himself led the funeral prayer, and the remains of the Prophet Daniel who had died some 13,00 years earlier were buried by the side of the river.

BATTLE OF JUNDE SABUR

After the conquest of Sus, the only place of military importance in Khuzistan still left in the hands of the Persians was Junde Sabur. It lay to the north east of Sus.

Abu Musa wrote to Hadrat Umar seeking orders whether Junde Sabur should also be captured. Hadrat Umar approved the proposal for capturing Junde Sabur. He asked Abu Musa to send a column under Aswad bin Rabee'a to Junde Sabur. Aswad bin Rabee'a was a companion of the Holy Prophet and was nicknamed as 'Muqtarib' as he acted as a waiter on the Holy Prophet.

Aswad bin Rabee'a accordingly marched with a Muslim force from Sus to Junde Sabur. Like other Persian cities, Junde Sabur was also a walled city. When the Muslim forces reached Junde Sabur the Persian garrison shut themselves in the city.

The Muslims besieged the city, and set up military posts at all approaches to the city. The Persians made some attempts to sally forth and break through the Muslim lines but they failed. The Muslims also made some attempts to carry the city by assault but the attempts did not succeed.

One day the gates of the city were thrown open. The citizens came out unarmed, and attended to their normal functions as if the hostilities had ended. The Muslims were surprised at this, and enquired from the Persians as to how it was that they had ended hostilities.

The Persians said: "You offered us peace on the payment of Jizya and we have accepted the offer."

The Muslim Commander got in touch with the Persian Commander and said that he had not offered them any terms, and as such the war was not over.

The Persians thereupon brought an arrow along with a message that had been shot from the Muslim camp. The message had been shot with the arrow offering peace if the Persians were to surrender and pay the Jizya.

The Muslim Commander made an enquiry and it was revealed that from among the Muslim ranks a Muslim slave Mukannaf had on his own account shot the arrow offering peace to the Persians on the payment of Jizya.

That was followed by parleys between the Muslim and the Persian Commander. Aswad b. Rabee'a explained that the arrow with the message had been shot by a slave on his own account and carried no authority. The Persian view was that they had received the message from the Muslim side, and they accepted it. It was not for them to probe whether the message was backed with the necessary authority or not. The Persians said that they had accepted the message in good faith. If for any reason the Muslims wanted to go back on their pledge, it was open to them to do so, and in that case the hostilities could be resumed.

It was an embarrassing situation, and it was decided that the matter should be reported to Hadrat Umar, and his instructions should be awaited. Till then it was decided to observe truce.

Aswad bin Rabee'a accordingly reported the matter to Hadrat Umar. In reply Hadrat Umar said:

> "Allah be praised that He has given you the strength that the enemy surrenders even at the instance of a message that lacks authority. As the message was sent from the Muslim camp it has to be honoured even if it lacked due authority. Those who seek peace leave them in peace."

On receipt of these orders, peace was formally negotiated with the Persians, and their surrender was accepted on the payment of Jizya .

HORMUZAN

After the conquest of Sus and Junde Sabur the entire Khuzistan stretching to the foothills of the Zagros mountains now lay in Muslim hands.

Abu Musa forwarded the state share of the spoils of war captured at Sus and Junde Sabur to Madina. He also despatched Hormuzan to Madina with an escort. The escort included the companions Unas bin Malik and Ashraf bin Qais. Unas was the brother of Bara b. Malik who had been killed by Hormuzan at Sus.

As the party entered Madina, Hormuzan was dressed in the court regalia, robes of velvet and gold. He had on his head his coronet of gold studded with precious stones.

The party waited on Hadrat Umar who was found sleeping in a corner of the mosque. It was a strange scene—a richly dressed captive, and a poorly dressed Caliph. As Hadrat Umar woke, and many people gathered in the mosque, Hadrat Umar turning to the Muslims said:

> "Praise be to Allah who has used Islam to debase the prince of Persia. Muslims ! hold fast in this faith and be guided by the teachings of your Prophet. Let not this world lead you astray, for it is full of deceit."

Hadrat Umar ordered that Hormuzan should be stripped of his finery and presented before him in ordinary dress. Hormuzan retired and was presented before Hadrat Umar again dressed in ordinary clothes.

Addressing the captive, Hadrat Umar said, "You are Hormuzan, the rebellious Governor of Ahwaz".

Hormuzan said, "Yes, I am Hormuzan".

The Caliph said, "And you have over and over again broken your pledge with the Muslims."

Hormuzan said, "Unfortunately that is correct, but I was prompted by love for my own country, and I was always hoping that I would drive away the Muslims from my land".

Hadrat Umar said, "Now that you have been defeated, and your treachery has been established, do you know that the punishment for such crime is death."

Hormuzan said, "Yes, I know that. The law is on the side of the victor". Hadrat Umar said, "Then I order your death. Be prepared for your death."

Hormuzan said, "I am feeling thirsty; let me have a cup of water before I die."

Hadrat Umar ordered that a cup of water be brought and handed to the captive.

Taking the cup in his hand, Hormuzan said, "What if I am killed before I have drunk this water."

Hadrat Umar said, "Rest assured. You will not be killed until you have drunk this water."

Hormuzan laid aside the cup and said. "In that case, I will not drink, and you have given me promise that you will not kill me until I have drunk this water."

Annoyed the Caliph thundered, "O enemy of God, you have tricked me and I will kill you."

Hormuzan retorted, "You may do as you like but I have your promise of safety. You may break your promise if your religion teaches you to do so."

At this stage, other Muslims intervened and they said, "Promise is promise, and it must be kept."

Hadrat Umar turned to Unas bin Malik and asked for his view. Unas bin Malik said, "Although this man has killed my brother and I am burning for revenge, but I would not advise the Caliph to break his promise, trick or no trick."

Turning to Hormuzan, Hadrat Umar said, "Woe to you O clever Persian, I would allow you safety only on one condition and that is that you accept Islam".

Hormuzan said "I agree."

Thereupon Hormuzan declared the article of faith and became a Muslim.

Welcoming him to the fold of Islam, Hadrat Umar said, "You may remain with us as our guest a few days, and thereafter you have the option to return to Persia."

Hormuzan said that as a Muslim he would prefer to stay in Madina.

Thereafter Hormuzan settled down as a citizen of Madina, and Hadrat Umar awarded him an annual allowance of two thousand dirhams.

This episode forms the theme of a poem by Richard Chenevix French. The poem reads:

> "Now the third and fatal conflict for the Persian throne was done,
> And the Muslims' fiery valour had the crowning victory won,
> Hormuzan the last and boldest, the invader to defy,
> Captive, overborne by number, they were bringing forth to die.
> Then exclaimed that noble captive, "Lo I perish in my thirst;
> Give me but one drink of water, and let then arrive the worst ! '
> In his hand he took the goblet and while the draught forebore,
> Seeming doubtfully the purpose of the foeman to explore.
> Well might then have paused the bravest—for around him angry foes,
> With a hedge of naked weapons did that lonely man enclose.
> 'But what fear'st thou' cried the Caliph: Is it, friend a secret blow ?

Fear it not, our gallant Muslims no such treacherous dealing know.
Thou may'st quench thy thirst, securely for thou shall not die before,
Thou hast drunk this cup of water, this reprive is thine—no more'.
Quick, the satrap dashed the goblet down to earth with ready hand,
And the liquid sank for ever, lost amid the burning sand.
'Thou hast said that mine my life is, till the water of that cup.
I have drained then, bid thy servants that spilled water gather up!
For a moment stood the Caliph as by doubtfull passion stirred,
Then exclaimed: 'For ever sacred must remain a monarch's word,
Bring another cup, and straightaways to the noble Persian give'
'Drink ' I said before, 'and perish'—now I bid thee 'drink and live.

PERSIA ON THE WAR PATH

After the conquest of Khuzistan, the Muslims wanted peace. They wanted to leave rest of Persia to the Persians. Hadrat Umar said:

> "I wish there were a mountain of fire between us and the Persians, so that neither could they get to us, nor we to them."

But the Persians thought differently. The pride of the imperial Persians had been hurt by the conquest of their land by the Arabs. They could not acquiesce in the occupation of their lands by the Arabs.

After the battle of Jalaula the Persian emperor Yazdjurd went to Rayy and from there he moved to Khurasan where he set up his capital at Merv. From Merv, the emperor sent a call to his people to rise to a man to drive away the Muslims from their lands. In response to the call, hardened veterans and young volunteers from all parts of Persia marched in large numbers to join the imperial standard.

The Persian forces were required to assemble at Nihawand south of Hamadan. Mardan Shah the son of Hurmuz was appointed to the chief command of the Persian forces. The banner of Kaveh, regarded by the Persians as the harbinger of victory was unfurled and entrusted to Mardan Shah by the emperor.

As the Persian forces assembled at Nihawand their number exceeded 60,000. They were fully equiped, and were fired with the urge to drive away the Muslims from the Persian soil. As Mardan Shah surveyed the Persian forces, he thought that no power on earth could defeat them. He was very bitter against the Muslims. Addressing the Persian forces he said:

"Muhammad who brought the new religion to the Arabs, never troubled us. Then Abu Bakr became their ruler, and he too did not bother us except by taking plunder, and that only in the part of the Suwad which was adjacent to their land. Then after him came Umar, and his rule has become very long. He has taken the Suwad and Ahwaz and ridden rough shod over them. He is very ambitious and war-like, and it appears he will not rest content until he has conquered the whole of Persia and made you slaves. He is coming to you, if you do not go for him. He has already done us considerable damage. We cannot allow him any further liberty. We must take the initiative and drive the Muslims from our lands. We should recapture the entire territory that he has captured from us. I will not be satisfied till our forces drive away the aggressors to the desert and engage them in their own land."

There was great enthusiasm among the forces, and on sacred fire they took the oath to carry on the war against the Muslims to the bitter end.

The news of the Persian resolve to fight, and their preparations on a large scale were communicated by the Muslim scouts to Qubaz the Commander of the Muslim forward troops at the border post on Kirmanshah road. Qubaz reported the matter to Ammar bin Yasir, the Governor of Kufa. Ammar in turn addressed a letter to Hadrat Umar and sought his instructions. The letter was sent through a special messenger.

HADRAT UMAR'S CALL TO ARMS

When the messenger of Ammar bin Yasir arrived at Madina he immediately waited on Hadrat Umar. Hadrat Umar read the letter, looked to the Heaven and then turning to the messenger said, ' Well brother, what is your name."

The messenger said, "My name is Qareeb."

And what's your father's name asked Hadrat Umar.

"Zafar" said, the man.

Hadrat Umar said, "This is good augury. This means that victory is near."

Hadrat Umar immediately called a meeting of the faithful, and apprised them of the situation on the Persian front. Addressing the people Hadrat Umar said:

> "Brothers, we have to consider a matter of great moment. Listen to what I say, and then give me firm advice. Do not indulge in unnecessary controversy for that would weaken your resolve and sap your courage. O Arabs, Allah has helped you with Islam and created amity among you after discord; given you wealth after hunger; and blessed you with victory over your enemies on all fronts, both in the east and the west. Now your enemies are once again in the field and seek to overpower you. But Allah is with us, and no power on earth can extinguish the light of Allah. We have to accept the challenge of our enemy.

"Then he read the letter of the Governor of Kufa. He had written of the threat of the Persians to the Muslims at Basra and Kufa. Ammar had suggested that the Muslims should take the initiative, and attack the Persians at Nihawand, before the Persians gathered strength to march to Basra or Kufa. Hadrat Umar expressed the view that as the war with the Persians was going to be crucial, he might go the field himself to lead the Muslim forces.

Hadrat Usman suggested that all forces from Syria, Yemen, and elsewhere should assemble at Madina and then march against Persia. He was of the view that as the force thus assembled would be considerable that would demoralise the Persians.

Hadrat Umar then asked for the opinion of Hadrat Ali. Hadrat Ali said that it would be unsafe to remove all forces from Syria and elsewhere. That would provide an opportunity to the Byzantines to attack Syria or the Ethiopians to attack Yemen. He said that the forces at Kufa and Basra should march against the Persians. He also suggested that the reserves throughout the country should be called to arms and they should proceed to the front to reinforce the regular forces. Hadrat Ali also suggested that it was not necessary for Hadrat Umar to command the forces in the field. He should remain at Madina and direct the operations from the Headquarters as heretofore, and should nominate a General of his choice to command the forces in the field.

After discussion it was decided to follow the course of action suggested by Hadrat Ali.

NUMAN BIN MUQARRIN

In the campaign against the Persians concentrated at Nihawand, Hadrat Umar appointed Numan bin Muqarrin as the Commander-in-chief of the Muslim army.

Numan bin Muqarrin was the son of Ubaid bin Aus an Ansar of Madina. Ubaid participated in the battle of Badr, where he captured four infidels and tied them up in one chain. For this act of binding, the Holy Prophet gave him the name of Muqarrin, the Binder.

Numan had several brothers, and all of them were good Muslims and warriors. They played important roles in the apostasy wars under Hadrat Abu Bakr. They fought under Khalid bin Walid in the wars in Iraq. Later Numan fought under S'aad b. Abi Waqqas. After the battle of Kaskar, Numan was appointed as the Administrator of Kaskar district.

Numan was not happy with the civil appointment. He longed for active service. He wrote to Hadrat Umar that S'aad had appointed him to collect taxes, but he would personally prefer active service on some front to carry on the holy war.

When Hadrat Umar appointed Numan as the General to command the Muslim forces against the Persians, he addressed him a letter in the following terms:

> "In the name of Allah, the Beneficent, the Merciful.
>
> From the slave of Allah, Umar, Commander of the Faithful, to Numan bin Muqarrin. Peace be upon you ! I render praise unto Allah, and verily apart from Him there is no other god.
>
> I have come to know that a vast army of Persians has gathered at Nihawand to fight against the Muslims.

I appoint you the Chief Commander for the campaign. When you get this letter, go by order of Allah and with the help and support of Allah, along with those of the Muslims who are with you march against the enemy. You should halt at some well watered place near Nihawand. I have written to the people of Kufa to join you; and when your army is all together, advance to Nihawand.

In case you fall in battle, the commander of the army will be Hudhaifah bin Al-Yaman: if he falls, then Jareer bin Abdullah; if he falls, Mugheera bin Shu'ba; and if he falls, Athath bin Qais.

Do not ill-treat your men or be harsh with them, for then you will come to harm. And do not withhold from them their rights, for then you will be unjust. And do not put them in a position of loss, because every single one of the Muslims is dearer to me than a lac dinars.

Seek the help of Allah and repeat often 'There is no power to change and no strength except with Allah'.

And again peace be upon you."

Simultaneously Hadrat Umar addressed letters to other Commanders who were to participate in the campaign under the chief command of Numan bin Muqarrin. Hudhaifah bin Al-Yamān was required to march with the bulk of the forces from Kufa. Abu Musa was to proceed with one third of the Muslim army stationed at Basra. A fresh force to be raised at Madina including many Companions and Hadrat Umar's son Abdullah was to march to the front under the command of Mugheera bin Shu'ba.

Hadrat Umar also organised an irregular force and this force was required to operate as raiders across the hills to disrupt Persian communications from Fars and Isfahan to Nihawand.

MARCH TO NIHAWAND

When Numan bin Muqarrin received orders, he moved with his forces towards Nihawand and halted at Tazar. Here all forces from Kufa, Basra, and Madina also joined. All movements of the Muslim army were completed by December 641 when they were poised for an attack on the Persians.

After the troops had settled down at Tazar, Numan bin Muqarrin sent a reconnaisance party to locate the presence of the Persians. The party included Amr bin Maadi Karib and Taleaha. The party returned to report that they had found no Persians between Tazar and Nihawand.

Thereupon Numan ordered the march to Nihawand. After some days of marching the Muslim army arrived at Isbeezahan, eleven miles from Nihawand and here they halted.

The two armies now faced each other well poised for a life and death struggle. Mardanshah the Persian General sent words to Numan to depute some emissary to the Persian camp for talks. Numan chose Mugheera bin Shu'ba for the purpose.

When Mugheera appeared before Mardanshah, the Persian General adopted a haughty tone and said:

> "You Arabs are a people farthest of all from good, the most wretched, the most foul, and the most filthy. The only thing which prevents me from ordering my warriors to kill all of you is my aversion to the pollution which your corpses would cause, for you are unclean. If you go away, we will be rid of you and we may pay you something. And if you refuse to go, be prepared for your end."

In reply Mugheera after praising Allah said that his description of the Arabs applied to the Arabs before the advent of Islam. With the coming of the Holy Prophet and their conversion to Islam, things had changed. They were now the purest, and the cleanest. He added:

> "By Allah, we have not ceased to receive victory and success from our Lord ever since His Prophet came to us. Now we have come to you carrying the message of Allah. You accept Islam, and that will be the end of hostility. If you do not accept Islam, but want to be at peace with us, then pay Jizya. If both these alternatives are not acceptable to you then only the sword will decide the matter between you and us."

That annoyed Mardanshah, and he said:
"If that is that, let the sword arbitrate".

Thereupon Mugheera returned to the Muslim camp. After hearing the account of Mugheera as to what had transpired at the Persian camp, Numan bin Muqarrin asked the Muslim troops to be ready for the fight.

A message was received from Mardanshah enquiring whether the Muslims would like to cross to the Persian side, or should they cross over to their side. Numan keen to take the initiative sent the word that the Muslims would cross over to the Persian side.

BATTLE OF NIHAWAND (FIRST PHASE)

It was on a cold day in the third week of December 641 A.D. that the battle of Nihawand began. The Persian army numbered 60,000 while the Muslim army numbered 30,000.

The Persians had the advantage of holding the high ground. They had secured their right and left flanks. In front of their forward line they planted a belt of iron caltrops to lame the horses of the invader. The Persian infantry was bound to each other in chains. These chains held five to ten men together. Equipped with splendid weapons, and bound with shining chains, the Persian host looked like a mountain of iron.

The Muslim left was commanded by Numan's brother Naeem, while their right was commanded by Hudhaifa bin Al-Yaman. Qaqa bin Amr commanded the cavalry. The Persian wings were commanded by Zardaq and Bahman. Their reserve were commanded by Anushaq.

After saying the midday prayers, Numan gave the battle cry of 'Allaho-Akbar, and at the third call the Muslim army dashed forward. As the Muslim army advanced they came under withering fire from the Persian archers, and many Muslims leading the attack were wounded. As the Muslim cavalry moved forward many horses were lame by caltrops. In spite of these odds the Muslim army advanced to grapple with the enemy. The battle was severe. On both sides there were heavy casualties. The two armies disengaged themselves when the night set. The day's action proved unproductive. The Muslims did not feel satisfied at their performance.

The next day the battle was resumed. The dispositions of the Persian army left no room for the Muslims for any outflanking movement. There was no option with the Muslims but to launch the frontal attack. In spite of the severity of the Muslim attack, the Persian army remained unshaken. It was a grim battle leading to heavy casualties on both sides. At nightfall the two armies disengaged once again. The Muslims felt unhappy. The death roll on their side was sufficiently heavy, and yet no tangible results had been achieved.

Numan now felt that as the Persians stood secure in their fortifications, a frontal attack against them would not be productive.

The strategy of Numan was that the Persians should come forward outside the security of their fortifications, so that they might be engaged in the open. The Persians were cognizant of their advantageous position, and they did not move beyond their fortifications.

For the next two days there was no action. The Muslims hoped that the Persians would move forward but they chose to remain at their posts. This stalemate also worked to the advantage of the Persians. The weather was intensely cold. The Persians were used to the weather and moreover they were secure in their fortifications. The Muslims on the other hand were not used to such inclement weather. Moreover as they camped in the open they suffered from the inclemency of the weather. The Persians organised raiding parties which caused considerable damage to the Muslims. These parties were highly mobile and they could withdraw hastily to the protectionof their fortifications before the Muslims could take any counteraction.

In the meantime the Persian army continued to receive reinforcements almost every day. The Persian basewas at Hamadan from where supplies and reinforcements came regularly. The Muslim,s base was at Kufa which was considerably away, and that was also a disadvantage for the Muslims.

Thus in the first phase of the battle of Nihawand, the Muslims failed to produce results as all advantages lay with the Persians.

BATTLE OF NIHAWAND (SECOND PHASE)

After the unsuccessful attacks against the Persian front, Numan bin Muqarrin called a council of war to decide the future course of action for the Muslim army.

After discussion, it was decided that the following stratagem should be adopted:

1. A rumour should be spread that Hadrat Umar the Caliph was dead.
2. The Muslim army should start moving back giving the impression that it was withdrawing because of the death of the Caliph and resistance of the Persians.
3. When the Persians advance to pursue the Muslims, the Muslim army should turn round and fight.
4. In the meantime Qaqa with the cavalry should outflank the Persian army and try to reach the rear thus cutting the retreat of the Persians.

For a week there was no Muslim attack. Then the Persians heard reports of the death of the Caliph. The news spread like wild fire, and the Persians felt jubilant. As Mardanshah heard of the news he felt convinced that he would be in a position to take revenge from the Muslims for the previous Persian defeats.

And then the Persian scouts carried the news to Mardanshah that the Muslim army had struck their camps and were withdrawing. Mardanshah gave the call to arms, and dashed forward with his army in pursuit of the withdrawing Muslims.

When Numan came to know of the Persian advance, he quickly ordered the Muslim army into battle formation. Obscured from the Persian view Qaqa with his cavalry proceeded to outflank the Persian army.

Addressing the soldiers, Numan exhorted them to fight in the way of Allah. He prayed for the victory of the Muslims and for his own martyrdom. He willed that if he was to be martyred, Hudhaifah bin Al–Yaman was to take over the chief command.

As soon as the Persian army came in sight, the Muslim soldiers became uneasy for an attack. Numan, however, asked them to wait. Mugheera who commanded a wing came to Numan and said, "If I were in chief command I would have ordered action". Numan said that in keeping with the practice of the Holy Prophet he would order the attack after the midday prayers when the winds had begun to blow.

After the midday prayers, Numan gave the battle cry, and the Muslim army rushed headlong at the enemy. Under the fury of the Muslim attack the Persian army reeled back. It was a grim and bloody contest and the battlefield was soaked with blood. When the battle was at its climax, in an attempt to advance, the horse of Numan slipped in the blood soaked soil, and fell along with its rider in a pool of blood. Immediately Numan was struck by an arrow shot from the Persian camp. Numan though still alive became unconscious, and with the arrow embedded deep in his side, there was no hope of his survival. Naeem the brother of Numan held the army standard in the place of Numan, and the battle went on without the Muslim army knowing that their Commander had fallen.

Slowly and steadily the Muslim army advanced beating back the Persians. The Persians fought with the courage of desperation. Shortly before sunset, the Persian resistance began to weaken, and the Muslims struck against them with greater violence. The cavalry under Qaqaa struck against the flanks of the Persian army. Night fell but the Muslims continued the pursuit. In the process of withdrawal the belt of caltrops played havoc with the Persians. An arrow from the Muslim side struck Mardanshah, and covered with blood he fell in the belt of caltrops to die.

In the meantime the news of the death of Numan was reported to Hudhaifah. He took over the command, and in spite of gathering darkness the Muslims pressed on their relentless pursuit of the Persians. The pursuit was carried until the Persians reached a ravine, and here in a frantic effort to escape the pursuing Muslims, the Persians fell down the precipice in thousands.

Out of the 60,000 Persians who had fought at Nihawand, 40,000 were killed. The rest escaped to Hamadan.

The battle of Nihawand was over. The Muslims had once again won an historic victory.

It was midnight when the Muslim army gathered in their camp. The Muslim soldiers gathered around the body of Numan. He still breathed. They washed his face. He stirred and opened his eyes. He asked, "What is the result of the battle".

They said, "Rejoice for God has given us victory".

Numan said, "Praise be to Allah," and with these words he breathed his last.

BATTLE OF HAMADAN

On the morning following the battle of Nihawand, Hudhaifah bin Al–Yamãn marched with a strong contingent in pursuit of the Persians. Four miles from the battle-field, at Dareezed a small town, the Muslims found a contingent of the Persian army arrayed for battle. The Persian army was commanded by Dinar.

Hudhaifah deployed his army for battle and launched the attack. The Persians could not withstand the charge and they beat a retreat.

The battle of Nihawand was fought at a site eleven miles from Nihawand proper. The army of Dinar now found refuge in Nihawand proper. The Muslim army under Hudhaifah advanced and invested the city of Nihawand. The Persians made a few sallies, but they were pushed back each time with heavy losses. Seeing that he could not defend the town against the Muslim army, Dinar surrendered. The Persians agreed to pay Jizya, and a peace pact was drawn up accordingly.

At Nihawand town there was only a small contingent of the Persian army. The bulk of the survivors of the Persian force who had fought in the battle of Nihawand withdrew to Hamadan.

Hudhaifah deputed a column under Naeem bin Muqarrin and Qaqa bin Amr to pursue the Persian army to Hamadan. When the Persian army came to know that they were being pursued by the Muslims they quickened their pace, and got to Hamadan before the Muslim army could catch them. A huge mule train carrying baggage, however, fell into the hands of the Muslims.

Reaching Hamadan, the Muslims invested the city, and set up posts on all sides to block any aid reaching the besieged army at Hamadan. The Persian forces in Hamadan were commanded by Khusro Shanum. He soon found that the Persians were no match for the victorious Muslims. Khusro Shanum surrendered and sought terms. The usual terms were offered and the Persians agreed to pay Jizya. Khusro Shanum also undertook the responsibility to administer the region on behalf of the Muslims.

Khusro Shanum was accordingly appointed as the Governor of Hamadan under Muslim control. After taking over his office, Khusro Shanum called upon the people of the region to accept the Muslim rule and pay Jizya. They agreed, and peace was restored.

HADRAT UMAR AND THE BATTLE OF NIHAWAND

After the conquest of Nihawand and Hamadan, and the signing of peace pact with Khusro Shanum the battle of Nihawand was over. This war was as important and momentous as the war of Qadissiya. Qadissiya acted for the Muslims as the gateway to Iraq; Nihawand served as the gateway to Persia proper. It was at Nihawand that the Persians put up stiff resistance with the hope of re-conquest. It was one of the decisive battles of history which sealed the fate of the Persian empire, and paved the way to the rise of the Muslims as a world power.

The booty that the Muslims gathered as a result of the battles of Nihawand and Hamadan was very large. The booty was distributed among the Muslim soldiers by Sāib bin Al–Aqra. Each cavalryman got 6,000 dirhams, while each infantryman got 2,000 dirhams.

While the booty was being distributed, the Zoroastrian High Priest of Nihawand waited on the Muslim Commander and said that if he was afforded protection, as a token of his goodwill he would offer to the Muslims the Nakheerzan treasure. He was given the protection asked for and he presented two boxes filled with pearls and other precious stones.

This treasure belonged to Nakheerzan, a Persian General. He was a close companion of the Persian emperor Parwez, the grandfather of Yazdjurd. He had as his wife a lady who was the most beautiful woman in Persia. On the night of marriage the lady told Nakheerzan that she loved the emperor, and out of regard for the emperor, Nakheerzan should not consummate the marriage. Nakheerzan agreed and he stayed away from the lady.

The news was carried to Parwez that Nakheerzan had not consummated the marriage. One day the emperor asked Nakheerzan, "I hear that you have a spring of sweet water and do not drink from it". Nakheerzan said, "O emperor, I have heard that a lion has his eye on that spring, and for fear of that lion, I keep away from it". The emperor was much pleased with the loyalty of Nakheerzan. Nakheerzan divorced the lady and she was admitted to the royal harem. Parwez bestowed a treasure on the lady, and as a token of her gratitude to Nakheerzan for falling in with her wishes she named the treasure after Nakheerzan. The treasure remained with the children of the lady, who deposited it with the Zoroastrain High Priest.

The state share of the booty along with the Nakheerzan treasure was sent to Hadrat Umar at Madina through a special messenger. The messenger gave Hadrat Umar the good news of the victory of the Muslims.

Hadrat Umar enquired about Numan bin Muqarrin and the messenger said that he had met his martyrdom. Thereupon Hadrat Umar burst into tears, and prayed for the soul of Numan bin Muqarrin, the Victor of Nihawand.

Hadrat Umar next asked the names of other Muslims who had been martyred in the battle field of Nihawand. The messenger named a few persons, and added that there were many others whose names he did not know. Hadrat Umar said, "Never mind if you or I do not know their names. Allah knows them". Then he prayed for the souls of all the Muslims who had been martyred in the battle of Nihawand.

When Nakheerzan treasure was presented to the Caliph he said, "Take it back to Iraq, sell it and use the proceeds for the pay and sustenance of the Muslims". The messengers returned to Iraq and handed over the Nakheerzan treasure to Sāib bin Al-Aqra. Saib bin Al-Aqra sold the treasure at Kufa for two million dirhams and the amount was credited to Baitul Mal.

CONQUEST OF ISFAHAN

Before the battle of Nihawand the policy of Hadrat Umar was that the Muslims should be content with what they had acquired in Iraq, and should leave Persia proper to the Persians and their emperor Yazdjurd. The battle of Nihawand showed that as long as Yazdjurd was there and the Persians smarted under the pain of the loss of their empire, the danger of Persian confrontation was always there. It now came to be felt that in order to ensure the security of the territories that the Muslims had wrested from Persia, it was necessary that the Persian power should be crushed once for all, so that no danger could come to the Muslims from that quarter in the future.

The psychological moment for striking a blow at Persia was immediately after the battle of Nihawand when as a consequence of the defeat the Persians were paralysed. Under the circumstances Hadrat Umar agreed to change his policy with respect to Persia. Having adopted the forward policy, the problem before Hadrat Umar was: where should the Muslims launch the next attack against Persia. There were three alternatives: firstly, an attack against Fars in the south; secondly an attack against Azarbeijan in the north; and thirdly an attack against Isfahan in the centre. Hadrat Umar summoned Hormuzan and sought for his advice as to where the Muslims should launch the attack. Hormuzan said:

> "Fars and Azarbeijan are two arms and Isfahan is the head. If you cut off one arm, the head and the other arm will be there. If you cut off the head, the arms will fall by themselves. So better start with the head."

This advice appealed to Hadrat Umar, and he ordered that the first attack against Persia should be launched against Isfahan. Hadrat Umar appointed Abdullah bin Abdullah bin

Utban to the chief command of the force that was to launch the attack against Isfahan. Abdlullah b. Warqah al-Asdi was appointed to command the right wing, and the left wing was placed under the command of Asmata bin Abdullah. Abdullah bin Abdullah accordingly set off with an army from Iraq, and marching via Nihawand made straight for Isfahan.

In an outlying district town of Iṣfahan, the advance of the Muslim force was resisted by a Persian detachment. The Persian force was commanded by Shaḥr Baraz Jazwiah. He was a man advanced in age. He suggested that instead of a battle between the forces it would be enough if there was a personal duel between a champion from the Persian forces and a champion from the Muslim forces. The Muslim commander agreed to the proposal. Abdullah bin Warqah the right wing commander of the Muslim forces volunteered to fight the duel. Shahr Baraz Jazwiah and Abdullah bin Warqah fought the duel. Shahr Baraz was advanced in age while Abdullah was young. The Persian champion was more experienced and skilful. Ultimately the age factor prevailed and Abdullah bin Warqah succeeded in killing Shahr Baraz Jazwiah. There was a further fight and Astandar the ruler of the district surrendered. A peace pact was drawn whereunder the Persians agreed to pay Jizya.

Thereafter the Muslim forces marched to Rayy which was a suburb of Isfahan. Here the advance of the Muslims was resisted by a Persian force. The Muslims launched the attack. After some fight the Persians retreated to Isfahan. The Muslims advanced and laid siege to the city of Isfahan.

Here the Muslims received further reinforcement. One large corps came under Ahnaf bin Qais, and another column from Basra came under the command of Abu Musa. The Muslims blocked all points of access to the city of Isfahan. The position of the besieged soon became precarious. At this juncture the Commander of the Persian forces, Fazusfan suggested that instead of involving so many persons in bloodshed it would be advisable if the issue was decided between the two commanders by personal duel, the winner taking all.

Abdullah the Commander of the Muslim forces accepted the proposal. The two generals met on horseback in the plain outside Isfahan to fight a duel. Abdullah enquired of Fazusfan whether he would like to strike first. The Persian General said that he would strike first. The Persian General struck. As a result of his stroke the saddle on the horse of Abdullah broke. He slipped off the horse and landed on the ground. He immediately rose up to jump on the bare back of his horse.

Now it was the turn of Abdullah to strike, but before he could strike his adversary surrendered. The usual terms were offered and the Persian General agreed to pay Jizya. A peace pact was drawn accordingly.

From Isfahan, one Muslim contingent proceeded to Kashan and captured it. Another column proceeded to Qum and likewise captured it. Now Isfahan and the region around it was in the occupation of the Muslims. The Muslims had succeeded in severing the head of Persia and that was a great blow.

The Isfahan campaign came to a successful conclusion some time in the early months of 642 A.D.

CONQUEST OF RAYY

After the conquest of Hamadan the Muslims had appointed Khusro Shanum the Governor of the District under the suzerainty of the Muslims. The Governor betrayed his trust, and when the Muslims were campaigning against Isfahan, he acted in a way prejudicial to the interests of the Muslims.

Hadrat Umar ordered a campaign against Hamadan and Rayy. The command was entrusted to Nuaim bin Muqarrin. Some time in January 642 Nuaim bin Muqarrin marched with his forces from Nihawand to Hamadan. The city was invested. The Persians were defeated and the city was recaptured. Khusro Shanum was deposed and another Governor was appointed in his stead.

Leaving a detachment at Hamadan, Nuaim proceeded to Qazween. At Waj Ruz a few miles from Qazween the Muslims met a large Persian army led by Isfandiar, a brother of the late Rustam. A bloody battle followed in which the Persians were defeated and driven back. Some Persians fled to Rayy and some to Azarbaijan.

From Waj Ruz the Muslim army marched to Rayy. The city of Rayy was strongly fortified and heavily defended. The Muslims invested the city. The siege proceeded for about a week. One night Muslims discovered an opening in the city walls through which the Muslim forces entered. Taken by surprise the Persian garrison surrendered. Rayy was sacked and a considerable booty was taken. The Persians agreed to pay Jizya and peace was restored.

Nuaim established himself at Rayy and sent columns under his brother Suweid to subdue the adjoining region. Suweid marched to Demawand where after some show of resistance the Persians surrendered. From Demawand the Muslim army proceeded to Damaghan. There was a confrontation but the Persians were beaten, and they surrendered agreeing to pay Jizya. Then the Muslims marched to Gurgan. Here no resistance was offered, and the Persians surrendered agreeing to pay Jizya.

By April 642 the Rayy campaign had come to a successful close. By the conquest of Isfahan and Rayy the Muslims had succeeded in driving a broad wedge in the centre of Persia, severing the north from the south. The Persian empire now lay bleeding.

CONQUEST OF TABARISTAN

The province of Tabaristan bordered the south coast of the Caspian Sea. After the conquest of Rayy, Tabaristan was exposed to Muslim attack. From Rayy, Nuaim b. Muqarrin sent an expedition to Tabaristan led by his brother Suweid bin Muqarrin.

Suweid proceeded to Qumas. It was a large town in Tabaristan. The people did not choose to fight. On the approach of the Muslim force they opened their gates to them, and surrendered on the usual term of the payment of Jizya, Qumas then fell to the Muslims without a blow.

From Qumas the Muslim forces proceeded to Jurjan. It was an important town on the main highway to Merv. The Persian forces under the command of Rozban offered a feeble resistance, but considering further resistance useless asked for terms. The usual terms were offered and Rozban entered into a peace pact agreeing to pay Jizya.

From Jurjan, the Muslim forces marched to Dehistan. Realising that Jurjan had already surrendered the people of Dehistan could not have the courage to resist the Muslims. They surrendered and on their accepting the same terms as had been accepted by the people of Jurjan a treaty was drawn and peace was restored.

From Dehistan the Muslim forces marched to Amul. The Persian garrison at Amul was led by Siphedar. He was a seasoned warrior. He had prepared for defence. Amul had strong fortifications, and the first reaction of Siphedar was to close the gates of the city against the Muslims. The Muslims invested the city. The siege dragged on for a few days, and the citizens of Amul came to suffer from the shortage of water and provisions Siphedar soon realised that a fight against the Muslims would be like dashing against a rock. He opened negotiations with the Muslims. The set terms were offered by the Muslims and agreed by the Persians. With the signing of the treaty the whole of Tabaristan came under the ruzerainty of the Muslims.

CONQUEST OF KHURASAN

As the Muslims advanced in Persia, the Persian emperor Yazdjurd moved from province to province until he came to the outlying province Khurasan. It is related that while fleeing to Khurasan in the way he had a dream. In the dream he saw himself and the Holy Prophet of Islam presented before God. Allah decreed that the Muslims should have Persia for a hundred years. The Holy Prophet of Islam wanted that this period should be increased. Allah raised the period to 120 years. The Prophet of Islam represented again and Allah said "Alright let the Muslims have Persia for as much time as you like." When Yazdjurd was to represent his point of view to God, he was awakened by his servants. Yazdjurd felt disconsolate as the dream signified that he and his dynasty were to lose Persia for ever. In Khurasan the emperor Yazdjurd settled at Merv.

When other provinces had fallen, Hadrat Umar decided that the Muslims should launch the attack against Khurasan and drive the emperor out of the country. Hadrat Umar appointed Ahnaf bin Qais to the chief command in the campaign against Khurasan. Ahnaf bin Qais accordingly started with his army from Isfahan. From Isfahan two routes led to Khurasan. The main highway was via Rayy and Nishapur. The other route which was less frequented led to Herat by passing Nishapur, and then to Merv. Ahnaf chose to follow the less frequented route.

On the march to Herat the first encounter took place at Tabas. After a feeble resistance the Persian garrison surrendered.

The next encounter took place at Tun. Here too the Persian garrison surrendered.

On reaching Herat, the Muslim army besieged the town. Details of the campaign are not known. It is recorded in contemporary histories that the Persians put up stiff resistance but they were defeated and laid down arms. Herat was occupied by the Muslims and Ahnaf stayed there for some time to reorganise the administration.

From Herat, Ahnaf sent a column against Nishapur. Some resistance was offered but ultimately Nishapur was captured.

From Nishapur the Muslim forces proceeded to Tûs and occupied it after overpowering the Persian garrison.

After clearing these pockets the main Persian town of Merv was made as the target. Merv was the capital of Khurasan and here Yazdjurd held his court. On hearing of the Muslim advance, Yazdjurd left for Balkh. No resistance was offered at Merv, and the Muslims occupied the capital of Khurasan without firing a shot.

Ahnaf stayed at Merv for some time to reorganise the administration and to await further reinforcements from Kufa. In the meantime the Persian forces gathered in considerable strength at Balkh. Yazdjurd sought aid from the neighbouring state Farghana and the Khan of Farghana personally led a Turkish contingent to Balkh.

Having received reinforcements, Ahnaf led the Muslim forces to Balkh. The Muslims had experience of fight with the Persians but they had little experience of war with the Turks. Ahnaf wanted to avoid war with the Turks, and in this connection he thought of ways whereby the Turks should abandon the cause of Yazdjurd. It was reported to Ahnaf that the practice with the Turks were that in the morning three heralds blew bugles and then the Turhish force marched to the battle.

One night Ahnaf hid himself in a safe place outside the Turkish camp. As soon as the Turkish herald came out of the Turkish camp to blow the bugle, Ahnaf overpowered him and killed with his sword. When the second herald came he met the same fate. The third herald also met the same fate. That day the bugles did not blow for the Turkish army. When the bugles did not blow the Khan of Farghana came out of the camp to see what had happened to the heralds. When he saw that all of them were dead he regarded this as a bad omen. At the spur of the moment he decided that the Turks should not involve themselves with the Muslims. He ordered his force to withdraw and march back to Farghana.

When the battle began the Persians charged thinking that they would be supported by their allies the Turks. But the Turks were no longer there. The Muslims counter attacked and the Persian forces found safety in flight across the Oxus to Transoxiana. Balkh was occupied by the Muslims, and with this occupation the Persian war was over. The Muslims had now reached the outermost frontiers of Persia. Beyond that lay the lands of the Turks and still further lay China. The old mighty empire of the Sassanids had ceased to exist.

From Balkh, Ahnaf returned to Merv. From Merv, Ahnaf sent a detailed account of his operations to Hadrat Umar. He stated that the Muslims were now in occupation of the whole of Persia. He further sought the instructions of the Caliph whether the Oxus should be crossed, and operations carried in Transoxiana.

When Hadrat Umar received the report of the conquest of Khurasan he held a thanksgiving prayer to God for making the Muslims the heirs to the mighty Persian empire. The Holy Prophet had prophesied that the Muslims would occupy Persia. That prophesy stood fulfilled.

Addessing the people, Hadrat Umar said:

"Praise be to God Who has made the Muslims the heirs to the mighty empire of Persia. Allah has destroyed the Magian imperialism. Where once the fire-cult dominated there today the Muslims have enforced the cult of the unity of God. God has today chosen you as His instrument. You have to prove yourselves to be worthy of such trust. If you follow the injunctions of God you will prosper. If you falter or waver, God will choose some other people in your place. So that you may prosper let there be no wavering in your faith."

To Ahnaf Hadrat Umar wrote a letter of appreciation. He exhorted him to run the administration in such a way that the people should come to feel that the Muslim administration was more beneficent to them than the Persian imperial administration. As regards carrying campaigns in Transoxiana, Hadrat Umar observed with great emphasis and vehemence that the Oxus was not to be crossed on any account.

CAMPAIGN IN FARS

After the battle of Jalaula and Ahwaz, Hadrat Umar had ordered that there was to be no further advance in Persia. The orders of Hadrat Umar were that the Muslims could advance as far as the land route could carry but where some sea or body of water intervened that was not to be crossed.

When the Muslims overran Iraq, and won the battles of Qadissiya, Ctesiphon, Jalaula, and Ahwaz the spirits of the Muslims ran high and they dreamt of conquering distant lands.

At this time Ula b. Al–Hadrami was the Governor of Bahrain. He had led the apostasy campaign in Bahrain and had succeeded in restoring law and order. Between Bahrain and Persia lay the Persian Gulf and across the Persian Gulf was the Persian province of Fars which could boast of such cities as Persepolis and Shiraz.

Anxious to win glory in the name of Islam, Ula called the local Arabs to arms. The response was encouraging, and Ula mustered a considerable force. Ula thought that with this force he could easily capture a greater part of Fars.

He was aware of the command of Hadrat Umar that no further advance in Iran should be undertaken. Ula knew that if he sought permission from Hadrat Umar to undertake an expedition against Fars such permission would not be forthcoming. He thought that the best course would be to launch the attack, and when the Caliph would hear of his success he would approve the fait accomplish.

Thus notwithstanding the ban imposed by Hadrat Umar, Ula ordered a march to Fars. The force was divided into three columns, and placed under the command of Jarud b. Mualla;

Sawwar b. Hamam and Khuleid b. Mundhir. The Muslim forces were transported by boats across the Persian Gulf, and they landed on the eastern coast of the Persian Gulf.

The Muslim forces then started the march inland towards Shiraz and Persepolis. Half way at Tawoos they found their way barred by a sizable Persian force.

Both the sides deployed their forces for battle. The contest was violent. There were heavy casualties among the Persians, but the Muslims also suffered heavily. The two Muslim commanders Sawwar and Jarud fell fighting. The command was then taken over by Khuleid. He launched a counter attack against the Persians and after putting up a gallant fight, the Persians withdrew.

As Khuleid surveyed the position he felt that unless he was strongly reinforced further advance in Fars was not possible. He accordingly decided to return to the sea shore and await further reinforcements.

When the Muslims came to the shore of the Persian Gulf, they found that by a flanking movement the Persians had already burnt the boats by which the Muslims had crossed the Persian Gulf.

The Muslims now found themselves in a precarious situation. They were not strong enongh to march inland to Fars. With the burning of the boats they could not recross to Bahrain. The only alternative was to march along the east coast of the Persian Gulf to Ahwaz and then to Basra.

After a day's march the Muslims reached the town of Jannaveh, and here they found that their way was blocked by a large Persian force led by Shahrak the Governor of Fars. The Persian force was too large for the Muslims to attack. The Muslims accordingly went into camp and prepared for a defensive action.

Shahrak launched several attacks against the Muslims but he was not able to make any headway. He accordingly withheld further attacks, and decided to blockade the Muslims. In the meantime the commander of the stranded Muslim force managed to send a messenger to Hadrat Umar. When Hadrat Umar came to know that the campaign had been launched without his permission and that it had failed he felt very angry and unhappy. He, however, decided to take immediate action to relieve the stranded army.

Hadrat Umar wrote to Utba bin Ghazwan the Governor of Basra to send a force to the relief of the Muslims stranded in Fars. Utba sent a large force led by Asim b. Amr, and Abu Sabra b. Abi Ruhm. It moved along the coastal route. In the meantime Shahrak also got some reinforcement, and he was planning the assault of the Muslim camp. The Muslim relief force arrived at the nick of the time and that turned the balance in favour of the Muslims. In the confrontation that followed the Persians were defeated, and they took to flight after heavy losses. The Muslim forces marched back to Basra. That was the end of the campaign in Fars. It cost Ula b. Hazrami his governorship, from which office he was removed.

CONQUEST OF FARS AND SISTAN

After the conquest of Isfahan, when the north of Persia had been cut off from the south, Hadrat Umar ordered a march against Fars the southern province of Persia.

The operation against Fars was to be undertaken in a series of campaigns. In the first campaign a corps under Mujasha bin Masud advanced in the district of Ardsheer Khurra. There was a confrontation at Tawwaj where the Muslims defeated the Persian force.

From Tawwaj the Muslim army proceeded to the town of Sabur. The town was besieged. Brought to bay the Persians laid down their arms and submitted to Muslim rule.

In the second campaign led by Usman bin Abul Aas, and starting from where Mujasha bin Masud had left off the Muslim army advanced to Jor. It was a city to the south of Shiraz and some distance away from the Persian Gulf. The Persian garrison at Jor offered resistance but they were soon overwhelmed and the city submitted to the Muslim rule.

From Jor the Muslim army struck north and occupied the city of Shiraz. From Shiraz the Muslim army struck north east and occupied Persepolis the ancient capital of Persia.

The third campaign led by Sariyah bin Zuneim launched from Persepolis was directed against Fasa and Darab. It was a hilly region. At a place near Fasa the Muslim army was stranded and exposed to great danger. That day was Friday and at that time Hadrat Umar was delivering the Friday sermon in the Prophet's mosque at Madina. Suddenly in the course of the sermon, Hadrat Umar shouted 'Sariyah to the hill, to the hill'. When the prayer was over the people gathered round Hadrat Umar and enquired what was the significance of his word 'Sariyah to the hills' in the course of the sermon.

Hadrat Umar said that while he was delivering the sermon he saw that the Muslim army under Sariyah fighting on the Fasa front, was stranded. He advised them to seek the protection of the hills.

It is related that on the battledfield Sariyah heard the voice of Hadrat Umar and he took to the hill as desired. That turned the tide of the battle, and the Muslims won the day. When after many days the messenger from Sariyah reached Madina to convey the news of the victory of Fasa, he declared on oath that on the day of the battle at the time of Friday prayers they had actually heard the call of Hadrat Umar enjoining them to take to the protection of the hill, and that they had acted accordingly.

After Fasa, the Muslims marched to Darab and there too the Persians surrendered after offering feeble resistance.

The fourth campaign in this series was carried by Suhail bin Adi. A column under Suhail marched to Kirman. The Persians offered resistance but when their Commander was killed on the battlefield, they lost heart and submitted to the Muslims. With Kirman as the base, the Muslim force marched against the towns of Jiraft and Sirjan without any difficulty. The entire province of Fars now lay at the feet of the Muslims.

After the conquest of Fars the Muslims turned to the province of Sistan, the home of the legendary hero Rustam of Shahnama fame. The attack on Sistan was led by Asim bin Amr. At the border of Sistan, the army of Asim were obstructed by a Persian force. In a violent attack launched by the Muslims the Persian forces were scattered, and the Muslim forces advanced to Zaranj. It was a fortified town, and the Persian garrison shut itself in the fort. The town was besieged by the Muslims and then carried by assault. The persians surrendered, and the entire province of Sistan came under Muslim occupation.

CONQUEST OF AZARBAIJAN

After the conquest of Rayy and Central Persia, Hadrat Umar ordered the conquest of Azarbaijan. The province of Azarbaijan lay to the west of the Caspian Sea, and was so called because of large number of fire temples therein.

Hadrat Umar appointed Hudhaifah to the command of the campaign against Azarbaijan. Hudhaifah first marched to Zanjan. Here the local garrison put up resistance but they were overpowered and the city was carried by assault.

From Zanjan the Muslim forces proceeded to Ardabeel the capital of the province. The Persians did not offer any resistance and surrendered on the usual terms of Jizya. From Ardabeel the Muslim forces marched northward along the western coast of the Caspian Sea. There was a confrontation at Bab which was an important port on the Caspian Sea. The Muslims scored a victory.

At this stage Hudhaifah was recalled. The Persians launched a counter attack, and the Muslims abandoned their forward posts in Azarbaijan. Hadrat Umar now sent the expeditionary forces to Azarbaijan, one led by Bukair bin Abdullah and the other by Utba bin Farqad.

The contingent under Bukair had their first confrontation with the Persians at Jurmizan. The Persians were commanded by Isandiar. In the battle which was quite severe, the Persians were defeated and their commander Isandiar was captured alive. Isandiar asked Bukair, "Do you prefer war or peace." Bukair said that the Muslims preferred peace. Isfindiar thereupon said, "Then keep me with you till I can help you in negotiating peace with the people of Azarbaijan". There were many forts in the hills. The Persians went to these hills and shut themselve in the forts. The Muslims captured the entire area in the plains.

The other Muslim forces under Utba bin Farqad had their confrontation with a Persian force commanded by Bahram a brother of Isandiar. The Persians were defeated with heavy loss, and Bahram fled away.

When Isandiar came to know that Bahram had been defeated, he waited on Utba and negotiated for peace. In the peace pact that was drawn up, the people of the region agreed to accept the Muslim rule and to pay Jizya.

The Muslims amassed considerable booty. That was distributed among the soldiers. Utba b. Farqad carried the state share to Madina. Along with the other gifts that he carried were loads of 'Halwa', a speciality of Azarbaijan. When Hadrat Umar tasted the Halwa, he said that it was most delicious and sweet. He had the 'Halwa' distributed among all persons in Madina. All those who ate it felt that it was a sweet from the Heaven.

EXPEDITION TO ARMENIA

Armenia lay to the north of Azarbaijan and Jazira. It was bounded in the east by the Caspian Sea, and in the west by the Black Sea.

After the conquest of Azarbaijan, Hadrat Umar gave the call for a march to Armenia. From Azarbaijan, Bukair bin Abdullah moved at the head of a Muslim column along the west coast of the Caspian Sea.

Crossing the border the Muslim forces reached Bab. It was ruled by Shahrbaz, a Magian. The majority of the people were Armenians but Shahrbaz was a Persian and he owed allegiance to Persia. Having come to know of the conquests of the Muslims Shahrbaz was not in a mood to resist the Muslims. He waited on the Muslim commander Bukair and told him that he had little sympathy for the Armenians. He was a Persian and owed allegiance to Persia, but as Persia itself had submitted to the Muslims he was prepared to do the likewise and submit to Muslim rule. He was offered the usual alternative. He said that he had warlike people with him who would be an asset to the Muslims in their wars against other people. He pleaded that as they would be prepared to fight along with the Muslims, they should not be subjected the stigma of Jizya. The matter was referred to Hadrat Umar, and he agreed to the suggestion subject to the provisos that if in any year there was no war they would pay Jizya and also that those who did not participate in the war would pay Jizya. This was agreed to by Shahrbaz, and the peace treaty was drawn up accordingly.

Thereafter the Muslims continued their triumphant march forward. A column under Bukair conquered Qan, an important frontier town. A column under Habib b. Maslamah marched on Tiflis. A column under Hudhaifah marched to the Al-Lan mountains. Another column under Abdul Rahman bin Rabih reduced Baida.

This multi-pronged advance into Armenia came to a halt with the assassination of Hadrat Umar towards the fall of the year 644 A.D.

CONQUEST OF MAKRAN

From Persia the conquering Muslim forces crossed over into Makran district of Baluchistan. That was the first contact of the Muslims with the Indo-Pakistan sub-continent in 644 A.D.

Makran was then a part of the dominions of Raja Rasil. Raja Rasil is referred to in contemporary histories as the Raja of the Sind. When Rasil came to know of the advance of the Muslims he rushed his forces to Makran. He is reported to have crossed a river in Makran, and took his position on the western bank thereof. The name of the river or the exact site of the battle have not been mentioned in contemporary histories.

The Muslim forces were commanded by Hakim bin Amr Taghlabi. He was assisted by Suhail bin Adi. The details of the battle are not known- It is, however, related that the fighting was severe, and that ultimately Raja Rasil was defeated with considerable loss. He crossed the river in his rear, and withdrew to Sind.

Makran was annexed after the people surrendered on the usual terms. Considerable booty was gained and this included a number of war elephants. The state share of the spoils of war along with all the elephants captured were sent to Hadrat Umar. Suhar Abdi, a man of a poetic bent of mind carried the news of victory to Hadrat Umar.

When the messenger waited on Hadrat Umar, he was asked to describe the country. Suhar Abdi broke into rhyme:

"O Commander of the faithful !
It's a land where the plains are stony;
Where water is scanty;

Where the fruits are unsavoury
Where men are known for treachery;
Where plenty is unknown;
Where virtue is held of little account;
And where evil is dominant"

Hadrat Umar looked at Suhar Abdi and said:

"Are you a messenger or a poet."

He said that he was a messenger, and that he had merely described the things as they were.

Thereupon Hadrat Umar said, ‘; If what you say is true, it would be futile to advance in such a land."

Hadrat Umar instructed Hakim bin Amr Al-Taghlabi that for the time being Makran should be the easternmost frontier of the Muslim dominions, and that no further attempt should be made to extend the conquests.

PART IV

Conquest of Syria and Egypt

BATTLE OF BAIT LIHYA

In Syria, the siege of Damascus began on 21st August 634, and on 23rd August Hadrat Abu Bakr was dead and Hadrat Umar had become the Caliph though the army in Syria did not know of this change. Khalid bin Walid was the Commander-in-Chief of the Muslim forces in Syria.

When the siege of Damascus began, the effort of Khalid was to isolate Damascus, so that no relief could reach it from any side. The road to Emessa lay open, and there was the danger that a relief force might come from Emessa. Khalid sent a detachment to take up its position at Bait Lihya ten miles from Damascus on the road to Emessa. The Commander of the detachment was instructed by Khalid to send out scouts to look for the approach of the Byzantine relief columns.

On the 9th of September 634, news was brought to Khalid that a large Byzantine army was marching from Emessa and was likely to reach Damascus within a couple of days. Khalid organised a mounted force of 5,000 men under the command of Zarrar. Zarrar was instructed to intercept the Byzantine force at Bait Lihya. Reaching Bait Lihya, Zarrar organised an ambush near "Thaniyyat-ul-Uqab"—the pass of the Eagle.

When the Byzantine army reached the pass, Zarrar ordered the attack. The Byzantines were prepared for the attack, and they deployed themselves in battle formation almost immediately. In the battle that ensued many Byzantines were killed, and the rest of the Byzantine army fled from the battlefield. The Byzantines were, however, able to capture Zarrar alive. The loss of Zarrar had a depressing effect on the Muslim forces. The command was taken over by Rāfe, and word was sent to Khalid for further help.

Leaving the command of Damascus to Abu Ubaidah, Khalid set off to Bait Lihya with his mobile guard of 4,000 horse. As Khalid approached the battle-field, he saw a Muslim rider with a masked face gallop off towards the Byzantine front. This warrior would kill a number of the soldiers of the enemy, and then withdraw. He would after some time pounce upon the enemy once again and kill every one who came his way. Khalid wanted this warrior to tell him who he was. The warrior, however, dashed to the front again. As he returned from the attack after killing a number of the enemy, Khalid wanted the warrior to halt and identify himself. The warrior said "I am Khaula, sister of Zarrar. My brother has been captured by the Byzantines, and I am dashing against the enemy with a view to liberating Zarrar". Khalid praised the young girl for her bravery, and assured her that he would have her brother rescued.

Khalid launched the attack against the Byzantines with full force and by mid-day the Byzantines began to withdraw under the pressure of the Muslims. The scouts brought the news that they had seen a contingent of 100 Byzantines riding to Emessa with a half-naked man in their midst tied to his horse. Khalid ordered Rāfe to take one hundred picked horsemen, move forward along the flank of the Byzantines, get to the Emessa road, and intercept the escort taking Zarrar to Emessa. Rāfe set off at once on the mission with one hundred horsemen. Khaula accompanied the party.

Rāfe and his party got to the Emessa road at a point where the Byzantine escort had not yet reached, and there lay in ambush. When the Byzantines arrived at the spot, the Muslims fell on the Byzantines, killed most of them, and set Zarrar free.

Under the unrelenting pressure of the Muslims the force sent for the relief of Damascus was forced to retreat to Emessa in a state of disorder. As Zarrar came back to the camp of Bait Lihya, Khalid was much pleased to meet him. Khalid thanked Rāfe and Khaula for their services in freeing Zarrar.

Khalid had a mind to pursue the fleeing force of the Byzantines, but he could not do so as his presence was required at Damascus. Khalid left a detachment at Bait Lihya, and himself along with his mobile guard returned to Damascus.

CONQUEST OF DAMASCUS

The Muslim army besieging Damascus was divided into five corps each under a Commander. Each corps was required to guard one or two gates of the city. In the north there were two gates, namely the Thomas gate, and Paradees gate. The corps commanded by Shurahbeel was stationed outside Thomas gate, while the corps commanded by Amr bin Al-Aas was posted outside Paradees gate. In the east there was one gate. Here corps commanded by Khalid himself was posted. In the south there were two gates. Here the corps commanded by Yazid was posted to look after both the gates. In the west there was one gate, namely the Jabiya gate. Here the corps commanded by Abu Ubaidah was posted. The Byzantine force within the fort was commanded by Thomas who was a son-in-law of the Byzantine emperor Heraclius.

Thomas counted on the arrival of a relief force to be sent by Heraclius. When Thomas came to know that the relief force had been battered at Bait Lihya, he decided to sally forth from the fort and break through the besieging Muslim forces. On a September day mustering a strong force, Thomas broke out through the Thomas gate in the north. Here he was opposed by the force led by Shurahbeel. There was an exchange of shots leading to casualties on both sides. On the Muslim side, one of the soldiers killed was Aban bin Saeed bin Al-Aas. He had only been married a few days ago. As soon as his widow came to know of his death, she donned his uniform, took a bow and joined the Muslim archers, determined to seek revenge for the death of her husband.

The Byzantine soldiers rushed out of the Thomas gate and launched an attack on the Muslims. There was heavy fighting. Shurahbeel's corps was outnumbered, but the Muslims held their ground. Thomas commanded the Byzantine forces personally. In order to demoralise the Muslim forces, Thomas rushed forward to overpower the Muslim Commander Shurahbeel. Before Thomas could reach Shurahbeel, an arrow shot by the widow of Aban struck him. That made the Byzantines fall back to the fort leaving behind a large number of the dead.

The following night, the Byzantines sallied forth from all the gates simultaneously. There was hard fighting. The Byzantines tried their best to break through the Muslim forces. The Muslim forces withstood their ground. Seeing that there was no weakening in the Muslim front, the Byzantines returned to the fort, leaving hundreds of their soldiers dead on the battle-field.

The following day a young Greek Jonah by name slipped from the fort, and coming to the Muslim camp sought an audience of Khalid. He said that he was madly in love with a girl with whom he had been married, but the ceremony of handing over the bride had not taken place. He had asked his father-in law to perform the ceremony but he wanted him to wait till the war was over. Jonah stipulated that if the Muslims could help him in getting his bride, he would help the Muslims in winning the fort. Khalid promised to help, and Jonah the Greek youth pointed a place on the city walls which the Muslims could scale. That night Khalid and a picked band of his soldiers scaled the wall and entered the fort. Then they made for the gate and broke it open. Through the gate the Muslim army rushed in, and began to massacre the Byzantines.

When Thomas came to know of the entry of Khalid through the eastern gate, he waited on Abu Ubaidah at the western gate, and offered surrender on the usual terms of paying Jizya. Abu Ubaidah accepted the surrender and offered amnesty to the Byzantines. When the forces of Abu Ubaidah entered the city from the western gate they soon found that Khalid had already entered it from the eastern gate. Khalid and Abu Ubaidah met in the heart of the town. Abu Ubaidah told Khalid that the Byzantine Commander had surrendered and that he had offered the Byzantines amnesty. Khalid said that he had won Damascus and there was no question of allowing amnesty. A council of war of the Muslim Generals met, and it was ultimately decide that the guarantee given by Abu Ubaidah should be respected.

The Byzantines were allowed to move out of the fort. They were allowed to carry their belongings. It was further stipulated that there would be no pursuit for three days.

Jonah met his girl, and wanted her to come to him. She wanted him to accompany them on their flight from Damascus. He told her that he had become a Muslim and that he would stay in Damascus. Thereupon she refused to have any deal with him.

All the Byzantines left the fort, which was thereafter occupied by the Muslims. The Muslims conquered Damascus some time towards the end of September 634 A.D.

BATTLE OF THE MEADOW OF BROCADE

Khalid felt very bitter that while he had taken the city of Damascus by sword, the fruit of his labour had been snatched away by clever diplomacy of Thomas and the large heartedness of Abu Ubaidah. He was also sad that the Commander of the Byzantine forces Thomas and his Deputy Harbees had escaped. Khalid had wanted to kill them. The Muslim soldiers were also dissatisfied that the Byzantines had carried away all valuable property leaving no booty for the Muslim soldiers.

Jonah highly grieved at his rejection by his bride waited on Khalid in a state of desperation. He suggested that if the Muslims could help him in getting his bride, he could lead them by some short cuts where they could intercept the Byzantine convoy after three days, the period of grace allowed to the Byzantines. The idea appealed to Khalid. He mustered his mobile guard, and decided to follow the convoy.

When the truce allowed for three days was over, the Muslims caught up with the Byzantine convoy at Al-Abrash, a short distance from Antioch. Here rain had fallen, and the convoy had dispersed on the plateau seeking shelter from the inclement weather. Their goods lay in the open. So many bundles of brocade lay scattered on the ground that the plain came to be known as 'Marj-ud-Deebaj'—the Meadow of Brocade.

The Muslim forces attacked the convoy from all the four sides. There was much slaughter and bloodshed. Khalid duelled with Thomas and Harbees, and killed both of them. After some fighting the Byzantine resistance collapsed.

Jonah found his beloved, and wanted her to accompany him. She refused. She took out a dagger from the folds of her dress, and stabbed herself with it. She expired in the hands of Jonah. Jonah took the oath that he would remain faithful to the memory of his beloved, and would not marry any other girl.

Some ladies in the convoy were captured. Khalid offered the most beautiful lady out of these to Jonah to make his wife. Seeing the lady chosen for him by Khalid, Jonah said that the lady was the widow of Thomas, and the daughter of Heraclius, and he could not have her.

The Muslims marched back with their spoils and captives. When they were a day's march from Damascus, they met a small party of riders. From this party a Byzantine noble stepped forward and said:

> "I am the ambassador of Heraclius the Byzantine emperor. You have killed his son-in-law and captured his daughter. He requests you to return his daughter to him, either on the payment of ransom, or as a gift."

At this address, Khalid was touched. He said:

"Take her as a gift; there will be no ransom."

The ambassador took the daughter of Heraclius, offering profuse thanks. Thereafter the Byzantines marched back to Antioch.

The following day Khalid and his force reached Damascus loaded with spoils. The booty was distributed to the Muslim soldiers.

Thereafter Khalid sat to write a detailed report to the Caliph about the conquest of Damascus. The letter was addressed to Hadrat Abu Bakr, and therein Khalid reported as to how Damascus had been conquered, how Abu Ubaidah had been deceived by the Byzantines; and how he had taken the revenge by pouncing upon the convoy after three days, the period stipulated by the truce. When Khalid was about to hand this letter to a messenger to carry it to Madina,

Abu Ubaidah waited on Khalid to say that Hadrat Abu Bakr was dead, and that the new Caliph Hadrat Umar had passed orders deposing Khalid from the high command and vesting the command in him (Abu Ubaidah).

DEPOSITION OF KHALID

On assuming office as Caliph, the first official order that Hadrat Umar passed as the Caliph was to depose Khalid from the chief command of the Muslim forces in Syria.

Hadrat Umar addressed his order to Abu Ubaidah as follows:

> "I urge upon you the fear of Allah Who lives eternally while everything else perishes, Who has guided us away from wrong doing and taken us out of darkness into light.
>
> I appoint you Commander of the army instead of Khalid bin Waleed. So take charge from him as is your duty.
>
> Send not the Muslims to their destruction for the sake of plunder; and place not the Muslims in a camp without reconnoitring it and knowing what is there.
>
> Send not expeditions except in properly organised units. And beware of taking any steps which may lead to the annihilation of the Muslims.
>
> Allah has tried me with you, and tried you with me. Guard against the temptations of this world lest they destroy you as they have destroyed others before you; and you have seen how they fell."

The Caliph instructed the messenger to carry the letter to Syria and hand it over personally to Abu Ubaidah.

The messenger arrived with the letter at Damascus in the first week of September 634, and handed over the letter to Abu Ubaidah. Abu Ubaidah read the letter, but he felt that with the siege of Damascus in progress, that was not the opportune time for making a change in the command. He kept the letter with him as a closely guarded secret, and proceeded to act as if no orders had been received from Madina.

When Damascus fell, the pact with the Byzantines was signed by Khalid, Abu Ubaidah had offered amnesty to the Byzantines over the head of Khalid, but even when Khalid felt annoyed, Abu Ubaidah merely argued in conciliatory terms, and did not drop a hint that he had indeed acted with due authority.

After Khalid had returned from his campaign of the 'Meadow of the Brocade', and written a report addressed to Abu Bakr, Abu Ubaidah could no longer keep the letter of the Caliph as a secret. Reluctantly he handed over the letter of Hadrat Umar to Khalid. Khalid read the letter, and was shocked at its contents.

Turning to Abu Ubaidah, Khalid said, "This letter must have reached you about a month ago: why did you conceal it from me?" Abu Ubaidah said that he did not wish to weaken his authority while he was engaged with the enemy.

Khalid gave the charge of the command to Abu Ubaidah. The options before Khalid were to retire, or to seek transfer to some other front. Khalid did not avail of these options, and he chose to serve in Syria under the command of Abu Ubaidah. Khalid said that he was fighting in the name of Allah and it made no difference to him whether he held the command or fought under the command of someone else.

THE RAID OF ABUL QUDS

A week after Abu Ubaidah had assumed command of the Muslim army, a Christian Arab came to inform the new Commander that a fair was being held at Abul Quds, which if raided would promise the prospect of a great booty for the Muslims. Abu Ubaidah was attracted, and he asked for volunteers who would like to go to raid Abul Quds.

Abdullah a son of Jafar a cousin of the Holy Prophet of Islam offered to command the raid. The offer was accepted and Abdullah with a contingent of five hundred soldiers marched to Abul Quds. Abul Quds was at the eastern foothills of the Lebanon range, 40 miles from Damascus on the road to Baalbeck. The fair was guarded by a force of 5,000 Byzantine men. In a fit of vainglory, Abdullah ordered a charge on the Byzantines. After some heroic fighting the Muslims came to be surrounded by the Byzantine forces. A Muslim soldier escaped from the battle-field and brought news to Abu Ubaidah that the entire contingent of the Muslims at Abul Quds was faced with the danger of annihilation, and that help should be rushed for their relief immediately.

Abu Ubaidah felt much worried. Hadrat Umar had instructed that the Muslims should not be sent for mere plunder, and here he had transgressed such instructions. He had taken over the command recently, and if the Muslim contingent at Abul Quds was not saved that would very much prejudice the Muslim interests in Syria. The only person who could help him in that crisis was Khalid, but he felt that it would be embarrassing to request Khalid to come to his relief so soon after his deposition. But Abu Ubaidah had no option but to request Khalid. Hesitatingly Abu Ubaidah approached Khalid and requested him to come to the rescue of the Muslims at that critical juncture. Khalid agreed to rush to the relief of the contingent at Abul Quds.

Khalid rushed to Abul Quds with his mobile guard. He broke through the ranks of the Byzantines and saved the trapped Muslims. Some bitter fighting followed in which Khalid received many wounds. He, however, stood firm and ultimately the Byzantine garrison fled the fleld. That enabled Khalid attack the stalls at the fair and amass considerable booty.

Khalid returned to Damascus along with the liberated Muslims and the booty from the fair. Abu Ubaidah thanked Khalid profusely. That showed that in the mind of Khalid there was no bitterness about his deposition. Abu Ubaidah reported the matter to Hadrat Umar at Madina, and in the report he lavished most generous praise on Khalid. He wrote that but for Khalid the raid of Abul Quds would have ended in disaster for the Muslims. Hadrat Umar merely noted the contents, and had no word of praise for Khalid. On the other hand, he reprimanded Abu Ubaidah for having sent a raid party to Abul Quds contrary to his instructions. He observed in strong terms that such acts of foolhardiness should not be repeated.

BATTLE OF FAHL

After the Byzantines had lost Damascus, the emperor Heraclius planned a large scale action against the Muslims. His strategy was to cut off the Muslim forces in Syria from communication with Arabia. With this object, he ordered a large concentration of the Byzantine force at Beisan to the west of the Jordan river to the south of Damascus.

The Muslims had only a small garrison at Fahl to the east of Jordan at some distance from Beisan. When Abu Ubaidah came to know of the concentration of the Byzantine force at Beisan, he held a council of war. The concensus of opinion was that all the forces that the Muslims could muster should march to Fahl, and meet the Byzantine force before it could gather further strength. Abu Ubaidah left a corps under the command of Yazid at Damascus, and the rest of the Muslim forces marched to Fahl.

When the Byzantines came to know that the Muslims were marching southward they dammed the Jordan river, and thereby flooded the countryside around Fahl. The Muslim forces cantoned at Fahl. The Byzantine forces were led by Saqlar bin Makhraq. He asked the Commander of the Muslim forces to depute some representative for the purposes of negotiation. Abu Ubaidah deputed Muadh b. Jabal as the Muslim representative.

The Byzantines had a cloth of gold laid for Muadh to sit. Muadh, however, sat on the bare ground. When asked to explain his conduct he said:

> "It is the wont of slaves to sit on bare ground. I am the slave of God, and therefore I sit on the bare ground."

Addressing Muadh Saqlar advised the Muslims to attack Persia and Abyssinia where the chances of their success were greater. He said that in the case of the Byzantines, the Muslims were ill advised to wage war, for the Byzantine could muster forces as numerous as the stars in heaven.

Muadh said that they would launch a campaign against Persia in due course. He said that the Muslims were in no way afraid of the large strength of the Byzantine forces. They were fighting in the way of Allah and they were fortified with the faith that God would help them. Saqlar said that the Muslims could have Baqla and some other districts adjoining Arabia provided they withdrew from Syria. Muadh turned down the offer. He offered the Byzantines the usual three alternatives. Muadh then returned to the Muslim camp.

The following day a Byzantine representative came to the Muslim camp. He found the Muslim Commander-in-Chief Abu Ubaidah dressed as an ordinary soldier sitting on the bare ground examining arrows. He gave Abu Ubaidah a message from Saqlar that if the Muslims withdrew from Syria he would pay them a good deal of money. Abu Ubaidah rejected the offer, and said that the issue between the Muslims and the Byzantines would be decided on the battlefield.

The following day the Muslims decided to cross the river, and attack Beisan. Khalid led the advance guard. The Muslim forces had not proceeded very far when they got stuck in the mud, and had great difficulty in extricating themselves. They accordingly returned to Fahl and decided to wait.

The Byzantines were happy that their stratagem of flooding countryside had paid dividends. Byzantine had guides who assured them that they could negotiate the marsh. The Byzantine forces commanded by Saqlar crossed the Jordan river and proceeded to Fahl. They hoped to catch the Muslims unaware.

The Byzantines launched the attack on 23rd January 635. As the Byzantines advanced, all advantages lay with them. They were larger in strength, and they were better equipped. The topography was also in their favour. They could negotiate the marsh. They opend the attack with a rain of arrows. The Muslim cavalry was led by Khalid and they formed the Muslim vanguard. Due to the rain of arrows from the Byzantine side the Muslim forces had to fall back. They steadily withdrew until they were on firm ground beyond the flooded area. Then the Muslims charged. In the hand to hand fight that ensued the Muslims were superior to the Byzantines. The Commander-in-chief of the Byzantine forces Saqlar and many other commanders were killed. That demoralised the Byzantines. Overpowered the Byzantine forces pulled back and decided to withdraw to Beisan. The Muslims increased their pressure. Under the pressure of the Muslim assault the retreat of the Byzantines soon became a rout. The Muslims played havoc with the forces. The retreating Byzantine got bogged up in the mud, and the pursuing Muslims made mince meat of them. The marsh which the Byzantines had created to trap the Muslims became a death trap for the Byzantines themselves. Over ten thousand Byzantines perished in the battle of Fahl. The marsh came to be studded with the dead bodies of the Byzantine soldiers. The battle ended in victory for the Muslims. Because of the mud, the battle of Fahl came to be known in the Arab chronicles as the Battle of the Mud.

After the battle of Fahl, the main Muslim army under Abu Ubaidah and Khalid returned to Damascus. One contingent was left to conquer Beisan. Another contingent proceeded to capture Tabariyya.

The Muslims crossing the Jordan proceeded to Beisan. The Persians shut the gates of the city in the face of the Muslims, and the Muslims laid siege to the city. After a few days finding resistance futile the Byzantines surrendered and agreed to pay Jizya.

Tabariyya was eighteen miles from Beisan. It was the chief town of Jordan. The town was fortified and at the approach of the Muslims, the gates of the city were shut against them. The Muslims laid siege to the town, and blocked all routes to the town. After the fall of Beisan, the citizens of Tabariyya also found that any further resistance was useless. They, therefore, surrendered and agreed to pay Jizya. They vacated fifty per cent of the houses in the city which were occupied by the Muslims. With the fall of Tabariyya, the whole of Jordan came under the occupation of the Muslims. The campaigns in Jordan ended in February 635 and the Muslims settled down to administer the land.

BATTLE OF MARJ-UR-RUM

When the Muslims were busy operating in the Jordan sector, Heraclius thought that it was a good opportunity to attack Damascus and recapture it. Heraclius accordingly sent from Antioch a strong Byzantine force under a General named Theodorus to recapture Damascus.

When Abu Ubaidah came to know that a Byzantine force was marching to Damascus, the Muslim contingents led by Abu Ubaidah and Khalid left Fahl and moved northward to Damascus. When Heraclius came to know of the movements of the Muslim force, he ordered a detachment of the Byzantine forces stationed at Emessa north of Damascus to be sent to Damascus to reinforce the Byzantine forces under Theodorus.

The Muslim and Byzantine forces met in the plain of Marj-ur-Rum to the west of Damascus. As the two armies stood in battle formation, the Byzantine contingent from Emessa under the command of Shans faced the corps of Abu Ubaidah, while the corps of Khalid faced the main army commanded by Theodorus. The two armies remained in their battle positions, each waiting for the other to make the first move. No side made the move.

As night fell, leaving Shans to face the Muslims, Theodorus pulled back his corps under the cover of darkness, and by dawn the following day arrived at Damascus. The movement was carried out with great skill and it was only about dawn that the Muslims came to know that the bulk of the Byzantine army had left for Damascus.

The Muslim garrison at Damascus was under the command of Yazid. On coming to know that a Byzantine force had arrived under the command of Theodorus, Yazid immediately deployed his force outside the fort. Just after sunrise the battle began between the Muslims and the Byzantines. The Byzantines vastly outnumbered the Muslims, and in spite of the strong pressure of the Byzantines the Muslims held fast till noon. Thereafter the Byzantines increased their pressure and the force under Yazid began to fall back.

At that juncture Byzantines were struck in their rear by a furious mass of Muslim horsemen. This was the mobile guard led by Khalid. When Khalid came to know that the force under Theodorus facing him was no longer at Marj-ur-Rum he guessed that the force must have proceeded to Damascus. Khalid accordingly rushed with his mobile guard to the relief of Damascus. So great was the onslaught of the Muslim cavalry that the Byzantine forces wedged in between the forces of Yazid and Khalid were cut to pieces.

Khalid killed Theodorus. With his death the Byzantine forces lost nerve. They retired from the battle-field in great confusion. Thousands of them were killed. Only a few escaped to tell the tale of disaster. The battle of Damascus ended in a victory for the Muslims.

At Marj-ur-Rum the Muslims under Abu Ubaidah faced the Byzantines under Shans. The battle began with a personal duel between Abu Ubaidah and Shans. In this duel, Abu Ubaidah killed Shans. Thereafter the battle began, and both the sides appeared to be balanced. By afternoon news was received that in Damascus the Byzantine force had been shattered. That unnerved the Byzantine force fighting at Marj-ur-Rum. As night fell, the Byzantines fell back and retreated to Emessa. The battle of Marj-ur-Rum was fought in March 635 A.D.

BATTLE OF EMESSA

After the battle of Marj-ur-Rum, the Muslim forces under Khalid advanced to Emessa in the north and laid siege to the city. After some time, Abu Ubaidah also arrived at Emessa alongwith the rest of the Muslim army. The citizens of Emessa thereupon felt that they were no match for the Muslim forces. They asked for a truce which was allowed. The people of Emessa paid 10,000 dinars and 100 robes of brocade. The truce was stipulated for a period of one year during which period the Muslims were not to attack them. If Emessa received any reinforcement during this period, the citizens of Emessa could resume hostilities. After the truce was agreed upon, the gates of the city of Emessa were thrown open, and the Muslims were free to move in the city.

After the truce with Emessa, the Muslims attacked the neighbouring cities, and these cities also sought truce on the lines of the truce of Emessa. In the meantime the winter set in. Heraclius sent considerable force to reinforce the garrison of Emessa. With the arrival of reinforcement the truce ended and the hostilities were resumed.

The military Governor of Emessa was Harbees, and to him Heraclius wrote, "The Muslims cannot stand the cold of Syria. Fight them on every cold day so that none of them is left till the spring."

For some time the siege of Emessa continued with unbroken monotony. Every day there was an exchange of archery, but there was no major action. The Byzantines hoped that the severe cold of Syria would be enough to destroy the desert dwellers and drive them away. The Muslims, however, with stood the cold with great resoluteness. By March 636 the severity of the cold was over, and the hopes of the Byzantines that the cold would drive away the Muslims were dashed to the ground. The Byzantines now became desperate. One morning a gate of the city was flung open, and Harbees the Byzantine Commander led a surprise attack against the unsuspecting Muslims. In the momentum of the surprise attack the Byzantines moved forward and the Muslims were forced to fall back.

At this juncture, Abu Ubaidah commissioned Khalid to go to the relief of the Muslims. Khalid regrouped the Muslim army, and launched a counter attack. By sunset the Byzantines were forced back inside the city. The Byzantines had fought hard, and the Muslims felt that Harbees was no ordinary Commander; he was a force to be reckoned with.

The following morning, Abu Ubaidah held a council of war. Most of the Muslim soldiers were in a restrained mood. Khalid advised that they should stage a withdrawal. When the sun rose, the Muslims had packed their belongings, struck the tents and had begun the withdrawal, Harbees thought that his action during the previous day had unnerved the Muslims, and they had accordingly raised the siege.

Harbees felt elated and he thought of giving a beating to the retreating Muslims. Harbees launched his mounted force into a fast pursuit to catch up with the retreating Muslims. The Muslims increased their pace, and the Byzantines also quickened the pursuit. When they were sufficiently away from Emessa, Khalid gave the signal, and the Muslim forces rushed from all sides to surround the Byzantines. Steadily closing in from all sides, the Muslims struck the Byzantines with spears and swords. The Byzantines fought desperately but were slaughtered down in large numbers. Breaking through the Byzantine force, Khalid reached Harbees, and then a duel began between the two Generals. In this duel the sword of Khalid broke and for some time Khalid was at the mercy of Harbees. Khalid held Harbees tight in his grip and then with his steel like grip splintered his ribs. Harbees fell lifeless in the hands of Khalid. The death of Harbees was the signal for the end of the Byzantine resistance.

The Muslims marched back to Emessa triumphant. There was no further resistance at Emessa. The citizens surrendered on the usual terms and the city of Emessa was occupied by the Muslims towards the closing days of March 636.

BATTLE OF YERMUK

When Emessa was still under siege, Heraclius the Byzantine emperor made another bid to muster strength and drive away the Muslims from the land of Syria. This time he planned action on a massive scale. By May 636 A.D., a Byzantine army of 1,50,000 men had been put in arms and concentrated at Antioch .

At this time the Muslims were operating in four pockets. Amr b. Al-Aas was operating with his corps in Palestine; Shurahbeel was in Jordan; Yazid was in Caesara; while Abu Ubaidah and Khalid were at Emessa.

The plan of the Byzantines was that one Byzantine force was to march from Damascus from the west, and cut off the Muslim force at Emessa. Another force was to attack the Muslims at Emessa from the north. One force was to attack Emessa from the east and still another from the west. The plan was to recapture Emessa and Damascus.

When the Muslims came to know of the Byzantine plan they held a council of war. The Muslims decided that instead of being divided into four pockets, they should consolidate their forces at one point and face the Byzantines as a united force.

The next point for consideration was where should the Muslim forces concentrate? If the Muslims concentrated their forces in North Syria, they were apt to be surrounded by the Byzantine forces and their contact with the Arabian desert was likely to be cut off. The only strategy under the circumstances was that the Muslims should concentrate their forces in southern Syria where they could always maintain contact with Arabia. In accordance with this decision, the Muslims vacated Emessa, Damascus and other posts in North

Syria, and concentrated their forces at Jabiya in Yermuk valley to the south of Damascus.

When the Byzantine force reached Emessa they found that the Muslims had left. They found that Damascus had also been evacuated. The Byzantines marched to the south and reached the Yermuk valley some time in the third week of July 636. Here they settled down in camps, and began their preparations for a confrontation with the Muslims. The Byzantine camp was 18 miles long, and between the Byzantine camp and the Muslim camp lay the central parts of the plain of Yermuk. The Byzantine forces comprised of 2 lakh men fully equipped.

The Muslim army consisted of 40,000 men. Against every five Byzantine soldiers there was only one Muslim soldier. When the Byzantine Generals surveyed their army, they felt sure of their victory.

The Muslims were fired with their faith, and hoped that God would grant them victory in spite of the odds against them. Abu Ubaidah felt that it was going to be a tough battle. He thought that at that critical stage it was necessary to avail of the military skill of Khalid. Abu Ubaidah accordingly decided to remain the nominal Commander-in-Chief. He delegated his powers of field operations to Khalid.

For some time there were negotiations between the two parties. The Byzantines offered to pay the Muslims some money in case they left Syria and returned to Arabia. The Muslims spurned the offer. In return the Muslims offered the Byzantines the usual three alternatives, Islam, Jizya or the sword.

BATTLE OF YERMUK —THE FIRST TWO DAYS

After the failure of negotiations, the arbitration was left to the sword. The battle began in the third week of August 636.

Both the armies faced each other across the plain of Yermuk, about a mile apart.

Before the two armies clashed, a Byzantine General George emerged from the Byzantine centre and rode towards the Muslims. Approaching the Muslim centre he asked for Khalid. Khalid rode out thinking that George wanted to have a duel with him. But George had no intention to duel. Instead George asked a few questions about Islam, and the Holy Prophet. He also enquired as to why Khalid was called 'The Sword of Allah'. Khalid answered these questions, and George said that he was satisfied. Khalid thereupon invited George to accept Islam and declare the article of faith. Surprisingly enough, George accepted the invitation and was converted to Islam at the hands of Khalid. Then George rode to the Muslim side where he was welcomed with great enthusiasm.

The Commander-in-chief of the Byzantine force felt much annoyed at the walk over of his General George to the Muslim camp. He vowed vengeance against the Muslims as well as George. In a fit of fury he chose a few selected warriors from the Byzantine side, and they challenged the Muslims to duel. Scores of duels were fought on the plain of Yermuk. Practically all the Byzantine champions were killed in the combat. On the Muslim side honours went to Abdur Rahman the son of Hadrat Abu Bakr who killed five Byzantine champions one after the other.

After the duelling was over, Mahan the Commander-in-Chief of the Byzantine forces asked his forces to launch the assault. The Muslims withstood their ground. At sunset when the action ended, there were more casualties on the Byzantine side than on the side of the Muslims.

On the second day, the Muslims were still at morning prayer when the Byzantines launched the attack. The Muslims got into position immediately and the two armies clashed. The Byzantines did not press at the Muslim centre; they directed their pressure on the Muslim flanks. The Muslim right was led by Amr bin Aas. The Muslim corps on the right withstood two attacks, but at the third attack which was very severe they fell back in some disorder. The Muslim cavalry held up the Byzantine advance for some time, but they were unable to hold it for long. Repulsed by the Byzantines the Muslims fell back on their camp. Here they were greeted by Muslim women with stinging rebukes. That made the Muslim warriors turn back from the camp. The Muslims launched a counter attack and the Byzantines were pushed back.

The Muslim left flank was led by Yazid. The corps under Yazid withstood the first attack but fell back under the severity of the second attack. The Muslim cavalry launched the counter attack but it was repulsed, and the Muslims fell back to their camp. Here the Muslim women put the Muslim warriors to shame. They exhorted them to return to battle and show their courage. They returned to the battle and launched a counter attack.

Seeing the pressure on the flanks, Khalid decided to come to their help. First he turned to the right wing and struck at the flank of the Byzantine army. The Byzantines reeled under the pressure of these blows and beat a retreat. Thereupon the corps of Amr regained all the ground they had lost.

Khalid next turned to the left wing, and attacked the Byzantine corps. Here again the Byzantines withdrew under the force of the counter attacks launched by the Muslims from the front as well as the flank. The attack on the Muslim side was led by Zarrar. He killed Derjan, the Commander of the Byzantine corps.

By sunset the two flanking armies of the Byzantines had been pushed back. The Muslims had faced a critical situation, but they had managed to regain the lost ground. When the battle ended on the second day the result was still undecisive.

BATTLE OF YERMUK —THIRD AND FOURTH DAYS

On the third day, the Byzantines again launched the attack. The initial attacks were repulsed by the corps of Amr and Shurahbeel. But when the Byzantines increased their pressure, the Muslims fell back. The Byzantines broke through in several places, and the Muslims fell back to their camp. The corps of Shurahbeel was similarly pushed back to the camp. The Muslim women in the camp once again came into action with sharp tongues and tent poles. The Muslim warriors felt that it was easier to face the enemy than their women. That made the Muslim warriors return to the battle. Khalid again came to the rescue of these corps. The Byzantine opposition to the Muslim counter attack was very stiff but by dusk the Byzantines had been pushed back to the original position.

On the third day also the battle remained undecisive. The losses of the Byzantines outnumbered those of the Muslims. The Byzantine attacks had been beaten back by the Muslims. The Muslims were satisfied with their performance, but in the Byzantine camp, Mahan the Commander-in-chief was not satisfied with the performance of the Byzantines.

On the fourth day the Byzantines again started the battle with an attack on the corps of Amr bin Al-Aas and Shurahbeel. The corps of Amr was pushed back, but there they held up with drawn swords. In the sector of Shurahbeel the Byzantines broke through and pushed the Muslims to their camp. Seeing the predicament of Shurahbeel, Khalid came to his assistance with his reserve. At the same time Abu Ubaidah and Yazid launched a frontal attack in their sector to prevent the increase of further pressure in the sector of Shurahbeel. As the Byzantines advanced in the sector of

Shurahbeel, by a counter flank movement, Khalid attacked the Byzantines from two sides. The Byzantines broke under the blows of the Muslim cavalry and fell back to their original position, losing heavily in the process. The Byzantine archers now let loose a rain of arrows on the Muslim forces. Over 700 Muslims were hit in their eyes.

The fourth day's battle because of these arrows came to be known as "The Day of Lost Eyes". That was the worst day of the battle for the Muslims. Seeing the consternation in the Muslim ranks the Byzantines increased their pressure. Even the corps of Abu Ubaidah and Yazid were pushed back. At this critical hour, Ikramahh and his contingent refused to retreat. They took the oath of death, and fell upon the Byzantines with the fury and violence of desperate men. Under their blows the Byzantines pulled back. Of the four hundred dedicated men who took the oath of death almost all including Ikramahh died, but they saved the day for the Muslims. Seeing the plight of the Muslims the Muslim women rushed forward with tent poles to fight against the Byzantines. That inspired the Muslims to heroic effort, and when the day's action was over, both the armies stood once again on their original lines.

BATTLE OF YERMUK —FIFTH AND SIXTH DAYS

On the fifth day the two armies again lined up for action, but there was no assault. Then an emissary came forward from the Byzantine side proposing a truce for the next few days so that fresh negotiations could be held. The Muslims did not accept the proposal. They said that they were in a hurry to finish the business. That day there was no battle.

On the sixth day before the battle began, Gregory a General of the Byzantine army stepped forward and challenged the Muslim Commander-in-chief to a duel. Abu Ubaidah accepted the challenge. In the duel, Abu Ubaidah killed Gregory.

Thereafter Abu Ubaidah gave the signal for a Muslim attack, and the Muslim front surged forward. The Muslim cavalry led by Khalid intensified their blows against the Byzantine cavalry, and after a hard struggle the Byzantine cavalry was driven away from the field. The Byzantine infantry was now left without the support of the cavalry. By a flanking movement, Khalid attacked the Byzantines both from the front as well as the rear, and some sectors of the Byzantine army collapsed. The Byzantine infantry was now in full retreat, and the Muslims suffered it to retire.

The Byzantines retreated towards Qadi-ur-Raqqad. Here a Muslim contingent under Zarrar lay ambushed and they made mince meat of the flying Byzantines.

By the afternoon of the sixth day of the battle only a third of the Byzantine army remained in the battle-field; the rest had fled away. The Muslim army now fell on the Byzantines.

In the meantime a storm began to blow. It blew against the faces of the Byzantines, and provided a greater momentum to the Muslims to rush forward. In the confusion that followed the Byzantines lost their bearings. Panic stricken they fled and the pursuing Muslims killed thousands of Byzantines right and left. The battle of Yermuk ended in a great victory for the Muslims.

The Byzantine Commander-in-chief, Mahan with the remnants of his army fled towards Damascus. The Muslims pursued them, and overtook them a few miles short of Damascus. The Muslims attacked the Byzantine rearguard with great violence. In the scuffle that followed Mahan was killed. Many Byzantines were slaughtered, but some managed to escape to tell Heraclius the story of the disaster that the Byzantines had met at the battle-field of Yermuk.

The battle of Yermuk was the greatest battle that the Muslims had fought so far. That spelled the end of the Byzantine rule in Syria, and ushered in the Muslim rule.

EPISODES OF YERMUK

Some episodes of the battle of Yermuk highlighting the courage, and heroism of the Muslim warriors have passed into legend, and have come down to us. Some of these episodes are noticed hereunder.

It was the last day of the battle of Yermuk. The Byzantine soldiers furiously attacked the right wing of the Muslim army. The wing was commanded by Salama. He bravely defended his position and in his heroic effort to stem the advance of the enemy he received numerous wounds on his person.

Suddenly the horse of Salama was found running in the battle-field without its rider. Hudhaifah, a friend of Salama, set out to seek Salama. He ran here and there, and at last found the wounded warrior fallen on the ground in a state of utter exhaustion caused by profuse bleeding.

Salama parted his lips with great difficulty and asked Hudhaifah about the condition of the battle. Hudhaifah said that the Byzantine attack had been beaten and the Muslims were now on the offensive and there were already marks of confusion among the Byzantines.

On hearing this the pale face of the dying General flashed with joy. He collected his vanishing strength and shouted to his men "Comrades forward and forward. Victory is yours. Turning to Hudhaifah he said, "I wish to hear the news of victory before I die."

Utterly exhausted, Salama sank back on the ground and gasped for water. Hudhaifah went to the camp and brought a tumbler of water. Salama took up the tumbler and was to drink it when a wounded soldier Hisham by name who lay on the ground at some distance was heard crying for water. Salama said to Hudhaifah, "Take this water to that wounded soldier. His need is more than mine."

Hudhaifah went up to the wounded soldier Hisham and handed him the cup of water. He was about to drink it when from some distance a cry came for water. Hisham said to Hudhaifah, "Give it to him over there."

Hudhaifah ran to the third man with the cup in his hand but when he reached there the man was dead. Hudhaifah returned to Hisham, but he was dead. Hudhaifah next ran to Salama but in the meantime Salama had breathed his last.

Hudhaifah threw the tumbler of water and lifted his hands in prayers for the souls of the departed warriors who had preferred the needs of others to their own needs.

When the war was raging at its highest, Habash bin Qais a noted warrior fought most bravely in the thickest part. Some one from the enemy ranks struck him a blow with a scimitar on one of his feet which was severed clean away. Habash continued fighting unconscious of the fact that he had lost a foot. When the war was over he found that one of his feet was missing and he asked of the people around him whether they had seen his missing foot. Habash belonged to the Attab clan and this episode became a matter of pride for the tribe. A poet sang:

"Habash comes of us,
And of us cometh straight
The seeker of the foot,
He, who has made his clansmen great."

In 'Bang-i-Dara' in one of his poems, Iqbal has dramatised an episode of the battle of Yermuk. In this battle the total strength of the Muslim army was 40,000 while the forces of the enemy numbered two lakh. In spite of the smallness of their number, the Muslims were in no way overawed by the superior strength of the enemy. Each Muslim warrior was fired with the urge to win or die, to live as a Ghazi or die as a martyr.

As the Muslim forces stood ready for battle awaiting the signal of their General, a young Arab warrior stepped forward and addressing the General Abu Ubaidah said:

> "O Commander of the forces of the faithful, I am impatient for the martyrdom and I cannot afford to await your orders for advance. Kindly have pity on me, and allow me to fall on the enemy. The Holy Prophet is calling me, and I want to rush to him after seeking martyrdom. O Amir, if you have any message for the Holy Prophet, give me such message and I will convey it to him when I meet him after my martyrdom. But O Amir do not hesitate to give me the permission. I see the Holy Prophet yonder calling me and any delay will be sacrilegeous."

On hearing these words, tears trickled from the eyes of Abu Ubaidah. He embraced the young soldier and said:

> "Young man, your love for the Holy Prophet is so intense that it puts me to shame. I wish each one of us could burn in the flame of the love of the Holy Prophet in the same way as you do. I do not want to stay between you and the Holy Prophet. You have my permission to fall on the enemy and seek martyrdom. And when you meet the Holy Prophet offer my respectful greetings and say 'God has been very kind to your followers, and all the promises that God made about conquests for the Muslims have been fulfilled."

CONQUEST OF SYRIA

The battle of Yermuk was a historic battle which changed the course of history. When the news of the disaster of Yermuk were conveyed to the Byzantine emperor Heraclius at Antioch the capital of Syria, he at once decided to abandon Syria and withdraw to Constantinople. His parting words were "Farewell Syria ! It is with great pain that I part from you. My salutations to thee O beautiful land."

From Yermuk, Abu Ubaidah sent a detailed report of the victory of the Muslims to Hadrat Umar along with the state share of the spoils of war. The message was carried by a high-powered delegation led by Hudhaifah b. Al-Yamān. Hadrat Umar had not slept for many nights anxiously awaiting news from Yermuk. As the news of the victory of the Muslims at Yermuk was intimated to Hadrat Umar he had all the Muslims in Madina assemble at the Prophet's mosque, and a special thanks giving prayer was offered.

Hadrat Umar in a letter addressed to Abu Ubaidah congratulated him for the victory. He instructed that the cities in Syria like Damascus and Emessa which the Muslims had abandoned on the eve of the battle of Yermuk should be re-occupied. He further desired that after the withdrawal of the Byzantine emperor from Syria, the whole of Syria should be brought under Muslim control.

When the instructions of Hadrat Umar were received, Abu Ubaidah left a few contingents in Jordan and Palestine and with the rest of the army marched northward. The city of Damascus opened its gates to the Muslims, and their return was enthusiastically welcomed.

From Damascus the Muslim army proceeded to Emessa. The people of Emessa also welcomed the return of the Muslims.

From Emessa a column under Khalid marched to Qinnissrin. Here a Byzantine force under Minas offered resistance to the Muslims. Khalid defeated the Byzantine army with great slaughter, and demolished all defensive works. There were many Arab tribes in the city. Khalid offered them Islam and they became Muslims. The other citizens agreed to pay Jizya. When the exploits of Khalid were reported to Hadrat Umar, he acknowledged the services of Khalid in generous terms. He wrote "God bless Abu Bakr. He singled out Khalid for his favours and he was a better judge of men than me."

The victory of Qinnissrin cleared the way to Aleppo. Abu Ubaidah accordingly marched to Aleppo at the head of the Muslim army. In the ourskirts of Aleppo there were many settlements of Arab tribes. They were offered Islam and accepting the offer they were converted to Islam. There was a Byzantine garrison at Aleppo which chose to shut itself in the fortifications. The city was besieged, and the Byzantines were forced to capitulate on the usual term of paying the Jizya.

From Aleppo the Muslim army marched to Antioch. It was the capital of the Byzantines in Syria. Although the emperor Heraclius had left for Constantinople, there was a sizable Byzantine garrison at Antioch. There was a large concentration of the Christians in the city. On the approach of the Muslim army the citizens of Antioch and the Byzantine garrison shut themselves within the fortified city. The Muslims besieged the city and blocked all approaches to the city. Within a few days the citizens suffered from the shortage of foodgrains and other provisions, and they capitulated agreeing to pay Jizya. With the capitulation of Antioch the Muslims were the masters of Syria. So great was the awe of the Muslim forces that wherever a few Muslim soldiers appeared the Christians waited on them and sued for peace.

After reducing Antioch, Abu Ubaidah spread the Muslim forces in all directions. The neighbouring towns of Buqa, Jumah, Surmin, Tuzi, Quras, Tilghraz, Daluk and Ruban were captured one after the other without firing a shot. There was some show of resistance at Balis and Qasrin but such resistance was overcome by the Muslims without any difficulty. At Bughras a town on the border of Asia Minor there was a fierce conflict. The Muslim force under Habib b. Maslamah ultimately carried the town by assault. The people were killed in thousands and those who survived fled to seek shelter in Constantinople. Khalid led a campaign against Marash. Here too there was a sanguinary battle. Brought to bay the Christians said that they were prepared to leave the city to the Muslims provided they were allowed to depart in safety. Khalid accepted the offer, and the Christians were allowed to escape to Constantinople without taking any property.

As a result of these campaigns, the Byznatines completely disappeared and Syria became a province of the Muslim dominions.

Abu Ubaidah sent a detailed report to Hadrat Umar about the conquest of Syria. Writing about Antioch, Abu Ubaidah said:

> "O Commander of the faithful, Antioch is a very beautiful and attractive place. Our soldiers were so much enamoured of the place that they insisted on staying there. I was afraid lest by staying there the Muslims might be involved in a luxurious way of living. I have accordingly come back to Emessa along with the army. The Byzantine women are very handsome and the Muslim soldiers are very much attracted by them. They long to marry such women and that is a matter of headache for me".

In reply Hadrat Umar congratulated Abu Ubaidah for the victories that God had bestowed on the Muslims. Hadrat Umar appreciated Abu Ubaidah's views about Antioch and his anxiety to pull out the Muslim soldiers from such a beautiful place lest they might be involved in a luxurious way of life. Hadrat Umar, however, pointed out that God had not declared good things unlawful for the Muslims. God had said, "Avail of fine things, and do fine deeds. He also says, O ye faithful, out of the sustenance provided by Us eat delicious things, and offer thanks to Allah Who has provided you such delicacies." Hadrat Umar added that it would have been advisable if he had allowed his soldiers to rest at Antioch for some time, but as he had pulled the Muslims from the attractive surroundings of Antioch with good intentions whatever he did was good. As regards the Byzantine women Hadrat Umar said:

> "Those who are unmarried let them marry Byzantine women provided they accept Islam. If any Muslim wishes to purchase a Byzantine woman as a slave let him do that for that is permissible."

FALL OF JERUSALEM

After the battle of Yermuk, when the main Muslim army under Abu Ubaidah and Khalid left for the north of Syria, some Muslim contingents under Amr bin Al-Aas and Shurahbeel remained stationed in the southern sector comprising Jordan and Palestine.

Finding that the bulk of the Muslim army had left, Artabun the Byzantine Governor assembled a large force at Ajnadin in another bid to drive away the Muslims from the soil of Syria. The battle at Ajnadin fought towards the close of 636 was very bloody and gruesome. Both sides fought bravely but ultimately the Byzantines were defeated, Artabun defeated with heavy loss fled to Jerusalem with the remnant of his army.

After the victory of Ajnadin the Muslim forces spread in all directions in Jordan and Palestine. The towns of Sabtah, Gaza, Nablus, Bait-Jibrin and many other towns were captured one after the other. That cleared the way to Jerusalem. The city of Jerusalem sacred to the Jews and the Christians was strongly fortified. It was protected on every side by deep valleys and steep ascents. Military engines were mounted on the walls which were intended for playing havoc with the advancing invader. It was the winter season, and the severity of the winter added to the difficulties of the besieging Muslim force. The siege dragged on and the Byzantines offered very stiff resistance.

Amr b. Al-Aas the Muslim Commander in the southern sector wrote to Abu Ubaidah for reinforcement. By this time, northern Syria had fallen to the Muslims and Abu Ubaidah was able to spare many contingents which rushed to the aid of the Muslims fighting in the southern sector. When

1the citizens of Jerusalem came to know that the besieging Muslim forces had been considerably strengthened they lost heart. Finding further resistance futile the Patriarch of Jerusalem sued for peace. He said that it was written in their holy books that the city would surrender to the man who was the best among the Muslims. He accordingly desired that the Caliph Umar should come to Jerusalem personally to receive the surrender of the city.

Abu Ubaidah referred the matter to Hadrat Umar at Madina. Hadrat Umar called a meeting of his Consultative Council, and asked for their advice, Hadrat Usman expressed the view that it was not necessary for the Caliph to go, and that the defeated Byzantines would themselves surrender. Hadrat Ali said that Jerusalem was as much sacred to the Muslims as the Jews or the Christians, and that in view of the sanctity of the place it was desirable that its surrender should be received by the Caliph personally. Hadrat Umar decided to accept the advice of Hadrat Ali.

Leaving Hadrat Ali as his deputy at Madina, Hadrat Umar proceeded to Jerusalem. No retinue accompanied the Caliph. Hadrat Umar was accompanied by one slave only, and between these two persons they had only one camel which they rode turn by turn. As they neared Jabiya where the Muslim Commanders were to meet Hadrat Umar, it was the turn of the slave to ride. The slave wanted Hadrat Umar to ride the animal, but Hadrat Umar refused. As they came to Jabiya the people saw the strange spectacle of the slave riding the camel and the Caliph walking on foot.

At Jabiya the Muslim Commanders met Hadrat Umar. Abu Ubaidah was dressed in coarse garments, and Hadrat Umar was much pleased to meet him. Yazid b. Abu Sufiyan, Khalid bin Walid and some other commanders were dressed in fine clothes and Hadrat Umar expressed his displeasure at their gaudy dress. Abu Ubaidah explained in detail the situation in Syria. He elaborated how with the grace of God the Muslims had been able to overthrow the mighty Byzantine power in Syria. As Hadrat Umar saw the green fields, orchards and lofty buildings of Syria he was greatly moved and he recited from the Holy Qur'an:

"They have left many a garden, fountain, park, arbour, and riches which they used to enjoy. Thus it is that We put another community in possession thereof."

A deputation from Jerusalem waited on Hadrat Umar at Jabiya and a treaty was drawn up. According to the treaty security of life and property were guaranteed to all citizens of Jerusalem. The safety of churches and other religious buildings and places was provided for. The citizens were required to pay Jizya. Any one not agreeable to owe allegiance to the Muslims was given the option to leave the city.

After the treaty had been drawn up, Hadrat Umar decided to travel to Jerusalem. Again he travelled in a simple way as an ordinary traveller. No guard was suffered to accompany him. He rode on a poor horse, and refused to change it for a better charger.

At the gate of Jerusalem, Hadrat Umar was greeted by the Patriarch of Jerusalem, the elite of the city, and the Muslim Commanders. While those who had come to receive him wore costly dress, Hadrat Umar was dressed in a garment of coarse cloth ordinarily worn by an average Arab. When some one advised him to wear a better dress befitting the State occasion, Hadrat Umar turned down the suggestion saying that he derived his strength and status from his faith in Islam, and not from any dress. When the Patriarch of Jerusalem saw the ascetic simplicity of the Caliph of Islam, and then looked to his own costly dress, he said, "Verily Islam has excelled all other religions".

The Partriarch of Jerusalem handed over the keys of the city of Jerusalem to Hadrat Umar. The Muslims were now the masters of Jerusalem. That was a special divine favour of God to the Muslims. As Hadrat Umar entered the city he was greeted by the citizens with great enthusiasm. Hadrat Umar said that he wanted to be led to some place where he could offer thanksgiving prayer to God. He was led to a Church, but he refused to pray there, on the ground that that would set a precedent for the Muslims of the following generations to forcibly convert churches into mosques. He was thereafter led to a place where the Prophet David used to pray. Here Hadrat Umar offered special prayers of thanksgiving and all the Muslims joined him. As the Byzantines watched the Muslims at pray, they felt that such people so obedient to God were bound to command. The Patriarch said that he was not sorry for surrendering the city for he had surrendered it to a better people.

Hadrat Umar stayed in Jerusalem for a few days. He reorganised the administration, and made the necessary arrangements to look after the needs of the citizens. He founded a mosque at an elevated place in the city. This mosque came to be known as Umar's Mosque. On the inaugural occasion Hadrat Bilal was requested to give the call to prayer as he used to do in the time of the Holy Prophet. After the death of the Holy Prophet, Hadrat Bilal had ceased to give the 'Adhan.' At the request of Hadrat Umar he agreed to give the Adhan to mark the foundation of Umar's mosque. As Hadrat Bilal gave the call to pray in his stentorian voice, Hadrat Umar and the Muslims wept recalling the days when the Holy Prophet used to be in their midst. As the inspiring words of the Adhan resounded in the hills and dales, the people stood in awe realising that a new era had dawned in Syria.

HADRAT UMAR'S ADDRESS AT JABIYA

After receiving the surrender of Jerusalem and completing the tour of Syria when Hadrat Umar was returning to Madina he led the prayer at Jabiya. On this occasion he delivered an address which is preserved in history.

In the course of the address, Hadrat Umar said:

"O ye people I counsel you to read the Qur'an. Try to understand it and ponder over it. Imbibe the teachings of the Qur'an. Then practise what the Qur'an teaches. The Qur'an is not theoretical; i it is a practical code of life. The Qur'an does not bring you the message of the Hereafter only; it is primarily intended to guide you in this life. Mould your life in accordance with the teachings of Islam for that is the way of your well being. By following any other way you will be inviting destruction.

Fear Allah, and whatever you want seek from Him. All men are equal. Do not flatter those in authority. Do not seek favours from others. By such acts you demean yourself. And remember that you will get only that is ordained for you, and no one can give you anything against the will of God. Then why seek things from others over which they have no control? Only supplicate God for He alone is the sovereign.

And speak the truth. Do not hesitate to say what you consider to be the truth. Say what you feel. Let your conscience be your guide. Let your intentions be good, for verily God is aware of your intentions. In your deeds your intentions count. Fear God, and fear no one else. Why fear others when you know that whatever sustenance is ordained for you by God you will get under all circumstances? And again why fear when you know that death is ordained by God alone and will come only when He wills ?

Allah has for the time being made me your ruler. But I am one of you. No special privileges belong to me as a ruler. I have some responsibilities to discharge, and in this I seek your cooperation. Government is a sacred trust, and it is my endeavour not to betray the trust in any way. For the fulfilment of the trust I have to be a watchman. I have to be strict. I have to enforce discipline. I have to run the administration not on the basis of any personal idiosyncracies, I have to run it in public interest and for promoting the public good. For this we have the guidance in the Book of God. Whatever orders I issue in the course of day to day administration have to conform to the Qur'an. God has favoured us with Islam. He sent to us His Messenger. He has chosen us for a mission. Let us fulfil that mission. That mission is the promotion of Islam. In Islam lies our safety; if we err we are doomed."

PLAGUE

In the winter of 638-639 virulent plague broke out in Syria, Egypt and Iraq. The plague exacted its heaviest toll in Syria, particularly Amwas, and the plague came to be known as the Amwas plague.

When Hadrat Umar heard of the outbreak of plague he decided to proceed to Syria personally to watch the measures to be adopted to suppress the epidemic.

When Hadrat Umar reached Surgh a few stages from Madina, he met Abu Ubaidah and other officers of the Muslim army in Syria. He was told that the virulence of the plague was increasing and that people were dying in thousands.

Many persons advised Hadrat Umar that he should not proceed to the infected area. Hadrat Umar held a counsel. Abu Ubaidah suggested that Hadrat Umar should visit the infected areas. Abdul Rahman bin Auf quoted a tradition of the Holy Prophet according to which the Holy Prophet had enjoined that when plague was raging one should not go from the non-infected to infected area or vice versa. That sattled issue and Hadrat Umar decided to return to Madina.

Abu Ubaidah did not feel happy at the decision of Hadrat Umar. He said:

"O Amir-ul-Mumnin, why are you flying from God's will." Hadrat Umar replied that he merely moved from one will of God to another will.

On return to Madina, Hadrat Umar addressed a letter to Abu Ubaidah asking him to come to Madina as he wanted to consult him on some important matters. Abu Ubaidah guessed the purpose of the call and wrote back saying that

Fate ruled everything, and that he could not move away from Syria to save his own life leaving others in danger.

Hadrat Umar thereupon asked him to move the troops to a healthier place. Abu Ubaidah accordingly moved the troops to Jabiya which was noted for its good climate. A few days after the arrival of the troops at Jabiya, Abu Ubaidah caught plague and died. Before death he appointed Muadh b. Jabal as his successor.

Some Muslims held that the plague was a calamity. Addressing the troops on the occasion of the Friday prayer, Muadh said that the plague was not a calamity; it was a mercy of God. The son of Muadh caught plague. While his son lay on his death bed, Muadh addressing him said, "My son this is a visitation from God. Let there be no doubt in your heart on this account." The boy said, "You will find me resigned to the will of God" and with these words he breathed his last.

When Muadh returned after burying his son, he fell a prey to plague, and died a few days later. Amr bin Al-Aas succeeded him as the Commander-in-Chief of the Muslim forces in Syria. Amr bin Al-Aas shifted the troops to the hills. This measure proved satisfactory, and plague no longer menaced the troops.

When the fury of the plague was over, leaving Hadrat Ali in charge of Madina, Hadrat Umar travelled to Syria accompanied by his slave Yarfa. He first went to Ella in Palestine. A story is told that at Ella, he gave his shirt to the local priest to have it mended. The priest had the shirt mended. He also presented a new shirt to Hadrat Umar, but he did not accept the gift.

From Ella he proceeded to Damascus. He disbursed the salaries of the troops personally. Calling for the heirs of those who had died in the plague, he put them in possession of their inheritance. He established military outposts at strategic points and had the fortifications strengthened.

CONQUEST OF CAESAREA

Caesarea was an important town and port on the Mediterranean sea coast. Caesarea is now in ruins, but at the time of the invasion of Syria by the Muslims in the seventh century, it was a large city with three hundred busy streets. The city was populated by the Christians who were completly hellenised.

As Caesarea was a large port and had communications through sea with Constantinople as well as Alexandria, it continued to receive help from the Byzantines. As the Muslims had no navy they were unable to intercept such aid. As help could come to Caesarea through the sea, and mustered there as a menace to the Muslims, it was even at the early stages of campaigning in Syria felt by the Muslim high command that Caesarea should be captured by the Muslims.

The city was first invaded in 635 A.D under the command of Amr bin Al-Aas. The siege dragged on for several months without producing any result to the advantage of the Muslims. On the eve of the battle of Yermuk, the siege was lifted to enable all the Muslim forces concentrate at Yermuk.

After the conquest of Jerusalem, Hadrat Umar issued orders that as Caesarea was the only Byzantine pocket left in Palestine it should be conquered. Yazid bin Abu Sufyan was appointed to the command. He marched with an army 17,000 strong and invested the city. A few days later he caught plague and withdrew to Damascus where he died.

After the virulence of the plague was over, Hadrat Umar ordered that another campaign should be launched against Caesarea. This time Muawiyah bin Sufyan the brother of the former commander Yazid was appointed to the command. Muawiyah pressed the siege. There were occasional skirmishes but thanks to the help that could come to the besieged through the sea, the city held out.

The city was populated by the Christians but there was a sizable minority of the Jews in the city as well. Some disputes arose between the Christians and the Jews, and in order to seek vengeance from the Christians the Jews decided to help the Muslims in their fight against the Christians.

One day, a Jew Yusuf by name came to the Muslim commander Muawiyah and told him that if the Muslims granted amnesty to the Jews they would help the Muslims win the city. Muawiyah gave the Jews the amnesty they asked for. Yusuf accordingly told the Muslim commander of a subterranean passage that led to the citadel. At night a Muslim contingent crept into the city through the subterranean passage and overpowering the guards opened the gates of the city for the main Muslim army to enter.

The Christians fought to the last and they were killed in thousands. Brought to bay the Christians surrendered on the usual terms of paying the Jizya. Caesarea fell in 640 A.D., and that was the last Muslim campaign in Syria. With the fall of Caesarea the entire Syria came under the control of the Muslims.

THE MUSLIMS AND THE SEA

With the capture of Caesarea and other towns in Syria which were also ports, the Muslims stood on the shore of the Mediaterranean. The capture of Alexandria in Egypt brought the Muslims still closer to the sea.

With the sea stretching before them, some of the Muslim warriors and administrators came to feel that the Muslims should become the masters of the sea as they had become the masters of the land.

After the conquest of Syria, the country was divided into three provinces. These were Northern Syria; Central Syria; and Southern Syria,with capitals at Emessa, Damascus, and Jerusalem respectiveiy. Muawiyah was the Governor of Central Syria. He was an ambitious man, and he thought that the sea should be no barrier to the westward march of Islam. He also felt that even for the protection of Syria which was a coastal country, it was necessary that the Muslims should become a naval power. In order to protect the maritime frontiers of the Muslim dominions, Muawiyah was strongly of the view that the island of Cyprus in the Mediterranean should be captured by the Muslims so as to serve as a base for naval operations.

After a good deal of thinking, Muawiyah wrote to Hadrat Umar explaining his project, and seeking permission to lead an expedition to conquer Cyprus. Hadrat Umar was not as ambitious as Muawiyah. Hadrat Umar stood more for consolidation than expansion. He had his own prejudices against water. In all his instructions to his Generals Hadrat Umar repeatedly emphasised 'let there be no expanse of water between you and me'. Hadrat Umar had no idea of conquering any lands beyond the sea

On receipt of the letter of Muawiyah, Hadrat Umar

thought fit to obtain the advice of Amr bin Al-Aas, the Conqueror of Egypt whose province was also washed by the Mediterranean. Amr bin Al-Aas expressed his views in the following terms:

> "O Commanderof the Faithful. I have seen a numerous people, going upon the sea, overpowered by a few. When it is calm it tends the heart, and when it is in motion it twists the brain. It weakens confidence and streng thens doubt. There is nothing there but sky and water. People at sea are like a worm in a log of wood. If their boat inclines they sink, and if they survive they are dazed."

Amr bin Al-Aas assessed the matter in a poetic vein, and not as a military commander of a nation commissioned by Allah to carry His message to all corners of the world. In view of Hadrat Umar's own aversion to the sea this reply of Amr b. Al-Aas appealed to the Caliph, and on the basis of this letter, Hadrat Umar wrote to Mauwiyah as follows :

> "We have heard that the Syrian Sea rises higher than the highest thing on earth; and that it seeks Allah's permission day and night to spread over the earth and drown it. So how can I send forces over this terrible infidel. By Him who sent Muhammad with the truth, I shall never send any Muslim upon it. The Muslim is dearer to me than the Roman whale. Beware of asking me again."

SECOND BATTLE OF EMESSA

Jazira was the land in upper reaches of the Tigris and the Euphrates. It was populated by tribes professing the Christian faith. When Syria was lost to the Christian Byzantines, the Christian tribes of Jazira persuaded Heraclius the Byzantine emperor to make another attempt to drive away the Muslims Syrian soil. In this task the Christian tribes of Jazira offered to come to the assistance of the Byzantine forces.

Heraclius welcomed the offer. A large Byzantine army was assembled and it was led to Syria to have another confrontation with the Muslims. Large contingents of Christian tribes crossed over to Syria from Jazira. All these armies headed towards Emessa. The strategy of the Christians was to occupy Emessa which was the key to North Syria.

In the view of the Christian pressure, Abu Ubaidah mustered all Muslim forces in North Syria at Emessa, and decided to play the defensive role. When the Christian forces came to Emessa they found the gates of the city of Emessa shut against them.

Abu Ubaidah wrote to Hadrat Umar and asked for reinforcements. Hadrat Umar had established military contonments in important cities where reserves were available for tmobilisation in the case of emergency. Hadrat Umar despatched fleet couriers to selected cantonments requiring the commanders of the stations to despatch reinforcements to Emessa immediately.

Qaqa b. Amr was stationed at Kufa. Hadrat Umar directed him to hasten with 4,000 cavalry to Emessa. Hadrat Umar himself proceeded with some force from Madina. The Caliph himself stayed at Damascus, but he sent the force to Emessa.

As the Christian tribes from Jazira were the main component of the invading army, Hadrat Umar decided to taunch an attack against Jazira. Suhail b. Adi was directed to dash to Jazira and attack the Christian tribes at Emessa from the rear. Abdullah b. Utban was asked to lead a contingent to Nisibin and launch an attack at the heart of Jazira. Walid bin Uqbah was deputed on a diplomatic mission to Jazira to negotiate with the Arab tribes in Jazira, and persuade them to withdraw their support from the Byzantines.

At Emessa, Abu Ubaidah held a council of war. The point for consideration was whether the Muslims should sally forth from the city and give the enemy a fight, or whether they should remain locked up in the city and watch further developments. Khalid bin Walid was in favour of an offensive and giving the enemy a fight. The contrary view was that for the time being the Muslims should remain on the defensive, and an attack should be launched when an adequate reinforcement had been received. Abu Ubaidah decided to await further aid.

When Jazira itself was attacked by Muslim contingents under Suhail b. Adi and Abdullah b. Utban the warriors of the Christian tribes at Emessa decided to return to Jazira to protect their own homes and hearths. Negotiations with the Arab tribes at Jazira also bore fruit and they agreed to support their Arab brethren instead of the Byzantines.

At this stage the Muslim forces in the city of Emessa sallied forth from their fortification and dashed against the Christian forces that were still there. The Christians could not withstand the attack, and they beat retreat after suffering heavy losses. The Christian army was routed and they took to flight. That was the last battle of the Byzantines on the Syrian soil. Syria was now completely under the domination of the Muslims.

AMR BIN AL AAS

Abu Ubaidah the Commander-in-Chief of the Muslim forces in Syria died of plague in 639 A.D. Other Muslim Generals who fell victims to plague included Shurahbeel b. Hasana and Yazid bin Abi Sufyan. On the death of the senior Generals, Amr bin Al-Aas was appointed as the Commander-in-Chief of the Muslim forces in Syria.

Amr bin Al-Aas belonged to the Bani Sahm clan of the Quraish. Like the other Quraish chiefs, Amr opposed Islam in the early days. He commanded a Quraish contingent at the of battle of Uhud. In 630 A.D. in the company of Khalid bin Walid, Amr bin Al-Aas rode from Mecca to Madina and there both of them were converted to Islam. Thereafter Amr took part in all the campaigns fought by the Muslims.

There is a story that in the days of ignorance when Amr was young he travelled once to Palestine with a caravan. One day was the duty of Amr to shepherd the camels of the caravan in the plain outside Jerusalem. It was a hot day, and as Amr sat under the shade of a tree, he saw a weary traveller come that way. The traveller appeared to be in a bad state because of thirst. Amr placed his water skin at the disposal of traveller who drank to his fill. Having quenched his thirst the traveller lay to rest under a nearby tree and soon he was sleep.

A little later Amr saw a snake crawl out from a hole and proceed to the sleeping traveller. Amr took out his bow and shot an arrow at the snake which fell dead. After some time the traveller woke to find that a dead snake lay near him. He asked Amr as to what had happened, and Amr told him that he had shot at the snake.

Turning to Amr, the traveller said, "You have saved my life twice firstly when I was dying of thirst, and secondly when I was exposed to the danger of the snake". He said that he would pay him an amount equivalent to the blood money for two lives. He stated that he had come to Jerusalem on a pilgrimage from Egypt. He was a priest in Egypt. He wanted Amr to accompany him to Egypt where he would pay the blood money. Amr hesitated to visit Egypt but the Egyptian priest painted such a rosy picture of Egypt that the curiosity of Amr was excited and he ultimately agreed to accompany the Egyptian priest.

Amr and the Egyptian priest travelled to Egypt. Throughout the journey the priest looked after all the needs of Amr. When they reached Alexandria Amr was lodged in a magnificent mansion and treated as a royal guest. The host of Amr took him to attend the Festival at the Hippodrome. One of the rites performed at the Festival was the Golden Ball rite. A high priest struck a golden ball and sent it flying io the air. The belief was that he in whose sleeve the golden ball landed would be the ruler of Egypt. When the high priest struck the golden ball every one followed the path of the golden ball with tense expectation. As the ball curved in the air, it landed in the sleeve of Amr. The spectators were dumbstruck. They could not believe that an uncouth Arab from the desert could rule over Egypt. They thought that there had been some mistake somewhere in the shooting of the golden ball.

The host of Amr said to him, "Congratulations for one day you will rule over Egypt. How you will come to rule over Egypt I cannot say, but this omen from the gods on high can never be false. Strange are the ways of destiny and who knows some day you may come here as the ruler of Egypt."

Amr returned from Egypt loaded with gifts and money. The episode of the golden ball always remained fresh in the memory of Amr. He often tried to dismiss it as an idle dream, but in his heart of hearts there was a strong conviction that some day he would march to Egypt as its victor.

When Amr became the Commander-in-Chief of the Muslim forces in Syria, he incessantly thought of Egypt and his destiny to conquer it. Hadrat Umar visited Syria in 639. On this occasion Amr waited on Hadrat Umar and said:

> "O Commander of the Faithful, permit me to march on Egypt. It will be a source of strength and sustenance for Muslims. It is the richest of lands on earth".

Hadrat Umar was not favourably inclined to the proposal, but Amr persisted. Ultimately Hadrat Umar gave way and he said:

> "Go and I shall seek Allah's guidance in the matter of your going. If on your march you receive a letter from me and I wish you to turn back then turn back if you have not entered Egypt by that time. If you have crossed the frontier when you receive my letter, then you may proceed and may God help you."

Having wrung this conditional permission from Hadrat Umar Amr bin Al-Aas took a contingent of 4,000 picked soldiers and immediately took the road to Egypt.

MARCH TO EGYPT

After Amr b. Al-Aas had left for Egypt with 4,000 soldiers only, Hadrat Umar on second thought considered that it was idle to expect to conquer such a large country as Egypt with vast manpower and resources with a meagre force of 4,000. Hadrat Umar accordingly wrote a letter to Amr b. Al-Aas asking him to come back. A post script was however added:

> "If you receive this letter when you have already crossed into Egypt then you may proceed. Allah will help you and I will also send such reinforcement as may be needed."

The letter was sent through a special messenger Uqba bin Amr.

Uqba caught up Amr at Rafat a little short of the frontier. Guessing what might be in the letter, Amr ordered the army to quicken up its speed. Turning to Uqba, Amr said that he would receive the Caliph's letter from him when the army had halted after the day's journey. Uqba being not aware of the contents of the letter agreed and marched along with the army.

The Muslim army halted for the night at Shajratein. This was a place well within the Egyptian territory. Now the Caliph's letter was received and read. Amr consulted his companions as to the course of action to be adopted. The unanimous view was that as they had received the letter on the Egyptian soil, they had the permission to proceed. To the Caliph, Amr wrote:

> "We have received your letter when we have reached Egypt. Therefore in the fulfilment of destiny we proceed seeking Allah's blessing."

When Hadrat Umar received the reply, he decided to watch further developments.

From Shajratein, the Muslim army marched to Areesh.

It was a small town where there was no garrison. No resistance was offered and the citizens offered allegiance on the usual terms. That was the Eid-uz-Zuha day. The Muslims celebrated the Eid festival at Areesh and offered the usual sacrifices.

In the later part of December 639 the Muslim army reached Farma. It was a fortified town manned by a Byzantine garrison. The Muslims besieged the town. There were sallies and counter sallies with no decisive result. The siege dragged on for two months. Towards the fall of February 640 an assault group led by Useifa b. Wala assaulted the fort and captured the gate through which the rest of the Muslim army entered. Thereupon the Byzantine resistance collapsed and the city was captured by the Muslims.

After the fall of Farma the Muslims marched to Bilbeis 40 miles from Memphis. It was a fortified town, and the Muslims besieged it. The siege lasted for a month, and towards the end of March 640 the city surrendered to the Muslims.

From Bilbeis the Muslims marched to Babylon. Amr had visualised that the conquest of Egypt would be a walk over. This expectation was belied. Even at the outposts of Farma and Bilbeis the Muslims had to meet stiff resistance. The siege of Farma had lasted for two months and that of Bilbeis for one month.

Babylon was a larger and more important city and here resistance on a larger scale was expected. Amr nevertheless persevered and pushed on to Babylon.

BATTLE OF BABYLON

After the fall of Bilbeis the Muslims advanced to Babylon. It was the key city of Egypt. Close to it was Memphis the ancient capital of the Pharaohs. Modern Cairo is not far from what at one time was known as Babylon. The Muslims arrived before Babylon some time in May 640 A.D.

Babylon was a fortified city, and the Byzantines had prepared it for a siege. Outside the city, a ditch had been dug and a large force was positioned in the area between the ditch and the city walls. The fort of Babylon was a massive structure 60 ft. high with walls more than 6 ft. thick. The fort was studded with numerous towers and bastions.

As soon as Amr arrived at Babylon he formed up his force of 4,000 men in assault formation and attacked the Byzantine positions in front of him. It led to some hard fighting, and the attack was repulsed by the Byzantines. Amr pulled his men back and went into camp near the east bank of the Nile. The Byzantine force in Babylon was six times the strength of the Muslim force.

The Muslims launched attacks every now and then, but these were repulsed. For two months the confrontation wore on with the Byzantines sitting tight in their defences and repulsing the frequent Muslim attacks against the crossings of the ditch.

In July, Amr wrote to Hadrat Umar asking for reinforcement. In August a reinforcement 4,000 strong came from Syria. Thus reinforced the Muslims renewed their attacks with greater force, but their attacks were not able to make any headway against Byzantine resistance. In these desultry fightings, a good number of Byzantine soldiers was killed, but no dents were made in the defences of the city. The attacks were called off and Amr again wrote to Hadrat Umar for more help.

Hadrat Umar raised a force in Madina for despatch to Egypt. Among those who volunteered to fight on the Egyptian front was Zubair bin Al-Awam, a cousin of the Holy Prophet. Hadrat Umar indeed offered Zubair the chief command of Egypt. Zubair did not accept the chief command, but he agreed to go to the help of Amr bin Al-Aas.

Reinforcement, 4000 strong was thus despatched from Madina to Egypt. It comprised four columns each column one thousand strong. These columns were commanded by Zubair b. Al-Awwam; Miqdad bin Al-Aswad; Ubaidah bin As-Samit, and Kharija bin Hudhaifah. Each Commander was in military prowess equal to a thousand men, and was the counterpart of Persian 'Hazar Mard' or gladiators.

This reinforcement arrived at Babylon sometime in September 640. The total strength of the Muslim force now rose to 12,000 and this was quite a modest strength. The Muslims now renewed their attacks against the Byzantines. In the attack launched by the Muslims some hard fighting followed, and some Byzantine detachments posted in front of the ditch were driven behind the ditch. The Byzantine defences, however, remained unshaken.

Ten miles from Babylon was Heliopolis. It was the city of the Sun Temple of the Pharaohs. There was the danger that some Byzantine force from Heliopolis might attack the Muslims from the flank while it was engaged with the Byzantine army at Babylon. With some detachments Amr and Zubair marched to Heliopolis. There was a cavalry clash outside Heliopolis, and though many Byzantines were killed, the engagement was not decisive. At an unguarded point, Zubair and some of his picked soldiers scaled the wall of the city, and after overpowering the guards opened the gates for the Muslim army to enter. Thereupon the local Byzantine garrison laid down their arms, and the city was occupied by the Muslims.

From Heliopolis Amr and Zubair with their force returned to Babylon to press the siege against the Byzantines with greater force. The Byzantines now began to sally forth across the ditch and attack the Muslims. The Muslims invariably repulsed such attacks. The sallies increased in intensity and the Muslim counter charge also gained in intensity. It was a see-saw affair leading to a condition of stalemate with no side gaining a positive advantage.

To break this stalemate the Muslim high command approved a stratagem. The following day when the Byzantines launched the attack the Muslims fell back according to a determined plan. The Byzantines thought that they had overpowered the Muslims. They pressed the attack, and the Muslims continued to withdraw till the entire Byzantine army had crossed the ditch. At a signal of Amr, five hundred Muslim horsemen led by Kharija bin Huzafa broke cover and rode out in rear of the Byzantine army. The main Muslim army now turned back and charged the Byzantines with great violence. Reeling from Muslim blows the Byzantines moved back to be attacked in the rear by Kharija and his men.

The Byzantine forces were now thrown into confusion. Many Byzantines were killed, but the main Byzantine army managed to cross the ditch and seek shelter in the walled city. The Byzantines entered the city and shut the gates. The area between the ditch and the city came to be occupied by the Muslims and that was a tactical advantage. The Muslims brought some catapults into action and started hurling boulders inside the city. That caused considerable distress to the Byzantines locked up in the city. Maqauqas the Viceroy of Egypt and the High Priest of the Copts who had his headquarter in Babylon shifted his headquarter to the Isle of Rauda in the Nile which was a much safer place. The Byzantine General Theodorus remained in Babylon to conduct the operations.

From the Isle of Rauda, Maqauqas sent emissaries to the Muslim camp inviting negotiations. These emissaries remained in the Muslim camp for two days, and when they returned they were accompanied by some Muslim emissaries. The Muslim envoys saw Maqauqas, and they offered the Byzantines the usual three alternatives, Islam, Jizya, or arbitration by sword, Maqauqas wanted some time to consider the matter and the Muslim envoys returned.

Turning to his emissaries, Maqauqas asked as to what they had seen in the Muslim camp. The emissaries said: "We found a people to each of whom death is dearer than life, and humility dearer than pride. None of them has a desire or greed for this world." On hearing this Maqauqas thought that the Egyptians could not fight against such a people, and that the best course for them was to negotiate peace. He accordingly asked Amr to send another delegation for negotiating peace.

Amr accordingly sent a delegation of ten picked warriors led by Ubada bin Al-Samit. All of them were over six feet tall and Ubada was the giant of a man doing about seven feet tall. Maqauqas talked long of the might of the Byzantine empire. He said that Heraclius would be sending a very large force, and the Muslims could not be a match for the Byzantine force. He stressed that the best course for the Muslims was to withdraw from Egypt. He said that he would give as a gift an amount of two dinars to each soldier, an amount of 100 dinars to each Commander, and one thousand dinars to the Caliph.

Ubada made Maqauqas understand that the Muslims could not be frightened by the strength of the enemy, nor could they be bought with gold. They were fighting in the name of Allah, and if they won they would have all they wanted; if they died they would get paradise. Ubada offered the usual three alternatives Islam, Jizya, and sword. Maqauqas enquired whether a fourth alternative was possible, and Ubada said "No". Maqauqas consulted his men. He wanted them to accept the offer of Jizya, but they did not agree. Under the advice of his counsellors, Maqauqas repeated his offer of dinars, and doubled the amount. The Muslims rejected the offer contemptuously. Thereupon the negotiations broke down and the Muslim envoys returned from the Isle of Rauda.

In Babylon itself there was a round of negotiations between Theodorus the Byzantine Commander and Amr b. Al-Aas. Amr himself went to Theodorus to have the matter talked over. Theodorus adopted a patronising attitude and wanted the Muslims to retire after receiving a few dinars each. The offer was brushed aside by Amr, and when the usual three alternatives were offered to Theodorus he said that the Byzantines knew how to wield their swords. When the negotiations broke down, and Amr was to return, Theodorus said in a boastful mood: "You have entered, now see how you get out." Theodorus sent word to the guard at the gate that as Amr would cross the gate, something should fall on him to crush him. Amr shrewd as he was sensed the danger. At the time of parting handshake with Theodorus Amr said, "I go but I will return with some of my senior colleagues so that you may talk to them as you have talked to me, and let us hope we may reach a decision acceptable to both the parties." Theodorus took these words at their face value and he came personally to the gate to see off the Commander-in-Chief of the Muslim forces.

Theodorus waited in vain for another visit of Amr and his companions. Amr said that he would visit Babylon again but that would be as a victor after the city had been conquered. The siege of Babylon had begun in May and it had dragged on till December. The Muslims now became very much concerned at the delay in capturing the city. Zubair had a reconnaissance of the city and he came across a point which was unguarded. On the 20th of December when it was a moonless night, Zubair and some soldiers accompanying him managed to scale the wall. Then they rushed to the gate and killing the guards opened the gate for the Muslim army to enter. The Muslim army rushed inside the city. Some resistance was offered which was soon overcome. When it was day it was found that Theodorus and his army had slipped away to the Isle of Rauda by the river route. The city of Babylon was captured by the Muslims on 21st December 640.

On the 22nd December, Maqauqas entered into a treaty with the Muslims. By the treaty, Muslim suzerainty over the whole of Egypt was recognised, and the Egyptians agreed to pay Jizya at the rate of 2 dinars per male adult. The treaty was subject to the approval of the emperor Heraclius, but Maqauqas stipulated that even if the emperor repudiated the treaty, he and the Copts of whom he was the High Priest would honour the terms of the treaty, recognise the supremacy of the Muslims and pay them Jizya.

Maqauqas submitted a report to Heraclius and asked for his approval to the terms of the treaty. He also offered reasons in justification of the acceptance of the terms of the treaty.

Amr b. Al-Aas submitted a detailed report to Hadrat Umar and asked for his further instructions,

MARCH TO ALEXANDRIA

When Hadrat Umar received the report of Amr bin Al-Aas about the conquest of Babylon and the treaty with Maqauqas, he wrote back to say that he approved of the terms provided Heraclius agreed to submit to them. He desired that as soon as the reactions of Heraclius were known, he should be informed so that further necessary instructions might be issued.

Heraclius's reaction to the report of Maqauqas was violent. He remarked sarcastically that the Muslim force hardly numbered 12,000 while the Byzantine force in Egypt was five times as large leaving aside the Copts. Maqauqas was removed from the Viceroyship of Egypt, but he remained the Head of the Coptic Church. This was a matter in which the emperor could not interfere. Heraclius sent strict orders to the Commander-in-chief of the Byzantine forces in Egypt that the Muslims should be driven from the soil of Egypt.

Maqauqas waited on Amr and told him that Heraclius had repudiated the treaty of Babylon. Maqauqas assured Amr that so far as the Copts were concerned the terms of the treaty would be followed, but they were not responsible for the Byzantines. That was now an issue which the Muslims and the Byzantines might settle among themselves.

Maqauqas asked for three favours from the Muslims, namely:

1. Do not break your treaty with the Copts;
2. If the Byzantines after this repudiation ask for peace, do not make peace with them, but treat them as captives and slaves; and
3. When I am dead allow me to be buried in the Church of St. John at Alexandria.

This position was to the advantage of the Muslims. The Copts were the real natives of the land of Egypt. Both the Byzantines and the Muslims were strangers. Though some Copts from personal considerations continued to support the Byzantines, the sympathies of the Copts were now by and large with the Muslims. The Copts were not supposed to fight against the Byzantines on behalf of the Muslims but they undertook to help the Muslims in the promotion of war effort, help them in the provision of stores; build roads and bridges for them; and provide them moral support.

Under the circumstances the Muslim fight in Egypt was not against the Egyptians; it was against the Byzantines who were really intruders.

The Generals of the emperor mustered at Alexandria the capital of Egypt, and decided to wage a relentless war against the Muslims and drive them from Egypt.

Amr reported these developments to Hadrat Umar, and Hadrat Umar desired that before the Byzantines could gather further strength the Muslims should strike at them and drive them from Alexandria.

In February 641, Amr set off with his army from Babylon and the destination was Alexandria. On the third day of their march from Babylon the Muslims encountered a Byzantine detachment at Tarnut on the west bank of the Nile. Light action followed. The Byzantines could not hold the ground, and withdrew northwards to Alexandria.

While the main Muslim army halted at Tarnut, an advance guard under Shareek bin Sumayy was required to proceed forward. Twenty miles from Tarnut, Shareek came across a Byznatine detachment. The Byzantine force was very large, and it launched an attack on the Muslim advance guard thinking that they would be able to annihilate it. The Muslim advance guard fell back. The next day the Byzantine fell on the Muslim advance guard again, but in the meantime the main Muslim army had arrived and the Byzantines found safety in withdrawal.

The following day the Muslims resumed their march and reached Sulteis where they encountered a Byzantine detachment. Some hard fighting followed, but the Byzantine resistance soon broke down and they withdrew to Alexandria. The Muslims halted at Sulteis for a day and then resumed the march to Alexandria. Alexandria was still two day march from Sulteis.

After one day's march the Muslim forces arrived at Kirayun twelve miles from Alexandria. Here the Muslim advance to Alexandria was blocked up by a Byzantine detachment 20,000 strong. The strategy of the Byzantines was that the Muslims should be driven away before they actually arrived at Alexandria.

The two forces were deployed for action, and some hard fighting followed but the action remained indecisive. This state of affairs persisted for ten days. On the last day the Muslims launched a vigorous assault. The Byzantine resistance broke down, and they withdrew to Alexandria. The way to Alexandria having been cleared, the Muslim forces resumed the march from Kirayun and reached the outskirts of Alexandria some time in March 641 A.D.

BATTLE OF ALEXANDRIA

The Muslims appeared before Alexandria in March 641. Alexandria was heavily fortified. There were walls behind walls, and forts within forts. The Byzantine force within the city numbered 50,000 while the strength of the invading Muslim force was 12,000 only. There was no dearth of provisions and food supply in the city. The city had direct access to the sea, and through the sea route help from Constantinople in men and material could come any time.

As Amr surveyed the military situation, he felt that Alexandria would be a hard nut to crack. The Byzantines had high stakes in Alexandria, and they were determined to offer stiff resistance to the Muslims. Amr, however, felt that in spite of the heavy odds the Muslims would be able to conquer the city. The Muslims accordingly decided to lay siege to the city. The Byzantines mounted catapults on the walls of the city, and these engines pounded the Muslims with boulders. This caused considerable damage to the Muslims and Amr ordered his men back from the advance position so that they might be beyond the range of these missiles.

A see-saw war followed. When the Muslims tried to go close to the city they were pounded with missiles. When the Byzantines sallied from the fort, they were invariably beaten back by the Muslims.

Heraclius the Byzantine emperor collected a large reinforcement at Constantinople. He intended to march at the head of this reinforcement personally to Alexandria. Before he could finalise the arrangements he died. The reinforcement mustered at Constantinople dispersed, and no help came to Alexandria.

When the Muslims came to know that the Byzantine emperor had died and that no reinforcement was likely to come to Alexandria they intensified their attacks. In one of the assaults the Muslims got into one of the towers. On the Byzantine counter attack the Muslims withdrew. As the Byzantines closed the outer gate four Muslims were trapped inside. These four Muslims descended to an underground chamber. Because of the narrowness of the passage it was not possible for the Byzantines to descend to the chamber to capture these Muslims alive. Left to themselves these Muslims would have been starved to death within a few days. Among these four trapped Muslims were Amr b. Al-Aas the Commander-in-Chief of the Muslim force; Masalma bin Mukhallad a young stalwart, and two others. The Byzantines were not aware of the identity of these four Muslims. They took them to be ordinary soldiers of no particular significance.

In a playful mood the Byzantines asked these trapped Muslims to surrender for if they did not do so they would automatically die in the underground cellar within a few days. The Muslims refused to surrender. Thereupon the Byzantines said that they could be exchanged with Byzantine prisoners in the Muslim camp. This was also not agreed to by the trapped Muslims. Thereupon in a chivalrous mood the Byzantines said, ' Let us have a duel, one man out of you and one man from us. If your man kills our man, all of you can depart. If your man is killed the rest of you will be our captives". To this the Muslims agreed.

Amr wanted to offer himself for the duel, but Masalma a young man of great sinews prevailed upon him that he should let Masalma fight the duel. Amr ultimately agreed. The Byzantines gave a solemn undertaking in the terms of the agreement arrived at and the trapped Muslims came out of the cellar into the chamber where the duel was to be held.

The Byzantine champion stepped forward and he was met by Masalma from the Muslim side. The contest was hard and stiff, and it appeared as if the Byzantine champion would score. But ultimately Masalma scored and the Byzantine champion was killed. The Byzantines kept their word. After the duel was over they opened the gate of the tower and let the Muslims go in peace. Little did they know that these four included the Commander-in-Chief of the Muslim force.

The state of stalemate continued. The Muslims intensified their attacks but there was no slackening of the Byzantine resistance. The siege dragged on for six months, and in Madina Hadrat Umar got impatient. In a letter addressed to Amr the Caliph expressed his concern at the inordinate delay in the conquest of Egypt. Hadrat Umar wrote:

> "When you get this letter address the people and urge them to fight. Launch the attack in the early afternoon of a Friday for that is the hour of God's blessing."

Amr bin Al-Aas assembled his men, and read to them the letter of Hadrat Umar. Fiery speeches were held to inspire the Muslims to violent action. It was decided that after the ensuing Friday prayers an all-out assault would be launched on the enemy. Ubada was chosen to carry the standard and launch the assault.

The following Friday after the noon prayers, the Muslims marched to the battle-field with the coffins tied on their heads. They moved forward with the fury of a torrent, and all resistance was swept aside. Before the sun set the city was carried by the Muslims by storm. Over 20,000 Byzantines were killed or taken captive. The rest of the Byzantine army found safety in flight to Constantinople through ships that stood anchored in the port. Some wealthy traders also left.

On behalf of the Egyptians, Maqauqas sued for peace, and peace was allowed. In his report to the Caliph, Amr reported:

> "We have conquered Alexandria. In this city there are 4,000 palaces, 400 places of entertainment, and untold wealth."

The Muslim soldiers were keen to collect the war spoils and distribute them among themselves. Maqauqas pleaded that in pursuance of the terms of the treaty those Egyptians who had chosen to remain in the city could not be deprived of their belongings or property. Most of the Muslim soldiers were of the view that as Alexandria had been taken by sword the Muslims had the right to the spoils of war. The matter was referred to Hadrat Umar, and he decided that while the Muslims could appropriate all the property and assets of the former Government, the private property should not be touched if the owners were there.

With the fall of Alexandria the Muslims were the masters of Egypt.

After the fall of Alexandria, Amr bin Al-Aas deputed a fast rider Muawiyah bin Khudaij to carry the news of the victory of the Muslims to Hadrat Umar at Madina. When Muawiyah reached Madina it was noon. Muawiyah thought that Hadrat Umar would be resting at the time and it was inadvisable to disturb him. He accordingly went to the Prophet's mosque to await the arrival of the Caliph there to lead the afternoon prayers. A slave girl of Hadrat Umar who was passing that way happened to see the traveller. Her curiosity having been awakened she enquired from the traveller from where he had come and he said that he was coming from Alexandria. The slave girl knew how Hadrat Umar had been anxiously awaiting news from Alexandria. She accordingly rushed home and told Hadrat Umar that a man had come from Alexandria. Hadrat Umar asked the slave girl to go to the mosque to fetch the messenger from Alexandria.

As Muawiyah presented himself, Hadrat Umar anxiously enquired what news he had brought. Muawiyah said that he carried good news and that God in His mercy had given victory to the Muslims. Hadrat Umar then enquired from Muawiyah why did he not come straight to him. Muawiyiah said that he thought the Caliph would be resting and it was inadvisable to disturb him at that hour of the day. Thereupon Hadrat Umar said, "I am sorry that you have such a poor opinion of me. Who would bear the burden of the Caliphate, if I were to sleep during the days?"

THE NILE

It was an ancient custom with the Egyptians that some time in July a virgin decked in bridal clothes was thrown in the river as an offering to propitiate the God of the river Nile. Even when the Egyptians became Christians they continued to follow the ancient custom of sacrificing a virgin.

When Egypt came under Muslim rule, the Egyptian elders waited on Amr in July, and wanted his permission for continuing the old custom of throwing a virgin in the river to seek the pleasure of the God of the Nile.

Amr said that such a practice was repugnant to Islam and could not be permitted in an Islamic State. He argued that Islam knew of no God of the Nile and the question of any propitiation did not arise. Islam knew of only one God Allah and Allah did not stand in need of any propitiation.

The Egyptian elders listened to the argument but they did not feel satisfied. They warned Amr that unless the sacrifice was offered as heretofore the Nile would not rise in flood and the entire countryside would get arid.

Amr was however adamant that floods or no floods human sacrifice could not be permitted. The Egyptian leaders retired in a sullen mood.

The month of July passed away. No sacrifice was offered, and there was no rise in the level of the river. It was the month of August and still the river did not rise. The Egyptians shuddered at what would happen if the river did not rise. The month of August passed away and still there was no flood in the river. The Egyptian leaders sighed and said, "That is all due to Islam. The Muslims have brought this fate on us."

And even during September there was no sign of any rise in the level of the river. The Egyptians gave themselves to despair and most of them thought of migrating elsewhere.

That made Amr anxious. He reported the facts of the case to Hadrat Umar and wanted his instructions. Hadrat Umar approved of the action of Amr in not permitting the human sacrifice. Along with the letter, Umar sent a card on which it was written:

> "In the name of Allah the Beneficent, the Merciful. From the slave of Allah, Umar Commander of the Faithful to the Nile of Egypt.
>
> Everything in the Universe is subject to the will of Allah. The rise in your level is subject to the will of Allah, and we pray to Allah to command you to rise in level."

Hadrat Umar asked Amr that the card should be thrown in the middle of the river. On the eve of the Feast of the Christian Day of the Cross, Amr had the Christians assemble on the river bank and after reciting some verses from the Holy Qur'an and taking the name of God he threw the card of Hadrat Umar in the middle of the river. Then the Muslims assembled on the river bank lifted their hands in prayers seeking the blessings of God in making the river rise in level. The card of Hadrat Umar floated on the surface of the Nile for some distance and then it disappeared.

The next morning the river rose to its full flood height. Verily Allah had commanded the river to flow, and that was the end of the evil custom of sacrificing a virgin to secure a rise in the level of the river. That was the vindication of Islam. Many Egyptians now came to believe that Islam was a blessing and a true religion. They hastened to the Muslim camp and were converted to Islam.

FUSTAT

When the Muslims conquered Egypt, Alexandria was the capital of the country. When the Muslims conquered Alexandria, most of the Byzantine population evacuated the city. The vacant houses were occupied by the Muslims. Alexandria was the queen of cities. Amr bin Al-Aas and the other Muslims with him were much attracted by the city. Amr wanted to make Alexandria the capital of Muslim Egypt.

Amr wrote to Hadrat Umar seeking his permission to make Alexandria the capital of the province. Hadrat Umar was of the view that Alexandria being a maritime city would not be suitable for the Arabs. He did not give the permission asked for. He suggested that the capital should be established further inland at a central place, where no mass of water intervened between it and Arabia.

Amr accordingly proceeded to choose a suitable site for the capital of Egypt. His choice fell on the site where he had pitched his tent at the time of the battle of Babylon. His tent had been fixed about a quarter of a mile north east of the fort. After the battle was over, and the army was to march to Alexandria when the men began to pull down the tent and pack it for the journey it was found that a dove had nested on top of the tent and laid eggs. Amr ordered that the tent should remain standing where it was. The army marched away but the tent remained standing in the plain of Babylon.

In this unusual episode of the dove and its nest, Amr saw a sign from the Heaven. He decided " Where the dove laid its nest, let the people build their city". As Amr's tent was to be the focal point of the city, the city was called Fustat, which in Arabic means the tent.

The first structure to be built was the mosque which later became famous as Mosque of Amr bin Al-Aas. The plot for the mosque was so chosen that the Mihrab and the pulpit came to be located on the exact spot where the tent had stood. The mosque was completed in 642 A.D. The mosque had a pulpit from where Amr as the leader addressed the congregation. Hadrat Umar did not appreciate the idea of a pulpit. He wrote to Amr:

> "It has come to my notice that you have built a pulpit by means of which you stand above the shoulders of the Muslims, which is the same as your standing with the Muslims under your heel. I command you to dismantle the pulpit."

Amr complied with the order.

Amr built a house for himself next to the gate of the mosque. Adjoining this house were the houses of Companions including Zubair, Ubaidah, Abu Zar, Abu Ayub Ansari, Abdullah the son of Hadrat Umar and Abdullah the son of Amr bin Al- Aas. Amr reserved a plot for the construction of a house for Hadrat Umar. Hadrat Umar wrote that he had no idea of residing in Egypt. Under his orders the plot was utilised for the construction of a market.

All houses were of one storey. No one was allowed to construct a palatial building. Kharija bin Hudhaifah, however, constructed a two storeyed house. When this was brought to the notice of Hadrat Umar, he wrote to Amr:

> "It has come to my notice that Kharija bin Hudhaifah has built an upper storey. Perhaps Kharija wishes to see into the private apartments of his neighbours. When you get this letter demolish the upper storey".

The order was complied with.

The city of Fustat was built east of Babylon. In due course Fustat extended to include the old town of Babylon.

EXPEDITION TO NUBIA

The land of Nubia lay to the south of Egypt. It stretched from Aswan to Khartoum and from the Red Sea to the Libyan desert. The Nubians were Christians and were ruled by a king. The capital of the kingdom was Dumqula.

In the summer of 642, Amr bin Al-Aas sent an expedition to Nubia under the command of his cousin Uqba bin Nafe. The expedition was ordered by Amr bin Al-Aas on his own account, and it appears that the approval of Hadrat Umar to the undertaking of the expedition was not sought. Amr bin Al-Aas thought that the victory over the Nubians would be an easy affair and that he would inform the Caliph after he had conquered another land.

Uqba bin Nafe who later made a great name for himself as the Conqueror of Africa, and led his horse to the Atlantic complaining that there were no lands left for him to conquer in the way of Allah came in for an unhappy experience in Nubia.

In Nubia, no pitched battle was fought. There were only skirmishes and haphazard engagements and in such type of warfare the Nubians excelled the Muslims. The Nubians were skilful archers. We have it on the strength of Balazuri that they would shout to the Muslims where would they like to be hit by the arrow, and where the Muslims mockingly named some part of the body, the arrow invariably struck there to the great grief of the Muslims.

One day Uqba came across a concentration of the Nubians. Before the Muslims could attack the Nubians, the Nubians subjected the Muslims to a merciless barrage of arrows. The arrows were aimed at the eyes and in the encounter 250 Muslims lost their eyes.

The Nubians were very fast in their movements. The Muslim cavalry was known for its speed and mobility, but it was no match for the Nubian horse riders. The Nubians would strike hard against the Muslims, and then vanish before the Muslims could recover their balance and take counter action. The hit-and-run raids by the Nubians caused considerable damage to the Muslims.

Uqba wrote to Amr bin Al-Aas of the state of affairs. He said that the Nubians avoided pitched battle, and in the guerilla tactics that they followed the Muslims were the sufferers. Uqba further pointed out that Nubia was a poor land, and there was nothing therein worth fighting for or to tempt by way of booty.

Thereupon Amr bin Al-Aas asked Uqba to withdraw from Nubia. Uqba accordingly pulled out of Nubia with his forces. Muslims were not defeated, but it was a fact that their expedition had not succeeded. It was a drawn battle.

CONQUEST OF BURQA AND TRIPOLI

After the failure of the campaign of Nubia in the south Amr bin Al-Aas decided to undertake campaigns in the west. Some time in September 642, Amr led his troops to the west. After one month of marching the Muslim forces reached the city of Pentapolis. The country was nominally under the suzerainty of the Byzantines, but they had made no arrangements for the defence of the city. The Muslims accordingly occupied it without any resistance. The citizens sued for peace, and Amr gave them peace on the usual terms. A peace pact was drawn up whereunder the people agreed to pay Jizya. Two unusual conditions were at the instance of the people inserted in the treaty. The first was that in lieu of Jizya, it was open to the citizens to sell their children. The second was that no tax collector was to enter the city; they would themselves pay the Jizya at the appointed time. Amr stayed in the city for some time to reorganise the administration. The Muslims renamed the city of Pentapolis as Burqa.

From Burqa, Uqba bin Nafe was sent at the head of a column to undertake a campaign against Fezzan. Uqba marched to Zaweela the capital of Fezzan. No resistance was offered, and the entire district of Fezzan submitted to the Muslims. They agreed to pay Jizya, but they got a clause inserted in the treaty to the effect that a part of the Jizya coming in from the district was to be spent for the relief of the poor of the area.

After the conquest of Fezzan, Uqba returned to Burqa. Soon after the Muslim army marched westward from Burqa. They arrived at Tripoli in the spring of 643 A.D. Where was a Byzantine garrison here and they refused to surrender.

The Muslims accordingly laid siege to the city. Amr put his camp on a high ground and blocked all land routes to the city. The city however had free access to the sea, and the passage to the sea could not be blocked by the Muslims.

The Muslim army did not have siege equipment with them. The Byzantine garrison remained locked up within the fortifications and did not come out into the open. The siege accordingly dragged on for two months. One day a party of the Muslims accidentally discovered the passage that provided the city access to the sea. This party rushed into the city through this passage raising the shouts of 'Allah-o-Akbar.' The Byzantine garrison thought that the entire Muslim army had entered the city. There was panic in the city, and the Byzantine garrison sought refuge on board the ships that lay anchored in the harbour.

Hearing the shouts of 'Allah-o-Akbar' from inside the city, the Muslim army pressed the attack from outside, and after having scaled the walls got into the city. The Byzantine garrison fled to the ships and sailed away. The Muslims captured the city without resistance. The citizens surrendered on the usual terms.

From Tripoli, Amr sent a column to Sabrata a city forty miles from Tripoli. A feeble resistance was put up, and thereafter the city surrendered and agreed to pay Jizya.

From Tripoli Amr bin Al-Aas wrote to the Caliph, "We have conquered Burqa, Tripoli and Sabrata. The way to the west is clear, and if the Commander of the Faithful wishes to conquer more lands, we could do so with the grace of God."

Hadrat Umar replied, "It is not Afriqa, it is Mafriqa. Any further advance would be divisive and treacherous, Consolidate your position in Egypt, and there should be no further campaigning."

Amr bin Al-Aas accordingly abandoned Tripoli and Burqa and returned to Fustat. This was towards the close of the year 643 A.D.

PART V

Death, Assessment and Review

SHADOWS OF DEATH

Once the Holy Prophet saw in a dream that he was drawing water from a well. Then he stepped aside and asked Abu Bakr to draw water. Abu Bakr was able to draw two buckets only. While drawing the third bucket, he felt exhausted and stepped aside. Then Umar took the job, and he completed ten rounds. The Holy Prophet interpreted the dream to signify that after his death, Khilafat would vest in Abu Bakr, who would hold the office for two years and a few months. Thereafter Umar would succeed him, and his term of office would be ten years. When Hadrat Umar assumed office as Caliph, he had the conviction that he would die after ten years.

In the time of Hadrat Abu Bakr, Auf bin Malik Al-Shajjai a prominent companion had a dream in which it was indicated to him by an unknown power that Hadrat Umar was to be conspicuous for three things : firstly, that he would be a pillar of strength for Islam ; secondly, that he would be the Caliph; and thirdly, that he would die the death of a martyr. When the dream was narrated to Hadrat Umar in the time of Hadrat Abu Bakr, Hadrat Umar silenced Auf bin Malik saying "May Hadrat Abu Bakr live long ; do not talk of the caliphate of any one else. "When Hadrat Abu Bakr died and Hadrat Umar became the Caliph, he asked Auf bin Malik to narrate his dream. After hearing the dream, Hadrat Umar said, "How can I get martyrdom when I stay in Madina, and do not go to the field to take part in the battles against infidels. But then Hadrat Umar recalled that the Holy Prophet himself on more than one occasion had referred to him as 'Shahid'. He, therefore, felt that he might be blessed with martyrdom even in Madina.

In the battle of Nihawand, the Muslim forces by way of war strategy spread the news that the Caliph had died. That brought the enemy in the open and in the ensuing fight they were defeated, and the Muslims were victorious. When Hadrat Umar came to know of this, he said. "If with the death of Umar, Islam can be victorious, let Umar die a hundred times."

When the year 641 A.D. dawned, that being the tenth year of his rule, Hadrat Umar had the premonition that before the year ended, he would die.

That year the Hajj fell in the month of October. Hadrat Umar performed the Hajj in the company of all his wives and all the surviving wives of the Holy Prophet. Hadrat Umar had the feeling that that was his last Hajj. It is related that when Hadrat Umar stood at the mount of Arafat he heard a voice saying, "O Caliph, never again will you stand on the Mount of Arafat". When during the Hajj ceremony, Hadrat Umar threw pebbles at the devil, he once again heard a voice that that was to be his last Hajj".

Hadrat Ayesha who was present on the occasion of the pilgrimage has left on record that as the party treaded the path between Mina and Mecca, some unseen person addressing Hadrat Umar said :

" Upon such an Imam as thou be peace and blessings,
With your deeds you have prepared for the journey to the Heaven,
In this journey no one can outstrip you.
You brought glory to Islam ;
After you there will be distress,
But so is the will of God.
From God you came, and now to God return."

It is narrated by Said b. Al-Museeb that while at Mina, Hadrat Umar raised his hands and prayed :

"O Allah, I have now become old. I am feeling weakness in my limbs
O Allah I have done the mission entrusted to me to the best of my capacity. Now call me to Yourself before I feel imbecile to work in your cause. O Allah bless me with the death of a martyr, and may that be in Madina the city of your beloved."

Jabir bin Mutaam states that he was present at the time of the Hajj with Hadrat Umar. He relates :

> "We saw a man standing at the top of the hill and crying 'Verily that is the last Hajj of Umar. He will never come here again."

Abu Musa Ash'ari states that at that time he had a dream. In the dream he saw the Holy Prophet and Abu Bakr standing on a mountain. Hadrat Umar stood at the base. Hadrat Abu Bakr and the Holy Prophet asked him to come up and he climbed the mountain. The dream was interpreted to imply that the death of Hadrat Umar was imminent.

On the last Friday in October 644, while presiding at the Friday Prayers Hadrat Umar said that in a dream he had seen a bird peck at him and this implied that he was going to die. He said, "May be this is the last Friday prayer for me to preside, and thus ye faithful, farewell."

Kaab Ahbar, a soothsayer came to Hadrat Umar and said "O Caliph you are going to die within three days. You may nominate your successor if you like". Hadrat Umar enquired how he knew that he was to die within three days. He said that he knew that from the holy book Torah. Hadrat Umar enquired whether there was any reference to him in the Torah. Kaab said that Hadrat Umar was not mentioned as such in the Torah, but the Torah mentioned a king who was just like Hadrat Umar, Kaab said that when he read of that king, he always recalled Hadrat Umar.

About that king it was written in the Torah :

> "And he had with him a prophet who was inspired, and the Lord inspired the prophet to say to him "make thou the covenant, and write thy testament, for verily thou art a dead man within three days. The prophet therefore told him this, and when it was the third day, he fell down between the wall and the bed".

And as foretold by Kaab the soothsayer, Hadrat Umar was stabbed to death within three days.

A PERSIAN STABBED HADRAT UMAR

After the battle of Nihawand, many Persians, men, women, and children were taken as captives by the Muslims. The captives were sold as slaves. One of these slaves was Firoz Alias Abu Lulu. He was purchased by Mughira Shu'bah the Governor of Basra. This Firoz was a craftsman, a carpenter, an ironsmith and a painter. Hadrat Umar did not allow non-Muslim adult captives to reside in Madina. Mughira sought special permission for the residence of Firoz in Madina on the ground that as he was a skilled craftsman, he would be of service to the people. Hadrat Umar gave the permission as a special case.

One day, Firoz waited on Hadrat Umar and complained that the tax which his master Mughira was exacting from him was too high. He wanted the Caliph to reduce the levy. Hadrat Umar enquired what work did he do. He said that he worked as a carpenter, painter, and an ironsmith. He added that he could make windmills as well. Hadrat Umar next enquired as to the amount of the tax that he was required to pay to his master. He said that he had to pay two dirhams a day. Hadrat Umar said that keeping in view the lucrative nature of the jobs done by him, the levy of two dirhams a day was prima facie not excessive. Hadrat Umar said that he would, however, write to Mughira, and examine the question further in the light of what Mughira said. That did not satisfy Firoz, and he went away sulking.

Hadrat Umar wrote to Mughira, and in reply Mughira quoted facts and figures to establish that what he took from his slave was by no means excessive. When Firoz called on Hadrat Umar again, Hadrat Umar explained to him that as the levy was not excessive, no reduction therein was called for. That made Foroz angry. In order to humour Firoz, Hadrat Umar said, "I understand you make windmilis ; make one for me as well." In a sullen mood, Firoz said, "Verily I will make such a mill for you, that the world would talk about it." As Firoz went away, the Caliph told the people around him that the Persian slave had threatened him.

There were Persian children slaves in Madina. Seeing them, Firoz would say, "You have been enslaved at such a tender age. This Umar has eaten my heart. I will take his heart out". He made for himself a dagger with a very sharp edge and smeared it with poison.

On the 1st of November 644 A.D. at the time of the morning prayer, Firoz went with his dagger to the Prophet's mosque and hid himself in a corner in one of the recesses of the mosque. When the faithful stood for prayer after straightening the lines, and Hadrat Umar took up his position as the Imam to lead the prayer, Firoz emerged from his place of hiding and rushed at Hadrat Umar. Firoz struck Hadrat Umar six consecutive blows with his dagger, and Hadrat Umar fell on the floor profusely bleeding.

Other persons rushed at Firoz, but he had the fury and frenzy of a desperate man about him. He struck right and lefts, and thirteen Muslims were wounded, some of them fatally, before Firoz could be overpowered. At last realising that he could not escape, Firoz stabbed himself to death with his own dagger.

HADRAT UMAR ON DEATH BED

From the mosque Hadrat Umar was carried home. When he regained consciousness he asked who was his murderer. He was told that his murderer was the Persian slave Firoz. Thereupon Hadrat Umar said, "Praise be to God that I have not been murdered by a Muslim".

The physician administered him date cordial and milk. These could not be digested and gushed out of his wounds. That indicated that the wounds were fatal and that he could not survive for long.

The people around him praised him for his virtues and sterling qualities. He asked them not to praise him. He said:

> "All praise is to Allah. If all the treasures of the world were to be at my disposal, I would offer them as a ransom to be saved from the trial at the Day of Judgement."

He then recited the Arabic verse :
"I have been unjust to my soul,
Except that I am a Muslim,
Say my prayers and fast."

Hadrat Umar asked his son Abdullah to wait on Hadrat Ayesha and beg her permission for his burial by the side of the Holy Prophet and Hadrat Abu Bakr. Hadrat Ayesha wept as she came to know that Hadrat Umar was about to die. She said, "I had reserved this place for my own burial, but I give Hadrat Umar precedence over myself. Let him be buried there". When Hadrat Umar was told that Hadrat Ayesha had given the permission, he felt happy and said, "God bless Ayesha. She has fulfilled my greatest wish. Now I can die in peace."

Then he asked his son to estimate the debt that he had to pay. He was told that the debt amounted to eighty six thousand dirhams. This included the salary that he had drawn from the Baitul Mal during the period of his caliphate. He instructed that the debt should be paid by the sale of his property.

Thereafter Hadrat Umar gave detailed instructions to his son regarding his funeral. He said :

> "Be moderate in the expenses of my shroud, for verily if there is anything of good with God in my favour, He will give me in exchange what is better than it, and if I have been otherwise, He will strip me of all that I have. And be moderate in the grave that you dig for me, for verily if there be anything of good with God in my favour, He will widen it for me, and if I have been otherwise, He will make it narrow for me to squeeze my body. And let no woman go with my funeral. Praise me not for that which is not in me, for the Lord knows best what I am. Therefore when you carry me to the grave, hasten in your going, for if there is anything of good with God in my favour you will speed me to that which is good, and if I have been otherwise, you will cast from your necks an evil that you bear."

Thereafter Hadrat Umar turned his face to the Qibla and breathed his last. There was serene smile on his face as he lay dead.

HADRAT UMAR AND HIS SUCCESSOR

When Hadrat Umar was on his death bed, he was asked that he should nominate his successor. Hadrat Umar sighed and said, "Whom should I nominate my successor ? If Abu Ubaida had been alive, I would have nominated him as my successor for about him the Holy Prophet had said that he was the trustee of the Muslim community. If Salam the liberated slave of Abu Hudhaifah had been alive, I would have nominated him as my successor for about him the Holy Prophet had said that among the Muslims he loved Allah most."

Some one said, "I propose the name of your son Abdullah for the office.

Thereupon Hadrat Umar said :—

"May God curse you for tempting me to nepotism by nominating my son when I am going to meet my Creator. The Caliphate is an affair affecting the entire Muslim community, and I would not like to make it an hereditary office in my family. I swear it by God that I never coveted the caliphate for myself. Therefore what I never coveted for myself I would not like to pass on to my family. If the caliphate is something good then by holding the office for the last ten years, I have had the blessing for my family. If the caliphate is something bad then why should I pass on this bad thing to my family ? God is my witness that during my caliphate I showed no favour to my family members. On the other hand I was more hard with them than with the other Muslims. I have tried to fulfil the obligations of the office always under the shadow of the fear lest I may at any stage falter in the performance of my duties. I do not know whether I have succeeded in my purpose, but I will be happy if my achievements and failures just balance, so that I am neither rewarded nor punished for holding the office of the caliphate. Remember ye men, that if I nominate my successor, a better man than me (namely Hadrat Abu Bakr) also nominated his successor. And again if I do not nominate a successor, remember that the best of men, namely Hadrat Muhammad (peace be on him) did not nominate a successor. Whatever the case I am confident that Allah will Himself protect the interests of Islam."

At this, the persons around Hadrat Umar went away. Hadrat Umar had some sleep. Then the men came again and they said :—

"O Amirul Momnin, if you are not going to nominate a successor at least leave some instructions for the selection of your successor."

Thereupon Hadrat Umar said :

"After hearing you and weighing the pros and cons of the case carefully I had decided that I should nominate my successor who should lead the Muslims on the path of righteousness. But then I lost consciousness, and in that state of unconsciousness I had a dream. I saw that a man who had laid out the garden was plucking all ripe and unripe fruit from all the trees, and gathering it on the ground. I interpret this dream to mean that I will die, and Allah will Himself attend to the affairs of the Muslim community. I therefore refrain from nominating a successor for I do not wish that even after death I should continue to carry the burden of the caliphate."

When pressed to leave some guidance for the people to choose his successor, Hadrat Umar said that he would nominate a Committee comprising Hadrat Ali, Hadrat Usman, Hadrat Abdul Rahman b. Auf ; Saad bin Abi Waqas ; Zubair b. Awam ; and Abu Talha. All these were eminent Companions whom the Holy Prophet gave the tidings of Paradise in their life-time. Hadrat Umar said :

"I enjoin that this Committee should elect one of themselves as the Caliph."

The following day Hadrat Umar called the members of the Committee (except Abu Talha who was out of station) and enjoined them that they should deliberate and choose one from among themselve as the Caliph. The Committee retired to hold a meeting. It was soon found that there were strong dissensions among the members, and loud voices were raised highlighting the differences. Thereupon Abdul Rahman b. Auf addressing the members of the Committee said :

"The Amirul Momnin is not yet dead, and you have started quarrelling over the question of succossion."

When this state of affairs was brought to the notice of Hadrat Umar he instructed :

"Defer the consideration of this issue for the present. When I die you take up the issue and then settle it within three days. On the fourth day after my death the person chosen by you should take the oath of office. He should be some one out of you. Abdullah b. Umar will sit with the Committee as Adviser and Moderator, but he will have no vote, nor will he be eligible for election as the Caliph. If during this period Abu Talha joins you he will be a member. If he does not come within three days, the rest of the members of the Committee will have the authority to take the decision. During these three days, Suhaib will lead the prayers. Thereafter, whosoever, is elected as the Caliph will lead the prayers."

TESTAMENT OF HADRAT UMAR

On his death bed Hadrat Umar was requested to make a testament for the guidance of his successor. Hadrat Umar addressed the following testament to his successor :

"I enjoin upon you to have trust and faith in God, He Who has no peer.

Be kind and generous to the Muhajreen and the Ansar. Those out of them who are good, be good to them ; those who are bad overlook their lapses.

Be good to the people of the conquered lands. They are the outer line of our defence ; they are the target of the anger and distress of our enemies. They contribute to our revenues. They should be taxed only on their surplus wealth.

Be gracious to the Bedouins as they are the backbone of the Arab nation.

I instruct you to be good to the *Dhimmis* for they are your responsibility. Do not tax them beyond their capacity. Ensure that they pay the Jizya without undue inconvenience.

Fear God, and in all that you do keep His pleasure in view. In the matter of people fear God, and in the matter of Allah do not be afraid of the people.

With regard to the people, I enjoin upon you to administer justice with an even hand. See that all the legitimate requirements of the people are met. Be concerned for their welfare. Ensure the safety of their person and property.

See that the frontiers of our domains are not violated. Take strong steps to guard the frontiers.

In the matter of administration do not prefer the rich to the poor. Be hard against those who violate the law. Show them no mercy. Do not rest content until you have brought the miscreants to book.

Treat all the people as equal. Be a pillar of strength for those who are weak and oppressed. Those who are strong but do wrong, make them pay for their wrong-doings.

In the distribution of booty and other matters be above nepotism. Let no consideration of relationship or selfish interest weigh with you.

The Satan is at large ; it may tempt you. Rise above all temptations and perform your duties in accordance with the injunctions of Islam.

Get guidance from the Holy Qur'an and Sunnah. Freely consult the wise men around you. Apply your own mind in difficult cases, and seek light from God.

Be simple in your living and your habits. Let there be no show or ostentation about you. Lead life as a model Muslim. As you are the leader of the Muslims, justify your leadership by being the best among them all. May God bless you."

His son Abdullah also desired some words of parting advise. Hadrat Umar asked him to hold fast to the fundamentals of faith. Abdullah asked what these fundamentals were.

Hadrat Umar said that these were :

(1) Keep fast in the intense heat of the summer when the Ramadan falls in such a season.
(2) Kill the enemies of Islam with sword.
(3) In the event of any calamity or distress exercise patience.
(4) In the cold of the winter perform your ablutions in full.
(5) On a cloudy day hurry up in offering prayers.
(6) Abstain from the mud of destruction.

Abdullah enquired what was the mud of destruction, and Hadrat Umar said it was wine-bibbling.

ELEGIES AND TRIBUTES ON THE DEATH OF HADRAT UMAR

Atika the wife of Hadrat Umar burst into the following elegy on the death of Hadrat Umar :

"Eye, let thy tears and weeping be abundant, Death has afflicted me in the fall of a horseman Distinguished in the day of battle and of contumely,
The stay of faith, the defence against inclement fortune,
And a champion unto the afflicted and oppressed,
Say unto the hopeless die,
Since Death hath given us to drink the cup of dissolution."
She also said :
"Firoz has deprived us of such a fair complexioned, fair minded person.
Who was fastidious about his prayers
Who was regular in the recitation of the Holy Qur'an,
Who was a source of strength for the weak ;
And who was stern and harsh against the oppressors."

Another wife of Hadrat Umar mourned his death in the following terms :

"The death of Umar has overwhelmed me with such grief
That the entire world now appears to be a place of sorrow and distress."

Bint Abi Hashma said :

"We mourn the death of Umar
Who disentangled every knot,
Who solved every difficulty,
Who put an end to all mischief,

Who revived the Sunnat of the Holy Prophet,
He has departed from this world
Free from all blame."

Hadrat Hafsa expressed her grief in the following terms:

"I am bearing this bereavement with patience,
The Holy Qur'an condoles me,
You are not alone to die,
Every one is to die in turn."

A poet mournfully said :

"Because of the leadership of Umar,
The Muslims became a disciplined community,
Apparently it's impossible that after him,
Any one should carry the burden of the State
As effectively as he did."

Said bin Zaid, the brother-in-law of Hadrat Umar, wept grievously.

He was asked why he was weeping so profusely. He said:

"I am not weeping for Umar. I am weeping for Islam in which cracks will appear after his death."

Seeing the face of Hadrat Umar, Hadrat Ali said :

"Salutations of God to thee,
Verily, there is no man
Other than this shrouded one,
Whose deeds I envy."

Hadrat Usman seeing the face of Hadrat Umar said:

"Out of us! who can equal Umar ?"

DISTINCTIONS OF HADRAT UMAR

Hadrat Umar was a man of many distinctions. A study of his life shows that in many respects he had the unique distinction of being the first or foretmost. Hereunder an attempt is made to catalogue the matters in which Hadrat Umar was the foremost.

He was unique in his power of discrimination. The Holy Prophet conferred on him the title of *'Al-Farooq'*.

Among his contemporaries he was the foremost in the matter of knowledge and learning.

He had the unique distinction of having his views confirmed by the Holy Qur'an.

His superiority over his contemporaries was acknowledged when the Holy Prophet said that if there was to be a prophet after him, it would have been Umar.

He was the first Muslim ruler to be known by the title of *Amir-ul-Mo'minin.*

The conquests made by him exceeded in extent the conquests made by any other Muslim ruler throughout the course of history.

He was the first Muslim ruler to establish public treasury.

He was the first Muslim ruler to establish courts of justice and appoint judges.

He was the first Muslim ruler to establish the Army Department and assign regular salaries to the men in the armed forces.

He was the first to create army reserves.

He established the land revenue department for the first time.

He was the first ruler under whom the survey and assessment work of lands was undertaken.

He was the first Muslim ruler to take a census.

He was the first Muslim ruler to strike coins.

He was the first Muslim ruler to dig canals.

He was the first Muslim ruler to found cities.

He was the first Muslim ruler to divide the country into provinces and provinces into districts.

He imposed the customs duty for the first time.

He was the first to set up jails.

He was the first to organise the Police Department.

He was the first among the Muslim rulers to establish Military Centres and Military Cantonments at strategic points.

He established cavalry. He set up stables at strategic points. He created the distinction of pedigree and non-pedigree horses.

He established guest-houses in all cities. He established rest-houses on the road from Madina to Mecca for the comfort of travellers.

He provided for the care and bringing up of foundlings.

He laid down that no Arab could be made a slave.

He gave stipends to the poor.

He established schools throughout the country. He allowed liberal salaries to school teachers.

He was the first who instituted the prayers of *Tarawih* in congregation in the mosque in the month of Ramadan.

He was the first to formulate the principle of *Qiyas*.

He had the formula "Prayer is better than sleep" inserted in the call for morning prayers.

He was the first to provide light in mosques at nights.

He was the first to provide salaries for Imams and *Muezzins*.

He was the first to organise sermons in mosques.

He was the first to punish for writing satires and lampoons.

He was the first to prohibit the mention of women's names in lyric poems, an ancient custom in Arabia.

He was the first to inflict eighty stripes for indulgence in wine.

He was the first to prohibit *'Muta'ah'*—marriage for a limited term.

He was the first to forbid the sale of female slaves, who had borne children to their masters.

He was the first who assembled the people to prayers over the dead with four *Takbirs*.

He was the first to enlarge and pave the Prophet's mosque at Madina.

He was the first to expel non-Muslims from Arabia. The Jews from Hijaz were transferred to Syria, and the Christians from Najran were transferred to Kufa.

He was the first to place the law of inheritance on a sound basis.

He was the first to establish trusts.

HOLY PROPHET'S ASSESSMENT OF HADRAT UMAR

A number of traditions have come down to us which speak of the Holy Prophet's assessment of Hadrat Umar.

Before the conversion of Hadrat Umar to Islam, the prayer of the Holy Prophet is on record wherein he prayed "O God, glorify Thy faith by the conversion of Umar."

There is a tradition that when Hadrat Umar was converted to Islam the Holy Prophet said that Gabriel had visited him to say "O Muhammad, verily the dwellers in Heaven rejoice with you at the conversion of Umar."

According to Abu Huraira, the Holy Prophet once related a dream in the presence of Hadrat Umar. The Holy Prophet related, "While I was asleep, I saw myself in paradise, and beheld there a woman performing her ablutions by the side of a house. I enquired whose house it was, and I was told that it was Umar's. The lady said that she belonged to Umar. Then recollecting how jealous Umar was in the matter of women, I turned back, and thereafter I woke up". Hearing this, Hadrat Umar said, "O Prophet of God, everything of mine is at your service ; how can I be jealous of you in any matter?"

On another occasion, the Holy Prophet had another dream. He related :

> "While I was asleep, I dreamt that I drank milk. Then that milk began to flow from my fingers. That milk I asked Umar to drink, and he drank to his fill." The Holy Prophet was asked to interpret the dream and he said that the dream signified that among his followers, Hadrat Umar would excel every one in knowledge.

According to another tradition, the Holy Prophet said, "While I was asleep, I saw the people presented to me. These people wore garments. Some had garments reaching to their breasts, and some had garments which reached their toes. Then Umar was presented, and upon him was a garment which was so long that he dragged it as he moved". The Holy Prophet was requested to interpret the dream. The Holy Prophet said that the significance of the dream was that Umar would be a source of strength and service to Islam.

Al-Bukhari carries a tradition according to which the Holy Prophet said that there was to be no prophet after him, but if there were to be no bar to such prophethood, Umar would have been the prophet. That was the highest tribute that the Holy Prophet could pay to Hadrat Umar.

According to another tradition the Holy Prophet said, "Verily God has placed truth upon the tongue of Umar, and upon his heart." According to an allied tradition, the Holy Prophet said, "Never did a thing come upon the people, and they said one thing regarding it, and Umar another, but the Qur'an revealed it after the manner that Umar had said. The greatest tribute was paid to Hadrat Umar, when the Holy Prophet said, "God speaks through the tongue of Umar."

There is a tradition that Gabriel once came to the Holy Prophet and said, "Greet Umar with a salutation, and tell him that his anger is glory and his approval, command."

According to a tradition, the Holy Prophet said, "Umar is the lamp of the dwellers in paradise."

A tradition is on record according to which pointing to Hadrat Umar the Holy Prophet said, "Umar is a strongly bolted gate against discord. As long as he lives in your midst, there will be no discord among the Muslims."

We have it on the authority of Hadrat Ayesha that the Holy Prophet said, "Verily I behold the evil spirits among genii and men, fleeing from Umar". In the same strain the Holy Prophet said, "Verily Satan avoideth Umar."

There is another tradition according to which the Holy Prophet said, "There is not an angel in Heaven, but he revereth Umar, and not a demon on earth but he fleeth from Umar."

On the occasion of the last pilgrimage the Holy Prophet said, "Verily God approved of the conduct of the pilgrims at Arafat in general and Umar in particular".

There is a tradition that in the days of his illness the Holy Prophet said, "The Truth after me is with Umar, wherever he may be."

About Umar's victory against Satan, the Holy Prophet said, "Verily Satan hath never met Umar since his conversion, but he hath fallen prostrate on his face."

According to a tradition the Holy Prophet said, "Gabriel said to me, Verily Islam will weep at the death of Umar."

According to a tradition the Holy Prophet expressed his attachment to Hadrat Umar in the following terms : "He who hateth Umar hates me, and he who loveth Umar loves me".

THE HOLY PROPHET'S JOINT TRIBUTES TO HADRAT ABU BAKR AND HADRAT UMAR

Some traditions have come down to us whereunder the Holy Prophet paid joint tributes to Hadrat Abu Bakr and Hadrat Umar.

Abu Hurraira said :

"I heard the Holy Prophet say, 'while a shepherd was in the midst of his flock, a wolf rushed upon it and carried from it a sheep and the shepherd pursued it, the wolf turned to him and said, who will be a protector to it on the day of resurrection—the day when there will be no other shepherd than myself. As a man was driving an ox which he had laden, it turned to him and said, Verily I was not created for this but for tillage."

The companions cried, "Good God ! Should an ox talk !". The Holy Prophet said :

"I believe in it, and likewise Abu Bakr and Umar."

This is indicative of the Holy Prophet's trust in the faith of Abu Bakr and Umar.

The Holy Prophet said :

"There was never a prophet but he had two Ministers from the dwellers in heaven and two Ministers from among the dwellers on earth. My two Ministers of the dwellers of heaven are Gabriel and Michael, and of the earth Abu Bakr and Umar."

It is related in a tradition that one day the Holy Prophet entered the mosque with Abu Bakr and Umar, one of them on his right hand, and the other upon his left. He held their hands and said :

"Thus shall we arise on the Day of Judgment."

According to another tradition, the Holy Prophet looked on Hadrat Abu Bakr and Hadrat Umar and said :

"They are my hearing and my sight."

There is another tradition according to which turning to Hadrat Abu Bakr and Hadrat Umar, the Holy Prophet said :

"Praise be to God, Who has strengthened me with ye two."

On one occasion, addressing Hadrat Abu Bakr and Hadrat Umar, the Holy Prophet said :

"If you two are agreed upon any matter, I would not oppose you."

The Holy Prophet also said :

"Every prophet has chosen ones among his people and verily my elect from among my companions are Abu Bakr and Umar."

The Holy Prophet said :

"Love towards Abu Bakr and Umar is faith ; hatred towards them is infidelity."

The Holy Prophet said on another occasion :

"Love towards Abu Bakr and Umar, and a knowledge of them is an injunction of the law."

The Holy Prophet also said :

"Verily I hope for the same benefit for my people by their profession of love towards Abu Bakr and Umar that I hope for them by their profession of faith 'thereis no god but God'."

ASSESSMENT OF HADRAT UMAR BY THE COMPANIONS

Hadrat Abu Bakr said about Hadrat Umar, "There is not upon the face of the earth a man dearer to me than Umar." When Hadrat Abu Bakr was on his death bed, it was said to him, "What will you say to God, now that you have appointed Umar as your successor ?" Hadrat Abu Bakr said, "I will say to Him that I appointed over His people the man who was the best among them all."

After the death of Hadrat Umar, Hadrat Ali said in the course of one of his sermons :

> "When Hadrat Umar became the Caliph, there were some people who approved of his caliphate and there were some who disagreed. During his caliphate he administered the affairs of the State strictly on the lines laid down by the Holy Prophet and his successor Abu Bakr. He followed them in the same way as a child follows its mother. Verily he was a pillar of strength for the weak, the poor, and the aggrieved. He was for the Muslims a source of honour, prosperity and victory. Nothing stood in his way in promoting the cause of Truth. He was so discriminating in truth that we come to believe that the angel spoke through his tongue. By being converted to Islam, he became a source of honour and strength for Islam. His migration was a cause of strengthening the religion of Islam. God made the infidels fear Umar, and the pious Muslims love him. As he was very harsh with the enemies of Islam, the Holy Prophet compared Umar to Gabriel. As he had a fiery temper the Holy Prophet compared him to Hadrat Nuh, O ye Muslims bear in mind that after the Holy Prophet, among his

followers the two best persons were Hadrat Abu Bakr, and Hadrat Umar."

Hadrat Ali used to say, "When the righteous are mentioned, then be quick and mention Umar." Hadrat Ali also said "We used to say not without reason that the Divine Presence spoke by the tongue of Umar."

Hadrat Abu Ubaida bin Al-Jarah, the Commander-in-Chief of the Muslim forces in Syria said :

"When Hadrat Umar will die, Islam will be disgraced. I do not wish that I should survive Umar. I wish to die during the life-time of Umar."

'Abdullah bin Abbas said :

"May God bless the soul of Umar. By God he was a pillar of strength for Islam. He was the shelter for the orphans and the widows. By his conduct he fortified the faith of others. He was a model Muslim. The weak relied on him for the redress of their grievances. He was a great helper of the people. As a Caliph he promoted the interests of Islam. Under him the standard of Islam was carried east and west, and the call to prayers could be heard in plains and on hills even in distant lands. In the states when he was hard or humble he maintained the dignity of Islam. He remembered God at all times. He was indeed the gem of a man. May Allah humilitate the person who talks ill of Hadrat Umar, or bears him any enmity."

Ibn Masud said :

"If the wisdom of Umar were placed in the scale of a balance, and the wisdom of living things upon the earth in the other scale, the wisdom of Umar would outweigh them, and verily the people used to think that Hadrat Umar carried nine-tenth of the wisdom of the world."

Ibn Mas'ud on another occasion said :

"Verily Umar was the most learned of us all in the Book of God, and most profoundly versed in the religious ordinances of Allah."

On the death of Hadrat Umar, Ibn Masud said :

"Umar was the fort of Islam. The people could enter the fort but could not come out of it. With the death of Umar that fort has fallen and now people would come out of it."

Hadrat Abbas said about Hadrat Umar :

"I was a neighbour of Umar. After the Holy Prophet I have not found any person superior to Umar in the love of God. He spent the greater part of night in prayer. Throughout the day he worked hard to win the pleasure of Allah".

On the death of Hadrat Umar, Saeed b. Zaid said :

"With the death of Umar, Islam has come to grief. His death has caused a breach in the citadel of Islam which would not be filled up."

Abu Hudhaifah said :

"It is as if the wisdom of mankind lay hidden in the bossom of Umar. By Allah I know not a man whom the reproof of the censurer in what relateth to the service of God, does not touch, but Umar". He also said, "In the time of Hadrat Umar Islam attained the climax of glory. After his death Islam will have to face difficulties."

Hadrat Ayesha said of him "By Allah, Umar was active in affairs, singly undertaking their management."

Abu Talha Ansari said, "By God, there is no Muslim household which has not suffered because of the death of Umar."

Ibn Umar said, "I never saw any one after the Holy Prophet, from the time that he died, any person more vehement and yet more beneficent than Umar."

Ibn Abbas was asked about Hadrat Umar, and he said, "Hadrat Umar was like a wary bird who apprehended a snare at every step to trap it.".

Amir Muawiyah said, "Abu Bakr sought not the world, and the world sought him not. In the case of Umar, the world sought him, but he sought it not."

ASSESSMENT BY WESTERN WRITERS

In his book "Lives of Successors of Muhammad", Washington Irving estimates the achievements of Hadrat Umar in the following terms :

> "The whole history of Umar shows him to have been a man of great powers of mind, inflexible integrity and rigid justice. He was more than any one else the founder of the Islamic empire; confirming and carrying out the inspirations of the Prophet; aiding Abu Bakr with his counsels during his brief Caliphate; and establishing wise regulations for the strict administration of the law throughout the rapidly-extending bounds of the Muslim conquests. The rigid hand which he kept upon his most popular generals in the midst of their armies, and in the most distant scenes of their triumphs, gives signal evidence of his extra-ordinary capacity to rule. In the simplicity of his habits, and his contempt for all pomp and luxury, he emulated the example of the Prophet and Abu Bakr. He endeavoured incessantly to impress the merit and policy of the same in his letters to his generals. Beware' he would say of Persian luxury both in food and raiment. Keep to the simple habits of your country, and Allah will continue you victorious ; depart from them and He will reverse your fortunes'. It was his strong conviction of the truth of this policy which made him so severe in punishing all ostentatious style and luxurious indulgence in his officers. Some of his ordinances do credit to his heart as well as his head. He forbade that any female captive who had borne a child should be sold as a slave. In his weekly distributions of the surplus money of his treasury, he proportioned

them to the wants, not the merits of the applicants. 'God' said, 'the has bestowed the good things of this world to relieve our necessities, not to reward our virtues : those will be rewarded in another world'."

In his book "The Caliphate, its Rise, Decline and Fall" Sir William Muir says as follows about Hadrat Umar :

"Umar's life requires but few lines to sketch. Simplicity and duty were his guiding principles ; impartiality and devotion the leading features of his administration. Responsibility so weighed upon him that he was heard to exclaim 'O that my mother had not borne me ; would that I had been this stalk of grass instead !' In early life, of a fiery and impatient temper, he was known, even in the later days of the Prophet, as the stern advocate of vengeance. Ever ready to unsheathe the sword, it was he who at Badr advised that the prisoners should be put to death. But age, as well as office, had now mellowed this asperity. His sense of justice was strong. And except it be the treatment of Khalid, whom according to some accounts, he pursued with an ungenerous resentment, no act of tyranny or injustice is recorded against him ; and even in this matter, his enmity took its rise in Khalid's unscrupulous treatment of fallen foe. The choice of his captains and governors was free from favouritism and (Al-Mughira and Ammar excepted) singularly fortunate. The various tribes and bodies in the empire, representing interests the most diverse, reposed in his integrity implicit confidence, and his strong arm maintained the discipline of law and empire. Whip in hand, he would perambulate the streets and markets of Madina, ready to punish offenders on the spot ; and so the proverb Umar's whip is more terribe than another's sword'. But with all this he was tender hearted, and numberless acts of kindness are recorded of him, such as relieving the wants of the widows and the fatherless."

In his classical work "The Decline and Fall of the Roman Empire, Gibbon refers to Hadrat Umar in the following terms:

"Yet the abstinence and humility of Umar were not inferior to the virtues of Abu Bakr : his food consisted of barley bread or dates; his drink was water; he preached in a gown that was torn or tattered in twelve places ; and a Persian satrap, who paid his homage as to the conqueror, found him asleep among the beggars on the steps of the mosque of Muslims. Economy is the source of liberality, and the increases of the revenue enabled Umar to establish a just and perpetual reward for the past and present services of the faithful. Careless of his own emolument, he assigned to Abbas, the uncle of the Prophet, the first and most ample allowance of twenty-five thousand dirhams of pieces of silver. Five thousand were allotted to each of the aged warriors, the relics of the field of Badr, and the last and the meanest of the companions of Mohammad was idstinguished by the annual reward of three thousand pieces. . . .Under his reign and that of his predecessors, the conquerors of the East were the trusty servants of God and the people, the mass of public treasure was consecrated to the expenses of peace and war; a prudent mixture of justice and bounty maintained the discipline of the Saracens, and then united, by a rare felicity, the despatch and execution of despotism with the equal and frugal maxims of a republican government."

In his book "History of the Arabs" Professor Philip K. Hitti has assessed the achivements of Hadrat Umar in the following terms:

"Simple and frugal in manner the energetic and talented Umar (634-644) who was of towering height, strong physique and bald headed, continued at least for some time after becoming the Caliph to support himself by trade and lived throughout his life in a style as unostentatious as that of a Bedouin Sheikh. In fact, Umar, whose name according to Muslim tradition is the greates in early Islam, after that of Mohammad, has been idolised by Muslim writers for his piety, justice and patriarchal simplicity and treated as the personification of all the virtues a Caliph ought to possess. His irreproachable character became an exemplar for all conscientious successors to follow. He owned, we are told, one shirt and one mantle only, both conspicuous for their patchwork, slept on a bed of palm leaves, and had no concern other than the maintenance of the purity of the faith, the upholding of justice and the ascendancy and security of Islam and the Arabians. Arabic literature is replete with anecdotes extolling Umar's stern character. He is said to have scourged his own son to death for drunkenness. Having in a fit of anger inflicted a number of stripes on a Bedouin who came seeking his succour against an oppressor, the Caliph soon repented and asked the Bedouin to inflict the same number on him. But the latter refused. So Umar retired to his home with the following soliloquy: 'O son of al-Khattab humble thou wert and Allah has elevated thee, thou went astray, and Allah hath guided thee; thou were weak, and Allah hath strengthened thee. Then He caused thee to rule over the necks of thy people, and when one of them came seeking thy aid thou didst strike him! What wilt thou have to say to thy Lord when thou presentest thyself before Him'. The one who fixed the Hijrah as the commencement of the Muslim era, presided over the conquest of large portions of the then known world, instituted the state register and organised the government of the new empire, met a tragic and sudden death at the very zenith of his life when he was struck down by the poisoned dagger of a Christian Persian slave in the midst of his own congregation."

"The Encyclopaedia Britannica" remarks about Hadrat Umar :

> "To Umar's ten years' Caliphate belong, for the most part, the great conquests. He himself did not take the field, but remained in Madina; he never, however, suffered the reins to slip from his grasp, so powerful was the influence of his personality and the Muslim community of feeling. His political insight is shown by the fact that he endeavoured to limit the indefinite extension of Muslim conquest, to maintain and strengthen the national Arabian character of the commonwealth of Islam, also by making it his foremost task to promote law and order in its internal affairs.

The saying with which he began his reign will never grow antiquated: 'By God, he that is weakest among you shall be in my eye the strongest, until I have vindicated for him his rights; he that is strongest I will treat as the weakest, until he complies with the law'. It would be impossible to give a better general definition of the function of the State."

ASSESSMENT OF HADRAT UMAR BY ORIENTAL WRITERS

In his book "History of Egypt", Jurji Zaidan, a Christian historian has paid a tribute to Hadrat Umar in the following words:

> "In his time various countries were conquered, spoils were multiplied, the treasures of the Persian and Roman Emperors were poured in streams before his troops, nevertheless he himself manifested a degree of abstemiousness and moderation which was never surpassed. He addressed the people clad in a garment patched with leather. He was himself the first to practise what he preached. He kept a vigilant eye over the Governors and Generals and enquired strictly into their conduct. Even the great Khalid bin Walid was not spared. He was just to all mankind and was kindly even to non-Muslims. Iron discipline was maintained every where during his reign."

In his well known book "History of the Saracens", Justice Syed Amir Ali has rated Hadrat Umar in the following terms:

> "The death of Umar was a real calamity to Islam. Stern, but just, far-sighted, thoroughly versed in the character of his people, he was especially fitted for the leadership of the unruly Arabs. He had held the helm with a strong hand and severely repressed the natural tendency to demoralisation among nomadic tribes and semi-civilised people when coming in contact with the luxury and vices of cities. He had established the Diwan or the Department of Finance, to which was entrusted

> the administration of the revenues; and had introduced fixed rules for the government of the provinces. He was a man of towering height, strong build, and fair complexion. Of simple habits, austere and frugal, always accessible to the meanest of his subjects, wandering about at night to inquire into the condition of the people, without any guard of court, such was the greatest and the most powerful ruler of the time."

Shah Wali Ullah has described the talents and achievements of Hadrat Umar graphically in the following terms:

> "Imagine the heart of Umar as a house with many gates. At each gate is seated a noble genius. At one gate stands Alexander the Great with all his genius for conquering countries, commanding armies and vanquishing foes. At another gates sits Anushirwan with all his genteleness, magnanimity, justice, and love of his subjects. And yet at another gate sits a spiritual leader like Syed Abdul Qadir Gilani or Khawaja Bahauddin. At another gate sits Hadith specialists like Abu Huraira and Ibn Umar, and yet at another gate sit thinkers of the calibre of Maulana Jalaluddin Rumi and Sheikh Fariduddin Attar. And people are standing around this house and every needy one represents his need to the Imam of his branch of knowledge and goes away satisfied."

Put in simpler words, this tribute means that:

(1) Hadrat Umar was a great Conqueror, greater than Alexander;
(2) Hadrat Umar excelled Anushirwan in justice;
(3) Hadrat Umar was a great spiritual leader;
(4) Hadrat Umar was a specialist in Hadith;
(5) Hadrat Umar was a great thinker;
(6) Hadrat Umar excelled in all branches of knowledge.

SAYINGS OF HADRAT UMAR

Hadrat Umar was known for his great knowledge and wisdom. He often expressed his thoughts in words conspicuous for their wisdom. A number of his sayings have come down to us, and these show the depths and dimensions of his thoughts and expressions. We give hereunder the various sayings attributed to Hadrat Umar, which we have been able to gather from various sources:

"He who keeps his own counsel keeps his affairs in his own hands."

"Fear him, whom you hate".

"The wisest man is he who can account for his actions."
"Do not put off today's work for tomorrow."

"Money cannot help lifting its head."

"What regresses, never progresses."

"He who does not know evil will fall into it."

"When a man puts me a question, I judge of his intelligence."

"Don't forget your own self while preaching to others."
"The less of the world, the freer you live."

"Avoidance of sin is lighter than the pain of remorse."

"On every dishonest man, there are two watchmen, his possessions, and his way of living."

"If patience and gratitude had been two she camels, it would have mattered little on which I rode."

"May God have mercy on him who sends me my faults as a present ."

"Preserve the sayings of those people who are indifferent to the world. They say only that what God wishes them to say."

"Fear God, for He alone lives; all other things are liable to perish."

"The wisest among you is he whose sustenance is the fear of God."

"Praise God, for by praise His blessings multiply."

"Fear God, for that is fortune; indifference to God is misfortune."

"Be patient; patience is a pillar of faith."

"Acquire knowledge and teach it to the people."

"Be dignified, honest, and truthful."

"Do not be an arrogant scholar, for scholarship cannot subsist with arrogance."

"When you see that any scholar loves the world, then his scholarship is in doubt."

"God forbid, men should be jealous of knowledge as they are jealous of women."

"May God bless the man who says less and does more."

"The criterion of action is that to-day's work should not be deferred till the following day."

"Trust is that there should be no difference between what you do and say and what you think."

"Learn the Arabic language; it will sharpen your wisdom."

"Luxury is an obstacle, and so is the fatness of the body."

"A man may be as straight as an arrow, but even then he will have some critics."

"O Allah do not give me in excess lest I may be disobedient to You, and do not give me less, lest I may forget You."

"Allah loves moderation and hates extravagance and excess."

"He who went to the kings to seek favours went away from God."

"Sit with those who love God, for that enlightens the mind."

"Before Allah that is the best dinner which people eat together."

"As long as you are pure of heart, you speak the truth."

"The pilgrims are the delegations of God."

"If your ruler is just, praise God; if he is unjust, pray to God to rid you of him."

"Allah is happy with such rulers whose slaves are under their control."

"Forgive the people so that God may forgive you."

"For the people prefer that which you prefer for yourself. Which you do not wish for yourself, do not impose on others."

"In the eyes ot God he is the best ruler who has secured prosperity and comfort for the people."

"That ruler is most accursed whose misconduct leads to the distress of the people."

"Every ruler should keep his door open to the people."

"Understand the teachings of the Holy Qur'an for that is the source of knowledge."

"Relate as few traditions as possible, lest by being involved in traditions the people overlook the Qur'an."

"All the injunctions of Islam are based on reason."

"The way to express gratitude to God is to give Zakat out of the property that He has bestowed on you."

"In my view your greatest obligation is to offer prayers.

He who fulfils this obligation with great regularity will be secure in his religion."

"He who sleeps without offering the night prayer, may he never enjoy a sound sleep."

"Women should offer Zakat on their ornaments."

"Blessed are those who are martyred in the way of Allah."

"In the preparation of Islam, commit no excess."

"Without consultation, the caliphate is unlawful."

"The ruler whose intention is good will have the help of God in the administration of his affairs; he whose intention is bad will come to disgrace."

"Do not accept gifts; that is bribery."

"The Judge should always uphold the principle of equality before law."

"May God curse the people who hesitate to dine with the slaves."

"Do not be misled by a person's prayers and fasting; look to his sincerity and wisdom."

"Do not be misled by hearing of any one's reputation."

"He trusts in God who sows seed in the ground then depends on God."

"Earning of livelihood by following some profession is better than living on charity."

"He who has any public responsibility should perform his duties without caring for criticism."

"He is to be preferred who has the urge to sin, but does not sin.

"Do not depend upon the morality of a person until you have seen him behave while in anger."

"I am surprised at three things. Man runs from death while death is inevitable. One sees minor faults of others, but overlooks his own major faults. When there is any defect to one's cattle he tries to cure it, but does not cure his own defects."

"To flatter is to slaughter."

"He, who pretends to be what he is not, is a hypocrite."

"If a person has ten habits out of which nine are good and one bad, that bad one will destroy the good ones."

"Do not overeat; that invites disease."

"He who wins through fraud is no winner."

"He who wants paradise should hold fast to the community."

"The efficacy of a prayer depends not on the words but on the sincerity of intention."

"In the narration of facts refrain from poetising."

"When you do not know of a thing say so plainly."

"O I am not worried about the poverty of the Muslims. I am afraid lest by getting rich they might become proud and thereby invite destruction."

"In the performance of your duties neither be over zealous, nor indifferent."

HADRAT UMAR AND SUFISM

In "Kashful Mahjub", Hadrat Ali Hajveri has assessed Hadrat Umar as a Sufi. The assessment of Hadrat Ali Hajveri is in the following terms:

"He was specially distinguished by sagacity and resolution, and is the author of many fine sayings on Sufism."

The Holy Prophet said:

"The Truth speaks by the tongue of Umar", and again "There have been inspired Muhaddith in the peoples of antiquity, and if there be any such in my people it will be Umar."

Hadrat Umar said:

"Retirement is a means of relieving one's self of bad company." Retirement is of two sorts; firstly, turning one's back on mankind, and secondly, entire severance from them. Turning one's back on mankind implies choosing a solitary retreat, and renouncing the society of one's fellow creatures. It also lies in seeking release for one's self from intercourse with men, and in making all people secure from one's evil actions. But severance from mankind is a spiritual state, which is not connected with anything external. When a person is severed from mankind in spirit, he knows nothing of created beings and no thought thereof can take possession of his mind. Such a person, although he is living among the people, is isolated from them, and his spirit dwells apart from them. This is a very exalted station, and Hadrat Umar held that station.

Hadrat Umar held this station for externally he lived among the people as their Commander and Caliph, but his spirit dwelt apart from them. His words show clearly that although spiritualists may outwardly mix with mankind, their hearts always cling to God and return to Him in all circumstances. They regard any intercourse they may have with men as an affliction sent by God; and that intercourse does not divert them from God, since the world never becomes pure in the eyes of those whom God loves.

Hadrat Umar said:

> "An abode which is founded upon affliction cannot possibly be without affliction." The Sufis make Hadrat Umar their model in wearing a patched frock and rigorously performing the duties of religion."

We have it on the strength of Al-Baihaqi that in Sufist strain, Hadrat Umar often said:

> "Would that I were a ram, that my people might fatten me as it appeared good to them, so that when I became as fat as could be, those whom they loved might visit them, and they might kill me for them, and make part of me roast, and part of me dried flesh, and eat me, and that I were not a mortal man."

HADRAT UMAR'S GIFT OF FORECASTING

Hadrat Umar was blessed with the gift of forecasting events by playing upon the meaning of words.

When on the eve of the battle of Nihawand, the Governor of Kufa sent a messenger to Hadrat Umar, he forecast the coming events by asking the messenger his name and the name of his father. When the messenger said that his name was 'Qareeb' meaning 'near', and his father's name was 'Zafar' meaning 'victory', Hadrat Umar forecast that for the Muslims victory was near.

It is recorded that once a man waited on Hadrat Umar. He asked him what was his name. He said that his name was 'Jamrah', meaning a live coal.

Hadrat Umar then asked him about his father's name, and he said that his father's name was 'Shihab' meaning 'flame'.

Hadrat Umar then enquired to which tribe he belonged. He said that he belonged to the tribe of 'Al-Harrah', meaning 'heat'.

He was asked where did he live and he replied 'Al-Harqah' meaning 'warmth'.

Hadrat Umar asked him what was his clan and he said 'Dat Ladha' meaning 'blazing'.

Then Hadrat'Umar said:

"Go home, for all your people have been burnt."

When the man went home, he found that his family had been burnt to death.

It was a custom with the Egyptians that a virgin was thrown in the river Nile to secure a rise in the surface of the water. When the Muslims conquered Egypt this inhuman practise was stopped. Instead of a virgin a card written by Hadrat Umar was thrown in the river, and immediately the water rose in the river.

It is on record that when a contingent of the Muslim army under Sariyah fighting in Fars were exposed to danger, Hadrat Umar while delivering Friday sermon in the Prophet's mosque shouted 'Sariyah to the hills'. The command was listened to by the Muslims in the battlefie]d thousand miles away and was complied with resulting in victory for the Muslims.

Hadrat Umar had a highly developed sense of discriminating the truth from falsehood. Whenever a person spoke the truth, Hadrat Umar would listen to him attentively, but whenever a person spoke anything false, Hadrat Umar would promptly say "withhold that".

It is related that the people of Kufa pelted their Governor with stones. When Hadrat Umar heard of this he was much annoyed. He was distracted even in his prayer. When he came to the salutation he said:

> "O God verily they have put confusion on me. O Allah you put confusion Upon them, and place over them a youth of the Banu Thaqif who may rule over them after the manner of the rule of the time of Ignorance."

This forecast came true when al-Hajjaj came to rule over Iraq in the time of the Umayyads.

WHEN ALLAH CORROBORATE HADRAT UMAR

Many instances are on record when Hadrat Umar gave a particular opinion and that opinion was later on corroborated by Allah and confirmation thereof was communicated to the Holy Prophet through Gabriel. That is why the Holy Prophet repeatedly said:

"God speaks through the tongue of Umar."

Hadrat Umar suggested that the station of Abraham in Mecca should be used as a place of prayer. Later an injunction to this effect was revealed to the Holy Prophet.

Hadrat Umar suggested that the wives of the Holy Prophet should be veiled. Later a verse was revealed enjoining the wives of the Holy Prophet to be veiled.

Hadrat Umar suggested that the use of wine should be prohibited. Thereafter God enjoined the prohibition of wine.

'Abdullah b Ubbay though a Muslim was insincere in his professions and was the enemy of God and the Holy Prophet. When he died the Holy Prophet led his funeral prayer. Hadrat Umar suggested that the Holy Prophet should not pray at the funeral of those who were the enemies of God and the Prophet. A verse was later revealed enjoining the Holy Prophet not to pray at the funeral of those who were the enemies of God and His Prophet.

When there was an imputation against the conduct of Hadrat Ayesha, Hadrat Umar said that this was a grievous calumny. Later a verse was revealed declaring the episode as a calumny and establishing Hadrat Ayesha's innocence.

After the battle of Badr, it was decided that the prisoners of the Quraish should be released on ransom. Hadrat Umar said that the prisoners being the enemies of God should be killed. Later according to a revelation the Holy Prophet was enjoined that the enemies of God should be killed.

When the Azan was originally proposed the contents of the call were:

> "I testify that there is no god but Allah--come ye to prayers."

Hadrat Umar suggested, "The words 'I testify that Muhammad is the Messenger of God' should be added". A revelation corroborated this suggestion.

The practice was that people went to see the Holy Prophet unannounced. Hadrat;Umar suggested that all visitors should seek permission before being admitted to the presence of the Holy Prophet. A verse was later revealed enjoining the asking of permission before entering the presence of the Holy Prophet.

Once two persons to a dispute referred the case to the Holy Prophet and the Holy Prophet gave his verdict. One of them appealed against the decision of the Holy Prophet. Hadrat Umar slew him with his sword. A verse was revealed absolving Hadrat Umar from the death of the person who did not believe in the judgment of the Holy Prophet.

Once a Jew said to Hadrat Umar, "Verily Gabriel who speaks to your Master is our enemy." Hadrat Umar retorted, "Whosoever is an enemy to God, or His angels, or His Apostles, or Gabriel, or Michael, verily God is an enemy to the unbelievers." Later a verse was revealed declaring that God was the enemy of unbelievers.

WIVES AND CHILDREN OF HADRAT UMAR

Before his conversion to Islam, Hadrat Umar had three wives. These were:

(1) Zainab bint Mazaun Jamiah;

(2) Malaika bint Jarul Khuzai; and

(3) Qariba bint Umayya Makhzumi.

When Hadrat Umar was converted to Islam, Zainab alone accepted Islam. After the Hudaybiah pact when God sent the words that Muslims should not marry idolatresses, Hadrat Umar divorced Malaika and Qariba.

After the Hudaibia-pact the first Muslim woman who fled from the Quraish and sought shelter with the Muslims was Sabiha bint Al-Harith. Her husband did not accept Islam. When the Quraish came to demand the restoration of Sabiha, the Holy Prophet refused to return her saying that the condition in the pact applied to men only and not to women. The Holy Prophet had Sabiha married to Hadrat Umar.

In Madina, Hadrat Umar married an Ansar lady Asiah bint Sabat Ansari. On marriage Hadrat Umar changed her name to Jamila. Hadrat Umar resided with her at Quba, and it is reported that there was great love between Hadrat Umar and Jamila. A few years later Hadrat Umar divorced her and shifted tc Madina.

'Atika bint Zaid was a cousin of Hadrat Umar. She was married to Abdullah a son of Hadrat Abu Bakr. When her husband died, Atika felt very disconsolate. In sympathy, Hadrat Umar married her in the first year of his caliphate.

Umm Hakim was the wife of 'Ikramahh the son of Abu Jahl. Ikramahh died fighting and thereafter Umm Hakim married Khalid bin Sa'id. Khalid bin Saeed was also martyred on the Syrian front. Umm Hakim doubly bereaved was much grieved, and Hadrat Umar consoled her by marrying her.

In 639 A.D., Hadrat Umar married Umm Kulsum the daughter of Hadrat 'Ali and Hadrat Fatima. Till his death in 644 A. D., Umm Kulsum remained his favourite wife.

Besides these wives, Hadrat Umar had two slave girls who bore him children. These were Fakiah and Layiah.

Hadrat Umar's sons included: 'Abdullah; 'Asim; Abu Shahma; 'Abdur Rahman; Zaid; 'Iyad and Mujir. Abdullah became a convert to Islam at an early age along with his father. He made a great name for himself as an expert in *Fiqh* and *Hadis*. 'Ubaidullah was well known for his bravery and fighting qualities. In revenge for the assassination of Hadrat Umar, 'Ubaidullah killed Hormuzan and some other persons. 'Asim was known for his poetry and piety. Umar bin 'Abul 'Aziz the puritan Umayyad Caliph was his daughter's son. Abu Shahma was flogged to death by Hadrat Umar for the offence of drinking.

The daughters of Hadrat Umar included: Hadrat Hafsa Fatima, Ruqayya and Zainab. Of these Hadrat Hafsa was the most well-known as she was the wife of the Holy Prophet.

'Abdullah, Abdur Rahman Akbar, and Hadrat Hafsa, were born to Zainab bint Mazaun.

'Ubaidullah and Zaid Asghar were the sons of Umm Kulsum who was divorced after the Hudaibiya pact.

Umm Hakim was the mother of Fatima.
'Asim was the son of Jamila bint Sabat Ansari
Umm Kulsum bint Ali was the mother of Zaid and Ruqayya,
'Iyad was the son of Atika.
Layiah was the mother of Abdur Rahman al-Wast.
Fatimah was the daughter of Umm Hakim.
Zainab was the daughter of Fakiah.

THE COARSE FOOD THAT HADRAT UMAR ATE

It is related that once Utba bin Abi Farqad came to see Hadrat Umar at his house. Utba was an eminent Companion. When he was announced Hadrat Umar was taking his meals. Utba was asked to come in. Hadrat Umar wanted Utba to share his food with him. Utba started eating, but the bread was so coarse that he could not swallow it.

Hadrat Umar watched Utba and then said:

" Utba, what is the matter ?"

'Utba sighed and said:

"O Commander of the Faithful why are you imposing such austerities on your self ? Why dont you use finer flour for your bread ? You can certainly afford it."

Hadrat Umar said:

"Fie on you Utba, you are seducing me to the devil's way."

'Utba said:

"So many Muslims eat fine bread. Do you think they are the followers of the devil ?"

Hadrat Umar said:

" Utba tell me, can every Muslim afford fine bread ?" Utbh said:

"Of course every Muslim cannot afford such bread, but many can."

Hadrat Umar said:

> "When I am the Commander of the Faithful and supposed to watch over the interests of all Muslims, how will I be true to my office when I eat fine bread, while most of the Muslims have to remain content with coarse bread ? Verily I will not eat bread of fine flour unless I am sure that all the Muslims are assured of such bread."

To this Utba had no reply and Hadrat Umar put him another question:

"Utba are you aware of the food of the Holy Prophet?"

'Utba said that the Holy Prophet ate coarse bread.

Why was that asked Hadrat Umar.

'Utba said that he might better answer the question himself.

Hadrat Umar said:

> "The Holy Prophet held the keys of the treasures of the world. He could have enjoyed untold wealth and availed of any pleasure, but he purposely refrained to do so. He did not wish to exhaust all such pleasures in this world. He wanted them to be kept in reserve for the next world."

Then Hadrat Umar elaborated "Look Utba, we are the followers of the Holy Prophet. It is incumbent on us to follow in the footsteps of the Holy Prophet. As the Holy Prophet did not wish to exhaust all the pleasures in this world, so as his followers it should be our endeavour to live a life of austerity and cut down our pleasures in this world, so that we may be loaded with pleasant things in the world to come."

Having spoken these words and shuddering as to what might happen to him on the Day of Judgment, Hadrat Umar began to weep. That made Utba weep as well.

When Utba left, he was fully resolved that henceforward he would eat coarse food, and avoid luxurious living. And thanks to the example set by Hadrat Umar, Utba kept his resolve.

It is related that one day Hadrat Hafsa (the daughter of Hadrat Umar) and Abdullah his son expostulated with Hadrat Umar, and tried to prevail upon him to eat good food. They argued that if he were to eat good food that would give him the strength to maintain the truth.

Hadrat Umar said:

> "I understand your counsel. My difficulty is that I have left my two companions, the Holy Prophet and Hadrat Abu Bakr upon a road, and if I depart from their road, I shall not find them at the journey's end. Under the circumstances I am under an obligation not to eat richer or better food than what my two esteemed companions ate."

It is related that once Hadrat Umar felt the desire to eat fish. Fish was not available in Madina. Yarfa the slave of Hadrat Umar went to the ponds outside Madina and there purchased some fish. The fish was cooked and presented to Hadrat Umar at his meals. Turning to Yarfa, Hadrat Umar said:

> "Why this dish of fish ?" Yarfa said that as he had expressed the wish to eat fish, he had procured it. Hadrat Umar said, "Fie on you Yarfa. Do you think I should succumb to sensual desires.? Take away this dish, By Allah I will not eat it."

HADRAT UMAR'S STANDARDS OF INTEGRITY FOR HIS FAMILY MEMBERS

Hadrat Umar set up very high standards of integrity for himself and his family members. He took particular care to see that such standards were followed strictly. Whenever Hadrat Umar issued any instructions for the people to follow, he brought home to his family members that he expected them to conform to such instructions strictly.

He issued strict orders that no member of his family should accept any gift from any person. Once Hadrat Umar found a new carpet with his wife Atika. He wanted to know from where the carpet had come. She said that it had been presented by Abu Musa Ashari, the Governor of Basra. Hadrat Umar had the carpet immediately returned to Abu Musa. Abu Musa was reprimanded in strong terms for sending a gift to the wife of the Caliph.

'Abdullah the son of Hadrat Umar purchased some camels. They were lean and were purchased cheaply. Hadrat 'Abdullah sent these camels to the state pasture where they fattened. These were then sold in the market and fetched a high price. When this was brought to the notice of Hadrat Umar he ordered that as the camels had been fed at the state pasture whatever profit had accrued in the sale of the camels should be deposited in the state treasury.

Once Hadrat Umar saw a small girl who was lean, thin, and emaciated. Hadrat Umar enquired who the girl was. 'Abdullah the son of Hadrat Umar said that she was his daughter, and that she had lost weight because with the allowance that Hadrat Umar allowed to his family nourishing food could not be provided. Hadrat Umar said that he was giving them what he gave to other families and he could not give his family anything more than what he did to other families.

Once 'Abdullah and 'Ubaidullah two sons of Hadrat Umar went to Basra. There they obtained a loan from Abu Musa on the condition that the amount would be paid to the state treasury at Madina. With this amount they purchased some merchandise and sold it at Madina. They earned considerable profit which they kept for themselves and credited the principal amount in the state treasury. When Hadrat Umar came to know of this transaction he wanted his sons to credit the entire profit to the state treasury as the money with which they had traded was state money. 'Abdullah kept quiet but 'Ubaidullah protested. He said that if there had been a loss the state would not have shared it. Hadrat Umar stuck to his decision, but 'Ubaidullah protested again. Some other companions intervened and it was decided that it should be treated as a case of partnership. Hadrat Umar allowed his sons to retain one half of the profit and to deposit the other half in the state treasury.

Once Hadrat Umar received a considerable quantity of musk. It had to be weighed and then distributed. Hadrat Umar was in search of a person who could weigh musk with meticulous care. Atika the wife of Hadrat Umar offered to do so as she was expert in the job. Hadrat Umar did not accept the offer on the ground that when she weighed and distributed it some musk would be attached to her hands and clothes and that would be misappropriation in state property.

Once Umm Kulsum a wife of Hadrat Umar purchased perfume for one dirham and sent it as a gift to the Byzantine empress. The Byzantine empress returned the empty phials of perfume filled with gems. When Hadrat Umar came to know of this he sold the gems. Out of the sale proceeds he handed over one dirham to his wife and the rest was deposited in the state treasury.

Once some gifts were received in the Baitul Mal. Hadrat Hafsa waited on Hadrat Umar and wanted a share. Hadrat Umar said:

"Dear, you have a share in my personal property, but I cannot give you a special share out of the property that belongs to the Muslims as a whole. You can get only what other Muslims get."

His son-in-law once waited on him and wanted some assistance from the Baitul Mal. Hadrat Umar paid him some money from his own pocket, and did not give him anything from the Baitul Mal.

Once after distribution a ladies scarf was found surplus. The custodian of the Baitul Mal suggested that this might be offered to Umm Kulsum the wife of Hadrat Umar. Hadrat Umar said:

"No. Present it to Umm Salit the lady who carried the water skin on her back on the day of the battle of Uhud to distribute water among the Muslim warriors."

Once after accounting, one dirham was found surplus in the Baitul Mal. The treasurer gave the dirham to a small son of Hadrat Umar. When Hadrat Umar came to know of that he had the dirham returned immediately.

'Abdullah a son of Hadrat Umar fought in the battle of Jalaula. He got his share of the spoils and sold it on the spot. This fetched a high value. When Hadrat Umar came to know of that he said that he was allowed the high price because people thought that he was the Caliph's son. He ordered that the profit earned beyond the market value should be credited to the state treasury.

One of the sons of Hadrat Umar drank wine inadvertently in Egypt. He submitted himself voluntarily to the punishment of 80 stripes at Egypt. Hadrat Umar was not satisfied. He called the boy to Madina and flogged him to death. When the boy was on death bed Hadrat Umar said to him, "When you meet the Holy Prophet tell him that Umar is following his injunctions strictly."

HADRAT UMAR IN HISTORY

During the ten years of his rule from 634 to 644 A.D., Hadrat Umar changed the course of history. Emerging from the deserts of Arabia, the Arabs fortified with the faith of Islam overpowered the Byzantine power in the west and the mighty Persian empire in the east. During the short space of ten years the Muslims conquered countries comprising an area of 22,51,030 square miles. Under Hadrat Umar the Islamic dominions assumed the dimensions of a continent. These extended from Mecca 1,036 miles to the north, 1,087 miles to the east, and 483 miles to the south. These countries included Egypt, Syria, Iraq, Khuzistan, Fars, Isfahan, Azarbaijan; Armenia, Makran and Khurasan. The dominions extended from the Oxus to the Nile.

There have been many conquerors in the course of history and the record of the conquests of Hadrat Umar compares very favourably with the record of other conquerors. In one point the conquests of Hadrat Umar surpass the conquests of all other conquerors. Whereas the conquests of other conquerors did not endure for long, the conquests of Hadrat Umar in the name of Islam have endured for the last 1,400 years.

In the history of the world, Hadrat Umar accordingly occupies a prominent position. He is one of the greatest men of all times. The passage of time has in no way dimmed the glory of his greatness. The life-story of Hadrat Umar which we have tried to narrate in these pages projects in unmistakable terms all the qualities that make greatness. Hadrat Umar lives in history as a great conqueror, a great ruler and the founder of the Muslim state. Hadrat Umar lives in legend as an embodiment of all that a great ruler or a great man should be.

The qualities and characteristics of the personality of Hadrat Umar include: towering personality; robust constitution, great power of mind; inflexible integrity; strong sense of justice; simplicity of habits; contempt of pomp and luxury; strong faith in his mission; strong conviction for the truth; highly developed sense of duty; absolute impartiality; devotion to Islam; extreme sense of dedication; very strong sense of justice; sympathy for the aggrieved; courage against the oppressor; energy; piety; humility; discipline; frugality; morality; political insight; accessibility; vigilance; patience; perseverance; accountability before law; equality for all; and indeed all the virtues that a ruler or a leader of men should possess.

Hadrat Umar was a man of great knowledge and learning. He was a good orator. Every Friday he would address the faithful in the Prophet's mosque at Madina. Some of the addresses that he delivered on such occasions have come down to us and are masterpieces of religious teaching. While sending his forces on various expeditions he addressed them in very inspiring terms. He was a good writer and some of his letters which have come down to us show the skill of his penmanship. The instructions that he issued to his officers to regulate state business are very much modern in content. Many anecdotes about him have come down to us, and these project his greatness, wisdom, and foresightedness. He was a good judge of poetry. He could freely quote appropriate verses to suit the occasion. He was a good judge of men. He could discern the truth from falsehood. He always called a spade a spade, and would never mince matters. Whatever he regarded as the truth he spoke it even though it might appear to be bitter. He enjoyed the reputation of being hard and harsh, but that was primarily because he always valued the truth, and had no hesitation in expressing it even though it might be displeasing. Howsoever stern or angry he might be, if the verses of the Holy Qur'an were read before him be would at once soften, and even burst into sobs.

Physically as well as intellectually he was a man of towering personality. But he never tried to give the impression that he was in any way superior to the people around him.

He was a good critic, but his criticism was not meant for others; alone it was meant for himself as well. He listened to his critics with great respect and if such criticism was unfounded he tried to explain things to them. He subjected himself to rigorous self-criticism. Whenever there was any lapse on his part, he would shut himself in a room of his house and then loudly reprimand himself. If he beat any body with his whip inadvertently and such punishment was found to be unjustified he would ask the person concerned to beat him with the whip in the same way as he had beaten him. During the famine he refused to take ghee or meat simply because the people of average means could not afford such food. He was the ruler of vast dominions but he denied himself all privileges of rulership. The allowance that he drew was just enough for a person of average means. When the people around him insisted that his allowance should be raised, he refused to accept any increase. And when he died he willed that after the sale of his property the entire amount of the allowance that he had drawn should be refunded to the treasury.

He set very high standards of integrity, and was the first to practise what he preached. His son 'Abdullah was a very talented man but he refused to give him any office. One of his sons Abu Shahma was found guilty of drinking and Hadrat Umar had him flogged to death. Once a Governor gave some gift to one of his wives. Hadrat Umar returned the gift and rebuked the Governor. Once a wife of Hadrat Umar sent some perfume as a gift to the wife of the emperor of Byzantine. The wife of the emperor of Byzantine sent some gift in return Hadrat Umar sold the gift and credited the proceeds to the state treasury

He ate the coarsest of food, and wore clothes of the coarsest of cloth. Once he was late for the Friday prayer and the explanation that he offered was that he had his clothes washed, and they took some time to dry which delayed his departure for the mosque. Umar the ruler of the largest empire of the time had only one shirt in his wardrobe and that too was patched. When the envoy of the Byzantine emperor came to Madina, he expected that the Caliph would be living in a heavily guarded palace. The envoy found no palace and no guard. He found the Caliph sitting in the mosque in the company of ordinary people. Hadrat Umar was the living embodiment of the doctrine of equality before law. Once he appeared in a suit in a law court and when the Judge wanted to show him some respect for the office he held, he desired that no preference should be shown to him in any way and that the law must have its course. When a messenger riding a dromedary came from Iraq carrying the news of the victory of the Muslims at the battle of Qadissiya, Hadrat Umar met the messenger a few miles outside Madina and ran all the way by the side of the dromedary of the messenger hearing the news and without disclosing his identity to the man who had brought the news. When Hadrat Umar went to Palestine to receive the surrender of the city of Jerusalem the world witnessed the strange spectacle of Hadrat Umar's slave riding the camel, and Umar the mighty Caliph, walking on foot holding the reins of the camel .

Hadrat Umar would perambulate the streets of Madina at night carrying his whip in his hand. The whip would freely descend on any one found guilty of any lapse or excess regardless of his status. Once a chief was found passing through the streets of Madina at the head of a procession of his followers. Hadrat Umar whipped him for this display of arrogance. A prince of Syria who had accepted Islam and was staying at Madina and Mecca as a state guest slapped a man who accidentally trod on his feet in the course of the Hajj. Hadrat Umar laid down that the man who had been slapped could in turn slap the prince.

Hadrat Umar kept a watch over the people as a shepherd would keep a watch over his animals. A blind woman in Madina had no one to attend to her needs. Hadrat Umar visited her frequently and attended to her needs. In a cottage a woman was found cooking stone in a kettle merely to give the children the impression that food was being cooked for them whereas there was nothing in the house to be cooked. Hadrat Umar carried a bag of flour and other eatables on his own back and handed them over to the lady. A Bedouin and his wife came to Madina and were in a predicament as the lady suffered from the pains of childbirth. Hadrat Umar's wife acted as a midwife and Hadrat Umar sat all the time outside the tent awaiting the birth of a child.

He took particular care to appoint men of approved integrity to high offices under the state. He watched over them like a hawk, and as soon as any lapse on their part came to the notice of Hadrat Umar immediate action was taken. People were free to complain against their officers. Impartial enquiries were held and when any officer was found guilty he was removed and punished. All the Governors were required to assemble at Mecca on the occasion of the Hajj, and here any person could complain against any officer. Hadrat Umar exhorted all concerned to realise that the officers were not meant to rule; they were there to serve the people, and build up a welfare state. Hadrat Umar's concept of administration was:

> "By God he that is weakest among you shall be in my eyes the strongest until I have vindicated for him his right. He that is strongest I will treat as the weakest until he complies with law."

No political thinker or ruler since Hadrat Umar has been able to come forward with a better concept of the purpose of the state than the concept enunciated by Hadrat Umar. About the ruler and the ruled relationship, Hadrat Umar said:

> "People generally hate their ruler and I seek protection of Allah lest my people should entertain similar feelings about me. "

Some of his standing instructions to his executive were: "Avoid vain suspicions; keep away from malice; do not encourage people to cherish vain hopes; be careful in respect of Allah's property in your charge; be accessible to the people; guard yourself against evil men; seek the company of the righteous; attend to your job with due diligence; do not procrastinate in the despatch of state business; watch your subordinates; take immediate action against those who are corrupt or inefficient; and award merit." All these instructions given 1,400 years ago would be as true today as these were then.

Hadrat Umar stood for quick and impartial justice. Hadrat Umar appointed capable and upright persons as Judges. He instructed his Judges in the following terms:

> "Justice is an important obligation. Treat the people equally in your presence, in your company, and in your decisions, so that the weak despair not of justice and the high placed have no hope of your favour. When you are in doubt on a question and find nothing about it in the Qur'an or in the Sunna of the Prophet think over the question; ponder over the precedents and analogous cases and then decide by analogy."

Hadrat Umar took special pains to project Islam in the proper perspective as a living faith. There was a school of thought who held that religion was mystical and supra-rational and as such the injunctions of religion including Islam were not to be tested on the basis of intellect or reason. Hadrat Umar founded what later came to be called *Israr Ilmuddin*. He held that Islam was a rational religion and all its injunctions and practices could be tested and justified on the basis of reason and intellect. He was the first Muslim to undertake *Ijtihad*, and lay down new laws in keeping with the spirit of Islam. In the Holy Qur'an no punishment was laid down for drinking. Hadrat Umar laid down a penalty of 80 lashes in this behalf. The position about *Mut'ah* was not clear. Hadrat Umar forbade *Mut'ah*. The position about three divorces was not clear. Hadrat Umar held that even when three divorces were announced at one sitting the divorce was irrevocable. In the month of Ramdan Hadrat Umar enjoined upon the Muslims to offer *Tarawih* in congregation.

Hadrat Umar took pains to ensure that the faith of Islam should remain pure, and should have no characteristic of idolatry about it. The tree under which the Holy Prophet took the oath of allegiance on the occasion of the Hudaibiya pact came to be regarded by the people as something sacred. Hadrat Umar had the tree uprooted to avoid idolatrous veneration thereof. On the way from Madina to Mecca there was a mosque where the Holy Prophet had once said his prayers. It became the practice that the pilgrims offered extra prayers at the mosque. Hadrat Umar forbade the practice. The Black Stone at the Kaaba came to be held as sacred. Hadrat Umar held that it was just a stone. At one stage the Holy Prophet had ordered *Rummal* in Hajj, under which the first rounds in the case of the Kaaba were to be performed running. Hadrat Umar was of the view that *Rummal* had been provided under circumstances which no longer existed. He did not abrogate the practice but nevertheless held that if some body could not run that did not matter.

Hadrat Umar is known for his humanitarian reforms. He provided privileges for slaves. He emancipated girl slaves who bore their masters children. Full protection was afforded to the *Dhimmis*. In the matter of citizenship they were treated at par with other citizens.

In the social field Hadrat Umar took particular steps to build a social order according to the teachings of Islam. Prohibition was enforced with great strictness. It was the practice with Arab poets to mention the names of their beloveds in their poetry. Hadrat Umar prohibited the practice. The poets also indulged in satires and lampoons. Hadrat Umar issued strict instructions that no poet should write satires and lampoons. Hadrat Umar also ordered that in their verses the poets should not extol non-Islamic virtues. Hadrat Umar laid down that no person, howsoever rich should build a double storeyed house, and no house should comprise more than three rooms.

The political and social order that Hadrat Umar set up by applying the principles of Islam was more democratic than the democracies of today and more socialist than the socialist countries of today. That order has remained the ideal for all Muslim countries to revive.

Because of his achievements, Hadrat Umar occupies an outstanding place in the history of the world. We do not come across any other ruler in world history who led so simple a life and yet inspired awe and terror among his people and his foes alike. The awe and fear that Hadrat Umar commanded was because of his high moral character. People feared him because he feared God. Hadrat Umar was an embodiment of the virtues of Islam. About him the Holy Prophet said:

> "If God had wished that there should have been another prophet after me, he would have been Umar."

About Hadrat Umar we can appropriately say what Girami said of Iqbal, namely:

> "In the eyes of those who know the secret of things,
> He fulfilled a prophet's role, but he cannot be called a prophet."

CHRONOLOGY

Hadrat Umar led a very eventful life. We narrate hereunder in chronological order the main events in the life of Hadrat ' Umar.

Hadrat Umar was born in Mecca around 580 A.D. He started independent business around 600 A.D. He married in the first decade of the seventh century.

He was converted to Islam in 616 A.D. at the age of 26. He migrated to Madina in 622 A.D.

He participated in the battle of Badr in 623 A.D.

He participated in the battle of Uhud in 625 A.D. A few months after the battle of Uhud, Hadrat Hafsah the daughter of Hadrat Umar was married to the Holy Prophet of Islam.

In 627 Hadrat Umar participated in the battle of the Ditch and the campaign against Banu Mustaliq.

In 628 Hadrat Umar was present on the occasion of the Hudaybiah pact. Thereafter he participated in the Khybar campaign. He divorced his wives Qariba and Malaika who did not accept Islam. He married Sabiha and Jamila.

In 630 Hadrat Umar participated in the conquest of Mecca and in the campaigns of Hunain and Ta'if.

In 632 he participicted in the farewell pilgrimage. This year the Holy Prophet died Hadrat Umar played an important role in getting Hadrat Abu Bakr elected as the Caliph.

Hadrat Abu Bakr died in 634, and Hadrat Umar became the Caliph. During this year the Muslims captured Damascus on the Syrian front. On the Iraq front there was the battle of

Namaraq in September; the battle of Kaskar in October and the battle of the Bridge in November 634 A D.

In 635 Hadrat Umar married Atika. During the Ramadan Hadrat Umar organised *Tarawih* on congregation basis. On the Syrian front the battle of Fahl was fought in January. Beisan and Tabariyya were captured in March. The battle of Marj Rum was fought in March whereby Damascus was reoccupied. In April the Muslim forces reached Emessa and a truce was arrived at. In the Southern Iraq sector Ubala was captured in April. The region of Aburqubaz and Meisan was occupied in November.

In 636 Hadrat Umar introduced the Hijri calendar. In Central Syria the city of Emessa was captured in March. In Southern Syria the Muslims won the battle of Yermuk in August. The battle of Ajnadin was fought in December. On the Iraq front the battle of Qadissiya was won by the Muslims in November. Thereafter began the march to Al-Mada'in. The battles of Burs, Babylon and Sura on the way to Mada'in were fought in December.

In 637 Hadrat Umar married Umm Hakim. This year stipends and allowances were sanctioned for the Muslims. On the Syrian front Qinissrin, Aleppo, and Antioch were captured. The whole of North Syria was cleared of the Byzantines. On the Iraq front Mada'in was captured in April. Takeet and Mosul were occupied in May. The battle of Jalaula was won in November. Khanqueen and Qirqassia were occupied in December.

In 638 Hadrat Umar adopted the title of 'Amir-ul-Mumnin.' The Jews and Christians were expelled from Arabia proper and settled in Iraq and Syria. On the Syrian front Jerusalem and Caesaria were captured. On the Iraq front Hulwan, Masabzan, Heet and Ahwaz were captured. During the year the city of Kufa was established in Central Iraq, and the city of Basra in Southern Iraq.

In 639 Arabia was afflicted by a severe famine. Hadrat Umar organised relief measures on a large scale. Plague broke out in Syria and Iraq and caused considerable havoc.

Amr bin Al-Aas marched to Egypt. On the Iraq front Ahwaz, Dauraq and Ram Hormuz were occupied by the Muslims.

In 640 there were battles of Farma, Bilbeis and Babylon in Egypt which were won by the Muslims. On the Iraq front there was the battle of Tustar which was won by the Muslims.

In 641 the Muslims captured Alexandria on the Egyptian front. Sus was occupied on the Iraq front in January. On this front Jande Sabur was occupied in March. The historic battle of Nihawand was won by the Muslims in December.

In 642 an expedition was undertaken to Nubia. The Muslims advanced to Burqa and Fezzan in North Africa. During this year the city of Fustat was founded as the capital of Egypt. On the Persian front war was carried and the Muslims occupied Hamadan, Isfahan, Rayy, Tabaristan, Fars and Sistan.

In 643 the Muslims occupied Sabrata and Tripoli but these advance posts were subsequently abandoned and the Muslims withdrew to Egypt. On the Persian front Khurasan and Azerbaijan were occupied by the Muslims during the year.

During 644 Makran and Armenia were occupied. During this year Hadrat Umar was assassinated and that was the end of a glorious and eventful career.

BOOKS ABOUT HADRAT UMAR

When I started writing this book on Hadrat Umar my first effort was directed to collect as many books on Hadrat Umar as possible. Unfortunately I could not collect many books. In spite of the outstanding personality of Hadrat Umar, it is a matter of regret to realise that the number of books on Hadrat Umar available in Pakistan is very meagre.

The books in Urdu that I could collect in Pakistan included :

(1) "Al-Faruq" by Maulana Shibli Nu'mani,
(2) "Biography of Hadrat Umar" by Muhammad Hussain Haikal of Egypt;
(3) "Umar bin Khattab" by Tantawi, translated into Urdu by 'Abdul Samad Haram and published by 'Al-Bian' Lahore;
(4) "Hadrat Abu Bakr Siddiq and Farooq-i-'Azam" by Dr. Ta Hussain, translated by Shah Hasan 'Ata, and published by Nafis Academy, Karachi;
(5) "Fiqh-i-Umar" by Shaḥ Waliullah; translated by Maulana Abu Yahya Imam Khan; and published by Institute of Islamic Culture, Lahore.

The only book in English on Hadrat Umar to which I could have access is "Omar the Great: The Second Caliph of Islam". This is a translation of Shibli Nu'mani's book "Al-Farooq". The book has been published by Sh. Muhammad Ashraf in two volumes. The first volume is by Maulana Zafar Ali Khan while the second volume is by Muhammad Saleem. This means that no original work in English has been produced on Hadrat Umar so far. This appears to be very strange as well as surprising. Hadrat Umar is one of the greatest men of the world, and it is regrettable that no standard work in English has appeared about this great man so far.

In the book "The Early Heroes of Islam" by B. A. Salik and published by the Book House, Lahore there are some Chapters on Hadrat Umar.

"The Encyclopaedia of Islam" contains an article on Hadrat Umar (Umar Ibn Khattab).

Recently three books by Lt. Col. A. I. Akram have been published. These contain some useful material about the conquests made during the caliphate of Hadrat Umar. These books are:

(1) Khalid bin Walid, the Sword of Allah;
(2) The Muslim Conquest of Persia,
(3) The Muslim Conquest of Egypt and North Africa.

Some historical works by classical Muslim writers contain an account of Hadrat Umar and his times. These include:

(1) Al-Waqidi's "Book of the Battles" which consists of annals of the conquest of Iraq and Syria;
(2) Ibn Sa'd's "Tabqat" which deals with the life of the Holy Prophet and his companions including Hadrat Umar;
(3) Al-Baladhuri's "Book of Conquests" which is an account of the conquests of Islam;
(4) Tabari's "History" which is an history of Islam up to 915 A.D.;
(5) Mas'udi's "History of the Times";
(6) Ibn al-Athir's "The Lions of the Forests" containing the life stories of the Companions including Hadrat Umar;
(7) Ibn Khallikan's "The Demise of the Prominent People" containing the biographies of prominent Muslims including Hadrat Umar.
(8) Al-Suyuti's "History of the Caliphs" which contains a section on Hadrat Umar.

Urdu versions of most of the above books are available in Pakistan. An English version of Al-Suyuti's "History of the Caliphs" (translated by Major H. S. Jarrett) is available in Pakistan having been published by Karimsons, Karachi.

We get some material about the life of Hadrat Umar from the biographies of the Holy Prophet. These biographies may be considered under two heads, namely: western scholars and Muslim writers.

The western scholars include: Thomas Carlyle; N. Alcock; Revd. George Bush; Washington Irving; Murray Elgin; A. Spreger; William Muir; Bosworth Smith; J. W. H. Stabart; Dermanghan; A Guillaume; Margoliouth; Montgomery Watt; Murster; Col. Badly; Edith Holland; T. Andrae; R. E. Dibble; G. M. Draycott; H. Pirenne, etc.

The Muslim writers include such names as, Sir Syed Ahmad Khan; Ameer Ali; Maulana Muhammad Ali; Dr. Ata Muhyuddin; F. K. Durrani; Essed Bey; Sirdar Iqbal Shah; K. L. Gauba; Khurshid Ahmad; Hafiz Ghulam Sarwar; M. A. Rauf; Abdul Wahhab; Khalifa Abdul Hakim; Shibli Numani; Abdul Hamid Siddiqi; Faqir Waheeduddin; Sufi Mahbub Elahi, etc.

Some books in English on the history of Islam furnish some material about Hadrat Umar. These books include:

(1) Cambridge History of Islam;
(2) History of the Saracens by S. Ockley;
(3) The Saracens by A. Gilman;
(4) History of the Saracens by Syed Amir Ali;
(5) History of Mohammadanism by C. Mills;
(6) History of Mohammadanism by W. C. Taylor;
(7) History of the Islamic Peoples by Dr. Well;
(8) History of the Islamic Peoples by Brockelman;
(9) A Short History of Islam by S. F. Mahmud;
(10) Outline History of the Muslim World by Prof. Masudul Hasan;
(11) History of the Arabs by Philip K. Hitti;
(12) The Arabs in History by B. Lewis;
(13) Islam and the Arabs by R. Landau;

(14) Arab Kingdom and its Fall by Wellhausen
(15) Islam in History by Justice Muhammad Munir.

Some books on Hadrat Abu Bakr which contain some material on Hadrat Umar include:

(1) AbuBakr and His Times by Dr. Ata Mohyuddin;
(2) Abu Bakr by Dr. Mahbul Haqq;
(3) Sidiq-i-Akbar Hadrat Abu Bakr by Prof. Masudul Hasan.

Index

'N'